Council Daybook

Vatican II, Session 3

Council Daybook

Vatican II, Session 3

Edited by

FLOYD ANDERSON

DIRECTOR, PRESS DEPARTMENT

NATIONAL CATHOLIC WELFARE CONFERENCE

Price: $5

Published by

NATIONAL CATHOLIC WELFARE CONFERENCE

1312 MASSACHUSETTS AVE., N.W.

WASHINGTON, D. C. 20005

Nihil Obstat:

Rev. James J. O'Connor

Censor Librorum

Imprimatur:

+ Leo A. Pursley, D.D.

Bishop of Fort Wayne-South Bend

Library of Congress Catalog Card Number: 65–17303

Foreword

From various sources requests have come to the N.C.W.C. to gather as soon as possible into one volume whatever information is available covering the day-to-day proceedings of the Second Vatican Council. One of the distinctive features of the present council in contrast to all preceding ones was the prompt reporting of each day's activities, including a summary statement of each speech delivered in the aula of St. Peter's. The correspondents of the N.C.W.C. News Service had access to the official press releases each day by early afternoon, and were able to supplement the record by the discussions which took place at the meeting of the daily press panel. The representatives of the various international news media, especially those from the United States, queried the "periti" or experts who had been present at the morning congregations of the council, and were in consequence able to fill in any lacunae which might have occurred and also to clear up any obscurities in the official releases.

The bishops of the United States had the benefit of receiving each evening or early the next morning a mimeographed copy of these reports. It was the general, one might say even the unanimous, judgment of the United States hierarchy that this was an invaluable service. It enabled the bishops to review in substance the speeches or the interventions made each day, with more leisure to evaluate the various contributions made to the subject under debate. Without this assistance it would have been much more difficult to develop that ultimate consensus of opinion which gradually evolved out of the variety of viewpoints expressed by those who participated in the discussion.

In the aftermath of previous ecumenical councils there was a rather protracted interval before the record of the proceedings and speeches which led up to the adoption of the final decrees was available for students and the interested public. We think of the many years that historians had to wait before the works of Mansi and the Lacenses brought together the source material of the council proceedings. To avoid similar delays it was suggested to the officials of the N.C.W.C. that a journal of the proceedings might be produced which would serve as a temporary source book until such time as an authentic and definitive record could be published.

In consenting to make available now such a journal of press reports it was realized that a work of this nature would leave much to be desired. To meet the needs of serious students in the future the Secretariat of the Council will no doubt publish in due time the conciliar proceedings, including all speeches and interventions, with the final results of the votes; but it will be many years, in all probability, before this official and authentic record will be available. Meanwhile, a journal, printed for a limited circulation, will provide a record of what was released to the press and communicated to the public at the time that the council was in session.

We take the occasion to express our sincere thanks to Monsignor Paul Tanner, our General Secretary of the N.C.W.C., and to the members of the Press Department, for their valuable assistance in preparing the "Council Daybook" for the use of the Church here in the United States and throughout the world.

+ KARL J. ALTER
Secretary,
Administrative Board of Bishops
National Catholic Welfare Conference

Preface

Council Daybook is written, basically, by the members of the Rome Bureau of the N.C.W.C. News Service, plus the invaluable assistance of a long-time correspondent of the News Service, Father Placid Jordan, O.S.B. These are the daily stories they wrote of the Second Vatican Council's discussions and debates, the speeches made on the council floor and off it, the interviews and comments, the summaries and texts of the various council documents.

These are the "facts" of the third session of the Second Vatican Council, as free as we can make them from opinions. We have tried to be as objective as is humanly possible.

Some of the news stories do not carry a signature: these were usually a collaborative effort of two or more of the News Service staff. Most of them are signed, however; and you might like to know the background of these writers:

James C. O'Neill: Head of the Rome bureau of the N.C.W.C. News Service. A native of San Francisco, he has been on our staff in Rome since 1957. He was with the San Francisco bureau of United Press before joining N.C.W.C. News Service. He is a graduate of the University of Santa Clara in California, and of the Columbia University Graduate School of Journalism in New York.

Patrick Riley is a graduate of St. Paul's College at the Catholic University of America, Washington, and of the Columbia School of Journalism, New York. He has worked for the New York Times, Reuter's news service in London, and with the United Press in its London and Paris bureaus.

Father John P. Donnelly was director of the N.C.W.C. Bureau of Information in Washington when he joined the Rome staff of the N.C.W.C. News Service in 1964. He had been editor of the *Inland Register*, Spokane, Wash., from 1959 until 1963, when he became director of the Bureau of Information. He is a graduate of the University of Missouri School of Journalism.

Father Placid Jordan, O.S.B., has been an N.C.W.C. News Service correspondent since 1930. He was ordained a priest in 1951 at Beuron, Germany, after a distinguished career in news broadcasting and writing. He was the Central European representative for the National Broadcasting Company from 1931 to 1947, when he began his studies for the priesthood. He has won international renown as a conscientious and brilliant reporter and an alert observer.

FLOYD ANDERSON
Director, N.C.W.C. Press Department

Table of Contents

The cover design and lettering of *Council Daybook,* done by Martin E. Greven, is in Chancery Cursive. It is patterned after the style of Niccolo Niccoli, who established a school of writing in Florence in the 15th century. This style of cursive handwriting became known for its form, clarity and style, and was adopted by order of Pope Eugenius IV (1431-1447) as the official form of all papal briefs; hence its name, Chancery Cursive. The other calligraphic lines are lettered in the half-uncial style of writing developed during the fourth century for early Christian manuscripts.

Council Daybook was set in the Fairfield type face, and printed by Our Sunday Visitor press, Huntington, Ind.

First edition, February 1, 1965.

II Vatican Ecumenical Council

Convoked by Pope John XXIII through the Apostolic Constitution "Humanae Salutis," dated Dec. 25, 1961, and solemnly begun in the Vatican Basilica on Oct. 11, 1962.

Council of the Presidency.

Eugene Cardinal Tisserant, Bishop of Ostia and of Porto and
    St. Rufina, Dean
Achille Cardinal Lienart, Bishop of Lille
Ignace Gabriel Cardinal Tappouni, Patriarch of Antioch of the
    Syrians
Norman Thomas Cardinal Gilroy, Archbishop of Sydney
Francis Cardinal Spellman, Archbishop of New York
Joseph Cardinal Frings, Archbishop of Cologne
Ernesto Cardinal Ruffini, Archbishop of Palermo
Antonio Cardinal Caggiano, Archbishop of Buenos Aires
Giuseppe Cardinal Siri, Archbishop of Genoa
Stefan Cardinal Wyszynski, Archbishop of Gniezno and Warsaw
Albert Gregory Cardinal Meyer, Archbishop of Chicago
Bernard Jan Cardinal Alfrink, Archbishop of Utrecht

Delegates or Moderators

Gregorio Pietro Cardinal Agagianian
Giacomo Cardinal Lercaro, Archbishop of Bologna
Julius Cardinal Doepfner, Archbishop of Munich and Freising
Leo Josef Cardinal Suenens, Archbishop of Malines-Brussels

Commission for Coordination of Council Work

Chairman

Amleto Giovanni Cardinal Cicognani, Titular Bishop of Frascati,
    Secretary of State

Members

Achille Cardinal Lienart, Bishop of Lille
Gregorio Pietro Cardinal Agagianian
Francis Cardinal Spellman, Archbishop of New York
Giacomo Cardinal Lercaro, Archbishop of Bologna
Giovanni Cardinal Urbani, Patriarch of Venice
Carlo Cardinal Confalonieri
Julius Cardinal Doepfner, Archbishop of Munich and Freising
Leo Josef Cardinal Suenens, Archbishop of Malines-Brussels
Francisco Cardinal Roberti
    The following are members of the commission:
Most Rev. Pericle Felici, Titular Archbishop of Samosata, Council
    Secretary General
Most Rev. Philippe Nabaa, Archbishop of Beirut and Gibail for the
    Melkites, Council Undersecretary

Most Rev. Casimiro Morcillo Gonzalez, Archbishop of Madrid, Council
    Undersecretary
Most Rev. Jean Villot, Titular Archbishop of the Bosporus, Coadjutor
    of Lyon, Council Undersecretary
Most Rev. John Joseph Krol, Archbishop of Philadelphia, Council
    Undersecretary
Most Rev. Wilhelm Kempf, Bishop of Limburg, Council Undersecretary
Msgr. Vincenzo Fagiolo, Assistant

Secretariat General
Secretary General

Most Rev. Pericle Felici, Titular Archbishop of Samosata
Office: Rome, Via Serristori, 10 — tel. 698, ext. 42-35
             Vatican City, Ospizio S. Marta — tel. 698, ext. 43-02

Undersecretaries

Most Rev. Philippe Nabaa, Archbishop of Beirut and Gibail for the
    Melkites
Most Rev. Casimiro Morcillo Gonzalez, Archbishop of Madrid
Most Rev. Jean Villot, Archbishop of the Bosporus, Coadjutor of Lyon
Most Rev. John Joseph Krol, Archbishop of Philadelphia
Most Rev. Wilhelm Kempf, Bishop of Limburg
Office: Vatican City, Ospizio S. Marta — tel. 698, ext. 43-04; 43-02

Offices of the Secretariat General
Office I
On Sacred Rites

Most Rev. Enrico Dante, Titular Archbishop of Carpasia, Prefect of
    Pontifical Ceremonies
The Masters of Pontifical Ceremonies
Ushers

Office II
Concerning Pending Business
Notaries

Msgr. Annibale Ferretti
Msgr. Cesare Federici
Msgr. Raffaele Boyer
Msgr. Alfredo Parisella
Msgr. Luigi Piovesana

Protonotaries

Most Rev. Salvatore Natucci
Msgr. Giuseppe D'Ercole
Mr. Giovanni Carrara, professor, attorney, Knight of the Grand Cross

Reviewers

Msgr. Arturo De Jorio
Msgr. Gerardo M. Rogers
Msgr. Giuseppe Casoria
Msgr. Ernesto Civardi
Msgr. Giovanni Sessolo

Office III

Reports and Files

Section A

Msgr. Vincenzo Carbone
Rev. D. Nello Venturini

Section B

Msgr. Achille Lupi
Msgr. Mariano De Nicolo

Section C

Msgr. Vincenzo Fagiolo
Msgr. Marcello Venturi
Rev. D. Giannino Zuliani

Section D

Msgr. Emilio Governatori
Msgr. Nazareno Cinti
Rev. D. Luciano Tosti

Interpreters

Msgr. Achille Lupi
Msgr. Edmondo Ulinski
Msgr. Enrico Francesco Davis
Most Rev. Archpriest Alessandro Koulik
Rev. Giovanni Feiner
Rev. Francesco Thijssen
Rev. Giovanni Corbon
Very Rev. Emanuele Lanne, O.S.B.
Very Rev. Paolo Ananian, Mechitarist
Very Rev. Agostino da Hebo, O.F.M. Cap.
Very Rev. Gerardo Corr, O.S.M.
Very Rev. Maurizio Bevenot, S.J.

Latinists

Msgr. Amleto Tondini
Msgr. Giuseppe Del Ton
Msgr. Guglielmo Zannoni
Abbot Carlo Egger, C.R.L.
Msgr. Innocenzo Parisella
Msgr. Rodomonte Gallicani
Msgr. Giovanni Coppa

Office IV

Technicians

Very Rev. Antonio Stefanizzi, S.J.
Dr. Francesco Vacchini, Engineer
Mr. Mauro Ercole

Pope Paul's Letter on Council Reopening

This is a translation of Pope Paul's letter dated Sept. 1, 1964, to Eugene Cardinal Tisserant, dean of the council of presidents of the ecumenical council, asking that the whole Church join in prayer and penance for the council on Sept. 23, 25, 26 and 27.

To Our Venerable Brother: Health and Apostolic Benediction.

The resumption of the Second Vatican Ecumenical Council is now at hand. The third session, as already decided and announced, will begin on Sept. 14, the day which the liturgy devotes to the feast of the Exaltation of the Holy Cross of our Lord Jesus Christ. This date for the resumption of the conciliar work was not arrived at by chance, but, as it were, to indicate the source from whence springs our salvation and whence the Church draws its trust in the happy outcome of this great synod —that is to say, from the Passion of our most merciful and most beloved Redeemer.

We wish to give due honor to this great mystery, celebrating its perennial and salutary memory, by offering to God at the opening of the conciliar session the Holy Sacrifice of the Mass which represents and renews in an unbloody manner the work of our redemption. We intend to perform this sacred rite as a first and essential act of the ecumenical council, which is about to assemble again, by means of a solemn concelebration by 24 conciliar Fathers chosen from various orders and regions, and united to us.

We wish this for the council so that the infusion of hearts and souls may be more evident to all and more efficacious in the sight of God, forming "one heart and one soul" (Acts 4, 32) of all those who are taking part in the holy assembly. We wish also through it to implore divine assistance for our common labors—that assistance which is our supreme guide in the arduous and humble search for the divine will on the part of the whole Catholic Church. In fact, the ecumenical council convened around the successor of St. Peter is, as everyone knows, a true representation of the universal Church, a fact which was stated by the Council of Trent and the First Vatican Council.

We write this to you, our venerable brother and dean of the Sacred College, so that you whom we have confirmed in the very high office of first member of the Council of Presidents of the Second Vatican Council, may exhort, in our name and authority, the conciliar Fathers to come punctually to the ecumenical synod itself, and to prepare their souls for it, as for an exceptional moment in the life of the Church.

The Church can hope all the more to be inspired and led by the Holy Spirit the more intensely, the more harmoniously and the more humbly are souls mutually disposed to receive grace. Such an extraordinary moment must be lived with inner meditation, with intense fervor, with humble piety, with absolute faithfulness to the precepts of Christ, with vigilant attention to the needs of the Church and the world.

Nor should your exhortation be limited to the conciliar Fathers to celebrate the great event with spiritual fulness. We desire that you extend it also, through the pastors whom you address, to all the faithful: to priests first of all; to Religious men and women; to all the family of Catholics who aspire to live in conscious and close communion with the Church; also to those afflicted with disease of mind or body, who are already joined to the Church; and to innocent boys and girls—the joy and adornment of the Church.

It is necessary indeed that each member of the Mystical Body of Christ consider this singular and historic event of the ecumenical council as pertaining to himself, and that each participate in the council with an attentive and ardent fellowship. True, when the earlier sessions of the ecumenical council began, an invitation of this sort went out to the whole Church. However, it seems wise to reiterate it—on the one hand because people's interest can diminish the more accustomed they become to this assembly—and against this we must guard; and on the other hand because the gravity of the council's acts and decisions is increasing as the discussions of the various topics suggested for study and deliberation by that body are being brought to conclusion.

There are two forms, proven by usage as is evident, whereby the faithful as individuals as well as the Church in community can join spiritually in an event of such religious and moral value, and contribute to its success: penance and prayer. By the former, man is disposed to remove the obstacles from his soul—that is to say, sins and perverse tendencies—which stand in the way of his reconciliation with God. By the latter, he is prepared to receive the abundance of heavenly mercy.

Both are opportune to make way for the divine action of renewal, and each contributes to that ineffable meeting, so to speak, of two wills: the will of man which is purified when it submits itself in humility and is prompted urgently to ask and to hope; and the Will of God, which can penetrate freely the vacuum of man's heart and, in that encounter, infuses and inflames it with Love transcending nature.

We should like, therefore, that from your own voice, Venerable Brother, as if it were the voice of the whole council, the whole Catholic Church might be exhorted to some special acts of penance and of prayer.

This is our suggestion: This year, let the Ember days which fall on Sept. 23, 25 and 26 be sanctified. Let those who can fast on these days do so, and let everyone regard it as an obligation to practice some exercise of mortification and penance. And let all feel it a duty to address the Lord special prayers of expiation and supplication. And on Sunday, Sept. 27, throughout the world, in every gathering of the faithful and in every ecclesiastical community, universal prayers should be recited for the successful outcome of the ecumenical council. This could be accomplished significantly through a solemn recitation of the "Our Father."

As everyone knows, we regard as a happy outcome of the council the renewal of the spirit of Jesus Christ in His Church, the reincorporation into its unity of the brothers who are still separated from us, the reawakening of the religious conscience in the world, the strengthening of justice and peace among men. These are aims for the highest and general good. No one, we hope, will fail to share the strong desire for the fulfilment of these wishes, for which you, venerable Brother—a proponent as authoritative as you are benevolent—will certainly be given sincere and prompt adherence by pious and generous-hearted people.

For this understanding which we all share, we express our gratitude to you in advance, while we grant you, as well as to the universal Church and to the world, our apostolic benediction.

Opening General Congregation

September 14, 1964

Pope Paul VI opened the third session of the ecumenical council with a ringing reassertion of the role of the Church's bishops as "the teachers, rulers and sanctifiers of the Christian people."

As if to back up his words by a striking action, he concelebrated the session's opening Mass with 24 council Fathers, including two Americans, Archbishops Lawrence J. Shehan of Baltimore and John J. Krol of Philadelphia.

Several times and in several ways he said in his opening address that the principal task of the third session will be the central task of the Second Vatican Council itself—to round out the First Vatican Council's incomplete teaching on the nature of the Church by explaining the nature and function of the bishops as successors of the apostles.

(The First Vatican Council [1869-70] defined only the primacy and the infallibility of the Pope.)

"The present council's deliberations on this subject will certainly be what distinguishes this solemn and historic synod in the memory of future ages," Pope Paul declared.

The Second Vatican Council has already made history by the Pope's declared intention of bringing women into its deliberations and by the actual presence of delegated observers from other Christian churches and communities.

Although the Pope expressly welcomed these "first women in history to participate in a conciliar assembly" in his speech, their names had not yet been announced.

The Pope also addressed non-Catholic observers, begging them not "to take it in bad part" when he invited them to "enter into the fulness of truth and charity."

Just as the Second Vatican Council will balance the First Vatican Council's definition of papal primacy with a clarification of the role of the bishops in the universal Church, Pope Paul balanced his own affirmation of the authority of the bishops with a forthright assertion of the pope's authority and of the Church's need for centralization. He said:

"If our apostolic duty obliges us to impose restrictions, to define terms, to prescribe modes of action, to regulate the methods which concern the exercise of episcopal authority, you realize that this is done for the good of the entire Church, for the Church which has proportionately greater need of centralized leadership as its worldwide extension becomes more complete, as more serious dangers and more pressing needs threaten the Christian people in the varying circumstances of history, and, we may add, as more rapid means of communication become operative in modern times."

Before the session began, all the council Fathers—except the cardinals, members of the papal household and the 24 concelebrants of the Mass with the Pope—were in their places in the nave of St. Peter's basilica.

When the papal procession entered, the choir began to sing the papal salute, "Tu Es Petrus." The cardinals—about 50 of them—were followed by members of the papal household and then came the concelebrants who, like the Pope, were vested in miter and red chasuble. Only Father Anastasio Ballestrero, O.C.D., superior general of the Discalced Carmelites, wore his hood as he has no miter. He and Abbot Benno Gut, O.S.B., abbot primate of the Benedictine Confederation, led the procession of concelebrants.

Pope Paul opened his arms in greeting as he entered on the portable throne. His face remained serious. Clapping broke out, but he subdued it immediately with a decisive gesture, and began to bless the council Fathers as he was borne up the aisle.

But an irresistible storm of applause broke upon him when he came within view of the assembled lay people and lesser clergy. His gesture asking for quiet produced little perceptible result.

The Pope descended from the portable throne, doffed his miter and immediately began the Mass with the prayers at the foot of the altar. Behind him in a great semicircle were his concelebrants, including Eugene Cardinal Tisserant, who as first of the presidents of the council had been the celebrant of the Masses which opened the previous sessions of the council.

Although all 24 Fathers recited the prayers along with the Pope, only his rich and unmistakable voice was audible over the basilica's loudspeaking system.

The Pope, as is customary in his Masses in St. Peter's, faced the nave of the church from the Altar of the Confession. The entire congregation—bishops, priests and people—gave responses in Latin and also sang the Ordinary of the Mass in well-known Gregorian melodies.

Father Ballestrero, the lowest in precedence of the concelebrants, chanted the Epistle. Cardinal Tisserant, the highest in precedence next to the Pope, chanted the Gospel.

A high point of the Mass came with recitation of the "people's prayer" introduced into the liturgy by the council at its last session.

Pope Paul himself began this series of prayers: "We humbly beseech God the Father Almighty, beloved brothers, that He who has called together the pastors of the Church in the Holy Spirit, may pour forth abundantly on all of them the gifts of His holiness, through His only begotten Son."

The choir then took up the petitions, singing them in the chant made familiar in the litany of the saints. The congregation answered from the same litany.

The chant of petition rose up for the Church, the Pope, the bishops, the clerics, the Religious and the entire Christian people, for "those who do not yet believe in Christ," for civil officials and all peoples.

Immediately afterward, at the Offertory, the concelebrants mounted the altar and took places around the Pope. Archbishops Shehan and Krol stood next to each other at the Pope's right. Archbishop Krol was one of two concelebrants who presented bread and wine to the Pope.

All 25 voices joined in the words of consecration, with the Pope's voice slightly predominating because the microphone was nearer to him. At the celebrants' Communion, the 24 moved in procession to the Pope and each took a segment of the same consecrated Host.

Each concelebrant carried his fragment of the sacred Host back to his place, supporting it over a paten. At a given moment, all consumed the sacred fragment together.

Then they moved again to the side of the Pope to partake of the Precious Blood. All dipped into the chalice with the same golden spoon.

The Pope distributed Communion to the lay auditors, including James Norris, assistant to the director of Catholic Relief Services—National Catholic Welfare Conference.

The Pope gave the final blessing of the Mass. The concelebrants blessed themselves but did not give the final blessing with the Pope.

There was no last Gospel. This omission is prescribed when other ceremonies are to follow the Mass.

At the end of the Mass Archbishop Pericle Felici, general secretary of the ecumenical council, led the new council Fathers in the profession of faith, which is the oath against modernism.

Pope Paul then launched into his hour-long speech which, except for a final hymn, the Veni Creator Spiritus, and a final papal blessing, concluded the morning's ceremonies.

The Pope, addressing the council Fathers, began by pointing out that the session was opening "under the sign of the Holy Cross" (Sept. 14 is the feast of the Exaltation of the Holy Cross).

He then declared: "The Church is present here. We are the Church."

He explained, "We are the Church as members of the Mystical Body of Christ . . .

"We are the Church since we are ministers of the Church itself, priests invested with a special character. . . a hierarchy entrusted with functions meant to perpetuate in time and to extend on earth the saving mission of Christ.

"We are the Church, finally, because as teachers of the faith, pastors of souls . . . we represent here the entire Church, not representing it as delegates or deputies of the faithful . . . but as fathers and brothers who personify the communities entrusted to the care of each of us, and as a plenary assembly legitimately convoked by the Holy Father."

The Pope asserted that because the council recapitulates the universal Church "in our persons and in our functions" it is therefore ecumenical. He further declared that the Church's four marks—oneness, universality, holiness and apostolicity—are to be found in the council.

Further exploring the ramifications of his statement that "the Church is present here," the Pope said:

"Now if the Church is here, here also is the Spirit, the Advocate, whom Christ promised to His apostles for the building up of the Church . . . For there are, as we know, two factors which Christ has promised and disposed in different ways to continue His mission . . . These two factors are the apostolate and the Spirit . . .

"These two agents, the apostolate which is entrusted to the sacred hierarchy, and the Spirit of Jesus, which uses the hierarchy as its ordinary instrument in the ministry of the word and the sacraments, cooperate with one another."

For emphasis he repeated three times "the Spirit is here." He urged the council Fathers to reflect on "this present reality."

He said the Church, exploring its consciousness and uncovering the teaching of the Holy Spirit, must give a definition of itself.

"Thus must be completed the doctrine that the First Vatican Council was preparing to enunciate, but which external obstacles prevented it from defining, except in its first part dealing with the head of the Church, the Roman pontiff, and his sovereign prerogatives regarding primacy of jurisdiction and infallibility of teaching."

"The discussion on this doctrine," he continued, "remains to be completed in order to explain the mind of Christ on the whole of His Church and especially on the nature and function of the successors of the apostles, that is, of the episcopate . . .

"The council has many other important subjects to treat of, but this one seems to us to be the weightiest and most delicate. The council's deliberations on this subject will certainly be what distinguishes this solemn and historic synod in the memory of future ages."

Pope Paul said the council, in dealing with this subject, must take up some difficult theological issues:

—The nature and mission of the Church's pastors.

—The episcopate's "constitutional prerogatives."

—Relations between the world's bishops and the Holy See.

—The "constitutional idea of the Church under its differing Eastern and Western expressions."

—The hierarchical organization of the Church.

The Pope said the council must make this last point clear not only to Catholics "but also for the separated brethren."

The Pope then said the third session's "central objective" is "to investigate and clarify the doctrine of the nature of the Church." This clarification would integrate the work already done in the council's two previous sessions.

He said the "principal objective" of the council itself would be that of "describing and honoring the prerogatives of the episcopacy."

The "wholeness of Catholic truth," he said, calls for a clarification of the doctrine of the episcopacy, in consonance with the papacy.

But he pointed out that as the successor of Peter and therefore as possessor "of full power over the entire Church," he has "the duty of heading the body of the episcopate."

He emphasized that his position as pope "in no way defrauds you, our brother bishops, of your due authority."

After observing that the Church, as it extends throughout the world, has a greater need of centralized leadership, he said:

"No one should regard such centralization as a device put together by pride. It surely will always be tempered and balanced by an alert and timely delegation both of authority and of faculties for local pastors. We assure you, our brothers in the episcopate, that this centralization is rather a service and a manifestation of the unifying and hierarchical spirit of the Church."

The Pope added that centralization "strengthens rather than weakens the authority of bishops, whether that authority be considered in the individual bishop or in the collegiality of bishops."

It was recalled that on the eve of the council's second session, the Pope indicated his willingness to bring local bishops into the Church's central administration if the council expressed its desire for this.

The Pope wound up his speech by greeting all dioceses and parishes represented by the council Fathers, all priests, Religious, Catholic laity, the poor, the persecuted and the suffering, and especially "those whom the lack of freedom still prevents from coming to this council."

He also welcomed the lay auditors. Then he added his welcome to the as yet unnamed women among the auditors: "And we are delighted to welcome among the auditors our beloved daughters in Christ, the first women in history to participate in a conciliar assembly."

He said the invitation to the auditors was prompted by his "desire to give to the Christian community an ever-increasing sense of harmony, collaboration and charity."

He then turned to the non-Catholic observers "with reverence and esteem." He welcomed them and thanked them, and assured them of his intention of removing "every obstacle, every misunderstanding, every hesitancy."

He said that St. Paul's words, "all things to all men," might today be described as "pluralism in practice."

At the same time he drew attention to the same apostle's exhortation to "preserve the unity of the spirit in the bond of peace" because there is only "one Lord, one faith, one Baptism, one God and Father of all."

He continued: "We shall therefore strive, in loyalty to the unity of Christ's Church, to understand better and to welcome all that is genuine and admissible in the different Christian denominations that are distinct from us. And at the same time we beg them to try to understand the Catholic faith and life better and, when we invite them to enter into the fulness of truth and charity which, as an unmerited blessing but a formidable responsibility, Christ has charged us to preserve, we beg them not to take it in bad part, but as being prompted by respect and brotherly love."

The Pope then asked the observers to convey his greetings to the Christian communities they represent. He added: "May our respectful regard also reach those which are not represented here." He said the separated churches—"churches that are so far and yet so close to us"—are the churches of his "sleepless nights."

Finally he turned his thoughts "to the world about us, with its own interests, also with its indifference, perhaps even its hostility."

Before giving his apostolic blessing, he invited all the council Fathers to join him in invoking the help of the Holy Spirit on the labors that lie before them in the council's third session.   PATRICK RILEY

List of Concelebrants

Two Americans, a Canadian and a Mexican were among the 24 council Fathers who concelebrated Mass with Pope Paul VI to open the council's third session (Sept. 14). Three of the 24 were cardinals.

The Americans were Archbishop Lawrence J. Shehan of Baltimore and Archbishop John J. Krol of Philadelphia.

Also concelebrants were Archbishop Marie-Joseph Lemieux, O.P., of Ottawa and Archbishop Miguel Miranda y Gomez of Mexico City.

Others were:

Eugene Cardinal Tisserant, dean of the College of Cardinals; Giacomo Cardinal Lercaro of Bologna, Italy, and Arcadio Cardinal Larraona, C.M.F., prefect of the Congregation of Rites.

Archbishops Pericle Felici, general secretary of the ecumenical council; Matthew Beovich of Adelaide, Australia; Pedro Santos Songco of Caceres, Philippines; Jose de Almeida Batista of Brasilia, Brazil; Casimiro Morcillo Gonzalez of Madrid; Juan Aramburu of Tucuman, Argentina; Bernard Yago of Abidjan, Ivory Coast; Adrianus Djajasepoetra, S.J., of Jakarta, Indonesia; Pius Kerketta, S.J., of Ranchi, India, and Joseph Malula of Leopoldville, the Congo;

Coadjutor Archbishop Jean Villot of Lyons, France;

Bishops Wilhelm Kempf of Limburg, Germany; Policarpo da Costa Vaz of Guarda, Portugal; Laurentius Satoshi Nagae of Urawa, Japan, and Stanislaus Lokuang of Tainan, Formosa;

Abbot Benno Gut, O.S.B., abbot primate of the Benedictine Confederation, and Father Anastasio Ballestrero of the Most Holy Rosary, O.C.D., superior general of the Discalced Carmelites and president of the Roman Union of Religious Superiors.

Pope Paul's Speech

This is a translation of the Latin address delivered by Pope Paul VI to the opening meeting (Sept. 14) of the third session of the ecumenical council.

Under the sign of the Holy Cross, in whose honor we have concelebrated holy Mass, we open today the third session of the Second Vatican Ecumenical Council. The Church is present here. We are the Church. We are the Church as members of the Mystical Body of Christ, for God has granted us the inestimable favor of being baptized, of being believers united by love and constituting the consecrated and visible people of God. We are the Church since we are ministers of the Church herself, priests invested with a special character received at our sacramental ordination.

On us are conferred marvelous and tremendous powers, making of us a hierarchy entrusted with functions meant to perpetuate in time and to extend on earth the saving mission of Christ. We are the Church, finally, because as teachers of the Faith, pastors of souls, stewards of the mysteries of God (I Cor. 4, 1), we represent here the entire Church, not as delegates or deputies of the faithful toward whom our ministry is directed, but as fathers and brothers who personify the communities entrusted to the care of each one of us, and as a plenary assembly legitimately convoked by the Holy Father.

The Pope has called the council into session in his capacity, which links him with all of you, as your brother, the bishop of historic Rome, and as the humble but authentic successor of the Apostle Peter—before whose tomb we are devoutly gathered—and therefore as the unworthy but true head of the Catholic Church and Vicar of Christ, servant of the servants of God.

Recapitulating in our persons and in our functions the universal Church, we proclaim this council ecumenical. Here is the exercise of unity, here the exercise of that universality by which the Church gives evidence of her prodigious vitality, her marvelous capacity to make men brothers and to welcome within her embrace the most diverse civilizations and languages, the most individualized liturgies and types of spirituality, the most varied expressions of national, social and cultural genius, harmonizing all in felicitous union, yet always respecting legitimate variety and complexity.

Here is the exercise of the holiness of the Church because here she calls on the mercy of God for the weaknesses and deficiencies of the sinners that we are, and because here as nowhere else do we become aware of the power granted to our ministry to draw from the "unfathomable riches of Christ" (Eph. 3, 8) the treasures of salvation and sanctification for all men.

Here we realize that this ministry of ours has no other purpose than to "prepare for the Lord a perfect people" (Luke 1, 17). Here, finally, is made manifest the apostolicity of the Church, a prerogative which is a marvel even to us, to us who have experienced our own weakness and who know how history bears witness to the frailty of even the most powerful of human institutions.

And at the same time we know with what continuity and fidelity the mandate of Christ has been transmitted from the apostles to our lowly and ever astonished person. We know how inexplicably and how triumphantly the Church has endured throughout the ages, this Church which is ever living and always capable of finding in herself the irrepressible spirit of youth.

At this point we can repeat with Tertullian: "It is the whole Christian world which is here represented and which we venerate. And see how good it is that from all sides men are gathered because of faith in Christ! See how good and happy it is for brothers to dwell together!" (De Ieuniis, C. XIII; P.L. 11, 1024).

Now if the Church is here, here also is the Spirit, the Advocate, whom Christ promised to His apostles for the building up of the Church: "I will ask the Father and He will give you another Advocate to dwell with you forever, the Spirit of truth whom the world cannot receive, because it neither sees Him nor knows Him. But you shall know Him, because He will dwell with you, and be in you" (John 14, 16-17).

For there are, as we know, two factors which Christ has promised and arranged in different ways to continue His mission, to extend in time and on earth the kingdom He founded and to make of redeemed mankind His Church, His Mystical Body, His fulness, in expectation of His definitive and triumphant return at the end of time.

These two factors are the apostolate and the Spirit.

The apostolate is the external and objective factor. It forms the material body, so to speak, of the Church and is the source of her visible and social structures.

The Holy Spirit is the internal factor who acts within each person, as well as on the whole community, animating, vivifying, sanctifying.

These two agents, the apostolate which is entrusted to the sacred hierarchy, and the Spirit of Jesus, which uses the hierarchy as its ordinary instrument in the ministry of the word and the sacraments, cooperate with one another. Pentecost shows them wonderfully linked at the beginning of the great work of Jesus, who although invisible remains ever present in His apostles and their successors, "whom He set over His Church as His shepherds and vicars" (Preface, Mass of apostles). These two agents, differently yet harmoniously, bear equal witness to Christ the Lord in a combination that confers on apostolic activity its supernatural force (cf. 1 Pet. 1, 12).

May we believe that the salvific plan, by which the redemption of Christ reaches and is fulfilled in us,

is even now in action? Yes, my brethren, we may believe, indeed, that this plan is continued and actuated by our means, in virtue of a power and sufficiency that comes from God, "who has made us fit ministers of the new convenant, not of the letter but of the spirit . . . which gives life" (2 Cor. 3, 6). To doubt this would be an insult to Christ's faithfulness to His promises, a betrayal of our apostolic mandate, depriving the Church of her certainty, which the Divine Word has guaranteed and history has confirmed, and of her indefectibility.

The Spirit is here, not yet to confirm with sacramental grace the work which all of us, united in the council, are bringing to completion, but rather to illuminate and guide our labors to the benefit of the Church and all mankind. The Spirit is here. We call upon Him, wait for Him, follow Him. The Spirit is here.

Let us reflect on this doctrine and this present reality so that, above all, we may realize once more and in the fullest and most sublime degree possible our communion with the living Christ. It is the Spirit who joins us to Him. Let us reflect on this truth also that we may put ourselves before Him in trepidation, fully at His disposal; that we may become aware of the humiliating emptiness of our misery and the crying need we have of His help and mercy; that we may hear as if spoken in the secret recesses of our soul the words of the Apostle: "Discharging . . . this ministry in accordance with the mercy shown us, we do not lose heart" (2 Cor. 4, 1).

The council is for us a moment of deep interior docility, a moment of complete and filial adherence to the word of the Lord, a moment of fervent, earnest invocation and of love, a moment of spiritual exaltation. To this unique occasion the poetic words of St. Ambrose apply with a special aptness: "Let us drink in joy the sober inebriation of the Spirit" (Hymn at Lauds). Such for us should be this blessed time of council.

And finally we have this to say: The hour has sounded in history when the Church, which expresses herself in us and which from us receives structure and life, must say of herself what Christ intended and willed her to be, and what the age-long meditation of the Fathers, pontiffs and doctors in their wisdom has explored with piety and fidelity. The Church must give a definition of herself and bring out from her true consciousness the doctrine which the Holy Spirit teaches her, according to the Lord's promise: "but the Advocate, the Holy Spirit, whom the Father will send in my name, He will teach you all things and bring to your mind whatever I have said to you" (John 14, 26). "The Spirit Himself gives testimony to our spirit that we are sons of God" (Rom. 8, 16).

Thus must be completed the doctrine that the First Vatican Council was preparing to enunciate, but which external obstacles prevented it from defining, except in its first part dealing with the head of the Church, the Roman pontiff, and his sovereign prerogatives regarding primacy of jurisdiction and infallibility of teaching, which Christ was pleased to bestow upon the Apostle Peter, His visible vicar on earth, and upon those who succeed him in so sublime and tremendous an office.

The discussion on this doctrine remains to be completed, so as to explain the mind of Christ on the whole of His Church and especially on the nature and function of the successors of the apostles, that is of the episcopate, with which dignity and office the greater part of you, venerable Fathers, and we ourselves, most reverend brothers, are of God's good pleasure invested.

The council has many other important subjects to deal with, but this one seems to us to be the weightiest and most delicate. The council's deliberations on this subject will certainly be what distinguishes this solemn and historic synod in the memory of future ages. It must undertake a number of difficult theological discussions. It must determine the nature and mission of the pastors of the Church. It must discuss, and with the favor of the Holy Spirit, decide the constitutional prerogatives of the episcopate. It must delineate the relations between the episcopate and the Holy See. It must show how homogeneous is the constitutional idea of the Church under its differing Eastern and Western expressions. It must make clear for the faithful of the Catholic Church and also for the separated brethren the true notion of the hierarchical organs in which "the Holy Spirit has placed you as bishops to rule the Church of God" (Acts 20, 28), with unquestionably valid authority in the humble and patient service of the brethren, as becomes pastors—ministers, that is—of faith and charity.

These thoughts are all the more important for us, and certainly for you, venerable brothers, because of the fact that this third session of the ecumenical council has chosen from among its many concerns this central objective: to investigate and clarify the doctrine of the nature of the Church, thus resuming and integrating the work done in the first two sessions, and making this solemn synod the logical continuation of the First Vatican Council.

At this point the Church wants to study itself, or rather probe into the mind of Christ, its divine Founder: just what and how much to say in order to honor His wisdom and charity and, by restoring to Him the full practice of its faith and fidelity, to render itself an even more fit instrument in the work of salvation for which it was founded.

But in case anyone should think that in doing this the Church is closing in on itself in an attitude of complacency, forgetting on the one hand Christ, from whom it receives everything and to whom it owes everything, or on the other hand humanity, to whose service it is committed, it places itself between Him and the world, not satisfied with itself, not as a forbidding barrier, not as an end in itself, but deeply concerned to be completely the Church of Christ, in Christ and for Christ, as well as completely the Church of men, among men and for men, humble and yet glorious, the Church of the Saviour and yet reaching out to all men, preserving and yet diffusing the truth and the grace of the supernatural life.

In our time which seems to be blessed in a special way, this seems to be all the more true and important, for today the inquiry concerning the Church will have a point of great interest for us, and especially for you, namely the hierarchic structure of the Church itself, and consequently the origin, nature, function and power of the episcopate, which is a major part of the hierarchy, in which with us "the Holy Spirit has made you bishops . . . to keep watch . . . over God's Church" (cf. Acts 20, 28).

And so we have in mind to tune in with a plan of Divine Providence in celebrating this historic moment by giving to you, our venerated and beloved brothers in the episcopate, the honor which Our Lord desired to be shown to the apostles together with Peter.

The Fathers of the First Vatican Council defined and proclaimed the truly unique and supreme powers conferred by Christ on Peter and handed on to his successors. This recognition has appeared to some as having limited the authority of bishops, the successors of the apostles, and as having rendered superfluous and prevented the convocation of a subsequent ecumenical council, which, however, according to canon law has supreme authority over the entire Church.

The present ecumenical synod is certainly going to confirm the doctrine of the previous one regarding the prerogatives of the Roman pontiff. But it will also have as its principal objective the task of describing and honoring the prerogatives of the episcopate.

Let every one understand that the convocation of this council has been a free and spontaneous act on the part of our venerated predecessor of happy memory, John XXIII, an act which we have readily confirmed, knowing full well that the theme of this sovereign and sacred assembly would deal with the episcopate. It could not have been otherwise, taking into consideration not only the proper interconnection of the doctrines concerned but also because of a sincere determination to proclaim the glory, the mission, the merits and the friendship of our brothers entrusted with the work of instructing, sanctifying and governing the Church of God.

Let us repeat as our own those well-known words which our distant and saintly predecessor of immortal memory, Gregory the Great, wrote to Eulogius, Bishop of Alexandria: "My honor is the honor of the universal

Church. My honor is the strength of my brothers. I am thus truly honored when the honor due to each and every one of them is not denied to them" (8, 30, P.L., 77, 933).

The integrity of Catholic truth now calls for a clarification consonant with the doctrine of the papacy which will place in its splendid light the role and mandate of the episcopate. In its work of tracing the outlines of such a role and such a mandate, the council will be anxious about nothing except interpreting the thought of Jesus Christ at its true source and genuine origin.

We have already had the pleasure of recognizing in the bishops our true brothers, addressing them, as the Apostle Peter did, as "elders," and gladly claiming for ourselves the equivalent title of "fellow elder" (1 Pet. 5, 1). We have had the pleasure of addressing to them the words of the Apostle Paul: "My partners in tribulations and consolations" (cf. 2 Cor. 1, 7). We have been anxious to reassure them of those religious convictions that characterize our relations with them: esteem, affection, solidarity. We are bound by our duty to recognize them as the teachers, rulers and sanctifiers of the Christian people, the "stewards of the mysteries of God" (1 Cor. 4, 1), the witnesses to the Gospel, the ministers of the New Testament and, in a certain sense, the very reflection of the glory of the Lord (cf. 2 Cor. 3, 6-18).

As successors of Peter and, therefore, as possessors of full power over the entire Church, we have the duty of heading the body of the episcopate, although we are surely unworthy of this dignity. Nevertheless, our position in no way defrauds you, our brother bishops, of your due authority. On the contrary, we are among the first to respect that sacred authority. If our apostolic duty obliges us to impose restrictions, to define terminology, to prescribe modes of action, to regulate the methods which concern the exercise of episcopal authority, you realize that this is done for the good of the entire Church, for the unity of that Church which has proportionately greater need of centralized leadership as its worldwide extension becomes more complete, as more serious dangers and more pressing needs threaten the Christian people in the varying circumstances of history and, we may add, as more rapid means of communication become operative in modern times.

No one should regard such centralization as a device formulated by pride. Centralization will surely be always tempered and balanced by an alert and timely delegation both of authority and of facilities for local pastors. We assure you, our brothers in the episcopate, that this centralization is rather a service and a manifestation of the unifying and hierarchical spirit of the Church. It is the glory, the power, the beauty which Christ promised to His Church and which He gradually grants to it as the ages run their course.

Apropos of this topic, we can recall the words which Pius XII of happy memory addressed to a certain group of bishops: "This union and this timely communication with the Holy See arises, not from a kind of longing to achieve centralization and homogeneity, but rather from the divine law itself and from a truly fundamental principle affecting the very essence of the Church of Christ" (A.A.S., 1954, P. 676).

Such centralization strengthens rather than weakens the authority of bishops, whether that authority be considered in the individual bishop or in the collegiality of the bishops. O how deeply we admire, how staunchly we support the rights and duties proper to the sacred hierarchy, which is the very instrument, born of the charity of Christ, and fashioned by Him to complete, to communicate, and to safeguard the integral and fruitful transmission of the Treasures of Faith, of example, of precepts, and of favors bequeathed by Christ to His Church!

The hierarchy is the mother of the community of the faithful. It is the architect of its visible framework. It is the public representative which wins for the Church the titles of mother and teacher. It is the bearer of the riches of the sacraments, the conductor of the symphony of prayer, the inspiration of works of charity.

Placed at the head of the sacred institution, how could we fail to devote to it our solicitude, our trust, our support? How could we fail to defend it? What duty presses upon us with greater frequency, with graver consequence, or with deeper satisfaction than that of safeguarding the independence, the freedom, the dignity of sacred hierarchy throughout the world? Is it not true that this exhausting task has been the very fabric from which has been woven the tapestry of the history of the papacy, especially in these years of political upheavals?

Let us add one further thought to this tribute to the episcopate in order to show how much its intrinsic nobility and its effective charity are enhanced by the harmonious unity which must bind it in close union with the Apostolic See, and how much the Apostolic See needs you, venerable brothers.

For your part, dispersed as you are all over the world, if you are to give shape and substance to the true catholicity of the Church, you have need of a center, a principle of unity in faith and communion, a unifying power, such as, in fact, you find in this Chair of Peter. Similarly, we need to have you always nearby, to give more fully to the countenance of the Apostolic See its beauty, its human and historic reality, even to give harmony to its faith, to be an example in the fulfilment of its duties and a consolation in its times of stress.

So that, while we look forward to the clearer definition which the council's deliberations will give to the doctrine of the episcopacy, we here and now pay you honor, pledge to you our affection as brother and father, and ask of you cooperation and support. May the communion, which binds together the Catholic hierarchy in living faith and charity, emerge from this council deeper, stronger and more holy. It will be to the glory of Christ, the peace of the Church and the light of the world.

There is much more we would like to say on this question and on many others of the first importance which have been brought up for the attention of the council, but we do not wish to tax your patience.

However we cannot forego the pleasure of sending a special greeting at this moment from this Holy See to the various dioceses and parishes which you represent here; first of all to our beloved and esteemed priests who labor so unselfishly in collaboration with their bishops; and to Religious, striving for every perfection that will make them like Christ and of service to their fellow men; to the Catholic laity, working with the hierarchy for the good of the Church and for the good of society; to the poor, the persecuted and the suffering; and especially to those whom the lack of freedom still prevents from coming to this council.

We wish also to welcome the auditors here present. Their high ideals and outstanding merits are not secret to us. And we are delighted to welcome among the auditors our beloved daughters in Christ, the first women in history to participate in a conciliar assembly. The auditors—both men and women—will not be slow to realize that behind this welcome of ours lies our fatherly love for all groups who make up the people of God, our desire to give the Christian community an ever-increasing sense of harmony, collaboration and charity.

And now we turn to you, the observers, with reverence and esteem, for you have once more accepted our invitation to attend the council. We welcome and thank you. We wish to assure you once more of our purpose and hope to be able one day to remove every obstacle, every misunderstanding, every hesitancy that still prevents us from feeling fully "of one heart and one soul" in Christ, in His Church (Acts 4, 32).

For our part, we shall do everything possible to this end. We are fully aware that the restoration of this unity is something of no small moment, and we shall give it all the attention and the time that it calls for. It is something new, in contrast with the long, sad history which led up to the various separations, and we shall wait patiently for the conditions to ripen that will make possible a positive and friendly solution. It is something, too, of deepest significance, having its roots in the mysterious counsels of God, and we shall strive, in humility and faith, to dispose ourselves to deserve so great a grace.

We recall the words of the Apostle Paul, who brought the gift of the Gospel to all nations, seeking to become "all things to all men" (1 Cor. 9, 22), such an adaptability as we might today be tempted to call "pluralism in practice." At the same time we recall how the same apostle has exhorted us to "preserve the unity of the Spirit in the bond of peace" because there is only "One Lord, one faith, one Baptism, one God and Father of all" (Eph. 4, 2, 5-6).

We shall therefore strive, in loyalty to the unity of Christ's Church, to understand better and to welcome all that is genuine and admissible in the different Christian denominations that are distinct from us. And at the same time we beg of them to try to understand the Catholic Faith and life better and, when we invite them to enter into the fulness of truth and charity which, as an unmerited blessing but a formidable responsibility, Christ has charged us to preserve, we beg them not to take it in bad part, but as being prompted by respect and brotherly love. For that fulness of truth and charity will be made the more manifest when all those who profess the Name of Christ are reassembled into one.

Meanwhile, through you, our reverend and esteemed guests and observers in this council, we wish to send our cordial greetings to the various Christian communities which you represent. May our respectful regard also reach those which are not represented here. We gather together in our prayer and our affections all those members who are still parted from the full spiritual and visible wholeness of the Mystical Body of Christ; and in this yearning of our love and concern, our sorrow grows, our hopes increase.

O churches that are so far and yet so close to us, churches for whom our heart is filled with longing, churches that are the nostalgia of our sleepless nights, churches of our tears and of our desire to do you honor by our embrace in the sincere love of Christ!

O may you hear, sounding from this keystone of unity, the tomb of Peter, apostle and martyr, and from this ecumenical council of brotherhood and peace, the loving cry we send you! Maybe great distances still separate us, maybe it will be long before our full and effective meeting can be realized. But know for sure that already we hold you in our heart. May the God of mercies support our deeply felt yearning and hope.

And finally may our thoughts go out to the world about us, with its own interests, also with its indifference, perhaps even its hostility. We renew the greeting which we addressed to it from Bethlehem with our resolute purpose of placing the Church at the service of its spiritual salvation and of its social prosperity, to bring it peace and true happiness.

We invite you all now, venerable brothers, to call upon the Holy Spirit together, as we make ready to inaugurate the third session of this Second Vatican Council, and in the name of the Lord, with trust in the help of Mary Most Holy and of the holy apostles, Peter and Paul, we bestow upon you all our apostolic blessing.

80th General Congregation

September 15, 1964

The work of the third session of the ecumenical council got off to a fast start.

The council Fathers wound up debate on the seventh chapter of the schema on the nature of the Church on the very first day of deliberation. The chapter is entitled "The Eschatological Nature of Our Calling." It had been drawn up to express the wish of the late Pope John XXIII, who felt that a treatment of the Church would be incomplete without dealing with the members of the Church who are fully united with Christ in heaven while still united with the Church on earth, thus forming one Church.

Pope John's wish was pointed out by Michael Cardinal Browne, O.P., of the Roman curia, who presented the report on the draft chapter.

However, the chapter came under heavy fire from several sides.

Three speakers objected that although the chapter deals with eschatology—the doctrine of the last things, such as death, resurrection, immortality and judgment—it made no mention of hell.

Three other speakers objected that the chapter deals with the Church's calling from an individual and ascetic point of view, omitting the Church's social, historic and cosmic viewpoints.

A third criticism was that the role of the Holy Spirit was neglected. Both an Eastern-rite and a Latin-rite Father made this point.

The council meeting opened with a Mass of the feast of the Seven Sorrows of Mary, offered by Bishop Charles Vanuytven, O.Praem., a retired Belgian missionary in the Congo. He was celebrating the 40th anniversary of his consecration as a bishop.

During the Mass a group of lay auditors received Holy Communion.

Once the "extra omnes"—the call to all not officially entitled to be there during a meeting to leave the council hall — had sounded, Eugene Cardinal Tisserant, dean of the College of Cardinals, addressed the meeting as chairman of the Council of the Presidency. He urged the Fathers to heed Pope Paul VI's appeal for prayer and sacrifice for the council's success.

He also reminded the Fathers that the council's aim is pastoral rather than doctrinal and said that this has been the guiding norm in preparing all schemata.

He said he had observed "a very strong desire" on the part of many bishops that this should be the concluding session of the council. He said he could not make any predictions on this point, but he urged the Fathers to stick to the point in arguments and to avoid repetition.

As a further means of hastening debate he suggested that any Fathers with suggestions for revising canon law make them to the commission for the revision of canon law.

Cardinal Tisserant also spoke on the question of council secrecy. He expressed regret at "certain incidents" of past sessions involving a breach of secrecy and urged all present not only to be prudent and discreet but to observe their duty of secrecy concerning the council's discussions.

The moderator of the day, Gregorio Cardinal Agagianian, who is also president of the council's mission commission, said that the council must aim at concluding its deliberations as soon as possible but without compromising full liberty of expression.

Archbishop Pericle Felici, council general secretary, after making routine announcements about the distribution of documents, said that unless the council experts observe the regulations laid down for their conduct with the Pope's approval, they can be stripped of their status as experts. Therefore, he said, they should engage in no lobbying for any point of view, organize no factions, and take part in no publicity campaigns designed to spread a particular opinion.

Archbishop Felici also pointed out that the norms laid down for the conduct of experts give him power to stop the unauthorized distribution of documents in or near the council hall. He said he would be ready to use this power if the necessity arose.

He also asked the council Fathers to stay in their places throughout the morning session because there would be several communications about the council's work. The council hall's coffee shops would not open until 11 a.m., he said. He added that it would be "useless to knock on the doors."

Fourteen council Fathers then rose in succession to

offer their views—often critical—of the draft of chapter 7 on the Church.

Cardinal Agagianian then announced that since no other Fathers had asked for the floor on this chapter, debate on it was concluded.

This 80th general congregation of the Second Vatican Council, first of the third session, ended about 12:35 p.m. It had been announced that congregations would end at 12:30, half an hour later than in previous sessions.

Chapter 7, on which debate was concluded, consists of four paragraphs.

The first, entitled "On Our Call to Sanctification through Christ and Our Call to the Perfection of Holiness in Heaven," deals with the relation between the present life and eternal life.

The second notes that until the end of time the Church consists of some members in heaven, some undergoing purification (in Purgatory) and some still on earth.

The third states that the example of the saints encourages earthbound Christians in striving for heaven.

The fourth states that the union of Christians on earth with the blessed in heaven is a stimulus to the efforts of the former to glorify and love God—provided that these efforts are in union with the Church.

Cardinal Browne commented on this chapter, saying that it is a synthesis of the theology of the last things. He said the chapter makes generous use of the words of Christ and of the Apostles.

It asserts that the union with the saints does not hinder the love of the Blessed Trinity but rather fosters it.

The chapter aims at promoting union with the separated brethren, he said, pointing out that devotion to the saints has always been a characteristic of the Oriental Churches. This devotion, he said, is an aid to the appreciation of the common patrimony of the Faith. Even those who do not agree with this doctrine may at least recognize its riches, he said.

Speakers on the chapter were: Ernesto Cardinal Ruffini of Palermo, Italy; Giovanni Cardinal Urbani of Venice; Rufino Cardinal Santos of Manila; and Laurean Cardinal Rugambwa of Bukoba, Tanganyika;

Latin-rite Patriarch Alberto Gori, O.F.M., of Jerusalem;

Archbishops Enrico Nicodemo of Bari, Italy; Justin Darmajuwana of Semarang, Indonesia; Ignace Ziade of the Maronite Rite See of Beirut; and Maxim Hermaniuk, C.SS.R., of the Ukrainian Rite See of Winnipeg; Bishop Pont y Gol of Segorbe, Spain; Coadjutor Bishop Leon Elchinger of Strasbourg, France; Abbot Christopher Butler, O.S.B., of Downside, England; and Archbishops Segundo Garcia of Burgos, Spain, and Louis Mathias, S.D.B., of Madras and Mylapore, India.

Cardinal Ruffini said: "The chapter's use of Scripture is admirably generous but lamentably imprecise. The chapter lacks good structure and order and therefore needs recasting."

Cardinal Urbani said: The chapter is generally acceptable except for the points mentioned by Cardinal Ruffini.

Cardinal Santos said: The chapter completes and enriches the whole schema.

Patriarch Gori said: The text fails to speak about the possibility of eternal damnation—in other words, the existence and eternity of hell. This is needed to check today's hedonism.

Archbishop Nicodemo, in the name of the bishops of the Apulia region of Italy, said: The chapter's title is too long. The chapter should mention hell lest the council's presentation of the last things be incomplete.

Archbishop Darmajuwana said: The chapter should be omitted since it says nothing not already common knowledge.

Archbishop Ziade said: There can be no mention of the eschatology of our calling without mention of the Holy Spirit. The Latin rite is still an adolescent in its understanding of the Holy Spirit. The Eastern Churches would be displeased by this omission from a solemn document.

Archbishop Hermaniuk said: The chapter should emphasize the sacramental union of the faithful with Christ in the Eucharist. It should also stress the need for vigilance in awaiting the coming of Christ.

Bishop Pont said: The chapter gives the Church a transcendent coloring but the schema never gives a parallel exposition of the Church's immanent aspect—doctrinal base—of its presence in the world.

Bishop Elchinger said: The chapter explains the personal aspect of our vocation in relation to the last things but lacks a treatment of the social, historical and cosmic aspects of the Christian vocation.

Abbot Butler said: The chapter fails to mention the Holy Spirit except in a "calamitous" passage seeming to say we give adoration to the Father and the Son but not to the Holy Spirit.

Archbishop Garcia said: It is too diffuse in its expression and too thin in its substance.

Archbishop Mathias said on behalf of several bishops that the chapter is satisfactory.

* * * *

The U.S. Bishops' press panel started its daily meetings during the ecumenical council's third session amid confusion on the part of journalists over the role of experts and what was allowed them in the light of the panel's new rules.

One of the most popular sessions in Rome during the last sessions of the council, not only for journalists but for anyone else who could crowd into the basement of the USO club, the panel this session was limited "strictly to the working press." Obviously, though, concessions were made to former panel members and a few others.

Rumors that the panel would have a different look were borne out when introductions were made. Elmer Von Feldt, director of the panel, explained that changes were also made at the last session when four former panel members were not present. He said that the panel was chosen by Archbishop Joseph T. McGucken of San Francisco with a view to obtaining "the best possible team after consultation with several others."

The archbishop said others would be called upon from time to time to discuss aspects of their particular fields, but that the present panel would be the regulars.

Before beginning work, the journalists and panel members stood for a moment in private prayer for two members missing from the last time—Father Gustave Weigel, S.J., a member of the press panel in 1963, and Milton Bracker, correspondent of the New York Times, who covered the 1963 session of the council. Both died shortly after the 1963 session ended.

Some concern was expressed by several journalists over restrictions on the experts announced on Dec. 28, 1963, by the council's Coordinating Commission and reiterated at the opening meeting of the third session by Archbishop Pericle Felici, general secretary of the council.

Father Robert Trisco pointed out these were not new restrictions but that perhaps more stress was being placed on them this time. He said they were "never expressed quite so bluntly before."

The restrictions on the experts—called norms—are three:

1—Experts are restricted to answering questions put them by the commission or council Fathers.

2—They are forbidden to lobby, establish factions or currents of thought, or to divulge or defend their private opinions on council matters.

3—They are to abstain from criticizing the council or council Fathers and from instructing outsiders on the secret business of the commissions.

Not included in norms, but threatened by Archbishop Felici at the first meeting, was that experts failing to follow these directives would be liable to lose their status as experts. Father Trisco said this was something new, and had not been announced after the Coordinating Commission's meeting in December. But he said that Archbishop Felici announced that he had such power.

Others on the panel said they felt that the new rule would not impose new restrictions or change the method of operation for journalists, since the experts have always been bound to such secrecy. As for restrictions on

lobbying and expressing personal opinions, there did not seem to be much hope among the panel that this would be observed too strictly.

Von Feldt pointed out that the panel has always had it as its purpose to provide background, even though at times panelists have expressed their personal views. He said it is perhaps true that the purpose of the panel had not always been properly stressed, and thus the present guidelines have been drawn up.

Following are the "ground rules" under which the press panel of the U.S. Bishops is operating during the third session, a panel spokesman said:

1. The U.S. Bishops' Press Panel has been established through the National Catholic Welfare Conference, the secretariat of the American bishops, as a service for working reporters. Unfortunately, limitations of space demand that briefing sessions be limited to the working press, with the consequent exclusion of seminarians, guests and spectators.

2. The purpose of the press panel is to make available to newsmen the professional help of specialists who can provide factual, theological and background information and clarification, which may be desirable to develop fully their reports on the council. The panel is not designed to provide a forum to promote the personal opinions or projects of individuals, whether panel members or journalists. In view of this purpose, questions by reporters, aimed at soliciting the personal opinion of the panel members, will be ruled out of order.

3. Panel members may be quoted, but the clarifications and background information they provide should not be represented as coming from the universities, colleges or institutions to which these men are attached.

4. Reporters are free to ask any questions seeking clarification or background information on a subject currently being considered by the Council Fathers. If a reporter has questions which are not on the subject, he is asked to contact the panel director. Arrangements will be made for a panel member to answer his questions fully, but in private. This procedure will avoid wasting the time of other reporters.

5. All reporters should identify themselves and their publications before giving their questions.

The following is what the press release described as an "initial listing" of members of the press panel at the third session:

Father Francis J. Connell, C.SS.R., former dean of the School of Sacred Theology of the Catholic University of America. Moral Theology. From Boston.

Msgr. Mark J. Hurley, chancellor of the Stockton (Calif.) diocese. Education. From San Francisco.

Father John J. King, O.M.I., superior of the General House of Studies in Rome for Oblate priests. Dogmatic Theology. From Lowell, Mass.

Father Francis J. McCool, S.J., professor of introduction to the New Testament at the Pontifical Biblical Institute in Rome. Sacred Scripture. From New York.

Father Frederick McManus, professor of Canon Law at the Catholic University of America. Canon Law and Liturgy. From Boston.

Msgr. George W. Shea, rector of Immaculate Conception seminary, Darlington, N.J. Dogmatic Theology. From Belleville, N.J.

Father George Tavard, chairman of the theology department of Mount Mercy College, Pittsburgh. Theology and Ecumenism. From France.

Father Robert Trisco, professor of Church History at Catholic University of America, and editor of Catholic Historical Review. Church History. From Chicago.

81st General Congregation

September 16, 1964

Leo Cardinal Suenens of Malines-Brussels, Belgium, appealed to the ecumenical council to streamline and simplify the canonization procedure so that the Church may recognize persons of all classes, nations and callings as saints.

He also suggested that regional conferences of bishops be empowered to beatify holy persons and that canonizations by the Holy See be reserved for saints of international importance.

The cardinal spoke at the third council session's second working meeting. He was one of three speakers who continued debate on the seventh chapter of the schema on the nature of the Church, despite the previous day's announcement that all speakers had had their say on that chapter. The chapter deals with eschatology—the last things, such as death, resurrection, immortality and judgment.

Of the 14 council Fathers who spoke on the schema's eighth chapter—on the Virgin Mary—four said it would be better for various reasons to drop the term "mediatrix" from the council's treatment of her. Augustin Cardinal Bea, S.J., president of the Secretariat for Promoting Christian Unity, was among them.

Ernesto Cardinal Ruffini of Palermo, Italy, defended the use of this title and asked only that it be more fully explained.

Some speakers indicated that they were simply resigned to incorporating the former schema on the Blessed Virgin Mary into the schema on the nature of the Church as a simple chapter. They indicated they felt that the undertaking made by council authorities not to diminish the role of the Blessed Virgin Mary in this chapter had not been honored.

The 81st general congregation of the Second Vatican Council began with the votive Mass of the Holy Spirit celebrated by Archbishop Hyacinthe Thiandoum of Dakar, Senegal. Madrid's Archbishop Casimiro Morcillo Gonzalez enthroned the Gospel. Giacomo Cardinal Lercaro of Bologna, Italy, was the day's moderator.

Archbishop Pericle Felici, council general secretary, announced that all Fathers wishing to address the council on the schema on pastoral duties of bishops had to put their names in on that day (Sept. 16). It was announced that Sept. 18 would be the deadline for registering for debate on the council's declarations on the Jews and religious liberty.

By an overwhelming majority the council accepted a streamlined voting procedure for the schema on the nature of the Church. The vote was 2,170 to 32. Two ballots were null.

At the end of the session, a vote was taken on chapter one of the schema. The results were not immediately announced.

The day's meeting included two statements: one by Archbishop Maurice Roy of Quebec on chapter eight and one on the entire schema by Bishop Andre Charue of Namur, Belgium.

Archbishop Roy, who spoke when the final three speakers on chapter seven had finished, said chapter eight has its place in the schema on the Church because of the inner link between the Blessed Virgin and the mystery of Christ and the Church.

The chapter is aimed at presenting a broad view of Our Lady's role in the Church without entering into controversial points.

The first part of the chapter handles Mary's role as illuminated both by Scripture and Tradition. The second part speaks of her cooperation with Christ in the work of salvation. The third part applies this teaching to devotion to the Blessed Virgin Mary, and also applies it to preaching.

Archbishop Roy noted that the title "mediatrix" — mediator — which is used in the chapter is not acceptable to all members of the council's Theological Commission. He asserted however that the chapter explains the title in such a way as to avoid obscuring Christ's sole mediatorship.

Bishop Charue spoke toward the end of the discussion on Mary. He said his statement had been prepared for delivery at the last session of the council, but had been crowded out by other events.

He asked the Fathers to avoid voting on the schema "placet juxta modum," which means voting with specified reservations. Such voting, he said, would considerably slow the work of the revising commission. He assured the Fathers that the commission would take all criticism of the schema into consideration despite the hoped-for absence of "placet juxta modum" votes.

The speakers on chapter seven were Cardinal Suenens, Auxiliary Bishop Alfred Ancel of Lyons, France, and Bishop Biago D'Agostino of Vallo di Lucania, Italy.

Speakers on chapter eight were Cardinal Ruffini; Cardinal Bea; Stefan Cardinal Wyszynski, Primate of Poland; Julius Cardinal Doepfner of Munich and Freising, Germany; Paul Cardinal Leger of Montreal; Raul Cardinal Silva Henriquez of Santiago, Chile; Archbishop Adrianus Djajasepoetra, S.J., of Jakarta, Indonesia; Archbishop Octaviano Marquez Toriz of Puebla, Mexico; Archbishop Corrado Mingo of Monreale, Italy; Bishop Giuseppe Ruotolo of Ugento, Italy; Bishop John Abasolo y Lecue of Vijayapuram, India; Bishop Eduard Necsey of Nitra, Czechoslovakia; Bishop Juan Hervas y Benet of Ciudad Real, Spain; and Bishop Placido Maria Cambiaghi of Novara, Italy.

Cardinal Suenens said that the Church aims at producing saints and that canonizations provide officially recognized examples of sanctity. For effectiveness they should include persons from all nations, classes and callings, he said. But in fact, he added, since canonizations began in the eighth century, Religious have accounted for about 85% of all canonizations and three European nations have had 90% of them.

The canonization process should be revised for three reasons, he said.

First, they are too slow and thus are deprived of much of their effectiveness, since the person canonized has become a part of history instead of a living memory.

Second, they are too expensive, thus effectively excluding laymen.

Third, they are too centralized, thus causing delays.

The beatification process, Cardinal Suenens said, could be left to local conferences of bishops and the persons to be beatified could thus be honored in their own countries. Canonization, a strict preserve of the Holy See, would be for those with international reputation for holiness, he added.

The distinction between the saints and the blesseds was vague in the early Church, and the terms canonization and beatification did not come into use until the 12th century. Through the beatification process, which centers on determining the sanctity of a person who has died, the Church declares the person blessed and permits some restricted public veneration of him or her. Beatification is neither an infallible nor an irrevocable process.

Canonization on the other hand is a solemn declaration that the person is listed in the official canon, or roll, of the saints in heaven who are to be venerated on earth. Canonization is held by theologians to be an infallible act which requires—not simply permits, as in the case of beatification—that the saint be accorded public honor by the church.

Bishop Ancel said the text should clarify the fact that the eschatological character of our vocation extends into all activities of our life.

Bishop D'Agostino said the text of the chapter should stress the need for personal holiness and include a reminder of hell.

Cardinal Ruffini said that Mary's title of "mediatrix" should be explained to make it clear to non-Catholics that it takes nothing away from Christ, the only mediator before God. The text gives insufficient importance to Mary's association in the redemption, he said, and does not explain why Mary is our mother.

Cardinal Wyszynski, speaking in the name of all 70 bishops of Poland, said the Polish bishops have asked Pope Paul VI to make official acknowledgment of the spiritual motherhood of Mary for all men. They also want the council to call Mary the "Mother of the Church." The Polish people attribute their tenacity in keeping the Faith to their devotion to Mary, he stated.

Cardinal Leger said that clear and accurate terms should be used in describing Mary's vocation. He added that the text does not present positive correctives for the abuses it cites.

Cardinal Doepfner spoke in the name of 90 bishops of Germany and Scandinavia. He said the chapter should not say too much about Mary as mediatrix, since this could lead to controversy. He said objections could be anticipated by bolstering the text's assertions with Scriptural quotations, and urged that the text's terminology should be modified to show that Mary shared in our redempion but in a more sublime fashion.

Cardinal Silva called on Scripture scholars to reexamine the text. Too much is said of the mediation of Mary and not enough of Christ's, he said, speaking in the name of Jose Cardinal Quintero of Caracas, Venezuela, and 43 other Latin American bishops.

Cardinal Bea said that criticism of the chapter springs only from a desire to protect the Church's interests and should not be seen as a reflection on the devotion of the critic. The chapter fails, he stated, to keep the promise not to enter into theological controversies. He added that practical directives about abuses should be given and that the text should be more precise. The use of the word mediatrix causes very serious difficulties for the separated Christians, Cardinal Bea noted. He spoke overtime but asked permission to finish. It took one minute for this.

Archbishop Djajasepoetra pointed out that the text says Mary "appeared significantly in the public life of Christ." It would be more precise, he continued, to say she disappeared significantly. He said the term "mediatrix" should not be used because, although Catholics may be able to make proper distinctions in the matter, pagans cannot.

Archbishop Marquez declared that although the spiritual motherhood of Mary seems to be the basis for the chapter, it is not mentioned specifically. There should be such a declaration, though not a definition, he said.

Archbishop Mingo said the schema had not only been revised, but had been radically altered. Its omission of Mary's association in the work of redemption is not understandable, he stated.

Bishop Ruotolo said the chapter should stress the newness of life which devotion to Mary gives.

Bishop Cambiaghi was applauded when he said Cardinal Ruffini and others had made his points, so he would yield.

Bishop Hervas said the chapter should be given its old title "Mary, Mother of the Church." Despite assurance last year that incorporation of the schema on Mary as a chapter in the schema on the Church would not weaken it, it has been altered, he claimed.

Bishop Abasolo said Mary's marriage with Joseph should be mentioned since it would offer example to Christian couples.

Bishop Necsey said the chapter should stress that the internal renovation of the Church, which is the aim of the council, can be achieved through devotion to Mary. Such devotion would also be an antidote to nefarious modern trends such as abortion, which murders legions of children yearly, he said.

* * * *

The ecumenical council proposal of Leo Cardinal Suenens of Malines-Brussels that beatification be placed within the competence of local groups of bishops may have been a compromise proposal, according to Father Frederick McManus, American canon law expert.

Speaking at the U.S. bishops' press panel, Father McManus said that Cardinal Suenens proposed only that the beatification procedure be changed, leaving cases of canonization to the pope. Father Francis J. Connell, C.SS.R., moral theologian, pointed out the difficulty in giving bishops competence in canonizations in the light of the "common teaching of theologians that the declaration of canonization is infallible."

Father McManus explained that canonizations were formerly the responsibility of individual bishops. Only during the Middle Ages were they reserved to the pope, and in the 16th century the Congregation of Rites took over.

The 1917 Code of Canon Law laid down the procedures to be followed in beatifications and canonizations, which include elaborate procedures on the local level followed by thorough investigation by the Congregation of Rites.

Auxiliary Bishop Philip M. Hannan of Washington explained that the procedure is longer in the Western Church—the Latin rite—because emphasis is placed on virtues and miracles. He said that the Eastern rites' procedures for canonization place greater stress on the need for the candidates' bodies to remain incorrupted.

The panel experts agreed that Cardinal Suenens' proposal is definitely pastoral in nature, since the local bishops would be more competent to decide which beatifications would best stir the devotion of local populations.

82nd General Congregation

September 17, 1964

By an overwhelming majority the ecumenical council has passed what might be termed a "little statement on the Jews." It calls the Jews "the chosen people most dear to God."

This was included in chapter two of the schema on the nature of the Church. The council passed all eight articles of the chapter by very broad majorities.

In the same voting the council also approved an amendment strongly urged at the last session by Bishop Robert E. Tracy of Baton Rouge, La., making it clear that in the people of God, that is in the Church, there can be no distinction based on race.

Speaking on non-Catholics, the schema says "those who have not yet accepted the Gospel are in various ways oriented to the people of God.

"In the first place is that people to which the covenants and promises were given and from which Christ sprang, the chosen people most dear to God because of the patriarchs."

The council's highly publicized statement on the Jews will be debated in the council hall itself—following months of debate in the world press—after the council completes its discussion of the schema on the Church and the schema on the bishops and the government of dioceses.

Discussions on the third session's fourth day were focused on chapter eight of the schema on the Church, devoted to the Blessed Virgin Mary. The outstanding point at issue was the schema's use of the title "Mother of the Church."

The papal sacristan, Bishop Peter van Lierde, not only defended the title but even suggested the chapter itself should be called "Mary, Mother of the Church" or "Mary, Mother of All Believers."

Auxiliary Bishop Alfred Ancel of Lyons, France, said he would accept the title in a spirit of harmony, provided the council did not put too bold a stamp of approval upon it. He said he would accept the title "mediatrix" for Mary in the same spirit, even though the intervention the previous day by Augustin Cardinal Bea, S.J., head of the Secretariat for Promoting Christian Unity, had convinced him that the Church's teaching on this question had not sufficiently matured.

Bishop Primo Gasbarri, apostolic administrator of Grosseto, Italy, warned that Catholics would be scandalized if the council failed to adopt the term "Mother of the Church" used by Pope Paul VI.

Archbishop Rafael Garcia y Garcia de Castro of Granada, Spain, supported this argument by pointing to the use of such a term by Pope Benedict XIV. Speaking in the name of more than 80 bishops, he said he hoped the council would not take from Mary a title given her by the popes.

However, Bishop Sergio Mendez Arceo of Cuernavaca, Mexico, declared that Pope Leo XIII was the first pope to use this title. He said Pope St. Pius X cautiously referred to Mary as "the Mother of the members of the Mystical Body," and Pope Pius XII was equally careful. Pope John XXIII used the title, but Pope Paul always used it "conditionally," he said.

Considerable interest was aroused when Archbishop Jozef Gawlina, Polish member of the Roman curia, quoted Martin Luther. The prelate was arguing that devotion to Mary is not an obstacle to unity. He cited a sentence from Luther's exposition on St. Luke's Gospel, in which he stated: "Mary does not wish to lead us to herself, but through herself to God."

The 82nd general congregation of the council began with a votive Mass of Christ the High Priest offered by Bishop Giuseppe Angrisani of Casale Monferrato, Italy. Archbishop John J. Krol of Philadelphia enthroned the Gospel. Giacomo Cardinal Lercaro of Bologna, Italy, remained as moderator since debate was continuing on the same chapter of the schema.

Archbishop Pericle Felici, secretary general of the council, announced the results of the previous day's voting on the whole of chapter one of the schema on the Church. Out of 2,189 votes, there were 2,114 "yes" votes and 11 "no" votes. Sixty-three Fathers voted "yes" with reservations, and one vote was null.

Archbishop Felici said he hoped the Sept. 17 vote on chapter two would go quickly. The following day (Sept. 18), he said, the Fathers would receive schedules for the expedited vote on chapter three.

On Sept. 18, the council was to begin debate on the schema on bishops and the government of dioceses.

The archbishop announced in the names of the moderators that all summaries of speeches to be made dealing with the schema on revelation must be submitted by Sept. 25. The deadline for summaries of speeches on the lay apostolate was set at Sept. 28. Written criticism of schema 13 on the Church in the modern world or any other schema to be discussed would have to be submitted by Oct. 1.

Archbishop Gabriel Garrone of Toulouse, France, acted as "relator" for the third chapter of the schema on the Church, which was being readied for a vote. He said the text describes the Church in its actual situation as well as in its totality. The text shows that both the pastors and the laity belong to the people of God. The hierarchy springs from the faithful as a means of achieving the Church's purpose. Therefore, the text emphasizes that the hierarchy renders service to the people of God, he said.

The four votes on the second chapter, which includes article nine to article 17 of the schema, were:

Articles nine to 12: 2,173 "yes", 30 "no" and seven votes null.

Article 13: 2,186 "yes," 12 "no" and four votes null.

Articles 14 to 16: 2,048 "yes," 48 "no" and three votes null. This included the statement on the Jews.

Article 17: 2,106 "yes," 67 "no" and one vote null.

Other speakers during the session were Leo Cardinal Suenens of Malines-Brussels, Belgium; Bishop Francisco Rendeiro of Faro, Portugal; Archbishop Lorenz Jaeger of Paderborn, Germany; Bishop Andrea Sapelak, apostolic visitor for the Ukrainian-Rite Catholics in Argentina; Bishop Wilhelm Kempf of Limburg, Germany; Bishop Leon de Uriarte Bengoa, O.F.M., for San Ramon, Peru; Father Aniceto Fernandez, O.P., master general of the Dominican Order; Father Alfonso Maria Monta, O.S.M., prior general of the Servite Order; Bishop Julien Le Couedic of Troyes, France; and Archbishop Aurelio Signora, pontifical delegate for the sanctuary of Pompei.

Cardinal Suenens said that from a doctrinal point of view the schema says too little. He added that it does not put enough emphasis on Our Lady's spiritual motherhood and the modern Church. The text, he continued, is too prudent and timid, and places insufficient stress on the deep link between Mary and the work of Christ.

Making Christ the center of all things is good, he said, but this should not be carried to the point of denying Mary's role.

From a pastoral viewpoint, the cardinal stated, the text fails to show the connection between Mary's spiritual motherhood and the apostolate. Just as Christ historically was born of the Holy Spirit and the Virgin Mary, he said, so Christ mystically was born and grows through the Holy Spirit and Our Lady.

Bishop Rendeiro said the schema is afraid of being too superlative in praise of Mary, and should proclaim Mary's title as "mediatrix." The text on mediation, he went on, should be left as it is. It would be a scandal to Catholics, he said, if the council discusses mediation and then rejects the word "mediatrix" in its pronouncement.

Bishop Sapelak said more stress should be placed on Mary's role as the protector and helper of the Christian people because this is her most important role in the Church.

Bishop van Lierde said the chapter's title fails to show Mary's intimate relation with the Church. He said a new title could be "Mary, Mother of the Church" or "Mary, Mother of All Believers." He declared that there are several gaps in the text: no mention is made of Mary's resolve to lead a life of virginity, of her motherly influence in rearing the Child Jesus or of her cooperation with the Holy Spirit. He also said the text has whittled down her influence in the early Church to the help of her prayers.

Archbishop Gawlina said that far from being an obstacle to Christian unity, devotion to Mary promotes it. He called such devotion a "bridge to ecumenism." He cited Luther's statement on Mary and pointed out that separated Eastern-Rite Christians have a tender love for Our Lady. He added that when he was in the Soviet Union he was struck by the people's deep devotion to Mary. This, he continued, served as a bridge between himself and the Orthodox, who asked him for the sacraments.

Archbishop Jaeger said the text should make it clear that Mary, like the Church, is animated and vivified by the Holy Spirit who dwells in her as in a noble temple.

Bishop Ancel said Cardinal Bea's talk had changed his mind about the maturity of the teaching on the title of "mediatrix" for Mary, as well as the title "Mother of the Church." He said both these titles could be used in the text if this did not seem to give them theological approval.

Bishop Kempf said Mary's cooperation in the economy of salvation needs to be brought out of mere biography and interpreted with theological applications.

Bishop De Uriarte said the fact that Mary is the Mother of Jesus is the starting point for all other conclusions, but that the text mentions this fact only twice and then not as starting points for argument but as mere statements of fact. He said that Mary is the mother of Catholics, Orthodox, Protestants, Moslems and of all men, believers and non-believers alike. She is the mother of the Church, he said.

Father Fernandez said the schema protests too much that Mary should not be called equal to Christ. Leaving the text as it stands, he stated, could give future generations the impression that some Catholics of our time maintain that Mary is the equal of Christ and that the Second Vatican Council had to correct this error. For the same reason, he continued, the Fathers should delete the caution warning preachers against using expressions that could give separated Christians the wrong impression of the Church's teaching on Mary.

Father Monta said the text's argumentation must be examined closely since it seems to be going in a circle. Instead of saying that Mary is a supereminent member of the Church, it would be better to discuss her as a spiritual mother, he stated. The priest said the council must not fear stating Catholic beliefs about Mary because great harm has always come to the Church from any attempt to deemphasize doctrine on the mother of God.

Archbishop Garcia said Mary must be given the title of "Mother of God" in the text. Pope Paul and earlier popes used it, he noted. He said that arguments for the title can be found in the works of St. Ireaneus and St. Leo the Great. Council Fathers should either speak as the popes have spoken or keep silent, he said.

Archbishop Signora said there should be reference to the Rosary, which has been called the "breviary of the faithful."

Bishop Le Couedic said the council should avoid the use of titles such as "mediatrix" and "coredemptrix" lest confusion arise.

Bishop Mendez said the Fathers should agree on a text that will eliminate any danger that the Church will appear divided before the world. The title "Mother of the Church" is too foreign to the traditions of the Eastern Church, and too recent to have a place in the council's declarations, he said. Noting that Pope Leo XIII was the first to use the title, Bishop Mendez stated that if the Church is our mother, then Mary as mother of the Church would be our grandmother.

The simple fact of not using the title would not imply condemnation of it, he said. He noted that the Mexican bishops have asked for a definition of Mary's motherhood of all men, not of her spiritual maternity over the Church. Mary is a sign of unity in the Church, he added, and should not be turned into a sign of division.

Bishop Gasbarri said that if from the ecclesiological point of view Mary is the most noble member and the first-born daughter of the Church, then from a Christological point of view she is the Mother of the Church because she is the mother of Christ. Some ecumenists desire a minimal statement on Mary, he said, but the Church's chief duty is to keep and proclaim the deposit of faith. He said the existing text presents only a brief biography of the Blessed Virgin which is beneath the dignity of a council discussion.

* * * *

A statement giving the opinion of Biblical scholars in Rome indicating that there is not sufficient basis in the Bible for the doctrine of episcopal collegiality was distributed to the Fathers of the ecumenical council on the opening day of the third session.

It was disclosed at the meeting of the U.S. bishops' press panel that copies of the statement were distributed to the council members by Archbishop Pericle Felici, the council's general secretary.

The concept of episcopal collegiality has emerged as one of the most important doctrinal issues to be debated by the council Fathers.

In brief, the concept means that the bishops of the world with the pope form a body, or college, which is the successor to the 12 Apostles, and as such a divine institution responsible as a whole for the mission of the Church on earth.

Father Francis J. McCool, S.J., of New York, a member of the faculty of the Pontifical Biblical Institute here, said the Scripture scholars' opinion was requested by Archbishop Felici "at the command of the Pope" last May 27. The request was sent to the secretary of the Pontifical Commission for Biblical Studies. Since an urgent response was requested, in time for the meeting of the council coordinating commission on May 31, Father McCool said, only the consultors of the Biblical commission residing in Rome were consulted.

The American Jesuit said that the signers of the statement of opinion include one bishop and other priest consultors of various nationalities, but only those residing in Rome. (The current Vatican directory lists 12 residents of Rome among the total of 31 consultors to the Biblical commission.)

Asked the substance of the statement, technically labeled a "votum," Father McCool said:

"Its form seems negative, indicating there is not sufficient Scriptural basis for the doctrine of collegiality. The phrase used, 'non constat' (it is not clear), would give this impression. However, some exegetes [interpreters] might find Scriptural basis for collegiality from the very texts used in the votum."

Press panel members could offer no explanation as to why the May request for the Biblical scholars' statement was so urgent that there was no time to seek the opinion of members or consultors of the Biblical commission who were not in Rome. Some panelists voiced the thought that the idea to pinpoint the Scriptural basis for the doctrine of collegiality might have been a last-minute decision preceding the meeting of the Coordinating Commission four days later.

(It was explained later that the term "votum" as applied to the Biblical commission consultors' statement is not the same as the "votum" which is a pronouncement of the council Fathers.

(A council "votum" is the least important pronouncement by the council Fathers. Next comes a "proposition." Then a "decree." Then the most important type of conciliar pronouncement, a "constitution."

(Msgr. Mark Hurley, chancellor of the Stockton, Calif., diocese, a member of the American press panel, said that another form of conciliar statement is a "declaration." This does not fit into any of the other four categories, he said, but is treated in the same way as a decree or a constitution—that is, that it is debated, voted on tentatively, amended, and then given a final vote in the presence of the Pope, who in turn promulgates it in a plenary council session.

(Msgr. Hurley said that the council's celebrated statements on religious liberty and on Christian-Jewish relations have the status of declarations.)

* * * *

The schema on the status of the Church in the modern world in its present form was judged inadequate by a Dutch theological expert.

Father Edward Schillebeeckx, O.P., spoke at the opening of the Netherlands bishops' new documentation center here in the presence of Bernard Cardinal Alfrink of Utrecht and numerous bishops and guests.

Father Schillebeeckx charged that the schema is based on "a conception that is still too dualistic regarding the Church's relationship to the world, as if the latter were beyond the scope of her saving mission, while the historic task of humanity is stressed, but insufficiently, and not enough emphasis given to apostolic secularity and secular sanctity."

The speaker added that God's love for man implies the justification of all efforts tending toward the improvement of living conditions for all mankind and toward a better world generally. This should not lead to an underevaluation of the secular sphere of life, which not only should be seen under supernatural perspectives but should be accepted as a reality to be redeemed, he said.

Religious practice starting from different premises as a monologue rather than a dialogue, the speaker said, would disregard "the intrinsic autonomy of the world and be alien to the concept of the world created by divine will, a world given to man as implicitly Christian and destined to become humane and more in keeping with man's dignity as the image of God."

Another council theologian at the same time spoke out against what he called a "triumphalism alien to the Church" which "always remains on pilgrimage in its existence on this earth." He was Father Otto Semmelroth, S.J., of Frankfurt, Germany, who addressed the German bishops' council press center here.

He was referring particularly to the veneration of saints, which was under discussion on the council floor. He said such veneration sometimes may appear as "veiled polytheism," while in reality it only should be an expression of a proper tribute to heroes of the Faith and should not be exaggerated. It is in this sense that the intercession of saints in heaven should be understood as a "triumph" in heaven of which their earthly experience is but a sign indicating the potential of future glory.   FATHER PLACID JORDAN, O.S.B.

83rd General Congregation
September 18, 1964

Council Fathers began debate on one of the most sensitive areas of the Church's institutional life, the exemption of certain religious communities from the full authority of local bishops.

Three Jesuit bishops and a Dominican cardinal sprang to the defense of such exemptions at the council's third working meeting of the current session.

It became clear from their remarks that the schema on the pastoral duties of bishops attempts to give more power to local bishops over the work of priests who are members of exempt religious congregations, while leaving these congregations full autonomy in their internal life.

Debate on this schema began after three final speakers wound up debate on the chapter in the schema on the nature of the Church dealing with Our Lady.

Coadjutor Archbishop Pierre Veuillot of Paris, presenting the report of the Commission for Bishops and the Government of Dioceses, which had drawn up the schema, announced that it contained a new article on the appointment of bishops. This amounted to a declaration of independence from civil authorities in the matter of naming bishops.

The schema urges those who now have the power to name bishops to give it up. (This appeared to refer to the Spanish government. However, the Spanish government's power of naming bishops is closely circumscribed and qualified.)

The schema also makes it clear that it does not prejudice agreements giving certain governments the right to review episcopal appointments. (Most of the recently concluded pacts give governments the right to make objections to episcopal nominations before they are made public.)

Richard Cardinal Cushing of Boston was present at a meeting for the first time this session. He told a priest acquaintance that he had come especially to make interventions during the debate on the council's statements regarding the Jews and religious liberty.

The day's debate began with a speech by Joseph Cardinal Frings of Cologne, Germany. Through an error he was the first speaker to be called, although he had prepared to address the council's Theological Commission rather than the council itself. The topic at this point was the chapter on Mary.

Cardinal Frings said the debate on the chapter on the Blessed Virgin had shown it would be impossible to secure the necessary majority to approve it. Therefore, a compromise would be necessary, and all should be ready to sacrifice personal opinions, he said.

Two other speakers benefited from the regulation providing that a council Father may speak in the name of at least 70 other Fathers after the formal debate has ended.

Bernard Cardinal Alfrink of Utrecht, the Netherlands, said much confusion over the chapter on Mary stemmed from confusion over the chapter's purpose, which was doctrinal rather than devotional. The task of the council, he said, is to determine what is taught and not what is thought. In this regard, he continued, the Fathers must recall that the conciliar decree will be binding, and they must be aware that there is no question of stating too much or too little, but only of stating what is true.

Cardinal Alfrink, a Scripture scholar, said Mary is not mediatrix in the strict spiritual sense, although Catholics grant that she had a very personal role in the plan of God. He asked whether it is proper to retain a title that might cause confusion and widen the gap between the Church and non-Catholics.

The third speaker offered a rebuttal to an attack made the previous day by Bishop Sergio Mendez Arceo of Cuernavaca, Mexico, on Mary's title as "Mother of the Church."

Bishop Laureano Castan Lacoma of Siguenza, Spain, speaking in the name of 80 bishops, deplored Bishop Mendez' "levity" in asserting that if Mary is the Mother of the Church—which is in turn the mother of men—then Mary is our grandmother. He said the same sort of logic if applied to the hierarchical structure of the Church would make bishops grandfathers, since bishops are the fathers of priests and priests are fathers of the laity.

The council Fathers were deprived of some of the expected debate when arguments for and against the controversial chapter three of the schema were delivered in printed form. This chapter deals with the collegiality of the bishops, the central point at issue in the council.

Archbishop Pietro Parente, a top official of the Congregation of the Holy Office, presented the favorable arguments, and Bishop Frane Franic of Split, Yugoslavia, set forth the difficulties in the chapter.

The council also approved chapter two of the schema on the Church, which it had approved section by section the previous day, by a vote of 1,615 to 19. There were 553 who favored the chapter with reservations, and three votes were null. The total votes cast were 2,190.

Archbishop Pericle Felici, general secretary of the council, announced that although the vote of unqualified approval was well beyond the required two-thirds, the commission would carefully study all suggested changes offered by those who had reservations.

In his explanation of the schema on the pastoral duties of bishops, Archbishop Veuillot emphasized that the schema's theological doctrine was necessarily founded on the theology the bishops expounded in the schema on the nature of the Church. (Voting on the latter schema's chapter dealing with bishops was to open Sept. 21.) Archbishop Veuillot pointed out that if any pertinent part of this fundamental schema were changed by the council, then the text he was presenting would also have to be changed.

He said the schema distinguished between the power of bishops and their ministry.

The day's moderator, Julius Cardinal Doepfner of Munich and Freising, Germany, urged speakers to stick to the point. As events were to show, he was prepared to make them do so.

Paul Cardinal Richaud of Bordeaux, France, led the speakers' list. He complained that the schema left too many problems to the Commission for the Revision of Canon Law. The council, he said, should give the commission sufficient guidance on what is to be done and the go-ahead to do it. Among problems to be dealt with, he said, were the competence of national episcopal conferences and the use of archbishops as courts of appeal for disagreements in an individual diocese.

Michael Cardinal Browne, O.P., a member of the Roman curia, opened fire on the schema's treatment of exempt religious orders. A Dominican, he is a member of the first active order to be exempted from full authority of local bishops and made subject directly to the Holy See.

Cardinal Browne took the exact opposite tack from Cardinal Richaud, urging that all treatment of Religious should be left for the projected revision of canon law. The schema, he said, makes Religious too rigorously subject to local bishops. He asserted that the international apostolate carried out by Religious should not be confined by the authority of bishops.

Cardinal Browne objected to what he called the schema's presupposition that the mission of preaching comes from episcopal consecration.

Three Jesuits rallied around Cardinal Browne in his defense of the exemption of Religious: Archbishop Frederick Melendro, S.J., of Anking, China; Bishop James Corboy, S.J., of Monze, Northern Rhodesia; and Massachusetts-born Bishop John McEleney, S.J., of Kingston, Jamaica.

Archbishop Melendro asserted that Religious cannot have two superiors, their religious superior and the local bishop. He also urged that there be regular ecumenical councils.

Cardinal Doepfner stepped in when he judged Archbishop Melendro was getting off the subject under debate, and when Archbishop Melendro again wavered from the subject, Cardinal Doepfner asked him to step down and hand in his speech.

Bishop Corboy criticized the schema for speaking with too little force of the general authority of bishops and too much force of the particular authority of bishops over Religious. He said the fundamental weakness of the schema is its failure to provide an adequate justification for exemption. He said any weakening of exemptions would weaken the Church's missionary effort.

Bishop McEleney opened with the assertion that difficulties between Religious and bishops in matters of the apostolate cannot be avoided. He said he saw two ways of dealing with such unavoidable difficulties. One would be to diminish the pope's authority over Religious. This, he said, would lead to a crisis in religious life and consequent harm to both the Church and the diocese. Yet this was the method put forward by the schema, he stated. The other way would be to erect a special commission to handle such difficulties, he said, and suggested that the schema be recast along this line.

Bishop Luigi Carli of Segni, Italy, one of the council's most frequently heard bishops, attacked the handling of collegiality. He said the schema assumes that a bishop exists first for the whole Church and then for his own diocese, whereas the contrary is correct. He pointed out that persons exist first and organizations afterwards.

In support of his thesis that a bishop derives his relationship to the universal Church from his relationship to his own diocese, he pointed to the history of the institution of titular bishops. When the Church began creating titular bishops, it emphasized that they were attached to a real—though defunct—diocese. He also urged the council to beware of treating Our Lady with extreme caution and treating bishops with extreme liberality.

Bishop Jean Rupp of Monaco complained that the schema fails to take into account the modern phenomenon of migration which carries the people from diocese to diocese in numbers undreamed of in past ages.

Bishop Antonio Pildain Zapain of the Canary Islands asked that the Holy See be assured of complete freedom in the appointment of bishops. Cardinal Doepfner called him to order when he appeared to stray from the point at issue.

Archbishop Armando Fares of Catanzaro, Italy, urged that the schema declare that the chief pastoral duty of bishops is that of protecting their flock from error. He also complained that the schema, in abolishing a direct link between some dioceses and the Holy See and making all dependent upon metropolitan Sees, was not showing sufficient respect for the dignity of some of these Sees.

Bishop Maksimilijan Drzecnik of Maribor, Yugoslavia, asked for inclusion of a chapter on pastoral sociology. He said each diocese should have a commission on pastoral sociology to gather information on and study the religious life of the diocese.

Bishop Brian Foeley of Lancaster, England, asked for more emphasis on the pastoral care of souls. Recalling that L'Osservatore Romano, Vatican City daily, had praised a priest for visiting 620 families in a year, he said in his opinion that was nothing more than his simple duty. Cardinal Doepfner called him to order.

Bishop Federico Kaiser for Caraveli, Peru, asserted that bishops who feel they have too few priests to spare any for the missions should recall Christ's words about giving clothes to the poor: Christians were to give away one tunic not if they had many but if they had only two.

Archbishop Robert E. Lucey of San Antonio, Tex., recalled the statement of Pope St. Pius X that religious ignorance was so prevalent among the faithful that the duty of catechetical teaching must have been either poorly performed or entirely neglected. He urged the importance of the Confraternity of Christian Doctrine.

Cardinal Doepfner interrupted Archbishop Lucey to ask what points in the schema he would like to see changed. Archbishop Lucey replied simply, "dixi" (I have spoken), and returned to his place.

When asked later whether he thought Cardinal Doepfner had acted correctly, he replied smilingly: "Cardinals are never wrong."

Bishop Manuel Larrain Errazuriz of Talca, Chile, offered a votive Mass of the Holy Spirit at the opening of the meeting. The Gospel was enthroned by Bishop Wilhelm Kempf of Limburg, Germany.

* * * *

An American archbishop indicated here that the ecumenical council was in favor of establishing some kind of international body of bishops to cooperate with the Pope in the government of the universal Church, and said that thus it is up to the Pope to make the next move.

Archbishop Joseph T. McGucken of San Francisco, the prelate in charge of the American Hierarchy's press panel, spoke on this aspect of collegiality at a press panel session on the eve of the week designated for the council's vote on the third chapter of the schema, or draft statement, on the nature of the Church.

Archbishop McGucken told the press that this third chapter expresses the desire of the council Fathers to participate in the government of the whole Church.

"It would seem then," he said, "that the next move would be up to the Pope to set up a group of bishops for this purpose."

The San Francisco prelate also said:

"The improvement in communications, the proximity of peoples and the like demand more collaboration than was possible through the old practice of a periodic consistory in Rome. Nor is the Roman curia sufficiently international to know the needs of all areas of the Church. Besides, it is not an obligation of office for the curia, as it is for the bishops."

The consensus of the bishops that they desire to take part in the government of the whole Church is contained in the third chapter's 21st, 22nd and 23rd paragraphs, in which the doctrine of episcopal collegiality is expressed, it was revealed at the press panel session.

Various panel members indicated that while the chapter expressed the bishops' desire to cooperate with the Pope in the government of the Church, it was not clear what form of participation the bishops were seeking. Father Frederick R. McManus, canon law professor at the Catholic University of America, Washington, disclosed that the schema does not use the word "senate." He said the Latin word used is "coetus," which means "assembly" or "body" rather than "senate."

Father McManus said this word was previously approved by the council. It is contained in the second article of the schema's first chapter, which was voted on favorably, he said. He indicated he expected that since the word "coetus" is mentioned again in the third chapter, it would be approved there as well. But he reiterated that this provision for a bishops' "assembly" is not at all specific.

84th General Congregation

September 21, 1964

The pros and cons of collegiality—the supreme power of the College of Bishops to teach, rule and sanctify the Church—came vividly before the council Fathers in a capsule debate organized by officials of the council (Sept. 21).

The outstanding point at issue was whether this teaching would weaken or endanger the Pope's primacy in any way.

Bishop Frane Franic of Split, Yugoslavia, declared that it would. Archbishop Pietro Parente, No. 2 administrator of the Congregation of the Holy Office, denied this. Both men spoke on behalf of the council's Doctrinal Commission, which drew up the draft of the constitution "De Ecclesia" (On the Church), incorporating the concept of collegiality.

This departure from the customary procedure in presenting a schema was ordered by the council's coordinating commission, the presidents and moderators. Instead of the usual announcement explaining the commission's reasons for drafting or altering the schema, one spokesman presented objections to the schema and two others explained the schema as it stood.

Archbishop Parente presented the commission's defense on the subject of collegiality while Auxiliary Bishop Luis Henriquez Jimenez of Caracas presented the commission's defense of a permanent and noncelibate diaconate. This debate occupied so much of the council's time that only five council Fathers were able to continue regular debate and only four of an announced six votes could be taken.

The first speaker in the regular debate was Paul-Emile Cardinal Leger of Montreal who said paternalism in the hierarchy is outmoded. He got applause when he urged that the council consider revising the dress and titles of clerics.

The first vote was on the text stating that the bishops are the successors of the apostles and the pope is the successor of St. Peter. This was passed by 2,166 to 53 with one null.

The second vote was on a passage declaring that the apostles were organized in the manner of a college with Peter in charge, to exercise the mission of salvation in the world. This passed by a smaller majority—2,012 in favor, 191 against, with three null.

In the course of the meeting, Archbishop Parente informed the council Fathers that two of their number had died earlier that day—Archbishops Jozef Gawlina and Leone Nigris, both of the Roman curia. Recalling that Archbishop Gawlina had spoken before the council in praise of the Blessed Virgin only four days earlier, Archbishop Parente voiced a prayer that the Polish prelate would be received by her in heaven.

Eugene Cardinal Tisserant, dean of the College of Cardinals and chairman of the council of the presidency, complained that certain council experts were violating the restrictions imposed on them by giving conferences and that some members of the doctrinal commission had distributed literature criticizing the statements that were to be presented that day on collegiality.

Archbishop Pericle Felici announced that the doctrinal commission had requested that Bishop Franic's statement listing objections to chapter three of the schema be presented along with the statements in defense of it.

Franziskus Cardinal Koenig of Vienna, who introduced the statement defending the text, declared that the two statements, for and against, were not to be understood as majority and minority reports from the doctrinal commission. He said the entire commission had approved the text of both statements.

(However, Bishop John J. Wright of Pittsburgh, a member of the doctrinal commission, told newsmen at a meeting of the U.S. Bishops' Press Panel, that Bishop Franic "spoke in great part for himself. It was not a minority report. It was the mind of the commission unanimously that Archbishop Parente's relatio [statement] presented the mind of the commission."

(Bishop Wright said that Bishop Franic asked if he could state the "difficulties lingering in the mind of a few.")

Bishop Franic's objections were directed against the concepts of the sacramentality of the episcopate and episcopal collegiality and the restoration of a permanent diaconate, either married or celibate.

He admitted that most theologians agree the episcopacy has sacramentality with the impression of a distinct character. But he felt the question was not yet sufficiently settled for a conciliar statement.

Turning to collegiality, he said the doctrine stated in the schema does not safeguard the teaching on papal primacy of the First Vatican Council. If the bishops were to receive full and supreme power from Christ Himself by virtue of their episcopal consecration, and are sharers even on a subordinate level of this supreme power, a diminishing of the Pope's primacy would be inevitable, he held.

The schema uses Scripture and tradition to buttress its teaching that the episcopate has supreme power by divine institution, Bishop Franic said. But he asserted that the schema's basic Scriptural proof from St. Matthew (18, 18) fails to establish that the power there given to Peter was also given to the apostolic college united to its head. He said the Pontifical Biblical Commission, in its reply to a question on this very point, backed him up.

(In May Archbishop Felici asked the Biblical commission to give its opinion on whether the Bible offers sufficient basis for doctrine of collegiality. The commission had four days in which to reply. In an opinion signed only by those of its consultors who live in Rome, the commission said it is not clear that the Bible gives foundation for the doctrine of collegiality.)

Bishop Franic said "many Fathers" are convinced that tradition offers no proof for collegiality. All arguments marshaled from tradition in the schema were known to the early Church fathers and teachers, and especially to the popes, yet all affirm that only the pope has full power received immediately from Christ, while the bishops take power immediately from the pope and only indirectly from Christ.

Bishop Franic rejected the distinction that these popes were speaking only of the exercise of jurisdiction and not of the jurisdiction itself.

He admitted that the proposed doctrine could be true but he insisted that it is not ripe enough to warrant a decision.

He added that collegiality, unless fully explained, would restrict not only the Pope's power but even the power of individual bishops in their dioceses.

Bishop Franic raised no doctrinal arguments against restoration of a permanent diaconate. But he argued that to restore it without making celibacy binding upon deacons has already been understood as a first step to abolishing priestly celibacy.

Cardinal Koenig then explained the method followed by the doctrinal commission in altering the schema. He urged the council to vote for the text.

Archbishop Parente prefaced his argument by declaring that he spoke not as assessor of the Holy Office but as titular archbishop of Thebaide. He noted that the ancient African see of Thebaide now lies in a desert. He said he hoped he was speaking "only as a voice from the desert, not as a voice in the desert."

He asserted that the text should allay any fears that collegiality would rouse ancient ghosts of the conciliar heresy of Gallicanism.

Archbishop Parente then said that the Pontifical Biblical Commission had confirmed the text's assertion that collegiality is of divine institution according to the letter and spirit of the New Testament.

He said the continuance of collegiality in the successors of Peter and the other apostles follows logically from the continuance promised by Christ to His Church. This is confirmed by the documents of tradition, he said.

The schema insists, he said, that the college of bishops has no authority except in union with the pope, understood as its head. This, said Archbishop Parente, forestalls erroneous interpretations; the text reiterates that collegiality implies no lessening of papal primacy.

The text emphasizes the full, supreme and universal power of the Pope as the Vicar of Christ, he continued. It says the body of bishops succeeds the college of the apostles in the power to teach and govern. It states that the body of bishops, with the Roman Pontiff at its head, and never without this head, is likewise a subject of supreme and full power over the universal Church.

This assertion is based on the 28th chapter of St. Matthew, he said, in which Christ gave His commission to the college of the apostles as a whole. The assertion is supported by the 18th chapter of St. Matthew, he said, where the power of binding and loosing given to Peter is likewise conferred on the other apostles.

The schema avoids the question of whether the holder of this power is one or plural, Archbishop Parente said. He added that in any case there is still only one power.

He said there is no validity to the objection against the word "full" used to modify the power of the Pope alone, and then to the power of the Pope and bishops in union with him.

However, he did admit difficulty arising from the use of the word "supreme" in those two ways. He said both difficulties disappear upon consideration of the fact that Christ instituted not a twofold power in the Church but only one power, and that He conferred it upon the entire apostolic college composed of Peter and the other apostles. Hence, the supreme power of the Pope remains intact, he said.

He asserted that participation of the bishops in the government of the Church makes the Pope's primacy more solemn and "more palatable" (Latin suavior).

Archbishop Parente also said that the schema does not contradict the teaching of Pope Pius XII in "Mystici Corporis" that episcopal power is derived from Christ through the Roman Pontiff: "Our text sets forth clearly that this power, though derived from Christ, is understood only in dependence upon the Roman Pontiff, both as regards its existence, because of the organic structure of the Church, and as regards its exercise."

Bishop Henriquez Jimenez delivered the section of the statement dealing with the restoration of the diaconate as a permanent order. He said the schema does not prescribe such a re-establishment for the whole Church but contents itself with leaving such a restoration up to national episcopal conferences, with the Pope's approval. He said the same schema merely leaves the door open for married deacons.

At the end of statements the voting began. During the balloting, five council Fathers spoke on the schema under debate, that on the pastoral duties of bishops.

The speakers were Cardinal Leger of Montreal; Carlo Cardinal Confalonieri, Secretary of the Consistorial Congregation; Bishop Enrico Compagnone, O.C.D., of Anagni, Italy; Archbishop Agnelo Rossi of Ribeirao Preto, Brazil; and Bishop Rudolf Staverman, O.F.M., for Sukarnapura, Indonesia.

Following is the gist of their points:

Cardinal Leger: The council's aim is pastoral and therefore demands new methods of teaching and governing. Today's men have a different approach from that of a generation ago: they are technical-minded, they reject any paternalism in the hierarchy or clergy, their idea of obedience safeguards their personal responsibility. To be pastorally effective, bishops and priests must be personally present among their flock. Archaic ecclesiastical language may be one reason why we are like voices crying in the wilderness. Diocesan chanceries should be reorganized on more pastoral lines. There is room for reform in clerical dress and titles.

Cardinal Confalonieri: Pastors must pay special attention to people without a fixed residence such as immigrants and sailors.

Bishop Compagnone: The primary contribution of the Religious to the apostolate is prayer, expiation and example. The zeal for the apostolate should not make bishops focus attention exclusively on what merely appears to be a greater good. The danger of abusing the contribution of Religious to the apostolate must be forestalled by determining concrete legislation in the future code of canon law.

Archbishop Rossi: A fresh look might be taken at the ancient concept of what constitutes a diocese.

Bishop Staverman: While bishops must be Fathers, they must remember that not everybody in their flock is a child. Bishops should be the very first to give the cooperation that all desire; if they take the lead the clergy and laity will follow.

A bulletin paraphrased the rest of Bishop Staverman's speech: "It is encouraging to see in the text a reference to the need of showing merciful attention to fallen priests, but there is likewise an element of sadness when we realize the practical impossibility of doing much to relieve their unfortunate situation. We cannot hold out a really helping hand [without] a more farsighted solution to their problems, one which is free of worry over consequences, a worry which is a sign of weak faith. A solution must be found which will be in keeping with today's mentality. There will be differences according to nations and localities, but it seems necessary to set aside the unduly rigoristic approach which has heretofore characterized all handling of the question."

This 84th general congregation of the council had opened with the Mass of St. Matthew, the feast of the day, celebrated by Massachusetts-born Bishop Frederic Donaghy, M.M., exiled Bishop of Wuchow, China, who is now a missionary in Formosa and who is marking his silver jubilee as a bishop. The Gospel was enthroned by Illinos-born Bishop Adolph A. Noser, S.V.D., for Alexishafen, New Guinea. Julius Cardinal Doepfner of Munich was the moderator. PATRICK RILEY

* * * *

Will the constitution on the Church present an infallibly-defined doctrine on the place of bishops in the structure of the Church?

Not as presently stated, according to Bishop John J. Wright of Pittsburgh, a member of the theological commission, which framed the document.

The words used in the text of the schema are "the council solemnly teaches" but not "the council defines," Bishop Wright said. "So far, the council has not asked for a solemn definition with all its niceties and careful distinctions. What seems to be called for is an 'authentic teaching' of the Church on collegiality," he said.

Speaking at a press panel after the first voting on the crucial chapter three of the Church schema which deals with collegiality, Bishop Wright further pointed out that "it is not the business of the theological commission to impose doctrine on the council, but to fulfill the council's wishes in framing the text."

So far, it is still at the option of the council Fathers whether the constitution will include a solemn definition, said Msgr. George W. Shea, a member of the press panel and rector of Immaculate Conception seminary, Darlington, N.J.

Father George Tavard, chairman of the theology department at Mount Mercy College, Pittsburgh, added that he "would be surprised if this council did bring up a solemn definition.

"It does not seem to be in the pastoral spirit of the council," he said.

Taking the words used by Archbishop Pietro Parente, an official of the Congregation of the Holy Office, in presenting the schema, Bishop Wright described the chapter as "historic" for three reasons.

"First, it completes the work of the First Vatican Council," he said. "Second, it integrates the juridical and organizational structure of the Church into theology properly so-called. Third, it opens at an organic level of the Church the possibility of enormous intensification of the life of the Church on all levels of activity, including more corporate action on the part of all bishops, the pooling of energies in missionary endeavors and the passionate interest on the part of all bishops in the whole Church rather than merely in their own dioceses."

* * * *

Pope Paul VI disclosed the name of the first woman auditor to be authorized to attend the council's sessions as Marie Louise Monnet, president of the international movement for the apostolate among independent social circles.

The Pope made the disclosure after the Sunday Mass he celebrated (Sept. 20) in St. Peter's in the presence of delegates of the movement which is a form of the apostolate among non-working women. Miss Monnet is the sister of Jean Monnet, one of the fathers of the European unity movement.

Miss Monnet was born Sept. 25, 1902, at Cognac in southwestern France. At Cognac she started the movement of Catholic independent youth which was organized on the pattern of the Young Catholic Worker movement. It brought together young people of professional, middle class or aristocratic backgrounds and spread throughout France.

In 1941 she turned over the leadership of the movement to younger people and founded the Independent Catholic Action movement, with the support of Bishop Jean-Baptiste Megnin of Angouleme and later of Achille Cardinal Lienart of Lille. This movement centered on gathering together adults of the same social origin for apostolic work.

In 1949 Miss Monnet worked through Msgr. Giovanni Battista Montini of the Papal Secretariat of State —now Pope Paul VI—to develop the movement on an international level. Its first international congress was held in 1958 at Lourdes. In 1963 the Secretariat of State approved the statutes of the new international organization, which goes by the French title, Mouvement International pour l'Apostolat des Milieux Sociaux Independents.

85th General Congregation

September 22, 1964

By an overwhelming majority the Second Vatican Council voted to approve the teaching that all Catholic bishops today are successors of the apostles by divine institution and that they, with the pope as their head, make up a college like that which was formed by St. Peter and the apostles.

Thus at the 85th general meeting of the Second Vatican Council, the work of the First Vatican Council, begun almost 100 years ago, has been advanced significantly. The First Vatican Council defined the infallibility of the pope but was adjourned before the precise relation of the bishops among themselves and to the pope was worked out.

At the same time, while affirming the divine origin of the episcopate and of its intimate union with the pope in the College of Bishops, the council Fathers also affirmed by vote that the College of Bishops has no authority except with the Roman pontiff, the successor of St. Peter, as its head. It affirmed that his power of primacy over all, both bishops and faithful, remains intact.

During the Sept. 22 meeting eight votes were taken and eight passed with tremendous majorities. These votes approved the changes in the third chapter of the schema on the nature of the Church dealing specifically with the place of the bishops within the Church and their relations to each other and to the pope.

The voting at the 85th session brought to 12 the number of amendments to the project that have been approved. In all there are 39 amendments to be voted on. Among the remaining ones, the most significant is the one which states that the College of Bishops together with the pope and never without him have full teaching and ruling power over the universal Church.

The amendments and votes cast Sept. 22 — the totals of which are greater than the individual tallies because they do not include the "yes" votes with reservations, which are not supposed to be made on amendments — are as follows:

Fifth amendment — That bishops are the successors of the apostles by divine institution. Total votes, 2,448; "yes," 2,198; "no," 50; null ballots, 0.

Sixth amendment — That the episcopacy is a sacrament. Total votes, 2,246; "yes," 2,201; "no," 44; null ballots, 1.

Seventh amendment — That the fulness of the sacrament of Holy Orders is conferred through episcopal consecration. Total votes, 2,240; "yes," 2,117; "no," 123; null ballots, 0.

Eighth amendment — That episcopal consecration, together with the duty of sanctifying, also confers the powers of teaching and ruling, which by their nature can be exercised only in union with the head of the college and other bishops. Total votes, 2,247; "yes," 1,917; "no," 328; null ballots, 1.

Ninth amendment — That only bishops through conferring Holy Orders may assume new members into the episcopal body. Total votes, 2,243; "yes," 2,085; "no," 156; null ballots, 0.

Tenth amendment — That just as Christ willed that St. Peter and the other apostles made up one apostolic college, in the same way the Roman pontiff and the bishops as successors of St. Peter and the other apostles are joined together. Total votes, 2,243; "yes," 1,918; "no," 322; null ballots, 2.

Eleventh amendment — That a person is raised to the episcopacy by virtue of consecration by members of the college and with communion with the Roman pontiff. Total votes, 2,213; "yes," 1,898; "no," 313; null ballots, 1.

Twelfth amendment — That the College of Bishops has no authority except with the Roman pontiff, the successor of St. Peter, as its head, and that his power of primacy over all, both bishops and faithful, remains intact. Total votes, 2,205; "yes," 2,114; "no," 90; null ballots, 0.

In addition to the votes taken on Sept. 22, the results of two votes taken Sept. 21 on amendments three and four were announced. They were:

Third amendment — That the mission of the bishops endures until the end of time. Total votes, 2,211; "yes," 2,103; "no," 106; null ballots, 1.

Fourth amendment — That the mission of the apostles is the mission of the bishops as that of St. Peter is that of the popes. Total votes, 2,207; "yes," 2,091; "no," 115; null ballots, 1.

The council session opened with a Mass celebrated by Archbishop Maurice Roy of Quebec. The Gospel was enthroned by Coadjutor Bishop Geraldo Pellanda of Ponta Grossa, Brazil. Eighteen bishops spoke, including six Frenchmen. Debate continued on the schema on the pastoral duties of bishops.

It was announced that debate was to begin Sept. 23 on the declaration on religious liberty, although one more speaker was still scheduled to discuss the schema on bishops.

In general, the day's debate dealt with relations between priests and bishops and called for the use by bishops of more scientific sociological knowledge to meet the great changes of modern times, and for greater cooperation and understanding between bishops and Religious working in their dioceses.

Bishop Louis Guyot of Coutances, France, opened the session, speaking in part for all the bishops of France. In the name of the French bishops, he called for a reorganization of all texts dealing with priests and the priesthood. He said that at present references are scattered through several projects and propositions and that there is a lack of organization which does not make it easy to have a theological vision of the role of the priest.

Then speaking for himself alone, Bishop Guyot made a plea for closer relations between bishops and their priests. He asked for a pastoral dialogue and stated that bishops should not have just personal contacts with priests but that teamwork is vital. The day's moderator, Julius Cardinal Doepfner of Munich and Freising, Germany, informed him that his time was up.

Bishop Alexandre Renard of Versailles, France, stressed essentially the same idea as Bishop Guyot, saying that bishops and priests need each other and that a bishop should not be only an administrator to his priests.

Bishop Richard Guilly, S.J., of Georgetown, British Guiana, spoke in the name of 17 council Fathers. He criticized the schema for considering relations between bishops and Religious only in terms of the individual diocese. He stated that Religious should be at the disposition of the pope and that it would be well not to strike too deeply at the exemption of Religious from diocesan authority lest they not be available to the pope.

Archbishop Joseph Urtasun of Avignon, France, called for collaboration between bishops and Religious, saying they should form a single family. Teamwork was called for again and the Archbishop stressed particularly the need for it in terms of interparish activities.

Bishop Pablo Barrachina Estevan of Orihuela-Alicante, Spain, said it is basic from a pastoral viewpoint that the diocese be looked on as a model or miniature of the universal Church. He warned that bishops should not favor some priests more than others because of the income which comes with the individual's assignment.

To do away with this problem he recommended that bishops take steps to reduce differences and inequalities.

Archbishop Emile Guerry of Cambrai, France, urged that more stress be put on the bishops' duty of didactic preaching. He said that the modern world calls bishops to a new form of preaching because they are called on to appear in civil life and should be heard on civil and social problems. Bishops need to be aware of the social problems of the day and need the explicit knowledge of the social order they can gain from laymen, he said.

Archbishop Guerry admitted that this would take courage and humility and the gift of clarity.

Bishop Jean Sauvage of Annecy, France, said he felt the schema talked too much of the relation of priests to bishops and that it should also stress that of bishops to priests and the bond of unity which should exist between them.

Archbishop Eugene D'Souza of Bhopal, India, echoed the call for cooperation between bishops and Religious. Saying that in some cases Religious fear falling under a diocesan dictatorship, he warned that there must be give and take on both sides.

Religious should not push their privileges, he said. To safeguard their interests he suggested they be given a place on national episcopal conferences or that a mixed commission of bishops and Religious be set up. Lastly he warned against what St. John Chrysostom called "those icy words — yours and mine."

Another Frenchman, Auxiliary Bishop Marius Maziers of Lyons, deplored the lack of a pastoral tone in the schema and called for emphasis to be placed on poverty, simplicity, humility and the need for being near the people.

A similar note was sounded by Coadjutor Bishop Herbert Bednorz of Katowice, Poland, who wanted stress to be placed on the care of souls. He emphasized the need for a missionary spirit and said that a pastor must serve everyone, not just Catholics. He recommended a common life for all engaged in apostolic work.

Archbishop Miguel Miranda y Gomez of Mexico City devoted his talk to a plea to include material on vocations. Talking of the vocation crisis in Latin America, he urged cooperation of bishops and Religious in securing vocations.

Listen as well as speak: That was the advice of Bishop Juan Iriate of Reconquista, Argentina. Saying that since there had been a change in types of bishops from feudal times to the period after the Council of Trent, so too a change is now needed from the post-Trent era to today and bishops must convince rather than dominate. Cardinal Doepfner intervened to call him to matters under discussion.

Bishop Wilhelm Pluta for Gorzow, Poland, was

another to deplore the lack of a strong pastoral tone in the schema. He asked the council Fathers to issue a declaration to correct the lack of concern for pastoral theology.

Three bishops devoted their remarks to the need for bishops to use sociological studies and other scientific means of getting to know the needs and problems of their people.

Bishops Leonidas Proano Villalba of Riobamba, Ecuador; Samuele Ruiz Garcia of Chiapas, Mexico, and Charles-Marie Himmer of Tournai, Belgium, all stressed the fact that a bishop cannot know his people individually today, but that he must know about them. To do this he should use the instruments which science, and particularly sociology, give to him.

An Eastern-rite prelate took issue with the schema because, he said, he felt it was wholly directed to dioceses of the Latin rite. Maronite-rite Archbishop Ignace Ziade of Beirut, Lebanon, called for revision of the schema so that it will apply also to the Eastern-rite areas. In particular he called for abolition of multiple-rite dioceses with a mixture of rites and jurisdictions. He pointed out that the Holy See was careful not to appoint two men to the same titular See and asked why the same concern could not be shown toward living Sees.

Bishop Agostinho Lopes De Moura, C.S.Sp., of Portalegre-Castelo Branco, Portugal, suggested various technical changes.

He was followed by Archbishop Antoni Baraniak of Poznan, Poland, who read a statement of Polish Archbishop Jozef Gawlina, who had died the day before.

The last major concern of Archbishop Gawlina's life was the immigrants and refugees he had worked for so many years. His statement deplored the fact that the 58 articles dealing with immigration contained in the original draft had been omitted in the new one. He called for their restoration or at least reinsertion of the context of the articles.   JAMES C. O'NEILL

* * * *

At a discussion of the U.S. bishops' press panel it was agreed that the most important vote on the issue of the collegiality of bishops was the one which affirms that a college of bishops exists today in the same way as an apostolic college.

On Sept. 21 and 22, votes on 10 amendments to the chapter on the schema on the nature of the Church which deals with collegiality were taken. All favored the idea by a large majority.

Father Francis J. McCool, S.J., of the New York Jesuit province, an expert on Biblical studies, noted at the panel that with this act a new emphasis has been introduced. The First Vatican Council concentrated on the primacy of the pope and was adjourned before it could consider the relation of this primacy with the bishops. Theologians, therefore, gave more emphasis to papal primacy.

Now the emphasis is on the whole structure of the Church and its primacy.

Father George Tavard of Pittsburgh, theology expert, said that for Protestant churches it is important that the Church, in explaining the primacy of the pope, is now pointing out that this is not the only way authority is exercised in the Church. It shows the Church in a different light, he said.

It shows it not as the authority of one man, but as the authority of the Church exercised in two ways, by the pope and by the college of bishops, and that the two cannot be isolated from each other. This will orient conversation between Catholics and Protestants, Father Tavard said.

86th General Congregation

September 23, 1964

Three American cardinals spoke out strongly in support of the proposed council declaration on religious liberty.

Two of the Americans, Richard Cardinal Cushing of Boston and Albert Cardinal Meyer of Chicago, warmly favored approving the entire document with minor changes.

Joseph Cardinal Ritter of St. Louis, while giving full support to the substance of the document, declared he did not agree with some of the arguments advanced for various parts of the declaration. He proposed that when the council moderators ask the council Fathers to vote on accepting the present text as a basis for discussion, they take two votes—one on the acceptability of its substance and a second on the reasoning supporting it.

At the same council meeting the Fathers approved overwhelmingly a key amendment on the doctrine of collegiality, amendment 13. By a vote of 1,927 to 292, the council Fathers approved the statement that the order of bishops, which succeeds the College of the Apostles and in which the Apostolic College continues with the Roman pontiff as its head, is the subject of supreme and full power over the universal Church. One nonvalid vote and four null votes were cast.

Before the debate on religious liberty was opened, Bishop Charles P. Greco of Alexandria, La., spoke on the schema on bishops and the government of dioceses to ask that a reference to the Confraternity of Christian Doctrine be inserted, as well as an exhortation to the world's bishops to establish CCD centers where they are not already in existence.

Paul Cardinal Leger of Montreal gave strong support to the religious freedom declaration and even advocated freedom of non-belief. But Ernesto Cardinal Ruffini of Palermo, Italy, and Alfredo Cardinal Ottaviani, secretary of the Congregation of the Holy Office, were less enthusiastic. A Yugoslav, Bishop Smiljan Cekada of Skoplje, proposed that the council draft a proposal to be submitted to the United Nations, asking that it promulgate a declaration on religious liberty in all lands and nations, including freedom of all church activities.

The meeting opened with Pope Paul VI's entrance into St. Peter's basilica carrying a silver reliquary containing the head of St. Andrew, which the Pope is hav-

ing sent back to Patras, Greece, as a gesture of brotherhood with Orthodox Christians. The reliquary was placed on the altar and Paolo Cardinal Marella of the Roman curia celebrated the Mass of St. Andrew, while the Sistine choir sang. After Mass, the eulogy was delivered by Franziskus Cardinal Koenig of Vienna.

The business of the 86th council meeting got underway after the ceremonies, but the reliquary remained on the altar instead of the usual enthroned Gospel.

After two Fathers spoke on the schema on bishops, the day's moderator, Leo Cardinal Suenens of Malines-Brussels, opened the floor to the religious liberty declaration. Bishop Emile De Smedt of Bruges, Belgium, was the declaration's relator, informing the Fathers how the document was drawn up and what problems had been encountered and anticipated in its drafting.

Nine cardinals and one bishop took the floor in the opening day's discussion. Cardinal Cushing was the first American and the fourth cardinal to speak. Those present said the cardinal's Latin was clear and somewhat oratorical in style for his first speech of the council.

Both Cardinal Cushing and Cardinal Meyer announced they were speaking in the name of practically all the American bishops. It was explained that they spoke in the name of all U.S. bishops who had attended a recent meeting called to discuss the declaration.

Cardinal Cushing led off by expressing satisfaction that the declaration had finally come before the council. He said the declaration was much awaited by non-Catholics and dealt with a practical question of major importance.

He summed up its contents with the English-language phrase, "a decent respect for the opinions of mankind." He declared the Church must champion religious liberty and if any changes are to be made, they should strengthen rather than weaken the document.

Boston's cardinal pointed out that the Church has always championed freedom for its own activities, and that now it is up to the council to proclaim that what it asks for itself it also asks for every human being.

Toward the end of his speech, Cardinal Cushing again used English to quote the statement of Lord Acton, British political scientist, that "freedom is the highest political end." He also cited Pope John XXIII, who stated that every well ordered society seeks to guarantee its members a life according to truth, justice, love and freedom.

Each of these characteristics is reflected in the concept of religious liberty, Cardinal Cushing said.

Truth is reflected, he said, because all men have a right to human dignity, and society cannot discriminate against its members.

Justice is reflected, he went on, because it requires that all men enjoy the civil rights due to human nature and dignity.

Love is reflected because nothing is more destructive of unity, concord and fraternal charity than attacks on religion.

Lastly, freedom of civil liberty is reflected because it is a necessary means to achieve the higher ends of man.

Cardinal Meyer said in his address that the declaration is in accord with Pope John's teaching in the encyclical, Pacem in Terris. He added that its passage is absolutely necessary for five reasons:

First, men want from the Church the promotion of religious liberty.

Second, because it will give the Church the opportunity of giving example to governments as to how they should treat religious bodies within their borders.

Third, it will teach Catholics that true religion consists in the free, generous and conscious acceptance of God.

Fourth, the apostolate of the Church will be assisted by the demonstration that none can be led to the Faith by force but only by hearing, preaching and receiving the gift of God.

Finally, it will lead to a fruitful dialogue with non-Catholics and work for the cause of Christian unity.

Cardinal Meyer conceded that he thought some changes should be made in the text, but he warned that if the declaration is not passed, nothing else enacted by the council will make much difference.

Cardinal Ritter said there were good reasons for accepting the declaration and praised it for its pastoral character, its prudence and its adaptability. He said he agreed with its substance but disagreed with some of the reasoning advanced to support various parts of the document, and recommended the elimination of elements which would give rise to controversy among the council Fathers. Instead, he said, he would like to see adopted a simple statement affirming religious liberty.

He stated that it is not the duty of the council to demonstrate or argue but simply to declare; not to argue but to state. Moreover, a simple statement, he said, would be more to the point and have greater effect.

Finally, he warned that in his opinion some of the arguments advanced are not solid and would lead some Fathers to vote against the declaration even though they endorse the principle of religious freedom.

For this reason, he said, he was asking the moderators that when the general discussion is completed they do not present the entire document for a simple acceptance or rejection. He proposed that the Fathers be asked to vote first on the acceptability of the substance of the declaration and then on the acceptability of its arguments. This would leave the door open for another document if present arguments are rejected, he said.

Cardinal Leger, speaking for several Canadian bishops, stated that the text was very satisfactory. He praised the document as being a prudent and cautious one that sought to safeguard mens' rights.

But he criticized the text for referring to believers only and omitting non-believers. He said the Church must defend the freedom even of non-believers. He also noted that in the text, as it now stands, the foundation given for the right of religious freedom presupposes the existence of God. This is objectionable to non-believers, he continued, and does not provide for their protection. Instead of presupposing God's existence, he proposed that the foundation for the right of religious freedom should be based on the idea that religious freedom is the highest peak of human reason.

In his introduction, Bishop De Smedt noted that 380 written observations had been sent to the Secretariat for Promoting Christian Unity prior to the drafting of the declaration, and that all had been considered carefully.

He said several improvements had been made in the present text over the previous one. One of these is that the notion of religious freedom is more clearly expressed, he said. He added that the rights of religious groups are dealt with more explicitly, that there is more effort to show that religious freedom comes from divine law and that there are sections pointing out how religious freedom can be more effectively promoted.

Bishop De Smedt noted that the declaration speaks of religious freedom rather than of religious tolerance. The reason for this, he said, is that the Church is speaking to the modern world and it must use modern terms as used by all others.

He said that the present text avoided two difficulties—that of presenting simply a list of practical points and that of turning the declaration into a merely juridical treatise. He pointed out that the basic foundation of religious liberty is the nature of the human person as created by God. The right to religious liberty rests on the fact that under the guidance of his conscience, every human person must obey God's call and His will.

The Bishop said the text holds that men must try to learn God's will and, in the case of believing Catholics, they must not act as if the Church has not received its authority from God and must inquire into what the Church teaches.

Turning to the part of the text dealing with the

restriction of religious liberty, the Bishop pointed out that it does not appeal to the notion of the common good but goes more deeply to the end established by God for society. He added, however, that it is impossible to find any formula which cannot be distorted by abuse in the hands of ill-intentioned public authority.

Lastly, the Bishop reported that the text notes that public authority is not expected to be neutral, but must indirectly favor the religious life of its citizens. But the state does not have the power to pass a judgment on the religious life of its citizens or subordinate the life of religious groups to its own political ends, he continued. This means that the government is to have a lay character but is not to accept a secularism which would be offensive to religion and which is forbidden by the natural law.

The first Father to speak on the declaration was Cardinal Ruffini. He called for a change in its title, suggesting it be called "Freedom to Profess Religion" or "Free Exercise of Religion." He warned against confusing freedom with tolerance. Freedom is proper to truth, he said, and only truth has rights. Tolerance must be patient and kindly, he said.

He objected to the section dealing with public officials. He declared that these officials cannot be forbidden to accept a state religion which they believe to be true, although without prejudice to the religions of others. He said limiting this would mean repudiating concordats signed by the Holy See and other countries.

Fernando Cardinal Quiroga y Palacios of Santiago de Compostela, Spain, called for complete revision of the declaration. His objection was that while it furthers union with separated Christians, it ignores grave dangers to the faith and charity of Catholics. He said it seems to have been written for Protestant countries with no thought to the situation in Catholic countries.

Charging that the text deals more with new elements than traditional ones and does not maintain a balance between continuity and progress, he asked that it be rejected and a new declaration be drawn up by a new mixed commission of experts.

Jose Cardinal Bueno y Monreal of Seville, Spain, said the declaration was generally correct doctrinally but that one weakness was that it descended from the doctrinal level to the juridical or political level. He also stated that sometimes it is lawful to prohibit the spread of error when it can do harm to those who want to profess the faith they have received from Christ.

Raul Cardinal Silva Henriquez of Santiago, Chile, speaking for 58 Latin American bishops, said he liked the text and that it was better than the one of the 1963 session. He said the declaration will have special impact on the work of evangelization, particularly in Latin America. He stated that the Latin American people need a new Christianization and that this declaration will be a spur to purer apostolic activity and not stop at simple proselytism.

Cardinal Ottaviani was the last cardinal to speak. He said he found some exaggerations in the text. He took exception to the statement that man, even in error, is worthy of honor. He said that man in error is deserving of charity and kindness but it is not clear that he is entitled to honor.

Cardinal Ottaviani said the declaration contains elements beyond ecumenism and does not pay sufficient attention to non-Christian religions. He declared that attention must be paid not only to natural rights but also to supernatural rights, and added that those professing a revealed religion have rights over and above those coming from natural law.

Father Robert Trisco of Chicago, expert on Church history, told the U.S. bishops' press panel that Cardinal Ottaviani was making the point that those who have a religion revealed by God have both an objective and subjective right to religious freedom, while those professing a non-revealed religion have a subjective right only.

Cardinal Ottaviani said that Catholics must profess their faith no matter what the consequences. Like Cardinal Ruffini, he took issue with the section dealing with the establishment of state religions, and cited the effect this would have on concordats. Many benefits have come from these agreements, he said, such as the protection of marriage and religious education in the concordat with Italy.

The Cardinal further declared that it is not lawful to admit the freedom to spread a religion when this may harm the unity of a Catholic nation and culminate in weakening it. He also wanted all sections of the declaration dealing with proselytism omitted, warning that it could be used against the Church to oust it from mission territories. Let us take care not to arm our adversaries, he warned.

The last speaker of the day was the Yugoslav bishop, who said that no matter what the reasons given in the text, it is imperative to have a declaration on religious liberty. He noted that Marxism always strikes at religious freedom when it is in a position to do so and allows such freedom only when it is not opportune to suppress it.

Bishop Cekada called on the council Fathers to send an appeal to the United Nations to issue a declaration proclaiming solemnly the obligation of respecting religious freedom in any land or nation, including all forms of religious activity. He asked that a special commission of Fathers be appointed to draw up an appeal and told them it would not be beneath the council's dignity to do so.

Before the opening of debate on the declaration, the council business included the special Mass, voting on six amendments to the schema on bishops and two statements concluding debate on that schema.

In addition to the passage of amendment 13, which is regarded by many as the key amendment touching on the doctrine of collegiality, five others were passed by large majorities.

The text of amendment 13 said that the order of bishops, succeeding the College of Apostles in the teaching authority and pastoral government, in union with its head, the Roman pontiff, and never without this head, is likewise a subject of supreme and full power over the universal Church, but this power may never be exercised independently of the Roman pontiff.

The other five amendments and the results of the voting are:

Fourteenth — That the power of binding and loosing given to St. Peter personally was also given to the College of Apostles in union with its head. "Yes," 1,943; "no," 307.

Fifteenth — That with due respect for the primacy and authority of its head, bishops exercise their own power for the welfare of the faithful and even of the whole Church through the help of the Holy Spirit. "Yes," 2,096; "no," 152.

Sixteenth — That this supreme power is exercised in ecumenical councils. Only the Roman pontiff can invoke, preside over and confirm the councils. There can be no ecumenical council not confirmed or at least accepted by a successor of St. Peter. "Yes," 2,114; "no," 127.

Seventeenth — That this same collegial power in union with the pope can be exercised by bishops throughout the world provided that the head of the college calls them to collegial action or at least approves of their unified action freely. "Yes," 2,006; "no," 204.

Eighteenth — That the collegial union of the bishops is reflected in their relationships with their particular churches and with the Church universal. Individual bishops represent their churches and all of them together with the pope represent the entire Church in the bond of peace, love and unity. "Yes," 2,163; "no," 56.

In addition to Bishop Greco's statement on behalf of the Confraternity of Christian Doctrine, Auxiliary Bishop Rafael Gonzales Moralejo of Valencia, Spain, spoke on the schema on bishops. He spoke of the need for a clear statement on the Church's freedom in naming bishops.

He called on the council to formulate concrete principles on episcopal appointments. He said it must be stated clearly what the competent authority is, what aids this authority can count on and what is the role of apostolic nuncios in bringing about these appointments. He suggested that nominations should be left in the hands of national bishops' conferences after consulting with priests of the interested dioceses and taking into account the opinion of the laity. JAMES C. O'NEILL

Cardinal Cushing

This is a translation of the Latin address by Richard Cardinal Cushing of Boston, supporting the ecumenical council's draft declaration on religious liberty, at the council session of Sept. 23.

The declaration on religious liberty in general is acceptable. In saying this I speak not only in my own name but also in the name of almost all the bishops of the United States.

It is most gratifying to us that at long last a full and free discussion on this subject will take place in this council hall. For in our time this is a practical question of great importance, both for the life of the Church and for the social and civil life. It is also a doctrinal question. For the doctrine of the Church on religious liberty in modern civil society has not yet been declared clearly and unambiguously.

This clear declaration is owed to the whole world—both Catholic and non-Catholic—which is indeed awaiting it. Therefore, in making this declaration, this ecumenical council will manifest, if I may quote words famous in our American history, "a decent respect for the opinions of mankind."

As His Excellency, the relator has said, the text of the declaration as it stands needs amendment here and there. But it is earnestly hoped that the amendments be such that the declaration be stronger in the meaning it already expresses and not weaker. For the substance of the doctrine as we have it here is true and solid. And it is aptly appropriate for our times. Therefore the declaration must remain intact as to its essential meaning.

One thing is of the greatest importance. In this declaration the Church must show herself to the entire modern world as the champion of liberty, of human liberty and of civil liberty, specifically in the matter of religion.

On the one hand this whole question of religious liberty is somewhat complicated. On the other hand, it seems to me, the question is simple. The whole matter can be reduced to two propositions.

First: Throughout her history the Catholic Church

has ever insisted upon her own freedom in civil society and before the public powers. She has fought for the freedom of the Pope, of the bishops to teach and govern the people of God. She has fought for the freedom of this same people of God, who have the right to live in civil society according to the dictates of Christian conscience without interference. The first proposition, therefore, is contained in the traditional formula, "libertas Ecclesiae."

The second proposition is this: That same freedom in civil society which the Church has ever insisted upon for herself and her members, she now in this our age also champions for other churches and their members, indeed for every human person.

Let me present some reasons, briefly, for this statement. They are taken from the encyclical letter, Pacem in Terris, of Pope John XXIII, of most blessed memory.

For Pope John said in his encyclical that every well ordered society is grounded in truth, in justice, in love, in liberty. Now in the first place, equal and universal religious liberty is demanded by that fundamental truth according to which all men, in so far as they are human persons, are of equal dignity; equally endowed with the same human rights, among which Pope John specified the right to religious liberty.

Secondly, religious liberty is demanded by justice. For justice requires that all citizens equally enjoy the same civil rights which in our age are acknowledged as necessary for due civil dignity. And among these rights the first is the right to religious liberty.

Thirdly, religious liberty is demanded by love. For nothing is more violently destructive of unity and civic concord than coercion or discrimination, either legally or illegally, because of religious reasons.

Fourthly, religious liberty is demanded by the very principle of civil liberty. For as Lord Acton said, speaking in the tradition of Christian civilization: "Freedom is the highest political end." Now, as the highest political end, civil liberty is also the means necessary to attain the higher ends of the human person. And this is the mind of Pope John. In particular, religious freedom—or the immunity from all coercion in religious affairs—is a necessary means by which man, in a manner which is human and willed by God, can seek God, can find Him, can serve Him.

There are other arguments for the validity of the human and civil right to religious liberty in society, and these are stated in this declaration, which as I say "in general is acceptable." And so I praise and approve this declaration.

Summary of Text
On Religious Liberty

The ecumenical council's draft text of the celebrated declaration on religious liberty proclaims that the freedom to follow God's call is the peak of human dignity and the foundation and safeguard of other freedoms.

If adopted as it now stands the declaration would proclaim the right of every man to follow his own conscience even if it leads him into error, provided he forms his conscience under the guidance of prudence and sincerity.

Details of the proposed declaration, drafted by the Secretariat for Promoting Christian Unity, were released in summary form by the council press office as debate on the document began (Sept. 23). The text was introduced at the council during last year's session but failed to reach the floor for discussion. The "summary" runs to 5,000 words.

The text in defining the term religious liberty distinguishes between the freedom of the individual in his relations with God and his freedom in relation with other men. The declaration is concerned exclusively with the latter, "other men" being considered either as individuals or as members of religious groups.

It states that the foundation of man's religious freedom "comes from the very serious obligation of respecting human dignity and following the law of God according to the dictates of a conscience sincerely formed."

According to the press office summary, the declaration as it stands is reminiscent of the phrasing in Pope John XXIII's encyclical on peace, Pacem in Terris. The encyclical states in its first section: "Every human being has the right to honor God according to the dictates of an upright conscience, and the right to profess his religion privately and publicly."

The draft declaration recognizes for religious groups authentic religious liberty in those things which develop spiritual life among men, both private and public. It demands the establishment in society of the conditions necessary to guarantee this.

The problem is an urgent one, it states, noting that closer bonds between people of diverse cultures and religions as well as increased awareness of personal responsibility have resulted from the evolution of modern law and society.

It places emphasis on the objective truth—absolute and universal—of divine law "in such a way as to exclude all danger of subjectivism and indifferentism."

Regarding the question as to when religious rights may be restricted, the text states the principle that it is the duty of governments, in matters of religion, to reconcile and harmonize things so that the exercise of these rights by one group does not constitute an obstacle to the exercise of the rights of another.

In this connection it recognizes society's right to restrict religious freedom as legitimate only when this exercise is "in grave conflict with the purpose of society." It adds:

"Consequently, it is unlawful for state authorities to discriminate against religion in any way. It is on the contrary their duty to protect and encourage religious liberty.

"Civil authorities have no direct power to regulate relationships of citizens with God. Hence they may not subject religious groups to the temporal aims of the state. On the contrary, it contributes to the common welfare when conditions are created which will favor religious life."

The summary makes a distinction between the right to propogate one's own religion sincerely and honestly and abuses of this right when "dishonest means" are employed in religious propaganda.

Concerning missionary activity and the spreading of the Gospel according to the Church's mandate from Christ, the text urges "love, prudence and patience, in accordance with the ways of God." It condemns all coercion, direct or indirect, citing the traditional teaching of the Church that by its very nature an act of faith must be fully free.

Proselytism is condemned. Father Thomas Stransky, C.S.P., of the Christian unity secretariat, defined proselytism as using "bad means" to achieve conversion.

Among the "bad means" which were cited by the American priest were "cajolery, bribery, blackening the name of other religions, or whitewashing one's own."

(He also specified the luring of hungry persons into the Faith by giving them food—so-called "rice" Christianity. Father Stransky said that the terms used here are the same as those used by the World Council of Churches. He said that ecumenists are just beginning to discuss their implications.)

The text proclaims that religious liberty is to be respected "not only by Christians and for Christians, but by all and for all—persons, individuals and religious groups."

The press office summary states that the document ends with the ringing assertion: "There can be no peaceful coexistence in the human family in the world today without religious liberty in society."

The draft declaration is divided into seven articles still numbered 25 to 31—its position in the schema on ecumenism, from which it was removed last fall and made a separate declaration.

The press office in presenting the summary said it was taken out of the ecumenism schema because "its great importance did not permit it to be compressed into such compact form as would have permitted its insertion into Chapter I of the ecumenism schema, as some Fathers suggested.

"Thus according to the desire expressed by the Coordinating Commission in its meeting of April 18, 1964 . . . it is now submitted to the council as a declaration distinct from, but annexed to, the schema on ecumenism."

Following debate, the document will be sent to the Christian unity secretariat for consideration of the objections and suggestions made on the council floor. Then it will be returned to the council to be voted on, first article by article, then on the declaration as a whole.

FATHER JOHN P. DONNELLY

More Auditors Named

Eight women Religious and seven laywomen have been appointed by Pope Paul VI (Sept. 23) to serve as auditors at the ecumenical council.

At the same time, eight laymen were named as auditors in addition to the 13 selected last year.

The official release on the appointments said that those named were chosen as representatives of international Catholic groups. This time continents other than Europe were given special consideration. Appointed were physicians, workers, business executives and leaders of Catholic youth and lay apostolate organizations.

In regard to women, Religious superiors were picked who represent worldwide territories in order to do justice to all continents. Australia is being represented by a laywoman.

Among the laywomen, two war widows were chosen "to pay a special tribute to women who in their sorrow exemplify an eloquent condemnation of war and humanity's universal aspirations toward a just and Christian peace."

Women auditors will be eligible to attend council meetings dealing with topics particularly related to their activities.

The release added that in addition to the auditors, other lay people this year will be guests of the council for a restricted number of meetings. These will be people "able to render useful services because of their merits in the Catholic field and their special competences in special sectors of the Church's life."

Following is the list of the newly appointed auditors:

Mother Sabine de Valon, superior general of the Religious of the Sacred Heart and president of the Union of Superiors General in Rome; Mother Mary Luke, superior general of the Sisters of Loretto, Nerinx, Ky., and president of the Conference of Major Religious Superiors of Women's Institutes of America; Mother Marie de la Croix Khouzam, superior general of the Egyptian Sisters of the Sacred Heart and president of the Union of Teaching Religious in Egypt;

Mother Marie Henriette Ghanem, superior general of the Sisters of the Sacred Hearts of Jesus and Mary and president of the Assembly of Major Religious Superiors in Lebanon; Sister Mary Juliana of Our Lord Jesus Christ, secretary general of the Union of Major Religious Superiors in Germany; Mother Guillemin, of France, superior general of the Daughters of Charity;

Mother Estrada, superior general of the Servants of the Sacred Heart in Spain; Mother Baldinucci, superior general of the Institute of the Most Holy Child Mary, Italy.

Laywomen auditors:

Dr. Alda Micelli, president general of the Missionaries of the Kingdom of Christ; Miss Pilar Belosillo of Spain, president of the World Union of Catholic Women's Organizations; Miss Rosemary Goldie of Australia, executive secretary of the Permanent Committee for International Congresses of the Lay Apostolate; Miss Marie Louise Monnet of France, president of the international movement for the apostolate in independent social circles;

Miss Anna Maria Roeloffzen, secretary of the International Federation of Feminine Catholic Youth, the Netherlands; Marchioness Amalia Lanza, widow of Marquess Cordero di Montezemolo, president of the Patronate of Assistance to the Italian Armed Forces; Mrs. Iduccia Marenco, widow, of the Association of Women's Catholic Action of Italy.

New laymen auditors:

Baron Leon De Rosen of France, president of the International Union of Catholic Employers Associations; Dr. Luigi Gedda of Italy, president of the International Federation of Catholic Physicians; Patrick Keegan of Great Britain, president of the International Federation of Christian Workers' Movements; Bartolo Peres of Brazil, president of the Young Christian Workers' organization;

Eusebe Adjakpley of Togo, regional secretary for Africa of the International Federation of Catholic Youth; Stephan Roman, Byzantine-rite Catholic of Toronto, Ont.; John Chen, of Hong Kong, president of the Hong Kong diocesan council for the Lay Apostolate; and Dr. Jose Maria Hernandez, president of the Catholic Action organization of the Philippines.

87th General Congregation

September 24, 1964

An Austrian cardinal has urged the ecumenical council to speak in the name of all men to seek freedom of religion behind the Iron Curtain.

Franziskus Cardinal Koenig of Vienna appealed to the council during debate on the proposed declaration on religious liberty not to forget "the tragic fact" that many nations under atheistic communist rule are deprived of religious freedom and that in many such nations religious education is either impeded or punished.

Meanwhile, an American priest told the same meeting that unless the ecumenical council defends religious freedom, the Catholic Church can no longer be considered a champion of liberty.

Father Joseph Buckley, S.M., superior general of the Marist Fathers, said a declaration of religious liberty is necessary to complete the council's work. He urged the council Fathers, let us not disappoint the world!

Bishop Ernest J. Primeau of Manchester, N.H., defended the draft declaration against a criticism often directed against it by council conservatives. The conservatives argue that it is wrong to coerce conscience and that it is equally wrong to allow every conscience—even an erroneous conscience—freedom to express itself outwardly.

Bishop Primeau put this in more philosophical language, distinguishing between a liberty that is internal and personal (usually called freedom of conscience), on the one hand, and a liberty that is external and social (usually called free exercise of religion), on the other hand. Basing himself on the unity and indivisibility of each man and on man's essentially social nature, Bishop Primeau argued that to recognize freedom of conscience without recognizing the free exercise of religion is to cut man in two.

Cardinal Koenig's speech never mentioned communism, which rules nations just across the border from his native Austria. But his talk was aimed directly at the so-called scientific atheism enthroned in communist countries.

The cardinal pointed out that it is against the principles of science to force opinions on others, but said that is precisely what these so-called scientific atheists do.

He said scientific atheists in power end up by proclaiming themselves infallible.

He concluded his speech: "I ask that the council speak in the name of all men and ask for better means of removing the anomaly under which only atheists in such countries can take part in the government and the nation's social life."

Objections voiced at the 87th council meeting against the religious liberty draft declaration stated:

—That it seems to give the erroneous conscience the same rights as a true conscience.

—That instead of being based on the subjective rights of the person, the schema is based on the objective rights of error.

—That it runs counter to Pope Leo XIII's encyclical, Immortale Dei, and Pope Pius XII's address, Ci Riesci, to the national convention of Italian Catholic jurists in December, 1953, in which he discussed religious freedom.

—That it implies a denial of the right of the state to determine the requirements of the common good.

—That it fails to throw a clear light on the obligation of all to seek the truth.

Most of the day's 18 speakers had objections to the schema in its present form. Archbishop Pietro Parente, assessor of the Congregation of the Holy Office, was exceptionally outspoken against arguments the schema used to buttress the idea of religious liberty. He espoused a suggestion Joseph Cardinal Ritter of St. Louis had offered on the previous day: to dispense with all the whys of religious liberty and merely proclaim it as a principle.

While debate on religious liberty proceeded, council Fathers continued to mark their ballots for votes on the schema on the Church.

All six votes scheduled for Sept. 24 were completed. Most of these votes were related to the concept of collegiality or stemmed directly from it.

The first vote of the day—No. 19 in the official reckoning of votes on the schema—was on the assertion that individual bishops exercise their power over that part of the people of God assigned to them, but that as members of the episcopal college they are under obligation to be interested also in the universal Church. It was explained that this is not an expression of jurisdiction, but of interest, promoting the uniting of Christ's mission for the Church. The vote was 2,162 "yes" and 64 "no."

Amendment 20 asserted the obligation of individual bishops to be missionary-minded in helping to supply men and money for needy churches. The vote was 2,205 "yes" and 23 "no."

Amendment 21 approved and encouraged formation of episcopal conferences. The vote was 2,147 "yes" and 77 "no."

Amendment 22 insisted on the element of service in the discharge of the mission of teaching and preaching. The vote was 2,189 "yes" and 35 "no."

Amendment 23 said that bishops can be canonically established through customs approved by the Holy See, by local laws or by the Roman pontiff, but if in any case the pope refuses apostolic communion, the bishop in question cannot be regarded as a valid member of the episcopal body. The vote was 2,177 "yes" and 43 "no."

Amendment 24 said the principal duty of bishops is to preach the Gospel. The vote was 2,152 "yes" and 51 "no."

The meeting opened with the votive Mass of the Holy Spirit celebrated by Archbishop Joseph Cordeiro of Karachi, Pakistan. Bishop Joannes Holterman, O.P., of Willemstad, Netherlands West Indies, enthroned the Gospel.

During the Mass and the enthronement of the Gospel, choir boys from the town of Bresseto near Parma, Italy, sang Gregorian chant.

The day's moderator was Leo Cardinal Suenens of Malines-Brussels.

Archbishop Pericle Felici, council general secretary, explained that the Sept. 25 deadline previously fixed for the presentation of summaries of speeches to be given on the schema on Revelation referred only to the first part of the debate. The first part of the debate touches only on the introduction and chapters one and two.

The deadline for the second part (touching chapter three on the inspiration and interpretation of Holy Writ) will be Sept. 28, he said. He announced Sept. 30 as the deadline for the summaries of speeches on chapters four, five and six, dealing with the Old and New Testaments, and with Scripture in the life of the Church.

Speaking during the day's session were Cardinal Koenig and Michael Cardinal Browne, O.P., of the Roman curia; also Archbishops Parente, Pedro Cantero Cuadrado of Zaragoza, Spain; Enrico Nicodemo of Bari, Italy; and Marcel Dubois of Besancon, France.

Other speakers were Bishops Primeau, John Abasolo y Lecue of Vijayapuram, India; Jose Lopez Ortiz of Tuy-Vigos, Spain; Antonio de Castro Mayer of Campos, Brazil; Johannes Pohlschneider of Aachen, Germany; Peter Antoon Nierman of Groningen, the Netherlands; Angel Temino Saiz of Orense, Spain; Michael Klepacz of Lodz, Poland; Archbishop Marcel Lefebvre, C.S.Sp.,

superior general of the Holy Ghost Fathers; Bishop Giovanni Canmestri, auxiliary of the vicar general of Rome; Auxiliary Bishop Anastasio Granados of Toledo, Spain; and Father Buckley.

Cardinal Koenig called the religious freedom declaration altogether acceptable as it stood but deplored its silence regarding nations which have been deprived of religious freedom. Some modern governments are militantly atheistic, while others twist religious freedom to mean freedom from religion, he said.

In such countries, he continued, religious education is hobbled, barred from the use of any means of public communication, or even punished as a crime. This is contrary to the 1948 United Nations Declaration of Human Rights.

Cardinal Koenig said that such countries have two classes of citizens: Those who profess atheism and therefore have access to the highest offices of the land; and Christians, who are excluded from those offices. This can be easily proved, he said. Such states sin against tolerance and due respect for the human person, he declared.

They violate scientific principles since nothing is more unscientific than to force opinions on others, he continued.

They harm the society they rule since the refusal of religious freedom turns the hearts of citizens against rulers and makes them disinclined to cooperate in achieving the common purposes of the nation, he said.

The cardinal added that they offend human dignity, which is the foundation of freedom. He said freedom offends totalitarianism since it implies that the state's authority is limited. Then he made his plea that the council speak in the name of all mankind and ask for religious freedom behind the Iron Curtain.

Cardinal Browne said the declaration cannot be approved in its present form. This form is not even necessary for the peace and unity of the world's peoples, he said. It bases religious liberty on the rights of the conscience, but social rights of a sincere but erroneous conscience cannot be considered equal to social rights based on a conscience which is both sincere and right, he continued. He said Pope John XXIII's encyclical, Pacem in Terris, did not speak of the dictates of any conscience being a norm, but only the dictates of an upright conscience. The norm of an upright conscience is divine law itself, he stated.

Cardinal Browne noted that in his allocution to the prelates of Rome in 1946, Pius XII set forth an altogether different foundation for religious liberty; not the rights of the individual conscience but rather the demands of the common good.

Archbishop Parente said that the text cannot be approved as it stands. To the rights of God, it prefers the rights of man and his liberty and the rights of his conscience, he added. The text lacks a clear distinction between objective and subjective aspects of truth and error. It also lacks a forthright statement of the Church's mission and much of the text is liable to equivocation.

Archbishop Parente declared that it is unfortunate to ask the Church to make use of its extraordinary teaching office authority to proclaim absolute religious liberty. The text should be amended to safeguard basic principles, he said. It contains much truth and should be stripped of all argumentation, setting forth only what is uncontested. (On this last point Archbishop Parente was echoing one made the previous day by Cardinal Ritter.)

Archbishop Cantero said that the text is acceptable, but that the treatment should not descend from the juridical to the practical. The text fails to distinguish clearly between religious freedom and freedom of conscience. These differ in their subject, since the term religious liberty pertains both to the individual and to society, whereas liberty of conscience pertains to the individual alone, he stated.

Archbishop Cantero said also that the two differ in the matter they embrace—religious freedom concerning itself only with religious acts, while freedom of conscience has a broader scope. They also differ in that liberty of conscience means immunity from external coercion. But religious liberty must be conditioned by many circumstances since it must be reconciled with the rights of others, he concluded.

Bishop Abasolo said that more emphasis should be put on duty than on right when speaking of religion. Man's rights in matters of religion, such as freedom of worship, arise from man's duties toward God, he stated. Not all consciences have the same rights since the rights of a correct conscience are on a higher level than those of an invincibly erroneous conscience. Therefore he suggested the title of the declaration should be changed to "Duties and Rights of Individuals and Communities in Religious Matters." There can be no right to persuade men to error, he said.

Archbishop Nicodemo said that religious liberty is not based on any objective right inherent in error but on a subjective right of the human person to follow the dictates of his conscience. Where an erroneous conscience acts against the natural law, the public authority may intervene, he said.

Bishop Lopez stated that the declaration's passage saying that the state is incompetent to judge the truth regarding religious matters should be deleted from the text. He said it insinuates that no government can declare itself Catholic. When a government makes such a declaration, it is not passing judgment on religious truth but only manifesting its obedience to divine law, he continued. When the citizens of a nation with practical unanimity profess the true religion, then the state should act accordingly, he said.

Bishop De Castro said the declaration should be recast completely. He said it states equality of rights for all religions, true and false, whereas the public profession of religion is to be allowed only to the one true faith. Since human nature is perfected only in adherence to the good and the true, it can derive no dignity from error even when it is error in good faith, he declared. Mutual relationships in society must be based on the natural law and God's positive law. This law of God commands that all men accept the true faith, he stated.

Bishop Canestri said the foundation of religious liberty cannot always be conscience. It is wrong to proclaim neutrality of the state, he said, noting that Pope Leo XIII declared that despite certain advantages, such neutrality is not always the best solution to the problem.

Bishop Pohlschneider said this historic document, which will promote peace on earth, needs to be filled out by a reference, however brief, to freedom of education. Our affirmation of freedom of education should be directed not merely to communist governments but to governments of all nations. Complete freedom demands freedom of education, which is the gravest of all duties for parents, he stated. It is a basic right that no state monopoly should restrict. It is the duty of the state to enable parents to make a free choice of schools without this choice bringing additional burdens on the family, he declared. These rights are in some degree violated everywhere in the world today, the bishop concluded.

Archbishop Lefebvre said that the text would be dangerous unless it is broadly revised. The text should distinguish internal acts of conscience from external acts, which can scandalize and which always involve public authority. Affirmation of full religious liberty for all groups would in some cases condone immorality, since some groups make immoral acts a part of their religion, he said. It is likewise a mistake to formulate a doctrine in view of only one set of circumstances which might prevail in a particular country, such as the United States, he declared.

Father Buckley said that among a number of improvements which seem desirable in the text, one would deal with the very foundation of personal religious liberty. The document repeatedly bases the right of a sincere conscience to liberty on the principle of a call from God, he noted. According to this principle, every sincere conscience, even if erroneous, is a call from God, he went on. While Holy Writ refers to the Christian faith, holiness and heaven as divine vocations, and also refers to the priesthood as a divine vocation, the term has been extended to the married state and even to careers such as medicine, law and engineering. He said that this tendency reaches an absurd length in the present document, which makes an upright but erroneous conscience a divine vocation. Most talk of divine vocation is false mysticism, he stated.

The text might treat the obligation of conscience as the foundation of religious liberty, he said. It would be the categorical imperative of conscience, conscience under God for those who believe in God, and the simple categorical imperative of conscience for all men, he continued.

Man as a social person has a right to social worship, Father Buckley said. The exercise of the right of an individual or association can be limited by society, but only insofar as this exercise infringes on the rights of others. But such an infringement should not be supposed too readily, he stated.

Although the world does not regard the Church generally as a champion of liberty, it would welcome any sign that the Catholic Church is on liberty's side. The council must not disappoint the world, he concluded.

Bishop Primeau said the text should distinguish between a religious liberty which is internal and personal, and a religious liberty which is external and social. In modern parlance, the first is called liberty of conscience, while the second is known as freedom of worship, he continued. There is a commonly accepted bond between the two, he said.

He warned against the false concept of man which would make him first an individual and then a social being. Man is essentially social, he declared, and the Fathers should not allow any dichotomy in the human personality. Because of this, it is unlawful to recognize a man's right to freedom of conscience while restricting him in his freedom of worship, he said. Both freedoms are equally essential and pertain to the integrity and dignity of the human person.

Freedom of worship is not only a logical deduction from freedom of conscience, Bishop Primeau stated. Religious freedom must be regarded as a true and strict right. In this light it constitutes a guarantee of immunity from coercion, he said.

Bishop Nierman spoke for the Dutch bishops and some Indonesian bishops. He said the declaration has great value in its description of the nature of religious liberty and in its practical implications for the life of the Church. However, certain principles should be given practical applications in the schema. Canon law today safeguards the rights of the Catholic party to a mixed marriage but not the rights of the non-Catholic party, he noted. This should be corrected in future revision of canon law, he said.

Bishop Temino said man's first obligation is to heed God when He has spoken clearly. It would be bad to subject God publicly to individual reason, he said. The text must be revised drastically since it is based on the equality of all religions in society, he stated. At times it may be in the interests of the Church to permit broader religious liberty and the council should base its declaration of religious liberty on this fact, not on false principles smacking of humanism, he declared.

Bishop Klepacz said the text omits the important relationship between the individual on the one hand, and society, state, nation and the human race on the other hand.

Archbishop Dubois said the text is too philosophical and too juridical. He added that it should be given a tone more in keeping with Scripture and tradition. St. Augustine addressed a heritical bishop as "honorable brother," because he respected him as an individual, he said. Christ Himself commended religious liberty, as can be seen in the passages comparing the apostles to light and salt, comparisons which exclude coercion. Many other texts could be used appropriately, he said.

Bishop Granados said it is preferable just now to overlook the text's practical side and concentrate on its doctrinal side. He said that the principle defending the strict right of all religious groups to profess their own doctrines, whether true or false, calls for these observations:

First: This teaching is new in the Church, which traditionally has taught that error is treated with tolerance if this is demanded by the common good.

Second: This teaching is opposed to the mind of Pope Pius XII in the allocution, Ci Riesce.

Third: The declaration skips unlawfully from the subjective order to the objective order.

Fourth: This principle cannot be reconciled with the principle of religious liberty as set forth in the document itself.

PATRICK RILEY

* * * *

The exact point of controversy in the council on religious liberty is not whether it is rational in political and legal spheres, but whether the concept is mature enough at this point to link it up with the theological and moral spheres. The area of controversy is relatively narrow.

This assessment was made by Father John Courtney Murray, S.J., noted American author on Church-state affairs, during the U.S. bishops' press panel discussion of the council debate.

Father Murray said:

"The schema is both traditional and new, since the Catholic tradition is one of progress and new and deeper understanding, especially when new and deeper questions are asked. Bishop Emile De Smedt of Bruges, Belgium, the schema relator and chairman of the special subcommittee under the Secretariat for Promoting Christian Unity which drew it up, says we are confronting a new problem; the questions are not the same as those asked in the 19th century. The Church is searching her mind to find what answers to give to new questions.

"It is a large step from the 'freedom with which Christ has made us free' (Gal. 5, 1) and technical sense of freedom . . . . The council is preoccupied with linking the former with political structures and the whole problem of civil liberty."

A variety of questions that were asked of the expert on religious liberty indicated the interest the council discussion has aroused in the world press:

One questioner asked what would happen to the classic concept of "the Catholic state" if the declaration is accepted.

"Major changes would be required," Father Murray admitted, adding that the preoccupation of the Spanish bishops on this point is entirely legitimate. He said that "as held by these bishops, the concept involves two legal institutions: 1. Catholicism established by law; 2. Legal intolerance, by which other religions are excluded and denied the right to public worship, private property and the propagation of their faith. The latter would be severely curtailed by the document."

What of the fate of concordats (treaties) between the Holy See and individual nations if the declaration were passed?

"I find it difficult to see where any substantial change will be necessary in this practice," said Father Murray. "Many nations historically have ties with a religion—England with Anglicanism, for instance, and Sweden with Lutheranism. There is no contradiction between full religious liberty and the maintenance of these ties. Nor is there anything in the notion of religious liberty preventing a nation from proclaiming that a majority of its citizens are Catholic or Moslem. This would be a declaration of fact, and the people might set a great store by it because of their traditions.

"But we are concerned only when the establishment of religion includes intolerance and thus the exclusion of other religions from public existence by the coercive power of the state. This is where the changes would come as a result of the declaration," the American Jesuit said. He cited examples of concordats in Ecuador and Colombia.

What about concordats which for instance bar divorce by law, such as the Lateran treaty between the Holy See and Italy?

"This is an application of principle—not the principle itself," said Father Murray. "The declaration does not descend to application and it should not. The Church officially has no opinion on what the laws of the state are. This is a matter of jurisprudence, not for the Church to decide. The common good is involved and the people are competent to decide. The question would have to be solved on this basis."

What are the norms for the restriction of religious liberty in its external exercise?

"This is greatly debated," Father Murray answered. "Bishop De Smedt says the commission is not sure that it has found the right formula. The present formula is only one of the many possible.

"In the United States of America the free exercise of religion is governed by the order of society—that is, the public order. This is made up of three civil goods: one, public peace; two, public morality, including the notion of public health; three, harmony in the exercise of civil rights. Religious liberty is subject to the same norms."

Asked to assess the most difficult issues inherent in religious liberty, Father Murray listed three:

—The relation between the freedom of conscience and the free exercise of religion in the external and social realm.

—The competence of governments and the law in regard to religion.

—The criteria for restricting religious liberty.

He said the last two are so intimately related that they are impossible to separate.

Referring to the intervention of Cardinal Cushing of Boston on the opening day of the controversy, Father Murray pointed out that the cardinal made a distinction between the Church's right of religious liberty based on the divine law (since it is the true Church), and the Church's claim of the same right for other religions, prompted by conditions of the world today. The latter claim is not based on divine law, but on rational grounds of dignity, justice, truth, charity and civil freedom. This does not mean that the Church's claim is based on expediency, Father Murray added.

Father Buckley

This is a translation of the Latin address by Father Joseph Buckley, S.M., superior general of the Society of Mary (Marist Fathers), on the council's draft statement on religious liberty at its Sept. 24, 1964, session.

This intervention of mine is dictated by two main considerations. First, I am concerned that this ecumenical council should issue a declaration of the inalienable right of man to follow the dictates of a sincere conscience, especially in matters of religion.

In the second place, I am concerned that the council's affirmation of religious liberty should be set forth on a firm foundation—one that is also understandable and congenial to men generally.

While in the text which is now before us a number of ameliorations seem desirable, let me deal with just one which appears to merit public review, namely the very foundation of personal liberty in the religious order.

Throughout the document, repeatedly, the right to liberty of a sincere conscience (conscientia recta) is based on the principle of a "call from God" (vocatio divina). According to this principle, every sincere conscience, even if mistaken (erroneous), is a call from God: a divine vocation. Calling an erroneous conscience a divine vocation, even from the viewpoint that it is written in the "heart of nature," constitutes the ultimate point attained thus far in a most unhappy evolution of the concept of divine vocation.

Originally in the New Testament, a divine vocation was a call to follow Christ (Mark 3,13); to the Christian faith (II Thess. 1, 11); to heaven (Heb. 3, 1); and to the holiness which befits those who are so privileged (I Thess. 4, 7).

In the New Testament the priesthood is also called a divine vocation (Heb. 5, 4).

This is not a suitable occasion for a discussion of the idea of a divine vocation to the priesthood, but spare me, venerable Fathers, if I recall to mind for you a tendency to speak as if the call of God to the priesthood was recognizable to each of us in the human psychological order, as if each of us knew that he was called by God.

From the evolution of the idea of divine call it has become customary to speak also of a divine vocation even to the married state. So far has the term "divine vocation" been extended that we now read and hear of a divine vocation to become a doctor, a lawyer, an engineer, a nurse.

Finally, in the document before us, we have the reductio ad absurdum of this entire unfortunate evolution: the imperative of a conscience, right but erroneous, is a *divine vocation*.

This way of speaking is a long way from the teaching of the Common Doctor, St. Thomas, in the Summa Theologica (Ia IIae, q. 19, a. 10), where he asks: "For the human will to be good, is it necessary that it agree with God's will in the thing willed?" St. Thomas answers: ". . . In individual matters we are ignorant of what God wills. Hence in these things we are under no obligation of trying to make our will agree with God's."

Most talk of divine vocation and finding out God's will is a lot of pseudo-mysticism.

I suggest as the foundation of religious liberty not some divine vocation but the obligation of conscience: the categoric imperative of conscience itself, under God. *Under God* for those who believe in God, but for all men the categoric imperative of conscience.

The right to religious liberty, like all the other rights of man, springs from an obligation. In created things no right exists which is not founded in a prior obligation.

If a man feels that he should worship God in a particular way, he has a right to fulfill this obligation. If a man, as a social person, judges that he is obliged to worship God socially, he has a right to social worship. There is no authority superior to the individual conscience under God, unless it is an authority sincerely perceived by the conscience itself. This is how Catholics accept the authority of the Church over them.

The exercise of the right of an individual or association can be limited by society but only inasmuch as the exercise infringes on the rights of others. Such a conflict of obligations and of rights should not be supposed too readily.

It is on this solid basis that I hope to see the declaration on religious liberty erected by the Council.

Liberty is most precious to all men. Whatever we priests may like to think, the Catholic Church does not enjoy a very high reputation in the world generally for its sponsorship of liberty. Still, such is the esteem of the world for the Church that it welcomes any earnest indication that the Catholic Church is on the side of liberty. Witness the enthusiastic reception universally given to the encyclical of Pope John XXIII, Pacem in Terris.

The Council must not disappoint the world!

Council Observers

Following is the list of observers delegated by non-Catholic Christian communities for the third session of the Second Vatican Council, together with the list of guests of the Secretariat for Promoting Christian Unity.

Ecumenical Patriarchate of Constantinople—Archimandrite Andre Scrima, rector of the Greek Orthodox church in Rome and personal representative of Patriarch Athenagoras I of Constantinople; Archimandrite Panteleimon Rodopoulos, dean of Holy Cross Greek Orthodox Theological School, Brookline, Mass., and Father John S. Romanides, professor of dogmatics and the history of theology at the same seminary.

Russian Orthodox Church (Patriarchate of Moscow)—Archpriest Vitaly Borovoy, professor at the Leningrad theological school and head of the Russian Orthodox delegation to the World Council of Churches, and Archpriest Vivery Voronov, also a professor at the Leningrad theological school.

Orthodox Church of Georgia—(Father Borovoy is concurrently an official representative of this autonomous church, whose two million members are concentrated in the Soviet Republic of Georgia in the Caucasus mountains).

Coptic Orthodox Church of Egypt—Bishop Amba Samuil, who is in charge of social services in the Patriarchate of Alexandria, and Father Marcos Elias Abdel Messih, pastor of Egyptian Copts in the United States and Canada.

Syrian Orthodox Church—Father Saliba Shamoon, secretary to Patriarch Theodosios VI of Antioch.

Syrian Orthodox Church of India—Chorepiscopus T. S. Abraham, former Singapore pastor.

Apostolic Armenian Church (Holy See of Etchmiadzin)—Bishop Parkev Kevorkian, delegate in Moscow of the Catholicos of Etchmiadzin and bishop of the Armenian community in Moscow; and member of the supreme spiritual council of the Etchmiadzin Catholicate.

Apostolic Armenian Church (Catholicate of Cilicia) —The Rt. Rev. Karekin Sarkissian, head of the patriarchal seminary in Lebanon, near Beirut, and Bishop Ardavazt Terterian of the Armenian Church of Marseilles, France, former professor of the patriarchal seminary in Lebanon.

Assyrian Catholicate-Patriarchate of the East (headquarters of the Patriarch-Catholicos now in California)—Father Isaac Rehana and George W. Lamsa.

Russian Orthodox Church Outside of Russia—Archpriest Igor Troyanoff, rector of the Russian Orthodox church in Lausanne, Switzerland, and Archimandrite Ambrose Pogodin of Rome. Substitute: Dr. Serge Grotoff of the University of Rome.

Old Catholic Church (Union of Utrecht)—Canon Peter Maan, professor of New Testament studies at the Old Catholic seminary at Amersfoort, the Netherlands, and vicar of the Old Catholic cathedral at Utrecht. Substitute: the Rev. Herwig Aldenhoven of the parish of Wallbach, Switzerland.

Mar Thomas Syrian Church of Malabar (India)—Missionary Bishop Philipose Chrysostom.

Anglican Communion—The Rt. Rev. John R. H. Moorman, Bishop of Ripon, England; the Rev. Eugene Fairweather, professor of Divinity, Trinity College, University of Toronto of the Anglican Church of Canada; the Rev. Ernest John of the Church of India, Burma and Ceylon, vicar of the Cathedral Church of the Redemption, New Delhi. Substitutes: The Rev. Howard Root, dean of Emmanuel College, Cambridge University, England, and Rev. Massey H. Shepherd, Jr., professor of liturgies, Church Divinity School of the Pacific, Berkeley, Calif. The Rev. Bernard C. Pawley, canon of Ely (England) cathedral, is representative of the Archbishops of Canterbury and York.

Lutheran World Federation—The Rev. Kristen E. Skydsgaard, professor of systematic theology at the University of Copenhagen, Denmark; the Rev. Warren A. Quanbeck of the Lutheran Theological Seminary of St. Paul, Minn., and the Rt. Rev. Sven Silen, Bishop of Vasteras, Sweden. Substitutes: Dr. George Lindbeck, professor of the history of theology at the Yale University Divinity School, New Haven, Conn., and the Rev. Dr. Vilmos Vajta, director of the theological department of the Lutheran World Federation, Geneva, Switzerland.

World Presbyterian Alliance—The Rev. Vittorio Subilia, dean of the Waldensian Theological Faculty, Rome; the Rev. Dr. A. Allan McArthur of the Presbyterian Church of Scotland, minister of Pollokshields-Titwood parish, Glasgow; and the Rev. John Newton Thomas of the United Presbyterian Church, professor of systematic theology at Union Theological Seminary, Richmond, Va.

Evangelical (Lutheran) Church of Germany—Dr. Edmund Schlink, professor of dogmatics at the University of Heidelberg. Substitute: The Rev. Wolfgang Dietzfelbinger, pastor of Erbendorf, Germany.

World Methodist Council—The Rev. Harold Roberts, head of Divinity School, Richmond College, Richmond, England; the Rev. Walter G. Muelder, dean and professor of social ethics at Boston University School of Theology, and the Rev. Albert C. Outler, professor of theology at Southern Methodist University, Dallas, Tex. Substitutes: The Rev. William R. Cannon, dean of the Candler School of Theology at Emory University, Atlanta; the Rev. Robert E. Cushman, dean of the Duke University Divinity School, Durham, N.C.; the Rev. Philip Potter, of the Methodist Missionary Society, London; the Rev. David Alan Keighley of Rome, representative in Italy of the British Methodist Church and of the Methodist Missionary Society; the Rev. Max Woodward, secretary of the World Methodist Council, London; and the Rev. Franklin H. Littell, professor at the Chicago Theological Seminary.

International Congregational Council—The Rev. Dr. Douglas Horton of Randolph, N.H., former moderator of the International Congregational Council; and the Rev. George B. Caird, senior tutor at Mansfield College, Oxford, England. Substitutes: The Rev. Bard Thompson, professor of church history at the Lancaster Theological Seminary, Lancaster, Pa.; the Rev. John R. Von Rohr, professor of historical theology at the Pacific School of Religion, Berkeley, Calif.; and the Rev. Heiko A. Oberman, professor of church history at Harvard University Divinity School.

Friends World Committee—Dr. Douglas V. Steere, professor of philosophy at Haverford College, Haverford, Pa., and Dr. A. Burns Chalmers of Washington, D.C., director of the Davis House and education secretary of the American Friends Service Committee.

World Convention of Churches of Christ (Disciples) —Dr. William George Baker, professor of practical theology at the Scottish Congregational College, Edinburgh; Dr. William B. Blakemore, dean of the Disciples' Divinity House at the University of Chicago. Substitute: The Rev. Dr. Howard E. Short, editor of The Christian, St. Louis.

International Association for Liberal Christianity—Dr. L. J. Van Holk, professor at the University of Leiden, the Netherlands.

Church of South India—The Rt. Rev. A. H. Legg, Bishop and Moderator of the Synod of the Church of South India, Trivandrum.

World Council of Churches—The Rev. Dr. Lukas Vischer, Geneva, research secretary of the World Council's Commission on Faith and Order; Dr. Nikos A. Nissiotis, associate director of the World Council's Ecumenical Institute at Bossey, Switzerland; Dr. Z. K. Matthews, in charge of the Division of Inter-Church Aid, World Service and Refugees of the World Council of Churches, Geneva; and Dr. Jerald C. Brauer, dean and professor of church history of the federated theological faculty of the University of Chicago.

The following are guests of the Secretariat for Promoting Christian Unity:

Bishop Cassien, director of the Orthodox Theological Institute of St. Serge, Paris; Pastor Marc Boegner, honorary president of the Protestant Federation of France, Paris; Dr. Theodore Mosconas, secretary of the Council of Churches of Alexandria, Egypt, archivist and librarian for the Greek Orthodox Patriarchate of Alexandria; the Rev. G. C. Berkouwer, professor of the Free Protestant University of Amsterdam; the Rev. Oscar Cullmann, professor at the University of Basel (Switzerland) and Paris; Dr. Masatoshi Doi, of the United Church of Christ in Japan, professor of systematic theology and ecumenism at Doshisha University of Kyoto, Japan; Dr. David Du Plessis, Pentecostal, minister, of both South Africa and California; Dr. Oswald C. J. Hoffmann of the Missouri Synod of the Lutheran Church, St. Louis; Pastor Wilhelm Schmidt, vicar of St. Michael's Evangelical Brotherhood, Bremen-Horn, Germany; the Rev. William A. Norgren, New York, director of Faith and Order studies of the National Council of Churches of Christ in the United States; Pastor Roger Schutz, prior of the Protestant religious community of Taize, France; and Pastor Max Thurian, subprior of the same community.

Marian Questions

The last chapter of the schema on the Church has presented the council Fathers with a thorny problem.

It is devoted to the Virgin Mary, under the title: "The Blessed Virgin Mary, Bearer of God (Deipara), in the Mystery of Christ and the Church." It replaces the formerly independent schema on Mary.

Discussion of the new text occupied more than two days of debate by the council Fathers. The debate centered on two points: Can Mary be called "Mother of the Church"? Should the schema speak of her as "Mediatrix"?

The sharp divergence of opinion expressed on the chapter must now be reconciled by the Theological Commission and brought back to the council for a vote.

The question of the motherhood of Mary in rela-

tion to the Church is not raised by the present text of the schema, but by the absence of that expression from its title. For the phrase, "Mother of the Church," appeared in the last version of the formerly separate schema on Mary. It was not in the original version, but only in the second, and it has now been omitted. The new title corresponds to the votes of the bishops during the second council session, when it was decided to treat the topic of Mariology in the context of the mystery of the Church.

However, Mariologists follow two main tendencies, called "Christo-typical" and "Ecclesio-typical."

The first sees Mary as a beautiful imitation of Christ and describes her holiness, her function and her privileges on the pattern of the corresponding qualities and functions of Jesus.

The second sees her as the image of the Church, and understands her meaning in the history of salvation on the model of the meaning and place of the Church.

The current title of the chapter therefore shows one purpose of the text: To follow a middle way between Christo-typical and Ecclesio-typical Mariologies by drawing on the insights of both. The fact that the bishops' speeches have not been concerned with this, indicates that the synthesis of the two points of view has been fairly successful.

The bishops who have asked for a return to the title of Mary as "Mother of the Church" have done it on two grounds.

On the one hand, this title seems to them likely to increase the devotion of Catholics. But Augustin Cardinal Bea, president of the Secretariat for Promoting Christian Unity, felt it necessary to state that the question before the council is not the devotion of anybody but the accuracy of doctrine.

On the other hand, this title has been advocated because it has been found by some speakers to be identical with the title, universally recognized, of Mary "Mother of the Faithful."

Among the more doubtful arguments used to support the title, "Mother of the Church," it has been said that the Church is the family of God, in which there must be a mother. Obviously, this literal understanding of the word "family" takes no account of the symbolic or analogical use of theological terms. It has also been said that Mary must be the "Mother of the Church," since she is already the "Mother of all men, the Mother of Protestants, of Mohammedans, of unbelievers," and so forth.

Reduced to its theological proportions, the problem is simple. Does such a title correspond to the Church's tradition?

As was pointed out by Bishop Sergio Mendez Arceo of Cuernavaca, Mexico, there are two known instances of this title being used in the 9th and the 10th centuries. The bishop could not find other uses of it until the end of the 19th century, with Pope Leo XIII. Recently Pope Paul VI invited theologians to find out if this appellation could be used meaningfully. An invitation to study this title implies at least that its legitimacy is not obvious to the Pope.

The contents of such a title depend primarily on one's understanding of the Church. If the Church is seen simply as an aggregate of all faithful or even as the organ and channel of salvation, Mary could be called Mother of the Church. By bringing Christ into the world, she was made the spiritual Mother of all those who will be saved by Him, and she became a central element in the salvation of mankind.

But to see the Church only in this individualistic perspective does not do full justice to the mystery of the Incarnation. The Church is also the holy community of God and man communing with each other in mutual indwelling. Coming down from heaven as the New Jerusalem, the Church brings to men, and first of all to Mary in the mystery of the Annunciation, the fulfilment of the promises of God and the implementation of His covenant with man.

Of such a Church, Mary can only be the daughter. And it is a notable fact that the title "Mother," from the time of the early Fathers to ours, has been given to the Church, mother of all the redeemed, who have been reborn in her through the waters of baptism.

After the bishops' exchange on this question, it seems unlikely that the title "Mother of the Church" will be restored in the final text of the constitution on the Church.

The other major point on which the bishops have disagreed in relation to the chapter on Mary concerns the title "Mediatrix."

The schema is very careful here. It does not itself call Mary "Mediatrix," but it states the fact that custom has given her this title. And it cautions that this word must not be understood as taking away from, or adding to, the dignity of Christ as the only Mediator.

In spite of this prudence, several cardinals and bishops, some of them speaking in the name of a large number of their colleagues, have asked for the total removal of the word "Mediatrix" from the schema. Others, on the contrary, have insisted that it be kept and, if possible, reinforced.

This question arises originally from the Catholic (and also the Orthodox) practice of praying frequently to Mary, asking for her intercession in our favor. Orthodox devotion has done this for centuries. Yet Orthodox theology has never tried to express this by building up a speculative system concerning the place of the Virgin Mary in the plan of salvation.

But the trend of Latin theology has always been to rationalize the broad assumptions of Christian piety and to organize them into a rational system of thought. Piety, both liturgical and private, tends to see Mary in the halo of poetry, and most of the titles given to Mary first arose in the lyrical context of Marian piety.

Thus Mary has been called, not only "Mother of Jesus" and "the Virgin," as in the New Testament, not only "Forthbringer of God" (Theotokos), as at the Council of Ephesus, which employed this expression to safeguard the integrity of the belief in the Incarnation, but also "Intercessor," "Auxiliatrix," "Advocate," "Mother of the Faithful," "Mediatrix."

In their popular use, these titles are without a well-defined theological meaning. And the Litanies of Loretto provide a source-list of poetic titles of the Virgin which have never been studied theologically and probably never can be.

The difficulty arises when one tries to give a precise theological content to these devotional titles. The name in question, "Mediatrix," clearly refers to Mary's prayer with and for all Christians. It is sometimes qualified as "Mediatrix of All Grace" (singular). All grace being summed up in Christ, this means no more than the traditional names "Forthbringer of Christ" or "Christ-bearing Virgin."

It has also been qualified as "Mediatrix of All Graces" (plural), which would seem to imply something quite different, namely that all graces do in fact come to men through Mary. At this point, theology, and with it the council, runs into difficulties.

It is of course impossible to conceive that all graces without exception must come through Mary. For the grace of God was already given in the Old Testament, before she was born. And Mary herself received grace, of which surely she could not be the "Mediatrix" in her own favor.

In view of this, the extreme school of Mariology, for which Mary's mediation is not only a fact of Christian life but also a necessity in God's plan for the salvation of the world, places itself at the limits of orthodoxy. For were such a necessity taken literally, it would follow that Mary is not only redeemed by Christ, as implied in the definition of her Immaculate Conception, but also self-redeemed. And it would follow that she must have been somehow pre-existent to her own birth.

It is in keeping with the logic of this extreme type of Mariology that the title "Co-redemptrix" prolongs that of "Mediatrix." Thus, the mediation of Mary does not remain posterior to Redemption, being the outcome of Mary's elevation to heaven by her Assumption, but it becomes intrinsic to Redemption itself.

The chapter on Mary does not mention co-redemption but only mediation. It neither recommends nor condemns it, but simply warns not to take it in a way that would be detrimental to faith in Christ, the only Mediator.

The immediate question, then, is: Should this title remain in the council's constitution, or should it not?

Some practical difficulties militate against its retention: How can one explain to Mohammedans and others, Archbishop Adrianus Djajasepoetra of Jakarta, Indonesia, asked, that we believe in only one Mediator between God and man, and also in a second Mediator subordinate to the first? How can we be certain that our own people, especially in regions where Marian devotion has a tendency to run wild, make no mistake about the only mediation of Christ, when they proclaim Mary "Mediatrix"?

The gravity of the situation was indirectly pointed out by Bishop Francisco Rendeiro of Faro, Portugal. He complained that removal of the word "Mediatrix" would scandalize Catholics in many parts of the world, who believe that all graces come to them through Mary. The statement implies that Catholics in other parts of the world do not hold such a belief. The question then is why should these be scandalized by retention of the name.

Among the arguments for keeping the word "Mediatrix," several bishops have mentioned its use by recent popes, especially Leo XIII, Pius X and Pius XI. This raises an issue that has been basic to all the Council's work: Is the use of an expression, a theological point of view or an explanation in a recent papal document a valid reason for an ecumenical council to do the same? If the council's function were to provide a digest of papal documents, it would limit its work to the culling of papal writings, which would restrict its authority to that of the documents cited or referred to.

As was pointed out by Cardinal Bea, a conciliar constitution must be a more solemn document than a papal encyclical. An encyclical, written for the circumstances of the day, may use the transitory language of its period. This commits the pope who publishes it, but not the whole Church.

On the contrary, a solemn proclamation by an ecumenical council is expected to stand for centuries, inspiring and regulating Christian life and theology for a long time. For the same reason, it should look for its sources, not in the recent past, but in the oldest Tradition, and specifically in the writings of the Church Fathers and the decisions of previous ecumenical councils.

A council should also be consistent. It should therefore take care that what it says in one place is in line with the contents of its other constitutions, decrees and declarations. Now the already promulgated Constitution on the Liturgy, the proposed Constitution on the Church in its first chapters, the proposed Constitution on Revelation, which is scheduled to be debated later in the third session, center all piety and doctrine on the testimony of Sacred Scripture.

It would be inconsistent for the council to approve in its chapter on the Virgin Mary the use of a term which contradicts the New Testament.

As several speakers have pointed out, the term "Mediatrix" as applied to Mary is incompatible with the teaching of St. Paul: "As there is only one God, so there is only one Mediator between God and men, the man Jesus Christ, who gave himself as a ransom for all" (1 Tim., 2:5-6).

Admittedly, a strong expression is used in Orthodox piety: "Christ is the only Mediator, and Mary the only Mediatrix after Him." This could set a precedent for a doctrine of "Mary Mediatrix," if it were a doctrine in the Orthodox Church. But it is only a pious ejaculation. A council should not endorse an expression, however poetical and devotional, which runs counter to the New Testament.

In defense, the upholders of the title assert that the two are compatible. It is only under Christ that Mary mediates; she mediates as "Servant of Christ the Redeemer." But this begs the question, for it assumes that Christ has such a servant in the work of Redemption itself. That the Church, Mary and also all Christians are, in their task of spreading the Gospel, associated to the Redemption of the world is undoubted. That such a contribution to the work of Christ and the Holy Spirit is intrinsic to Redemption itself and makes a creature into a secondary mediator is a totally different conclusion that many bishops feel unwarranted by the premise.

One cannot foresee how the council will finally decide on the hotly debated question of the legitimacy of the word "Mediatrix." It is recognized that it does correspond to something which is true of the Virgin Mary, and not necessarily of her alone. But many contend that, in spite of this, the appellation remains unbiblical and misleading. Nevertheless others maintain that the name of "Mediatrix" should be kept because it extols the glory of the Mother of God.

The Doctrinal Commission of the council must decide what to do in view of the contradictory positions adopted by the council Fathers. Where the majority will lie if the matter is put to a vote is not certain.

But it is certain that if the constitution retains the title of "Mediatrix," it will do so by way of description, without recommending its use and with a strong warning not to explain it against the basic faith in the unique Mediation of Christ.

At any rate, it seems likely that theology, if not piety, will learn from the debates at the council to be more sober in borrowing Marian titles from the language of popular devotion. FATHER GEORGE H. TAVARD

Father Tavard is author of a number of theological works, chairman of the theology department of Mount Mercy College, Pittsburgh, an official consultor for the Second Vatican Council, and a member of the U.S. bishops' press panel in Rome.

Meaning of Concelebration

When Pope Paul VI and more than 20 bishops concelebrated the opening Mass of the Second Vatican Council's third session, two points were made clear.

The pope and all the other bishops together make up a body, called a "college," with a common responsibility to serve, teach and make holy the universal Church. And the liturgical reform decreed in December, 1963, by the council is well under way.

According to the 1963 Constitution on the Liturgy, the Church's real nature is perfectly manifested when the whole body assembles at the altar: the bishop surrounded by his priests, ministers and all the faithful taking part in the celebration of the Eucharist. On the occasion of the first Mass of the council's third session (Sept. 14), it was the chief bishop, the pope, surrounded by the other bishops who make up the apostolic college, by the priests and other members of the clergy, and by a huge crowd of the faithful all taking their full part.

This form of Mass, with a chief celebrant presiding and with other concelebrating bishops (or priests), is a concrete symbol of what the ecumenical council will proclaim in its doctrinal pronouncement on the Church, expected in the next few weeks. Central to this is the council's teaching on the "collegiality" of bishops: all the bishops as a body or college succeed the band of apostles, as the chief one among them, the pope, succeeds the chief apostle, Peter.

This doctrine, agreed upon by four-fifths of the bishops at the 1963 session, strongly supported by Pope Paul in his opening address, and voted for overwhelmingly by council Fathers at the meetings of Sept. 22 and 23, is re-

flected on the diocesan level in the collaboration of the priests with the bishop, on the parish level in the collaboration of assistant priests with the pastor and, finally, in the common action of all the Church's members, lay and clerical.

In the Mass concelebrated in St. Peter's basilica the community nature of the Church was a little obscured by the almost inevitable grandeur of the occasion. The altar was practically hidden from view by the concelebrating bishops gathered around it, there was a multiplicity of prayers said in common by the concelebrants, the reception of Communion and other rites were complex in appearance, and only a handful of the laity received Communion.

But none of this can obscure the powerful teaching effect of concelebration, showing the order of bishops united to the priests and other clergy, united to all the people, in the Church's life of prayer and work. It was a sign of the unity of the priesthood, but above all a sign of the unity of the Church. All attention was focused on the celebration of the "same Eucharist, the single prayer, at one altar." Clergy and faithful sang the sacred chants and refrains to psalms. The role of the chief celebrant, in this case Pope Paul, and of the other celebrants, in this case other bishops, was made clear: to preside over and serve the whole Church.

Last January, the Pope set up a new commission to revise the Church's liturgy in accordance with the council's commands. In the spring, the commission announced that a new rite of concelebration was being prepared. Next Holy Thursday it should become a common parish

54

experience. And, wherever there is an abundance of priests, the practice of celebrating Masses individually and privately should gradually give way to the single community Mass concelebrated as a sign of unity.

The Mass in St. Peter's also gave indications of revisions which, when officially decreed, will affect all Masses celebrated publicly, not merely concelebrations. These include, for example, the service of God's word (from the Epistle through the Creed) with the celebrating priest seated away from the altar and listening to the readings along with the people; the few invocations of a litany after the Creed; the "prayer of the people" for the needs of the Church and of all mankind; the simple ending of Mass with the dismissal and blessing.

If there had been any doubt about liturgical—and other—renewal in the Church, it was dispelled by the concelebrated Mass. Concrete reforms are under way. Their purpose is a fuller, sounder proclamation of doctrine and the spiritual renewal of the Church's members.

FATHER FREDERICK R. McMANUS

Father McManus is a priest of the Boston archdiocese who is president of the National Liturgical Conference, professor of canon law at the Catholic University of America, an official consultor for the ecumenical council, and a member of the U.S. bishops' press panel in Rome.

88th General Congregation

September 25, 1964

Debate of the Second Vatican Council on the important declaration on religious liberty was brought to a close after three days of praise and criticism.

One of the last to speak in its favor was Archbishop Karl J. Alter of Cincinnati. Another was a former personal theologian of Pope Paul VI.

Several other bishops, including some Americans who had been scheduled to speak, did not take the floor because the moderator, Leo Cardinal Suenens of Malines-Brussels, moved that debate had been sufficient to expose the areas of opinions on the document. A vast majority of the council favored closing debate.

A few more interventions would be heard later if the bishops can secure the signatures showing that each speaks in the name of 70 or more council Fathers.

Archbishop Alter told the council that the declaration does not affirm a personal right of any individual to teach error or to do harm. He insisted that the declaration does not speak at all of the possible senses in which religious freedom can be understood, but only refers to the right of every human being to be free from outside force in his worship of God.

Archbishop Alter noted that persons do not have a personal right to teach error or to do harm. What the declaration claims for the individual is only freedom from social coercion, he said.

The prelate said that peace and harmony would be promoted if the council issues a clear declaration on this point, especially in areas where the Church is living in a pluralistic society.

Because Catholics have been accused of inconsistency and even of insincerity, as though they shifted their stand on religious liberty according to their majority or minority in social society, the text should be so formulated as to forestall any repetition of these doubts and suspicions, he said.

Archbishop Alter added that the Fathers should affirm the absolute incompetence of public officials to judge religious matters, and should reiterate that these officials have the obligation to use all appropriate means to insure free practice of religion with safety to the individual.

This declaration, said the archbishop, is good for the Church. It does not say that men enjoy an absolute right to independence from all authority on earth, including the Church, he added.

But without liberty for the Church's individual members, that liberty which the Church has always claimed for herself would be useless and meaningless, he said.

Archbishop Alter also rejected the frequent criticism that the schema jumps illicitly from the subjective order (conscience) to the objective order (social rights).

Support of the declaration also came from Bishop Carlo Colombo, head of the theological faculty of the Milan archdiocesan seminary, who was Pope Paul's theologian when the Pontiff was Archbishop of Milan and who remains a close friend of the Pope.

Bishop Colombo defended the doctrinal character of the text and said it should be retained. He said the text, although pastoral in intent, cannot avoid being doctrinal at the same time and it should set forth principles governing relationships of persons with moral and religious truth.

Offering a number of principles to guide in drawing up this doctrine, Bishop Colombo noted that problems offered by the exercise of freedom of religion cannot be solved always and everywhere in the same way. Solutions will differ according to circumstance.

Not all of the day's 11 speakers were so in favor. Bishop Ubaldo Cibrian Fernandez, C.P., for Corocoro. Bolivia, called the declaration unacceptable. He gave as his reason his belief that it was not based on adequate doctrinal principles.

As it stands now, he said, its teaching is in conflict with the magisterium [teaching authority] of the Church.

The Master General of the Dominicans, Father Aniceto Fernandez, O.P., also criticized the declaration. He called it a sign of our times in that it shows a desire to avoid all division and criticism. He called it weak because it affirms merely the subject principle as the basis for freedom of religion, and because, by leaving too much to the dictates of conscience, it obscures the principal fonts of Christian doctrine.

The 88th session opened with Mass in the Syro-Antiochene rite celebrated by Archbishop Cyrille Emmanuel Benni of Mossul, Iraq, with Aramaic, the language of Our Lord, used in the rite and singing. Bishop

Jean Karroum of Hassake, Syria, enthroned the Gospel.

Archbishop Felici announced the distribution of the declaration on the Jews, and also that the Pope has granted all council Fathers who are not bishops the same powers to hear confessions in Rome as were granted to the Bishops last December.

It was also announced that the six schemata which have been reduced to propositions and which were only to be voted on without debate will now be accompanied by a brief discussion in the council hall before voting. Archbishop Felici said this was in response to requests from many bishops.

During the session votes were taken on six more amendments to the schema on the Church, dealing largely with aspects of infallibility.

The first speaker of the day was Francesco Cardinal Roberti, president of the Commission on the Reform of the Roman Curia. This identification was given in the council press bulletin and was the first disclosure of this title, although it had been known generally that he had been named to the post earlier by the Pope.

Cardinal Roberti stated that a clear distinction was needed between freedom of conscience and freedom of consciences. As freedom of conscience is often understood today, he said, it means conferring on an individual right of free personal choice, even when confronted with the law of God. The Church cannot admit freedom of conscience in its present-day sense because the Church could thereby be in contradiction with itself. However, the Church can admit freedom of consciences, he said, because this implies freedom from all external coercion in the belief and exercise of religion.

Archbishop Denis E. Hurley of Durban, South Africa, made a speech which was a vigorous attempt to refute the classic argument for a state's right to intervene in religious matters. He pointed out that if the state has such a right, then the schema should be altered.

He reduced this classic argument to skeletal form. It begins with the premise that man is a social being and is therefore obliged to worship in a social way. Therefore, society should worship God in the way God points out.

Archbishop Hurley said that the flaw of this argument is that it jumps from its premise to the unwarranted conclusion that civil society as such must be concerned with this worship.

He said that if God founded a special society for this purpose, then the "famous principle of subsidiarity" releases civil society from competence over religious matters. But God did found such a society, the Church.

He said the classical argument holds that the Church has direct power over civil society, and not merely in what pertains to worship but even in the civil constitution itself. But this, he said, is no longer admitted.

He said that a declaration that civil society has no obligation or authority in religious matters would not harm the Church. On the contrary, it could pave the way for the Church's broader influence in a society that is not resentful against the Church on account of any authoritarianism.

Spanish-born Bishop Cibrian Fernandez followed the South African prelate. He objected to the text on the grounds that its foundation should be in God and the nature of truth. He warned the council that the declaration cannot be in conflict with the Church's magisterium. Basically we should declare simply that religious liberty must be implemented in practice and with all due respect for the rights of others, he said.

Exiled Archbishop Frederick Melendro, S.J., of Anking, China, another Spaniard, also called for textual reorganization and suggested it would be best if the whole discussion of the subject were postponed to allow the matter to mature.

Objecting that the declaration bases religious liberty on the norm of the dictates of conscience, he stated that it is not sufficient to say that men are invited to embrace the true faith. Rather, they are bound to do so by the divine law, he said.

Polish Archbishop Karol Wojtyla of Cracow declared that all should make ceaseless efforts to secure full religious liberty from the state, because no state has the power to dominate religion. A declaration of this kind is expected from the council by peoples of all faiths, he said.

Archbishop Gabriel Garrone of Toulouse, France, said the apparent contradiction between the declaration's doctrine and the actual practice of the Church is not a real one. Noting the profound changes which have taken place in the past century, he indicated that the Church formerly emphasized what it saw as the threat from doctrinaire liberalism. Today, he said, it stresses the rights of man in his daily life. There have been regrettable incidents in the past, and for these the Church is humbly penitent, he said. But he added that the doctrine of the declaration should point out that no real contradiction exists.

Vietnamese Bishop Simon Hoa Nguyen van Hien of Dalat said the declaration is of immense importance for dialogues with other Christians and in areas where Christians are a minority. He called for a change in the title to "Basic Principles of Religious Liberty," and asked for a new paragraph treating of man's objective calling from God and of the mission and function of the Church in relation to civil society.

Archbishop Alter was next on the roster of speakers, and he was followed by the Dominican superior general, who warned that the text could cause confusion.

In the text, he said, religious liberty arises from below, namely from the consciences of men, whereas its real source is from above. He added that the text proceeds in a manner which is too worldly and naturalistic, and that the council document should not reflect only the present day.

Ireland's Bishop Cornelius Lucey of Cork and Ross declared that the liberty of conscience is a human right and is not to be understood as a personal moral right. There is a universal obligation to respect good faith no matter where it may be found, he said. There are even atheists in good faith, he said, and added that while man's personal acts of religion are always acceptable to God, this gives no right to interfere with the acts of religion performed by others.

Last speaker of the day was Bishop Colombo, who suggested some principles concerning relationships of humans with moral and religious truth. First of these was that the foundation of all religious liberty is two-fold, first a natural right to investigate moral and religious truth and to follow it according to the dictates of conscience; and second, the freedom of the act of Christian and Catholic faith.

The second principle he offered was that the council should insist on two other principles, the obligation to investigate truth and to follow it, and to investigate it through adequate means, chief among which is the doctrinal authority of the Church and secondly the special value of truth among the benefits of society. He offered a third idea, that of the relationship of personal rights and freedom of faith with the demands of the common good. This problem cannot be solved always and everywhere in the same way, he warned.

With that debate was closed. Amendments and votes cast that day on the schema on the Church follow:

Amendment 25 — that bishops do not have the gift of infallibility as individuals, but that the universal body of bishops is infallible when it teaches solemnly, in union with the successor of Peter, especially in ecumenical councils. The vote was, 2,134 "yes" and 63 "no."

Amendment 26 — that the scope of this infallibility is coterminus with the deposit of divine revelation. The vote was 2,059 "yes" and 32 "no."

Amendment 27 — that the Roman Pontiff is infallible when he definitively proclaims a point of faith or morals as pastor and teacher of the faithful of Christ. His infallibility does not depend on the consent of the Church. This is because he does not declare his opinions as a private person but as supreme teacher of the universal Church. The vote was 2,140 "yes" and 45 "no."

Amendment 28 — that the infallibility promised to the Church is found in the body of bishops when it exercises the supreme magisterium in union with the successor of Peter. Such definitions always have the assent of the Church because of the action of the Holy Spirit. The vote was 2,139 "yes" and 46 "no."

Amendment 29 — that when the Roman Pontiff or the council issues a definition, this is in keeping with Revelation, which all are bound to accept. In the investigation and formulation of definitions, the Roman Pontiff and the bishops, according to circumstances, cooperate but they can never proclaim a new public revelation as belonging to the divine deposit of faith. The vote was 2,155 "yes" and 25 "no."

Amendment 30 — that the bishops' office of sanctifying is exercised especially through the celebration of the Holy Eucharist. The vote was 2,139 "yes" and 21 "no."

JAMES C. O'NEILL

* * * *

What has happened to the proposed council statement on the Jews and other non-Christians since the first version which was released to the public press last year?

Answering questions at the American bishops' press panel meeting following the introduction of the schema on the floor of the council (Sept. 25), Father Thomas Stransky, C.S.P., of the Secretariat for Promoting Christian Unity, pointed out that the new version which was leaked to the press a few weeks earlier obviously omits some items contained in the first one. He also revealed that a second version prepared after the March meeting of the unity secretariat has never been released and is still under council secrecy.

Father Stransky, a Paulist Father from Milwaukee, said the third version, now on the council floor, omits two statements contained in the original:

1. The theological explanation, based on the Council of Trent, that all men are guilty of the death of Christ.

2. A historical explanation of the instrumentality of Christ's death which eliminates from the responsibility of deicide the Jewish people as a whole at the time of Christ.

He said the text has retained the original statement exonerating the Jewish people of the present time from any responsibility. Father Stransky pointed out, as had Cardinal Bea in the statement introducing the text, that there were four and one-half million Jews outside Jerusalem at the time of Christ, which was then a majority of the Jews, and that even those who were directly involved in the death of Christ could not have been formally responsible since, as Christ said from the cross, "They know not what they do."

Father Stransky said both points of the original are omitted in the present version, but were included in the second text prepared in March. He said that it is no secret that since the unity secretariat had no time to call together the bishops of the commission to discuss eliminations after the March meeting, the only body competent to make changes was the Coordinating Commission. Why they did it had not been explained yet, but there was no point in speculating why, he said, adding: "The council Fathers will have to decide whether these statements should be returned to the text."

In defense of the new version, Msgr. John M. Oesterreicher, of the Institute of Judaeo-Christian Studies at Seton Hall University, South Orange, N.J., told the press panel: "It meets many of the concerns of Jews today. If the original had not been revealed to the press, the present version would have been quite satisfactory to many. The public is not generally aware that all schemas have undergone many changes since their original versions were drawn up. They are aware of this one because of the leak."

Msgr. Oesterreicher added: "Many wrong conclusions and misstatements have followed the publication of the present version. For one, there is no invitation to Jews to join the Church. No talk of coming back. No proselytism intended. The word 'adunatio' [drawing together] used in the present text is a supple and tender one. It implies eschatological hope for the final union of all people in the people of God and is an exact counterpart of the Jewish hope for the same union envisioned by the prophets."

Father Stransky added that the council will not settle the problem of what is meant by "adunatio" — whether this "calling together" will take place in the pilgrim church on earth or only in heaven.

Father Francis J. McCool, of the New York province of Jesuits and stationed at Rome's Biblical Institute, pointed out that St. Paul's struggle with this notion (in Romans 9, 11) was prompted by his conviction that God's promises to Abraham and the prophets for the salvation of the chosen people could not fail to be fulfilled. Hence salvation must come to the Jews in some way.

FATHER JOHN P. DONNELLY

* * * *

The length of debate in the Second Vatican Council on the proposed religious liberty declaration should not occasion surprise, Archbishop Karl J. Alter of Cincinnati said here.

Speaking as a press panelist after participating in the council debate, the archbishop reminded newsmen that debate in the U.S. Constitutional convention lasted from June to September in 1787 before settling on a simple statement contained in the First Amendment, which guarantees freedom of religion.

Archbishop Alter, a pioneer in the religious liberty field, recalled that he wrote an article on the subject 30 years ago for the American Ecclesiastical Review.

He said much of the difficulty involved concerns the definition of religious liberty, which means different things to different people. Some approach the issue from the logical sphere, others from the practical side favored by the U.S. hierarchy, concerned with the juridical order, Archbishop Alter said.

Declaration on Jews Presented to Council

The Church's unity cardinal put the draft declaration on the Jews before the Second Vatican Council with the warning that it is "plainly impossible" for the council to sidestep this issue.

Augustin Cardinal Bea, S.J., raised his voice in emphasizing that the council's declaration on the Jews is not political in any way. The president of the Secretariat for Promoting Christian Unity said that it is "purely religious" and does not concern itself with the Zionist movement or the state of Israel but simply with the followers of the Mosaic law.

Referring to the much-publicized omission from the text of an original passage denying that the Jews can be charged with deicide, Cardinal Bea told the council that his secretariat had had nothing to do with this omission. This was accomplished without the secretariat's cooperation, he said.

However, he added, the idea that the Jews were a deicide or God-killing people could not be considered the taproot of anti-Semitism. He conceded that history

produced examples where individuals and peoples were led to despise or persecute Jews on the grounds that the Jews were deicides. But he affirmed that there are many different causes of anti-Semitism, in the social, political and economic spheres.

Cardinal Bea disclaimed any knowledge of how the text of the revised schema on the Jews had gotten into the newspapers.

He said the revised text was better organized than the original text, which was presented to the council toward the end of the previous session but never voted upon.

The slight, stooped Jesuit was greeted with warm applause as he approached the speakers' stand. Sustained applause filled the council hall again when he concluded with the affirmation that the schema's potential contribution to the world is so great that the council should proclaim it regardless of whatever political accusations might follow.

Leo Cardinal Suenens of Malines-Brussels, the

moderator of the day, prefaced Cardinal Bea's address with the explanation that Cardinal Bea was delivering it then instead of on Sept. 28 as originally scheduled, because Cardinal Bea would be away in Greece. Cardinal Bea is delivering the relic of the head of St. Andrew to Orthodox Metropolitan Constantine of Patras on behalf of Pope Paul VI.

Cardinal Bea began by drawing attention to "the vast interest" aroused by this declaration on the Jews. Not only is the world watching for this declaration on the Jews, he said, but many people will judge the council solely according to how it handles this matter.

But he asserted that this interest alone would not justify the council's action.

"The primary reason is that the Church must follow the example of Christ and the apostles in their love for the Jewish people," he said. Hence, it is "plainly impossible" to strike this question from the council's agenda.

He said that not only had the draft declaration been reorganized more logically, but that certain texts had been added on the prerogatives of the chosen people and on the Christian hope for the eventual coming together of the Jewish people with the chosen people of the New Testament.

Cardinal Bea styled the deicide issue as the "crucial" point — whether and in what way the condemnation and death of Christ can be said to be the fault of the Jewish people as such.

He then denied that a notion of this kind is the chief reason for anti-Semitism, though conceding it had indeed been responsible at times for contempt and persecution of the Jews.

He examined the problem in some detail. He pointed out that although leaders of the Sanhedrin were not democratically elected, they were nonetheless regarded as the legitimate authority of the people.

Cardinal Bea then asked whether the leaders of the Jewish people were so fully aware of the divinity of Jesus that they could be called formal deicides. In answer, he pointed to Christ's words on the Cross: "They know not what they do," and to Peter's words, "through ignorance you acted, just like your princes." He also cited similar words of St. Paul.

He asked whether the entire Jewish people of that time could be held responsible for Christ's death. In reply he pointed out that the Jews of the Roman Empire outside Palestine numbered about four and one-half million, which was more than the entire population of Palestine in that era.

He asked rhetorically whether all these Jews could be held equally guilty. But he said that in any event there are no grounds for attributing any responsibility for Christ's death to today's Jewish people as a people.

Cardinal Bea said his secretariat had considered many ways of stating this difficult matter. He said a text was finally agreed upon but that lack of time made it impossible to submit it to all the members of the secretariat.

Presumably this meant the secretariat has a formula ready for insertion in the schema, which had been stripped of all mention of the innocence of the Jews in the death of Jesus.

Cardinal Bea said that many council Fathers had specifically requested that the schema come to grips with the issue of deicide.

He turned to the second part of the declaration, which deals with other non-Christian religions.

He let it be known that some council Fathers had asked that the Moslems receive special treatment in the declaration. It is widely held in Rome that the Moslems received specific mention in the schema to smoothe over whatever Moslem feelings may have been ruffled by the council's draft declaration on the Jews.

Cardinal Bea said the schema's passages on the Moslems had been checked and approved by specialists on the Islamic question, both among the Dominican Fathers in Jerusalem and the White Fathers in Tunis.

Cardinal Bea attributed great importance to this section on other non-Christian religions because many of today's non-Christians who believe in God find themselves surrounded by practical irreligion and militant atheism. A statement from the council would comfort and encourage them, he said.

He said this section of the schema stresses three points: (1) God is the Father of all men and they are His children; (2) All men are brothers; (3) All discrimination, violence and persecution prompted by race or national origin should be condemned.

Cardinal Bea recalled that many Fathers had felt that a declaration on the Jews was out of place in the schema on ecumenism, which, properly speaking, deals with the promotion of Christian unity. On the other hand, he pointed to a close connection between all Christians and the chosen people of the Old Testament, conceding that this tie is less strong than among Christians themselves.

But a compromise was reached, he said. The subject was treated in a distinct document which was, however, connected with the schema on ecumenism.

He replied to criticisms of the schema which center around its lack of some of the more severe judgments which Christ Himself made on His fellow Jews. We must not forget Christ's love for the Jews, and the love of the Apostles for the Jews, he said.

Winding up his speech, Cardinal Bea insisted "most vigorously" that the draft declaration on the Jews is a purely religious document. He said the declaration's aim is to imitate the "sublime example" of Christ's charity on the cross.

He concluded by saying that "the renovation of

the Church" is of such supreme importance that the Church must be ready to expose itself to the accusations of pursuing political ends in its declaration on the Jews and other non-Christians.   PATRICK RILEY

* * * *

British Archbishop John Heenan of Westminster declared here that it is "fitting that the compassion of the council be expressed" in stating its abhorrence of the treatment Jews have suffered in the present generation.

The British prelate, vice president of the Secretariat for Promoting Christian Unity, spoke at a press conference (Sept. 26) in the presence of American Archbishop Martin J. O'Connor, president of the conciliar press committee. He also made a strong plea for adoption "by an impressive majority" of the council Fathers of the statement on religious liberty to show the world "where Catholics stand on the question of freedom."

"It is important," Archbishop Heenan said, "that the council speak in unequivocal fashion to show that all men should be free to practice their religion and that no man be penalized because of his religious beliefs."

He warned, however, that "freedom is not easy to define, for it is not mere tolerance which is passive and negative. It is active and positive."

Regarding the statement on the Jews, Archbishop Heenan again stressed that the motives for including it in the ecumenism schema are "exclusively theological

and spiritual, and the chief reason why the Jews are singled out is because of their unique relationship with Christianity." At the same time, he said, the unity secretariat felt the opportunity should be taken to condemn anti-Semitism and all racial and religious intolerance.

It would be a misunderstanding of the whole nature of ecumenism to assume that the object of the statement is the conversion either of non-Catholics or non-Christians, the archbishop said.

"Ecumenism is an essay not in polemics but in charity," he said. "Its intention is not for one side to score a victory but for each side to emerge with a deeper knowledge of the other."

He explained that "ecumenism for the Church of Rome is not a plot to destroy the faith of Protestants or Jews or any other believers."

Regarding the revision of the original text of the Jewish statement, Archbishop Heenan said he did not know why the sentence about the Jews being innocent of deicide had been removed.

"It is a matter of faith that Christ is the victim of sin," he said, "and that all sinners are in this sense responsible for His death." He said Christ's condemnation by the Sanhedrin (the supreme council of Jews in Jerusalem) is a historical fact, "but this is not to say that the Jews, having recognized Christ as God, resolved to kill Him. For had they accepted Christ's claim to be God, obviously they would not have put Him to death."

Cardinal Bea

This is an unofficial English translation of the Sept. 25 speech of Augustin Cardinal Bea in which he presented the proposed declaration on the Jews to council Fathers.

1. In speaking on the schema of the declaration, "Jews and Non-Christians," I can only begin with the fact that this declaration certainly must be counted among the matters in which public opinion has shown the greatest concern. Scarcely any other schema has been written up so much and so widely in periodicals. Whatever the reasons for this interest and whatever judgment may be given concerning its value, the very fact of the concern shows clearly that precisely in this matter public opinion has turned its eyes toward the Church and many will judge the council good or bad by its approval or disapproval of the declaration.

Certainly this is not the only or even the principal reason why the declaration is necessary. In the first place it is required by the Church's fidelity in following the example of Christ and the apostles in their love for this people. Nonetheless, on the other hand, these external reasons must not be neglected. They make it entirely evident that it is quite impossible to do what some

of the Fathers have asked, namely, remove the question completely from the agenda.

Our Secretariat [for Promoting Christian Unity] has examined seriously the reasons proposed by these Fathers and has made every effort to revise the text of the declaration in accordance with the proposals made thus far by the Fathers of the council. In addition, the members of the Commission for the Coordination of the Work of the Council know that it was necessary to spend a great deal of time on this brief text.

2. The revision was done in this way. First of all, in accord with the proposals expressed in the hall during the second session of the council, the brief introduction, which was given at the beginning of the chapter in the earlier version, has been enlarged and made the second part of the declaration. Thus the schema now consists of two parts, almost equal in length, one concerning the Jews, the other concerning non-Christians.

3. With regard to the first part concerning the

Jews, the text was arranged in a somewhat better order, so that the progress of ideas is better expressed. Similarly, some new ideas were added, principally two texts from the Epistle to the Romans, on the prerogatives of the chosen people (9, 4) and on the Christian hope for the final gathering together of this people with the chosen people of the New Testament, that is, the Church (11, 25).

4. The central point on which major changes were introduced is the question of "deicide," as it is called. It should be noted that the question has been very fully discussed in the periodicals, but that this was done without any cooperation or intervention of the secretariat. The principal elements of the question should therefore be indicated to you: whether and in what manner the condemnation and death of Christ the Lord are to be attributed to the culpability of the Jewish people as such.

Many Jews today assert that the belief in a culpability of the Jewish people as such is the principal basis of anti-Semitism, as it is called, and thus the source of the many evils and persecutions to which the Jews have been subjected through the centuries. This assertion does not stand up in any way. In the report already given last year on the schema I stated clearly in this hall: "Do we not know very well that there are many reasons for anti-Semitism which are not of the religious order but are political-national, or psychological or social or economic?"

Nevertheless there are many historical instances from various nations which cannot be denied. In these instances, this belief concerning the culpability of the Jewish people as such has led Christians to consider and to call the Jews with whom they lived a "deicide" people, reprobated and cursed by God, and therefore to look down upon them and indeed to persecute them. For this reason, the Jews of today are trying in every way to have the council publicly and solemnly pronounce the contrary, namely, that the death of the Lord is in no way to be attributed to the Jewish people as such. Now the question may be put this way: Is a declaration to this effect on the part of the council possible? If it is possible, how is it to be made and what should its tenor be?

As is evident, there is no question here, nor can there be any question, of denying a single point of doctrine found in the Gospels. Rather the question is: Certainly the leaders of the Jewish Sanhedrin, even if not democratically chosen by the people, were considered and are to be considered as the lawful authority of the people, in accord with the mentality of the times and of Sacred Scripture itself. The gravity and tragedy of what this authority did in regard to the condemnation and death of Christ the Lord comes from the fact that it was the lawful authority.

But we must ask what is the gravity of this act? The leaders of the people in Jerusalem did not fully understand the divinity of Christ in such a way that they could be formally called deicides. On the cross the Lord prayed to His Father and said: "Father, forgive them, for they know not what they do" (Luke 23, 34). This manner of speech is not an empty formula — surely a false supposition — it certainly means that the Jews did not fully understand their crime. St. Peter also, speaking to the Jewish people about the Lord's crucifixion, said: "I know that you acted through ignorance, as did your leaders. . ." (Acts 3,17). Thus St. Peter in some way excuses the leaders as well. And St. Paul speaks in similar fashion in Acts 13, 27.

Besides, whatever we may say of the knowledge of the leaders in Jerusalem, the whole Jewish people of that time as such never can be charged with what was done by the leaders in Jerusalem to bring about the death of Christ. It is a statistical fact that in apostolic times the Jewish diaspora in the Roman Empire numbered about 4,500,000. Are all these to be accused of the deeds done by the members of the Sanhedrin on that sad Friday?

And even if we granted, which we do not, that those acts could be attributed to the whole people of that time as such, by what right may they be blamed on the Jewish people of today? We may never, in any case, attach blame to any people for deeds of its ancestors or leaders of 19 centuries past.

5. Our secretariat has tried to take into account these conditions. On the one hand, the guilt of those who decreed the crucifixion of Christ the Lord should be asserted in accord with the Gospel accounts themselves. On the other hand, the guilt should not be ascribed to the people as such, much less to the people of today.

In this connection, however, it is of no help to point out that Christ the Lord died for all men. This fact does not mean that guilt for the Lord's death in the historic order — which alone is at issue — is to be transferred to all men or that all men in the historic order were the effective cause of the Lord's death. At the time the Jewish people as such — both of the time of Christ and, even more, of our time — should never be accused of guilt which is not theirs. I therefore ask that this problem and its several parts be considered in judging this section of the declaration.

Because of the difficulty of the question, it will be understood that one formula after another has been tried in order to satisfy the desires and the difficulties proposed by the Fathers. Thus many consultations have been undertaken which, as many of you realize, have become known even publicly, I do not know in what way. In view of this, both the Fathers of the council and others, including non-Catholics and non-Christians, have respectfully requested that the issue of "deicide" be somehow treated in the declaration.

It would take too long to mention these discussions individually. It is enough to indicate the way in which the text in your hands has come about. But one point may be added. These discussions have consumed a long period of time. It was therefore not permitted to submit this part of the declaration to the members of the secretariat for their examination. Since the secretariat had completed all other matters at its meeting last March, it did not seem that the members should be called to Rome again to examine this part only. It now remains only to submit the schema for your examination and discussion, venerable Fathers. As you see, it is a question of great importance, at the same time extremely difficult.

6. Something must now be said about the second part of the declaration, which deals with our relationship to non-Christian religions. As I stated already, in the general discussion of the schema on ecumenism last year, many wish a fuller treatment of our relationship toward the followers of non-Christian religions; some Fathers also asked that explicit mention be made of Mohammedans.

Everyone appreciates the significance of this question in the circumstances of today, when representatives of various non-Christian religions on occasion seek contacts with the Catholic Church and when all religions are today surrounded by concrete evidences of irreligion and also by the proponents of theoretical atheism.

When our secretariat first dealt with this topic — in fact until last May—there was no other commission or secretariat to undertake it. (The Secretariat for Non-Christian Religions was not established until around the feast of Pentecost this year.) Thus there was nothing for our secretariat to do but take charge of the question.

With the assistance of some experts of the council we attempted to work out a first schema. After examining this schema, the Coordinating Commission, in a letter dated April 18, decreed that three ideas in particular should be expressed: that God is the Father of all men and that they are His children; that all men are brothers; and that therefore every kind of discrimination, force and persecution on the basis of nationality or race is to be condemned. The secretariat tried to follow this decision to the best of its ability.

In the development of the schema explicit mention of the Mohammedans was made as had been the desire of many Fathers. On this matter we may say that the text has been praised by experts, especially by the Dominican Institute for Oriental Studies in Cairo and by the White Fathers of the Pontifical Institute of Oriental Studies in Tunisia.

Since all the other matters to be treated by the secretariat had been completed by the beginning of March, it was not permitted to submit this part of the declaration to the judgment of the members of the secretariat, but this may now be done, venerable Fathers, after you have expressed your views on the schema.

7. Before I conclude, a word may be added about the relation of this declaration to the schema on ecumenism. As you recall from the debate here last year, the inclusion of this material in the schema on ecumenism was unsatisfactory to many Fathers. This is easily understood from the fact that ecumenism in a strict sense means activity to promote the unity of Christians. Nevertheless, because a profound and special relationship between the chosen people of the New Covenant, that is, the Church, and the chosen people of the Old Covenant is common to all Christians, clearly there is a bond between the ecumenical movement and the question treated in this declaration. But the bond between Christians and the Jewish people is not so close as the relations among Christians. The question of our relationship to the Jews therefore is not dealt with in a chapter of the schema on ecumenism, but separately in a declaration, which is instead added rather, and this only externally, to the schema on ecumenism. In this fashion perhaps all may be satisfied the more easily because the question of the location of the topic is not of major importance.

In conclusion I may speak of the nature and significance of the questions treated in this brief schema. They are matters of the greatest importance for the Church and for the world today. So far as the relationship to non-Christians is concerned, its importance is evident from the fact that the topic is dealt with for the first time in the history of the Church by any council and also from the Holy See's establishment of a special agency to foster relations with non-Christian religions. The same fact is abundantly clear in the program of the encyclical, Ecclesiam Suam, of the Supreme Pontiff, who speaks there of non-Christians and of the dialogue with them. Let us reflect, moreover, that this is a question of the relation of Catholics to hundreds of millions of men, of our love for them, of our fraternal assistance and cooperation with them.

So far as the Jewish people are concerned, it is necessary to say, again and again, that we do not treat here any political question whatever, but a purely religious question. We do not speak here of Zionism or of the political state of Israel, but of the followers of the Mosaic religion, wherever they live throughout the world. Nor is it a matter of heaping honors and praise upon the Jewish people, of extolling them above other nations, or of attributing privileges to them.

Some feel that the schema is drawn up so that it does not mention all the severe things — and they are not few — which Christ the Lord said to the Jews or about them, and that it forgets what blessings of God this people lost because of its unbelief. Therefore, it is said, the schema does not provide a sufficiently balanced picture of the real situation of this people. If this is the view of many of the Fathers, evidently we must again subject the question to thorough examination.

Nonetheless it may be stated now that in no sense is it the aim of the declaration to offer a picture of the Jewish people complete and absolute in all its parts. Otherwise how much would have to be said, how many doctrinal and historical testimonies brought forth. Certainly the Lord Jesus Himself spoke with the greatest severity of this people and to this people, as we know, for example, from the Gospel of St. Matthew, but He did all this out of love, to show them that the hour was at hand, that "they might know the time of their visitation" (cf. Luke 19,44), and accept the graces offered them, and so be saved. St. Paul also wrote of the Jews to the Thessalonians: "They killed the Lord Jesus and the prophets and have persecuted us. They are displeasing to God, and are hostile to all men, because they hinder us from speaking to the gentiles that they may be saved. Thus they are always filling up the measure of their sins" (1 Thess. 2,15 ff). But the same apostle on the other hand affirms: "I speak the truth in Christ . . . I have great sadness and continuous sorrow in my heart. For I could wish to be anathema myself from Christ for the sake of my brethren" (Rom. 9,1-3).

This is the purpose and the scope of the declaration, that the Church may imitate Christ and be apostles in this love and may be renewed by this imitation, reflecting on the way God has worked his salvation, reflecting on the blessing conferred on the Church through this people.

When there is question of the condemnation and death of the Lord in Jerusalem through the deeds of the leaders of the Jews, it is again for us to imitate the love of Christ the Lord on the cross, when He prayed to the Father for them and excused His persecutors in these words: "They know not what they do." It is for us to imitate the love of the Prince of the Apostles and the Apostle of the Gentiles. If the Lord, while He suffered persecution, acted thus toward His persecutors, how much more must we foster love for the Jewish people of today, who have no guilt in this matter.

While the Church, then, is eager for her own renewal in the council and, according to the famous expression of the Supreme Pontiff, John XXIII, tries to renew herself in the greater fervor of her youth, it seems that our hands must turn to this issue, that the Church may also be renewed in it. This renewal is of such importance that we must pay the price of accepting the danger that some may perhaps misuse this declaration for political purposes. For there is question here of our obligations to truth and to justice, of our duty of gratitude to God, of our duty to imitate faithfully and most closely Christ the Lord Himself and His Apostles Peter and Paul. In doing this the Church and this council cannot in any way permit the consideration of any political authority or political reason.

Archbishop Heenan

Following are two statements by Archbishop John C. Heenan of Westminster, England, on the ecumenical council's declarations on the Jews and on religious liberty, made at a Vatican City press conference Sept. 26.

1. The Jews

I propose for a moment to ignore current controversies in order to inquire how, in the first place, the council came to consider the question of the Jews. This came about in the context of ecumenism. It is impossible to study Catholic theology in isolation from the Old Testament. The new law cannot be interpreted without the old. It was natural, therefore, to extend Christian ecumenism to include the Jews. It is important to stress that the motives for including the Jews in the schema on ecumenism were exclusively theological and spiritual.

It was only after the publication of the original schema that the Secretariat for Christian Unity was made to face controversial issues. Bishops living in pre-dominantly Moslem areas made it plain that there was some danger lest Moslems should become aggrieved that the Jews alone were given consideration at the Vatican council. Those bishops living in areas where Buddhists or Hindus predominate similarly maintained that the faithful in Asia might suffer unless others besides Jews were mentioned.

The secretariat has met these objections by introducing a second part to the Declaration dealing with non-Christians who are not Jews. It must be said, however, that the demand for the inclusion of non-Jews may have been based on a misconception. We had no political motive of any kind for introducing the Jews into the schema on ecumenism. The chief reason why the Jews were singled out is because of their unique relationship with Christianity.

There was another reason why the secretariat felt it proper to introduce a section on the Jews. In our generation no race has suffered more violent and widespread persecution than the Jews. Millions of Jews during this century have been tortured and put to death for reasons of race or religion. It seemed fitting that the compassion of the great assembly of council Fathers should be expressed. The opportunity was taken of declaring our abhorrence of this treatment and of condemning anti-Semitism and all racial and religious intolerance.

At the last session it was hoped that the whole schema on ecumenism might have been approved. But it became clear during the debate that many of the Fathers had reservations. Cardinal Bea, therefore, wisely refrained from pressing the matter to a vote. Many of the Fathers in the Middle East and Asia might have voted against the schema for the reasons explained above. But if a considerable number of votes had been cast against the schema "De Judaeis," the world might have thought that many bishops are, in fact, anti-Semitic. This would have been deplorable. It was wise to postpone the voting until mention could be made of other non-Christian religions and so prevent any adverse reaction.

The reformed schema has created a great deal of misunderstanding, especially in England and in the United States of America. The headline in the Jewish Chronicle for Sept. 11 reads: "REVISED CHAPTER ON JEWS CAUSES DEEP DISMAY." There are two chief objections. The first is the quotation from St. Paul's Epistle to the Romans (Ch.11 v. 25): "I must not fail, brethren, to make this revelation known to you, or else you might have too good a conceit of yourselves. Blindness has fallen upon a part of Israel, but only until the tale of the gentile nations is complete; then the whole of Israel will find salvation. . . ." From this it was assumed that the main motive of including the Jews in the schema on ecumenism was to convert them.

This was to misunderstand the whole nature of ecumenism. Its object is not the conversion either of non-Catholics or of non-Christians. Ecumenism sets out to break down barriers between religious denominations in order that each may come to know and better understand the other. Ecumenism is an essay not in polemics but in charity. The dialogue is not a battle of wits. Its intention is not for one side to score a victory, but for each side to emerge with deeper knowledge of the other.

It must be admitted, however, that the ultimate end of all ecumenical activity is the unity of the sons of God. All Christians — whether of East or West, Protestant and Catholic — work and pray for reunion in the one Holy Catholic Church. The unity of all the brethren of Christ is the hope of every Christian. But ecumenism for the Church of Rome is not a plot to destroy the faith of Protestants, Jews or any other believers.

It is difficult to understand how the motives of the secretariat came to have been misinterpreted. There is no more reason for Jews than for Protestants to accuse the secretariat of proselytism. Rabbi Hechel is reported in the Jewish Chronicle as saying that he "would be ready to go to Auschwitz if faced with the alternative of conversion or death." This is, of course, rhetorical language. True conversion means the free acceptance of the Faith. It was far from the mind of the secretariate to use the statement "De Judaeis" to attack the beliefs of our Jewish brethren.

The second objection to the new draft is that it omits any reference to deicide. In the former schema these words were used: "Although a large part of the chosen people remains separated from Christ it would be unjust . . . to call it a deicide people since the Lord by His Passion and death has atoned for the sins of all men, which were the cause of the Passion and death of Jesus Christ (Luke 23: 34, Acts 3: 17, I Cor. 2, 8); the death of Christ was not caused by a whole people then living and much less than by a people of today."

The new schema reduces this paragraph to a single sentence: ". . . Equally all should be on their guard not to impute to the Jews of our time that which was perpetrated in the Passion of Christ."

I understand why the Jews feel aggrieved. To have removed the reference absolving the Jewish people from deicide at first sight appears equivalent to repeating the accusation. I do not know why the wording was changed. Perhaps the reason will be revealed during the debate in the council. To me personally the expression "deicide" has always seemed rather odd. That Jesus Christ was condemned to death by the Sanhedrin is a fact of history. In that sense it is correct to say that Jesus Christ was killed by Jews.

But this is not to say, or even to suggest, that the Jews, having recognized Christ as God, resolved to kill Him. If the Jews had accepted Christ's claim to be God they obviously would not have put Him to death.

What really needed to be stated is that the Jewish people as such cannot be held guilty for the death of Christ. This was not true of the main body of the Jewish people even at the time when Christ was crucified. It is even more obviously untrue to impute responsibility for the death of Our Lord to the Jews of a later age and of our own time.

It is important to say that the question of the culpability of the Jews for the death of Jesus has been given an altogether exaggerated importance. I do not believe that most Christians think of the Jews when thinking of the Passion and death of Our Lord. Every Catholic in the world has been taught to recite daily the Act of Contrition. In this prayer these words occur:

"I beg pardon for all my sins because they (my sins) have crucified my loving Saviour, Jesus Christ. . . ." It is part of Catholic theology that the Son of God died to redeem mankind from sin. It is of Faith that Christ is the victim of sin and that all sinners — Christians as well as non-Christians — are in this sense responsible for His death.

It is not for me to anticipate the debate in St. Peter's on the new draft of "De Judaeis." I can only hope that it will be passed with an impressive majority. I am quite certain that there is no anti-Jewish feeling among the Fathers of the council.

2. Religious Liberty

At the beginning of the declaration on religious liberty it is made clear that the work of ecumenism cannot prosper if any doubt exists that all Christians share a belief in religious liberty. That is why religious liberty is being discussed under the guidance of the Secretariat for Christian Unity. But it is evident that even if there were no talk of Christian unity, any council called in the middle of the 20th century would have to take account of the question of liberty. It may seem strange that never before has religious liberty been the subject of discussion in a general council. But the fact is that the need for the Church to protect liberty has become really urgent only in recent years.

Liberty has been threatened in our times in a way hitherto unknown to history. There have been absolute monarchs and tyrannical rulers in past centuries. What is new is making a cult of tyranny under the name of ideology. This is one of the reasons why the Church has been forced to turn its attention to the whole question of freedom. The threat to liberty is now epidemic and the time has come for a solemn proclamation from an ecumenical council.

The inviolability of a man's conscience is a fundamental requirement for all freedom. It is not new for the Church to make a plea for religious freedom. There have probably been more Christians put to death for their faith in the last 50 years than in any comparable period in history. The Church has tirelessly protested against the suppression of religious freedom in nazi and communist states throughout the world. But the statement does not seem to be primarily concerned with the persecution of religion. Cardinal Koenig, in a most moving speech on Thursday, was severely critical of the statement because it passes over almost in silence the crucifixion of liberty which is part of the communist creed.

The statement is concerned to proclaim the Church's belief in religious freedom for all mankind. It has often been alleged of Catholics that they believe in tolerance only when they themselves are in a minor-
ity. It is said that in countries where the overwhelming majority of citizens is Catholic the same view is not upheld. The statement is obviously more concerned to correct this view than to make a fresh protest against the persecution of the Church by atheistic communism. In the notes which accompany the statement the development of the Church's doctrine on liberty is outlined. In his encyclical Pacem in Terris, Pope John had a great deal to say about the dignity and liberty of the human person. He reminded us that while condemning error we must always cherish the person who errs. This was typical of the kindly attitude of Pope John but it was by no means a new departure in Catholic theology. The distinction between the sin and the sinner has always been traditional in the Church.

Pope John was following the example of his predecessor, Pope Pius XII, who had not remained silent on the question of religious freedom. Both in audiences and encyclicals he made reference to this subject. Thus in his encyclical Mystici Corporis, having spoken of his desire for the return of all to the one fold of Christ, he said: "It is absolutely necessary that this must come about because men freely desire to enter the Church. For no one can believe unless he wishes to do so. Those who do not believe should never be forced to enter the Church, to approach the altar or to receive the sacraments. The faith must be completely free because it is the submission of the mind and the will."

The subject matter of the statement has been described as delicate and difficult. One of the reasons for this is that the traditions of different countries tend to give people opposite concepts of freedom. Freedom itself is not easy to define. It is not mere tolerance which is passive and negative. Freedom is active and positive. Some countries are regarded as being more devoted to freedom than others. Citizens of the United States, for example, as members of a fairly new nation, are inspired by the ideals of liberty written into the United States constitution. But this constitution is, in fact, a modern version of ideas deeply rooted not only in Christian, but in Jewish and classical traditions. Above all, these ideas of liberty are embedded in the common law of England. Magna Carta is much more than a name to the British people.

Whatever principles be laid down by the council, the actual exercise of freedom ultimately depends upon those who hold authority in the state. It is not difficult to frame laws which give the impression of freedom although, in fact, they may mask intolerance. Let me take the example of Stalin's constitution for Soviet Russia. Article 124 reads: "Freedom of worship and freedom of anti-religious propaganda are guaranteed to all citizens." This meant, in effect, that citizens could attack religion but — since religious propaganda is illegal — the believer could be punished for preaching the Gospel.

Although without the good will of those in authority liberty cannot be enjoyed, it is nevertheless right for the Church to lay down the principles. It is important to remember that the idea of freedom as the right of all men is a fairly modern notion. For centuries civilized states took slavery for granted. Therefore we should not be too surprised that it has been left to a general council in the 20th century to consider the subject of liberty.

But it is important that the council should speak in an unequivocal fashion, because not only Christians but all believers and even non-believers await the council's pronouncement with deep concern. Pope Paul VI is conscious of the need for a conciliar statement and has stressed its importance. He said, according to L'Osservatore Romano of April 18, 1964, during an audience the previous day, "The Church is preoccupied with the question of religious liberty. It is a question of far-reaching importance and the council realizes it. We have every right to hope for the promulgation of a text which will have significance not only for the Church but for the countless number of people who will feel affected by an official pronouncement on this question."

Since a statement of this kind at a general council is unprecedented, it is not easy to know in what terms the decree should be made. The statement could easily have been allowed to grow into a politico-philosophical treatise. Equally it could have become a dogmatic thesis on the nature of truth and the right of man to be intolerant of error. But the Vatican council is pastoral and therefore has based its decisions on the nature and dignity of human personality. A man has the duty — and therefore the right — of obeying his conscience. But notice that the expression "liberty of conscience," like the expression "liberty of thought," is not strictly speaking accurate. A man can refuse to follow his conscience — just as he can refuse to admit the evidence of his senses — but conscience itself is a dictator — hence the common expression "dictates of conscience." Freedom of conscience really means that a man must be left free in choosing to accept or reject what his conscience tells him is right and good.

The council is setting out to show that all men should be free to practice their religion and that no man should be penalized because of his religious beliefs. This is a principle easy enough to lay down but not always easy to follow in practice. There are some religious sects which normal men regard as fanatical. Their creed may be founded, for example, upon hatred of those who differ from them in religion. It might be the duty of the state to curb the activities of sects of this kind. In this event the adherents of the sect would claim that they were being persecuted — whereas the state is merely doing its duty by protecting other citizens. It is part of the religious instinct of man to be a crusader. In Christian terms we call this the "missionary spirit." One of the most delicate problems of religious freedom is to know what limits, if any, should be set on missionary activity. This can be put another way by asking — what is the difference between conversion and proselytism? There is no easy formula to use in reply to this question. The difficulty is faced by a state whose citizens are subjected to missionary activities. Is it possible to say that Catholics everywhere must always have the right to attempt to make converts, if we deny the same right to others who are conscientiously following their beliefs?

Conscience must be a man's guide but — and here is the most delicate aspect of the problem — his conscience may be in error. For the individual Catholic the problem is not serious because the Church gives infallible guidance in faith and morals. But most of mankind is not within the Catholic Church and is without this infallible guidance. If Catholics are in authority in a state, have they the right or duty to allow non-Catholic missionaries to propagate what the Catholic Church declares to be false doctrine? The schema answers affirmatively but bishops from Catholic areas where unrest has been stirred up by Protestant missionaries may give no more than a juxta modum to this view. [A juxta modum vote is one that is favorable but with reservations.]

What should be the attitude of the state to religion? It is fashionable now to talk about the pluralistic society in which there is no one moral code binding all citizens. It is clear that the state has no right to suppress religion — but has she the right to support one religion more than another? Is it against the principles of religious liberty to have an established church in different states?

Not all are agreed on what is meant by state neutrality in matters of religion. It need not mean that the state must stand apart from religion. It could mean that the state is willing to give support to the various religions of their citizens. We know, for example, how differently states interpret their duty toward denominational schools. Although in England the Anglican is the established church, Catholic schools receive precisely the same generous grants as are given to Anglican schools. In other countries state aid of every kind is withheld from church schools. These I give as examples of the difficulty and delicacy of the Vatican council in making a detailed statement on religious freedom.

The matter is now under debate and we can only say that it is a welcome sign that the Catholic Church should stand so strongly for religious freedom. The reputation of the Church has often been attacked on the grounds of her intolerance. I hope and believe that this conciliar document will be passed by an impressive majority so that the world may see where Catholics stand on the question of freedom.

89th General Congregation
September 28, 1964

Strong support for a clear and positive statement of the Church's relation with the Jewish people was championed by four North American cardinals as the council opened discussion of the declaration on the Jews at the beginning of the third week of the third session.

Among 14 speakers to take the floor on the declaration were Richard Cardinal Cushing of Boston, Albert Cardinal Meyer of Chicago, Joseph Cardinal Ritter of St. Louis and Paul-Emile Cardinal Leger of Montreal, all of them throwing weight behind a strong statement.

Another member of the American hierarchy to speak at this 89th session was Bishop John J. Wright of Pittsburgh who, speaking in the name of more than 70 bishops, intervened to comment on the already-debated religious liberty declaration. He was joined by Archbishop John C. Heenan of Westminster, who spoke on the same subject in the name of the hierarchy of England and Wales, as well as many bishops of Scotland, Ireland, Australia, New Zealand, France and Belgium. Also speaking out on the religious liberty declaration were Archbishop Jean Zoa of Yaounde, Cameroun—in the name of the bishops of Africa—and Bishop Hadrianus Ddungu of Masaka, Uganda.

Included in the day's business was approval of six amendments to the schema on the nature of the Church. Among these was the general approval of the principle of the reestablishment of the diaconate as a separate order rather than as a stepping stone to the priesthood. No reference in the amendment was made to the question of a married diaconate or to the actual role deacons would have in the ministry.

Cardinal Cushing was the first of the American hierarchy to speak on the declaration on the Jews. The Bostonian said that the declaration of esteem for the Jews should be clearer, stronger, and more charitable. He specifically called for a denial by the text of the culpability of the Jews as a people for the death of Jesus.

Rejection of Christ by the Jewish people is a mystery and is to serve to instruct us, not to inflate us, he said. He declared that we cannot judge the ancient judges of the Jews, as that is for God to do. At the same time, he said, Christians must be aware of the universal guilt of all men who by sin crucified and are crucifying Christ.

Chicago's Cardinal Meyer called for restoration of the original text, which had been introduced during the last council session and which has been redrafted and presented in a different and altered form. The first text, he said, was better and more ecumenical. He stated that it is not enough for the Church to deplore any injustice against the Jewish people. It must also point out the close relationship of the Jews with the Church, he said.

Cardinal Meyer pointed out that St. Thomas Aquinas taught that the Jews were not formally guilty of deicide. He also stated that he felt there were reasons for restricting the declaration to the Jews alone and eliminating references to other non-Christian religions. He suggested these references could be included in schema 13, on the Church in the modern world.

The Chicago cardinal also called for a clear statement on the declaration against discrimination of any kind on the grounds of race, color or creed.

Cardinal Ritter took the floor to declare that the reason for the issuing of such a document is that it answers a need of the present time. Political considerations are not at stake, he declared, but the declaration would repair injustices of past centuries.

He noted that it is often assumed that God abandoned the Jews and the Jews were rightly to be accused of condemnation of Christ. Now, he said, an opportunity has been offered to remedy these errors and to remove these injustices.

The St. Louis cardinal suggested several changes. He suggested the text could make more fully and more explicitly clear how religious bonds join Jews and Christians today, how divine love has been extended to each in a special way and that there is a union in that love.

Cardinal Ritter objected to the phrase referring to a gathering together of the Jews in the Church and said it sounds as if the Church envisions conversion. He pointed out that the text does not speak of the Moslems and pagans in the same respect. Therefore, he suggested a choice of less offensive wording, and held that a paragraph expressing hope of the union of all men, extending to all men, be placed at the end of the document.

Cardinal Ritter also said that he preferred the first text and that the present one is only half-hearted in some of its statements and does not touch the heart of the

Jewish question. What is not said is sometimes more important than what is said, he declared.

To Cardinal Leger the declaration was all important. The Canadian cardinal called it a necessary act of the Church's renewal. He labeled unfortunate the fact that it is not stated explicitly that the Jewish people were not guilty of deicide.

The strongest voice against the declaration in the day's session came from Ignace Cardinal Tappouni, Syrian Rite Patriarch of Antioch. Speaking in the name of several Eastern rite prelates, he repeated their objections of the second session to any statement on the Jews whatsoever and called for its complete omission from the acts of the council.

The 89th session of the council opened with Mass celebrated by Bishop Frantisek Tomasek, a titular bishop from Czechoslovakia. Bishop Emilio Gaona Sosa, S.D.B., retired bishop of Concepcion, Paraguay, enthroned the Gospel book. It was his 80th birthday.

Archbishop Pericle Felici, council general secretary, announced that when the third chapter of the schema on the Church came to be voted on as a whole, it would be divided into two parts. Division had been requested by the council's doctrinal commission because it said that if this were not done, so many bishops would vote with reservations that an immense amount of work would be created for the commission.

(Commenting on this division of the vote on the third chapter, Father John King, O.M.I., pointed out at the American bishops' press panel session that the first part deals with the collegiality of the apostles and of the bishops as their successors. The second part would deal with the function of the bishops in ruling, teaching and sanctifying the Church, he said. He said the first would include the first 21 amendments, and the second would include amendments 22 through 39.)

Then Archbishop Heenan took the floor to outline the religious history of the Church in the British Isles and said that it is clear to both Protestants and Catholics in England that liberty and equality of treatment for all is the only way of promoting peaceful relations among citizens. He said this is why the declaration deserves praise and approval without reservation.

Archbishop Heenan rejected the proposal that only the principle of religious liberty be enunciated in the declaration. He said the reasons behind such principles must be spelled out, and asked the council to declare to the whole world once and for all the heartfelt belief of Catholics in the full liberty of all the sons of God.

Bishop Wright said he feared that discussion of the declaration had been too pragmatic. The text is too cautious, he said, because it does not point out sufficiently the link of religious liberty with the inseparable concept of the common good.

Bishop Wright declared that elimination of religious freedom does more harm than the preaching of error can do to the common good. The common good should not be confused with a sort of passive and forced conformity which is found in police states, nor is it just a grab bag of functions and services of the state such as social security, pension programs and police protection.

Therefore, he stated that a pragmatic approach is not worthy of the dignity and seriousness of the subject. Citing the philosopher Jacques Maritain, Bishop Wright said common good is founded not on force but on justice.

Finally, he urged the council to work for religious liberty of all men. We need religious liberty now more than ever before, he declared.

Bishop Ddungu of Masaka, speaking for 70 African bishops, said the declaration is satisfactory and is especially needed in Africa with its many new nations. Such a declaration would have a great effect on African countries, he said. Moreover, since most of Africa is not Christian, he said, an example of restriction of this freedom by Christians could lead African leaders to apply the same restrictions to Christians themselves.

Archbishop Zoa also expressed fear that the reasons advanced for defense of religious liberty were too pragmatic and called for pastoral and doctrinal reasons as well. The document should be concerned with man as such and not with man in any particular country or circumstance.

Debate on the Jewish declaration began with Achille Cardinal Lienart of Lille, France, taking the floor. He expressed his satisfaction with the document's treatment of the common heritage shared by the Jews and Christians, but wanted more pastoral notes to be incorporated into the text.

Cardinal Tappouni spoke in the name of Coptic Rite Patriarch Stephanos I Sidarouss of Alexandria, Melkite Rite Patriarch Maximos IV Saigh of Antioch, Chaldean Rite Patriarch Paul II Cheikho of Babylon, and Armenian Rite Patriarch Ignace Pierre XVI Batanian of Cilicia.

He repeated solemnly the grave objections which the Eastern patriarchs had made at the council last fall. He warned that the Church would find itself in serious difficulties if anything concerning the Jews were passed, and said the declaration is most inopportune. He asked that it be omitted completely.

Cardinal Tappouni held that if the declaration were passed it would cause trouble for the Catholics of the Near East because of the hostility of the Arab world to such a statement. His own opposition and that of others was not based on any opposition to Judaism as a religion or to the Jews as people, he said, but rather on the grounds that the council would be promoting political ends if it were to approve such a declaration.

Joseph Cardinal Frings of Cologne, Germany, expressed special pleasure with the document's wording concerning the Moslems. But he asked that the original text be restored because of its wording concerning the Jews. Christ's death cannot be attributed to a whole people, he said. He also asked that the declaration include reference to St. Paul's treatment of the relationship between the people of the Old and the New Testaments, as found in the second chapter of his letter to the Ephesians.

Ernesto Cardinal Ruffini of Palermo, Sicily, told the council he is in favor of the good things said about the Jews in the text, but asked that the declaration also exhort the Jews to love Christians. He held that Jews have traditionally followed Talmudic teachings which hold Christians in contempt and despise them as animals.

In the course of his talk Cardinal Ruffini charged that Jewish people have supported Freemasonry, which the Church has condemned. Finally, he asked why there is no mention in the text of the redemption of the Jews.

(At the American bishops' press panel session following the day's council meeting, it was brought out that the Talmud—the compilation of the oral teaching of the Jews, which dates from the early centuries of the Christian era—uses words for Christians which are subject to various interpretations.

(Msgr. John M. Oesterreicher, head of the Institute of Judaeo-Christian Studies at Seton Hall University, South Orange, N.J., said that Talmudic references which appear to slur Christians may refer only to Jews who become Christians. He said it is difficult to quote the Talmud because it is like a newspaper recording of all types of conflicting opinions, and almost anything can be proved from it. Thus one rabbi can be quoted against another.

(Concerning Cardinal Ruffini's plea that Jews take a better view of Christians, Msgr. Oesterreicher said, "I hope and believe that Jews in general take a favorable view of Christians."

(Msgr. Mark Hurley, chancellor of the diocese of Stockton, Calif., spoke at the briefing session on Cardinal Ruffini's reference to "pernicious" Freemasonry. The American priest said that a radical distinction must be made between the European Masonry of the Grand Orient Lodge variety and American and British Masonry. The Grand Orient is atheistic, he said, but it should also be kept in mind that a great part of Masonry bars Jews from membership.)

Giacomo Cardinal Lercaro of Bologna addressed the council after Cardinal Ruffini. He sought to answer the question as to why the Church is only now coming to the point of making a declaration concerning the Jews. The basic reason cannot be found in the nazi war of genocide against the Jews, nor in what he called

political reasons, he said. Instead, he insisted, it arises from the Church's developing a deeper knowledge of herself and of her essential mystery.

The declaration grows out of the Constitution on the Liturgy and from the nature of the Church, Cardinal Lercaro said, and should be further amended to suggest Biblical discussion with the Jews. He said the Jewish people should not be regarded as having value only in the past. But the heritage of Israel, the institution of the Eucharist within the Jewish paschal cycle, the relationship between the Passover meal and the Mass, the common fatherhood of Abraham—all these should be emphasized in the text, he said, in order to give witness in a Biblical and pastoral way and to foster piety.

He said that the Jews of today should not be called an accursed or a deicide people, but rather that we should recognize that all of us "have strayed like sheep."

Cardinals Leger and Cushing spoke after Cardinal Lercaro. In addition to his other points, Cardinal Cushing stressed that Christians should reject and repudiate persecution and hatred. In this solemn moment, he said, there is no Christian reason for hatred or persecution against our brothers, the Jews. He added that the New World has great hopes that the council will approve a good statement on Christian-Jewish relations.

Cardinal Cushing also said that Christians should confess humbly that they have not been truly Christian in their treatment of the Jews. Christians should acknowledge how many Jews have suffered and died because of indifference and silence on the part of Christians. If not very many Christian voices cried out in the past, he said, let our voices cry out humbly now.

Franziskus Cardinal Koenig of Vienna said he was pleased with the specific mention of the Moslems in the text because of their belief in the One Merciful God. Concerning the declaration's references to the Jews, he raised the question as to why the revised text, in condemning persecution of the Jews, omits the words "formerly or in our own times." He also made several other detailed suggestions which he said would improve the text.

Archbishop Lorenz Jaeger of Paderborn, Germany, said that the council statement should be entitled a "Declaration on the Jews and Other Non-Christians," inasmuch as the Jews are also non-Christians. He asked for inclusion in the declaration of some other Scriptural references which he said would improve the text, as well as requesting the elimination of some references which he said are not to the point.

Coadjutor Archbishop Philip F. Pocock of Toronto said that the Church must acquit the Jewish people of all false accusations made in the past through the abuse of truth and charity. The harsh words used by Christ, by St. Stephen and by St. Paul, who were all Jews, he noted, were used as exhortations to conversion. They cannot be taken as objective descriptions of a whole people, he said. He noted that St. John does not refer to the Jews often, but rather to the enemies of Christ, and this applies only to a few.

Bishop Pieter Nierman of Groningen, speaking in the name of the bishops of the Netherlands, said the declaration is most acceptable. He gave as his reason the fact that it shows on the part of the Church an increasingly clear perception of the religious values of the Jewish people and of other religions, in all of which there are some elements of truth coming from the Father of Light. He also suggested some changes for the sake of harmony and strength.

The last speaker of the day was Bishop Jules Daem of Antwerp, Belgium. He called the text acceptable, but said that it could be made to reflect more perfectly the conditions of the Church's present-day dialogue with Judaism. He said that today's dialogue with the Jews is based on an antinomy—the opposition of one law to another law—found in Scripture.

On the one hand, he said, there is a condemnation of the Jews, while on the other, God's will to save all men. Thus our dialogue today is taking place according to the plan of God, he said.

Following this discussion, the council Fathers turned again to the voting on amendments to the schema on the nature of the Church. Six were voted on in all:

Amendment 31—dealing with the bishops' power to govern. The vote was 2,088 "yes" and 86 "no."

Amendment 32—citing the obligation of bishops to imitate the Good Shepherd. The vote was 2,145 "yes" and 14 "no."

Amendment 33—dealing with priests and their relationship to Christ, to the bishops, and to the Christian people. The vote was 2,125 "yes" and 38 "no."

Amendment 34—on the brotherly union among priests. The vote was 2,157 "yes" and 11 "no."

Amendment 35—discussing the place of deacons in the Church. The vote was 2,055 "yes" and 94 "no."

Amendment 36—providing for the restoration of the diaconate as a permanent order. The vote was 1,903 "yes" and 242 "no."

Three more amendments remained to be voted on for completion of the voting on the amendments on the document on the nature of the Church.

JAMES C. O'NEILL

* * * *

Archbishop Pericle Felici, general secretary of the ecumenical council, called a halt to a movement among council Fathers to cut down the number of "yes-but" votes on documents under debate.

Such votes are known technically as "placet juxta modum." This means the document is acceptable but with certain changes, which the voter submits along with his vote.

Father Yves Congar, O.P., a French theologian, has suggested to many council Fathers that like-thinking groups of them meet outside the council hall to decide on a single change for a document. This change would be submitted by one council Father only in the vote, the rest voting simply "placet," which is an unqualified affirmative.

Archbishop Felici told the council Fathers (Sept. 28) this arrangement was against the council's regulations.

Father John King, O.M.I., of the U.S. bishops' press panel, said Father Congar had been suggesting the modification as a means of ensuring broad majorities of affirmative votes in the council.

Father Frederick R. McManus, professor of canon law at the Catholic University of America, said some bishops had espoused this idea to avoid the appearance of disunity in the council. But he said this line of thought was based on a misunderstanding of the principle of the "juxta modum" vote, which is not a part of normal parliamentary or congressional procedure.

He said part of the very purpose of the "juxta modum" vote is to help insure unanimity in the final vote, in which no "juxta modum" votes are permitted. "Juxta modum" votes are needed in the preliminary voting, he said, precisely because the council is not a simple parliament, but a body that gives witness to the unity of Christian truth.

Cardinal Cushing

This is a translation of the Latin address by Richard Cardinal Cushing of Boston on the council's draft declaration on the Jews at the council session of Sept. 28, 1964.

The declaration on the Jews and non-Christians is acceptable, in general. Through this Ecumenical Council the Church must manifest to the whole world, and to all men, a concern which is genuine, an esteem all embracing, a sincere charity—in a word, it must show forth Christ. And in this schema "De Ecumenismo," with its declarations on religious liberty and on the Jews and non-Christians, in a certain sense it does just that. I would propose, however, three amendments specifically on the Jews.

First: We must make our statement about the Jews more positive, less timid, more charitable. Our text well illustrates the priceless patrimony which the new Israel has received from the law and the prophets.

And it well illustrates what the Jews and Christians share in common. But surely we ought to indicate the fact that we sons of Abraham according to the spirit must show a special esteem and particular love for the sons of Abraham according to the flesh because of this common patrimony. As sons of Adam, they are our brothers: As sons of Abraham, they are the blood brothers of Christ.

The fourth paragraph of this declaration should manifest this and our obligation of special esteem, as a conclusion which logically flows from the first section.

Secondly: On the culpability of the Jews for the death of our Saviour, as we read in Sacred Scriptures, the rejection of the Messiah by His own people is a mystery: a mystery which is indeed for our instruction, not for exaltation.

The parables and prophecies of Our Lord teach us this. We cannot judge the leaders of ancient Israel—God alone is their judge. And most certainly we cannot dare attribute to later generations of Jews the guilt of the crucifixion of the Lord Jesus or the death of the Saviour of the world, except in the sense of the universal guilt in which all of us men share.

We know and we believe that Christ died freely, and He died for all men and because of the sins of all men, Jews and gentiles.

Therefore, in this declaration in clear and evident words we must deny that the Jews are guilty of the death of our Saviour, except insofar as all men have sinned and on that account crucified Him and, indeed, still crucify Him. And especially, we must condemn any who would attempt to justify inequities, hatred, or even persecution of the Jews as Christian actions.

All of us have seen the evil fruit of this kind of false reasoning. In this august assembly, in this solemn moment, we must cry out. There is no Christian rationale—neither theological nor historical—for any inequity, hatred or persecution of our Jewish brothers.

Great is the hope, both among Catholics and among our separated Christian brothers, as well as among our Jewish friends in the New World, that this sacred synod will make such a fitting declaration.

Thirdly and finally, I ask, venerable brothers, whether we ought not to confess humbly before the world that Christians, too frequently, have not shown themselves as true Christians, as faithful to Christ, in their relations with their Jewish brothers? In this our age, how many have suffered! How many have died because of the indifference of Christians, because of silence! There is no need to enumerate the crimes committed in our own time. If not many Christian voices were lifted in recent years against the great injustices, yet let our voices humbly cry out now.

90th General Congregation

September 29, 1964

The two-day debate on the historic declaration on the Church's relations with the Jewish people closed at the council's 90th meeting with a majority of the day's 21 speakers favoring a strong positive council statement.

At the same meeting, a proposal to allow young men to be ordained deacons without an obligation of celibacy failed to gain the two-thirds majority needed. In fact, for the first time in the council's history the "no" votes of the Fathers were a majority. In this case, only 839 Fathers voted "yes," while 1,364 voted "no."

However, two other votes on the diaconate were passed by slender majorities. One approved locating authority for the introduction of the separate order of deacons in national conferences of bishops with the approval of the Holy See. The other approved conferring the order of deacon on older married men.

Among the speakers on the closing day of discussion of the Jewish declaration were three Americans, one of whom won applause when he declared he was yielding his right to speak because his points had been adequately covered by other speeches. He was Archbishop Lawrence J. Shehan of Baltimore. The other Americans who spoke were Auxiliary Bishop Stephen A. Leven of San Antonio, Tex., and Archbishop Patrick A. O'Boyle of Washington.

With completion of the debate—unless some bishops secured the signatures of 70 of their colleagues so that they could speak later on the Jewish declaration—the next schema on the council agenda was scheduled to be the one on Divine Revelation. This was to be introduced Sept. 30.

Bishop Leven launched a strong appeal for the insertion of a clear statement that the Jews should never be called deicides or killers of God. He said that perhaps this statement had been eliminated from the present text on the basis that, as a philosophical or theological consideration, it is impossible to kill God.

But he pointed out that what the council is considering is not a matter of words. Rather it is a question of a sad reality, he said. The Fathers must make sure that the term "God-killer" is never again used against the Jews. Any silence on this would be an offense against justice, he declared.

Bishop Leven said that he was speaking in the name of almost all U.S. bishops and proposed two textual changes in their name.

The first was the clear repudiation of the charge of deicide against the Jews. Secondly, he asked that the present text be revised and called for a return to the earlier text. The present text says deicide must not be attributed to the Jews of modern times. The earlier text favored by Bishop Leven states that the crime cannot be attributed to the Jewish people as a whole of all times.

Archbishop O'Boyle took the floor to speak as a council Father from the country which has the largest Jewish population of any nation in the world. While supporting the declaration, he made a number of recommendations aimed at clarifying and strengthening the document.

He stated that the text should be ecumenical in spirit and that it should be intelligible to the Jews. It must be precise, accurate and inspired by wisdom and charity, he said. He added that it is directed to an ecumenical end and consequently, without hiding any facts, it should avoid giving offense without cause.

As it stands, he said, the document does not comply with this norm. As an example, he cited the passage in which is expressed the concept of the ultimate joining together of Jews and Christians. This, he said, immediately brings to the minds of many Jews the memories of past persecutions, forced conversions and forced rejection of their faith. This raises the prospect of proselytism in Jewish minds, he said.

Archbishop O'Boyle stated that certainly conversion is an object of the Church, but that this aim should be stated in a sober manner and in a way that does not offend. There should be no hint of pressure or other means that would disrupt fruitful dialogue between the Church and the Jewish people.

Moreover, he said, the text seems to be lacking in truth and charity in its partial absolution of the Jews of modern times of deicide. It does not mention the innocence of the Jews at the time of Christ, he said.

Archbishop O'Boyle asked that the full truth be set forth in clear terms and said that only by doing this would the Jews be freed of all injustice of this accusation.

A great majority of the day's 21 speakers favored the statement on the Jews, although many had various suggested changes to make.

Archbishop Joseph Descuffi of Izmir, Turkey, however, asked that the declaration be dropped and that the council simply issue an anti-Semitism statement.

Archbishop Descuffi and Archbishop Pierre Sfair, ordaining prelate in Rome for the Maronite rite, both warned of the consequences in the Arab world if too great attention is centered on the Jews. He said he issued his warning in view of the long aversion between the two peoples.

Bishop Yves Plumey of Garoua, Cameroun, joined them in turning attention to the Moslem considerations. The African prelate proposed setting up a separate secretariat for dealing with the Moslems.

Archbishop John C. Heenan of Westminster, England, supported the removal of the passage from the text that has been interpreted as a proposal of conversion. He also asked for a clear statement against the deicide charge.

The archbishop, who is a member of the Secretariat for Promoting Christian Unity and who helped draw up the original text, told the Fathers: "The wording of the document now in your hands is not precisely ours. I have no idea which theologians were charged with drawing up the final draft of this declaration."

While not questioning the good will of the theologians who drew up the final text, Archbishop Heenan said they possibly had little experience in ecumenical matters, which require great delicacy, especially when "dealing with the Jews, whom frequent persecution has made particularly sensitive."

Archbishop Heenan rejected the notion that the text's citing of St. Paul was a call for direct conversion. He said: "It is my view that the Jews are mistaken in regarding this text as a summons to give up their religion." However, since it has been badly taken by the Jews, Archbishop Heenan continued, "for me this is sufficient reason for removing the quotation from the declaration."

Archbishop Heenan warned that the original text on deicide was clear and publicly known, and that to temporize or water it down would be a great mistake. "I humbly plead that this declaration of ours shall openly proclaim that the Jewish people as such are not guilty of the death of Our Lord," he said.

The 90th council meeting opened with Mass celebrated by Archbishop John Kodwo Amissah of Cape Coast, Ghana. The Gospel was enthroned by Bishop Leon Lommel of Luxembourg. Since he is the only bishop of his tiny country, there was joking comment that it was the first time the Gospel had been enthroned by an entire national episcopal conference.

At the meeting's outset Archbishop Pericle Felici,

council general secretary, announced the distribution of the introductions on chapters four, five and six of the schema on the nature of the Church. These concern the laity, the universal vocation to sanctity and Religious.

On Sept. 30 two votes were scheduled to be taken on chapter three on the hierarchical constitution of the Church. The wisdom of the decision to split that vote into two was obvious from Sept. 29's three votes, which revealed widespread disagreement with the amendments having to do with the diaconate.

Amendments and votes were as follows:

Amendment 37—that the authority to introduce the diaconate is entrusted to national conferences of bishops with the approval of the Holy See—"yes," 1,523; "no," 702.

Amendment 38—that the diaconate may be conferred on older married men—"yes," 1,598, "no," 629.

Amendment 39—that the diaconate can be conferred on younger men without the obligation of celibacy—"yes," 839, "no," 1,364.

Archbishop Felici told the council that all written statements of objections or suggestions that will be submitted with the voting on each chapter will be read very carefully, even if they treat of matters which have already won a two-thirds majority approval. He also made the point that even when a matter is approved by a vote of the council, it is improper to speak as if it were closed, since the council's act can only be considered carried when it is voted on in its final form in the presence of the pope and with his approval.

The day's first speaker was Jose Cardinal Bueno y Monreal of Seville, Spain. He said that since the dialogue of the Church should not exclude anyone, it would be deplorable if the declaration were not adopted.

Referring to the observation by Ignace Cardinal Tappouni, Syrian-rite Patriarch of Antioch, at the previous session regarding the difficulties the Church would encounter in the Arab and Moslem world if the declaration were approved, Cardinal Bueno said they were worthy of grave consideration. However, he declared that if the council makes it clear that political considerations are not involved, it does its duty and must proceed even if some accuse it of taking sides.

He also asked that the title be changed to include all non-Christians and also that the text be altered to stress the closeness of the Jews to Christianity. As for references to guilt and deicide charges, he asked that they be omitted altogether because the very idea is offensive.

Archbishop Franjo Seper of Zagreb, Yugoslovia, also rejected the political charges and said that persecution against the Jews demands the action of the council. He also called for revision of the text to provide a basis for more contemporary dialogue with the Jews, since Christians and Jews alike have the same history of salvation. As practical steps, he suggested drawing up a directory or guidebook covering Church-Jewish relations and establishing a permanent Jewish section within the Secretariat for Promoting Christian Unity.

Bishop Plumey said the Moslems should be discussed immediately after the Jews. Noting that they adore the one God, venerate Christ as a prophet, refer to the Patriarch Abraham as Father and Mary as the highest and noblest daughter of Abraham, he said the Church and the council should hold Moslems in the greatest respect.

Bishop Sergio Mendez Arceo of Cuernavaca, Mexico, stated he preferred the earlier text and asked that an explanation of the passages of Sacred Scripture which are used and abused by anti-Semites be inserted. He also called for clarification of the condemnation of persecution.

Japanese Bishop Laurentius Satoshi Nagae of Urawa, speaking in the name of all the Japanese Bishops, asked that the declaration's title be changed to include all non-Christians. He warned against a completely negative attitude toward paganism and asked Fathers not to reject all the elements found in pagan culture and to pay attention to the way in which the Church treats non-Christians.

Bishop Edmund Nowicki of Gdansk, Poland, called for changes in the terminology of the Latin words used in the text. He pointed out that it uses "vexatio" instead of "persecutio" for the word "persecution." He spurned the explanation that Cicero used "persecutio" in a legally restricted sense. "Vexatio," he said, means badgering and does not give the weight of persecution. He also called for complete omission of the question of guilt or non-guilt of deicide because it can cause either confusion or bitter reaction.

Vietnamese Bishop Nguyen van Hien of Dalat said the consideration of non-Christians is not only timely but also urgent. He pointed out that a majority of the world is neither Christian nor Jewish. He also said that there should be some reference to Moses, the law giver. Urging the Church to respect good elements in non-Christian religions and countries, Bishop Hien said that many missionary magazines publish pictures and articles reflecting no honor in the countries they are writing about.

Bishop Leven, in his statement on deicide, said: "We are not dealing here with some philosophical entity but with a word of infamy and execration which was invented by Christians and used to blame and persecute the Jews. For many centuries and even in our own, Christians have hurled this word against the Jews and because of it they have justified every kind of horrible excess and even their slaughter."

Bishop Leven then declared: "It is not up to us to make a declaration about something philosophical but

to reprobate and damn a word which has furnished so many occasions of persecution through the centuries. We must tear this word out of the Christian vocabulary so that it may never again be used against the Jews."

Referring to limiting the lack of guilt to the Jews of modern times, Bishop Leven said: "Obviously many of the Jews of the time of Christ, especially in the diaspora, never heard of Him nor could they have consented to His death. It is as absurd to accuse all the Jews of the time of Christ of His death as it would be to blame all Romans of that time for His death, because the Roman, Pilate, delivered Him up and Roman soldiers nailed Him to the cross."

Coadjutor Bishop Leon Elchinger of Strasbourg stressed that many Jews today are authentic witnesses of Sacred Scripture and practice the virtues of the Bible. Cooperation between Jews and Christians could be a great means to combat atheism, he said.

He added that the council should ask forgiveness from the Jews for past injuries. Lastly, he said, he favored the original text rather than the present one.

Auxiliary Bishop Bernhard Stein of Trier, Germany, argued that there is no Scriptural basis for proposing the divine fatherhood of all men. All men are related to God as their Creator, he said, but in the proper sense God is the Father of the Jewish people and through Christ of Christians.

Bishop Antonio Anoveros of Cadiz and Ceuta, Spain, warned that Catholic publications should beware of offensive treatment of other religions, and that Catholics should work with others in the fields of brotherhood, social work and civil order as a prerequisite to real dialogue.

Archbishop Heenan's intervention came next, and he was followed by Archbishop O'Boyle of Washington. Archbishop Sfair insisted on positive relationships between Islam and Christianity. He cited the teaching of St. John Damascene, who called Islam a Christian heresy, and warned against glorifying Jews and thereby arousing Arab animosity and difficulties for bishops in their lands.

At this point Archbishop Shehan won applause for passing his turn to speak and submitting his comments in writing to the secretariat.

Two Indian archbishops urged more development of the declaration's treatment of non-Christian religions.

Malabar-rite Archbishop Joseph Parecattil of Ernakulam noted that remote longings for Christ can be found in the sacred books of Hinduism which speak of God as director and liberator. The Church, he said, must affiliate to itself whatever is good in every culture.

Archbishop Joseph Attipetty of Verapoly wanted the declaration to state that Christians owe the same charity not only to themselves, but also to all men of all religions according to the spirit and command of Christ.

Stressing the non-political nature of the declaration, Bishop Donal Lamont of Umtali, Southern Rhodesia, said it should be clarified that the declaration is a result of the earlier one on religious liberty.

He asked that the Secretariat for Promoting Christian Unity be made a permanent body at the end of the council. He also objected to an impression of anti-Semitism in the Church which, he said, could result from the text's warning to preachers and to catechists to avoid injurious expressions.

Argentine Bishop Jeronimo Podesta of Avellaneda stressed the religious significance of the declaration and its lack of political significance.

Bishop Joseph Tawil, patriarchal vicar for Damascus, Syria, of the Melkite-rite patriarchate of Antioch, said he wanted the council to scrap the declaration. He suggested that it substitute a simple statement on anti-Semitism.

He said that the pastoral aims of the council demand that the declaration be suppressed as a source of harm to the Church.

The last speaker of the day was Archbishop Descuffi. He said the declaration would help vindicate the memory of Pope Pius XII, and that it comes from the inspiration of divine faith and should not give rise to any bitterness.

He stressed points of contact between Christianity and Islam and said the document should reflect this. He said Islam was closer in many things to Christianity than Judaism. JAMES C. O'NEILL

A member of the American bishops' press panel, commenting on the council Fathers' rejection of the ordination of young deacons not obliged to remain unmarried, recalled that some bishops had feared that if deacons were free to marry then priests might seek the same freedom.

Father Francis J. McCool, S.J., said the council's Sept. 29 decision to admit older married men to the diaconate would be unlikely to lead to a relaxation of priestly celibacy.

The day before paving the way for ordination of married older deacons, the council Fathers gave initial approval to a statement on the function of deacons within the Church. By a vote of 2,055 to 94, they went on record as holding that deacons may administer Baptism solemnly, give Holy Communion, solemnly witness the sacrament of Matrimony, give the nuptial blessing when there is no wedding Mass, bring the Viaticum to persons in danger of death, read and explain the Holy Scriptures, and officiate at burials. Elsewhere, council documents refer to deacons as administering certain of the temporal affairs of the Church, as in the Acts of the Apostles.

A member of the Christian Unity Secretariat, Father John F. Long, S.J., cited the problem arising in the Eastern Churches, in which a strong tradition allows men to marry before being ordained priests but not afterwards. He said the death of a priest's wife often means that their children must be raised in a motherless household.

Pope Paul Meets Non-Catholic Observers

"An abyss of distrust and skepticism has largely been overcome," said Pope Paul VI, addressing non-Catholic observers to the ecumenical council during a special audience in the Sistine chapel.

Present at the reception were Augustin Cardinal Bea, president of the Secretariat for Promoting Christian Unity, and Bishop Jan Willebrands, secretary of the unity secretariat.

Replying to remarks by Greek Orthodox Archimandrite Panteleimon Rodopoulos of Brookline, Mass., one of the three representatives of Orthodox Patriarch Athanagoras of Constantinople (Istanbul), the Pope said he was happy and honored by their presence. He expressed the hope that efforts would be undertaken to become "more vivid and more confidant in aspiring to the joint goal of full and true unity in Christ." He continued:

"Your physical proximity proves and favors a spiritual proximity which formerly we did not know."

"A new method has asserted itself. A friendship was born, a hope was engendered, a movement is on the way," he said.

Defining what he called "our position," the Pope said:

"You will have noticed that the council has had only words of respect and joy for your presence and for the Christian communities you represent, words of charity and hope in regard to you. This is no little matter when we think of the polemics of the past, and if we are aware that our mutual behavior is sincere, cordial and even profound."

Pope Paul said observers could see for themselves that the Catholic Church "is disposed toward an honorable and serene dialogue and ready to examine how difficulties may be eliminated, and misunderstandings done away with, even though it cannot disregard certain doctrinal requirements it must uphold," respecting all the while "the authentic treasures of truth and spirituality you possess."

"Love, not egoism, prompts us," the Pope added, quoting II Corinthians 5, 14. He also repeated his willingness to cooperate in the establishment of an institute for the study of the history of salvation, as proposed by the observers last year.

He said he was willing to continue sending Catholic observers to gatherings of other churches.

"We beg you," he concluded, "not to be satisfied only with a passive presence here, but also try to understand and pray with us so as to contribute to progressively closer contacts in Christ Our Lord. All this, as you see, is but a beginning, but that it may someday bear fruit in its results we now invite you to pray jointly with us the Our Father."

The observers had been presented to the Pope by Cardinal Bea, who pointed out that this year their number had increased from 66 to 75, and the number of churches they represent from 22 to 23. One church represented at the last session dropped out, but two new ones are represented—the Orthodox Patriarchate of Constantinople and the Assyrian Catholicate-Patriarchate of the East.

Speaking on behalf of the observers, Archimandrite Rodopoulos, dean of the Holy Cross Greek Orthodox Theological School in Brookline, said the decisions of the council "will have influence beyond its limits."

He added, however: "We have no illusions. We realize there are essential questions that separate us, and we realize that these questions probably will not be solved in the near future. But these difficulties do not lead us to discouragement or abandonment of the effort for ultimate unity."

Prior to the reception, all jointly recited the Gloria of the Mass, each in his own language. Those using English took the text from the Anglican Book of Common Prayer.

Pope's Talk to Non-Catholic Observers

This is the text of Pope Paul VI's address on Sept. 29, 1964, at the reception for non-Catholic observers at the ecumenical council.

Gentlemen, beloved and venerable brothers!

1. This new meeting of your group with the Bishop of Rome, successor of the Apostle Peter, on the occasion of the third session of the Second Ecumenical Vatican Council, is a new motive for spiritual joy, which we like to believe to be reciprocal. We are made happy and honored by your presence; and the words just now addressed to us give assurance that your feelings resemble ours. We feel the necessity of expressing our gratitude to you for the favorable reception accorded our invitation, and for your attendance, with such dignity and edification, at the conciliar congregations. The fact that our mutual satisfaction over these repeated meetings of ours shows no signs of fatigue or disappointment, but is now more lively and trusting than ever, seems to us to be already an excellent result; this is a historic fact; and its value cannot be other than positive in regard to the supreme common aim, that of full and true unity in Jesus Christ. An abyss, of diffidence and skepticism, has been mostly bridged over; this our physical nearness manifests and favors a spiritual drawing-together, which was formerly unknown to us. A new method has been affirmed. A friendship has been born. A hope has been enkindled. A movement is under way.

Praise be to God Who, we like to believe, "has given His Holy Spirit to us" (I Thess. iv. 3).

2. Here we are, then, once again seeking, on one side and on the other, the definition of our respective positions. As to our position, you already know it quite well.

(a) You will have noted that the council has had only words of respect and of joy for your presence, and that of the Christian communities which you represent. Nay more, words of honor, of charity and of hope in your regard. This is no small matter, if we think of the polemics of the past, and if we observe also that this changed attitude of ours is sincere and cordial, pious and profound.

(b) Moreover, you can note how the Catholic Church is disposed toward honorable and serene dialogue. She is not in haste, but desires only to begin it, leaving it to divine goodness to bring it to a conclusion, in the manner and time God pleases. We still cherish the memory of the proposal you made to us last year, on an occasion similar to this; that of founding an institute of studies on the history of salvation, to be carried on in a common collaboration; and we hope to bring this initiative to reality, as a memorial of our journey to the Holy Land last January; we are now studying the possibility of this.

(c) This shows you, gentlemen and brothers, that the Catholic Church, while unable to abandon certain doctrinal exigencies to which she has the duty in Christ to remain faithful, is nevertheless disposed to study how difficulties can be removed, misunderstandings dissipated, and the authentic treasures of truth and spirituality which you possess be respected; how certain canonical forms can be enlarged and adapted, to facilitate a recomposition in unity of the great and, by now, centuries-old Christian communities still separated from us. It is love, not egoism, which inspires us: "For the love of Christ impels us" (II Cor. v. 14).

(d) In this order of ideas, we are happy and grateful that our Secretariat for Unity has been invited, on various occasions, to send observers to the conferences and meetings of your Churches and your organizations. We will gladly continue to do this, so that our Catholic organizations and our representatives may, on their side, acquire a knowledge, corresponding to truth and to charity, which are a prerequisite of a deeper union in the Lord.

3. As for you, gentlemen and brothers, we ask you kindly to continue in your functions as sincere and amiable observers; and to this end, not to content yourselves with a simple passive presence, but kindly to try to understand and to pray with us, so that you can then communicate to your respective communities the best and most exact news of this council, thereby favoring a progressive drawing-together of minds in Christ Our Lord.

In this regard, we would ask you now to bring to your communities and to your institutions our thanks, our greetings, our wishes of every good and perfect gift in the Lord.

All this, you can see, is only a beginning; but, in order that it may be correct in its inspiration, and fruitful one day in its results, we invite you to conclude this meeting of ours by the common recitation of the prayer which Jesus taught us: the "Our Father."

Summary of Statement On the Jews

This is the summary of the proposed ecumenical council declaration on the Jews released by the council press office.

The History of This Declaration.

In the 63rd general congregation of the Second Ecumenical Vatican Council (Nov. 8, 1963) there was distributed to the council Fathers a text covering 42 lines, which was presented as chapter 4 of the schema on ecumenism, and having as its title: "The Attitude of Catholics toward non-Christians and Particularly toward the Jews."

After a brief mention of other monotheistic religions, the chapter then went on to treat especially of the Jews, who have particular relationships with the Church of Christ. At the same time a communique from the Secretariat for Promoting Christian Unity explained that this chapter, which had been drawn up two years earlier by the secretariat, was exclusively religious in content and was inspired by solely spiritual considerations. Hence, the secretariat vigorously opposed any attempt to give the document a political interpretation.

The council began the discussion of the schema on ecumenism in the 69th general congregation (Nov. 18, 1963), and on the following day Cardinal Bea, in the 70th general congregation, read a four-page report to clarify the significance, the content, and the scope of the chapter on the Jews in the schema on ecumenism.

In the general debate on the schema some misgivings were voiced on the chapter on the Jews. Some felt that the chapter was out of place in the treatment of ecumenism strictly so-called, while others observed that if the council is to treat of the Jews, then it must likewise speak of the Moslems and of the other non-Christian religions. The council Fathers from the Arab world were particularly vigorous in affirming the inopportuneness of a chapter on the Jews in view of the particularly tense circumstances now prevailing.

In the 72nd general congregation (Nov. 21, 1963) the first three chapters of the schema on ecumenism were approved by a vote of 1,966 to 86. In the 79th and last general congregation, Cardinal Bea gave assurance to the council Fathers that although the chapter on the Jews had not been brought up for discussion, there was question only of a temporary postponement, and in the meantime the chapter would be carefully reworked.

At the beginning of the plenary meeting of the Secretariat for Promoting Christian Unity (Feb. 27-March 7, 1964) the proposals on the chapter on the Jews presented by the Fathers either in the oral discussion in the previous session or in writing, filled a booklet of 72 pages. As the result of its deliberations the secretariat reached the following conclusions: (1) the schema on ecumenism strictly so-called will, as is logical, discuss only the question of unity among Christians; (2) the revised chapter on the Jews will be retained both for internal reasons and for its importance and because of the universal expectation which it has aroused; (3) because of the special bonds uniting the people of the Old Covenant with the Church, the document on the Jews will be an appendix to the text on ecumenism, but not a chapter, because, strictly speaking, ecumenism deals only with relationships between Christians; (4) this same appendix will touch on the relationships of Christians with non-Christian religions, with special emphasis on Islamism.

The Declaration on the Jews and Non-Christians.

The new text is composed of approximately 70 lines unaccompanied by notes. The text is two pages long. It is subdivided into three paragraphs, treating of the common religious patrimony of Christians and Jews, of the universal Fatherhood of God, and of the inadmissibility of any and all discrimination.

A. The Common Religious Patrimony of Christians and Jews.

The Church of Christ recognizes gladly that, according to the divine mystery of salvation, the beginnings of its Faith and of its election are rooted in the patriarchs and the prophets. As a new creation of Christ and the people of the New Covenant, the Church can never forget that she is a continuation of that people with which God in His ineffable mercy established the Old Covenant and to which He entrusted the Revelation contained in the books of the Old Testament. Nor does the Church forget that Christ according to the flesh was born of the Hebrew people, as also the Mother of Christ and the apostles, the foundation and the columns of the Church. The Church also bears in mind the words of the Apostle Paul to the Hebrews "who have the adoption as sons, and the glory and the covenants" (Rom. 9, 4).

Because of this heritage passed on to the Christians by the Jewish people, the council aims to encourage and to recommend mutual knowledge of one another, which will be deepened through theological research and in fraternal dialogue, and in addition the council deplores and condemns all injustices ever committed anywhere against human beings, and particularly the hatred and persecutions against the Jews.

It is also to be remembered that the union of the Hebrew people with the Church is part of Christian hope. According to the doctrine of the Apostle Paul (Rom. 11, 25), the Church awaits in faith and with desire the entrance of this people into the fulness of the people of God restored by Christ.

Consequently, let all take care in catechetical teaching, in preaching and in everyday conversation not to present the Hebrew people as a rejected people, and also take care neither to say or to do anything which may alienate minds against the Jews. In addition, all should be careful not to attribute to the Jews of our time what was committed during the Passion of Christ.

B. God is the Father of all men.

This truth, already taught by the Old Testament, was confirmed in a new light by Christ. We cannot proclaim or invoke God as the Father of all men if we maintain an attitude of hostility in regard to other men created according to the image of God. Whoever expects pardon from God must be disposed to pardon his neighbor, and whoever does not love his brother whom he sees, cannot boast of loving God who is invisible.

In our spirit of love toward our brethren, we wish to consider with great respect the opinions and doctrines which, although they differ from our own in many respects, nevertheless in many elements reflect a ray of that light which illumines all men. Thus we seek to have an understanding also of the Moslems who adore one God, personal, and the rewarder of the actions of this life, and who with their religious sense are in some degree close to us.

C. Condemnation of any kind of discrimination.

Hence there disappears any foundation for the theory which established between man and man, between people and people, differences in human dignity or in the rights flowing therefrom.

All honest men, and Christians particularly, must refrain from any act of discrimination or of harassment for reasons of race, color, social condition or religion. Christians are ardently summoned by the council, as far as lies in their power, to live in peace with all men, to love all men, even those who may one day be their enemies, in order that they may all be sons of our Father in Heaven, who makes His sun to rise on all men without distinction.

Bishop Leven

This is the text of the address delivered by Auxiliary Bishop Stephen A. Leven of San Antonio, Tex., at the ecumenical council on Sept. 29 on the proposed council declaration on the Jews.

In general the declaration is satisfactory, but I wish to propose three emendations. Proposing the first and second I speak in the name of nearly all the archbishops and bishops of the United States; proposing the third I speak in my own name.

1. To paragraph 32, line 22 should be added, "The Jews must never be called a deicide people." This monitum was set forth plainly in the first version of this document, that is, in chapter four of the schema on ecumenism given to us last year. It was said in that text that the Jews were not guilty of deicide. Now this statement is not in the present text.

Some say this statement was suppressed because the word deicide is philosophically and theologically absurd, per se contradictory, and therefore not worthy of a conciliar document.

Fathers of the council, we are not dealing here with some philosophical entity but with a word of infamy and execration which was invented by Christians and used to blame and persecute the Jews. For so many centuries, and even in our own, Christians have hurled this word against Jews and because of it they have justified every kind of horrible excess and even their slaughter and destruction. It is not up to us to make a declaration about something philosophical but to reprobate and damn a word which has furnished so many occasions of persecution through the centuries. We must tear this word out of the Christian vocabulary so that it may never again be used against the Jews.

The Council of Trent declared that all men and their sins were the cause of the death of Christ. Therefore, we are all guilty and we must confess that we have sinned and procured the death of Christ. This death is not to be attributed to any one people.

There is another reason why this sentence should be restored in the text of our declaration. The whole world knows the history of anti-Semitism among Christians. So many horrible things have been perpetrated against the Jews. Now the world awaits and expects an absolute and irrefutable sign of our good faith in this matter of justice. We must repudiate the Machiavellian spirit by which we would demand justice for ourselves alone. We, as Fathers of the council, must seek justice for all men according to the necessities of situation and time. Our time and our situation now demand this repudiation and reprobation. Precisely because this was in the earlier document does its omission here seem a refusal of the justice we must render to the Jews.

2. My second emendation: in paragraph 32 after line 32 should be inserted, "Not all the Jews of the time of Christ are to be blamed for the death of Christ."

Obviously, many of the Jews of the time of Christ, especially in the diaspora, never heard of Him, nor could they have consented to His death. It is as absurd to accuse all the Jews of the time of Christ of His death as it would be to blame all the Romans of that time for His death because the Roman Pilate delivered Him up and Roman soldiers nailed Him to the Cross.

3. The third and final emendation I make in my own name. To paragraph 33, line 2 there should be added an expression of our eschatological hope that all men of every race and people, Jews and gentiles, will be gathered together with God, as St. Paul wrote (I Tim. 2, 4): "It is the will of God that all men should be saved and come to the knowledge of the truth." Thus also we will apply in this context the beautiful words of the Constitution on the Church, chapter 1, paragraph 2, lines 10-15, "But at that time, as we read in the holy Fathers, all the just from the time of Adam 'from Abel the just even to the last of the elect' will be gathered together with the Father in the universal church."

Archbishop Heenan

*These are the texts of addresses delivered by Archbishop John Heenan of West-
minster, England, at the ecumenical council on its draft declarations on religious
liberty and the Jews. The former address was made on Sept. 28 in the name of the
English bishops. The latter address was delivered on Sept. 29.*

1. On Religious Freedom:

I dare to make a short intervention because the
hierarchy of England and Wales, many Bishops in Scotland, Ireland, Australia and New Zealand, as well as
some of our neighbors in France and Belgium, think it
opportune for me to tell the Fathers of the council how
the principles laid down in the Declaration on Religious
Liberty have already been reduced to practice in our
country.

It is well known that in England during the 16th
century a bitter fight was joined between Protestants
and Catholics. Religious liberty was soon banished from
the land. The Blessed Martyrs of England and Wales by
their death are witnesses to the ferocity of this persecution. To be honest we must also confess that when the
Catholic Queen Mary was on the throne, Protestants
suffered a similar fate. By the end of the century the
Protestants had triumphed and the Church of our forefathers had almost ceased to exist in Britain. The few
who remained faithful to the Holy See were harassed
and penalized. But persecution gradually relaxed and in
the year 1828 Parliament passed the Catholic Emanci-
pation Act freeing Catholics from most if not quite
all of their civil disabilities.

Great Britain today can in no sense be described
as Catholic. The Church of England is the Established
Church and our Queen is its head. It is true that many
of our fellow-citizens do not actively practice any religion. Most Englishmen would nevertheless call themselves Christians. Infants born in England are usually
baptized, couples generally prefer to be married in
church and almost all who die are given Christian burial.
There are also, of course, many who profess no religion
of any kind.

There is a picture of a pluralist society in which,
nevertheless, religion is honored both publicly and in
private. Although the Church of England is the Established Church, full religious liberty is granted to citizens of other faiths. Thus, for example, the state makes
a substantial contribution for the provision of Church
schools and pays full salaries to their teachers, even to
those who are priests, Brothers or nuns. But—and this
is the real point—precisely the same rights and privileges

are granted to Catholic schools as to those belonging to
the Church of England. It is clear to both Protestants
and Catholics in England that liberty and equality of
treatment for all is the only way of promoting peaceful
relations among citizens.

That is why we praise and unreservedly approve
the proposals in this Schema on Religious Freedom. Pope
Pius XII once said that the common good might impose
a moral obligation in what are described as Catholic
countries to respect the freedom of other religions. Today the world is small. What happens in one state can
have consequences all over the world. For the sake of
the common good freedom of religion must flourish in
every nation in the world.

Some fear the danger of allowing unrestricted scope
to the propagation of error. These fears are real and not
to be despised. No one can feel happy at the prospect
of allowing the young or ignorant to be led into error.
One of the great dangers of our time is contempt for
all restraint. Liberty all too easily degenerates into law-
lessness. Liberty nevertheless is precious. Despite all
dangers it must be boldly defended.

If restrictions are to be applied, who is going to
apply them? Only the state has the physical power to do
so and all man's experience shows that the less the
state interferes in religious matters the better. We are
persuaded that the external practice of religion should
be subject only to those restrictions which are absolutely
necessary to safeguard public order.

The authors of this schema are to be praised for
attempting to base it on something more positive than
tolerance and the common good.

To bring this about, patience, charity and firm-
ness are needed in the practice of the Faith. Otherwise there is a danger of indifference.

It has been said in this debate that only the principles need be set down and that no attempt should be
made to explain the underlying Catholic doctrine. This
argument to me seems faulty. In a pastoral document of
this kind it is necessary to give some indication of the
methods by which we have reached our conclusions.
This at least is certain that many outside the Church
hold that Catholics do not sincerely believe in religious
freedom. Let us declare to the whole world, once and

for all, our heartfelt belief as Catholics in the full liberty of all the sons of God.

2. On the Jews:

It is not surprising that the Jews have received the new version of the declaration "De Judaeis" without marked pleasure. The earlier pronouncement about the Jews in the schema on ecumenism was made public during the second session of the council and in consequence its terms are well known to the Jews. It is natural that they should now be asking why certain changes have been made. It is impossible not to notice a subtle difference in the tone and spirit of the new version. In its present form the declaration seems less forthcoming and less friendly. We of the Secretariat for Promoting Christian Unity prepared our text keeping in mind the hundreds of comments made between sessions by the Fathers of the council. The wording of the document now in your hands is not precisely ours.

I have no idea which theologians were charged with drawing up the final draft of this declaration. Let me say quite plainly that I have no suspicion of any kind that they set out to make our words less warm or our approach less generous. It is quite possible that these theologians have had little experience in ecumenical affairs. Such delicate material has to be handled with great care and even subtlety. This is especially true when dealing with the Jews, whom frequent persecution has made particularly sensitive.

This sensitivity may well be the reason why the Jewish newspapers have complained so bitterly about the quotation from the Epistle of St. Paul to the Romans: "I would not have you ignorant, brethren, of this mystery . . . blindness has fallen upon a part of Israel but only until the tale of the gentile nations is complete; then the whole of Israel will find salvation . . ." The Apostle of the Gentiles is here using what we call eschatological language. He is referring, in other words, to the end of the world when, it is hoped, all men, including the Jews, will return to the unity of the true people of God. I have no doubt in my own mind that this quotation was deliberately chosen as a proof of our brotherly love and desire for union with all the other sons of God. It is my view that the Jews are mistaken in regarding this text as a summons forthwith to give up their religion.

I must add, however, that the question of conversion, whether of individuals or of whole communities, really has no place in the context of ecumenism. The object of the ecumenical movement is to lead people of different religions to examine each other's beliefs. Neither party in the dialogue has any ambition to score victories. Its object is for all to grow in mutual understanding and esteem. That is why in discussing Christian unity, the schema made no mention of conversion either of the Orthodox in the East or of non-Catholics in the West. Our hope, nevertheless, of the return of all the brethren of Christ to the one fold remains strong. Our separated brethren pray no less earnestly than ourselves that led by the Holy Spirit all will eventually be united in one Church.

However good the intentions of those who inserted this quotation from St. Paul's Epistle to the Romans, the fact is that it has been taken badly by the Jews. For me this is a sufficient reason for removing the quotation from the declaration. Notice that in the same declaration when talking about other non-Christian believers—such as the Moslems—no word is said about converting them. Here are the exact words of the text: "Although their opinions and doctrines differ from ours in many ways, nevertheless in many things they show a ray of that Truth which enlightens every man coming into this world." But surely if these other non-Christian religions possess a ray of truth, the Jewish religion has much more since it is in a way the root of our own Faith. Pope Pius XI once said: "We are all Semites."

I want to end with a word about the famous question of deicide. In the earlier version of our document the Jewish people was absolved from the crime of deicide. We must never forget that the text was published to the whole world. If, therefore, this absolution is deleted the interpretation will be made that the Fathers of the council, having had a year to think it over, now solemnly judge that the whole Jewish people—at least those alive at the time of Christ's death—are, in fact, guilty of the crime of deicide.

The Jews during this century have suffered grave and, indeed, inhuman injuries. In the name of Jesus Christ Our Lord Who from the cross forgave His executioners, I humbly plead that this declaration of ours shall openly proclaim that the Jewish people as such is not guilty of the death of Our Lord. It would certainly be unjust in our own day if all the Christians of Europe were judged guilty of the death of millions of Jews in Germany and Poland. I maintain that it is no less unjust to condemn the whole Jewish people for the death of Christ.

91st General Congregation

September 30, 1964

The ecumenical council has opened debate on the schema on Divine Revelation with reports setting forth two diverse approaches to the problems of tradition and the Bible.

Because the 91st council meeting was taken up with reports on various matters to be voted on and with the double report on the Revelation schema, only four speakers took the floor. The first speaker did not begin until noon and the last speaker of the day was Albert Cardinal Meyer of Chicago.

Bishop John J. Wright of Pittsburgh, as a member of the Theological Commission, delivered a report on chapter four of the schema on the nature of the Church which was then voted on. Chapter four is on the laity.

Chapter three of the same schema, which deals with collegiality and the diaconate, was voted on in two votes and all of its 19 articles were approved.

Chapters four, five and six were also voted on affirmatively. Chapters five and six deal with the universal vocation to sanctify and Religious. This left only two more chapters of the schema to be voted on. These deal with the last things—death, immortality, resurrection—and Our Lady.

The schema as a whole still has to be voted on at a plenary meeting and promulgated by Pope Paul VI before it becomes an official council act.

Introducing the schema on Revelation, a majority and minority report representing two views of the 24 members of the Theological Commission were read.

The majority view of 17 members was read by Archbishop Ermenegildo Florit of Florence, Italy. The minority report, representing seven others, was read by Bishop Frane Franic of Split, Yugoslavia.

The essential point of division centered on the question of whether tradition has a broader scope or extension than Scripture or, to put it another way, whether everything contained in the tradition of the Church is found in some way in the Bible or whether tradition extends beyond Scripture and includes elements not to be found in it.

The majority view of the Theological Commission, which the text of the present schema reflects, takes the position that it is best to avoid deliberately taking a definitive stand on the question at this point. The ma-

jority maintained it is best to leave the door open on the matter and await the development of theology on this point before making a council pronouncement.

The minority sought to affirm the broader extension of tradition.

Cardinal Meyer sided with the open door approach in general, but warned that while tradition is broader in scope than the Bible, the living tradition of the Church is not always free of human defects.

He said the text is acceptable in general. But he called for clarification of Divine Revelation in the light of modern Scripture research and cautioned against defining the faith in overly intellectual terms.

He pointed out that living tradition arises not only from definitions but also by means of reflection by the faithful on God as found in Scripture. The text says it grows from contemplation of God. But the cardinal objected, saying it is proper to speak of the faithful seeing God through Scripture but that the faithful can only contemplate God in heaven.

Cardinal Meyer held that tradition is extended beyond the limits of the infallible teachings of the Church and that living tradition is subject to failings and defects, since the Church is still a pilgrim in the world. He said it would be an exaggeration to speak of tradition as if there were only a constant progress toward the higher and better.

As examples of where this tradition has deviated from the ideal, he cited the exaggerated moralism of the past centuries, private pious practices which have grown away from the spirit of the liturgy, neglect of the Bible, and even the active discouragement of Bible reading among Catholics that occurred in other eras.

He said we must realize that these defects are always possible. He suggested that it can be said that tradition grows through contemplation, yet, since the Church is still a pilgrim in the world, this tradition can also have faults. The value of the Bible in relation to tradition is that the Bible can serve as a corrective norm by which tradition can be judged, he said.

Bishop Wright took the floor at the council to read the "relatio" or report on the changes that have been made in chapter four of the schema on the Church, which deals with the role of the laity in the Church.

The chapter was approved by a vote of 2,152 to 8, with only 76 votes "juxta modum," that is, favorable but with reservations.

The subcommission charged with the task of amending the chapter tried to incorporate the views of the Fathers which could generally be reduced to three main points:

First, that the chapter was too negative in its conception of the layman.

Second, that it was insufficient and inexact in its presentation of the hierarchy's role in regards to the laity.

Third, that clarification had been asked of the notion of the "royal" priesthood of the laity mentioned by St. Peter, and of the laity's part in the apostolic work of the Church, particularly in the consecration of the world.

Bishop Wright said that efforts had been made to give a positive expression to the layman in conceptual and doctrinal terms. He said the text does not present a definition of the layman as much as it tries to describe him.

Dealing with the role of the hierarchy and how the Church is formed, Bishop Wright said that an attempt had been made to steer a middle course and to avoid identifying the laity and the Church's ministers as one but also to avoid the chasm separating one from the other too absolutely.

Lastly, a new paragraph had been inserted dealing with the layman's participation in the Church and its worship and as a witness of Christ. There is also greater stress on the dignity of the layman as being one of the people of God and note is paid to the apostolic significance of Christian marriage and family life. Other points that were clarified were the rights and duties of laymen toward their superiors in the Church, Christian liberty and obedience, and free cooperation and loyalty to pastors.

The meeting opened with Mass celebrated by Bishop Manuel Rodriguez Rozas of Pinar del Rio, Cuba. The Gospel was enthroned by Archbishop Francois Marty of Rhiems, France. Giacomo Cardinal Lercaro of Bologna, Italy, was the moderator of the day.

Archbishop Pericle Felici, council general secretary, announced that the Fathers were to receive a special booklet explaining parts of the schema on the Church in the world. Contents of the booklet are not for discussion, but only to illustrate and clarify, he said.

At the request of Valerian Cardinal Gracias of Bombay, India, he also denied false reports that the Nov. 28 opening date of the International Eucharistic Congress in Bombay had been changed.

A standing vote by the Fathers approved the council moderators' decision to divide the vote on chapter three of the schema on the Church into two parts. The vote was taken when it was objected that the moderators' decision was not in conformity with the council procedure. Archbishop Felici said it was not permissible, as some requested, to vote "yes" on a proposal and then to send in observations separately. A "yes" vote, he said, means acceptance without reservation, and if reservations exist they must accompany a "juxta modum" vote.

The first vote on chapter three—articles 11 to 23, dealing with the nature of the episcopate—was 1,624 "yes," 42 "no," 572 "juxta modum" and 4 null. (Articles 1 through 10 are parts of chapters one and two.)

The second part of the vote—on articles 24 to 29 dealing with the ministry of the episcopate, but without inclusion of the approval of the diaconate for younger men without the obligation of celibacy—was 1,704 "yes," 53 "no," 481 "juxta modum" and 2 null.

A special vote was taken on whether there should be a separate chapter on Religious distinct from the chapter on sanctity, into which the Religious had been incorporated. A separate chapter won by a large majority.

Chapter five on the universal vocation to sanctity was passed by 1,856 "yes" votes to 17 "no." There were 302 "juxta modum" votes.

Chapter six on Religious was passed 1,736 "yes" to 12 "no," with 438 "juxta modum" votes. All "juxta modum" votes are to be carefully examined by the commission, even though the majorities are won.

Bishop Wright, in concluding his report on chapter four on the laity, said: "This entire treatment is of the utmost importance. As has been said, everyone forms his judgment about a race track according to how his own horse performs. Consequently for the mass majority of the Church, namely the body of the laity, the image of the Second Vatican Council will depend largely on the chapter dealing with the laity."

At the U.S. bishops' press panel later in the day Bishop Wright expanded his remarks on the laity's relations with bishops, saying:

"Bishops must recognize and encourage the Christian liberty and intitiative of the laity so that they may plan a proper part in the consecration of the world. The laity must recognize the rights and obligation of the hierarchy to exercise the office of teaching."

He said he referred specifically to the bishops' teaching authority because it is from its exercise that the laity are given principles of action.

Abbot Benno Gut, O.S.B., abbot primate of the Benedictine Confederation, had presented 679 recommendations submitted on the chapters voted on during the day, with the result that numerous important changes had been made.

There is now greater emphasis on the objective and moral sanctity which the Church has from God and Christ, Abbot Gut said at the council, and more stress on the universal vocation to sanctity. The text makes it clear that although sanctity is substantially one, nevertheless it varies according to degrees of cooperation on the part of man's free will.

The chapter on Religious sets down the divine origin of the counsels of poverty, chastity and obedience and there is greater emphasis on the Christ-like form of the Religious state. A more detailed explanation of the relation of the Religious state to the Church has been introduced, he said. In general, the Religious state has been treated from the theological aspect rather than the jurisdictional one.

Bishop Franic, in presenting the minority report on the Revelation schema, said that the minority of the Theological Commission felt the schema will be basically defective unless a clear stand is taken on whether certain doctrines could be held by the Church in virtue of tradition alone, even though they were not based on the Bible. He argued ecumenically, saying that the affirmation of this would have value in the Church's relations with the Orthodox Churches and the Protestants want a clear statement on the matter. He also cited various references, including the First Vatican Council, which he said have affirmed this position.

Failure to take this stand could lead to confusion, Bishop Franic declared. It would seem that Catholic doctrine on this point had been changed, he added. Catholic Biblical scholars would be forced to an insincere exegesis, trying to trace various traditions to the Bible. He cited, for instance, the sacraments and said there is not a Biblical basis for all seven of them. Lastly, he noted that the minority view did not hold that the schema was in error, but that it suffered from substantial defects.

Archbishop Florit disclosed that the present schema, which succeeds the one withdrawn by orders of Pope John XXIII, was drawn up with the aid of 280 observations submitted during the first council session. The schema is divided into six chapters. It is the second chapter that the minority object to.

The first chapter was approved without difficulty and treats of the nature and object of Revelation, preparation of the Revelation of the Gospel through the Old Testament, Christ as Consummator of Revelation, the credence to be given to Revelation and lastly, revealed truths.

Chapter two deals with the transmission of Revelation under four headings. They are the apostles and their successors as heralds of the Gospel, tradition, the mutual relationship of tradition and Scripture and, lastly, the deposit of Revelation in its relationship to the entire Church and to the Church's teaching power.

Before debate on the Revelation schema opened, Bishop Jean Gahamanyi of Butare, Rwanda, speaking in the name of 70 African bishops, spoke on the declaration on the Jews. His point was that though much has been said of the similiarities between Christians and Jews and between Christians and Moslems, there still remain points on which they are far apart. At the same time, much in the animistic religions of Africa have points of similiarity to Christianity and it would be offensive if only the Jews and Moslems were mentioned. Instead, the declaration should deal with all non-Christians and devote sections to the Jews and Moslems.

The first speaker on Revelation was a Biblical scholar, Ernesto Cardinal Ruffini of Palermo, Italy, who declared himself in agreement with the minority view, and said this was the constant teaching of the ordinary teaching authority of the Church up to the present time. He also questioned the use of some of the Biblical citations in the schema.

Julius Cardinal Doepfner of Munich and Freising, Germany, speaking in the name of the German and Scandinavian bishops, said the text was acceptable because it provides an adequate relation between Scripture and tradition without involving itself in the question raised by the minority. He said this problem should be left open in all revisions of the text and that changes are needed to eliminate doubts, avoid repetition and achieve clarity.

Cardinal Meyer closed the session.

At the U.S. bishops' press panel, Bishop Wright, commenting on the Revelation schema, stated: "We should keep it always in clear focus that the sum and living center of all Revelation is the living Christ, the word made flesh. It may be that some schools of thought concerning the channels of Revelation have tended to be overformalized and institutionalized."

He warned that there has been a tendency for some people to be "prisoners of tradition with a capital T or prisoners of the Bible with a capital B."

Bishop Wright said: "These rigid patterns tend to take on deeper meaning when seen in terms of their relationship to the person of Jesus Christ. It is Christ, eternal and incarnate word, who is the living source of Revelation. The Bible and tradition have their significance only in terms of what they tell us about Him and His thoughts. He is the sole full witness to God's truth, and other sources of that truth have their validity and veracity as a result of their demonstrable relationship to Him."

JAMES C. O'NEILL

Summary of Revelation Schema

At the heart of the first day's debate on Revelation at the ecumenical council are the introduction and the first two of the six chapters of the schema.

The introduction sets down briefly the link between the schema and Sacred Scripture and its relation to the First Vatican Council. It is stated that the present document is a continuation of the earlier council.

Chapter one deals in general with what Revelation is and what its effect is on man. In short, Revelation is the opening of God to man in a plan of salvation. It consists of both action and words.

The action of Revelation, according to a summary of the document made public by the council press office, is the salvific action of God in history and gives validity to the revealed word, that is, to the Bible. The Bible interprets the divine action which, without the word to explain it, would remain mute and obscure in its meaning. God speaks when He acts in history, and with His word He explains His action, the schema summary states.

Salvific will is unfolded gradually through history. Salvation was promised after Adam and Eve had sinned, and the plan becomes clearer through Abraham, Moses, and ultimately through Christ. The Christian era is not merely a historical period of religion or salvation, but it unfolds as an epoch of eschatological hope.

Then the text discusses man's faith in Revelation, and chapter one ends with a series of definitions regarding Revelation adopted by the First Vatican Council.

The second chapter deals with the transmission of Divine Revelation. Here the document is concerned with the difficult problem of relating Scripture and tradition. The schema has tried to leave the question open, pending the development of more mature theological thought. This approach has drawn some fire in the council hall already, and is among the most controversial problems in the schema.

The text states that there are not two parallel sources with no mutual connection. Rather there are two modes of transmission in which one mystery of salvation continues to live in the Church.

The document tells how Christ commanded the apostles to proclaim the message of salvation. Revelation as it exists stems from the tradition of the living Christian communities at the outset of the Christian era and in the Scripture which was born of this tradition. Through these two the Church finds God in Revelation.

The document defines tradition as the total being and the action of the Church, in its life, in its doctrine, and in its worship, whereby the mystery of salvation is implicit and is passed on to all ages. Scripture is not outside of tradition, but forms part of it and contains it in a very special manner.

The document says from the living connection between the Church and tradition there also flows the possibility of the development of tradition. This statement has drawn much fire. Many maintain that there is a distinction between apostolic tradition and the tradition or traditions of the post-apostolic period.

The document explains that there is no increase of new content, but that there is a progressive comprehension of the mystery of salvation under the constant influence of the Holy Spirit.

Finally, chapter two states that tradition lives in all members of the Church but that its authentic interpretation is entrusted to the teaching authority of the Church. This does not mean that the Church has any power over the word of God, but that it has the mandate to conserve and to announce the word of God with fidelity and vigilance.

Chapter three is entitled the Inspiration and Interpretation of Sacred Scripture. The chapter, following the directives of pontifical documents and avoiding all controverted questions, states the Church's basic teaching on inspiration.

It emphasizes two truths:

1. That the sacred books were composed under the Holy Spirit's influence in such a way that God is their author and they are immune from error.

2. That they were written by men endowed with certain human talents, and had their origin in a determined human context.

Chapter three says that the proper interpretation of Holy Scripture requires two investigations: one into the intention of the author in writing the text and, secondly, into what God Himself intended to say through the human author.

The first investigation, the chapter says, requires a study of the "literary forms" of Holy Scripture. Our historical, prophetical, poetical, didactic and apocalyptical books express truth in different forms. Attention must also be paid to literary usage in Biblical times.

But interpretation should not be limited to a literary analysis of individual texts, the chapter continues. Only by a thorough understanding of the whole mystery of salvation can we uncover the full meaning of Scripture.

The remaining chapters deal with the Old and New Testaments and with Sacred Scripture in the life of the Church.

Chapter four, on the Old Testament, is brief. It traces the history of salvation in the Old Testament: God choosing the people of Israel, making promises to them and making Himself known through His intervention in their history. The prophets interpreted God's words and deeds.

The chapter explains that the history of Israel's salvation is a preparation for the final salvation offered by Christ. Despite the imperfect and impermanent character of many of the details in the books of the Old Testament, these books are of permanent value for the Church since they illuminate God's paths toward salvation in Christ and also bear witness to God's holiness and goodness.

Chapter five, On the New Testament, has kept this title despite the complaints of many council Fathers that it indicates that the text would deal with the Gospels almost exclusively. The commission decided to retain the title but to incorporate a new article (17) dealing with the entire content of the New Testament.

Articles 18 and 19 examine the Gospels in closer detail. Article 19 refers to the "historical character of the Gospels." Article 20 deals with other books of the New Testament.

Though the text was drawn up in April, the council press office says it is in "complete harmony" with the Pontifical Biblical Commission's instruction of the following month.

Chapter six bears the new title, "The Sacred Scripture in the Life of the Church." There had been objections to the previous title, which referred to "the use" of Sacred Scripture, based on the notion that there is something irreverent in "using" God's word.

The chapter's contents were also altered in the light of a schema "On the Word of God" drafted by the Secretariat for Promoting Christian Unity before the council opened in 1962.

It not only urges that accurate translations of the Bible be made but that they be undertaken in collaboration with separated Christians wherever possible.

The schema urges another type of cooperation: between Scripture scholars and dogmatic and moral theologians. Article 23 both praises Scripture scholars for their past work and encourages them to continue confidently, so that the Church's judgment may ripen through their assistance.

The schema says that the study of Sacred Scripture is the heart of theological formation. It recommends Scripture reading, especially for priests but for all faithful as well.

Bishops should see to the preparation of editions of the Bible equipped with explanatory notes. Other editions should be prepared for non-Christians with notes suitable for their needs.

The schema finally expresses the hope that the faithful may delve deeply into riches of the Sacred Scripture, drawing fresh incentives for a fuller Christian life.

JAMES C. O'NEILL

92nd General Congregation

October 1, 1964

Sidestepping the problem of whether tradition is broader than Scripture and contains truths not found in the Bible won support and opposition as the ecumenical council debate on the Revelation schema entered its second day.

Twenty speakers took the floor at the 92nd council meeting, including Fathers speaking for 45 Peruvian bishops, 67 African bishops and another representing the entire hierarchy of Poland.

Bishop Kazimierz Kowalski of Chelmno, Poland, called on the council in the Polish bishops' name to issue a condemnation of atheism as the "enemy of reason, science, the human person and Revelation."

Archbishop Lawrence J. Shehan of Baltimore stressed the part played by man in the process of Revelation. He offered an amendment to the text which emphasizes that the action of Revelation by God to men was broader than the mere presentation of certain propositions to be believed and that Revelation was received by man and recorded by him.

Early at the meeting, Archbishop Pericle Felici, council general secretary, announced to the Fathers that Father Jean Janssens, S.J., general of the Society of Jesus, was dying and asked for prayers for him.

The meeting opened with Mass celebrated by Bishop Raffaele Campelli of Cagli and Pergola, Italy. The Gospel was enthroned by Archbishop Alberto Ramos of Belem do Para, Brazil, on the 25th anniversary of his consecration as a bishop.

No votes were taken at the meeting, at which Giacomo Cardinal Lercaro of Bologna, Italy, presided as the day's moderator.

Paul Cardinal Leger of Montreal, the day's first speaker, praised the decision of the council's Theological Commission, which drew up the Revelation schema, to avoid making a matter of council definition the question of the extension of tradition. However, during the debate three bishops—one Italian and two Indians—warned that to do this would be to reverse the Church's position and teachings as pronounced by the Council of Trent and the First Vatican Council.

The cardinal also stated that it should be recognized that there have been at times certain indiscretions in regard to the insistence on infallibility without making all

the necessary distinctions. This sets up a wall of separation with separated Christians, he said. He added that council Fathers should distinguish between the infallibility which is strictly proper to Revelation and that which is proper to the teaching authority of the Church.

Before debate got underway, Archbishop Felici announced that another attempt to speed the council's progress would be introduced on Oct. 2. He said it was planned to distribute three chapters on the ecumenism schema and then propose new plans of voting. Details were not given.

Voting on the amended ecumenism schema begins Oct. 5. Archbishop Felici said that he was asked what value could be attributed to the booklet on schema 13 on the Church in the modern world distributed the previous day. He at first said it was compiled and issued by the Lay Apostolate Commission and was a private document explaining various points in the schema.

Later in the meeting he said that it was the work of a mixed commission of members of the Lay Apostolate Commission and of the Theological Commission and was not merely private, although it still has no conciliar value.

Cardinal Leger's support of the draft schema on Revelation was straightforward. He called it excellent and in accord with the spirit of the modern Biblical movement. He termed wise the decision to avoid the problem of tradition's extension.

As debate continued, it became clear that various Fathers were using the word tradition in two senses. Some Fathers restricted the word to the apostolic tradition and took the position, as Cardinal Leger did in his speech, that it is wrong to speak of tradition as living and always evolving. Others, as Albert Cardinal Meyer of Chicago had done on the previous day, used the word in a broader sense to include other elements not of the apostolic period.

Cardinal Leger stressed the difference between apostolic and post-apostolic tradition, and said the word should be used carefully. He said the text itself skips from one usage of the word to another and back again without distinguishing. He asked that this defect be cleared up.

He further stressed the transcendence of Revelation

and declared that Revelation is above and superior to post-apostolic traditions. He said it also transcends the teaching authority of the Church. Likewise, he declared, there is a distinction between the teaching office of the apostles, who were eyewitnesses of Christ, and the teaching office of their successors, the bishops, which is to safeguard and hand down what the apostles gave them as witnesses of Christ's life and teaching.

If these distinctions are clear, he said, it will do much to foster the spirit of Christian unity.

Bishop Enrico Compagnone of Anagni, Italy, and two Indians, Bishop Michael Arattukulam of Alleppey and Archbishop Joseph Attipetty of Verapoly, disagreed completely with Cardinal Leger in urging avoidance of the tradition problem.

Bishop Compagnone said he thought the wider extension of tradition was a very firm teaching of the Church. Citing the Council of Trent and the First Vatican Council, he warned that to sidestep the problem would make it appear that the present council is reversing established teaching.

Bishop Arattukulam agreed that the schema as it stands is in conflict with the Council of Trent, which stated that the Bible and tradition are to be received with an equal feeling of piety. He said that the Council of Trent was clearly referring to two different things.

He warned that such practices as infant baptism and the existence of all seven sacraments are endangered if it is insisted that tradition can be found in the Bible.

Archbishop Attipetty said a stand must be made, since the two views are mutually contradictory. Any hesitating on this, he stated, leaves the council and the Church's dogmas open to ridicule.

Archbishop Attipetty suggested that if the council does not take a stand on the breadth of tradition, it should be referred to Pope Paul VI for a decision in view of his supreme teaching authority.

In essence, the council Fathers were rearguing the problem which ultimately led Pope John XXIII to have the whole schema on the two sources of Revelation removed from the first session and redrafted.

Juan Cardinal Landazuri Ricketts of Lima, speaking for Peru's bishops, agreed with Cardinal Meyer, holding that Revelation is not a closed deposit but a living one. He urged clarification of the text in several instances.

Irish-born Michael Cardinal Browne, O.P., of the Roman curia, a theologian, deplored the lack of a provision for the role of theologians in treating Revelation. His view was that tradition does not grow; rather it evolves in regard to its expression, but not in regard to its substance.

Following Cardinal Browne the floor was taken by Armenian-rite Patriarch Ignace Pierre XVI Batanian of Cilicia, who called the schema excellent. He said he was pleased with the link given to tradition and Scripture.

An impassioned plea for a council statement condemning atheism was delivered by Bishop Kowalski, who called it a grave moral duty. He said such a statement would be welcomed by all men of good will.

Bishop Vittorio Costantini of Sessa Aurunca, Italy, praised the text and said it was clearer than the first one. But he called for some changes to forestall worries and anxieties.

Archbishop Lorenz Jaeger of Paderborn, Germany, agreed with Cardinal Browne that tradition does not grow. He also called for a fuller concept of Revelation, which he described as a colloquy of God with man through Christ.

The same stress on this point was given by Archbishop Shehan, who said he thought that the text is not complete enough and is not sufficiently explicit because there is a certain task left to the subject of Revelation, which is the human mind.

Supernatural Revelation is really the communication of God to men by which God manifests Himself to men, he said. There should be inserted in the text, he stated, both parts of the process of Revelation—one, that action of God which is broader than the mere presentation of certain propositions to be believed, and, two, that reception of this action and its interpretation by men. This interpretation depends on objective deeds in history and therefore is not completely subjective. The role that man played in the reception of Revelation should not be ignored, he concluded.

Two council Fathers called for insertion of a reference to Moses in the text, as had other pleas on the previous day. Bishop Felix Romero Menjibar of Jaen, Spain, said more emphasis should be given to Moses, who together with Abraham and Christ were great communicators of Revelation. Italian Archbishop Antonio Vuccino, former Ordinary of Corfu, Greece, also wanted Moses referred to.

Auxiliary Bishop Joseph Reuss of Mainz, Germany, objected to the text's treatment of the act of faith which Catholics have toward Revelation as insufficient. He said it does not sufficiently stress the act as an act of the whole man.

Bishop Emilio Guano of Leghorn, Italy, objected to what he felt was too much emphasis on the separation of tradition and Scripture. He said they were not two rivulets, but rather one stream.

Bishop Tomasz Wilczynski for Olsztyn, Poland, said he was pleased that the schema did not close the door on further theological research, thus siding with the open door approach to the tradition question.

African Archbishop Paul Zoungrana of Ouagadougou, Upper Volta, spoke in the name of 67 bishops. He asked that a statement be inserted in the text saying that the person of Christ is a fact of Revelation, that Jesus Christ as a historical person is a fact of divine Revelation.

Italian Archbishop Armando Fares of Catanzaro said he wanted clarification of the criteria to be used in the arguments for the historicity of the Gospels.

The day's last speaker was Bishop Pierre Rouge of Nimes, France, who praised the text. He expressed his satisfaction that the great effort of the past to enhance tradition is not reflected in the present text. He said stress should be on the action of the Holy Spirit in guiding and developing the Church's life and customs.

JAMES C. O'NEILL

Religious Liberty Declaration Summarized

This is the text of the ecumenical council press office's summary of the proposed declaration on religious freedom.

Introductory note:

The revised text ON RELIGIOUS LIBERTY comprises five pages and appendix to the schema DE ECUMENISMO with the indication DECLARATIO I, along with another DECLARATIO II, dealing with the Jews and non-Christians. The declaration on religious liberty is accompanied by five pages of Notes, a relatio, and a brief summary. The text was transmitted to the Council Fathers on April 27, 1964.

The genesis of the amended text on religious liberty.

In the second session of the council, on Nov. 19, 1963, the Fathers were given the fascicule on religious liberty as chapter 5 of the schema "De Ecumenismo," and in the 70th general congregation held on that same day, Bishop De Smedt, of Bruges, member of the Secretariat for Christan Unity, read to the council an explanatory and introductory relatio. Conflicting opinions were immediately evident among the council Fathers, ranging from enthusiasm to severe criticism. The text was not brought up for discussion on the council floor for want of sufficient time.

Up to Feb. 27, 1964, the Secretariat for Christian Unity accepted observations from the council Fathers and incorporated them into a volume of some 280 pages. Some of the Fathers wanted the text on religious liberty incorporated into the schema of ecumenism, inasmuch as the recognition of religious liberty forms part of the foundation of ecumenism. According to certain other Fathers, however, the text in question should constitute a distinct chapter of the schema on ecumenism. Still others would have abbreviated the presentation and included it in chapter I of the schema, treating of the basic principles of ecumenism. Lastly, others proposed the presentation of the subject as a decree distinct from

that on ecumenism, considering the fact that, notwithstanding its ecumenical importance, the subject matter exceeds the limits of ecumenism strictly so called.

The text was amended by the Secretariat for Christian Unity according to the recommendations made by many of the Fathers, but its great importance did not permit it to be compressed into such compact form as would have permitted its insertion into chapter I of the schema on ecumenism. Thus, according to the desire expressed by the Coordinating Commission in its meeting of April 18, 1964, the text on religious liberty, like that on the Jews and non-Christians, is now submitted to the council as a "declaration" distinct from, but annexed to the schema on ecumenism.

The criteria followed in the revision of the text.

After a careful study of all the observations sent in by the council Fathers concerning the revision of the text, the Secretariat for Christian Unity saw fit to retain five principal points:

a) *A clearer expression of the concept of religious liberty.*

The purpose of this clarification is to forestall any fallacious or equivocal interpretations of the text. Consequently, at the very beginning of the new text, an additional paragraph explains the exact significance of the concept of "religious liberty." A distinction must be made between freedom as far as relations with God are concerned, and freedom in relations with men. The text is concerned exclusively with religious liberty *in relation with other men,* considered either as individuals (or) as members of religious groups. The foundation of these rights comes from the very serious obligation of respecting human dignity and following the law of God according to the dictates of a conscience sincerely formed. Freedom to follow one's own religious conscience is the greatest advantage of every person and for this reason it is a strictly personal right in social association, and there must be respect for freedom for following the call of God, in which we behold the peak of the dignity of the human person.

b) *Explicit indications of the rights of religious groups.*

To these groups is recognized authentic religious liberty in those things which develop spiritual life among men.

c) *A better explanation of the principle by which our rights can be restricted.*

The aim of society is the complexus of those conditions of social life which aid men to achieve the more fully and the more expeditiously the perfection at which they are aiming. It is thus the duty of public authority in matters of religion to reconcile and to harmonize among themselves the exercise of the rights of both, in such wise that the exercise of the rights of one group will not constitute an obstacle to the exercise of the rights of the other.

A distinction must also be made between the right to propagate sincerely and honestly one's own religion and the abuses of this right when dishonest means are employed in religious propaganda.

d) *Emphasis on the objective truth of the Divine Law with all its exigencies.*

This is done in such a way as to exclude all danger of subjectivism and indifferentism.

e) *Present-day circumstances confirm the necessity and the rights of religious liberty.*

The urgency of this problem becomes all the more evident because of the closer bonds created among men of diverse cultures and religions, along with the increased consciousness of personal responsibility, with the evolution of the juridical structures of civil institutions.

SUMMARY OF THE DECLARATION ON RELIGIOUS LIBERTY

The numbering of the articles follows that of the schema on ecumenism, which comprises 24 numbers. Hence the articles of this declaration begin with No. 25.

No. 25 — The consideration of the problem of religious liberty favors contacts among Christians. This emphasized its ecumenical aspect.

No. 26 — *The nature of religious liberty.*

a) Its foundation: In the religious field, it is both a duty and an honor for man to follow the will of God, according to the dictates of conscience. This is the very root of the right to religious liberty.

b) The right to religious liberty in society puts men in a position to be able to practice privately and publicly their own religion, and no restriction must be placed on this religious practice.

c) Religious liberty demands that there should be established in society the conditions required to guarantee it.

d) The council, in its affirmation of man's dependence on God, proclaims that *religious liberty in society must be recognized and respected by all and everywhere.*

No. 27 — *The task of the Church.*

According to the mandate received from the Lord, the Church propagates the Word of God and prays for the salvation of all men, exhorting her own children to spread the life-giving light of the Gospel.

No. 28 — *No one can be forced to embrace the Faith.*

With love, prudence and patience, in accordance with the ways of God, contact is established with those who do not have the true Faith. But all coercion, direct or indirect, is to be excluded from the preaching of the Truth, because according to the traditional norm of the Church, based on the very nature of the act of Faith, the acceptance of Faith must be fully free.

No. 29 — *The religious liberty of the individual in human society.*

In human society, religious liberty is to be respected not only by Christians and for Christians, but by all and for all—persons, individuals, and religious groups.

Freedom to follow God's call is the peak of human dignity, and consequently this liberty in social coexistence is a right in the truest sense of the term, and is the foundation and safeguard of other freedoms.

The objective, absolute and universal Divine Law is the norm of our relationships with God, whence there derives man's obligation to acquire diligently the knowledge of this law. But man can follow the Divine Law only through the judgment of his own conscience which he forms for himself under the guidance of prudence. In sincere obedience to conscience, a man implicitly obeys God. If, in his attempts to know the Will of God, a man falls into an erroneous interpretation of that Will, no man and no power has the right to induce him to act contrary to the dictate of his conscience.

An essential element of religious liberty is the right to practice one's religion publicly. Hence the Church proclaims not only the right to one's opinion and freedom to practice the rites of one's own religion, but also an individual's genuine right to observe and to witness his private and public worship before God and men, whether individuals or groups, and to organize according to the precepts of his religion the whole of his own individual, family, educational, cultural, social and charitable life.

The *exercise* of this right must be adapted to the exigencies of the social nature of man. Hence it can be subject to restrictions. But it can be restricted legitimately only when it is in grave conflict with the end of society. Consequently, it is unlawful for state authorities to discriminate in any way against religion. It is, on the contrary, their duty to protect and to encourage religious liberty.

No. 30 — *The freedom of religious groups in social coexistence.*

Men have the right of free assembly in groups, which groups in turn, within the limits determined by the end of society, have the right to govern themselves according to their own laws, to honor God with public worship, to assist their members in their religious life, and to create institutions of social character based on religious principles.

The Catholic Church expects from state authorities a recognition of the right of religious liberty in social coexistence.

Any violent oppression of religion itself or of the religion of a determined religious group is in opposition with the Divine Will and with human rights.

Religious groups are entitled to carry on sincere and honest propagation of their religion, but they must refrain from any "proselytism" which would employ dishonest means.

Civil authorities have no direct power to regulate the relationships of their citizens with God. Consequently, they may not subject religious groups to the temporal aims of the state. On the contrary, it contributes to the common welfare when conditions are created which will favor religious life.

No. 31 — *Religious life in the world today.*

Today in particular, the problem of religious liberty is of greater urgency because of the more extended contacts which exist between men of different cultures and different religions, because of an increased consciousness of personal responsibility, because of the juridical organization of today's civil order—all of which set off in a clearer light the incompetence of the state to establish itself as a judge of religious truth.

There can be no peaceful coexistence in the human family in the world today without religious liberty in society.

93rd General Congregation

October 2, 1964

Cooperation with non-Catholic Christians in producing translations of the Bible has been proposed to the ecumenical council.

At its 93rd general meeting the last four chapters of the Revelation schema were distributed and reported on by the Theological Commission, which had drawn them up. In chapter six, which deals with the Bible's role in the life of the Church, it was proposed that translations in various languages be undertaken with the aim of producing a common set of Scriptures in cooperation with non-Catholic churches.

The text of chapter six, as revealed at the U.S. bishops' press panel, stated that "if these translations were **made in a common** effort with the separated brethren, they could be used by all Christians." The proposal will not come up for debate until chapters one through five are discussed.

During the day, 16 speakers continued discussion on the schema's first two chapters. Chapter one deals with the nature and object of Revelation. Chapter two deals with Revelation's transmission under four headings: the apostles and their successors as heralds of the Gospels, tradition, the mutual relation of tradition and Scripture, and the deposit of Revelation in its relation to the whole Church and the Church's teaching authority.

For the most part, speakers engaged for the third day in a debate on whether or not the council should deal with the question of whether tradition contains revealed truths not found in the Bible, and on whether tradition stopped with the death of the apostles, or whether it is to be understood in a broader meaning and therefore is still developing even today.

Abbot Christopher Butler, O.S.B., president of the Benedictine Confederation of England, denied that it is a defined dogma of the Church that Sacred Scripture is deficient and that tradition contains elements not found in it. He supported the majority view of the Theological Commission, which had proposed avoiding the entire question since it is not theologically mature.

Almost all of the day's speakers, however, if not directly in favor of a specific treatment of the problem, expressed dissatisfaction with the treatment of tradition **in the schema.**

After 16 Fathers had spoken on the subject, discussion on the third chapter—on the inspiration and interpretation of the Bible—was begun. A short introduction was made by Bishop Jan van Dodewaard of Haarlem, the Netherlands, a member of the Theological Commission. He presented briefly the background and general contents of chapters three, four, five and six. But discussion by two speakers, who took opposite positions, was limited to chapter three. The speakers were Ernesto Cardinal Ruffini of Palermo, Italy, and Franziskus Cardinal Koenig of Vienna.

Cardinal Ruffini, usually the first to speak when any new subject comes up in debates because of his seniority, took issue with several portions of the third chapter.

He objected that too much freedom had been given to Catholic Biblical scholars and rejected the view that the Church's understanding of the Bible is not complete.

On the other hand, Cardinal Koenig said there is great need for use of recent developments in scientific and natural history which have opened new doors to Biblical scholars. At the same time, he said, it should be stated that there are some geographical and historical mistakes in the Bible which only prove that God used men in their limited state.

The day opened with Mass celebrated by Bishop Niel Farren of Derry, Ireland, on the 25th anniversary of his consecration. Bishop Paul Hagarty of Nassau, Bahama Islands, enthroned the Gospels. Giacomo Cardinal Lercaro of Bologna, Italy, moderated the discussion of chapter two and Julius Cardinal Doepfner of Munich and Freising, Germany, moderated the third chapter debate.

At the meeting's outset Archbishop Pericle Felici, council general secretary, outlined the method of voting proposed for the three chapters on the ecumenism schema. The voting is to begin Oct. 5. A standing vote later approved the proposed voting process.

Archbishop Felici also said that for the schemata on the lay apostolate and on the Church in the modern world there would be the usual general discussion first, followed by a vote to accept or reject each schema as a basis for detailed debate chapter by chapter.

Bishop van Dodewaard, speaking in the name of the

Dutch bishops, was the first to speak on chapter two. He said that while it proclaims the apostles as the foundation of the episcopate, it should be made clear that the successors of the apostles do not have all the rights the apostles had in regard to Revelation. He said this distinction would be ecumenically pleasing.

Archbishop Casimiro Morcillo Gonzalez of Madrid objected to the interpretation given in the text to a quote from St. John, "The truth shall come to you," as being too broad. He said this can be interpreted as referring to the apostles or to the faithful as a whole, but cannot be applied to individuals because of the possible confusion that could arise.

The day's first speaker to touch on the question of tradition was Archbishop Octavio Beras of Santo Domingo, Dominican Republic. His attitude was that the postponement of discussion of the question should be based on opportuneness instead of on the idea that there is a doctrinal problem. As far as he is concerned, he said, it is within the scope of the council to confirm the traditional teaching on the subject, otherwise the council endangers the Marian dogmas of the Assumption and Immaculate Conception. He overran his time and was cut off.

Auxiliary Bishop Antonio de Castro Monteiro of Vila Real, Portugal, said the definition of tradition in the text was acceptable, but that he wanted more stress on the infallibility of tradition and also a clear statement that tradition's teaching on faith and morals has been passed on without any corruption.

Bishop Angel Temino Saiz of Orense, Spain, objected to chapter two's treatment of the transmission of Revelation because it ignores the role of reason. He stated further that it is clear that tradition encompasses more than what is found in the Bible.

Another Spaniard, Bishop Jacinto Argaya Goicoechea of Mondonedo-Ferrol, affirmed that tradition is certainly at work in the Church, guided by the Holy Spirit. He said it should be clear that Revelation is above the teaching authority of the Church.

Italian Archbishop Enrico Nicodemo of Bari said he wanted some listing of the elements contained in tradition. He added that many truths are not found in Revelation, including all of the seven sacraments, the Assumption, and valid baptism by heretics, as well as what are the true Scriptures and what are not.

Bishop Jose Alba Palacios of Tehauntepec, Mexico, asked that the title be changed from sacred tradition to divine tradition and said the text is not strong enough in stating the fact that preaching is the main form of transmitting the word of God. He also warned that St. Thomas should not be cited as the ultimate argument on all things, as his opinions have actually been ruled against by popes in various instances.

Bishop Jean Rupp of Monaco objected that two concepts of tradition were used interchangeably in the text. One is the concept of tradition as the revelation of truth. The other is the idea of tradition as the transmission of that truth. The word of God does not grow, he said, but its transmission develops. Therefore, there must be a distinction between the deposit of faith and its transmission in the world.

Archbishop Salvatore Baldassarri of Ravenna, Italy, maintained that the text, by its silence and by direct reference in its appended notes, implicitly affirms that the concept of the two sources of revelation is not mature. This is only a tradition, he said, and the council should act in this matter.

The prior general of the Order of St. Augustine, Father Luciano Rubio, called the text's silence on the extension of tradition disturbing. He asked how it could be passed over since not all doctrines are in the Bible.

Abbot Butler took the opposite view. He stated that the Council of Trent did not intend to declare the Bible insufficient when it affirmed the equality of tradition and the Bible. This affirmation was repeated by the First Vatican Council, he said, and, if it pleases the Fathers, it can be repeated again at the Second Vatican Council.

But he said that it is wrong to affirm that the ordinary teaching authority of the Church defines that there are two separate sources of Revelation as a doctrine. Such a solemn doctrinal definition is proper only to the Church's extraordinary teaching authority, he said.

In treating of both the Bible and tradition, Abbot Butler said the ordinary teaching authority of the Church has wanted to affirm that, in the spirit of these sources, what the Church has handed down is true. The question of whether there are two separate sources, or only two aspects of one source, of Revelation is a secondary question, he stated.

Abbot Butler said the Church's teaching on the Bible in past centuries has been static rather than dynamic, that it has sought more to conserve and preserve than to explore. Today the approach is a dynamic one and things are being seen in the Bible that were not obvious previously, he continued.

Therefore the intent of the ordinary teaching authority of the Church is not to affirm a deficiency in Sacred Scripture, he said. Rather it merely reflects the state of exegesis of that past time.

Abbot Butler said the discussion shows that the matter is not theologically mature, and stated that those who hold there are two separate sources still do not understand the arguments of their opposites.

Italian Archbishop Raffaele Calabria of Benevento said the text is acceptable but wanted a clear statement on the providential mission of the Church's teaching authority in the transmission of tradition.

Archbishop Francois Marty of Rheims, France, said it is true that living tradition grows with time, but that the text fails to identify the source of this growth. He said that for missionary purposes, he wanted emphasis placed on the connection with the Church's living tradition and the concrete history of peoples and cultures where the Church takes root.

The last speaker on chapter two was Archbishop George B. Flahiff of Winnipeg, Man. He pointed out that divine tradition should not be identified with everything handed down by the Church and agreed with the statements on the previous day by Albert Cardinal Meyer of Chicago, Paul Cardinal Leger of Montreal and Juan Cardinal Landazuri Ricketts of Lima, Peru, that the Church is not automatically preserved in the purity and integrity of its doctrine, but must constantly examine its life in the light of the Bible and guided by tradition as already by the Church's teaching authority.

The introduction on the remaining four chapters of the Revelation schema were made by Bishop van Dodewaard.

The bishop said in his report that the text had been carefully amended. He said it draws attention to the problems of modern exegesis and the extent to which certain systems can provide reliable guidance for understanding God's word.

Chapter four on the Old Testament has been recast to show it as the history of salvation rather than the history of the chosen people only, he stated. He added that it shows that inspiration of the Old Testament gives it lasting value.

Chapter five on the New Testament, he said, has been revised to include all the books of the New Testament rather than the Gospels alone. He said it discusses the historical character of the New Testament.

Chapter five on the New Testament also refers to the Pontifical Commission for Biblical Studies' instruction of May 14, 1964, which urged Catholic scholars to apply both traditional and modern means to discover the full meaning and significance of Relevation. The instruction dealt specifically with the three stages of the development of the Gospels: first, what Christ said and did; second, how the apostles represented this to fit the conditions of the listeners of the time; and third, how the evangelists reproduced this for their readers.

Chapter six had been entitled, Use of the Word of God, and is now called Sacred Scripture in the Life of the Church. It recommends preparation of accurate translations of the Bible in various languages, he noted.

Chapter six further recommends that such translations of the Bible be made in collaboration with separated Christians.

It also touches on the duties of Catholic scholars and on the importance of Holy Writ for the study and teaching of theology, the bishop said.

Cardinal Ruffini began debate on chapter three by criticizing the text for ignoring the usual norms laid down to guide the research of Catholic Biblical scholars.

He said there is no reference to the norm of the analogy of faith, which in general means the fittingness and consistency of various teachings. Nor is there a reference to the teaching of the Fathers of the Church on specific matters, nor to the need of following the sense of the Church, he went on.

Cardinal Ruffini objected to what he called the exaggerated degree of freedom given Catholic Biblical scholars in the text and said he disagreed that the Church is only now learning about literary forms and the role they play in the way Scripture was written. He said it would be an exaggeration to think that the sacred books have not been understood up to now.

Cardinal Koenig said that great progress has been made by modern scholars in Eastern studies and that this must be taken into account when interpreting the Bible. Pointing to some factual errors in the Bible, he said they do not deprive the Bible of its authority, but show that God used men who were limited as to historical and other facts. Inspiration works in a very human way, he said.   JAMES C. O'NEILL

* * * *

The schema on revelation currently before the ecumenical council "rises above all discussions of conflicting schools of theology on Scripture and tradition and the opposition between the Reformation and counter-Reformation," a leading Belgian prelate said.

Bishop Andre Charue of Namur, a member of the doctrinal commission which helped frame the new schema, told a press conference (Oct. 3) that the welcome accorded the text has been generally positive.

"Nevertheless there is still some opposition to it," he said. "Some Fathers would want to open debate again on the problem of two sources of revelation. But one may wonder if it is opportune to begin anew the discussion which caused so much disagreement in the first session. Especially since the very expression lends itself to confusion.

"Whether there is one source or two is not so important as affirming that Scripture and tradition together transmit to us the one Gospel preached by the apostles. In this way the Church is certain of remaining in close contact with the 'living voice of the Gospel' and of being able to make this voice heard."

The opposition to the first text was so strong in the council's first session that the majority voted on Nov. 20, 1962, to return it for revision. Although the majority vote was not the required two-thirds, Pope John XXIII intervened and directed the text to be reworked by a mixed commission.

Bishop Charue said the present schema provides an "irenic, positive and constructive explanation of the question to serve as a starting point for a better understanding of both revelation and tradition."

Referring to the controversy over the relation between Scripture and tradition, Bishop Charue said "tradition refers without a break in continuity to Scripture, and Scripture in turn is made present in tradition. Neither can be had without the other, and together both work toward the same goal—the building up of the Mystical Body of Christ.

"The tradition of the Church is in contact with the tradition of the apostles. It was the apostles who opened to us the understanding of the Old Testament in its tendency toward Christ. Then came the books of the New Testament enriching apostolic tradition. The inspired character of Scripture guarantees its infallibility. Scripture permits us to situate the coming of Christ in the general picture of the history of salvation and provides a witness which prevents the people of God from wandering along aimlessly."

Bishop Charue concluded by stressing the Christological perspective of the schema which "gives it its true unity and the reason for its richness."

94th General Congregation
October 5, 1964

By overwhelming majorities the ecumenical council has initially approved the principles that lay the foundation for a more definite and fervent drive for Christian unity among the world's Catholics.

The council Fathers, in approving the first four changes in the proposed decree on ecumenism, have affirmed that the restoration of unity among all Christians is one of the principal objects of the Second Vatican Council.

They also affirmed that the Church as Christ desired it has unity and uniqueness as one of its main characteristics, that separated Christians in their Churches and communities have many and precious Christian elements in not a few of which there can be a life of grace leading to salvation, and that the council exhorts Catholics to recognize the signs of our times and engage actively in the ecumenical movement.

Although the votes were only the first four of a total of 14 which will be taken on the three chapters of the ecumenism schema, they indicated a forward step toward the beginning of the drive to end the divisions among Christians.

At the 94th council meeting, 15 speakers also commented on chapters three through six of the schema on Revelation. The chief point at issue was the treatment of the historicity of the Gospels or what use is to be made of modern scientific research in interpreting the Gospels.

Among those favoring the use of modern research were Albert Cardinal Meyer of Chicago and Auxiliary Bishop Charles G. Maloney of Louisville, Ky. But bishops from Ireland and Italy expressed fear that the treatment of some modern scholars weakens the authority of the Sacred Books and is harmful to the faithful.

Among other events of the day was the announcement of the death of Father Jean Janssens, S.J., general of the Jesuit Fathers, who died shortly after a morning visit from Pope Paul VI.

The day's opening Mass was celebrated by Archbishop Peter McKeefry of Wellington, New Zealand. The Gospel was enthroned by Father Joseph Malenfant, O.F.M.Cap., apostolic prefect of Benares-Gorakhpu, India.

Before the Fathers voted on the amendments of chapter one of the ecumenism schema, Archbishop Joseph Martin of Rouen read a report on the chapter, outlining the thinking of the commissions which had drafted it.

Aside from Cardinal Meyer, Augustin Cardinal Bea, S.J., was the only other Cardinal to speak. The president of the Secretariat for Promoting Christian Unity called for more stress on the Old Testament and criticized the text for its vagueness and obscurity.

Voting on the ecumenism schema changes was as follows:

By a majority of 2,094 "yes" to 16 "no," the Fathers accepted an amendment to add an introductory paragraph to the original text of the schema which was first discussed during the second council session last year.

The introduction stated that the restoration of Christian unity is one of the principal objects of the Second Vatican Council and extols the need of that unity among Christians. It noted that many men have been disturbed by the divisions among Christians and that a movement has arisen among them to restore the lost unity.

This movement is the ecumenical movement, the introduction stated, and it embraces all who call upon the Triune God and follow Christ as their Lord.

Archbishop Martin, in his report on the changes in the schema, stated that the original title of the first chapter had been changed. Originally it had been called "On the Principles of Catholic Ecumenism." Now it is called "On Catholic Principles of Ecumenism." The change acknowledges that there is only one ecumenical movement and not a special movement limited to Catholics.

The second amendment, approved by a vote of 2,081 to 30, proclaimed the unity and uniqueness of the Church founded by Christ and said that the mystery of the Church founded by Christ is the one fold of God, like a sign among nations bringing the Gospel of peace to the whole human race.

The third amendment, approved by a vote of 2,051 to 57, treated of the relationship of the Christian churches and communities separated from the Catholic Church. Noting that divisions have occurred over the centuries, not without fault on both sides, it stated that people belonging in good faith to these bodies cannot be blamed for the sin of separation and that those who believe in

Christ and are baptized are in some way united with the Catholic Church, though not perfectly.

It also stated that in these bodies many precious elements of Christianity such as the word of God, grace, faith, hope and charity exist and that not a few of the sacred actions which are performed by them can generate the life of grace and that this is capable of leading to a communion of salvation.

The fourth change, approved by a vote of 2,056 to 50, said that under the guidance of the Holy Spirit efforts are being made through prayer, words and deeds to approach the unity desired by Christ. It was stated that the council exhorts Catholics to recognize the signs of the times and engage actively in the ecumenical movement.

The amendment encouraged individual ecumenical efforts through prayer and the dialogue of experts of the various churches. It also said that there is no opposition between ecumenical activity and the apostolate of conversion since both works are inspired by the Holy Spirit.

Archbishop Martin's explanation was given prior to the voting. He said the views expressed by the Fathers when the text was first presented at last year's sessions, as well as more than 500 written observations, were taken into account in reworking the schema.

He noted that there is greater attention paid to the Holy Spirit's role in ecumenism, and that ecumenism is not a static formula but a movement aroused by the Holy Spirit, which can take turns no one can foresee.

Archbishop Martin stated that the new text does not overlook difficulties and does not presume to solve them all. But the council can give impetus to the movement since the hour of unity is now approaching, he stated.

Cardinal Meyer was the first of the day's 15 speakers. He said he found the text's summary of the principles of interpretation excellent and that they show respect for Holy Writ. However, he said, he does not accept the fact that inspiration should be treated only in terms of freedom from error or Biblical infallibility.

He said the interpretation should be examined in the light of the word of God and that words go beyond their immediate meaning. As effects or offshoots of words, the Cardinal listed three—conveying ideas, revealing the nature of the speaker or writer, and producing a reaction among others.

The word of God admirably fulfills these three functions, he said. If we approach our appreciation of Scripture along these lines, then we will be able to understand Revelation correctly as something much more than a series of disjointed propositions setting forth the truth. We will express not only the negative element of freedom from error, but will put strong emphasis on Scripture in a genuinely positive light. Finally, he said, this approach will provide a better context for a clearer understanding of the idea of inerrancy itself.

Cardinal Bea said he feels the text does not sufficiently stress the value of the Old Testament.

Cardinal Bea also said the text was vague and obscure in some places, particularly in alluding to citations from the Bible without actually printing them. He called for a change in one section of the text which urges Catholics and especially Religious to read the Bible. He said he objected to this since it would leave the impression that Religious do not read the Bible.

Bishop Jean Weber of Strasbourg, France, called for emphasis on the richness, unity and fulness to be found in Scripture. The Bible is not just a book dropped from heaven, he said, and in spite of its diversity, the books of the Bible have an affinity, since all bring Revelation within the reach of man.

The problem of the Bible's freedom from error also concerned Bishop Francis Simons of Indore, India. He said the text makes freedom from error a consequence of Revelation. But what is important is what God wants to say, not what the writer wanted to say. God used the errors of the man who writes Scripture and gradually reveals Himself. There is nothing to show that God wished to free the sacred writers from the errors of their time, he stated.

Italian Bishop Primo Gasbarri, apostolic administrator of the Grosseto diocese, called for a reconfirmation of the historical character of the Gospels and objected to chapter five, which deals with the New Testament. He also cited three documents of the Holy See dealing with Biblical criticism, warning against various dangers arising from historical criticism and the use of form or literary criticism. He said the chapter now is ambiguous and dangerous and must be altered so that scholars do not hurt the consciences of Catholics or weaken the authority of the Sacred Scriptures.

Bishop Jaime Flores Martin of Barbastro, Spain, altered the usual opening salutation of "venerable brothers" by saying "venerable Church of God." He asked for a clear declaration that the writers of the Bible are genuinely the authors of the Bible and that they are instruments of God.

Bishop Maloney said it is the duty of the council, as it proposes old things and new, to leave doors open as it pursues the goal of the inner unity of the Church. In the field of Scripture, literary forms were known in the early Church, as can be demonstrated from the writings of St. Augustine and St. John Chrysostom, he said. The Church now can make use of new discoveries to corroborate the things it has been teaching and to obtain more explicit knowledge of other elements.

The historical method can make genuine contribution to a right knowledge of Scripture if this method is correctly understood and applied, he said. Citing the recent instruction of the Pontifical Biblical Commission, he stated that instead of saying that the sacred writers used "all their faculties and powers," it would be more exact to say they used "their human faculties and powers."

A comprehension of chapter three seems to restrict the sense of Sacred Scripture to what the human sacred writer understood, the bishop declared. It would be wrong to conclude that the understanding of the text on the part of the Church is always restricted to the degree of understanding of the human author, he stated.

Archbishop Casimiro Morcillo Gonzalez of Madrid said the text lacks emphasis on the law as found in the Old Testament and that Christ came to fulfill that law. He said he wanted it stressed that the law and the Ten Commandments were elements of the Old Testament. He also objected that Revelation is treated as a progressive experience and fails to say anything of the demands Revelation makes on man.

An Eastern rite prelate took a completely different tack, finding fault with the text's basic treatment because it deals with the matter from the viewpoint of the Latin rite of the West.

Melkite-rite Archbishop Neophytos Edelby, consultor of the Patriarchate of Antioch, although approving the provisions for including the findings of modern research in interpretation, said the text was too timid and weak on presenting theological interpretation. The Western Church, he said, has a tendency to the juridical approach, splitting things such as the primacy and episcopate, Scripture and tradition.

This results in a loss of unity, he said; we must come back to the mystery of the Church and realize we cannot separate tradition and Scripture from living the life of the Church. Without tradition, Scripture is a dead letter, he stated. Revelation was lived in the mystery of the Church before it was written and what is needed is a total vision of the action of the Holy Spirit, he declared.

Auxiliary Bishop Eduard Shick of Fulda, Germany, speaking in the name of the German and Scandinavian bishops, expressed pleasure that the text calls for Bible reading by the faithful, since this will end the old accusation that the Church does not favor such reading.

Archbishop Rafael Garcia y Garcia De Castro of Granada, Spain, called for an amendment of several articles for the sake of clarity.

Irish Bishop William Philbin of Down and Connor wanted more emphasis given to the traditional means of Biblical interpretation and not have everything centered on modern means. He complained that there is no synthesis between the two means and also called for greater stress on the ordinary teaching authority of the Church in interpreting the Bible. Lastly, he pointed out that the text says the words and deeds of Jesus in the Bible are true, but what about those of others?

Auxiliary Bishop Joseph Heuschen of Liege, Belgium, said the text protects the historical character of the Gospel and also is satisfactory to the demands of modern Biblical interpretation. By using modern research we can achieve a clearer knowledge of the written Gospels, he said.

Archbishop Joseph Cordeiro of Karachi, Pakistan, said the text should agree with the teaching contained in an instruction issued this year by the Pontifical Biblical Commission. At the same time, he said that the epistles of the New Testament are slighted by the text since it refers to them only as "other apostolic writings." He asked this be changed to give honor to them and particularly to the Church's greatest theologian, St. Paul.

The day's last speaker was Bishop Manuel del Rosario of Malolos, Philippines. He said a distinction between apostolic tradition and traditionalism, a source of errors, should be made. This must be clear, he said, otherwise we may be accused of using tradition as a means of explaining away skeletons in the closets of the Church.

JAMES C. O'NEILL

95th General Congregation

October 6, 1964

The ecumenical council ended debate on the schema on Revelation at its 95th meeting and introduced a new one on the lay apostolate, which emphasizes that laymen are not only in the Church but are the Church.

At the same meeting, the council Fathers passed with great majorities additional changes in the ecumenism schema, including an expression of regret for past faults toward other Churches. The council also pardoned those who have offended the Catholic Church and authorized the holding of some interfaith prayers and services.

During the meeting it was announced that some specially chosen priests will be admitted to the council during the discussion of the council proposition on the priesthood at Pope Paul VI's request.

Thirteen speakers took the floor to discuss the Revelation schema at the meeting. Following them, Fernando Cardinal Cento of the Roman curia gave a 15-minute introduction to the lay apostolate schema.

Before the votes on the ecumenism schema were taken, Bishop Charles H. Helmsing of Kansas City-St. Joseph, Mo., gave a report on chapter two in which he disclosed that the Secretariat for Promoting Christian Unity will draw up an ecumenical directory to guide the world's bishops in ecumenical matters. He urged the bishops to submit their suggestions and advice to the secretary of the secretariat, Bishop Jan Willebrands.

During the meeting five ballots were taken.

The first vote was on the ecumenism schema's introduction and first chapter as a whole. The day before the council Fathers had voted on four separate amendments to the introduction and chapter one, that is, on articles one through four. On Oct. 6 both were approved as a whole by a vote of 1,926 to 30, with 209 Fathers voting favorably but with reservations.

The next four votes were on chapter two of the ecumenism schema, which deals with the practice of ecumenism and indicates how Catholics can participate in it.

The first of these four votes was on articles five and six. (The articles, or amendments, are numbered successively for the whole schema rather than chapter by chapter.) Article five says that the restoration of Christian unity is the concern of the whole Church, of

both laymen and pastors. Article six says the Church must be ever more faithful to its calling in order to work best for unity and must be ready to reform itself. The vote was 2,120 "yes" to 46 "no."

The next vote was on article seven, which says that without heartfelt adherence to God's call there can be little progress in the ecumenical movement. It says this has special meaning for those in authority and that all of us in some way have a responsibility for the sins of disunity.

It states that the Fathers ask pardon of God and of separated Christians and likewise give pardon.

The vote was 2,076 "yes" to 92 "no."

The following vote was on article eight, which stresses the need of prayer for Christian unity. It speaks of Catholics and non-Catholics praying together under certain circumstances, which are to be determined in concrete cases by episcopal authority (which is not further defined as local or regional).

The vote was 1,872 "yes" to 292 "no."

The final vote was on articles 9, 10, 11, and 12.

Article 9 deals with mutual knowledge and the means to it: dialogue, willingness to learn, and meetings between theologians with participants on an equal footing.

Article 10 deals with ecumenical training, especially in the seminary.

Article 11 deals with the way in which the truths of the Faith are to be expressed and warns against false irenicism.

Article 12 deals with cooperation with separated Christians in such things as social action in the emerging regions of the world, work for peace, and attempts to bring a Christian spirit into the arts and sciences.

The vote on articles 9 through 12 was 2,099 "yes" to 62 "no."

During the day's debate on the Revelation schema, one bishop appealed for the establishment of an international Biblical society by the Holy See similar to the Protestants' very successful Biblical societies. Another warned the council against an indiscriminate recommendation that Catholics read the Bible when they are not prepared for the problems it can pose.

But as on previous days, comment centered on the

relation of the Bible and tradition, the problem of the use of form criticism in Biblical interpretation and the historical accuracy of the Gospels.

Abbot Christopher Butler, O.S.B., president of the Benedictine Confederation of England, summed up the historical accuracy problem as follows:

"Everyone knows that anxieties have been felt in this field from two sides. Some fear that we are in the process of losing the necessary historical foundation of our Faith. Others want our scholars to have all rightful liberty in pursuing their task, which is of such great service to the Church."

Abbot Butler's position was solidly in favor of historical research by many Catholic Biblical scholars, for "either there is a worldwide conspiracy of scholars to undermine the bases of Christian faith (and a man who can believe that can believe anything), or the aim of our scholars is to reach the full, objective and real truth of the Gospel tradition."

Many of the day's speakers, however, expressed fear that literary and form criticism is greatly threatening the authority of the Gospels and endangering the faith of Catholics.

The meeting opened with Mass celebrated by Archbishop Hector Santos of Tegucigalpa, Honduras. The Gospel was enthroned by Bishop Edmund Nowicki of Gdansk, Poland. Julius Cardinal Doepfner of Munich and Freising, Germany, was the moderator.

Bishop Helmsing's report on chapter two of the ecumenism schema stressed that the desire for deeper unity among Christians is a part of the renewal of the Church sought by the council.

To achieve success in the field of unity, he said, it is admitted that a conversion of the heart is required of all Catholics, freely regretting past errors and pardoning past offenses. This can be expressed in approving some forms of inter-faith religious activity. But, he noted, the schema gives only general directives which are to be used by either individual bishops or by national conferences according to the circumstances.

Bishop Helmsing noted that chapter two seeks to avoid not only a false irenicism, but also hardness of heart and intellectual pride. He concluded that approval of the amended articles could signify a great step forward for the Church in its ecumenical relations with other Christian bodies.

In his introduction of the lay apostolate schema, Cardinal Cento said that part of its intent has already been realized since the doors of St. Peter's basilica have swung open to admit laymen and laywomen as council auditors. This is a symbol of the highest esteem in which the hierarchy hold the laity, he said.

He added that it has been one of the council's efforts to increase the sense of responsibility on the laity's part for the welfare of the Church in keeping

with the desire of Pope John XXIII. The apostolate of the laity and that of the hierarchy are "one thing," he said. While there is a distinction between the hierarchy and the laity, there is not a distance, he continued.

The laity are not only in the Church but are the Church, he said, and it is increasingly necessary that the laity work effectively in a cooperative spirit with the hierarchy to spread the Church throughout the world.

The day's first speaker on the Revelation schema was Italian Archbishop Armando Fares of Catanzaro. He said he wanted the text to recognize the work of scholars, but at the same time to safeguard the veracity of the Scriptures from some of the results that could come from the use of various methods which could cast doubt on the historical truth of the Gospels.

He asked for greater collaboration between Scripture scholars and theologians and said that such collaboration should be based on the freedom from error of the Sacred Books. Lastly, he urged that various means of spreading the reading of the Gospels be advocated by the text.

Another Italian prelate, Bishop Luigi Carli of Segni, insisted that the text sound a warning against the perils of form criticism and assure Catholics that the Bible gives them genuine history, especially in reference to Gospel reports on the birth and childhood of Christ. Many Biblical scholars today hold that not all details of this period of Christ's life are to be taken literally as found in the Gospels, he said.

Bishop Carli also stated that tradition is virtually excluded from the text. He said he wanted this rectified.

A third Italian, Bishop Costantino Caminada of Ferentino, warned that indiscriminate circulation of the Bible among Catholics is not without dangers. Stating that Catholics are not ready to read the Bible without instruction and commentaries, he recommended that Catholic anthologies of the Biblical text be compiled with commentaries explaining the texts. He asked that an obligation for clerics to read the Bible daily be inserted in the new Code of Canon Law.

An exactly opposite view was expressed later by Yugoslavian Bishop Smiljan Cekada of Skoplje, who declared that the Biblical problem today is that of insuring the widest possible distribution of the Bible in cheap and easily readable editions.

Citing the success of Protestant editions of the Bible, he noted that some Catholic missionaries use these editions because no Catholic editions are available.

To remedy this he suggested that the Holy See set up an international Bible society for translations in all languages and for distribution to all parts of the world.

Bishop Cekada, however, expressed doubts about the possibility of producing a common translation of the Bible with non-Catholics. He asked what books of the

Bible will be chosen and whether they will be printed with or without commentaries. All these problems have to be answered, he went on. He said some of the ecumenical spirit seems to be infantilism and romanticism. He gave as an example the fact that one of his diocesan priests, after an earthquake had destroyed his cathedral, suggested that in its place there be erected an interdenominational cathedral. One must beware of pan-Christianism and syncretism, Bishop Cekada concluded.

Spanish Bishop Pablo Barrachina Estevan of Orihuela-Alicante objected to the schema as it stands because it is not well organized and fails to put sufficient stress on the pastoral aim.

Bishop Hermann Volk of Mainz, Germany, said he wanted more emphasis on the fact that Scripture is not only the font of truth but is also a personal colloquy between God and man, that faith is not only the intellectual act of believing but also a total dedication of all human faculties to God.

Father Joao Ferreira, O.F.M., apostolic prefect of Portuguese Guinea, criticized the sixth chapter of the schema dealing with Scripture in the world for lacking a pastoral spirit. Asking that direct quotes from the Bible be used, he said he also desired that the practical aspect of faithful reading of the Bible be stressed.

Bishop Pierre Boillon of Verdun, France, said he wanted inserted in the text a statement that definitions of the ordinary teaching authority of the Church must be understood in the light of Sacred Scripture and also that Scripture has a great importance for theologians. He said there is no problem about a dogma's being based on tradition but not found specifically in Scripture. A specific text is not necessary, he stated. What is sufficient is that it can be related to the general context of the Bible.

Italian Bishop Carlo Maccari of Mondovi asked that the title of the sixth chapter be changed to read "the Word of God in the Life of the Church," because the word of God is not restricted to the Bible but is the whole content of Revelation, Scripture and tradition. He warned against soft-pedaling the entire content of Revelation.

Dealing with problems posed by the discussion of the historical character of the Gospels, Abbot Butler said that from the point of view of faith "there is no doubt that the Gospels along with the other books of the Bible are inspired. It is, however, certain that the notion of 'literary types' is applicable to the Gospels, as it is to the other inspired books."

Abbot Butler suggested various changes in the wording of the text concerning how the evangelists wrote the Gospels and then stated: "Let us not be afraid of scholarly and historical truth. Let us not be afraid that one truth may tell against another truth. Let us not be afraid that our scholars may be lacking in loyalty to the Church and to traditional doctrine . . .

"Doubtless some will turn liberty into license—but we must risk this for the sake of the greater good. Doubtless mistakes are made and will be made in this field—but it is one where trial and error are the road to truth."

Spain's Bishop Eduardo Martinez Gonzalez of Zamora said he found it difficult to distinguish between what is to be regarded as inspired and what errors that exist are due to later copyists.

Colombian Archbishop Anibal Munoz Duque of Nueva Pamplona objected that the text, if taken literally, would mean that Scripture and only Scripture is the work of God, thus excluding tradition. To correct this he suggested that Scripture be described as the word of God in writing.

The day's last speaker was retired Archbishop Juan Gonzalez Arbelaez of Popayan, Colombia, who also objected to saying that nothing is revealed except what is in Scripture. He said the text should be revised. He also said the text on inspiration is not clear. It cannot be proved that the writer of Scripture always wished to express objective truth, he stated.

Precisely what "episcopal authority" is to decide when, where and how Catholics may worship in common with non-Catholics was left deliberately vague in the schema on ecumenism. This was stated at the U.S. bishops' press panel after the council meeting by Father Thomas Stransky, C.S.P., American official of the unity secretariat which drafted the schema.

Father Stransky said some bishops feared that different policies on common worship in adjoining dioceses might cause confusion.

Father Robert Trisco of Chicago, professor of Church history at the Catholic University of America, said some bishops feared their authority in this matter might be infringed upon if such decisions were entrusted to a regional conference of bishops.

Bishop Helmsing in his official explanation of the schema to the council Fathers explicitly referred to this episcopal authority as either local bishops or regional conferences of bishops.

However, Father Stransky said, the schema left room for putting really big decisions on common worship into the hands of a future senate of bishops, which the council, acting with the pope, might set up to assist the pope in the central administration of the Church.

Father John Long, S.J., another U.S. priest in the unity secretariat, pointed out that during the 17th and 18th centuries Catholic priests often administered the sacraments in Orthodox churches at the request of Orthodox bishops. He said this was suppressed by the Congregation of the Holy Office in the 18th century.

He said conditions that might indicate common

worship or a real sharing in the sacramental life vary widely from region to region. He pointed out that Catholics in some parts of the East must either receive the sacraments from the Orthodox clergy or not at all.

Concerning the projected directory on ecumenism, Father Stransky said the unity secretariat has "no idea of what will be in it." He said it would offer more precise details on ecumenical action and "might be much more difficult to put together than the schema."

Msgr. George G. Higgins, director of the social action department of the National Catholic Welfare Conference, recalled that the Commission on the Lay Apostolate considered putting together a directory, "but it was voted down, I think rightly." JAMES C. O'NEILL

Summary of Schema on the Lay Apostolate

This is the text of the summary of the schema on the lay apostolate released by the council press office.

INTRODUCTION:

After recalling that the dogmatic Constitution De Ecclesia treats of the place of the laity in the Church, the introduction points out that the schema aims to recall the value and the necessity of their apostolic activity, enunciate the principles governing it, and provide pastoral directives which can make this apostolate more effective.

The apostolate of the laity has always existed in the Church, but the need for it is being increasingly felt in our own day and age. Scientific and technical progress, the increase in population, as well as increased relationships among men of all nations widen the field of the apostolate and pose new problems. It is not merely the scarcity of priests, but it is especially the fact that numerous sectors of human activity have become foreign to religion and morality, which makes this apostolate more necessary. The action of the Holy Spirit is visible in the manner in which the laity are responding to this need.

The schema is made up of five sections, divided into paragraphs:

I—The apostolic vocation of the laity.
Share of the laity in the mission of the Church.
Apostolic tasks are the duty of each and every one.
Training for the apostolate.
II—Communities and situations.
The fields for the apostolate.
In the family.
In ecclesial communities.
In different milieux.
In groups with open membership.
III—The aims to be achieved.
Distinctions.
The conversion of men and their progress toward God.
The Christian restoration of the temporal order.
The exercise of charity toward one's neighbor.

IV—Associations.
Importance of the organized apostolate.
Multiple forms of the organized apostolate.
Juridical recognition.
Catholic Action.
The esteem accorded to associations.
V—Sound organization.
Relationships with the hierarchy.
Pastors and the apostolate of the laity.
Mutual cooperation.
Cooperation with other Christians and with non-Christians.
Final exhortation.

I. THE APOSTOLIC VOCATION OF THE LAITY

All the members of the Church must *cooperate actively, each in his own manner, in the mission of the Church,* which is to continue the work of Christ on earth. The term "apostolate" indicates the action of announcing the Gospel and impregnating the life of men with its spirit. The exercise of this apostolate is both a right and a duty which flows from union with Christ in the sacraments. The apostolate of the laity is as vast as the mission of the Church, and thus takes in the whole of the temporal order. The only activities excluded from the apostolate of the laity are those which require the powers of either Holy Orders or of jurisdiction.

Cooperating in the salvation of all men is the *honor and the duty of each and every member of the Church.* This cooperation, whose fruitfulness will be measured by the holiness of each individual member, is first exercised in prayer (especially participation in the liturgy), by the way in which one bears up under the burdens and the sufferings of life, and by acts of sacrifice offered for others. But the apostolic spirit must animate the whole of human activity, and it is by their lives that Christians are to witness to the presence of Christ within them. In a special manner, their attitude toward the poor is an especial symbol for our times. In this way there must be created in society conditions which will make human life possible and easy. Lastly, apostolic zeal will make men seize opportunities to speak of Christ, to make known the doctrine of the Church. This apostolate of the laity is essential for the witness of the Church.

Training for the apostolate must necessarily form part of all Christian education. It comprises both spiritual and doctrinal elements, as also a knowledge of the social sciences according to individual capacities. This training must be provided not only through education but likewise through practical experience. This training must last a lifetime. The first ones responsible for it are parents, priests, catechists, teachers, and also associations. Educational institutions must do their part. The priest must have an interest in it in his apostolic and pastoral activities. Lastly, each individual must be aware of his responsibility for his own formation. In addition, the schema expresses the hope that specialized centers will be organized for more advanced training of the laity.

II—COMMUNITIES AND SITUATIONS

The second section considers *the different fields of the apostolate*: the family, ecclesial communities (parish, diocese, Universal Church), situations proper to the laity. It then studies, in particular, activities within groups or associations within which the lay Catholic finds himself along with non-Catholic Christians or with non-Christians.

The *family* is not merely a field for the apostolate (for relatives among themselves, for parents toward their children). The family, as such, exercises an apostolate through the radiating of its example. Family circles, in addition, can be useful in preparing for marriage or in bringing assistance to families in spiritual or material distress. Lastly, family groups can aid in the defense of family rights, and make it possible for families to assist one another in their apostolic activity.

The next paragraph shows how the apostolate of the laity *contributes to parochial and diocesan life,* in close collaboration with priests and in close union with the bishop, the head of the diocese. At the same time the text stresses the necessity of interparochial cooperation, in order to meet the pastoral needs of large cities and rural areas. Then it points out that, like clerics, the laity must accomplish their mission *with a deep consciousness of belonging to the Universal Church.* This sense of "belonging" must be accompanied with concern for the needs of the entire Church, interest in whatever may promote the unity of the human race in justice and charity, and in the union of Christians, of all those who believe in God and of all men of good will. Those living outside their own country must remember that among men there must be a brotherly exchange in which each one gives and receives.

The Christian must promote "whatever is true, just and holy." This phrase of St. Paul must guide the laity engaged in *associations with open membership.* Catholics engaged in such groups would do well to organize in view of mutual enlightenment and assistance in this apostolate.

III—THE AIMS TO BE ACHIEVED

The schema first calls attention to the *distinction* between the evangelization and sanctification of men and the Christian inspiration of the temporal order, and observes that it is one and the same Christian conscience which inspires the Christian toward the attainment of this twofold goal.

To work for the *conversion of men to lead them to God,* the Church has never been without the assistance of the laity, acting as laymen filially united with the hierarchy. Today the laity assists the Church in reaching those who are far away. Their experience and their assistance permits the Church to fulfil more effectively the mission entrusted to her in the complex circumstances of present-day life. The laity are invited to reflect on their potentialities in this regard and to reply generously to the appeals of the popes and the bishops. Their activity must be the expression of their interior life, of their sense of the Church, and they must show forth humility and charity and be on their guard against any spirit of human domination.

The Christian impregnation of the temporal order achieves the goal of creation, which must be in its entirety recapitulated in Christ for the glory of God. This penetration is carried out without modifying the nature of the temporal order, through the observance of the moral law dictated by charity. The schema remarks that modern progress makes men more capable of corresponding to their vocation while at the same time it increases the danger of losing sight of the genuine nature and meaning of the temporal order. The text emphasizes the necessity of Revelation for a clearer and surer understanding of human values and their relationship with the supernatural order and the grace of God. The Christian restoration of the temporal order is the concern of the entire Church. But inasmuch as the action of the hierarchy does not reach this temporal order directly, the laity have a special role to play and must act on their own responsibility. Forms and methods of action vary according to circumstances. The schema insists on the necessity of knowing and observing the laws proper to the temporal order. It insists likewise on the importance of those human qualities which are demanded by Christian love and the effectiveness of the apostolate (probity, sincerity, courage, prudence, kindliness, competence, civic sense).

Lastly, the schema considers *the works of mercy and charity toward one's neighbor* performed in the spirit reflected in the words of Christ: "What you have done

to the least of mine, it is to me that you have done it."
Activities organized for the relief of all kinds of needs
are a powerful contribution to the efficacy of the two
above-mentioned forms of the apostolate. The text points
out that such works receive their apostolic effectiveness
in the degree in which they respect the dignity of the
human person, freedom of conscience and the image
of God and Christ imprinted in each one. Charity must
rule out all appearance of domination, must promote
justice, contribute to bettering living conditions and
reach all men.

IV—ASSOCIATIONS

The schema stresses *the importance of the organized apostolate*. The individual apostolate is undoubtedly
effective, and in certain cases it is the only one possible.
But in our modern world, the existence of organized activity in every sector of lay activity is absolutely necessary.
Only a closely knit union of forces can make it possible
to attain the goals of the apostolate today.

There are actually in existence *varied forms of organized apostolate*. The laity remain free to organize associations and to become members of associations. Still,
it is important to avoid a dispersal of forces. The universality of the mission of the Church and the evolution
of modern society make it imperative to develop associations on an international level. Nevertheless, when a
determined form of lay activity has been tried in one
country, it is not always advisable to want to apply it to
another country.

Canon law recognizes and regulates the existence
of a certain number of associations which do not all have
an end which is immediately apostolic. Bishops and other
authorities shall take care to instil into their members a
genuinely apostolic spirit and to coordinate their activities. The council asks the Commission for the Revision
of Canon Law to provide a juridical basis for the apostolate of the laity and to adapt existing legislation on associations to the needs of the modern apostolate.

For several years now associations have been set up
with an apostolic goal, and to them both popes and bishops have given the name "Catholic Action." Structures
and names differ according to countries, but they are all
characterized by the presence of the following notes, all
of which must be verified simultaneously in order for a
movement to be called "Catholic Action," which title
must be received from the hierarchy:

a) Their immediate aim is the very apostolate of the
Church, namely, the evangelization and the sanctification of men, and the formation of their conscience so that
they can impregnate their milieu with the spirit of the
Gospel.

b) Cooperating in their own proper fashion, the
laity assume the responsibility for the organization of the
group, the evaluation of the situations in which their
activity is to be exercised, and for the drawing up and
the execution of their programs.

c) In these associations the laity act as an organized
group. This is a clearer manifestation of the ecclesial
community and renders the apostolate more effective.

d) They act under the higher direction of the hierarchy itself, which can sanction this collaboration by
means of an explicit mandate.

V—PRINCIPLES OF ORGANIZATION

*Relations between the hierarchy and the lay apos-
tolate* take on different forms. In every case, the hierarchy must encourage this apostolate, formulate its principles, provide spiritual assistance, issue eventual directives and exercise a role of vigilance. When there is a
question of temporal activity, the role of the hierarchy is
to formulate moral principles. It will also pertain to the
hierarchy, if such be the case, to decide if a particular
undertaking is in keeping with the principles of the organization, or if a particular project can produce useful
results from the supernatural viewpoint.

The schema takes up four different types of relationship:

a) Certain movements are organized by the laity on
their own initiative and under their own responsibility.
The hierarchy sometimes praises or recommends them.
They cannot be called "Catholic" without the implicit or
explicit agreement of the hierarchy.

b) Other movements are recognized by canon law.

c) In other cases, the hierarchy assumes the responsibility for apostolic activity by the laity by associating
this activity closely with its own proper apostolate, without changing its nature and without taking initiative out
of the hands of the laity. This act of the hierarchy is
called the "mandate."

d) Lastly, the hierarchy can turn over to the laity
certain duties normally performed by clerics (in the
liturgy, in preaching, and in pastoral activity, as also
catechists in the missions). In such cases the laity participate in the apostolate proper to the hierarchy and are
completely subjected to ecclesiastical authority. This
status is known as the "canonical mission."

The schema exhorts pastors, bishops and priests, to
recognize the place which belongs to the laity, to be interested in cooperation with them, and to show an interest particularly in those actively engaged in such activity. It recommends special care in the appointment of
chaplains, who represent the hierarchy before these organizations and assure collaboration with it. These chaplains are for the laity spiritual inspirers, counselors in
activity, collaborators in seeking out the most effective
means for the attainment of the goal desired. They must
help to develop unity of spirit in each association and also the spirit of teamwork with other groups. Religious
men and women who are not priests should also cooper-

ate. There is special mention in the text of those members of the laity who dedicate themselves entirely to the apostolate and are entitled to special spiritual assistance as also to a normal material life and a precise juridical status.

Then the schema emphasizes the necessity of the overall coordination of apostolic efforts. Different activities and projects should be collaborating in diocesan councils, and these councils can be helpful on the parochial, interparochial, interdiocesan, national or international level. The schema provides for organizing a secretariat in Rome to function as a consultative organ and a center of research at the service of the hierarchy and the laity, with the collaboration of clerics, religious and lay persons, both men and women.

Lastly, the schema recommends collaboration with others, Christians and non-Christians alike, to stress the value of the common patrimony, which is either the Gospels or human values.

A final exhortation invites all the laity to carry out actively their role in the Church and to work also with Christ for the salvation of the world.

96th General Congregation

October 7, 1964

The long-awaited schema on the lay apostolate in the modern world came under heavy fire on the first day it was discussed in the council hall.

Joseph Cardinal Ritter of St. Louis led off the debate and called for a complete revision of the text. However, he asked the council Fathers to accept the text as a basis of discussion because of the importance of the subject.

Only four Fathers had spoken before the day's moderator, Leo Cardinal Suenens of Malines-Brussels, asked the Fathers if they wanted to accept the present text as a basis for discussion. A standing vote approved this.

During the 96th meeting, the Fathers approved the ecumenism schema's chapter two as a whole by a vote of 2,174 to 32, with 564 Fathers voting in favor of the chapter with reservations.

The Fathers also approved by overwhelming majorities three sections of proposed amendments to chapter three of the schema and its newly written introduction after two bishops had presented reports on it.

The first of the votes on chapter three was on article 13. It concerned the introduction, which speaks of the two principal categories of the rift in Christian unity: The rifts in the East (which started at the Councils of Ephesus and Chalcedon) and the rifts in the West (mainly those started during the Reformation). In some Church groups of the West, Catholic traditions continue to exist in part, the amendment noted.

This was approved by a vote of 2,154 "yes" to 21 "no."

The second vote was on a section dealing specifically with the Eastern Churches. It gives a historical outline of relations between Rome and the East and notes that they were happy for many centuries despite cultural and other difficulties. It says that proper consideration should be given this healthy variety in the Church's daily life.

The section also considers the sacraments and worship in the Eastern Churches. It notes that the Catholic and Eastern Churches have the same Eucharist and venerate Our Lady and the same saints, many of whom are doctors of the Universal Church. It points to the possibility of "communicatio in sacris"—Catholics actively and publicly joining in worship with non-Catholics of the separated Oriental Churches—since there is a common priesthood and the same Eucharist. In proper circumstances such intercommunion is even recommended. The section emphasizes points of similarity between the Roman and Eastern Churches.

It also deals with discipline in the Eastern Church and the development of theology in the East, with emphasis on the idea that it is complementary to that of the West. It urges consideration of all these factors, and says the reestablishment of unity should not involve needless burdens. It calls for cooperation between the Roman Catholics and Orthodox both in the East and West.

The vote on this section (articles 14 to 18) was 2,119 "yes" to 39 "no."

The third vote was on articles 19 to 24 dealing with the separated Churches and ecclesiastical communities of the West. This section refrains from attempting to describe these Churches and communities. It indicates points of dialogue and contact: faith in Christ, love and veneration of Holy Scripture and sacramental life (Baptism and Holy Eucharist which, despite the differences of belief surrounding these sacaments, could serve as a basis of dialogue).

The section also points out that much of the social action of these Churches and communities stems from their Christian beliefs. It says there should be no imprudent zeal, but confidence in the Holy Spirit.

The vote on this section was 2,088 "yes" to 43 "no."

The day's opening Mass was celebrated by Archbishop Aurelio Signora, head of the independent prelature of Pompei, Italy. The Gospel was enthroned by the master general of the Dominican Order, Father Aniceto Fernandez, O.P.

Because most of the meeting was taken up by the reports presented on chapter three of the ecumenism schema and on the lay apostolate schema, only nine Fathers were able to speak.

Two separate reports were made on chapter three. The first was by Ukrainian-rite Archbishop Maxim Hermaniuk of Winnipeg, Man., and dealt with the chapter section treating of Eastern Churches. The second was by Archbishop John C. Heenan of Westminster, England,

and dealt with non-Catholic Churches and communities in the West.

Bishop Franz Hengsbach of Essen, Germany, presented a detailed report on the lay apostolate schema before the speakers took the floor.

Cardinal Ritter, as the lead-off speaker, said the schema as it now stands includes almost all the necessary elements for a good and effective council document on the laity. But, he said, he felt it should be revised for three reasons.

First, he asked that flaws in the text be omitted. Among these he listed a clerical spirit which seems to have a patronizing tone, as if the highest role of the laity were to aid the clergy and not to pursue its own proper role. He also criticized the document's juridical tone as being improper and nonpastoral in treating relationships between the laity and the hierarchy. Another flaw he cited was the favoritism shown toward Catholic Action to the detriment of many other forms of the apostolate.

The second reason for the revision Cardinal Ritter gave was that the text's real values should be strengthened and reinforced, while other non-essential elements should be eliminated. There is too much scattered and unconnected material, and the lay apostolate should be presented in its essential relationship to the life of the Church, he said.

Cardinal Ritter added that a distinction between the hierarchy and the laity should be brought out in the light of their different ends and the means they have to attain these ends.

Lastly, he said, a new arrangement is needed to include the theological basis of the lay apostolate that is now expressed in chapter four of the schema on the Church. For this new arrangement he suggested an introduction setting forth the theological basis and then sections dealing with the essence of the lay apostolate, its forms and its sanctification. He said the introduction would conclude with an exhortation to the laity.

Despite his objections to the text, Cardinal Ritter still urged that it be accepted as a basis for discussion because of its importance and the danger that if it were not discussed now, it might be some time before it could be considered.

Michael Cardinal Browne, O.P., Irish member of the Roman curia, expressed his general satisfaction with the schema but objected to the terminology it uses and made a series of detailed suggestions for changes.

After the cardinals, two Canadians—Bishops Remi De Roo of Victoria, B.C., and Paul Charbonneau of Hull, Que.—took the floor. Bishop De Roo stated that the text fails to set forth the essential principles of the lay apostolate and, though acceptable as a basis for discussion, it is doctrinally insufficient. Bishop Charbonneau criticized the tone of the document and said it must be declericalized. It must be made clear that the lay

apostolate is not merely a remedy for the priest shortage, he said.

Archbishop Hermaniuk in his report on the first part of chapter three of the ecumenism schema said that the aim of the Secretariat for Promoting Christian Unity was to show Catholics that the institutions and forms of both the Eastern and Western churches are of the same essential nature.

Archbishop Hermaniuk stated that it must be remembered that the cardinal legate who excommunicated an Eastern patriarch in 1054 gratuitously attributed all known heresies in the Church to the Byzantine leader. Archbishop Hermaniuk added that today it is recognized that no dogmatic truth was actually involved at that time.

He noted that the role of Catholic Eastern rites in the East is a double one: to be faithful to St. Peter's successors and to be faithful to their own tradition. Thus they will open the way to dialogue with the separated churches of the East, he said.

He noted, too, that in article 15 provisions for prayers and services in common are provided for.

Archbishop Heenan in his report on the Western separated Christians noted that "separated Christians in the West are not just groups of individual Christians but communities, each with its own tradition and character as a Church." He said some of these groups refuse to call themselves Churches, so that the schema speaks both of Churches and ecclesiastical communities, but without touching on what is necessary for a Christian community to fulfill the theological definition of a Church.

Archbishop Heenan said the schema describes members of these communities and Churches simply as "separated brethren in the West." He noted that the schema calls attention to what these have in common with the Catholic Church, including belief in Christ as mediator, veneration of the Bible, the sacrament of Baptism and, lastly, the following of Christ in daily life.

Archbishop Heenan also stated that the text mentions divisive doctrines, but that its aim is to foster unity.

In his report on the lay apostolate schema, Bishop Hengsbach said it did not attempt a treatment of the entire question of the laity in the Church, since a portion of this is found in the schemas on the Church and on the Church's role in the modern world. He admitted the schema was far from perfect and expressed confidence the Fathers would work to perfect it in the following debate.

Drawing up of a postconciliar directory on the lay apostolate has been left to national conferences of bishops and to the laity, he said.

All interventions and suggestions submitted by the Fathers have been considered in drafting the text, he said, adding that it has been drastically reduced from its original size. After outlining its contents, he noted that the International Commission on the Lay Apostolate to be set up is to assist and help the laity and hierarchy, not to direct activities.

Cardinal Browne said the schema was among the most important to come to the council floor. He said he felt the text universalizes too greatly the concept of the duty of the laity to carry out a specific apostolate. He said he also wanted stress laid on the respect due pastors of individual parishes, of which the laity should be conscious in assisting pastors.

Bishop De Roo insisted on a stronger view of the laity's role and said laymen should not be considered as mere assistants to the hierarchy, for laymen can enter certain sections of the world where the hierarchy cannot go.

Bishop Charbonneau said what the laity needs to know is the structure and goals of the lay apostolate in the modern world. The Church is a transcendent society within the world, he said, and must show concern for famine, racism and injustice. He said he also disliked the emphasis given to Catholic Action and suggested that seminarians be imbued with real respect for the laity.

Bishop Paul Sani of Den Pasar, Indonesia, speaking for the Indonesian Episcopal Conference, called for better and clearer language. He objected that the temporal order which the laity is called on to restore in Christ is not defined nor is its restoration explained. The lay apostolate is not separate from Catholics' own daily lives, he stated.

Coadjutor Archbishop Angelo Fernandes of Delhi, India, also said he wanted the doctrinal foundation of the lay apostolate included in the text, and asked that attention be paid to the double life of the Christian who lives in the world, but in a higher world as well. He further urged that the text be in a language which Catholic laymen can understand and that it pay attention to the economic and social problems of Catholics.

Archbishop Leon Duval of Algiers, Algeria, said he thought the text is too individualistic and lacks sufficient stress on the concept of the laity as part of the Mystical Body of Christ and on the mystical and spiritual character of the laity's cooperation with the hierarchy.

Spanish Bishop Mario Rubio Repulles of Salamanca again called for a doctrinal description of the laity's role and its twofold vocation in the Church and in the world. He called for active methods as the foundation for apostolic training and said he wanted a clear treatment of the nature and various forms of the lay apostolate.

Complete revision of the text was urged by the day's last speaker, Archbishop Carlo Maccari, Bishop of Mondovi, Italy. He said the text disappointed the world's expectations, particularly because of insufficient treatment of Catholic Action. A former ecclesiastical assistant of Italian Catholic Action, Archbishop Maccari said the special apostolate of Catholic Action is almost belittled in the text and that it changes the hitherto accepted notion of Catholic Action in the Church. He warned that was playing into the hands of the Church's enemies.

JAMES C. O'NEILL

97th General Congregation

October 8, 1964

Bishops from the U.S., India, South Africa, Lebanon and Germany rose in the council hall during the second day of debate on the lay apostolate's role in the Church to urge that their fellow bishops and priests have greater confidence and trust in the laity.

Bishops must treat "laymen as adults," was the way the day's first speaker put it. He was Archbishop Eugene D'Souza of Bhopal, India. He asked the Fathers if they were ready to declericalize their attitude toward laymen and to treat them as brothers.

Auxiliary Bishop Stephen A. Leven of San Antonio, Tex., declared in English that the lay apostolate schema should "be streamlined and given more punch." There can be no dialogue with the laity if the laity is expected to listen only, he said.

Both prelates suggested practical ways of showing this clear confidence.

Archbishop D'Souza suggested that laymen could represent the Holy See on international commissions and councils, that they could fill offices in the Roman curia and staff the diplomatic corps of the Holy See, even serving as apostolic nuncios.

Bishop Leven called for the establishment in every diocese of a senate similar to the one which, it has been suggested, might be established after the council to assist the pope.

Bishop Leven said that bishops cannot know what laymen are thinking and what they want if they consult only a few people or if they talk only to their doctor and housekeeper.

Auxiliary Bishop Heinrich Tenhumberg of Muenster, Germany, speaking for 83 German-language Fathers, suggested laymen could be placed in diocesan curias to assist the bishops.

The 97th council meeting opened with a Mass celebrated by Bishop Gioacchino Pedicini of Avellino, Italy. The Gospel was enthroned by Bishop Cornelius Chitsulo of Dedza, Malawi. Archbishop Pericle Felici, council secretary general, reminded the Fathers that Oct. 10 was the anniversary of Pope Pius XII's death and asked for prayers.

During the meeting the Fathers voted 1,843 to 24 to approve the ecumenism schema's chapter three as a whole. There were also 296 votes in favor but with

reservations. The day before the Fathers had approved three sections of amendments to the chapter, which deals with separated Christians. The day's ballot ended voting on the ecumenism schema.

Eighteen bishops took the floor in the following debate.

Archbishop D'Souza took issue with the statement in the draft text that nothing in the lay apostolate field can be undertaken without the bishops. He said this implied that no initiative or project could be begun without a bishop's expressed approval. This, he said, is not the case. Granting that nothing should be done against the will of a bishop, bishops should not subject everything to their immediate control, he stated.

Bishops, he said, must be careful not to usurp the responsibilities of the laity in such areas as education, social services and the administration of temporal goods. Nothing will be accomplished, he warned, if there is not a radical change of attitudes in the Church. Admitting that some abuses and mistakes could occur, he said these must be endured as the price of growth.

Bishop Leven expressed happiness that the role of the laity has finally come before an ecumenical council. This shows that the Church is not merely a juridical entity but is the living Body of Christ, he said.

The lay apostolate is not a concession made to the faithful but is their right, he said. Every Christian has the cause of Christ at heart and this constitutes the apostolate of Christians, the majority of whom are in the ranks of the laity, he continued.

Bishops can direct this apostolate, but may not forbid it or so hem it in with restrictions as to make it meaningless, he declared. A real dialogue between the bishops and the laity is needed, he said, adding that no dialogue is possible if the laity is expected only to listen.

He said the schema is actually too timid and hesitant. It needs to be streamlined and given more punch. This is most important for areas where laymen are generally educated and are ready to dedicate their time and efforts to the cause of the Church, he said.

There will be little gained if a bishop consults only a few persons, especially if these few are only his doctor and his housekeeper.

It would be desirable, he said, for every diocese to

have a kind of diocesan senate, perhaps modeled on the one suggested for the Pope. This group would make it possible for a bishop to maintain contact with different trends in his diocese and give consideration to all reasonable suggestions, he noted. There may be problems because fanatics and crackpots are to be found everywhere, he said, but still it is necessary to take chances because the trend to the lay apostolate is one of the signs of our times.

South African Archbishop Owen McCann of Cape Town declared that laymen are mature and that there is a need for mutual trust between the clergy and the laity. He deplored the text for lacking the inspiration expected of it and said the laity had looked for a Magna Carta, but did not get one.

He suggested that priests should be given special preparation for dealing with the laity and its apostolate, and asked for the establishment of a post-council commission and a director of the lay apostolate.

Maronite-rite Archbishop Ignace Ziade of Beirut, Lebanon, also urged priests to have greater confidence in their people. He also asked that all references to canon law and the Commission for the Revision of Canon Law be removed from the text because these excluded the Eastern rites.

Bishop Tenhumberg declared that the lay apostolate is necessary but should not be looked on merely as a solution of the priest shortage. He also objected to the text's phrase "canonical mandate" in referring to the apostolate as smacking of a juridical and clericalistic outlook.

Belgian Bishop Emile De Smedt of Bruges spoke on a different aspect of the text, asking that there be insistence on the religious freedom of non-Catholics with whom lay apostles are in contact. He warned against the use of pressure or moral force and against injudicious zeal and exaggeration in dealing with non-Catholics by the lay apostolate. The task of the lay apostle is to assist non-Catholics in reaching the truth and to help them to come to their own conclusions, he said.

Bishop Biagio D'Agostino of Vallo di Lucania, Italy, echoed a demand heard several times in the opening debate of the previous day — that a clearer statement of the theological basis of the lay apostolate be incorporated into the text. He said he also wanted stress on the idea that the lay apostolate really depends on the action of priests, because laymen get their spiritual training from priests.

This idea found support from Archbishop Cesar Mosquera Corral of Guayaquil, Ecuador, who complained that the text did not give sufficient attention to the special spirituality of the laity and that priests must guide laymen in achieving a deep spirituality as a basis for their action.

Two Polish prelates were among the day's speakers.

Bishop Stefan Barela of Czestochowa said he wanted more and better use of quotations from the Bible. He said those now in the text are mostly ornamental. He also asked for a clarification of the section of the text dealing with the lay apostolate's possible cooperation with non-Catholics in certain fields. He said he wanted to know exactly how this was to apply to atheists whose ultimate aim is the destruction of human and religious values.

Obviously referring to circumstances in his communist-dominated country, Polish Archbishop Karol Wojtyla of Cracow said he was pleased with the schema for dealing with the universality of the apostolate and not with its forms and organization. He said this pleased him because a personal sense of the apostolate is necessary in regions where organization is not possible. He said there should be insistence on the natural right of Catholics to exercise the apostolate and that care should be taken to exclude from the apostolate those who are using it for their own ends.

The spiritual foundation necessary for the lay apostolate was discussed by Auxiliary Bishop Luigi Bettazzi of Bologna, Italy, who said laymen must give spiritual witness. He also said bishops must be inclined to overcome some of their personal ideas regarding the lay apostolate and recognize that there has been too great a sense of guardianship over the laity.

Pointing out that two-thirds of the world's population are younger than the council Fathers, he stressed the need for providing for the training of those who will govern the Church in the future.

Bishop Antoine Caillot of Evreux, France, stressed the apostolate's close connection with the daily life of Catholics and said Catholics' example can open the way to the conversion of nonbelievers. Catholic Action can be regarded as a means of conversion, he said.

Speaking in the name of the Dutch bishops, Bishop Gerardus De Vet of Breda said that the text should allude to the fact that the lay apostolate is already being carried out and that it should not be regarded as a necessary evil. The world is the proper place for the laity to work in because they are of it, he said.

Concentration on youth was the special concern of Irish Archbishop William Conway of Armagh. He objected that the text overlooks youth completely and fails to be aware of the restlessness of today's youth, which reflects the world's restlessness.

Youth demands ideals, not material satisfaction, he said. Let the council give them the ideals they crave, he added. Sanctification is the basis of the lay apostolate and the world has respect for genuine sanctity, he concluded.

Bishop Albert de Vito of Lucknow, India, declared that laymen have to some degree a share in the task of teaching, governing and sanctifying the Church. But he complained that the doctrine on the apostolate in the text is insufficiently presented and is too brief.

Pope Paul VI's private sacristan and the vicar general of Vatican City, Bishop Peter van Lierde, objected to omissions in the text. He said there are no references to the use of free time, to the practice of justice, to true patriotism and to the apostolate of the intellectuals. He also asked why the council has not treated at all the status and role of the secular institutes which have sprung up in recent years.

Spanish Archbishop Vicente Enrique y Tarancon of Oviedo claimed the text is confused in many things and said he wanted it stated that laymen who dedicate themselves to the apostolate are doing it in their own right and not by virtue of a benign concession from authority. He said he also wanted it clearly stated that the activity of the laity differs from the activity of the clergy.

The day's last speaker was Coadjutor Archbishop Pierre Veuillot of Paris, who said the schema was acceptable but called for a clear definition of the word "apostolate." He also asked that a special effort be made to clarify the proper responsibility of the laity. This responsibility differs from that of bishops, which is on a higher level. Yet both types of authority should be reconciled, he said.

* * * *

Archbishop D'Souza's speech roused something like a debate at the U.S. bishops' press panel following the day's meeting.

Msgr. George G. Higgins, director of the Social Action Department of the National Catholic Welfare Conference, asserted that while he agreed with the speech, most of what the Archbishop said had already been incorporated into the treatment of the laity in the schema on the Church. He pointed out that where Archbishop D'Souza urged bishops to look upon laymen as brothers, this very exhortation came from the Church schema.

Msgr. Mark J. Hurley, chancellor of the Stockton, Calif., diocese, taking up Archbishop D'Souza's suggestion that laymen be employed in many offices of the Roman curia and diocesan chanceries, pointed out that many of the larger dioceses are moving to appoint laymen to fulltime jobs. He said the major obstacle is cost, since laymen's salaries are bigger than priests' salaries.

Father Robert Trisco of Chicago, professor of Church History at the Catholic University of America, said the number of jobs laymen might hold in the Roman curia is limited by the nature of the work itself, which often involves judgments about sacraments and other things proper to the clergy. Father Trisco also picked up Archbishop D'Souza's suggestion that apostolic nuncios and other diplomats of the Holy See could be chosen from the laity. He said this would involve difficulties since a nuncio is not only the pope's diplomatic representative to a political state, but also the pope's representative to a nation's hierarchy.

Bishop De Smedt's warning that Catholics in the apostolate should avoid anything remotely resembling moral coercion elicited comment from Bishop Allen J. Babcock of Grand Rapids, Mich., who said: "We are continually warning our people against interfering in things that do not have any real relationship to moral matters."

Martin Work, executive director of the National Council of Catholic Men, commented that lots of Catholic Action groups in the U.S. have "gone much too far in pressuring theaters and bookshops."

Where the council debate touched the question of when and how the Church and its bishops should speak out on social questions, Msgr. Higgins commented: "I would be very suspicious of anyone who claims he has an absolute answer to that dilemma."

He said this is the problem of the schema on the Church in the modern world. He said it was his impression that most of the pressure on bishops to speak out on social problems comes from the laity, while most of the reluctance to speak out comes from the clergy. He styled this as "inverted clericalism."

Msgr. Higgins cited the problem of race relations. He said that if the Church fails to make a statement on the moral issues involved, it is charged with dereliction of duty. He said the same question has risen lately concerning the problems of war and peace. "The hierarchy is in the delicate position of not wanting to interfere in the temporal order, yet of being expected to speak where moral principles are involved," he said.

Bishop Leven, commenting on his council speech suggesting diocesan and parish parliaments where bishops could keep in touch with trends in their dioceses, said that in his experience the diocesan boards of the National Council of Catholic Men and the National Council of Catholic Women "work out as very good senates."

Bishop Leven pointed out that South Carolina's pioneer Bishop John England wrote a constitution for his diocese with a House of the Clergy and a House of the Laity. He said Bishop England did this at a time when bishops elsewhere in the U.S. were having troubles with the system of lay trustees. He said he has suggested to the dean of a non-Catholic history faculty that an investigation be made into this phase of Church history.

Martin Work said just one state north in North Carolina, Bishop Vincent S. Waters of Raleigh has created an advisory committee of 100 laymen. He said there are also lay-coordinating committees in New York and Los Angeles.

"The question is what these bodies conceive

their task to be and how the bishop himself looks at it," Work said.

Msgr. Higgins took up the plea by Bishop Leven and Archbishop Wojtyla for more dialogue within the Church between the clergy and the laity. He said that while he welcomed this idea, he warned that too much emphasis on dialogue between the laity and clergy in the schema on the lay apostolate could imply that the task of the lay apostolate is to help the clergy.

He also said: "I want to say emphatically that whatever the defects of the schema, they are not the result of any deliberate attempt on the part of the curia to weaken the schema. I think the schema will be radically revised."

Bishop Leven

This is the text of the address delivered Oct. 8 at the ecumenical council by Auxiliary Bishop Stephen A. Leven of San Antonio, Tex.

That there should be a schema on the apostolate of the laity is certainly pleasing. This sacred synod which for the first time in conciliar history has spoken of the laity in a positive way calling them the people of God; which teaches us again to think of the Church not as an organization held together by authority and canon law but as the Body of Christ structured by the sacrament of the episcopacy and living by the charismata given by the Holy Spirit to each member according to His mysterious will; rightly turns its attention to the laity as part in the apostolate.

The schema should therefore say more plainly and forcefully and fully that the apostolate of the laity is of the essential nature of the Church. The apostolate is not something conceded and mandated to the laity by the bishop or the pastor, but the working out in practice of the gifts of the Holy Spirit. It is the duty of those who receive the charismata of authority and administration to moderate and guide the apostolate of the laity, but they may not suppress it. If Jesus said in the parable of the talents it is a sin to wrap one's talent in a napkin and bury it, can the bishop or the pastor who by his ineptitude causes the entire body of the laity to keep their charismata fruitless be without fault?

What the schema says of the apostolate, it says too repetitiously and too timidly. It should be streamlined and shortened and given more strength.

The schema should emphasize more the necessity of a real and meaningful dialogue between the bishop and the pastor and the laity. This is especially true where there is an educated laity. There is no dialogue if the laity are only invited to listen. Nor is there dialogue if the bishop listens only to individuals, such as his doctor or his housekeeper, rather than to truly representative laymen and laywomen.

If the schema cannot set out a detailed method of dialogue, because it is concerned only with general principles, and specific details are left to a post-conciliar commission, then we, as council Fathers, should instruct such a commission to make adequate plans for a sort of parliament, perhaps on the order of the rumored senate of bishops to assist the pope. Obviously, the laity cannot do in the Church the things that require the power of orders or jurisdiction. Obviously, the bishop cannot engage in conversation with every layman in his diocese. Obviously, there are some fanatic and unbalanced people with whom the bishop should not lose much time. But of all the desires of an intelligent and well instructed and dedicated laity, the first is for true and meaningful and respectful dialogue. The post-conciliar commission is earnestly asked to include in its directory the setting up of machinery through which every reasonable suggestion from the laity may reach the bishop, receive consideration, and be given an honorable acknowledgment.

Our laity look to us for acceptance as full and mature members in the Body of Christ. They ask only to be allowed to exercise the charismata the Holy Spirit has given them.

98th General Congregation

October 9, 1964

Warnings against clericalism, divergent views of the nature and forms of Catholic Action, and concern for missionary countries were the dominant notes of the third day of the council debate on the lay apostles' role in the Church.

Nineteen speakers took the floor during the 98th council meeting and most were critical of the lay apostolate schema that the Fathers have accepted as a basis for discussion.

By far the most critical speaker of the day was Canadian Bishop Alexander Carter of Sault Sainte Marie, Ont., who called for a complete revision of the text which, he said, was "conceived in the sin of clericalism." Agreeing in general with him were Fathers from Yugoslavia and Syria.

The role and nature of Catholic Action found Antonio Cardinal Caggiano of Buenos Aires and Leo Cardinal Suenens of Malines-Brussels taking different points of view. Cardinal Caggiano called for a strict definition of this form of the apostolate. Cardinal Suenens urged that the term "Catholic Action" be used generically and not be limited only to those organizations that have been given that title in the past.

Insistence on references in the text to the lay apostolate's particular importance in missionary countries came from Bishop Stanislaus Lokuang of Tainan, Formosa, and Bishop Sebastiao Soares De Resende of Beira, Mozambique.

Two practical suggestions were proposed. Bishop Soares De Resende called for the establishment of an international training center for laymen and priests, particularly those from missionary countries, and Yugoslav Archbishop Franjo Seper of Zagreb suggested that every parish should have an obligatory weekly meeting of all adults of the parish to provide training in the lay apostolate and foster an exchange of opinions between the clergy and the laity.

The meeting opened with a Sacred Liturgy celebrated by Chaldean-rite Archbishop Zaya Dachtou of Urmya and Salmas, Iran. The Gospel was enthroned by Chaldean-rite Bishop Stephane Bello of Aleppo, Syria. Cardinal Suenens was the day's moderator.

Discussing Catholic Action, the day's first speaker, Argentine Cardinal Caggiano asked for the inclusion of the definition of Catholic Action given by Pope Pius XI and perfected by Pope Pius XII. This would stress the necessity of Catholic Action. Its omission from the text is unjust and out of order, Cardinal Caggiano said.

Training for the lay apostolate and Catholic Action must be complete and begin early and be well grounded in theology, he added. It must be presented not only as theory but also in its practical aspect. This requires effective and reciprocal trust between the clergy and the laity, he said.

Cardinal Suenens, on the other hand, said he did not want Catholic Action to be limited to a few organizations that have already been given that title. He said he wanted many of the newer forms of the apostolate to be included under the title of Catholic Action or, if not, then a new title should be evolved covering all forms of the lay apostolate. He also stated he thought bishops are free to accept or reject various forms of the apostolate in their dioceses, but that once they accept one form or another they are not free to change its nature or essence.

A third prince of the Church, Laurian Cardinal Rugambwa of Bukoba, Tanganyika, said it is necessary for the text to explain further the freedom, spontaneity and initiative that are to be guaranteed to Catholics in the lay apostolate. It is necessary to avoid the twin excesses of authoritarianism and monarchism, which in past centuries have been like pestilences in the Church, the African Cardinal declared.

He said it must be acknowledged that the Holy Spirit can act as He wishes even outside of organizations. Catholics should not be treated like minors, for each has his responsibility and must be free to carry it out, he stated.

Bishop Carter said he called for a complete revision of the schema, principally because its text is lacking in unity and its doctrinal basis is not clear. He said this was due to the great reduction of the original text. He added: It was not compressed, it was gutted.

The clerical tone of the text is due, he said, to the fact that the original commission was composed of clerics and that, when laymen were finally added, it was too little and too late. He said the present text does not respond to the expectations of the people and no dialogue is provided for. Rather, there is too much emphasis on organizations and organizational forms, he concluded.

Archbishop Seper agreed with Bishop Carter and said the text does not exclude that horror of the laity which has been behind clerical thinking of recent years. He said the text seems to be referring only to an elite, whereas training for the apostolate is for all laymen. There should be opportunities for dialogue between the hierarchy and the laity, but these are not provided for by the text, he said.

Regarding his suggestion for a weekly parish meeting for adults that would be obligatory like Sunday Mass, he said such meetings are necessary in countries where religious freedom is restricted to permit a priest to form his people.

Another Father reacting to the clerical tone of the document was Father Hilaire Capucci, superior general of the Aleppine Melkite Order of St. Basil, who stated that in the Eastern rites there has always existed an intimate association between the clergy and the laity not marked by the distance between an aristocratic-like hierarchy and a laity bound to it by obedience. The whole Church is missionary, he said. The whole Church is under the influence of the Holy Spirit. The Church must be careful to turn away from clericalism and open its doors wide, he said.

Another Father who called for a complete revision of the text was Archbishop Denis Hurley of Durban, South Africa. Calling the text disordered, verbose and lacking a logical process of thought, he said that various concepts are confused in it as a result. He asked that theological references to the lay apostolate found in the schemata on the nature of the Church and on the Church in the modern world be brought together in an introduction to avoid factions and disagreements in the future.

Archbishop Adam Kozlowiecki of Lusaka, Northern Rhodesia, said the text's definition of the apostolate is narrow, one-sided and inaccurate, since it gives the impression that the laity's role is only to help the clergy in preaching the Gospel. The laity's works of suffering, sacrifice and prayer are true actions of the apostolate and it would be best to avoid reducing the lay apostolate to too great a dependence on the hierarchy, he said.

Italian Bishop Luigi Barbero of Vigevano distinguished two senses of the apostolate. In the wider sense, he said, it means the fulfilment of one's duties. In the stricter sense, it means collaboration with the hierarchy and assisting it in special tasks. The latter sense implies gifts of God such as intelligence and zeal and also requires at least an implicit call or summons on the part of the hierarchy, he stated.

Panama's Bishop Marco McGrath of Santiago-Veraguas, speaking for more than 30 Latin American bishops, said the mission of the laity is not clear in the text

and that there is a need for clearer insistence on the divine foundation of the lay apostolate. Since the laity are involved in secular matters, it is up to them to establish Christian points of reference within the secular life and at the same time it is up to priests to form the Christian conscience of the laity, he said.

Formosa's Bishop Lohuang wanted inserts on the missionary requirement for the lay apostolate because they had been omitted from the new text and because the council missionary proposition, which is still to be considered, omits any such references. This is important, he said, because stress on the laity's role is needed for those countries where the Church is not free or is in sad circumstances.

Bishop Bernardo Cazzaro for Aysen, Chile, asked for an insert saying that the lay apostolate is a consequence of the spiritual life. He also said it is necessary that the laity work hand-in-hand with the clergy and not at a distance.

France's Bishop Louis Rastouil of Limoges was the first of two bishops to stress that the lay apostolate's role comes as a consequence of Baptism and Confirmation. He said he wanted a clearer statement on the rights, duties and powers of the laity in the Church.

The same idea was expressed by Bishop Antonio Quarracino of Neuve de Julio, Argentina, who cited Baptism and Confirmation as a source of the role of the laity in the Church's apostolate. He also suggested that the laity could be given some representation in the election of Church officials and in the administration of its temporal goods.

Applause greeted the announcement by Bishop Ignacio de Orbegozo y Giocoes of Vauyos, Peru, that everything he intended to say had been said and therefore he was relinquishing his turn.

Auxiliary Bishop Eduardo Pironio of La Plata, Argentina, urged that the text be written in a more Biblical and patristic style. He objected that there is not enough stress on the prophetic mission of the laity nor on the value of the liturgy.

A warning that the present text may disappoint many was voiced by Bishop Stefan Laszlo of Einsenstadt, Austria. He complained that the text gives the impression that the Church appreciates only those works and activities that contribute directly to its own mission and that there should be a better explanation of the laity's role in the restoration of the temporal order.

The last speaker of the day, Bishop Giuseppe Ruotolo of Ugento-Santa Maria Di Leuca, Italy, said the text should state clearly the obligation of the laity to become members of apostolic associations. After tracing the rise of the lay apostolate to combat hostile secret societies, he said the text should emphasize the value of meetings and annual retreats to perfect apostolic training.

JAMES C. O'NEILL

Constitution on the Church 'Memorable Achievement'

The forthcoming Constitution on the Church will become the most memorable achievement of the Second Vatican Council and will launch a totally new era in Catholic thought.

The constitution has already received the basic approval of the council Fathers through an affirmative vote on the first six chapters, although it will not become official until its promulgation by Pope Paul VI.

The modifications still to be made on the text as a result of the suggestions of the council Fathers will not be substantial and will be designed to perfect the present text rather than change its basic content.

While the new constitution cannot be expected to have an immediate sensational effect in theology, its ultimate result will be revolutionary.

It will mark a new stage in theological reflection, in pastoral initiative and in the development of spiritual life. Since the 16th century, ecclesiology, or reflection on the Church, has gone in the one-sided direction of self-defense against the real or imaginary assaults of Protestants, deists, rationalists, modernists, materialists and atheists. This did strengthen the Church's interior discipline and coherence, but it also hastened her loss of contact with the masses of many countries and with the intellectual concerns of the educated.

The institution of the Church and its hierarchy came out of this immeasurably more powerful than before in their narrow confines, yet considerably weakened in their impact on society and on the shape of modern thought.

As a result, the Church became increasingly irrelevant to the concrete problems of men. It is this fatal trend that Pope John XXIII wanted to stop by calling a council for a profound renovation of the Church.

The Constitution on the Church, especially once it is completed by a decree on "The Church in the World," should be the main factor in making the tide turn, by changing Catholics' view of their Church.

The faith will not change. But the practical conception of what the Church is and does and of how to be a Christian in today's world, will grow, perhaps out of recognition.

The constitution, which is solid ground for this growth, can be summed up in the following points:

1) It brings Catholics back to a more Biblical understanding of the Church as a community of love in which God communicates to man the mystery of his own life. Thus the Church is essentially turned outward in service rather than inward in complacency.

2) It restores the concept of the Church as the people to whom God has passed His covenant. This is the principle of the laity's awakening to the spiritual responsibility which is theirs as a result of Baptism.

3) The hierarchy is no longer presented as a mainly administrative body, but rather as the repository of the Apostles' function of preaching the Gospel and of their spiritual authority. This will make the bishops, in the long run, better pastors and leaders, more respectful of the responsibility of both laity and clergy. Above all, it will give them a stronger desire to serve, not only their small territory, but the whole Church.

This should enable Catholics everywhere to share their problems and to reach solutions in common. By associating the bishops to the Pope's solicitude for all the world, it will considerably extend and deepen the Church's catholicity, and give all her members a deeper awareness of the need to enlarge their soul to the scope of the universe, above all barriers of nationality, citizenship, race, color or religion.

4) The chapters on the call to holiness and on Religious orders should start a renewal of the life of prayer and give shape to a modern type of sanctity adapted to our world. Religious orders themselves should reflect on their calling in the light of the constitution, and thereby make their way of life more relevant to our times and more meaningful to our contemporaries—without which their survival is questionable.

5) The last two chapters, by focusing attention on the eschatological dimension of Christian life and on the meaning of Mary as the image of the Church should restore among Catholics a sense of commitment to the spiritual realities and to the invisible world which familiarity with a materialist civilization tends to overshadow.

The Constitution on the Church will be the longest document of the council. It has been the work of more teams of theologians and bishops than any other. When one compares its present form with what was presented at the start of the first session of the council, one can also see that a considerable distance has been covered, and that a stupendous task of theological updating has been achieved.

The constitution contains eight chapters, including that on the Virgin Mary, which concludes it. The votes that have recently been made cover the first six chapters, the last two being under revision by the Doctrinal Commission.

On account of the difficulties felt by many bishops on matters treated in the third chapter (on the Church's hierarchy), the voting on this was much more detailed than on the other sections of the draft. Thus, there were one vote for chapter 1, four for chapter 2, 39 for chapter 3, one for chapter 4 and one for chapter 5.

This variance reflects differences in the numbers of difficulties that the debates had revealed. To respect the bishops' freedom to accept one section of a chapter and to reject another, the text of chapter 3 was divided into 39 articles, each with a separate vote.

The votes on a chapter in general need not be absolute. One may vote for or against it; but one may also approve it with a proviso, which has to be explained in writing so that the competent commission may, if advisable, alter the text in the sense indicated. The votes on parts of a chapter, on the contrary, do not allow for a qualified approval.

The negative votes on chapters one and two were negligible, but the votes on chapter three were much more complicated.

For the 39 successive votes of chapter 3, the negative vote varied between 11 and 1,364. Apart from the texts on the diaconate (where the highest negative vote was cast), the passages that raised an opposition of more than 100 votes all contain some allusion to the episcopal college or to the powers conferred by episcopal consecration. The highest negative vote about the episcopacy (328) was cast against the idea that episcopal consecration confers the powers of sanctifying, teaching and ruling.

The reason for these minorities of 100 to 300 votes lies in the fact that the notion of an episcopal college was new to many bishops. Contrary to reports, these nays do not come from any special nation, although there seems to be a rather high concentration of them in Italy and Spain. This is understandable: the Italian episcopate has always had close ties with the papacy; and, since the reconquest of Spain from the Moslems, the Spanish episcopate has enjoyed privileges which are held to come graciously from the pope rather than to belong to the Spanish bishops by right as members of the episcopal college.

The meaning of these negative votes is therefore that the concept of collegiality has not yet been fully grasped by a minority of bishops. These have therefore felt it their duty to defend the pope's supremacy by voting against texts which, as they read them, detract somewhat from what they consider to be the authority of the bishop of Rome. The majority, on the contrary, felt that to assert collegial episcopal authority does not take away anything from the primatial authority of the bishop of Rome.

The five votes on the restoration of a permanent diaconate are in a category of their own. The question was not one of doctrine, but of discipline: Should a permanent diaconate be restored? If so, who will have authority to do it? And may these permanent deacons be married?

A text describing the diaconate and its functions was accepted by 2,055 votes against 94. The wisdom of its restoration as a permanent degree of the hierarchy was recognized by 1,903 against 242. By 1,553 votes against 702, it was decided that episcopal conferences, with the approval of the pope, are competent to do so in their territory. That the diaconate may be given to "mature married men" was carried by 1,598 ayes against 629 nays. That it could be given to younger men, who would not be bound to celibacy, was rejected: 839 voting yes, and 1,364 no.

These votes indicate that 242 bishops were definitely opposed to the principle of the permanent diaconate. The second vote shows that, besides these, approximately 450 objected to the power given, in this matter, to episcopal conferences. Many of these votes must have been cast by the 328 bishops who had previously opposed the very principle of collegiality. The last two votes, on the question of a married diaconate, are more puzzling. Clearly, only 629 did not want married deacons at all. To reject the ordination of younger men who would be allowed to marry (as opposed to mature and already married men), they must have been joined by others, who may have been motivated by any of the following reasons:

Some did not want to depart from the traditional practice of the Eastern Churches, where a married man may be ordained, but a celibate or widowed priest or deacon may not marry. Others could not see the practicality of introducing this new kind of deacon into the structure of their dioceses. Finally, a number of council Fathers feared that lifting the law of celibacy in favor of younger men would cause a slump in the vocations to the celibate priesthood, and this slowly would make it necessary to suspend, at least in part, the law of celibacy for the priesthood of the Latin Rite.

We must evidently wait several years before we can see if the limited kind of married diaconate that has been approved is sufficient to fulfil one of its primary purposes, namely, to counterbalance the lack of vocations to the priesthood in Latin America.

Chapters 4, 5 and 6 of the draft were adopted with very few negative votes. However, there was a substantial number of qualified approving votes for chapters 5 (302) and 6 (438). These qualifications affect the sections on the universal call to sanctity and on the relationship between the religious orders and the bishops.

The Doctrinal Commission which will examine all these qualifications need pay attention only to those which tend to better the text. Those still aimed at changing the text are ruled out by the fact that it now has been accepted by the required majority. The purpose of the revision is to accept the best suggestions of those who are in favor of the ideas expressed in the text.

Thus few changes can be expected in the text at this stage. The vocabulary will be improved and the thought clarified and completed in some points. But the text as it finally will be promulgated will be essentially the same as that accepted in the chapter by chapter vote by the Fathers.   FATHER GEORGE H. TAVARD

Father Tavard is the author of a number of theological works, chairman of the theology department of Mount Mercy College, Pittsburgh, an official consultor for the Second Vatican Council and a member of the U.S. bishops' press panel in Rome.

99th General Congregation

October 12, 1964

Attempts to balance the layman's individual call to the apostolate with the need for lay organizations on the national and international level to bring the Gospel to the world and the world to Christ characterized the ecumenical council's last scheduled day of debate on the lay apostolate schema.

After 17 speakers had taken the floor, Archbishop Pericle Felici, council secretary general, called for a standing vote to close debate. This was greeted with loud applause and overwhelming acceptance.

Several speakers continued debate on the role of Catholic Action in the lay apostolate, some asking for a stronger statement of its unique position in the Church, others asking that "the door be left open" as to what form the apostolate will take in each nation.

Referring to the draft's call for a secretariat for the lay apostolate to be set up in Rome, Archbishop John Heenan of Westminster, England, said: "It is bound to fail unless the laity is fully consulted.

"This secretariat will be unique among secretariats of the Holy See. It would be a disaster to model it on any of the departments already existing in the Roman curia. Most of its members must be chosen from the laity."

Five speakers devoted most of their talks to the spiritual formation required of the lay apostle. Several others stressed the need not only to Christianize individuals but also, as Bishop Henry Donze of Tulle, France, said, the need for a "collective apostolate aimed at the whole social order, since evangelization of the world belongs to groups as well as to individuals. Men are not only individuals, but also part of groups."

Bishop William Pluta for Gorzow, Poland, said the draft does not state clearly enough the nature of the formation required of the lay apostle. He said intellectual formation as well as spiritual formation is required and asked for a statement of four principles for such formation: holiness of life; ascetical formation, including the ideas of brotherhood, kindness and charity, which he called "humane virtues so rare in the world that they are prized highly;" formation for and with the Church; and the "golden rule" of religious and catechetical instruction—that is, that they be primarily spiritual as well as ascetical.

Bishop William Power of Antigonish, N.S., stressed

that the spiritual life presupposes the order of nature, which must always be taken into account. He said that laymen must learn how to make the Church active and present in the world.

He suggested five principles for the layman's formation:

1. The development of human gifts and talents, including a keen sense of justice, the responsibility of charity and a sense of the problems facing the world.

2. The "insertion" of the layman into the real situation in the world so that he will have a real interest in it and conceive it in the light of the Faith.

3. His insertion into the reality of Christ.

4. Emphasis on united action, which is demanded by the evolution of society in which the law of solidarity applies to spiritual as well as human affairs.

5. Development of contact between laymen and the hierarchy with a realization of competence on each side.

Bishop Andre Fougerat of Grenoble, France, chaplain of the Conference of International Catholic Organizations, emphasized the right and duty of lay Catholics to organize international movements. He asked that these be interested not only in spiritual works but also in education, culture, world health, medical-moral problems and the like. He said he was turning in an amendment to this effect which he hoped would be included in the final draft.

He cited Pope John XXIII's encyclicals in support of his proposal and said the Pope had specifically praised the effectiveness of such international organizations as the United Nations and its specialized agencies.

He said it was for the same reason that the majority of lay auditors were chosen from international organizations. He added that the "whole Christian world is turning its eyes to these men."

Warning against "institutionalism," on the other hand, Bishop Manuel Larrain Errazuriz of Talca, Chile, president of the Latin American Bishops' Council, said the lay apostolate must be "incarnated in the world, but it surpasses all institutions." An exaggerated form of institutionalism, he said, would stifle the fiery zeal of apostles and might have the effect of closing Catholics off in "ghettos."

Taking up the theme of Bishop Donze on the social

aspects of the apostolate, Bishop Luigi Civardi of the Roman curia said that the lack of such a treatment in the draft might disillusion many. The Church cannot omit a strong teaching on justice as a necessary means in the apostolate, he said.

"We must not only preach against misery, but dry up the fonts of misery," he stated. He added that many have become communists because of social needs and wants rather than through intellectual conviction, and thus the Church must be careful not to forget stomachs while it develops social consciences.

Bishop Joseph Hoeffner of Muenster, Germany, deplored the omission of any mention of original sin in the draft, and also said that there is too close a connection in the text between the cooperation of the Church with non-Catholic Christians and its cooperation with non-Christians, which he said must be different because the Church has the common bond of Christ with the former.

The bishop said that the whole treatment of the social order was too optimistic. He also said that order never can be restored fully because of the fact of original sin and that the Church should make this clear.

The 99th general meeting opened with Mass celebrated by Coadjutor Archbishop Antonio Ferreira de Macedo of Aparecida, Brazil. The Gospel was enthroned by Archbishop Guido Bentivoglio of Cantania, Italy. Since Leo Cardinal Suenens of Malines-Brussels, moderator for the debate on the lay apostolate, was out of town, Gregorio Cardinal Agagianian took his place.

During the session, Archbishop Felici announced the deaths of three council Fathers, including Bishop John P. Treacy of La Crosse, Wis., who had not attended this session and died at home (Oct. 11). The others were retired Bishop Michael Rodrigues of Belguam, India, and retired Bishop Alphonse Verwimp of Kisantu, the Congo, who died in Belgium.

Archbishop Felici also announced that the following day a lay auditor would address the council on the lay apostolate, even though that debate had closed during this meeting. He is Patrick Keegan of England, chosen by other lay auditors to represent them.

Reports on the long-awaited schema 13 on the Church in the modern world, scheduled next on the agenda, was not yet ready, Archbishop Felici said. Therefore, the next discussion will be on the proposition on the priestly life and ministry, formerly schema on the priesthood. If schema 13 is still not ready when discussion on the priesthood is ended, then the proposition (formerly the schema) on the Eastern Churches will be debated.

The only cardinal to speak was Achille Cardinal Lienart of Lille, France. He said that the schema was quite correct in stressing that the apostolate is not the exclusive preserve of the clergy. Through Baptism and Confirmation, as through their share in the universal priesthood, the faithful necessarily participate in the apostolate. The text should emphasize the importance of formation to real responsibility, he said, and make possible the use of large numbers of the laity who are ready to dedicate themselves selflessly to the sanctification of their neighbors.

The Church has a great gift in the ardor of youth, the cardinal said, and this should be used in every way possible.

Continuing the extended debate, Cardinal Lienart said that Catholic Action deserves special mention in the schema because it is a specialized form of the apostolate of the laity. He said that the name Catholic Action has a well determined meaning, and that arguments for widening its scope are not very conclusive. The basis of Catholic Action, he said, is the mandate of the bishop; hence the term should not be used indiscriminately to cover all forms of Catholic activity. But nothing prevents bishops from putting under this heading all groups which fulfil the requirements, he said.

Auxiliary Bishop Candido Padin of Rio de Janeiro, speaking for 40 Brazilian bishops, said that the text should consider the evolution of Catholic Action. Not all nations have proceeded in the same way, he said, and in some nations results have been spectacular, while in others they have not.

"Our policy should be to open doors, not to close them, and we should make every effort to avoid fossilizing categories . . . If we wanted to raise questions on names, the Jesuits could not call themselves the Society of Jesus because all Christians are called to life in the society of Jesus. Likewise there could be no such name as the Holy Office, because all ecclesiastical offices are holy."

He said that the style of the passage dealing with the future secretariat is too clericalistic, and that in a thing touching them so intimately, the faithful should not merely be invited to cooperate, but summoned to a position of direct responsibility in its functions.

Bishop Alexandre Renard of Versailles, France, said that the text fails to give a clear definition of the lay apostolate. The apostolate of the Church is the proclamation of Christ, and all have a share in this, he said.

Spanish Bishop Manuel Llopis Ivorra of Coria-Caceres said that the apostolate should be proposed not as something demanded by the extrinsic needs of the Church, but as flowing from its intrinsic needs. It should stress also the need for a perfect human formation of lay apostles, who no less than the priest are "taken from among men and appointed for men in things that are of God."

Archbishop Heenan called upon lay apostle candidates to put themselves "humbly in the hands of their priests for training." He said that even though priests' training may be defective in some areas and must be revised, it is still true that "even young priests from the seminary have finished the course of sacred studies and are capable of providing the laity with the spiritual guidance they need.

"It is well known that the enemies of the Church are doing all in their power to create divisions between the clergy and the faithful. It would be most unfortunate if the apostolate of the laity were seen as something in opposition to the apostolate of the clergy."

Regarding Catholic Action, Archbishop Heenan said it is better if the expression is not used in some countries, since it has acquired political overtones in them. He asked that regional conferences of bishops be left free to speak of the apostolate rather than of Catholic Action.

The archbishop also asked that when the proposed lay secretariat be set up, it include not only "old gentlemen loaded down with ecclesiastical honors, but also some of our young men and women who have to earn their daily bread."

Bishop Larrain said that laymen must be the bridge bringing world problems to the Church and taking back the Gospel of the Church to the world. This can be no "angelism." It must be a real incarnation in the world, he said. We should listen not only to prophets, he said, but also to the voice of God heard in the voice of our times.

Bishop Stefan Baeuerlein of Srijem, Yugoslavia, asked that in the treatment of the special apostolate of the Christian family, it be stated that the family's chief function is the procreation and education of children.

He said that the norm that lay organizations may not be called Catholic unless authorized by the bishop should also apply to organizations of priests and Religious. Bishop Baeuerlein said that in discussions of mutual cooperation, stress should be placed on the advantages of free discussion on a parish level, and on the right of recourse to public opinion, but always in the proper form. He cited in defense of this St. Gregory the Great's dictum: "It is better to allow scandal to be born than to abandon truth."

Auxiliary Bishop Paul Cheng of Taipei, Formosa, said that the Christian mission is to bring the charity of Christ into the world, that is, into the family, city, nation and world. Basic to all apostolic activity, he said, must be great esteem for and confidence in one's neighbor. The task of the apostolate is not only to preach to individuals but to Christianize the world.

Archbishop Enrico Nicodemo of Bari, Italy, suggested that Catholic Action should not be listed among the forms of the organized apostolate, but rather that the council should emphasize the specific difference between Catholic Action and other forms of the apostolate. The difference lies in the fact of Catholic Action participation in the apostolate of the hierarchy and its strict dependence on the hierarchy. Precisely because of this, it integrates the pastoral action proper to priests and bishops, he said.

Other speakers were Bishop Aurelio Del Pino Gomez of Lerida, Spain, and Archbishop Luis Monoyerro, military vicar of Spanish armed forces. Among the four speakers listed to speak but cut off by the cloture vote was Auxiliary Bishop Philip M. Hannan of Washington.

FATHER JOHN P. DONNELLY

Pastors Invited

Four United States pastors have been invited to attend the rest of this session of the ecumenical council along with priests from several other countries.

Pope Paul VI asked them to be on hand for discussions on the council's draft statement on "The Priestly Life and Ministry." According to the current timetable, deliberation of this document is to follow debate on schema 13 on the Church in the modern world.

Of the four American priests invited, two were already present in Rome: Msgr. Walter J. Tappe, pastor of St. Rose's parish in Santa Rosa, Calif., and vicar general of the Santa Rosa diocese; and Msgr. Joseph E. Emmenegger, pastor of St. Andrew's parish, Delavan, Wis., and former superior of the graduate house of the North American College in Rome.

The other two American priests are Msgr. Gerard L. Frey, pastor of St. Francis de Sales parish, Houma, La., and director of the Confraternity of Christian Doctrine for the New Orleans archdiocese; and Father Thomas B. Falls, pastor of Sacred Heart parish, Manoa, Pa., and director of the Legion of Mary in the archdiocese of Philadelphia.

100th General Congregation

October 13, 1964

The ecumenical council's 100th general meeting was marked by discussion of a wide range of topics dealing with the priestly life and ministry and by the first speech delivered to a formal working session by a layman.

Subjects dealing with the priesthood ran the gamut from the spirituality required of a priest to the salaries of rectory housekeepers. Pleas were made for abolishing Church benefices, and paying priests adequate salaries and providing medical care and retirement benefits. A special tribute was paid to the country priest, forgotten in a mass urban society.

Patrick Keegan, council auditor from England, addressed the Fathers on the lay apostolate schema even though debate on it had been formally closed by a cloture vote the previous day. He was greeted by a round of applause after he had told the Fathers, in an attempt to "voice the sentiments of the faithful laity throughout the world," that the document was most warmly welcomed, "giving us a new vision of our active participation in the whole mission of the Church."

After Archbishop Francois Marty of Rheims, France, had given a report on the proposition "On the Priestly Life and Ministry," Albert Cardinal Meyer of Chicago led off the discussion. He rejected the draft as unacceptable and called for a full schema and full discussion of the subject, just as there had been for the bishops and the laity.

Though originally scheduled as a schema, it had been reduced to a "proposition" during the interim preceding the present council session. Only recently by a vote of the council Fathers was it decided to give it any discussion prior to voting. Propositions, unlike schemas, are not scheduled to be fully debated by the Fathers.

Another American prelate who spoke was Auxiliary Bishop John A. Donovan of Detroit. He made a strong plea for understanding and care of psychologically disturbed and psychotic priests. He asked that they be given modern treatment rather than confined in "ecclesiastical prisons."

Twelve other speakers discussed the priesthood after three, invoking the 70-signature rule to speak after a cloture vote, continued the debate on the lay apostolate.

Announcing the 100th meeting, Archbishop Pericle Felici, council secretary general, said that "while the council has reached the centenary mark, it is not growing older—but always growing younger."

The meeting began with Mass celebrated by Bishop Edoardo Mason for El Obeid, the Sudan. The Gospel was enthroned by Bishop Johann Gunnarson for Iceland. The moderator of the day was Gregorio Cardinal Agagianian, prefect of the Congregation for the Propagation of the Faith.

Archbishop Felici recognized the presence of pastors chosen from various countries to sit in on the discussion of the priesthood at the personal request of Pope Paul VI. He gave them a cordial welcome which was seconded by the applause of the council Fathers.

The Americans present were Msgr. Walter J. Tappe of Santa Rosa, Calif., and Msgr. Joseph E. Emmenegger of Delavan, Wis. Msgr. Gerard L. Frey of Houma, La., and Father Thomas B. Falls of Manoa, Pa., the other two U.S. priests called to the council, had not yet arrived.

In his report on the proposition on the priesthood, Archbishop Marty explained that the title had been changed from "The Priesthood" because its material had been reduced so drastically that such a title was too vast for a simple proposition. He also said the change was dictated by the incorporation of a treatment on the priesthood in the schema on the Church and other council drafts.

The proposition, he said, is the fruit of extensive and concentrated work. The criteria used in drawing it up, he said, were the pastoral needs of the ministry and a positive approach. It stresses the relationship between the priest and the faithful, not only as Fathers and teachers, but as brothers among brothers, since both are members of the Mystical Body of Christ, he said.

Not only are the supernatural virtues required of the priest stressed, but the natural virtues are also emphasized, since the priest must deal with the world, Archbishop Marty stated.

The text confirms the law of celibacy and its application to the priest, he said, "in response to various rumors to the contrary." It also extols the value of the three evangelical counsels of poverty, charity and obedience in the life of a priest, and exhorts them to become men of virtue and prayer. It recommends conferences on pastoral problems and life in common where possible, he stated. It asks for a complete revision of the system of benefices "lest the Church be accused of feudalism and lest it lead to setting up of social classes among priests," he declared.

Archbishop Marty said the text also encourages personal exercises of piety and interest in vocations. Lastly, he said, since the source of the whole priestly life is the priest's intimate union with Christ, priests are exhorted to conform their whole lives to this divine model in a spirit of ministration and service. He said it was hoped that the interest thus manifested by the council will be for all priests a great incentive for zeal and the pursuit of holiness.

Cardinal Meyer said that the text is "not too acceptable" because it is not too clear what its aim is. It does not correspond to the aim set forth in Archbishop Marty's report—"the pastoral needs of the Church today" —since there is no general discussion of this important matter, Cardinal Meyer said. Pointing out that there was a discussion on the apostolate of the bishop and of the laity, he said the latter depends so much on the apostolate of the priest that to do justice to the topic of the apostolate, a full schema on the priest is required, covering all necessary points. This should be accompanied by free discussion, which will show the genuineness and depth of the council's interest in priests and their needs, he stated.

He also said that the proposition seems to deal only with priests' obligations, and this in a way will hardly encourage them or inspire them to higher things. There should be an encouragement for their efforts, he said.

His talk was greeted with applause.

Bishop Donovan said that he was happy with the proposition's reference to proper medical care for priests, and asked that Religious superiors be given the same exhortation.

"Only after a sick priest has had all available expert care can a bishop rest with an easy conscience," he said.

Referring to priests with mental illnesses which require long treatment, or are even sometimes incurable, he noted that such priests often become the occasion of scandal to Catholics, even though they are not morally responsible for their actions. He said the practice of imposing canonical penalties on such priests, or sending them off to houses of penance, should be stopped.

Bishop Donovan also objected to the text's reference to the desirability of common life for all priests, pointing out that some choose the diocesan priesthood precisely because they do not feel called to a common life.

Archbishop Leonardo Rodriguez Ballon of Arequipa, Peru, paid a special tribute to the contributions of missionary priests in Latin America and asked that national and international organizations be set up to coordinate the work of providing priests for needy dioceses. He said it is important to assure careful training of priests going to strange lands, and said that groups from the same countries should work together in the same areas, provided they do not cut themselves off from others.

He insisted that missionaries acquaint themselves with the customs of the countries in which they work, and not try to impose their form of Catholicism on them, but rather to build on what is there. He also asked that missionaries work more closely with the native clergy and help to foster native vocations.

Auxiliary Bishop Joseph Hiltl of Regensburg, Germany, called for more adequate salaries for parish housekeepers. These, he said, are demanded by justice and prudence—the latter since the good domestic who is poorly paid will be inclined to find a job elsewhere. He said that he wants norms laid down in canon law to this effect, observing that where the bodily needs of the priest are not taken care of, his pastoral and apostolic works are likely to decline.

Archbishop Joseph Evangelisti, Bishop of Meerut, India, called for more adequate salaries for priests themselves so they can have an opportunity to do works of charity for the whole Church.

He pointed out what he called an inconsistency in the text, saying it speaks of a priest devoting his whole life to souls and then elsewhere treats of retirement pensions. He said it is not proper to talk about the retirement of priests, since so few retire. Instead, he said, the text should discuss pensions only for disabled priests.

He called for intensification of the missionary spirit as part of the priests' spirituality. He said the Church is essentially missionary. Bishops, by virtue of collegiality, are expected to look out for the welfare of the whole Church. If this is true for bishops, then it is true also for priests, who participate in the episcopal office, he said.

Rejoicing at the presence of at least one rural pastor in the council chamber, Archbishop Giovanni Perris of Naxos, Greece, pointed out that nothing was said in the proposition about country pastors, and urged a new proposition extolling their value. Almost all such pastors are diocesan priests rather than religious, he pointed out, and often they are overlooked or slighted as the lowest form of the priesthood.

The archbishop said that the Church has always loved rural and farming people, just as Christ did, Who chose His apostles from among them. He said that we are sometimes so involved in converting pagans that we overlook those who are working to keep the Faith among the baptized.

He also said that migration to the cities often leaves the rural pastor in solitude and poverty. He asked that bishops visit them more frequently, and also provide substitute priests so that the rural pastors can have a chance to come to cities more often to renew their spiritual life and pastoral knowledge. Archbishop Perris expressed the hope that international organizations would be set up for the relief of poor parishes and that richer nations would give a giant share.

Bishop Pierre Theas of Tarbes and Lourdes, France, deplored the increased weakness in faith which causes people to look upon priests as ecclesiastical functionaries, rather than "other Christs." Laymen, he said, are always in increasing need of the priest for their spiritual life, and the text should emphasize that they have the same apostolic mission as bishops and share with them the priesthood of Christ.

Archbishop Julio Rosales of Cebu, the Philippines, in the name of the bishops of the Philippines, said that the proposition was "very pleasing . . . containing much in little," and said that its proposals should be implemented in an eventual pastoral directory or in a revision of canon law.

Bishop Antonio Anoveros Ataun of Cadiz and Ceutra, Spain, said that the schema has been too drastically reduced. He called on the Commission for Revising the Code of Canon Law to provide for a better distribution of clergy throughout the world, and to revise completely the system of ecclesiastical benefices, particularly in cathedral parishes, which often are more tourist attractions than real parishes with a proper liturgical life.

Contrary to the views of Bishop Donovan, Archbishop Armando Fares of Catanzaro and Squillace, Italy, stressed the value of the common life for all priests, but especially younger priests. He also asked that emphasis be placed on keeping up with the times in the study of pastoral theology.

Maronite Archbishop Francois Ayoub of Aleppo, Syria, labeled the common effort of bishops and priests in promoting the Kingdom of God as "concelebration."

He said that the text will not respond to the expectations of the clergy and recommended the omission from it of such questions as distribution of the clergy, adequate compensation, and funds in common, since these are more in the domain of the bishop.

Auxiliary Bishop Jacobus Komba for Peramiho, Tanganyika, wanted more stress placed on the value of suffering in the priesthood. He also said that it is not fair to urge priests to avoid vanity in dress and titles when there is no such reference in the draft on bishops.

Returning to the theme of Archbishop Fares, Auxiliary Bishop Guido Casullo for Pinheiro, Brazil, asked that priests keep abreast of modern means in the apostolate, especially for psychological, ascetical, cultural and pastoral reasons.

The day's final speaker on the priesthood was Auxiliary Bishop Franjo Kuharic of Zagreb, Yugoslavia, who asked that each diocese have a spiritual advisor who would provide unity and stimulus to the priestly spiritual life. He also called on the canon law commission to make it mandatory that priests in their last wills leave their property not to their families but to the good works in the diocese. He also recommended that the system of benefices be abandoned for all those engaged in the care of souls.

Speaking on the lay apostolate, before the discussion began on the priesthood, were Archbishop Emile Guerry of Cambrai, France; Auxiliary Bishop Santo Quadri of Penerolo, Italy; and Melchite Patriarchal Vicar for Egypt, Archbishop Elie Zoghbi.

Bishop Franz Hengsbach of Essen, Germany, who had given the report on the lay apostolate, then made final observations and thanked the speakers for their suggestions, remarking that many of their observations were based more on the choice of wording than on the intention of the draft. FATHER JOHN P. DONNELLY

Patrick Keegan

This is the text of the address delivered by Patrick Keegan, lay council auditor from England and first layman to speak at a formal working session of the council.

In the name of the lay auditors, men and women, present in Rome, I thank the cardinal moderators for the honor and opportunity of addressing this great assembly. I would assure you, venerable Fathers, that we are very conscious of our responsibility at this historic moment to try, however inadequately, to voice the sentiments of the faithful laity throughout the world.

We have welcomed most warmly the chapter of the document on the Church dealing with the laity, giving us a new vision of our active participation in the whole mission of the Church. We have welcomed also the

Constitution on the Liturgy which has vitalized our share in the public worship of the Church.

We offer the assurance of our loyal cooperation in fulfilling the noble aims of the document on Christian unity. And now we have been following with the greatest attention your debate on the lay apostolate.

This schema marks for us a point of fulfilment in the historical development of the lay apostolate. We sincerely hope that it marks also the beginning of a whole new stage of development.

The schema is the natural outcome of the Church's

new awareness of herself. It is also the result of the progressive discovery by men and women of their responsibility and role within the whole apostolate of the Church. All those who work in the different fields of the apostolate will welcome the present debate as a powerful recognition of their efforts. The very existence of the document under discussion is proof that the apostolate of the laity is no luxury nor passing fashion. It means that this apostolate is incorporated into the new dynamism of the Church, seeking new ways to implement the message of the Gospel, seeking new means better adapted to the different social, economic and cultural situations of modern man.

No document could have provided a codification of all that is being done in the different fields of the apostolate. Nor would one have wished that it should. This schema leaves the field open for further developments and at the same time points to the common ground in apostolic endeavor. Because circumstances and needs will differ, precise forms and structures cannot be universally imposed.

In the general report on the schema, we heard with great interest of the commission's intention to link this schema with other conciliar documents which directly affect the laity: with, for example, the chapter on the laity in "De Ecclesia"; with the decree on means of communication. In particular, we anxiously await the debate on the Church in the modern world. All this will have immense implications for the responsible activity of the laity both in the spiritual and in the temporal orders.

It is clear that an apostolic lay action must be rooted in the actual situation and needs of the world. And, as we all know, these needs, both spiritual and temporal, are very great.

Yet, whilst it is true that all Christians are called through Baptism and Confirmation to the apostolate, we must face the fact that few answer that call.

How are the vast majority of Catholics to be made aware of their apostolic responsibility to bear witness in their daily life, as members of a family, as members of the community of the Church and of the whole community? This is the challenge for all those who bear responsibility for Christian formation—for parents, teachers, priests and for leaders of Catholic groups and organizations. It is here that we see the first role of our organizations. It is clear that association provides the most favorable conditions for Christian formation and for sustaining the individual in the development of his creative potential and in the witness he must bear to the world. The establishment and development of organized groupings should therefore be strongly encouraged.

To help us to fulfil our role, venerable Fathers, may we presume to appeal through you for priests to give us their indispensable help. It is the priest who brings Christ to us through the sacraments and the Gospels. It is the priest who equips us spiritually to "consecrate the world." Those of us especially who work in lay movements know how much we owe to our brotherly cooperation with our chaplains.

The lay apostolate cannot be an isolated entity in the Church. It reaches its fulness in close collaboration with all the other members of the Church. By its very nature it demands a constant and regular exchange between the hierarchy and the laity. It is for us as lay people to bring to our pastors our experience of the needs of the world in which we live, and to seek from them guidance in our endeavor to respond to these needs. In simple terms, there must be the "family dialogue" of which our Holy Father, Pope Paul, has spoken so frequently and emphasized in his recent letter, "Ecclesiam Suam."

His Eminence Cardinal Cento, to whom our thanks, as to all members of his commission, are due, told us in his introduction to this debate that there is, by wish of her Divine Founder, a distinction within the Church between the hierarchy and the laity. But this distinction implies no distance. This debate in the council has done much to bind us together inseparably in the single mission of the Church.

101st General Congregation
October 14, 1964

A kind word for assistant pastors and a stern warning against modernism and secularism among the clergy marked the ecumenical council's second day of debate on the proposition on "Priestly Life and Ministry."

Two council Fathers called for the establishment of advisory councils of priests to aid bishops in their work. Several spoke of the need for advanced training in spiritual life and in modern pastoral methods for priests who are years removed from seminary life. Encouragement was given associations designed to help priests in their personal spiritual life and in developing a missionary spirit.

Speaking in the name of 112 bishops of Brazil and other nations, Archbishop Fernando Gomes dos Santos of Goiania, Brazil, called for a complete revision of the text, calling it "too little too poorly done" and claiming that in its present form it would be an "insult to the priesthood." He warned against too much rush in the progress of the council and said "haste should not be an obstacle to perfection of the heart." His plea was met with applause alternating with good-natured groans when he further suggested that all voting be put off "until the next session of the council."

Though it is generally known that a fourth session is in the works, this was the first public reference to it in the council hall.

In all 19 bishops took the floor. Archbishop Pericle Felici, council secretary general, announced that reports on schema 13 were ready but still to be printed. He said discussion of the proposition on the Eastern churches would begin on Oct. 15 with the end of the debate on the priesthood. He speculated that discussion of schema 13 would begin either Oct. 16 or 19.

Auxiliary Bishop-elect Jozsef Bank of Gyor, Hungary, asked for clarification of the relationship between pastors and their assistants. Sometimes assistants "bear the burden of days and nights of labor" without proportionate compensation, he said. He asked that pastors work to establish with assistants "that unity of mind and heart so necessary for the smooth operation of the Church and for domestic peace."

Recalling the teaching of the social encyclicals on just wages and other aspects of justice, he said that sometimes these documents "remain voices crying in the wilderness, hardly observed even by ecclesiastics."

Returning to the previous day's criticism of benefices—income dervied from the capital of a given parish or church post—Bishop-elect Bank said these must be revised since they are obstacles to justice and equity and make the Church immobile, fixed in a certain pattern.

This, he said, often results in harm to souls. He also called for revision of the practice of stole fees— charges for administering the sacraments—as offensive to modern ears. Bishop-elect Bank said the payment of stole fees smacks of business and if it cannot be abolished, at least it should be changed completely, with the assurance that no distinction is to be made in providing Church services based on the classes of people involved or on their ability to pay.

Warning against secularism and modernism creeping into the priesthood in some places, Bishop Smiljan Cekada of Skoplje, Yugoslavia, cited several characteristic and dangerous "signs of the times." Among these he listed instances of priests in confessional work "trying to reform moral theology on their own authority—particularly regarding the Sixth Commandment."

He also mentioned cases of priests who have called the need for auricular confession into doubt and who have maintained that all precepts of a purely ecclesiastical nature should be abolished.

He deplored the modern tendency of priests to lay aside clerical clothing in favor of lay garb and said that although there is no direct relation between clothing and holiness, "the cassock has always been a protection for us against the world."

Spanish Bishop Marcello Gonzales Martin of Astorga called the practice of rejecting candidates for the priesthood because they are not needed in a diocese "scandalous." He said that in Spain from 1,000 to 2,000 such candidates are turned away every year, "while countless other dioceses are encountering almost insurmountable difficulties in their efforts to provide for even the most basic spiritual needs of the people."

He suggested that national and international seminaries under the auspices of episcopal conferences be set up to remedy the situation and also that funds be distributed to avoid instances where vocations are available but material means to develop them are not.

He asked that institutions be erected for further training of priests even several years after ordination and cited reasons why these are necessary:

1) The era of the laity makes it imperative that as the layman's spiritual life becomes more intense, priests' capacity to serve their needs should expand.

2) Such training would strengthen priests' convictions if they wane in later years, and thus "lamentable defections" could be avoided.

3) Bishops cannot be content to let priests live their difficult lives without offering them fitting means to cope with their difficulties.

Jaime Cardinal de Barros Camera of Rio de Janeiro also called for better distribution of priests, but suggested that only dioceses be helped in which there is evidence of internal vitality and genuine efforts to recruit vocations on their own. He applied the same principle of helping those who help themselves to the distribution of financial aid.

Admitting that not all bishops are gifted with administrative ability—"I am one of them," he said—he asked such bishops not to hesitate to make use of diocesan administrative councils. He also stressed the importance of annual retreats and monthly days of recollection for priests and suggested, since many Religious priests are in parish work, that the text should include them in its exhortations.

A formal petition that one of the pastors who were attending the discussions on the priesthood at the invitation of Pope Paul VI be invited to address the council was made by Archbishop Salvatore Baldassarri of Ravenna, Italy. He also said the text should be completely revised to avoid treating bishops' "main collaborators in a second rate manner." He asked for recognition of priests' spiritual and economic rights, leaving details to national episcopal conferences.

Bishop Kazimierz Kowalski of Chelmno, Poland, said that 100 years of experience in his country has proved the usefulness of such associations of priests as the Apostolic Union of the Clergy and the Union of the Clergy for the Missions. These were likewise praised by Bishop Laureano Castan Lacoma of Siguenza-Guadalajara, Spain, who also recommended other associations, such as those which encourage ecclesiastical studies and those which pool funds for social security for priests. He asked that the council take steps to assure priests of freedom to join such organizations.

The 101st general council meeting opened with Mass celebrated by Auxiliary Bishop Vincentas Brizgys of Kaunas, Lithuania, now a resident of Chicago. The Gospel was enthroned by Archbishop Michele Gonzi of Malta. The day's moderator was Gregorio Cardinal Agagianian.

Archbishop Felici announced the procedure to be followed in voting on the proposition on the priesthood. The introduction and 12 articles were to be covered in eight votes. A report on the proposition dealing with seminary training was distributed during the meeting.

The Fathers were informed that the Commission on the Discipline of Clergy and the Faithful was preparing a proclamation for the priests of the world to serve as a supplement to the proposition under discussion. It will be a revised version of the original schema on the priesthood distributed at the last session. The council would be asked to signify its approval according to a procedure to be determined by the council presidency and moderators.

Ernesto Cardinal Ruffini of Palermo, Italy, said the text contained many fine points and reflected the wisdom and prudence of the commission that framed it. He asked, however, for more emphasis on the dignity and sublimity of the priesthood. He said this is particularly necessary since the text now consists largely of admonitions and gives the impression that abuses are rampant. The text should not fail to express a word of appreciation to the countless priests whose lives are genuine models of a Christ-like priestly spirit, he said. He also said that special mention should be made of the pre-eminence of the parochial ministry.

The only other cardinal to speak was Fernando Cardinal Quiroga y Palacios of Santiago de Compostela, Spain, who said that the text suffers weaknesses of internal structure and should include more stress on the holiness of the priesthood.

Asking for a modification of the text's absolute prohibition against priests' engaging in commercial activities, Coadjutor Archbishop Antonio Ferreira de Macedo of Aparecida, Brazil, observed that in certain localities some activity of this kind is absolutely essential as a means of livelihood. He said he also wanted the text to stress humility, love of the Cross, and self-denial to remedy the basic lack of supernatural motivation in its treatment of priestly virtues.

Auxiliary Bishop Luigi Sanchez-Moreno Lira of Chiclayo, Peru, listed three great needs in the priestly ministry today: contact with the faithful, a knowledge of modern times and pastoral needs, and more mobility and specialization to assure greater adaptability in the approach to present-day needs. He asked priests to break down the "wall of separation" which tends to cut them off from the people and not to wait for the people to come to them, but to go out in search of the lost sheep.

Auxiliary Bishop Paul Latusek of Gniezno, Poland, asked that more attention be given to the spirituality proper to the diocesan priesthood. This, he said, should include a dynamic apostolic spirit, a missionary spirit toward Catholics and non-Catholics alike, an ecumenical spirit and one of collaboration with the laity. Stress on the diocesan priest's spirituality is necessary, he said, because retreat preachers in seminaries and dioceses are often Religious without much pastoral experience.

According to Auxiliary Bishop Manuel Pereira of Coimbra, Portugal, the provisions of the text regarding the use of material goods seem to contradict the accepted teaching of moral theology and canon law and could give rise to scruples. He suggested that a distinction be made between money gained from the spiritual ministry and that coming from benefices. The former should be used in the service of the Church, but the latter as the priest desires, he said.

He suggested that the faculties for hearing confessions granted by a bishop be automatically valid for a whole nation.

Bishop Victor Garaygordobil Berrizbeitia for Los Rios, Ecuador, said he felt priests should be protected against the "arbitrariness of bishops, who are neither confirmed in grace nor infallible." He suggested following the example provided by the early Church where priests were regarded "not merely as executors of episcopal desires nor mechanical instruments in their hands, but human and personal collaborators."

Seconding Cardinal de Barros Camera's suggestion of a board of priests to act in a consultative capacity, he said such a board should be composed of priests "who really represent their fellow priests."

Bishop Leonidas Proano Villalba of Riobamba, Ecuador, called for the elimination of all honorary ecclesiastical titles for priests.

Mexican Bishop Ernesto Corripio Ahumada of Tampico also urged abolishing the benefice system, which results in many "flagrant inequalities in the financial order." He said it is not rare to find some priests with much more money than they need, while others, perhaps even their neighbors, are on the verge of starvation. He asked that all priests be provided with social security and health insurance and said this could perhaps best be done by setting up a common fund in every diocese.

Bishop Demetrio Mansilla Reoyo of Ciudad Rodrigo, Spain, and Bishop Edmund Nowicki of Gdansk, Poland, completed the day's discussion, the latter calling for an amendment to the text dealing with the priest's attitude on political questions and his mentality in dealing with economic problems.

Since some Fathers on the list of registered speakers on the subject had not yet been heard, Archbishop Felici said that voting on the proposition, scheduled for Oct. 15, would be postponed to a day to be determined by the council moderators. FATHER JOHN P. DONNELLY

* * * *

The council proposition on the priestly life and ministry consists of 12 individual propositions covering the practical aspects of the priesthood.

Bishop Charles P. Greco of Alexandria, La., a member of the commission which drew up the propositions, told the U.S. bishops' press panel that as they stand the propositions are the end result of a long period of preparation and represent only a fraction of the total work his commission had been engaged in for the past several years.

Much of the commission's work has been transferred to other schemata and the remainder has been reduced to certain essential points, he said.

"No schema comes out perfectly, but we felt that what was wanted was something practical. The result is 12 propositions which cover the practical side of the priest's life and work," Bishop Greco stated.

Before the third council session opened on Sept. 14, there were only 10 propositions, but the commission added two others in response to suggestions by council Fathers, he said.

Following are the 12 propositions:

1—Priests' relations with the laity are stressed, with insistence on the fact that priests must be not only fathers and teachers but also brothers among brothers. This was one of the two later additions.

2—Priests must feel the need for holiness and, because they are Christ's representatives among men, they must reflect Christ's sanctity.

3—The exercise of the priesthood increases and sustains sanctity by its very nature, but priests are also admonished on the need for spiritual exercises, such as daily mental prayer.

4—Priests must base their lives on the Gospel, observe the evangelical counsels of poverty, chastity and obedience and avoid all vanity whether in clothing or in titles, to bring the Gospel more effectively to the poor. The insistence on celibacy is given greater stress in the proposition's final draft than in the earlier one to reaffirm the Church's view of the matter. It is also stated that priests should live in common as much as possible.

5—Priests must continuously deepen their knowledge of priestly studies and also of nonpriestly sciences insofar as they contribute to making priests' work more effective.

6—Centers should be organized for the study of catechetics, the liturgy and sociology. Special libraries should be established to help priests in their mission.

7—Priests must have a concern for churches outside of their parish and must share in the bishop's concern for the Church as a whole. Priests should even serve outside their own diocese if necessary. This was the second of the two later additions.

8—Canon law should be altered to insure a better distribution of the clergy. This does not apply only within a single diocese but applies to improving the supply of priests in whole regions, nations and continents. Steps are to be taken to establish international seminaries.

9—Goods which priests acquire through exercising their ministry are destined for purposes of worship, necessary support, and apostolic and charitable work.

10—The present system of benefices must be revamped.

11—Priests are to receive normal compensation for their work.

12—The richer dioceses should aid the poorer ones and a common fund should be established for assistance.

A member of the press panel, Father Frederick R. McManus of Boston, professor of canon law at the Catholic University of America, defined benefices as ecclesiastical offices to which an income is attached and said the proposition seeks to put the stress on the sacredness of the office rather than what it offers as income, so as to get away from any impression of gain-seeking on the part of the clergy.

Referring to a query as to what constitutes normal compensation for the clergy, Bishop Greco said it varies widely from area to area and nation to nation. But the ideal is to establish a regional norm.

102nd General Congregation

October 15, 1964

If it is passed as drafted, the council's proposition on the Eastern Churches will allow Catholics of Eastern rites to receive the sacraments from and pronounce marriage vows before Orthodox priests.

Recognizing the "special circumstances" existing in the Near East and in the relationship between the Catholic Eastern rites and Orthodox Churches, the draft presented for discussion at the 102nd meeting of the council points out that Orthodox priests are validly ordained and thus can effect valid sacraments. It provides that Catholics can make use of these when no Catholic priest is available.

The severest criticism of the draft from the three Fathers who spoke on it concerned the section on Eastern-rite patriarchs. Two such patriarchs arose to plead for the restoration of the ancient rights of their office and the recognition of their preeminence in the Church. One called the present treatment "totally inadmissible."

The proposition was introduced by Amleto Cardinal Cicognani, head of the Council Commission on the Eastern Churches, which drafted it. The report on the draft was given by Archbishop Gabriel Bukatko of Belgrade, Yugoslavia, after eight speakers had continued the discussion of the proposition on the priesthood and the council Fathers voted cloture by a narrow majority.

The proposition on the Eastern Churches contains an introduction and six parts, divided roughly into two overall considerations: the discipline of Eastern Churches and their unity.

In presenting the text, Cardinal Cicognani said that its framing was guided by "reverence and fraternal esteem for the Eastern Churches and motives of charity toward the separated brethren of the Near East." He said that such a document was demanded by history and by recognition of the dignity of this branch of the Church.

The text caused difficulty for the commission particularly in three areas, Cardinal Cicognani said, and the majority reached on these points was far from unanimous. The points included these:

1. Eastern Christians converted to Catholicism should be received into the Catholic rite corresponding to the Orthodox one they leave, with provision made for recourse to the Holy See to change;

2. A Catholic priest's presence at a mixed marriage between Eastern Christians is required for a marriage within the law (liceity) unless a dispensation is granted, but not for a valid marriage.

3. Permission for Eastern-rite Catholics to make use of Orthodox sacraments provided no Catholic priest is available.

Presenting the report on the proposition, Archbishop Bukatko said that the present draft was the last of several that had been prepared and was adopted at the commission meeting in April, 1963. It is not the result of theological or theoretical speculation, he said, but is based solely on recommendations submitted by council Fathers, which were worked out exclusively in plenary sessions without recourse to any subcommissions.

Because of the great condensation and contraction of the text in its present form, he said, it will be difficult to make changes. In fact, all recommendations sent in by council Fathers since Oct. 1 have been included as appendices at the end of the text rather than incorporated into it. Reiterating Cardinal Cicognani's remarks, Archbishop Bukatko said that the proposition is necessary as an act of homage to the Christian East and out of consideration for the separated Eastern Christians.

Perhaps the major difficulty the commission had, according to Archbishop Bukatko, concerned mixed marriages. Eight plenary sessions were held on this subject alone and the solution contained in the text was a "last-minute effort," he said. But even this solution is not satisfactory, he stated. At a plenary session held on Sept. 30, just 15 days earlier, a more radical solution was adopted by a vote of 14 to 7. This is included in the appendix, he reported.

The text in question states: "To avoid an invalid marriage when Eastern-rite Catholics and (Eastern) non-Catholics marry, and to insure the solidity and sanctity of marriage and domestic peace, the faculty is granted to hierarchs to dispense their subjects from the canonical form if it cannot be observed, providing the necessary promises (required in all mixed marriages) are made at least by the Catholic party."

Since the papal decree of Feb. 22, 1949, it has been required that a Catholic priest be present for a valid mixed marriage. This is the "canonical form" which would be changed by the present text.

The "more radical solution" contained in the appendix would amend the text to the effect that dispensations from hierarchs, though still required for a lawful marriage, would not be required for the validity of a marriage in the eyes of the Church. For this, the presence of a validly ordained priest, even an Orthodox priest, would be sufficient.

Melkite-rite Patriarch Maximos IV Saigh of Antioch commended the text as showing evidence of real progress over previous ones. But he said the weakest chapter is the one dealing with patriarchs, which is "absolutely inadmissible."

It is false to state that the patriarchate is a purely Eastern institution, he said. The first patriarch of the Catholic Church is the bishop of Rome—the pope himself—and history shows the patriarchal idea was dominant for centuries, even in the West. The very basilica in which the council is being held is called a "patriarchal basilica," he noted.

He discounted the notion that the title of patriarch in any way diminishes the primacy of the pope, any more than does his title of bishop of Rome. He observed that in the early Church a newly elected pope sent his profession of faith to the four patriarchs of the East and they returned theirs.

It is no use to shower patriarchs with praise and reverence in the text, he observed, and then reduce them to the position of subordinates, obliging them to check with various offices of the Roman curia for many administrative details best left to their own competence.

The patriarch objected also to the opening words of the proposition's introduction which expresses the great esteem of the Catholic Church for Eastern rites. In this he said he saw the implication that the Eastern rites are something other than Catholic.

He called for the restoration of ancient dignity and prerogatives of the patriarchate and asked that the honorary patriarchates in the West be abolished, since they demean the dignity of the office.

"Let us not close the circle of Catholicity in the West—retaining only small appendages from the East," he said.

Coptic-rite Patriarch Stephanos I Sidarouss of Alexandria also asked for the restoration of patriarchal dignity. He said he preferred the whole treatment on the Eastern churches to be included in the Constitution on the Nature of the Church since, although they have different rites, they are not, strictly speaking, particular churches.

The day's only other speaker on the Eastern churches was Franziskus Cardinal Koenig of Vienna, who spoke in the name of all the Eastern-rite council Fathers from Austria. He said the text should be revised so as to harmonize more fully with the schema on ecumenism and asked that the treatment on patriarchs be included as background in the schema on the pastoral duties of bishops. As for the treatment on the discipline of the sacraments, he said, if it is common to the Universal Church, then it is out of place in this treatment, and if it is not, then it belongs to the legislative authority of the interested rites.

The meeting began with the Mass for the feast of St. Teresa of Avila, celebrated by Bishop Santos Moro Briz of Avila, Spain. The Gospel was enthroned by Archbishop Gabriel Garrone of Toulouse, France. Gregorio Cardinal Agagianian, prefect of the Congregation for the Propagation of the Faith, presided during the continuance of the debate on the priesthood proposition. He was replaced by Giacomo Cardinal Lercaro of Bologna, Italy, for debate on the Eastern Churches.

First to speak on the priesthood was Bernard Cardinal Alfrink of Utrecht, the Netherlands, who accused the text of "superficial treatment" and said it cannot be published in its present form without frustrating the hopes of priests. He said it does not clarify the image of either the priest or of the priesthood. The apostolate in modern times calls for new thinking on the mission of the priest and that of the Church, he said.

Cardinal Alfrink called for a more extended treatment of celibacy to answer the need of the modern Church, "which amounts to a crisis" as a result of publicity and discussion on the subject. This treatment, he continued, should include a firm foundation for celibacy based on both the Bible and tradition.

Archbishop Gregorio Modrego y Casaus of Barcelona, Spain, said he also wanted a fuller treatment of celibacy based on the Gospels, with an expanded emphasis on the positive aspects of priestly consecration, "which alone can provide for the priest strong support in his difficulties and valid protection in his dangers."

Auxiliary Bishop John Gugic of Dubrovnik, Yugoslavia, adding further criticism to the already severely attacked system of benefices, said that in some localities priests have gone to the extreme of concluding that where there is no benefice there is no work to be done and they refuse their bishop's assignment. He asked that the council reaffirm the obligation of all priests to accept assignments even if no benefice is attached.

Bishop Jaime Flores Martin of Barbastro, Spain, added that where the system of benefices has been abolished, the generosity of Catholics has had to compensate. This has opened the door to a spirit of avarice among some, he said, even to the point that they try to prevent division of parishes for financial considerations.

He called for a complete revision of the method of clerical support, providing for equal distribution of funds through a diocesan administrative commission. All priests should share equally in this, he said, because "all are priests to the same degree."

Retired Archbishop Victor Sartre of Tananarive, Malagasy Republic, called for a complete revision of the text to state that priestly ordination is the basis for a whole spiritual life, which life is intimately bound up with the ministry.

Two other speakers took the floor before the cloture vote. They were Bishop Josef Koestner of Gurk, Austria, and Auxiliary Bishop Henri Jenny of Cambrai, France.

After cloture, Joseph Cardinal Lefebvre of Bourges, France, invoking the 70 signature rule, rose to ask that the whole presentation of the text be considered more in the light of theology.

Closing remarks on the debate were made by Archbishop Francois Marty of Rheims, France, who had given a report on the proposition at the beginning of the debate.

FATHER JOHN P. DONNELLY

Lasting Impact in Revelation Document

Because of its solidly doctrinal character, the Second Vatican Council's document on Revelation will have a powerful and lasting impact, which will be felt in many fields.

The discussion of the Revelation schema which has ended here indicates that it will receive a preponderant vote of acceptance. Though many suggestions were offered for its improvement, almost all the bishops spoke of it as adequate, balanced and well-informed—a worthy product of the long, careful labor spent in its preparation.

The opening chapters emphasize a dimension in Revelation which many have overlooked, its primary character as a vital communication of God to man. In the past few centuries common teaching has concentrated on an analysis of the separate truths which form the contents of Revelation. Doctrines have been presented as a monolithic deposit coming down from an ancient past to form a body of truths which men must accept with a predominantly intellectual assent of faith.

Somehow, St. Thomas' emphasis on the self-manifestation of First Truth in every truth it utters was lost sight of, probably because the concept was too rarified for most teachers to grasp. In the schema, however, this primary factor is once more reaffirmed. The speaking of God, like the speaking of man, is presented as a self-revelation. Through His living word God enters into contact with those whom He addresses, revealing Himself and manifesting the secrets of His inward life and love.

Through this emphasis the schema restores a perspective which brings all Revelation into focus and binds its separate truths into unity. Each truth is now seen as resonant with the voice of God manifesting Himself to every man, past or present, who opens his heart through faith.

Recognition of this perennial dynamism of God's Revelation is bound to infuse new vitality into the Church's teaching on faith. Far from being a merely intellectual assent to the separate doctrines God has revealed, faith involves a vital response of the whole man to the living God who gives Himself in the here and now to all who hear His word.

Ever since the Council of Trent took measures to safeguard the necessary intellectual element in faith, many teachers have tended to emphasize this aspect alone. It is time now to enlarge this concept with a fuller and more dynamic stress on man's total response to God. Several bishops, in fact, asked that this be explicitly stated in the schema's treatment of faith.

Those vital elements which St. Paul and the early Fathers stressed in the act of faith once more will come to the fore as a primary dimension in Christian life. Systematic teaching of the separate truths of Revelation will continue, but there will be a new awareness of God speaking. Emphasis will shift from the system which tends to separate truths and will turn to the revealing God whose self-manifestation unites them. Man's faith in the truths of Revelation will be seen in the terms of a "you and I" dialogue between the loving Father who speaks and the devoted son who responds.

The schema, therefore, is bound to exert a strong impact on the liturgical life of the Church where systems and divisions melt away before the presence of God. In the liturgy the Christian family draws near with love to the Father and Brother who have prepared a family feast. There God speaks in the midst of His very own, and men who are His children respond with wholehearted faith. Far from being merely a Church service, the liturgy provides man's best opportunity for intimate encounter with God.

This renewed attitude in Christian living will be greatly strengthened by the schema's teaching on tradition. For the first time a conciliar document has dealt at length with the concept of tradition as something far more extensive than the teaching of the Fathers and of the teaching authority of the Church.

Tradition is now presented as embracing the whole life of the Church, its teaching, its cult, its practice. God is always speaking to everyone in the Church through the truths of Revelation and through the illumination of His Holy Spirit; and the Church is always responding with a faith which can never fail. Tradition, therefore, far from being merely a tenacious memory of the past, is a living reality in the present; for the word of God never changes and the voice of His Son, responding through the Church, His Mystical Body, is always the same—"yesterday, today, yes, and forever" (Heb. 13:8).

This concept of tradition spells a new dignity for every Christian, giving him a full role to play in the perennially vital transmission of God's word to the world. This means, too, a new urgency for full Christian living, intelligent and wholehearted. Each man must realize that he is part of a living tradition. In his weakness he will always need the light and control of the Church's teaching authority. But what he himself is and lives by, his belief, his prayer, his conduct—all this enters into the Church's full tradition. Each Christian is a living echo of the voice of God.

It is hardly needful to say what this means for the apostolate of the laity. Previously our laity have been called the "hands of the Church," reaching into areas where otherwise the Church's teaching would have no influence. The schema shows the profound reason why the laity are so necessary and how it is possible for them to perform so great a task. They, like everyone else in the Church, are living voices of tradition. In their lives other men hear God speaking and God's son responding. For the world at large, that world of men who know nothing of Pope or bishop or priest, the voice of God will be heard chiefly through its resonant echo in the lives of our Catholic laity.

These emphases of the schema cannot fail to make a deep impression on the non-Catholic mind. The whole background of Protestantism has conditioned non-Catholics of our day to think of religion as something eminently vital. God speaking and man responding, this alone is true religion for most non-Catholics.

The formidable and tightly wrought structure of the Church, its emphasis on an unchanging moral code and its highly systematized theology, its seeming impersonality and its multitudinous rites—all this strikes the average non-Catholic as something foreign to the Biblical concept of religion as a dialogue with God.

Now, with a new thrust, the Church itself has brought to the fore that essential feature of her life which, in the mind of non-Catholics, was often obscured by elements which, though necessary to secure the integrity of personal religion, are often open to misunderstanding.

The schema thus dissolves a wall of separation. Reading it, the non-Catholic will discover in the Church the very values which have always formed for him the heart of true religion.

The schema does more than affirm these principles. It implements them. In its treatment of Revelation in Sacred Scripture the document makes provision that God's voice will be heard in all its rich fulness. The chapters on interpretation of the Bible, and on the Old and New Testaments, present directives which incorporate what is best in modern scholarship.

As many bishops pointed out, these chapters need perfecting. But, even as they stand, these sections show a competent awareness of all those factors which must be a feature of the Biblical scholar who has at his command tools for investigating the riches of Scripture which were unknown in previous centuries.

The principles of Bible interpretation described by Pope Pius XII in Divino Afflante Spiritu and by the Pontifical-Biblical Commission in its recent letter now come to the fore with the full authority of a conciliar document.

These directives spell full encouragement for the Biblical scholar to walk with confidence in the intricate ways of his own specialized field. Even more, the debates of the bishops on the concept of inerrancy, the nature of inspiration, and the relation between Scripture and tradition indicate that these are still open questions, presenting a challenge to scholars and rendering imperative their conscientious and fruitful labor. The council has lifted the shadow of suspicion which for so long a time has pressed heavily on the souls of some of the Church's most loyal and devoted sons. Many, in reading this schema, will breathe a fervent "Deo gratias."

These directives will also shape the teaching of Scripture in seminaries, the conduct of adult study clubs, the whole course of Scripture teaching.

Little by little the new insights will filter down to those who are not specialists in the field of Scripture study. They will gradually become familiar with the only true way in which Scripture may be read—under the guiding light of the mentality of those who first heard the words of Revelation and who formed the first rank in that living tradition which embraces their day and ours.

But all these facts are secondary to the council's prime purpose. The conciliar schema is preeminently concerned with the need to make God's voice resound through the world. God speaking and man responding form the unifying theme of this document.

If, then, the Fathers have spoken of Biblical studies, if they have enunciated guiding principles, it was not simply to help the Biblical scholar, to direct the course of seminary studies, or to encourage the work of Bible study clubs. All these factors, though real and very necessary, must be seen in proper perspective.

If they feature in the schema, it is because they are needful to discover the full message of God that men may hear His voice fully and perfectly and may respond wholeheartedly to His word which is "living and efficient and keener than any two-edged sword" (Heb. 4:12).

FATHER BARNABAS AHERN, C.P.

The author is professor of Scripture at the Passionist Seminary in Louisville, Ky., editor of the magazine, Bible Today, and a consultant for the council.

103rd General Congregation

October 16, 1964

The proposition on the Eastern Churches got sparse praise and severe criticism, particularly from Eastern-rite prelates, during its second day on the council floor.

The spiritual leader of Rumanians in exile made an eloquent plea for six million persecuted Eastern-rite Catholics and called on the council Fathers to make their plight known to the United Nations.

"Reading the text of the document on the Eastern Churches," said Bishop Michael Doumith of Sarba, Lebanon, "one finds all hopes for the Eastern Christians vanishing into thin air."

Bishop Joseph Stangl of Wurzburg, Germany, in an apparent reference to the recent speed in the council deliberations, observed: "Posterity will not ask if we were in session three years or four—but what did we accomplish."

Four prelates debated whether converts from Eastern Orthodoxy should be allowed to choose their rite when entering the Catholic Church or required to enter the corresponding rite of Catholicism. Two favored freedom, two were opposed. One pointed out that such freedom could lead to "pastoral anarchy" in the administration of the Church.

In the name of the bishops of the Ukraine, exiled Archbishop Josyf Slipyj of Lvov warned Latin-rite Catholics of the dangers of "proselytizing" members of Eastern rites. He said the Eastern rites have suffered much from the attempts by "Latinizers" to make them fit into the cultural pattern of the West.

The 103rd general meeting of the council opened with the concelebration of a Melkite-rite Liturgy (Mass). Concelebrants included Bishop Georges Hakim of Acre, Israel, and two archimandrites: Father Hilaire Capucci, superior general of the Melkite-rite Order of St. Basil of Aleppo, and Father Atanasio Hage, superior general of the Melkite Basilian Order of St. John the Baptist. Presiding at the Liturgy was Melkite-rite Patriarch Maximos IV Saigh of Antioch. The Gospel was enthroned by Melkite-rite Archbishop Paolo Achkar of Lattakia, Syria. The day's moderator was Giacomo Cardinal Lercaro of Bologna, Italy.

The plea for persecuted Eastern-rite Catholics was made by Bishop Basilio Cristea, delegate of the Congregation for Oriental Church to Rumanian Catholics in exile. He said the six million Eastern-rite Catholics in Rumania and the Ukraine have been subjected to religious persecution and to the deprivation for their rights for years. They are not permitted to practice their religion publicly and many have been deported or forced into labor camps, he said. Their churches have been turned over to secular uses and their schools seized by the state, he added.

Since the suppression of religion by law in Rumania in 1948, he said, six bishops who resisted have been jailed and five of these have since died. Now, not a single Eastern-rite bishop is left there, and other bishops are forbidden to exercise their office, he added.

These Eastern-rite Catholics have "always given brilliant witness to their Faith wherever they have lived, and have made important contributions to the culture of their host nations," he said.

He asked the council Fathers to keep the plight of these peoples in mind when they discuss religious liberty. He also asked for the institution of a "Day of Prayer for the Suffering Church" as proof of how much the rest of the Church esteems them.

Regarding criticism from some quarters that communities of Eastern-rite Catholics are an impediment to reunion with separated Eastern Christians, he said that those who talk this way fail to recognize the value of the Eastern rites. "What will the separated brethren become after reunion? Is it not what we already are?" he asked.

Bishop Doumith observed that the text of the proposition was completely silent on the "most crucial problem" facing the Eastern Church today—the presence of more than one jurisdiction within the territorial limits of the same diocese. He said that though this system was introduced to solve problems, it has turned out to be against the best interests of the Church, and unless the council corrects this difficulty now, it will be accused of having shelved it forever.

He said the proposition fails to correct long-standing prejudices, such as the insinuation that Eastern rites are "just individual Churches" instead of part of the Universal Church. He said he also felt that much of the text is useless and repetitive and that many of the points treated have been better handled already in other schemas. He said the text was adopted to help the separated Christians—"but it does not work."

Bishop Stangl said he saw no disrespect for the Eastern rites in treating them separately, but regretted this treatment had been reduced to a mere series of propositions. "Nothing is left of the original text but a skeleton, where there should be a well-built body."

He wanted the text to be revised so it will not be a mere compilation of canons and directives, but rather a genuine expression of esteem and brotherly love for Eastern brethren. It should also include more on the separated Eastern Christians, he said.

As it stands, the tone of the text is marked by a fear of exceptions, dangers and abuses. It should be one that echos magnanimity and the kindness of the love of Christ, he declared.

The real question for the Eastern rites today is "to be or not to be," Archbishop Slipyj said, quoting the famous Shakespearian line in English. Many fine things are said in the propositions, but they do not represent the Eastern rites in the light of the Catholicity of the whole Church.

These Churches have suffered from persecutions in recent years, a fact of which we are all aware, he said. But we must not forget they have also suffered much and often from the imprudence of "over-zealous Latinizers" trying to force Eastern-rite Catholics into the Latin Church. Such pressure not only ruins these rites, but also does great harm to the Latin Church itself, he said.

Archbishop Charles De Provencheres of Aix, France, said he saw a special vocation for the Eastern rites today in promoting Christian unity. He said the Latin rites could also learn much from their manifestation of universality and from their patrimony of liturgy, spirituality, theology and ecclesiastical institutions.

Regarding the exchange of the sacraments between Eastern-rite Catholics and the Orthodox, he said that some degree of this is necessary for the good of souls otherwise deprived of the sacraments.

The Melkite-rite patriarchal vicar for Egypt, Archbishop Elie Zoghbi, agreed with this. He added that legislation on participation in non-Catholic services is based on a false interpretation of decrees of the Council of Trent by those not familiar with the East. He said the new provisions of the proposition meet a concrete spiritual need.

Archbishop Zoghbi called for new thinking on the validity of the patriarchal system by the Western Church. Tracing its history from the earliest times, he noted that although the system has been supplanted in the West, still Latin patriarchs were set up in various Eastern Sees. These were generally regarded as intruders and "shadows of the Roman pontiff" and their presence was a constant source of friction, he stated.

He said that until the First Vatican Council, the primacy of the pope, which was the chief source of division between the East and the West, was regarded in the East only as a legislative structure, although the pope was always considered the first bishop of the Church. The decision to proclaim papal infallibility as a dogma was made at a council [Vatican Council I] in which representatives from the East were conspicuously absent, he said.

When the separated Eastern Christians broke from Rome, he said, they attributed no special theological value to the papal primacy, nor did they regard themselves as separated from the Universal Church, whose head is the pope.

The question of what Catholic rite converts from Orthodoxy would be asked to join was given considerable attention during the discussions. Jaime Cardinal De Barros Camera of Rio de Janeiro and Latin-rite Patriarch Alberto Gori, O.F.M., of Jerusalem, both asked that converts be left free to choose their rite.

Patriarch Gori said he felt that the appeal to Rome required for a change of rite hardly takes into account individual needs in matters of such importance to the individual. He said such a "right of appeal" is almost a suppression of freedom in practice.

"It would be ironical that the convert wishing to change rites should be obliged to appeal to the authority of Rome, which he has always been taught to distrust and suspect." He asked the council to establish the principle that all converts retain their former rite, but leave intact the freedom of individuals to change rites at the time of conversion if they wish.

Two other prelates asked for retention of the provision requiring converts to enter the Catholic rite corresponding to the Orthodox one they leave. Bishop Isaac Ghattas of Thebes, Egypt, said he saw only "pastoral anarchy" in the alternative, since it would intensify the problem of plurality of jurisdictions in the same diocese. With Bishop Doumith he called this situation the gravest problem facing the Eastern rites.

The other council Father to speak against freedom of choice in rites was Armenian-rite Patriarch Ignace Pierre XVI Batanian of Cilicia. He said the individual converted to Catholicism from Orthodoxy is like a "son who has wandered away from the family home. When he returns to his native city, it is natural that he go not to just any family, but to his own."

Individual freedom is safeguarded, he said, by the section providing for recourse to the Holy See.

Referring to the rule in the Eastern Churches that Catholics can marry merely by mutual consent when no Catholic priest is available, since the Church would not allow an Orthodox priest to perform the ceremony, he said such a practice renders the Church odious in the eyes of the Orthodox clergy and faithful. He called for the adoption of a provision in the appendix of the proposition which would allow an Orthodox priest to perform the ceremony in such cases, since marriage without a priest is "unthinkable" for an Eastern Christian.

Cardinal De Barros Camara called for the recognition by the council of the fact that there are millions of Eastern-rite Catholics living in non-Eastern countries and thus dispersed among Latin-rite Catholics. The Brazilian cardinal, who for 11 years has served as Ordinary of the eight Eastern rites in his country, expressed concern for Eastern-rite Catholics who marry Latin-rite Catholics. He asked that marriage legislation concerning this difficulty be included in the proposition's text.

He said he wanted all Latin-rite bishops who have Eastern-rite Catholics in their dioceses to show toward them the "same sentiments of esteem and paternal love they show the faithful of their own rite. They should never be simply tolerated as immigrants. Should difficulties, major or minor, arise, the interested parties should get together in a spirit of mutual understanding and settle these questions among themselves."

During the meeting Archbishop Pericle Felici, council secretary general, announced the distribution of the new liturgical instruction to implement the Constitution on the Liturgy, the first document completed by the council. His announcement was greeted by widespread and warm applause throughout St. Peter's. The instruction was drawn up by the Vatican Liturgy Commission and issued by the Congregation of Rites.

A report on schema 13 on the Church in the modern world was also distributed, together with an amended text on chapter seven of the schema on the nature of the Church, which deals with the final vocation of Christians to heaven. It was announced that a vote on this chapter would be taken Oct. 19.

In accordance with the decision of the Coordinating Commission, Archbishop Felici said that all schemas reduced to propositions would be voted on immediately after discussion if more than half the council Fathers so

decide in standing vote. Otherwise they will be returned to the competent commission for revision and then returned to the council floor for a vote. This was decided in response to many requests from the council Fathers, Archbishop Felici said. FATHER JOHN P. DONNELLY

✻   ✻   ✻   ✻

While the new changes enacted by the post-conciliar liturgy commission become mandatory and must be observed as of next March 7, the first Sunday of Lent, national bishops' conferences could get permission to put them into effect earlier, according to Father Frederick R. McManus.

The Boston priest told a meeting of the U.S. press panel that a national body of bishops would only have to apply to the commission for the permission to put all of the changes into effect prior to the effective date.

Father McManus noted in his explanation to journalists that the instruction of the commission involves only changes which can be made easily, without having to alter the existing liturgical books to a major extent. He said, however, that in the future there are to be a number of structural changes which will be much more radical in restoring the purity of the celebration of the Eucharist.

Father McManus noted that while the instruction is the work of the new liturgy commission, it was issued by the Congregation of Rites after review by that body.

The priest pointed out that the instruction provides for use of the vernacular in the Mass whenever there is a congregation. But if a priest is celebrating Mass by himself with only an altar boy present, Latin is to be the language of the Mass.

Father McManus also stated that instructions regarding concelebration of Mass and Communion under both species have been drawn up but have not yet been published. No reference is made to these two aspects of the liturgy in the present instruction, he said.

Ecumenism Schema Clarifies Church's Stand

The newly approved decree on ecumenism gives a clear and authoritative decision on the future posture of the Church toward non-Catholic Christians.

The decree, which received the overwhelming approval of the Second Vatican Council in detailed voting completed here, tries to correct four major misunderstandings about the grace-filled movement toward Christian unity.

First, there is not a "Catholic ecumenism" pushing behind, alongside of, or ahead of Orthodox, Anglican and Protestant types. We are witnessing today one Christian movement, and each church is asked to contribute, ac-

cording to its conscience, whatever can bring about, among all Christians, that full invisible and visible unity that Christ has willed for His Church.

The cause of Christian unity is not best served as it had been in the past: by the traditional refusal of serious contact with other Christian communities. The lack of such contact is no longer an obvious anomaly or a salutary punishment but an added obstacle insofar as it perpetuates and strengthens mutual ignorance and apathy.

Our common concern is not eventually to erect a ghetto of united Christians, set apart from the rest of men. Rather, our concern is to eliminate the scandal of a Christian family which appears to the non-Christian not as a united body of men and women proclaiming the Good News of Christ which can save the world from itself, but a chorus of voices hotly arguing about what the Gospel of Christ really is. We wish to be one in order that through our united witness in word and act the world may believe.

Secondly, ecumenism concerns a movement, not the static stance of Church to Church. Since the Catholic Church is involved in this dynamic movement, the conciliar decree does not attempt to define ecumenism, but only provisionally to describe the ecumenical situation in the mid-1960s.

Thirdly, the Catholic contribution to Christian unity is not confined to specialists or "professional dialogists." Ecumenical work is the faithful service of the whole Church—layman, Sister, Brother, seminarian, priest, bishop, and pope—in the face of a divided Christian world. The decree tries to discover what God expects of all Catholics while 400,000,000 brothers in Christ remain, in varying degrees, united with us, yet separated from us; how we can better determine and respect what makes non-Catholic Christians our brothers and how we can help heal the tragic wounds that make them separated.

Fourthly, the Catholic involvement in the ecumenical movement presupposes "the continuing reform" of the Church—yes, the decree is not afraid to use the term.

This Church renewal is now being expressed in various movements: a deepening appreciation of the Church as the people of God sent by Christ to serve both Him and His world; the liturgical and Biblical revivals; a worldwide missionary apostolate which embraces every layman; social action; the catechetical and homiletic movement; the formation of seminarians and Sisters.

True, the council is trying to formulate in clear terms and thus to develop these reforming movements. But the council is not the Church and the council's immediate aim is not to reform the Church but to enable the Church to reform itself. Even the best of conciliar decisions do not automatically grip the members of the Church as living truths to be put into practice immediately. The Church is not composed of IBM machines.

As with ecumenism, so with the other renewals: we all are asked to shorten the inevitable time lag while the council's decisions filter through the Church—in diocesan chanceries, seminaries, sermons, catechisms, and Catholic homes. Thus, the future ecumenical life of a diocese cannot be judged solely by the number of specific Catholic-

Protestant-Orthodox joint-projects which are organized by an official ecumenical committee.

With these points in mind, it may become clear why it is so difficult to play the role of a prophet in predicting the exact course of the ecumenical movement or the role of a bureaucrat in detailing rigid programs of action. The movement for Christian unity is only in its initial stage. It would be unfortunate to bind the Church too rigorously today to programs that soon may be dated.

Future postures and actions by Catholics will depend also on the developments in attitudes and activities by other Christians.

For example, the council has determined to allow, at times urge, some forms of worship in common between Catholics and other Christians. But what kind of service and what degree of participation will depend largely on how deeply correct, nonsuperficial ecumenical and liturgical attitudes have caught on among both Catholic and non-Catholic Christians.

Accordingly, the decree states only brief principles for prohibiting and recommending common worship services, in order to give elasticity and freedom for prudent experimentation on local and national levels.

The future ecumenical life of the Church will see a gradual change of what is presently predominating in our attitudes toward other Christians. We will take more seriously the words of Pope Paul VI in his first encyclical: "Let us stress what we have in common rather than what divides us." Teachers and scholars will be more alert to understand the doctrine and history, the spiritual and cultural life, and the thinking patterns of non-Catholic Christians. This will be greatly aided not only by a confrontation in print, but also by person-to-person dialogue.

We will be more on the lookout to seize opportunities for a common Christian witness in realistic action against nuclear warfare, the plight of the homeless, illiteracy, unequal distribution of wealth, and the effects of rapidly expanding populations in some areas of the world.

If one is allowed to predict what is most needed in the future, I would not hesitate to write: a feet-on-the-ground realism about the theological and pastoral difficulties which will continue to plague divided Christians and a deeply spiritual hope that if we Christians serve God's will while we are divided, our service will result in that unity God wishes through the means and ways He wishes and gives, and when He wishes to give it.

FATHER THOMAS F. STRANSKY, C.S.P.

Father Stransky is a staff member of the Secretariat for Promoting Christian Unity and has long been active in ecumenical work.

Council Auditor

Mrs. Catherine McCarthy, 60, president of the National Council of Catholic Women, has been named America's second woman auditor at the ecumenical council. Her appointment was made public in Vatican City Oct. 16.

A resident of San Francisco, Mrs. McCarthy has been president of the 10-million-member women's organization since 1962.

Previously named as a council auditor by Pope Paul VI was Sister Mary Luke, of Nerinx, Ky., superior general of the Sisters of Loretto, and president of the American Conference of Major Superiors of Women.

Mrs. McCarthy was born in Worcester, Mass. She attended Worcester State Teachers College, Clark University in Worcester and Boston College. She taught at junior and senior high schools in Auburn and Whitinsville, Mass., and was married to the late Joseph McCarthy in 1935.

After moving to San Francisco, Mrs. McCarthy became president of the Archdiocesan Council of Catholic Women. She became a national director in 1960. Last February she was awarded the Pro Ecclesia et Pontifice medal by Pope Paul.

Mrs. McCarthy is the mother of two daughters, Catherine, now Mrs. Frank Filice of San Francisco, and Winifred, a teacher in San Francisco public schools. She is a member of the Citizens' Advisory Council of the Food and Drug Administration and of the President's Committee on Employment of the Physically Handicapped.

Instruction on the Liturgy

This is an English translation of the Vatican Liturgy Commission's instruction implementing changes in the Mass and other forms of the liturgy recommended in the Vatican council's Constitution on the Sacred Liturgy. The instruction was issued by the Sacred Congregation of Rites with the date of Sept. 26, 1964, but made public Oct. 16, 1964.

INTRODUCTION

I. *Nature of this Instruction*

1. The Constitution on the Sacred Liturgy is deservedly counted among the first fruits of the Second Ecumenical Vatican Council, since it governs the most excellent part of the Church's activity. It will bear more abundant fruit the more profoundly the pastors and the faithful of Christ perceive its genuine spirit and put it into practice with good will.

2. The Commission for the Implementation of the Constitution on the Sacred Liturgy, established by the Supreme Pontiff, Paul VI, in the apostolic letter Sacram Liturgiam has already speedily undertaken the task entrusted to it, to bring the directives of the Constitution and of the apostolic letter to a proper fulfillment and to provide for the interpretation and execution of these documents.

· 3. It is of the greatest importance that the documents, from the very beginning, should be properly applied everywhere, with doubts, if there are any, concerning its interpretation being removed. Therefore, the Commission, by mandate of the Supreme Pontiff, has prepared this Instruction, in which the functions of the bodies of bishops in liturgical matters are more clearly defined, some principles given in general words in the above-mentioned documents are explained more precisely, and finally some matters, which can be put into practice now, before the restoration of the liturgical books, are allowed or required.

II. *Some principles to be noted*

4. What is now defined as to be put into practice has the purpose of making the liturgy correspond always more perfectly to the mind of the council concerning the promotion of active participation of the faithful.

The general reform of the sacred liturgy, moreover, will be accepted more readily by the faithful if it proceeds gradually and by stages and if the reform is proposed to the faithful and explained to them by the pastors by means required of the catechesis.

5. Nevertheless, it is necessary first that all be persuaded of the intention of the Constitution on the Sacred Liturgy of the Second Vatican Council: not only to change liturgical forms and texts, but rather to stir up that formation of the faithful and pastoral activity which has the sacred liturgy as summit and fount (cf. Const., Art. 10). The changes thus far introduced and to be introduced into the sacred liturgy in the future are directed toward this end.

6. The power of pastoral-liturgical activity rests in this, that the Christian life may express the paschal mystery in which the Son of God, incarnate and made obedient even to the death on the cross, is so exalted in His resurrection and ascension that He may share His divine life with the world. By this life men, dead to sin and conformed to Christ, "may live no longer for themselves but for him who died for them and rose again" (2 Cor. 5:15).

This is done through faith and through the sacraments of faith, that is, chiefly through baptism (cf. Const., Art. 6) and the most sacred mystery of the Eucharist (cf. Const., Art. 47). Around the Eucharist are ranged the other sacraments and the sacramentals (cf. Const., Art. 61) and the cycle of celebrations by which the paschal mystery of Christ is unfolded in the Church during the course of the year (cf. Const., Art. 102-107).

7. Therefore, even if the liturgy does not exhaust the entire action of the Church (cf. Const., Art. 9), nevertheless the greatest attention must be paid to the necessary connection between pastoral works and the sacred liturgy, so that pastoral-liturgical action is not exercised as if separate and abstract, but as intimately joined to other pastoral activities.

It is especially necessary that there be a close union between the liturgy and catechesis, religious formation, and preaching.

III. *Fruits to be hoped for*

8. Thus, the bishops and their assistants in the priesthood should relate their entire pastoral ministry ever more closely to the liturgy. In this way the faithful may derive the divine life in abundance from the perfect participation in the sacred celebrations and, made the ferment of Christ and the salt of the earth, will proclaim the divine life and communicate it to others.

CHAPTER I

Some General Norms

I. *Application of these norms*

9. The practical norms, found in the Constitution or in this Instruction, and whatever is permitted or determined now by this Instruction before the restoration of the liturgical books, even if they pertain to the Roman rite alone, may nevertheless be applied to the other Latin rites, the provisions of law being observed.

10. Those matters which are entrusted to the competent territorial ecclesiastical authority in this Instruction may and should be put into effect by that authority alone through legitimate decrees.

In individual cases, the time and the circumstances in which these decrees will take effect shall be defined, always with a reasonable interval of time for the faithful to be instructed and prepared for their observance.

II. *Liturgical formation of clerics* (Const., Arts. 15-16 and 18)

11. With regard to the liturgical formation of clerics:

a) In theological faculties there shall be a chair of liturgy, so that all the students may receive the necessary liturgical instruction; in seminaries and in the houses of studies of Religious, local Ordinaries and major superiors shall see to it that as soon as possible there be a special and properly prepared teacher of liturgy.

b) Professors who are appointed to teach sacred liturgy shall be prepared as soon as possible, in accordance with the norm of Art. 15 of the Constitution.

c) For the further liturgical instruction of clerics, particularly of those who are already working in the Lord's vineyard, pastoral-liturgical institutes shall be established where possible.

12. The liturgy shall be taught for a suitable period of time, to be indicated in the curriculum of studies by the competent authority, and according to an appropriate method in accordance with the norm of Art. 16 of the Constitution.

13. Liturgical services shall be celebrated as perfectly as possible. Therefore:

a) The directions shall be carefully observed and the ceremonies performed with dignity, under the diligent vigilance of the seminary directors, with the necessary preparations beforehand.

b) Clerics shall frequently fulfil the liturgical functions of their order, that is, of deacon, subdeacon, acolyte, lector, and, in addition, of commentator and cantor.

c) The churches and oratories, the sacred furnishings in general, and sacred vestments shall afford an example of genuine Christian art, including contemporary art.

III. *Liturgical formation of the spiritual life of clerics* (Const., Art. 17)

14. In order that clerics may be formed for the full participation in liturgical celebrations and for the spiritual life to be derived from these celebrations, while being prepared to share this participation and life with others, the Constitution on the Sacred Liturgy shall be put into full effect in seminaries and houses of studies of religious, in accordance with the norm of documents from the Apostolic See, with the unanimous and harmonious cooperation of all the directors and teachers to this end. A suitable formation in the sacred liturgy shall be provided for the clerics together with the recommenda-

tion of books dealing with the liturgy, especially under its theological and spiritual aspect, which should be available in the library in sufficient numbers; as well as by meditations and conferences which shall be drawn above all from the fount of sacred Scripture and the liturgy (cf. Const., Art. 35, 2); and by common exercises, in accord with Christian custom and usage, but suited to the various seasons of the liturgical year.

15. The Eucharist, the center of the entire spiritual life, shall be celebrated daily with the use of different and appropriate forms which best correspond to the condition of the participants (cf. Const., Art. 19).

On Sundays, however, and on other major feast days, a sung Mass shall be celebrated with the participation of all who are in the seminary or house of studies, with a homily and, as far as possible, with the sacramental communion of those who are not priests. The priests may concelebrate, especially on the more solemn feast days, if the needs of the faithful do not require that they celebrate individually, and after the new rite of concelebration has been published.

It is desirable that, at least on major feast days, the students should participate in the celebration of the Eucharist assembled around the bishop in the cathedral church (cf. Const., Art. 41).

16. It is most fitting that the clerics, even if they are not yet bound by the obligation of the divine office, should each day recite or chant in common lauds, in the morning as morning prayer, and vespers, in the evening as evening prayer, or compline, at the end of the day. The directors themselves shall take part in this common recitation, as far as possible. In addition, sufficient time shall be provided in the order of the day for clerics in sacred orders to pray the divine office.

It is desirable that, as least on major feast days, the students should chant vespers in the cathedral church, where possible.

17. Exercises of piety, arranged according to the laws or customs of each place or institute, shall be held in due esteem. Nevertheless, care should be taken, especially if these exercises are celebrated in common, that they be in harmony with the sacred liturgy, according to the purpose of Art. 13, and that they be related to the seasons of the liturgical year.

IV. *Liturgical formation of members of institutes dedicated to acquiring perfection*

18. What has been said in the preceding articles concerning the liturgical formation of the spiritual life of clerics must be applied also to the members, both men and women, of institutes dedicated to acquiring perfection, with the necessary adaptations.

V. *Liturgical formation of the faithful* (Const., Art. 19)

19. Pastors of souls shall strive diligently and

patiently to carry out the command of the Constitution concerning the liturgical formation of the faithful and their active participation, both internal and external, "according to their age and condition, their way of life, and standard of religious culture" (Const., Art. 19). They should be especially concerned about the liturgical formation and the active participation of those who are engaged in religious associations of the laity, since it is the latter's duty to share more intimately in the life of the Church and also to assist the pastors of souls in properly promoting the liturgical life of the parish (cf. Const., Art. 42).

VI. *Competent authority in liturgical matters* (Const., Art. 22)

20. Regulation of the sacred liturgy pertains to the authority of the Church: therefore, no other person shall proceed in this matter on his own authority to the detriment, as may often happen, of the liturgy itself and of its restoration by the competent authority.

21. It pertains to the Apostolic See to reform and to approve the general liturgical books; to order the sacred liturgy in those matters which affect the universal Church; to approve, that is, confirm the acts and deliberations of the territorial authority; and to receive the proposals and petitions of the same territorial authority.

22. It pertains to the bishop to regulate the liturgy within the limits of his diocese, in accordance with the norms and spirit of the Constitution on the Sacred Liturgy as well as the decrees of the Apostolic See and of the competent territorial authority.

23. The various kinds of territorial bodies of bishops, to which the regulation of the liturgy pertains in virtue of Art. 22, 2, of the Constitution, must be understood to be, for the interim:

a) either the body of all the bishops of a nation, in accordance with the norm of the apostolic letter Sacram Liturgiam, n. X;

b) or a body already lawfully constituted which consists of the bishops, or of the bishops and other local Ordinaries, of several nations;

c) or a body to be established, with the permission of the Apostolic See, consisting of the bishops or of the bishops and the local Ordinaries of several nations, especially if in the individual nations the bishops are so few that they may convene more profitably from various nations of the same language or of the same culture.

If the particular local conditions suggest another solution, the matter should be proposed to the Apostolic See.

24. The following must be invited to the above-mentioned bodies:

a) residential bishops;

b)   abbots and prelates nullius;

c)   vicars and prefects apostolic;

d)   apostolic administrators of dioceses who have been appointed permanently;

e)   all other local Ordinaries except vicars general.

Coadjutor and auxiliary bishops may be invited by the president, with the consent of the majority of those who take part in the body with deliberative vote.

25.   Unless the law provides otherwise for certain places in view of particular circumstances, the convocation of the body must be made:

a)   by the respective president, in the case of bodies already lawfully established;

b)   in other cases, by the archbishop or bishop who has the right of precedence in accordance with the norm of law.

26.   The president, with the consent of the Fathers, determines the order to be followed in the examination of questions, and opens, transfers, prorogues, and closes the conference.

27.   A deliberative vote belongs to all who are named in n. 24, including coadjutor and auxiliary bishops, unless a different provision is expressly made in the document of convocation.

28.   For the lawful enactment of decrees, two-thirds of the votes, taken by secret ballot, are required.

29.   The acts of the competent territorial authority which are to be transmitted to the Apostolic See for approval, that is, confirmation, should contain the following:

a)   the names of those who took part in the session;

b)   a report of matters taken up;

c)   the result of voting for the individual decrees.

Two copies of these acts, signed by the president and the secretary of the body, and with the proper seal, shall be sent to the Commission for the Implementation of the Constitution on the Sacred Liturgy.

30.   When, however, it is a question of acts in which there are decrees concerning the use and extent of the vernacular language to be admitted in the liturgy, besides what is enumerated in n. 29, in accordance with Art. 36, 3, of the Constitution and the apostolic letter Sacram Liturgiam, n. IX, the acts should also contain:

a)   an indication of the individual parts of the liturgy which are to be said in the vernacular;

b)   two copies of the liturgical texts prepared in the vernacular, one copy of which will be returned to the body of bishops;

c)   a brief report concerning the criteria upon which the work of translation was based.

31.   The decrees of the territorial authority which need the approval, that is, the confirmation of the Apostolic See, shall be promulgated and put into practice only when they have been approved, that is, confirmed by the Apostolic See.

VII.   *The office of individuals in the liturgy* (Const., Art. 28)

32.   The parts which pertain to the schola or to the people, if they are sung or recited by them, are not said privately by the celebrant.

33.   Likewise the celebrant does not say privately the lessons which are recited or chanted by a competent minister or by a server.

VIII.   *Avoiding distinctions of person* (Const., Art. 32)

34.   The individual bishops or, if it seems opportune, the regional or national conference of bishops shall see to it that the prescription of the holy Council which forbids any favor to private persons or any favor on the basis of social distinctions, either in ceremonies or in external pomp, shall be put into effect in their territories.

35.   In addition, pastors of souls shall work with prudence and charity so that, in the liturgical services and, more especially, in the celebration of Mass and the administration of sacraments and sacramentals, the equality of the faithful shall be evident even outwardly and that, further, all appearance of money-seeking be avoided.

IX.   *Simplification of certain rites* (Const., Art. 34)

36.   In order that the liturgical services may exhibit a noble simplicity in harmony with the mentality of our times:

a)   The salutations to the choir on the part of the celebrant and the ministers shall be made only at the beginning and at the end of the sacred rite;

b)   The incensation of the clergy, apart from those who are bishops, shall be done once for each part of the choir, with three swings of the thurible;

c)   The incensation of the altar shall be done only at that altar where the liturgical service is being celebrated;

d)   The kisses of the hand and of objects which are being presented or received shall be omitted.

X.   *Sacred celebrations of the word of God* (Const., Art. 35, 4)

37.   In places which lack a priest, if no priest is available for the celebration of Mass on Sundays and feast days of precept, the sacred celebration of the word of God shall be fostered, according to the judgment of the local Ordinary, with a deacon or even a layman, authorized for this purpose, presiding over the service.

The pattern of this celebration shall be almost the same as the liturgy of the word in Mass: ordinarily the Epistle and Gospel of the Mass of the day shall be read in the vernacular, with chants, especially from the psalms, before the lessons and between them; the one who presides shall give a homily, if he is a deacon; if not a deacon, he shall read a homily indicated by the bishop or the pastor; and the whole celebration shall be closed with the "common prayer" or "prayer of the faithful" and with the Lord's Prayer.

38. It is also fitting that sacred celebrations of the word of God, which are to be encouraged on the vigils of the more solemn feasts, on some weekdays in Advent and Lent, and on Sundays and feast days, should take into account the pattern of the liturgy of the word in Mass, although there may be only a single reading.

In the arrangement of several readings, however, in order that the history of salvation may be clearly discerned, the reading from the Old Testament shall generally precede the reading from the New Testament, and the reading of the Holy Gospel shall appear as the climax.

39. In order that these celebrations may be held with dignity and piety, it shall be the task of the liturgical commissions in the individual dioceses to indicate and provide appropriate aids.

XI. *Vernacular translations of liturgical texts* (Const., Art. 36, 3)

40. In vernacular translations of liturgical texts prepared in accordance with the norm of Art. 36, 3, it is fitting that the following be observed:

a) The vernacular translations of liturgical texts shall be made from the Latin liturgical text. The version of the biblical pericopes, however, should conform to the Latin liturgical text, but with the possibility of revising this translation, if deemed advisable in accordance with the original text or some other clearer translation.

b) The preparation of the translation of liturgical texts should be entrusted, as a special concern, to the liturgical commission mentioned in Art. 44 of the Constitution and in n. 44 of this Instruction. So far as possible the institute of pastoral liturgy should assist the commission. But if there is no such commission, the supervision of the translation should be entrusted to two or three bishops, who will choose persons, including lay persons, expert in Scripture, liturgy, biblical languages, Latin, the vernacular language, and music. For the perfect translation of the liturgical text into the language of the people must necessarily and properly fulfill many conditions at the same time.

c) Whenever it is called for, there should be consultation concerning translations with the bishops of neighboring regions which have the same language.

d) In nations which have several languages, different vernacular translations should be prepared for these languages and submitted to the special examination of the bishops concerned.

e) Consideration should be given to the dignity of the books from which the liturgical text is read to the people in the vernacular language, so that the dignity of the book itself may move the faithful to a greater reverence for the word of God and for sacred things.

41. In liturgical services which are celebrated in some places with people of another language, it is lawful with the consent of the local Ordinary to use the vernacular language known to these faithful, especially in the case of groups of immigrants, or of members of a personal parish, or similar instances. This shall be done in accordance with the extent of the use of the vernacular and its translation as legitimately approved by a competent territorial ecclesiastical authority of the respective language.

42. New melodies for parts to be sung in the vernacular language by the celebrant and the ministers must be approved by the competent territorial ecclesiastical authority.

43. Particular liturgical books which were lawfully approved before the promulgation of the Constitution on the Sacred Liturgy and indults conceded up to that day retain their force, unless they are opposed to the Constitution, until other provision is made in the liturgical restoration, as it will be completed in whole or in part.

XII. *The liturgical commission of the body of bishops* (Const., Art. 44)

44. The liturgical commission, which it is desirable that the territorial authority establish, shall be chosen from among the bishops themselves, as far as possible. At least it shall consist of one or other bishop, with the addition of some priests expert in liturgical and pastoral matters, who are designated by name for this office.

It is desirable that the members of this Commission be convened several times a year with the consultors of the Commission that they may deal with questions together.

45. The territorial authority may, as circumstances suggest, entrust the following to this Commission:

a) studies and experiments to be promoted in accordance with the norm of Art. 40, 1 and 2 of the Constitution;

b) practical initiatives to be undertaken for the entire territory, by which the liturgy and the application of the Constitution on the Liturgy may be encouraged;

c) studies and the preparation of aids which become necessary in virtue of the decrees of the plenary body of bishops;

d) the office of regulating the pastoral-liturgical action in the entire nation, supervising the application of the decrees of the plenary body, and reporting concerning all these matters to the body;

e) consultations to be undertaken frequently and common initiatives to be promoted with associations in the same region which are concerned with Scripture, catechetics, pastoral care, music, and sacred art, and with every kind of religious association of the laity.

46. The members of the institute of pastoral liturgy as well as individual experts who are called to assist the liturgical commission shall also freely offer their assistance to individual bishops for the more effective promotion of pastoral-liturgical action in their territory.

XIII. *The diocesan liturgical commission* (Const., Art. 45)

47. The following duties pertain to the diocesan liturgical commission, under the direction of the bishop:

a) to be informed about the state of pastoral-liturgical action in the diocese;

b) to implement carefully what is proposed in liturgical matters by the competent authority, and to obtain information concerning studies and programs which are taking place elsewhere in this field;

c) to suggest and promote practical undertakings of every kind which may help to promote the liturgy, especially those which will assist priests already working in the Lord's vineyard;

d) in individual cases, or also for the entire diocese, to suggest opportune and progressive steps in the work of pastoral liturgy; to indicate and also to call upon suitable persons who on occasion may help priests in this matter; and to propose suitable materials and aids;

e) to see to it that programs in the diocese to promote the liturgy progress with a harmonious spirit and with the assistance of other associations, in a way similar to that indicated for the commission established within the body of bishops (n.45e).

CHAPTER II

The Most Holy Mystery of the Eucharist

I. *The rite of the Mass* (Const., Art. 50)

48. Until the entire rite of the Mass is restored, the following shall be observed.

a) The parts of the Proper which are sung or recited by the schola or by the people are not said privately by the celebrant.

b) The celebrant may sing or recite the parts of the Ordinary together with people or the schola.

c) In the prayers to be said at the foot of the altar at the beginning of Mass, psalm 42 is omitted. All the prayers at the foot of the altar are omitted whenever another liturgical service immediately precedes the Mass.

d) In solemn Masses the paten is not held by the subdeacon, but is left upon the altar.

e) The secret prayer or prayer over the offerings shall be chanted in sung Masses, and recited in a loud voice in other Masses.

f) The doxology at the end of the Canon, from the words "Per ipsum" up to "Per omnia saecula saeculorum. R. Amen," inclusively, shall be chanted or recited in a loud voice. Throughout the entire doxology the celebrant lifts up the chalice and the host for the little elevation, omitting the signs of the cross, and at the end genuflects only after the response "Amen" is given by the people.

g) In low Masses the *Lord's Prayer* may be recited by the people together with the celebrant in the vernacular language; in sung Masses it may be chanted by the people together with the celebrant in the Latin language and, if the territorial ecclesiastical authority shall so decree, also in the vernacular language, to melodies approved by the same authority.

h) The embolism after the *Lord's Prayer* shall be chanted or recited in a loud voice.

i) In distributing Holy Communion the formula, "Corpus Christi," shall be used. The celebrant, as he says these words, lifts up the Host a little above the ciborium to show it to the communicant, who responds: "Amen," and afterward is communicated by the celebrant. The sign of the cross with the host is omitted.

j) The Last Gospel is omitted; the Leonine prayers are suppressed.

k) It is lawful to celebrate a sung Mass with a deacon only.

l) It is lawful for bishops, if necessary, to celebrate a sung Mass according to the form used by priests.

II. *Lessons and Chants between the lessons* (Const., Art. 51)

49. In Masses celebrated with the people, the lessons, Epistle, and Gospel shall be read or chanted facing the people:

a) in solemn Mass, at the ambo or at the edge of the sanctuary area;

b) in high Mass or in low Mass, if they are read or chanted by the celebrant, either at the altar or at the ambo or at the edge of the sanctuary area, as may be more convenient; if they are read or chanted by another, at the ambo or at the edge of the sanctuary area.

50. In Masses celebrated with the people which are not solemn Masses, the lessons and Epistle, together with the intervenient chants, may be read by a qualified lector or server, while the celebrant sits and listens. The Gospel, however, may be read by a deacon or by a second priest, who says "Munda cor meum," seeks the blessing, and at the end presents the book of Gospels for the celebrant to kiss.

51. In sung Masses, the lessons, Epistle, and Gospel, if they are proclaimed in the vernacular, may be recited without chant.

52. In reciting or chanting the lessons, Epistle, the chants which occur after them, and the Gospel, the order is as follows:

a) In solemn Mass, the celebrant sits and listens to the lessons and Epistle as well as to the intervenient chants. After the Epistle has been chanted or recited, the subdeacon goes to the celebrant and is blessed by him. Then the celebrant, seated, places incense in the thurible and blesses it. While the Alleluia and its verse are being chanted or toward the end of other chants following the Epistle, the celebrant rises to bless the deacon. At his seat he listens to the Gospel, kisses the book of Gospels, and, after the homily, intones the Creed, if the latter is to be said. At the end of the Creed he returns to the altar with the ministers, unless he is to direct the prayer of the faithful.

b) In high or low Masses in which the lessons, Epistle, the chants following them, and the Gospel are sung or recited by the minister mentioned in n. 50, the celebrant acts in the manner described above.

c) In high or low Masses in which the Gospel is chanted or read by the celebrant, while the Alleluia and its verse are being chanted or recited or toward the end of other chants following the Epistle, he goes to the lowest step of the altar and there bows deeply while saying Munda cor meum. Then he goes to the ambo or to the edge of the sanctuary area to chant or recite the Gospel.

d) But if, in a high Mass or low Mass, all the lessons are chanted or recited by the celebrant at the ambo or at the edge of the sanctuary area, then, standing in the same place, he also recites the chants occurring after the lessons and the Epistle, if this is necessary; he says Munda cor meum turned toward the altar.

III. The homily (Const., Art. 52)

53. There shall be a homily on Sundays and feast days of precept in all Masses which are celebrated with the people present. No exception may be made for conventual, sung, or pontifical Masses.

On other days, a homily is recommended, especially on some of the weekdays of Advent and Lent, as well as in other circumstances when the people come to church in larger numbers.

54. By a homily from the sacred text is understood an explanation either of some aspect of the readings from holy Scripture or of another text from the Ordinary or Proper of the Mass of the day, taking into account the mystery which is being celebrated and the particular needs of the hearers.

55. If plans of preaching within Mass are proposed for certain periods, the intimate connection with at least the principal seasons and feasts of the liturgical year (cf. Const., Art. 102-104), that is, with the mystery of the Redemption, is to be harmoniously preserved: for the homily is part of the liturgy of the day.

IV. The common prayer or prayer of the faithful (Const., Art. 53)

56. In places where the custom is already in force of having the common prayer or prayer of the faithful, for the interim it shall take place before the offertory, after the word Oremus, according to the formulas now in use in the individual regions. The celebrant shall direct the prayer either from his seat, from the altar, from the ambo, or from the edge of the sanctuary area.

The intentions or invocations may be chanted by a deacon or a cantor or other qualified server, reserving to the celebrant the words of introduction and the concluding prayer. This latter will ordinarily be: Deus, refugium nostrum et virtus (cf. Missale Romanum, Orationes diversae, n. 20) or another prayer which corresponds better to a particular need.

In places where the common prayer or prayer of the faithful is not in use, the competent territorial authority may decree that it be done in the manner indicated above, with formulas approved for the interim by that authority.

V. The place which may be granted to the vernacular language in the Mass (Const., Art. 54)

57. In Masses, whether sung or low, which are celebrated with the people, the competent territorial ecclesiastical authority may admit the vernacular language, the decrees having been approved, that is, confirmed, by the Apostolic See:

a) especially in proclaiming the lessons, Epistle, and Gospel, as well as in the common prayer or prayer of the faithful;

b) according to the circumstances of the place, also in the chants of the Ordinary of the Mass, namely, Kyrie, Gloria, Creed, Sanctus-Benedictus, and Agnus Dei, and in the antiphons at the Introit, offertory, and communion, as well as in the chants that occur between the lessons.

c) Moreover, in the acclamations, salutations, and dialogue formulas, together with the formulas at the communion of the faithful: Ecce Agnus Dei, Domine, non sum dignus, and Corpus Christi, and in the Lord's Prayer with its introduction and embolism.

Missals for liturgical use, however, should contain the Latin text in addition to the vernacular translation.

58. It pertains solely to the Apostolic See to concede the vernacular language in other parts of the Mass which are chanted or recited by the celebrant alone.

59. Pastors of souls shall carefully see to it that the faithful, more particularly the members of lay religious associations, also know how to say or to sing together in the Latin language those parts of the Ordinary of the Mass which pertains to them, especially with the use of simpler melodies.

VI. *The faculty of repeating Communion on the same day* (Const., Art. 55)

60. The faithful who communicate in the Mass of the Easter Vigil or in the midnight Mass of Christmas may also receive Communion again in the second Mass of Easter and in one of the Masses which is celebrated on Christmas in the daytime.

CHAPTER III

The Other Sacraments and the Sacramentals

I. *The place which may be granted to the vernacular language* (Const., Art. 63)

61. The competent territorial authority may admit the vernacular language, the decrees having been approved, that is, confirmed, by the Apostolic See;

a) in the rites of Baptism, Confirmation, Penance, Anointing of the Sick, and Matrimony, including the essential forms, as well as in the distribution of Holy Communion;

b) in the conferral of orders: in the allocutions at the beginning of each ordination or consecration, as well as in the examination of the bishop-elect in episcopal consecration, and in the instructions;

c) in the sacramentals;

d) in funeral rites.

Wherever a more extended use of the vernacular language appear desirable, the regulation of Art. 40 of the Constitution is to be observed.

II. *Things to be suppressed in the rite for supplying omissions in Baptism* (Const., Art. 69)

62. In the rite for supplying omissions in the case of a baptized infant, which is given in the Roman Ritual, tit. II, cap. 5, those exorcisms shall be omitted which are found under n. 6 (Exi ab eo), 10 (Exorcizo te, immunde spiritus — Ergo maledicte diabole), and 15 (Exorcizo te, omnis spiritus).

63. In the rite for supplying omissions in the case of a baptized adult, which is given in the Roman Ritual, tit. II, cap. 6, those exorcisms shall be omitted which are found under n. 5 (Exi ab eo) 15, (Ergo, maledicte diabole), 17 (Audi maledicte satana), 19 (Exorcizo te, Ergo, maledicte diabole), 21 (Ergo, maledicte diabole), 23 (Ergo, maledicte diabole), 25 (Exorcizo te — Ergo maledicte diabole), 31 (Nec te lateat), and 35 (Exi, immunde spiritus).

III. *Confirmation* (Const., Art. 71)

64. If Confirmation is conferred within Mass, it is fitting that the Mass be celebrated by the bishop himself. In this case he confers Confirmation while vested in the Mass vestments.

The Mass within which Confirmation is conferred may be celebrated as a votive Mass of class II, of the Holy Spirit.

65. After the Gospel and homily, before the reception of Confirmation, it is praiseworthy that those to be confirmed should renew the promises of baptism, according to the rite legitimately in use in the individual regions, unless this has already taken place before Mass.

66. If the Mass is celebrated by another, it is fitting that the bishop assist at the Mass wearing the vestments prescribed for the conferral of Confirmation, which may be either the color of the Mass or white. The bishop himself shall give the homily, and the celebrant shall resume the Mass only after Confirmation.

67. Confirmation is conferred according to the rite prescribed in the Roman Pontifical, but at the words In nomine Patris, et Filii, et Spiritus Sancti which follow the formula Signo Te, a single sign of the cross shall be made.

IV. *Continuous rite for anointing of the sick and viaticum* (Const., Art. 74)

68. When Anointing of the Sick and Viaticum are administered at the same time, unless a continuous rite is already found in a particular ritual, the rite shall be arranged as follows: after the sprinkling with holy water and the prayers of entrance which are given in the rite of anointing, the priest shall hear the confession of the sick person, if necessary, then administer anointing, and finally give Viaticum, omitting the sprinkling with its formulas and the Confiteor and absolution.

If, however, the apostolic blessing with a plenary indulgence at the hour of death is to be imparted on the same occasion, this shall be given immediately before anointing, omitting the sprinkling with its formulas and the Confiteor and absolution.

V. *Imposition of hands in episcopal consecration* (Const., Art. 76)

69. All the bishops present at an episcopal consecration may impose hands; they vest in choir dress. The words Accipe Spiritum Sanctum, however, shall be said

only by the bishop consecrator and by the two co-consecrating bishops.

VI. *Rite of matrimony* (Const., Art. 78)

70. Matrimony, unless a just cause excuses from the celebration of Mass, shall be celebrated within Mass after the Gospel and the homily. The latter is never omitted.

71. Whenever Matrimony is celebrated within Mass, the votive Mass for the spouses shall always be celebrated or a commemoration made of it, according to the rubrics, even during the prohibited season.

72. As far as possible, the pastor or his delegate who assists at the marriage shall celebrate the Mass; but if another priest assists, the celebrant shall not continue the Mass until the rite of Matrimony has been completed.

The priest who assists at the marriage but does not celebrate the Mass shall be vested in surplice and white stole and, according to the local custom, also in cope, and shall give the homily. The blessing after the Lord's Prayer and before the Placeat, however, is always to be imparted by the priest who celebrates the Mass.

73. The nuptial blessing shall always be imparted within the Mass, even in the prohibited season and even if one or both of the spouses is entering a second marriage.

74. In the celebration of Matrimony without Mass:

a) At the beginning of the rite, according to the apostolic letter Sacram Liturgiam, n. V, a brief admonition shall be given. This is not a homily, but only a simple instruction for the celebration of marriage (cf. Const., Art. 35,3). There shall be, however, a sermon or homily drawn from the sacred text (cf. Const., Art. 52), after the reading of the Epistle and Gospel from the Mass for the spouses, so that the order of the whole rite shall be: brief admonition, reading of the Epistle and Gospel in the vernacular language, homily, celebration of marriage, nuptial blessing.

b) For the reading of the Epistle and Gospel from the Mass for the spouses, in the absence of a vernacular text approved by the competent territorial ecclesiastical authority, it is lawful for the interim to use a text approved by the local Ordinary.

c) A chant may be sung between the Epistle and the Gospel. Likewise the prayer of the faithful is highly recommended after the completion of the rite of Matrimony, according to a formula approved by the local Ordinary, in which petitions for the spouses are also to be included.

d) At the end of the rite the blessing shall always be imparted to the spouses, even in the prohibited season and even if one or both of the spouses is entering a second marriage, according to the formula which is found in the Roman Ritual, tit. VIII, cap. III, unless another blessing is given in particular rituals.

75. If marriage is celebrated during the prohibited season, the pastor shall advise the spouses to take into account the special character of this liturgical season.

VI. *Savramentals* (Const., Art. 79)

76. In the blessing of candles on Feb. 2 and in the blessing of ashes at the beginning of Lent, a single prayer from among the prayers which are found in the Roman Missal for these blessings may be said.

77. Blessings which have been reserved up to the present time and which are contained in the Roman Ritual, tit. IX, cap. 9, 10, 11, may be given by any priest, with the exception of the blessing of a bell for the use of a blessed church or oratory (cap.9, n.11), the blessing of the first stone for the building of a church (cap.9, n.16), the blessing of a new church or public oratory (cap.9, n.17), the blessing of an antimension (cap.9, n.21), the blessing of a new cemetery (cap.9, n.22), the papal blessings (cap.10, n.1-3), and the blessing and erection of the stations of the Way of the Cross (cap.11, n.1) inasmuch as this is reserved to the bishop.

CHAPTER IV

The Divine Office

I. *The celebration of the divine office by those bound to the obligation of choir* (Const., Art. 95)

78. Until the restoration of the divine office is completed:

a) Communities of canons, monks, nuns, and other regulars or Religious bound to choir by law or constitutions must celebrate the entire divine office daily in choir, in addition to the conventual Mass.

Individual members of these communities who are in major orders or are solemnly professed, except for the conversi, even if they are lawfully dispensed from choir, must recite individually each day the canonical hours which they do not celebrate in choir.

b) Cathedral and collegiate chapters must celebrate those parts of the office in choir which are imposed upon them by the common law or by particular law, in addition to the conventual Mass.

Individual members of these chapters, in addition to the canonical hours which all clerics in major orders are bound to celebrate (cf. Const., Art. 96 and 89), must recite individually those hours which are celebrated by their chapter.

c) In mission lands, however, while preserving the religious or capitular choral discipline established by law, religious or members of chapters who are lawfully absent from choir by reason of the pastoral ministry may enjoy the concession made in the apostolic letter Sacram Liturgiam, n.VI, with the permission of the local Ordinary, but not of the vicar general or delegate.

II. *Faculty of dispensing from or commuting the divine office* (Const., Art. 97)

79. The faculty conceded to all Ordinaries of dispensing their subjects, in individual cases and for a just cause, from the obligation of the divine office in whole or in part or of commuting it, is also extended to major superiors of non-exempt clerical religious institutes and of societies of clerics who live the common life without vows.

III. *Short offices* (Const., Art. 98)

80. No short office is considered as drawn up after the pattern of the divine office which does not consist of psalms, lessons, hymns, and prayers and which does not take into some account the hours of the day and the respective liturgical seasons.

81. In order to celebrate the public prayer of the Church, for the interim those short offices may be used which have been lawfully approved up to the present time, provided that they have been drawn up according to the requirements enumerated in no. 80.

New short offices, however, must be approved by the Apostolic See in order to be used for the public prayer of the Church.

82. The translation of the text of a short office into the vernacular language for use as the public prayer of the Church must be approved by the competent territorial ecclesiastical authority, the decrees having been approved, that is, confirmed by the Apostolic See.

83. The competent authority for conceding the vernacular in the recitation of a short office to those who are bound to this office by the constitutions, or for dispensing from or commuting the obligation of recitation, is the Ordinary or the major superior of the respective subject.

IV. *Divine office or short offices celebrated in common by members of institutes dedicated to acquiring perfection* (Const., Art. 99)

84. The obligation of celebrating in common the divine office or a short office or parts of either imposed by their constitutions on members of institutes dedicated to acquiring perfection does not take away the faculty of omitting the hour of prime and of selecting from among the other minor hours one that best suits the time of day (cf. apostolic letter Sacram Liturgiam, n. VI).

V. *The language to be used in the recitation of the divine office* (Const., Art. 101)

85. In the celebration of the divine office in choir, clerics are bound to retain the Latin language.

86. The faculty granted to the Ordinary of conceding the use of the vernacular language, in individual cases, to those clerics for whom the use of Latin constitutes a grave impediment to their praying the office properly, is extended also to the major superiors of non-exempt clerical religious institutes and of societies of clerics who live the common life without vows.

87. The grave obstacle which is required for the grant of the preceding concession must be weighed by taking into consideration the physical, moral, intellectual and spiritual condition of the petitioner.

Nevertheless, this faculty, which is granted solely to make the recitation of the divine office easier and more devout, is in no way intended to detract from the obligation incumbent upon priests of the Latin rite to learn the Latin language.

88. The vernacular translation of the divine office according to a rite other than the Roman rite shall be prepared and approved by the respective Ordinaries of that language, employing for elements common to both rites those translations approved by the territorial authority, and then proposed for the confirmation of the Apostolic See.

89. Breviaries to be used by clerics to whom the use of the vernacular language in the celebration of the divine office is conceded in accordance with Art. 101, #1, of the Constitution, should contain the Latin text in addition to the vernacular translation.

CHAPTER V

The Proper Construction of Churches and Altars in Order To Facilitate the Active Participation of the Faithful

I. *The arrangement of churches*

90. In the new construction, repair, or adaptation of churches great care shall be taken that they are suitable for the celebration of divine services according to the true nature of the services and for the active participation of the faithful (cf. Const., Art. 124).

II. *The main altar*

91. It is proper that the main altar be constructed separately from the wall, so that one may go around it with ease and so that celebration may take place facing

the people; it shall occupy a place in the sacred building which is truly central, so that the attention of the whole congregation of the faithful is spontaneously turned to it.

In choosing the materials for the construction or ornamentation of the altar, the prescriptions of law shall be observed.

Moreover, the presbyterium or sanctuary area around the altar shall be of sufficient size that the sacred rites may be conveniently celebrated.

III. *The seat of the celebrant and ministers*

92. The seat for the celebrant and ministers, according to the structure of individual churches, shall be so placed that it may be easily seen by the faithful and that the celebrant may truly appear to preside over the entire community of the faithful.

Nevertheless, if the seat is placed behind the altar, the form of a throne is to be avoided, as this belongs to the bishop alone.

IV. *Minor altars*

93. The minor altars shall be few in number. In fact, to the extent permitted by the structure of the building, it is highly suitable that they be placed in chapels in some way separated from the principal part of the church.

V. *Ornamentation of altars*

94. The cross and candlesticks, which are required on the altar for the individual liturgical services, may also, in accordance with the judgment of the local Ordinary, be placed next to it.

VI. *The reservation of the most holy Eucharist*

95. The most holy Eucharist shall be reserved in a solid and inviolable tabernacle placed in the middle of the main altar or of a minor, but truly outstanding, altar, or, according to lawful customs and in particular cases to be approved by the local Ordinary, also in some other noble and properly adorned part of the church.

It is lawful to celebrate Mass facing the people even if there is a tabernacle, small but suitable, on the altar.

VII. *The ambo*

96. It is fitting that there be an ambo for the proclamation of the sacred readings, so arranged that the ministers can be easily seen and heard by the faithful.

VIII. *The place of the schola and organ*

97. The places for the schola and the organ shall be so arranged that it will be clearly evident that the singers and the organist form a part of the united community of the faithful and so that they may fulfil their liturgical function more suitably.

IX. *The places of the faithful*

98. The places for the faithful shall be arranged with particular care, so that they may participate in the sacred celebration visually and with proper spirit. It is desirable that ordinarily benches or seats be provided for their use. Nevertheless, the custom of reserving seats for certain private persons is to be reprobated, in accordance with Art. 32 of the Constitution.

Care shall also be taken that the faithful may not only see the celebrant and the other ministers but may also hear them easily, with the use of present-day technical means.

X. *Baptistry*

99. In the construction and ornamentation of the baptistry, care shall be taken that the dignity of the sacrament of Baptism is clearly apparent and that the place is suitable for the community celebration of the sacrament (cf. Const., Art. 27).

* * * *

The present Instruction, prepared at the command of Pope Paul VI, by the Commission for the Implementation of the Constitution on the Sacred Liturgy, was presented to His Holiness by James Cardinal Lercaro, president of the Commission.

The Holy Father, after having given due consideration to this Instruction, with the help of the abovementioned Commission and of this Sacred Congregation of Rites, in audience granted to Arcadio Maria Cardinal Larraona, prefect of the Congregation, on Sept. 26, 1964, approved it in a special way as a whole and in its parts, confirmed it by his authority, and ordered it to be published, and to be diligently observed by all concerned, beginning the First Sunday of Lent, March 7, 1965.

All things to the contrary notwithstanding.

Rome, Sept. 26, 1964.

James Cardinal Lercaro
Archbishop of Bologna
President of the Commission for the
  Implementation of the Constitution
  on the Sacred Liturgy.

Arcadio M. Cardinal Larraona
Prefect of S.R.C.

✠ Henry Dante
Titular Archbishop of Carpasia
Secretary of S.R.C.

156

Father McManus Discusses Instruction on Liturgy

The striking new changes in the Mass made by the instruction of the Vatican Liturgy Commission aim at stressing the community nature of Christian worship and taking full advantage of the liturgy's educational or formative possibilities.

The new changes, which go into effect March 7, 1965, the first Sunday of Lent, must be regarded as a preliminary step in the overall liturgical reform decreed last December by the Second Vatican Council.

In the Constitution on the Liturgy the council gave broad mandates for reforms to be worked out in detail by a commission drawn from all over the world. Early this year, Pope Paul VI set up the commission with the major task of revising the official missal, ritual, breviary and so forth. Although complete reform is expected to take several years, the Vatican Liturgy Commission has prepared an interim instruction concerning the Mass and other services. It was made public Oct. 16 by the Congregation of Rites, the Vatican agency which has dealt with liturgical matters since the 16th century.

Unlike the changes of liturgical texts into various languages, which are questions entrusted by the council to the bishops of each country, the new instruction is obligatory throughout the Latin rites of the Church by the expressed direction of Pope Paul.

The instruction has simplified the beginning and the end of Mass. Psalm 42 in the preparatory prayers as said by the priest and the server will be dropped. The Mass will end at the blessing, with the last Gospel and prayers after Mass entirely eliminated.

These omissions will not shorten the Mass very much, nor is this the intention of the change. The time saved is needed for the preaching insisted upon by the council as an integral part of Mass and also for the new "Prayer of the People." The latter brief series of invocations or petitions is to be said or sung at the completion of the Service of God's Word (readings, homily, creed) just after the priest says: "Let us pray." The actual text of the prayer of the faithful, however, has been left to the decision of national conferences of bishops.

One contradiction in the rite of the Mass has been partially corrected. Three of the most solemn and public prayers recited quietly by the priest up to the present will be sung or said aloud for all to hear and to respond to. They are:

1. The prayer over the offerings, called the secret prayer, which completes the preparation of bread and wine.

2. The concluding doxology of canon or Eucharistic prayer.

3. The prayer for deliverance from evil and for peace which is added to the Lord's Prayer.

Of the "public" prayers of the Mass which the whole congregation should read and follow, only the body of the canon, which still awaits revision, will be said quietly.

Broader changes are also indicated. On principle, the celebrating priest will no longer recite privately or quietly any text of a prayer or reading that is said or sung by others, whether by the people, or by the choir in case of chants and hymns, or by the lector in case of readings. This eliminates a curious duplication. In the past the rule prevailed that the priest should recite the Gloria, for example, even though the hymn was sung by the people.

This change, making specific a decision of the council, is not intended to relieve the priest of a small burden. It is intended to make clear the distinction of roles or parts in the liturgy, with each one—priest or minister or layman—taking his own part.

In countries where parts of the Mass are already said in the vernacular or where this change will be introduced soon, the Epistle and Gospel should, of course, be proclaimed or announced facing the people to whom the words are addressed. The new instruction goes further, however, and describes the whole new rite for this "Liturgy of Word of God."

At low Mass, for example, it is preferable that the lector, whether cleric or layman, should read the Epistle while the celebrant listens. The same lector may read the chants which follow the Epistle unless these are sung or recited by others. The Gospel reading is reserved to the deacon, second priest or celebrant himself. Even at low Mass, the celebrant may remain at his seat through these readings, thus emphasizing his office of presiding over the service, and take his place at the altar only for the celebration of the Eucharist itself, beginning at the Offertory.

Various possibilities are provided for readings: at the lectern or the pulpit, at the edge of the sanctuary area, the railing, even at the altar. The alternatives are a step toward breaking down the rigidity and formalism of ceremonial directives or rubrics. Great flexibility is provided, according to the circumstances, so that reading to the people will be well planned beforehand and not conducted routinely according to a rigid pattern.

To help popular participation and to show that the Mass is a sacrificial banquet or meal, the instruction allows and prefers, but does not require, that the altars be arranged, for Mass with the celebrant facing the people. It is made very clear that Mass may be celebrated in this way even if there is a small tabernacle on the altar.

Few directions are given on church building and planning to encourage the congregation to participate with understanding. The widest freedom is given in locating the tabernacle, which has sometimes appeared to be an obstacle to the celebration of Mass toward the people. The tabernacle may be on the main altar or on another altar (ideally in a separate chapel or other such area, according to the instruction). But it may even be, according to local custom, and in particular cases with approval of the bishop, in some other fitting place in the church.

The instruction, which contains 99 sections, deals with many details. Some are technical, such as the procedure when national bodies of bishops enact legislation on the liturgy in virtue of the 1963 constitution. The responsibilities of liturgical commissions, national and diocesan, are also spelled out at length.

Most details have pastoral value and importance: the possibility of a sung Mass with a deacon but without a subdeacon; the elimination of restrictions formerly placed upon priests in giving certain blessings; reprobation of any distinction among persons, for example, church seating arrangements in church on a basis of social or economic condition.

One welcome concession allows the faithful who receive Holy Communion at the Easter Vigil Mass or at Christmas Midnight Mass to receive Communion again at Mass on Easter Sunday morning and Christmas Day.

The instruction devotes much space to seminary training and especially to the long overdue integration of the whole spiritual life of clerical students with the liturgy. The popular Bible services are encouraged in parishes, but with their pattern left flexible. Details of Confirmation and marriage rites within the Mass itself are worked out.

Since the homily is part of the Mass and not a catechetical instruction or occasional sermon, a general statement of the council has made specific: where plans for Mass sermons are set up, they must be in harmony with the mystery of the Redemption.

In some matters the instruction is more restrictive than the council's Constitution on the Liturgy. The altar missals and breviaries used by the clergy should contain Latin as well as the vernacular texts, even when the latter are allowed. Ordination rites must remain in Latin except for introductory sections. In general, however, the openness of the council has been preserved even in a document which necessarily deals in directives and norms.

The spirit of liturgical renewal shines through in the significant opening paragraphs of the instruction. The whole import of the reform does not lie in the novelty but in pastoral action to express the "paschal mystery" better. This mystery of the Death, Resurrection and Ascension of Jesus is celebrated in the Church "through the sacraments of faith, that is, chiefly through Baptism and the . . . Eucharist." And around the celebration of the Holy Eucharist "are ranged the other sacraments and sacramentals by which the paschal mystery of Christ is unfolded in the course of each Church year."

Some will be disappointed that this or that change has not been achieved at once. But the instruction points out repeatedly its provisional character and the necessity for gradualism mentioned in the case of liturgical education and instruction, formation and participation. This task, according to the instruction, is the responsibility of all pastors of souls, "in the words of Vatican Council II."

FATHER FREDERICK R. McMANUS

Father McManus is a priest of the Boston archdiocese who is president of the National Liturgical Conference, professor of canon law at the Catholic University of America, an official consultor for the ecumenical council and a member of the U.S. bishops' press panel in Rome.

Highlight of the opening of the third session of Vatican Council II Sept. 14, 1964, was a Mass concelebrated by Pope Paul VI with 24 Council Fathers from nations round the world. Archbishop John J. Krol of Philadelphia and Archbishop Lawrence J. Shehan of Baltimore are seen in the lower lefthand corner, facing the Pope.

104th General Congregation

October 19, 1964

The council Fathers gave overwhelming approval at their 104th meeting to chapter seven of the schema on the nature of the Church which concerns the Christian vocation to the happiness of heaven.

They also voted to send the proposition on the priesthood back to commission for revision.

In continuing debate on the Eastern churches, several Fathers reacted to strong criticism at the previous meeting of the schema's treatment of patriarchs. In the name of the Patriarchal Conference of the Chaldean Rite, Bishop Raphael Bidawid of Amadiya, Iraq, said that the present document is "entirely satisfactory, combining pastoral solicitude with an ecumenical spirit." He said the section on patriarchs is especially gratifying since it sets forth their dignity "as truth, justice and ecumenism demand."

Armenian-rite Bishop Raphael Bayan of Alexandria, Egypt, called the patriarchates an anachronism and asked that they be eliminated, though with the provision that their synods and system of government be honored.

Regarding the document's provision that converts from the Orthodox churches must join the corresponding rite of the Catholic Church, Auxiliary Bishop Gerald V. McDevitt of Philadelphia called this an "undue restriction of freedom, contrary to the whole spirit of the council in its expressions of concern for religious freedom and the care of souls." He said the provision for recourse to the Holy See to change the rite is not a sufficient safeguard of liberty and would be looked upon as surprising and cruel—"as if the grace of God could await such recourse."

According to a new procedure adopted the previous week, the Fathers are now able to decide by lot whether to vote for a proposition immediately after it is discussed on the council floor or to send it back first to the appropriate commission for revision. The latter was the decision reached regarding the proposition on the priesthood. The vote was 1,199 to 930. Archbishop Pericle Felici, council secretary general, announced the Fathers would have three more days to send in further written observations on the text to guide the commission on its revision.

The four articles included in chapter seven of the schema on the nature of the Church all received virtually unanimous approval.

The vote on the first article—giving a description of the Church with emphasis on its completion in heaven —was 2,099 to 20.

The article showing the relation of the Church triumphant to the Church on earth received 2,121 favorable votes.

The one describing the relation of the Church on earth to that in heaven got 2,104 favorable votes.

The favorable vote on the article giving pastoral directives, including proper perspectives in the veneration of saints, was 2,067.

The last three articles each received only 8 negative votes.

During the council meeting, a report on the proposition dealing with Catholic schools was distributed. But discussion on this was not scheduled until after debate on schema 13 on the Church in the Modern World.

Bishop Bayan said in his talk that it is important to distinguish between the dignity and honor of patriarchs and that of the patriarchal synods. He asked that care be taken not to exaggerate the personal power of patriarchs and said that their restoration, on the evidence of history, "would undoubtedly lead to greater abuses than those it is intended to remedy."

He agreed with the proposition's provision that converts to Catholicism retain the rite corresponding to the Orthodox rite they leave.

Bishop McDevitt, on the other hand, saw great danger in this provision. He admitted that recourse to the Holy See to change the rite is quite proper for those who are already Catholics, since it avoids bickering and tends to safeguard the preservation of these rites. But in the case of non-Catholics it is basically different, he said. "They stand at the door knocking. Why should the council put obstacles in their path? Why should there be a change in the new canon law promulgated for the Eastern rites as late as 1958?"

The code for the Eastern rites provides that converts are free to choose whichever rite they wish when entering the Church.

Referring to the fact that he spent a decade working in the Apostolic Delegation in Washington, Bishop McDevitt said he is aware that recourse to the Holy See in such matters takes a long time—often from six months to a year.

"Why make the grace of the Spirit wait while recourse is being acted on?" he said.

He referred to a private communication circulated among the council Fathers suggesting that there be a provision that a prospective convert's rite is to be maintained unless he makes a change of rite a condition of his conversion, in which case no recourse would be needed. Such a suggestion is dangerous, he said, since the condition would impose a burden on the conscience of the convert. He said he wondered if an individual could propose such a condition without sinful bad faith.

He also said he wanted a choice of rite to be available to converts from Protestantism as well as Orthodoxy.

The meeting began with Mass celebrated by Archbishop Joseph Descuffi of Izmir, Turkey. Bishop Peter Saburo Hirata of Oita, Japan, enthroned the Gospel. Giacomo Cardinal Lercaro of Bologna, Italy, continued as moderator of the debate on the Eastern churches.

Francis Cardinal Spellman of New York was present in the council hall for the first time this session. He had arrived in Rome the previous weekend after an extended recuperation from a recent operation.

Rufino Cardinal Santos of Manila presented the report on the amended text of chapter seven of the Schema on the Church before the council voted on its four articles. He pointed out that 17 Fathers had spoken on the subject and another 28 had presented their views in writing to the commission. All but one agreed that this new chapter belongs in a constitution on the Church, he said, which otherwise would be "mutilated and defective."

He said the amendments added by the commission include greater stress on the function of the Holy Spirit and more ample treatment of the four last things—death, judgment, heaven and hell—with an introduction of statements on purgatory and hell at the suggestion of several council Fathers. Another amendment calls for Catholics to contribute to the progress of the world and the effective restoration of all things in Christ, even before the final glory of heaven.

Leading off the discussion on the Eastern churches, Cardinal Lercaro said this is a question which touches the life of the universal Church. Many of the points in the text, although good and practical in themselves, are not points for universal legislation, he said. There is no need for a council decree in such matters because Eastern-rite Catholics have their own Ordinaries and synods, he added. The council should do nothing which might interfere with their own proper legislative power, he said.

Melkite-rite Archbishop Joseph Tawil, patriarchal vicar for Damascus, Syria, said he felt that the text should be revised to bring it into closer harmony with the schema on ecumenism.

The Latin Church was governed under the patriarchal system for more than 1,000 years, he observed, and like the Eastern-rite bodies, it too is quite a particular church.

He objected to the presence of a Latin patriarch in Jerusalem. In the eyes of Eastern-rite Catholics, he said, "it is the last word in the Latinization of the East, and in this patriarchate, this Latinization seems to have been embodied in an institution." He asked the council to take precise steps to remedy this situation, and called for a post-conciliar commission to work out the details.

In the opinion of Archbishop Alexandre Scandar of Assiut, Egypt, the text forgets one of the chief purposes of the Eastern rites—to promote union with the Orthodox. He asked that seminaries emphasize the study of Eastern-rite matters, enriching their theology and spirituality from Eastern sources. He also asked that the council order reform in the Eastern-rite sacramental discipline. He said he thought the degree of participation in Orthodox services permitted in the text constitutes a definite danger of indifferentism and a threat to faith and unity.

The president of the Bavarian Congregation of the Benedictine Order, Abbot Johannes Hoeck, strongly supported the patriarchal system as of cardinal importance to the Eastern church and to ecumenism. In any discussion of unity, he said, the great Orthodox churches of the East will want to know what would be their position within the Catholic Church. "Will they be subordinated to the Roman curia, especially the Congregation for the Oriental Church, and will they be given a secondary role alongside the college of cardinals?"

He said it was a historical fact that for 1,000 years the churches of the East enjoyed full freedom to choose patriarchs and bishops, and to organize their liturgy and law. The right of intervention by Rome was always recognized but verified only in rare cases. "If this system worked well for 1,000 years, why would not it be feasible today? Any attempt to restore unity with the Orthodox churches must start from the premise that this unity will be on the same principles which existed before the break. It is not a question of recognizing favors or privileges, but of the fundamental structure of the entire Church."

Bishop Vittorio Costantini of Sessa Aurunca, Italy, urged the Eastern-rite Catholics to make a greater organized effort at educating the world in the riches of their religious and historical patrimony. He called for an institute for the joint study and propagation of Eastern theology to be established in Jerusalem "as a lasting memorial to the kiss of peace exchanged between East and West, between Paul VI and Athenagoras I."

Retired Archbishop Antonio Vuccino of Corfu, Greece, called the text "basically a disappointment." He said the initial statement that the Church has always shown great esteem for the Eastern churches is in open conflict with many historical facts. He also asserted that it is a grave mistake to refer to the Orthodox churches as "separated brethren."

Bishop Stephen J. Kocisko of the Byzantine-rite diocese of Passaic, N.J., said he thought the text should emphasize inter-ritual esteem and cooperation. He suggested that seminarians and laymen be trained in rites and practical norms for the field of inter-ritual contacts.

This, he said, would encourage mutual esteem and lasting charity, and would facilitate contacts with separated Christians.

Melkite-rite Archbishop Neophytos Edelby, counselor of the Antioch patriarchate, called for the establishment of an Eastern hierarchy wherever the good of souls demands it, as a vital means of safeguarding the patrimony and traditions of the Eastern churches.

FATHER JOHN P. DONNELLY

105th General Congregation

October 20, 1964

In an attempt to understand the modern world and to interpret the Church's message to that world, the council Fathers began discussion of one of the most talked-about and long-awaited schemas on its agenda.

Eight cardinals took the floor and all but one expressed general satisfaction with the text of schema 13 on the Church in the modern world. They asked the council to accept it as a basis for discussion.

Francis Cardinal Spellman of New York hailed it as "representing the basic hopes of the Second Vatican Council" and asked that in recommending changes, council Fathers take care not to weaken but rather to strengthen the text and improve its clarity.

Both Julius Cardinal Doepfner of Munich, Germany, and Giacomo Cardinal Lercaro of Bologna, Italy, cautioned against speed in deliberations. The latter observed that "perhaps there is not even time enough left in this session—especially if there is going to be a fourth session next year."

Saying he was unhappy with the impression given by the text that the Church "fears contagion from associating with the world," Albert Cardinal Meyer of Chicago called for a deeper understanding of the role of the world in the plan of salvation. He cited Scripture and tradition to support his contention that the world itself, and not only the soul of man, is the proper object of Redemption.

By a vote of 1,921 to 29, the council approved the whole of chapter seven of the schema on the nature of the Church. Various parts of the chapter had been approved separately on the previous day. The chapter concerns the four last things—death, judgment, heaven and hell—and affirms the final vocation of everyone to paradise. There were 233 votes of qualified approval.

After three speakers completed debate on the proposition on the Eastern churches, the council decided by a vote of 1,911 to take a final vote on it the following day (Oct. 21) rather than to send it back to commission for revision. Opposing this were 265 Fathers.

In the name of the mixed commission of members of the council's Theological Commission and the Commission on the Apostolate of the Laity, of which he is president, Fernando Cardinal Cento introduced schema 13. He said it was offered with a great deal of "trepida-

tion" and a consciousness of the extreme gravity of the task at hand. This task, he said, is to make the Church stand out as the "light of nations," according to the words of Pope John XXIII.

The Church is conscious that it is not growing old, but ever younger, he said, because of the presence in its midst of its Divine Founder.

"The Church must find answers in Christ for a world living in constant fear of an apocalyptic conflagration," he said. It must try to understand man and his problems, but it must also seek the supernatural order. It must frame a message which can be sent not only to believers, but to atheists as well.

He explained that the text was drafted by the mixed commission through a special subcommission headed by Bishop Emilio Guano of Leghorn, Italy, with Father Bernard Haering, C.SS.R., as its secretary. Father Haering is professor of moral theology at the Redemptorist Fathers' Rome institute of higher studies.

Bishop Guano then gave a report on schema 13. He said the Church stands between Christ and human society, never as an end unto itself, but with a concern and desire to belong to Christ, to act for and with Him, and to belong to men and to act for and with them.

Men are concerned about earning their daily bread, about peace in the world and about human dignity, he said. Some are hostile and others indifferent to the message of Christ, he noted. But, he added, the Church has something for all men and it must remember that it can never remain closed up in a fortress protecting only its own members. It must speak with all and try to answer their questions, he said, and added that the council is the symbol of this dialogue.

Bishop Guano said the aim of schema 13 is different from that of all the other schemas. It does not concern doctrine or theoretical principles, he stated, so much as the transition of the council to the treatment of the problems that concern man today. It is an attempt to promote a dialogue in which man can know more about the Church and at the same time the Church can gain a deeper understanding of man and his problems. It is difficult to find the proper equilibrium between the principles of the Gospel and the practical lives of men, but this is the job now set before the council, he said.

All men feel the need of some absolute, he said, and the Church must live up to the task of providing what answers it can. The Church loves the world just as God did giving His only Son for its Redemption, he continued. But the Church also recognizes the presence of original sin in the world and it condemns sin and intends to liberate the world from sin, Bishop Guano concluded.

In his talk, Cardinal Spellman emphasized the obedience of Church members to the authority of the hierarchy and asked that this obedience be not merely a legal compliance with commands, but rather a Christian obedience which remains consonant with freedom.

He said the text is good, clear and sincere and that it rightly calls for Catholics to act on their own responsibility when there are no specific directives to follow. But, he said, the essential condition for a dialogue with the modern world is fidelity and obedience to the Church.

Calling for a "compenetration" between the world and the Church, Cardinal Meyer cited proofs from Scripture and tradition that the world itself, and not only man, is the proper object of Redemption. Quoting St. Paul's statement that "all things are created through Him and unto Him," Cardinal Meyer observed that work here on earth pertains not only to the temporal order but to the everlasting as well. By his labors, man "prepares the way for the final transformation of all things into a new heaven and a new earth," he said. At the end of his talk he was greeted with enthusiastic applause.

The opening Mass of the 105th general council meeting was celebrated by Archbishop Karol Wojtyla of Cracow, Poland. The day's feast was that of one of Poland's patrons, St. John Cantius of Cracow. The Gospel was enthroned by Bishop Michael Arattukulam of Alleppey, India. The moderator was Cardinal Doepfner.

The council's secretary general, Archbishop Pericle Felici, announced that after some debate on the general principles of schema 13, a vote would be taken to determine whether the Fathers were ready to open discussion of the individual points. Contrary to previous procedure, he said, this vote would be secret. If favorable, discussion would proceed in three parts: on the introduction and first chapter, on chapters two and three together, and then on chapter four which, since it contains much detailed material, would be discussed one topic at a time. These topics include the dignity of the human person, marriage and the family, the right promotion of culture, economic and social life, human solidarity and peace.

The first speaker on schema 13 was Achille Cardinal Lienart of Lille, France. He said he welcomed the schema as an important one as well as one unique in the history of ecumenical councils. He said the text is ac-

ceptable in substance but not in its present form, which in many cases is illogical.

Observing that the text is an exhortation to Christians to aid the world, he said it should not be addressed only to Christians. He added: "The world carries on its life and activity in the natural order which, with the supernatural order, is the work of God. We must make it clear that elevating man to the dignity of a son of God makes him more of a man." He suggested that the Church declare clearly its esteem for the natural order.

The lone dissenter to the general acceptability of the text was Ernesto Cardinal Ruffini of Palermo, Italy, who called it obscure in many ways, filled with flaws and weakened by repetition. One of the obscurities, he said, was its stress on the humanitarian mission of the Church almost to the exclusion of its main mission to procure eternal salvation. He said he also saw an exaggeration in dealing with ecumenism. He asked for a complete revision of the text based on the encyclicals of modern popes, beginning with Leo XIII.

Cardinal Lercaro cautioned the Fathers not to fear difficulties in the present discussion, adding that the council has committed itself to schema 13 and must keep its word.

"We must expect contradictory viewpoints and we must face them," the cardinal said.

He urged the Fathers not to send the text back to the commission, because then the commission would not have the benefit of their opinions to guide it. He said a thoroughgoing discussion is essential, especially since the text admittedly has not achieved the proper balance on many delicate points. One of its chief weaknesses, he said, is its European and Western outlook, which must be corrected during the discussion.

He cautioned against haste so that the council can obviate the danger of fastening on concrete situations which may soon be obsolete.

Again there was applause in the council hall.

Paul Cardinal Leger of Montreal asked the council to avoid all "sterile condemnations" and work positively, showing how the construction of the world is a task to which Christians can make a very special contribution. He asked that the council use the experience of recognized experts in the specialized fields covered by the text, mentioning specifically the problem of world hunger.

Cardinal Doepfner called for a clearer concept of "the world" and the "service" to be given by the Church to the world. He asked for more attention to the problem of atheism and men not yet reached by Revelation, lest "as we direct our text to the entire world, we still seem to be talking only to ourselves."

He said he wanted Scripture scholars to examine the text's use of Biblical references to make sure they correspond with the demands of modern exegesis, and asked that all the text's arguments be put on a stronger Scriptural basis.

The day's last speaker was Raul Cardinal Silva Henriquez of Santiago, Chile, who listed four reasons why schema 13 was important:

1. Because of the mission of the Church.

2. Because of the secular character of the laity whose orientation would be incomplete without a discussion of their temporal mission in the world.

3. Because we must demonstrate the effectiveness of the Church's doctrine, since the Church is accused of being interested only in heaven. We need a "Christian cosmology." We are denying no temporal values.

4. Because of the necessity of dialogue with present-day humanism, often atheistic. We must try to understand atheism and get to the roots of its error.

Preceding the introduction of schema 13, three final speakers ended the discussion on the proposition on the Eastern churches—Archbishops Maurice Baudoux of St. Boniface, Man., and Dominic Athaide of Agra, India, and Melkite-rite Bishop Georges Hakim of Acre, Israel.

Bishop Hakim asked for an affirmative vote on the proposition. Although he admitted the text was not perfect, he added, "only God is perfect." He also asked that an extension of faculties for concelebration between the different Catholic rites be granted to local authorities, not only for pilgrimage centers, but also on the occasion of national and international gatherings.

Archbishop Baudoux called for ecclesiastical discipline to insure that the Catholics do not change their own rites. He said he felt this would provide a safeguard against social pressure to change.

He said any diminution or belittling of the patriarchal system would be an "injury to the Church and will constitute a real obstacle to effective dialogue."

Archbishop Athaide asked that to avoid "jurisdictional pluralism," the text should provide that in every territory there be only one diocesan bishop responsible for the welfare of all souls in his territory. This obligation could be fulfilled either through special parishes or through the appointment of vicars with appropriate faculties. Only if this fails should special hierarchies be set up for various rites, he said.

He said he felt that Eastern-rite patriarchs should be shown no less honor than that given to cardinals.

The final summary on the Eastern churches was given by Archbishop Gabriel Bukatko of Belgrade, Yugoslavia, who had given the introductory report. He observed that the text could still be perfected, but that this would be possible only if the council first approved it in a vote the following day.

The council press bulletin reported the statements of Cardinals Spellman and Meyer as follows:

Cardinal Spellman said that the schema is good, clear and sincere.

The commission has done an admirable piece of work. Any modifications of the text should be careful not to weaken it. Our only altering of the text will be to increase its clarity. The council's aim in this schema is to listen and to be listened to as we try to help the entire human race. All the faithful are rightly called to the full dignity of sons of God and to open dialogue with all men.

Frequently when ecclesiastical directives are wanting, the faithful must act on their own responsibility. The essential condition of all fruitful dialogue is fidelity to the Church and to its authority. There is danger of an obedience which will be only juridical. This text gives hope for a new impulse to dialogue and will serve to increase the vigor and sanctity of the Mystical Body of Christ. It should serve to direct all our thoughts and our hopes.

Cardinal Meyer of Chicago said that:

We must make men realize that their daily work is an essential part of the plan of salvation.

The text seems to fear contagion from the world. Nevertheless, the material world is part of the whole plan of redemption.

We must teach how the perfection of the natural order helps the perfection of man in the supernatural order. St. Paul teaches this eloquently when he speaks of the hope of the world and the redemption of the body. Both body and soul are to be freed from the slavery of sin. Material work is to be transformed into the new heaven and new earth of which St. John speaks. All things must contribute to the restoration of the world in Christ.

FATHER JOHN P. DONNELLY

*   *   *   *

Introduction of the famous schema 13 on the Church in the modern world almost automatically insures the fact that a fourth session of the ecumenical council will have to be held.

"Debate on this schema gives every reason to think that it will occupy many weeks of the council and it may occupy the whole rest of this session. I hope it does," declared Bishop John J. Wright of Pittsburgh, one of the members of the mixed commission which drew up the document, introduced at the 105th session of the council.

In brief, the schema consists of an introduction and four chapters. Chapter one deals with the vocation of the whole man as a Christian living in the world.

Chapter two treats of the Church in the service of God and men—what the Church can give to men and what the Church receives of men.

The third chapter deals with the Christian mode of life in the contemporary world, and the last chapter deals with the principal tasks of the Christian today.

This in substance forms the document which the

council Fathers will debate. Added to this, however, are five long appendices which cover a multitude of various practical and specific problems. These appendices will not be debated on the floor of the council, but the council Fathers have been asked to submit any comments they want to make on them in writing to the mixed commission.

At present, Bishop Wright said at the press panel of the American bishops, the appendices have no conciliar character, but are intended as an aid or means of helping debate on the draft.

Father Roberto Tucci, S.J., editor of Civilta Cattolica, Rome Jesuit review, explained how the document and appendices reached the form they are now in. After the first preparatory work had been done, a draft document of six chapters was produced. Leo Cardinal Suenens of Malines-Brussels, Belgium, then suggested it be reworked because it was unwieldly. This reworking is known among the mixed commission experts as the "Louvain text" since it was prepared by theologians of Louvain University in Belgium.

The product of this effort was the second text. This text was basically the first chapter of the original text presented in three chapters, which are the same as the first three chapters now before the council. The remaining five chapters were made appendices and stand as such in the latest draft.

The mixed commission was not satisfied with the so-called Louvain text, mainly because it felt that by putting all practical considerations in the appendices the text became too abstract and up in the air, Father Tucci said.

So a subcommission was appointed to rework the text for a third time. The result is the present schema, consisting of the essentials of the three chapters of the second draft and a new fourth chapter which seeks to synthesize the contents of the five appendices.

Bishop Wright explained that because the mixed commission never had time to study and officially approve the appendices, it could not present the appendices as conciliar documents. He estimated it would take a year to review and study sufficiently all the material contained in the appendices. The commission intends to do this in the coming months and may at a later date announce to the council Fathers their approval of the material.

Msgr. George G. Higgins, director of the Social Action Department of the National Catholic Welfare Conference, suggested that it would probably be a mistake for the appendices to be made acts of the council since they contain much material that may be altered by circumstances at some future time. Many Fathers would have serious misgivings if such material were made full conciliar acts, he said.

Regarding the over-all view, Bishop Wright summed it up by saying:

"What we have here in this text is at best and most —although I'm happy that we have this much—the basis of a document which we hope will be long and warmly discussed. It would be a disappointment for us of the mixed commission if it were only discussed briefly. The document is offered for a long, detailed and fierce discussion that will hammer out a final draft of great importance and significance." JAMES C. O'NEILL

106th General Congregation

October 21, 1964

Should the Church speak to the world more from its treasury of Divine Revelation or should it depend more on rational arguments in helping the world to understand itself?

This was the central point of debate at the council's 106th general meeting. Eleven Fathers asked the council to accept schema 13 on the Church in the modern world as a basis for discussion. Only one speaker asked for its rejection.

Augustin Cardinal Bea, president of the Secretariat for Promoting Christian Unity, said he wanted a more Scriptural foundation for the schema, observing that the text is addressed primarily to believers. He called for a declaration of the universal dominion of Christ over all created things and an expression of man's twofold life, natural and supernatural.

Following the lead given by Albert Cardinal Meyer of Chicago in his address the previous day, Maronite-rite Patriarch Paul Pierre Meouchi of Antioch said he wanted a clearer theological foundation for the text based on the notion that the world itself is the proper object of salvation.

Archbishop Karol Wojtyla of Cracow, Poland, on the other hand, said he felt that the draft stated sufficiently the Church's treasury from Scripture and tradition. He asked rather that it speak not only from authority, but give clear and intelligent arguments from natural law and reason, leading the world to discover its own answers.

The council voted on five of the seven sections of the already debated proposition on the Eastern Churches, accepting all of it but the section concerning the choice of Catholic rites for converts from Orthodoxy. The present text would have insisted that they keep the same rite on entering the Church. A majority of speakers had pleaded for freedom in the choice of rite. Because it failed to receive a two-thirds vote of approval, this section will be returned to commission for reworking and revoting at a later date.

Coadjutor Bishop Leon Elchinger of Strasbourg, France, also wanted a more theological footing for the text. The Church should state clearly, he said, that its mission first of all consists of the obligation of preserving what is essentially human in life. "You cannot implant

the Gospel in men who have been reduced almost to the state of inhuman machines," he said. Rather than being subjected to undue organization, men should be given the right to act in a spontaneous and creative way, he stated.

It is strange, said Archbishop William Conway of Armagh, Northern Ireland, that nothing is said about the serious root of so many evils today, such as the vast commercialization of sex. Such corruption of morals, particularly of the young, would have been a capital offense in the ancient world, he stated. In the modern world it is a most profitable business, he said.

Another omission that he said he found surprising was the lack of mention of suffering Christians who are denied their freedom because of their religion. No doubt mention of the Church of Silence has been omitted to avoid impeding the dialogue with the persecutors, he said, "but the first condition of dialogue is sincerity and honesty." Any other approach is "excessively timid," he declared.

In enumerating the signs of the times, Archbishop Casimiro Morcillo Gonzalez of Madrid observed that the text is incomplete since it omits any mention of the right of migration, modern overemphasis on sex, atheism and the problems of want and hunger. Because of these omissions, he said, the Church is far from really understanding the signs of the times and hence far from speaking to the world of today.

The meeting began with concelebration of a Rumanian-rite Liturgy (Mass) by Bishop Basilio Cristea, visitor delegate of the Congregation for the Oriental Church for Rumanians in exile, and five exiled Rumanian priests. It was announced that these priests represented the five dioceses of the Rumanian-rite Church at the time of its suppression in 1948, as well as the memory of the five bishops of these dioceses who died in prison. The Gospel was enthroned by Byzantine-rite Bishop Stephen J. Kocisko of Passaic, N.J. The day's moderator was Julius Cardinal Doepfner of Munich, Germany.

During the meeting a report on the proposition on the Church's missionary activity was distributed and it was announced this would be next on the agenda.

Voting on various parts of the proposition on the Eastern Churches was as follows:

The introduction, setting forth the value and importance of the rights and traditions of the Eastern Churches, was approved by 1,790 to 119. There were 265 votes cast favorably but with reservations.

The vote on articles two to four, dealing with particular Churches of the East and including the choice of rite by converts, was 1,373 for to 73 against, with 719 favorable with reservations. Since this part failed to receive a two-thirds majority of yes votes, it returns to the commission for revision and the incorporation of suggestions made by those voting with reservations.

Articles five and six, on the preservation of the spiritual patrimony of the Eastern Churches, were approved 2,005 to 31 with 136 favorable with reservations.

Articles seven to eleven, on Eastern-rite patriarchs, were passed 1,790 to 183, with 186 favorable with reservations.

Articles 12 to 18, on the discipline of the sacraments, were approved 1,920 to 103, with 118 favorable with reservations.

Two votes remained to be taken on the proposition's sections—one on divine worship and the other on contacts with the separated Christians.

The day's first speaker, Juan Cardinal Landazuri Ricketts of Lima, Peru, said the Church can no longer flee from the world but must be of service to it. The world has opened a dialogue with the Church on the things troubling it, and the Church must try to answer its questions.

This dialogue is delicate, he said, because it involves the application of eternal principles to temporal circumstances. With the speakers of the previous day he called for a clear definition of the "Church" and the "world" and a clearer explanation of the spiritual-temporal tensions so characteristic of man today.

Though the Church cannot multiply the loaves and fishes like Christ, it should have a greater concern for the problem of hunger, he said, pointing out that of the 50 million who die each year, 35 million die from malnutrition and starvation.

Leo Cardinal Suenens of Malines-Brussels said it would be a mistake to hide the Church's mission of evangelization under a bushel while waiting for a complete humanization of the world. Paraphrasing Pope Pius XI, he said the Church civilizes by evangelization, but does not evangelize by civilizing.

The open profession of atheism today cannot be ignored, he said, nor can it be simply condemned. The Church must show atheists who the God is whom they attack. Perhaps we will find, he said, that the God they reject is not the real God but only a caricature.

He called for the introduction into the schema's text of some of the material contained in its supplements, particularly the material on collaboration in international organizations, on marriage and on family life.

The Church is not like a doctor diagnosing illness from the outside, Bishop Alphonse Mathias of Chikmagalur, India, observed. It is rather a part of the world it is examining.

He said he wanted the wording of the text to be simpler and more practical, expressing the unity, fraternity and equality of man.

He asked for greater emphasis on the role of Divine Providence in the world as a bulwark against materialism and the denial of Providence, and called for a defense of the principles of natural ethics in both private and public life.

Bishop Giuseppe Vairo of Gravina and Irsina, Italy, said he thought the treatment of evolution, original sin and the primary end of marriage is "not entirely satisfactory." He said the schema has no clearcut statement on the position of the Church in the face of modern philosophies. The text should present a "Catholic synthesis" which will harmonize temporal and eternal values, he added.

Being a good shepherd is much more important than being a good administrator, said Archbishop Elie Zoghbi, Melkite-rite patriarchal vicar for Egypt. He said he wanted churchmen characterized as mediators between the world and the poor. "Bishops can no longer live as princes of the Church, withdrawn from everyone in their palaces in order to save face. The more we have to associate with the world and rich, the more we must be with the poor," he declared.

Ukrainian-rite Archbishop Maxim Hermaniuk of Winnipeg, Man., noted that he saw in the text an "unfortunate" introduction of a dualism between man's natural and supernatural vocation. It should be demonstrated clearly, he said, that the latter demands the perfection of the former.

Patriarch Meouchi accepted the text as a basis for discussion but said it needs "sweeping reorganization." There are numerous repetitions, ambiguities, lack of logic and inconsistencies in the use of terms, he stated. The mission of the Church is so closely linked with the solution of the world's problems that the impression is given that the Church would not exist if there were not works of charity to be performed or social and economic problems to be solved, he continued. He said he wanted a statement inserted on the sanctification of the world through men's work, and another on the evolution of the world into the kingdom of God.

"In a word, the text is individualistic, whereas the Church is essentially collective," he declared.

He called the text "immature" and said it must evolve the theology of the Incarnation and the theology of history. It must bring God closer to His creatures than they are to themselves, he said.

Archbishop Wojtyla spoke in the name of all the bishops of Poland. He said it must be borne in mind, in any document intended for men the world over, that part of that world welcomes the Church's presence and another part would prefer its absence.

While speaking to those outside the Church, he said, the text uses the mentality and language of the Church. The schema should be directed to all men, both Catholic and non-Catholic, and must consider the problem of the language to be used for both, he said. He added that the text is also defective because it fails to provide a close reasoning on moral issues and then attempts to bridge this gap with exhortations and moralizations. This, he said, is no way to carry on a dialogue.

Hitting what he called the "economic and biological idolatry" affecting many Christians today, Bishop Elchinger said the Church's mission is to fight against idolatry. It must point out the ambiguity of modern

progress, taking the values of the world as they are and putting them in a supernatural light, he declared.

"We can be witnesses to life only if we are genuine lovers of life. These problems must be treated not with the reasonings of a professor, but with the inspiration of a prophet," he said.

Archbishop Morcillo was the only speaker to reject the draft as a basis for discussion. He said it was completely unacceptable and wondered how it was ever hoped that it would reach those for whom it was intended. Its great weakness, he said, is that it uses the same language throughout, whether speaking to believers or nonbelievers. To Christians the Church speaks as a mother and teacher, he said, and to non-Christians it speaks as a religious group drawing on 20 centuries of experience and on the natural law for its authority. The Church cannot be properly understood if it speaks in the same way to both, he stated.

FATHER JOHN P. DONNELLY

Discusses Draft on Lay Apostolate

The draft on the lay apostolate which underwent five days of sharp debate has gone back to the Second Vatican Council's commission on the lay apostolate for complete revision.

The 64 speeches by council Fathers left not a single section of the draft untouched by criticism, some of it slashing.

Despite the great number of suggestions, the total rewriting indicated by the debate will be a difficult task for the commission. This stems in part from the fact that the work must be done by the same people who prepared the three major drafts on the lay apostolate to date. There is the added difficulty that much of the body of its original material has been eviscerated and given to other commissions.

Most notable of these was the original schema's section on the layman in the temporal order. This section was taken over entirely by the commission for schema 13 on the Church in the modern world.

The Commission on the Lay Apostolate is already at work, reassessing the wreckage left after five days of almost continuous attack. Five subcommissions are assessing the speeches on the council floor to determine how to meet the criticisms and make use of the many constructive suggestions.

No doubt they will succeed, but probably not in this session. Given a fourth session and therefore more time for reflection, and probably wider lay consultation, the final document has an excellent chance of meeting the Fathers' approval and, equally important, an enthusiastic acceptance by the laity themselves.

One of the knottiest problems to be solved relates to the organized form of the lay apostolate called "Catholic Action." Catholic Action is one of the earliest terms used to describe an organized form that closely collaborates in the hierarchical apostolate and has a strict dependence on the hierarchy. It is enshrined especially in Italy and some Spanish-speaking countries.

Many speakers criticized the schema as giving Catholic Action a preferential position. "Favoritism" was the word used by Joseph Cardinal Ritter of St. Louis. This group maintained that the lay apostolate has developed beyond the original limited "defense of the Church" concept of Catholic Action. Not only that, but Catholic Action has unfortunately taken on strong political overtones in some countries. If the name Catholic Action is to be used at all, they argued, it should be employed as a generic term for many types of the organized apostolate.

On the other hand, a number of voices attacked the schema on this same point but from the opposite point of view. The schema did not recognize adequately the special place that Catholic Action has earned, they said.

The resolution of this problem will not be an easy one, and an "open door" compromise will probably be reached.

Closely related to this controversy are several others. The accusation of "juridicism" was heard constantly during the debate. This seemed to center, but not exclusively, around the section which attempted to define the relationship of the laity to the hierarchy. Here too a reference to "canon law" annoyed many of the Fathers. So did the juridical terms "mandatum" (mandate) and "canonica missa" (canonical mission).

The Fathers had just completed debating and approving by an almost unanimous vote the magnificent chapter on the laity in the schema on the nature of the Church, which spoke so convincingly of the dignity, responsibility and "the blessed way of the liberty of the sons of God." The juridical and formal concept and language of the lay apostolate schema did not in their minds even remotely reflect the theology they had just approved.

The value of the organized apostolate in relation to the value of the individual apostolate was another point-and-counterpoint argument running through a number of the speeches. Some council Fathers strongly held that the former was overemphasized and that the right and duty of every member of the laity to be apostolic as a "natural and supernatural duty" was neglected. The lay apostolate schema was too narrow in approach and had to be broadened and left unlimited, they held.

On the other hand, there were those who seemed to hold that the organized apostolate was not sufficiently encouraged.

There seems to be no essential problem here because obviously both apostolates are of extreme importance in the modern day. Each complements the other. The problem will be one of balance.

A number of Fathers noted what they considered to be a serious omission in the schema, particularly in view of the chapter on the laity in the schema on the Church and the great discussion of the subject in recent years by the laity of the world. What was missing was what has been dubbed "the apostolate of public opinion in the Church." Their argument was based on the Church schema's statement that the laity are entitled to and indeed even have the duty to make known their opinions in matters concerned with the Church.

There was no appreciable opposition to this concept so it can be presumed that the Lay Apostolate Commission will see what can be done to meet this new apostolate of the dialogue within the Church. The right kind of a statement will go a long way toward meeting a long-felt need of the Church not only in the United States but around the world.

A fundamental problem facing the drafting sub-commissions will be that of giving the text the internal unity which it now lacks. This resulted from the evisceration that took place when parts of the original draft were distributed to half a dozen other schemata, and from the facts that the subject is completely new in conciliar agenda, and that the original broad outline was not appropriate. This outline was discarded, but the present draft still shows the remains of it.

Comparable in importance to internal unity is the problem of external unity. The criticism was leveled that the lay apostolate schema did not seem to have any organic connection with the schema on the nature of the Church (De Ecclesia) on the theological side and the schema on the Church in the modern world on the temporal side. One Father pointed out that if this connection is not made we shall have "apostles of De Ecclesia," "apostles of the Lay Apostolate," and "apostles of the Modern World."

This external linkage should not be difficult to supply now that De Ecclesia has been debated and discussion of schema 13 is underway. The Fathers of the council were reminded during the introduction to the schema that it was written before work had been completed on either of the other two.

Some of the strongest speeches on the floor were aimed at the "clericalism" of the document. This criticism was directed at the fundamental "top down approach" to the apostolate, the "lecturing and sermonizing," and the "paternalistic approach," the heavy concern with "relationship to the hierarchy," the reference to "nothing without the bishop" attitude, and the style of writing. The total effect of the document to many of the bishops spelled out "clericalism."

This will be difficult to handle for the commission because it is in many cases a very subtle matter. Perhaps one council Father highly sensitive to this matter could be asked to screen the next draft along with a few laymen not tied to any organization.

The word "disappointment" could probably be used to describe the basic reaction of the Fathers. Archbishop Owen McCann of Cape Town, South Africa, put it this way: "The text of the schema could hardly be called a magna carta." The Lay Apostolate Commission is in a much better position now to write a "magna carta." It must be remembered that this schema never before had been discussed on the council floor, that the commission itself listed in the introductory report some of the defects of the schema; and that the council Fathers have almost without exception indicated that they are "magna carta" minded.

In summary, it seems that all of the suggestions that have been made, with the possible exception of those recommending that a preeminent and favored position be given "Catholic Action," will be extremely helpful to the lay apostolate in all of its diverse forms, organized and individual in the United States. Together with the other documents of the council that relate to the laity it can be a "magna carta" for the future.

MARTIN H. WORK

Mr. Work is the executive director of the National Council of Catholic Men, who is attending the third session of the Second Vatican Council as an aggregate auditor.

107th General Congregation

October 22, 1964

Mild criticism but general acceptance of schema 13 on the Church in the modern world as a basis for discussion came to an abrupt end during the council's 107th general meeting.

In a violent attack couched in some of the strongest language the Fathers have heard to date, Britain's ranking prelate denounced the schema as a "dangerous . . . set of platitudes . . . unworthy of a council." He asked that the next session be postponed for perhaps four years until it is reworked.

"Having spent such a long time on theological niceties, this council will become a laughing-stock in the eyes of the world if it now rushes breathlessly through a debate on world hunger, nuclear war and family life," Archbishop John C. Heenan of Westminster said. "People will ask, ironically and with good reason, what do we really mean when we call this a pastoral council?"

He also had harsh words for some of the council's experts, or "periti." In what seemed to be a reference to recent widely publicized arguments on birth control, many of them coming from England, the Archbishop said: "The Church of God has suffered a great deal from the writings and speeches of some of the periti.

"These few specialists care nothing for the ordinary teaching authority of bishops — nor, I regret to say, for that of the pope."

In rejecting the text, he recommended it be given to a new commission including married couples, doctors, economists and scientists, as well as priests with long pastoral experience.

"Then after three or four years let the fourth and final session of the council be convened to discuss all these social problems," he said.

Several Fathers disagreed with many of his points during the day's discussion. One even came to the defense of the council experts. Only one of the other 15 speakers rejected the text as a basis for discussion.

Voting was completed on the last two of the seven parts of the proposition on the Eastern Churches. This cleared the way for a vote on the entire proposition after the commission reworks the one part — on the choice of a Catholic rite by converts from Orthodoxy — which was rejected the previous day.

The Fathers approved the part dealing with the Eastern-rite liturgy 2,104 to 22, with 27 voting qualified approval.

On the part concerning contact between Eastern-rite Catholics and Orthodox Christians, the Fathers voted 1,841 to 111 to accept the text. Qualified approval was expressed by 195 Fathers.

The theme of the criticism of the schema on the modern world's problems continued along the lines of two previous days of discussion. Some wanted a more fundamental theological foundation for the arguments presented. Others stressed the need for the proofs from natural law. The need for more attention to the world's poor was the preoccupation of one speaker, while two others asked the Church to grapple with the growing problem of atheism, which Bishop Raffaele Barbieri of Cassano all'Ionio, Italy, called the "dishonor of our age."

The only American speaker was Archbishop Lawrence J. Shehan of Baltimore, who said he accepted the text as satisfactory for discussion. He asked, however, that it be reworked with special emphasis on the first encyclical of Pope Paul VI, Ecclesiam Suam.

Though the deposit of faith and the fundamental structure of the Church cannot change, he said, the Church has progressed — and must continue to do so— both in its doctrine and structure. This is especially true in matters concerning religion in its relationship to man and the temporal order, he declared.

From the beginning, he said, the Church should state that it is considering the nature and destiny of man from a religious viewpoint and from the viewpoint of the revelation God has given concerning man.

Pope Paul's encyclical contains abundant riches not yet plumbed, Archbishop Shehan said. In it world problems are accurately set down in a profound way. The schema, on the other hand, in some of its expressions is too obscure and lofty in style and would do well to take the lead from the encyclical.

We should not fear if it is objected that we pervert the doctrine of the Church by setting up a dialogue with the world, he said. Authentic traditions must be preserved, but there must also be progress in the application of the Gospels to "signs of the times."

Quoting from the encyclical, he said: "The Church must progress in its own nature and in its consciousness of its own doctrine."

Bishop Josef Stimpfle of Augsburg, Germany, who spent several years in a Russian prison camp, cautioned against unreal optimism. Noting the "rapid progress of militant atheism, which has wrecked parishes, imprisoned and killed bishops and priests," he said the Church cannot afford to remain silent regarding these crimes. But he said that the aim of any dialogue, even with atheism, must be "not to conquer but to persuade."

Against Archbishop Heenan's suggestion, he recommended that at least the fourth chapter of the schema be given to the present commission, rather than a new one, and that the commission be given wider powers in dealing with its revision. The fourth chapter reportedly includes proposals regarding race discrimination, marriage, social and economic problems and nuclear warfare.

Bishop Sebastiao Soares de Resende of Beira, Mozambique, observed that genuine poverty would increase the credibility of the Church. If the Church presents itself not merely as the Church of the poor, but as a poor Church, then it will have a greater claim to being listened to, he said.

"This depends on all of us," he told the bishops at the council. "We could begin with the garments we bishops wear on various occasions. Why do we need all this dignity and all this show?"

He also asked that the laity be urged to take an active part in politics, "which is not to be regarded as forbidden fruit or something of little or no importance."

The day's meeting opened with Mass celebrated by Archbishop Benedictos Printesis of Athens. American-born Bishop John Taylor of Stockholm, Sweden, enthroned the Gospel. The day's moderator was Julius Cardinal Doepfner of Munich, Germany.

During the meeting, medals were distributed to council Fathers to commemorate the opening (Sept. 14) of the third council session.

Joining Archbishop Heenan in rejecting the text as a basis for discussion was Archbishop Denis Hurley of Durban, South Africa. Its basic defect, he said, is that it was composed before its purpose was clearly determined. It provides too theoretical a solution for problems which are extremely delicate in practice, and it contains at least apparent contradictions and obscurities, he said.

He cited the schema's statements that "defensive war is lawful" and that "nuclear warfare is criminal."

"Does this mean defensive nuclear warfare is condemned?" he wanted to know.

To put into proper light the true value of the natural order and its relation to man's final end, he suggested the use of the "splendid religious and scientific insight which characterized the illustrious and faithful son of the Church, Father Pierre Teilhard de Chardin."

It was an obvious reference to the fact that Jesuit Father Teilhard's works were for some time under a cloud of theological suspicion. Only after his death was permission granted to publish his scientific writings, and then permission to read them, even in his own order, was slow to come.

Archbishop Hurley had a kind word for council experts to counteract Archbishop Heenan's attack. Suggesting that a small group of them be organized to rework the schema, he admitted "there are still some good ones left."

In the name of 10 Hungarian bishops, Archbishop Endre Hamvas of Csanad departed from the prepared text to thank the Pope for the new accord between the Holy See and the Hungarian government which allows the Church more freedom to pursue its work in that communist-controlled country.

Regarding the schema, he said, it is encouraging to see the Church under Pope Paul VI continuing the difficult task of acting as mother and teacher of the world in the abiding spirit of Pope John XXIII. He said he saw schema 13 as opening the Church to the world, but asked for greater stress on the visibility of the people of God.

"We cannot wait four years," said Bishop Andre Charue of Namur, Belgium, in answer to Archbishop Heenan's proposed delay regarding the fourth session. "This schema must be published next year."

In his defense of the council experts, Bishop Charue said: "The commission has good periti at its disposal. If necessary, they can get others and work will proceed."

Bishop Charue then added that the human race has made more progress in the last 50 years than in the previous 2,000, and with this progress man becomes increasingly conscious that he is collaborating with his Creator.

It is wrong, he said, to insinuate that all evil comes from the body and all good from the soul. The Gospel ignores any such division. The world has its own law which the Church must observe.

Archbishop Maurice Roy of Quebec said he wanted the schema addressed not only to Catholics or Christians but to all men. Its language must be intelligible to everyone and be in the "language of man to man," he said.

"This means avoiding all pompous phrases," he added. We should start with what is better and more easily known, in regard to both fact and principle, and only then proceed to what is proper to Catholics. Among those things more easily known, he said, are the dignity of the human person, basic justice, and the nature of true progress.

The basic error of today, said Coadjutor Archbishop Pablo Munoz Vega of Quito, Ecuador, is disregard or contempt for the human person and human dignity. It is extremely important, therefore, to develop a high level of Catholic culture.

The text should not omit extolling the contribution made in the life of the Church by present-day martyrs, he said.

By failing to present the traditional doctrine of the subordination of civil society to the Church, Brazilian Bishop Antonio de Castro Mayer of Campos said, the text runs the risk of falling into secularism. Besides, he stated, the text presupposes good will in all men, and this does not correspond to fact. The schema should also warn against dangerous secret societies, and make some mention of the mass media, he said.

The master general of the Dominican Order, Father Aniceto Fernandez, O.P., said the greatest dignity of human nature is that it has been assumed by the Divine Person. With man thus lifted, the whole universe is brought along, he went on. He asked for an expansion of the schema's theology based on the theology of the Incarnate Word.

Archbishop Leon Duval of Algiers, Algeria, said he thought the text was too long, too scholastic and too ecclesiastical. He said he wanted it to include a condemnation of all social and racial discrimination and asked the Fathers to try to approve a text which would make war impossible in the future.

Archbishop George Beck of Liverpool, England, said the schema may well be the second most important document produced by the council and that it therefore merits full discussion, at least in general, as a basis for further consideration. With the council's most important document, that on the nature of the Church, it will constitute a double foundation for the updating of the Church so much desired by Pope John XXIII, he stated.

This work, he said, "is a pastoral duty which falls on the Fathers of the council as distinct from the periti. It is our duty to offer practical guidance in moral questions to all men, and with the full authority which serves to affirm and vindicate the objective moral law."

Bishop Frane Franic of Split and Makarska, Yugoslavia, said he felt the text lacks a clear purpose and should pinpoint specific errors such as atheism and materialism. This is of extreme pastoral importance for those living under Marxism, he said. Therefore, he continued, the schema should go into such things as the binding force of the natural law "because even some of our own people today seem unconvinced or uncertain."

Wider use of laymen and specialists in drawing up new council documents and in revising the ones already debated is a very likely result of such speeches as Archbishop Heenan's.

That was the opinion expressed by Msgr. Mark J. Hurley, chancellor of the Stockton, Calif., diocese, during a meeting of the U.S. bishops' press panel following the council meeting at which the British prelate said that true specialists did not play a big enough part in drawing up the directives on family life, nuclear warfare and world hunger. At the same time, the archbishop denounced too much reliance on the experts "who, since their youth, have spent their lives in monasteries, seminaries or universities."

Msgr. Hurley said it has been a mistake from the start to limit the experts almost completely to priests versed in theology or canon law. Msgr. Hurley, who is an expert for the commission which drafted the proposition on Catholic schools, said his commission is contemplating much greater use of educational specialists and other laymen when it comes time to rework the proposition, which has yet to be introduced before the council.

What is needed, he said, are more scientists, demographers, educators, chemists and other specialists, because the job before the commission dealing with the schema on the Church in the modern world is too big for canon lawyers and theologians alone.

Italian Father Roberto Tucci, S.J., director of the Jesuits' Rome periodical, Civilta Cattolica, agreed with Msgr. Hurley that work on the draft schema needs to be enlarged and that consultation with specialists needs to be extended. He said that a number of lay specialists were consulted in the early preparatory phases.

He stated that Archbishop Heenan's charge that the experts guiding the drafting of the text were inexperienced was not completely true and partly unjust.

The panel members commented at length on the British archbishop's fear that theologians and specialists would be the ones who would explain what the bishops mean in their council documents.

Father Frederick R. McManus of Boston, canon law professor at the Catholic University of America, and Msgr. George G. Higgins, director of the Social Action Department of the National Catholic Welfare Conference, pointed out that it was a mixed commission of members of the council's Theology Commission and Commission on the Lay Apostolate that drew up and approved the schema for presentation to the council. Therefore, they noted, an attack on the schema is an attack on the mixed commission, headed jointly by Alfredo Cardinal Ottaviani and Fernando Cardinal Cento.

English theologian Father Charles Davis, a temporary member of the press panel, pointed out that a great part of theologians' time is spent interpreting acts of past councils and popes.

Father Francis J. McCool, S.J., of New York, a professor at the Pontifical Biblical Institute, said that while it is the bishops who have the teaching power, they are forced in fact to rely on theologians, since it is the theologian's function to teach by the mandate of their superiors and to break new paths with prudence. A theologian has to see what Divine Revelation has to say on a particular point and, ultimately, it is often from the work of the theologian that bishops proceed to declarations and teachings.

FATHER JOHN P. DONNELLY

Marriage Problems, Atomic Warfare

Two of the burning issues raised in the ecumenical council's long-awaited schema 13, atomic warfare and birth control, were discussed here publicly by two prominent council figures.

Archbishop Thomas D. Roberts, S.J., former missionary Archbishop of Bombay, India, spoke at the Dutch documentation center here on problems related to both nuclear war and contraception. In the course of his talk he said that the Church should approve conscientious objection to military service in this nuclear age.

Father Bernard Haering, C.SS.R., German moral theologian who served as secretary to the committee which prepared schema 13 on the Church in the modern world, spoke at the German press center for the council. Dwelling on the schema's treatment of marriage, he said that its uppermost consideration is "the primacy of love." He said that the Church's marriage laws should be made less rigid and more flexible.

Both clerics spoke before capacity audiences.

Archbishop Roberts said that the Church needs to speak out more explicitly in regard to moral questions in the field of international relations. While self-defense is always permissible, the Jesuit prelate said, when it comes to using weapons that can destroy millions of innocent people, then "conscientious abstention" should be allowed and people should not be forced to fight.

Archbishop Roberts, one of the contributors to the newly published book, "Contraception and Holiness," said that the schema as it now stands is too vague in its treatment of birth control. It ought to be realized, he said, that the study of this question has barely begun, especially concerning its relevance to the natural law. Only when such study matures can proper definitions be feasible, he said.

The Archbishop said that since this is a question which has arisen in modern times only, tradition cannot be invoked for its solution. He added:

"There has been no real freedom to discuss it in the Church. But it should now be recognized that the principle of contraception is already accepted with the approval of certain regulatory methods to control fertility, only the machinery being (held) in question."

Above all, he continued, there must be respect for the freedom of the individual conscience. "Obedience, after all, is absolute in regard to God only, although we realize how difficult it can be to know what is the divine will," he said. "But in regard to man, obedience is relative only. Because of man's fallibility, therefore, it should never be blind, but guided by the individual conscience."

Father Haering in citing the schema's stress on the "primacy of love" in marriage, explained that while the marriage section of the document deals only with Church law on the subject, it recognizes marriage as a sacred bond of love.

"Ecclesiastical law does not stand beside divine law independently, but in the service of divine law," he said. Certain existing legal provisions, he went on, no longer correspond to present-day conditions of life. Therefore Church marriage legislation should be made more flexible and procedures concerning it should be simplified.

As for mixed marriages, Father Haering added that the pertinent provisions should keep in mind the developing ecumenical dialogue and the principle of religious freedom, which must be respected in regard to non-Catholic partners in mixed marriages as well as for others.

But the Redemptorist theologian said that the dispensation from the standing Church prohibition against mixed marriages should be given only if the Catholic partner is willing both to keep his faith and to provide for the Catholic education of the children — even though this latter point might not be "unconditionally divine law." Father Haering added that no absolute safeguards can be expected in this respect.

FATHER PLACID JORDAN, O.S.B.

Archbishop Heenan

This is an English translation of the speech by Archbishop John C. Heenan of Westminster, England, at the general session of the ecumenical council on Oct. 22 on the schema of the Church in the modern world.

It would be most ungracious if we were not to praise the efforts of the commission which has produced the document we are now considering. There can be no doubt that the council Fathers concerned and their advisers have worked hard and have done their best. It is nevertheless quite obvious that the document they have presented to us is unworthy of a general council of the Church.

If we are to speak at all about the Church in the world of today we must do so in clear, unmistakable and down-to-earth terms. For some years not only the faithful but non-Catholics and even unbelievers have been awaiting from this council wise advice on many grave problems. The Holy See itself has suggested that the Second Vatican Council will make some attempt to solve the complex social problems of our day. The document now before us will therefore be studied with eager hope.

What sort of judgment, venerable brothers, do you think the world will pass on this treatise? On some questions, as we know, it is better to say too little than too much. On the subject of world problems, however, it would have been much better to say nothing than produce a set of platitudes. I would like you to call to mind the number of sittings we had when the question of the sources of Revelation was so fiercely debated. The theologians, of course, rightly regarded this as a highly important topic. But to the citizens of the wide world, whether Catholic or non-Catholic, a debate of this kind seems like wasting time and beating the air. Having spent such a long time on theological niceties this council will become a laughing-stock in the eyes of the world if it now rushes breathlessly through a debate on world hunger, nuclear war and family life. People will ask ironically and with good reason what do we really mean when we call this a pastoral council?

I must speak plainly. This document is going to dash the hopes of everyone who has been awaiting it. Its authors do not seem to realize even to whom the message should be directed. Here is an example of their way of writing: "Christians," they say, "are ready to engage in a dialogue with all men of good will." But surely this a pointless thing to say. Christians should be ready to conduct a dialogue with anyone whether or not he is a man of good will. The whole treatise reads more like a sermon than a document of a council.

We have been given the schema itself together with certain supplements. The fact is that the schema, even read with the supplements, remains obscure and misleading; read on its own it is dangerous and could prove harmful. I would like the Fathers of the council to consider this question very seriously. We have been told to debate the schema and to pass over the rest without comment. But if we fail to scrutinize both documents with great care, the mind of the council will have to be interpreted to the world by the specialists who helped the Fathers of the commission to draw up the documents. God forbid that this should happen! I fear specialists when they are left to explain what the bishops meant.

Between sessions of this council, the Church of God has suffered a great deal from the writings and speeches of some of the specialists. They are few in number but their sound has gone forth to the ends of the earth. These few specialists care nothing for the ordinary teaching authority of the bishops — nor, I regret to say, for that of the pope. It is idle to show them a papal encyclical in which a point of Catholic doctrine is clearly laid down. They will immediately reply that a pope is not infallible when writing an encyclical. It really does not seem worthwhile for the pope to write any more encyclical letters since they can apparently no longer be quoted in support of the Faith.

We must protect the authority of the teaching Church. It is of no avail to talk about a college of bishops if specialists in articles, books and speeches contradict and pour scorn on what a body of bishops teaches. Until now it has not been a doctrine of the Church that the theologians admitted to the council are infallible. The theories of one or two must not be mistaken for a general agreement among theologians which has, of course, special authority.

Perhaps the commission (members) responsible for this document had no chance of success from the outset. They were, in fact, denied the help of experts who really knew their subjects. When you are dealing with the problems of social life you need to consult those who know and live in the world. Now let me ask how many parish priests, how many of the faithful, how many husbands and wives, how many doctors, economists, scientists (especially experts in biochemistry and nuclear physics) were at work on this commission? It is useless in these matters to seek advice only from those who since their youth have spent their lives in monasteries, seminaries or universities. These eminent men may hardly know the world as it really is. The world can be unpleasant and cruel. These scholars often have a childlike trust in the opinions of men in the world. Certainly they are simple as doves but they are not always wise as serpents.

If you are looking for examples of all this you need only study the section on matrimony. Everyone knows that doctors all over the world are busily trying to produce a satisfactory contraceptive pill. This special kind of pill is to be a panacea to solve all sexual problems between husbands and wives. Neither the treatise itself nor the supplements hesitate to prophesy that such a pill is just around the corner. Meanwhile, it is said, married couples and they alone must decide what is right and wrong. Everyone must be his own judge. But, the document adds, the couple must act according to the teaching of the Church. But this is precisely what married people want to be told — what *is* now the teaching of the Church? To this question our document gives no reply. For that very reason it could provide an argument from our silence to theologians after the council who wish to attack sound doctrine.

The document thus blandly addresses husbands and wives: "Some practical solutions have made their appearance and there are more to come." This is no way for a document of the Church to be composed. When our children ask us for bread we should not give them a stone.

I strongly appeal for this document to be given to a new commission. The treatise itself says that learned men and married couples must work out with theologians ways of understanding more thoroughly the mysteries of nature. But this should be done before and not after a conciliar document is drawn up.

I therefore propose that without delay a new commission be set up composed of specialists from the laity and priests with long pastoral experience. Then after three or four years let the fourth and final session of the council be convened to discuss all these social problems. It is true that some of us in this episcopal college will have gone to our reward. But perhaps we shall then be able to help the council more by our prayers than we do now by our speeches. One thing is quite certain. It would be a scandal to rush this debate now that we have at last come to really pastoral problems.

108th General Congregation

October 23, 1964

The ecumenical council's third session will end Nov. 21 with concelebration of the Mass by Pope Paul VI and 24 council Fathers.

The Saturday morning ceremony in St. Peter's on the feast of the Presentation of Mary in the Temple will be followed by formal closing ceremonies the same afternoon in the basilica of St. Mary Major in downtown Rome. Taking part in the morning Mass will be prelates in whose dioceses the world's major Marian sanctuaries are located.

In announcing the third session's closing date, Archbishop Pericle Felici, council secretary general, expressed hope that several documents already discussed in the council and now being reworked in commission would be ready for formal proclamation by the Pope at the closing ceremonies.

He said the fourth session will begin "whenever the Pope decides."

These announcements were made during the council's 108th congregation, at which the draft schema on the Church in the modern world was accepted as the basis for further discussion after three days of debate.

Three speakers—one in the name of 70 other Fathers—called for formal condemnation in the text of what was called the "total heresy of communism."

Seven speakers in all took the floor to defend the schema as the basis for discussion before the standing vote to close the discussion. The Fathers then decided to accept the schema by a secret vote of 1,579 to 296. Seven more speakers then began the discussion of the introduction and first chapter of the document.

One of the more colorful talks of the day was made by a monk who responded to the charge by England's Archbishop John C. Heenan of Westminster the previous day that monks and seminarians are out of contact with the world.

Remarking that he rose "trembling and afraid," Archabbot Benedict Reetz, O.S.B., superior general of the Benedictine Congregation of Beuron, Germany, made an eloquent defense of monks, who, he said, "carry the world on their shoulders." He referred to the legend of Pope St. Gregory the Great's commission to 40 monks to go to England and "make angels out of the

Angles"—the forefathers of the English. He also pointed out that the very next day at Monte Cassino, Pope Paul would proclaim a monk—St. Benedict—patron of Europe. These facts hardly indicate monks are out of contact with the world, he said.

Exiled Archbishop Paul Yu Pin of Nanking, China —now rector of Fu Jen Catholic University in Taipei, Formoso—asked in the name of 70 other Fathers that a new chapter on atheistic communism be added to the schema.

The Church cannot ignore this "accumulation of all the heresies," he said. It must defend truth and clear up confusion caused in the minds of the faithful by peaceful coexistence and talk of so-called Catholic communism.

The Church must consider this evil not only as one of "the signs of the times," but as the most prominent of all the signs in the modern world, Archbishop Yu Pin asserted. He said that as it is militantly atheistic and grossly materialistic, communism must be condemned for its denial of human freedom. Thus will the council satisfy the expectations and desires of all freedom-loving peoples, he said, especially those under communism's yoke.

Archbishop Guillermo Bolatti of Rosario, Argentina, took up the same theme. The Church cannot pass over the doctrine of communism in silence, he said, since one-third of the world is under its yoke and the rest is in danger.

This "reality of the world," however, should not be treated from a political or economic point of view, but rather as an ideology affecting the minds of men. Atheistic communism is obviously opposed to the Gospels, he said. It destroys men's sense of God as the Creator of the world and of Christ as its redeemer. For this reason, the Church must condemn it or at least warn men against it, since it is "intrinsically contrary to Catholic teaching," the archbishop said.

He added: "Do not say it is inopportune to act now. Pope Paul has thought otherwise, as witnessed in his encyclical, Ecclesiam Suam."

The third speaker to take up the same theme was Bishop Paul J. Schmitt of Metz, France. This is the first council ever held in the "age of atheism," he said,

178

and it is a "novelty" in the world to which the Church must give heed.

In the Middle Ages, the Church absorbed society and the "world" was something apart and condemned, he said. But this is not the "world" spoken of in this schema. "We mean rather the total complex of civilization of the last four centuries, and it is in this complex that we must make the actuality of the Gospel felt," said Bishop Schmitt.

Archbishop Raymond Tchidimbo of Conakry, Guinea, said the text was only partially satisfactory since it says nothing about one-third of the world. Apparently written with European and American orientation, he said, it leaves out problems of the vast continent of Africa, among others.

The statement on poverty is not enough, he continued. The Church must also express itself on the necessity of "socialization" in modern unified society, and declare its "solidarity with the poor." He asked that bishops from nations outside Europe and America be given a greater voice in reworking the document.

Summing up the arguments on the schema's general acceptability for discussion, Bishop Emilio Guano of Leghorn, Italy, said he was speaking in his own name since there was not time to convoke the mixed commission which framed the text. He said that he felt his remarks would nevertheless reflect the thinking of the commission.

He observed in answer to criticism expressed that a large number of specialists and experts had been consulted in the preparation of the schema. These included scientists, scholars and a number of the laity, as well as priests with pastoral experience and some council Fathers "who can be presumed to have some pastoral background." He said, however, that the ultimate responsibility rests with the council.

Many of the observations made were contradictory, Bishop Guano said—some calling for more doctrinal expression, others asking for more exhortation. These will have to be sifted by the commission, he said.

Regarding "some points of major importance," he said that the council cannot go into too much detail since the Pope "has made known that some of these points are being carefully examined by experts and he has reserved to himself the final judgment on their findings."

Although the speakers varied in their enthusiasm for the schema as drafted, Bishop Guano said, "only one damned the whole text to eternal fire." The reference was again obviously to Archbishop Heenan's strongly-worded attack the previous day.

The congregation opened with Mass celebrated by Archbishop Luc Sangare of Bamako, Mali, and the Gospel book was enthroned by Ukrainian-rite Bishop Nicholas T. Elko of Pittsburgh. Julius Cardinal Doepf-

ner of Munich, Germany, began as the moderator and was replaced by Belgium's Leo Cardinal Suenens of Malines-Brussels with the opening of the discussion on particular points of the introduction of the first chapter of Schema 13.

The amended text of the proposition dealing with religious life was distributed, together with a brochure of appendices to aid the discussion. The new title for these propositions is "Accommodated Adaptation of the Religious Life"—or as it was announced at a press briefing the same day, "The Renewal of the Religious Life in Modern Times."

Among those speaking before the cloture vote was Bishop Franz von Streng of Basel and Lugano, Switzerland, in the name of all the bishops of Switzerland. He said the schema could well be reduced to two chapters, one for the exposition of principles, the other for practical applications.

Some of the delicate problems of marriage and family life should not be treated by the full council, he said, but rather left to discussion by regional bishops' conferences. On the other hand, the schema should say something about business morals and the moral obligation to respect life and the integrity of others on the highways in the midst of increasing modern traffic. A statement should also be included, he said, declaring the inviolability of the life of unborn children.

Auxiliary Bishop Rafael Gonzalez Moralejo of Valencia, Spain, also wanted the text divided into two parts, one doctrinal and the other practical. Speaking for 60 Spanish-speaking bishops, he said the value of the schema is based on three considerations: doctrinal and conciliar aspect, the pastoral aspect, and the ecumenical aspect.

He referred to the intervention by Pope Paul in a speech during the first session of the Second Vatican Council when he was still Cardinal Montini. In his talk, the then Archbishop of Milan said the work of the council would be to answer two questions: What is the Church and what does the Church do? The present schema is an answer to the second of these questions dealing with the mission of the Church to the world, Bishop Gonzalez said.

The last speaker of the general discussion was Archbishop Justin Darmajuwana of Semarang, Indonesia, in the name of the Indonesian Bishops' Conference. He thought the schema does not answer the main question—what is the value of temporal activity in relation to the kingdom of God? It also fails to clarify the role of the laity in the solution of moral and religious problems encountered in the world. It fails, he said, to have a proper outlook on the true and living reality of the world.

Moving to a particular discussion on the introduction and the first chapter, Archbishop Paul Gouyon of Rennes, France, remarked that the text appears to have been composed by men living in peace, far removed from strife and from gripping, practical problems.

He said its vision of the world is limited, and only in passing does it seem to have a universal outlook. Its language shows no emotion like that of a mother speaking of joys or sorrows of her children. "We need a cosmic vision expressed in an ardent language," he said.

Bishop Felix Romero Menjibar of Jaen, Spain, wanted an explanation of the basic principles of dialogue between the Church and the world, which he said he thought should be the ideological theme of the entire schema. The world has to show competence, he said, and the building of an earthly city belongs to men of the world. It is a valid occupation in itself, and can lead men to salvation.

Nor is it possible to ignore the historical reality of sin, to which all men are subject, he said.

Bishop Gerard De Vet of Breda, the Netherlands, thought there was not enough place given to the good of men. The text seems to distrust the world and to be ill at ease trying to recognize its positive aspects. The Church stands out as above and beyond men and almost identified with the hierarchy. This should be corrected, he said.

Archbishop Luis del Rosario of Zamboanga, the Philippines, spoke in the name of his country's episcopal conference. He cautioned the Fathers to give the Chris-

tian mentality of Redemption as a countermeasure against the "squirrel-cage mentality" so common today—whereby men run and run and never arrive. It is important to explain to men the what, how and why of human existence so they will understand where they are heading. Since justice and charity are means of living and not ends in themselves, they cannot be the aim of Christian life.

One of the first themes to be expressed in the schema, according to Bishop Joseph Schoiswohl of Graz-Seckau, Austria, is the nature and immortality of the soul. Even many who believe in God are not too convinced of this. He called for arguments which would be not only philosophical, but would reach the hearts and "into the inner being of man."

The day's final speaker was Archbishop Segundo Garcia de Sierra y Mendez of Burgos, Spain. He asked that the text see everything in relation to man: "Not that man is a measure of all things, but because all things were made for him."

He wanted emphasis on such fundamental truths as man's creation to the image and likeness of God, and said the root of most presentday errors is a false concept of man viewed in purely natural light.

Man must also be taught, he said, to maintain a proper balance between technical progress and culture.

FATHER JOHN P. DONNELLY

Summary of Introduction and First Chapter Of Schema on Church in Modern World

This is the English-language summary of the introduction and first chapter of the ecumenical council's schema on the Church in the modern world. The council press office in releasing it said that summaries of subsequent chapters would follow "as the discussion develops in the council hall."

1. GENERAL INTRODUCTION:
a) *The story of the schema.*
On July 3, 1964, the Holy Father gave instructions that the schema "The Church in the World Today" should be sent to the Council Fathers in its present form.

This schema, after being re-worked by the Mixed Commission composed of members of the Theological Commission and of the Commission for the Apostolate of the Laity, speaks of the relationships of the Church and the modern world.

In its first version, the schema was composed of six

chapters treating of the following subjects: the grandeur of man's vocation, man in society, marriage and the family, the necessity of proper progress in culture, the economical order and social justice, the community of peoples and peace. Of this first version, only the first chapter has been retained, with its presentation of the doctrinal aspects of these points, while the other five chapters have been added to the present schema in an appendix.

This second revision of the schema was turned over to the Mixed Commission and to a special subcommission set up for this specific purpose. The five chapters of the appendix have been worked over by the different subcommissions of the Mixed Commission.

In June of this year, the final text was submitted to the Mixed Commission for discussion and approval. Thus the schema reached its present version, which will be discussed in the council hall and which comprises a synthesis of the various chapters which first made up the appendix to the schema.

b) *The subject matter.*

The schema takes up the general problems confronting the relationships of the Church and the world today. Its intention is not to work out a new theology, but rather to study and to penetrate temporal realities in the light of theological principles, both speculative and practical, in a perspective valid for all ages, considering the world in its actual situations, with all its elements of good and evil, with its anxieties and its hopes. In a word, the schema wants to demonstrate that the Church makes temporal problems its own, because she is the Mother of men living in the world. At the same time, she reminds all that the earth is not man's definitive dwelling-place, but a place where he passes by for a time.

c) *The form and style of the schema.*

The language used in the preparation of the schema is inspired by Sacred Scripture and remains always faithful to theology. It is a simple and modern language, and thus can be understood by men of today and particularly by men who have had no special theological training.

d) *The structure of the schema.*

The schema is made up of an introduction, four chapters and a conclusion. The appendix contains material distinct from the text.

The four chapters are as follows:
1. The vocation of the whole man.
2. The Church in the service of God and men.
3. The Christian mode of life in a contemporary world.
4. The principal task of the Christian today.

THE INTRODUCTION

As members of one same human family, we have all been created by God and placed on this earth where we all share the same destiny, whether in prosperity or in adversity. We are all called to form one same family of the sons of God in Jesus Christ, who came into this world to save all men and to form a kingdom of love, unity, and peace.

Time is a sign and a voice for the Church and for men. It is a sign of the presence or the absence of God, a voice for the man who invokes his God and the voice of God speaking to man.

The schema is addressed first of all to the sons of the Church, then to their brethren in the separated Christian churches, to the adorers of one God and, lastly, to all men of good will.

In explaining the relations of the Church and the modern world, the Council wishes only to present Christ as the Light and the Saviour of the world.

CHAPTER 1—THE VOCATION OF THE WHOLE MAN

The first chapter treats of the fundamental position which the Church must adopt in the face of the problems of the contemporary world, problems which hinge on one central point: man and his vocation.

Many consider man only from the temporal viewpoint. For these, the final end of salvation is regarded as something of a brake in the construction of the earthly city. Others, even among Christians, condemn temporal activities. For the Church all created things are "very good," as is stated in Genesis. All things have been created in the Word and through the Word. By means of the Incarnation the whole of human nature has been elevated.

Man was called by God to the dignity of being a citizen of the heavenly city, to participation as a son of God in divine life in this world by means of Faith and in the next world "face to face." Hope for a future life gives real meaning to the life of man and makes man live in charity toward God and his neighbor. The activities whereby man exercises his domination over nature is a social bond, a source of progress for culture, a perfecting of human nature, and it forms part of the plan of God.

For this reason the council exhorts the faithful to be aware of their vocation and to manifest it consistently, as well in private as in social life. At the same time the faithful are urged not to follow those who give life only earthly dimensions.

Man needs the Redeemer even for the building of his earthly city, because human nature was wounded by sin. Only Christ, born without sin and who died for sinners, restored to man eternal life and assists him in building the earthly city on the solid foundations of justice and love.

The will of God is that man may recognize God's domination over all things and that the Kingdom of Christ may spread over the entire earth. This will be realized in the degree in which man performs his duties toward God, his neighbor and the world, which belongs to God and to men.

Interview With Cardinal Koenig

"The switches are now thrown in the right direction." This was the comment of Austria's Franziskus Cardinal Koenig about the effect of the actions taken so far at the Second Vatican Council.

The Archbishop of Vienna used the metaphor in an interview here to emphasize his view that a fair appraisal of the council's work must be a long-range one, and that it should not be expected that its effects will be felt immediately in all directions.

"It would be a mistake to express judgments exclusively on the strength of the council decrees adopted, no matter how important they may be. We must appreciate the overall influence emanating from these deliberations, the impact resulting from them and we should realize that the gears certainly cannot be thrown into reverse any more," he said.

Cardinal Koenig said he believed his impression of the council's direction would be confirmed by most council Fathers. He mentioned the council votes on the draft proposals dealing with the Church and with the pastoral duties of the bishops as indicators of this.

"They showed that easily 80% of the council Fathers are fully behind the innovations now proposed, especially in regard to what has been called the collegial principle, which in practice implies a decentralization and internationalization of the Church," he explained.

Asked if this trend would lead to the widely discussed reform of the Roman curia, he responded: "It certainly will, inasmuch as that supreme council of bishops will be set up, which the Holy Father visualizes. As for the reform of the Roman curia the Holy Father has left no doubt about his intentions in this regard."

The question was then put to him about the capacity of a dissident minority to stall such changes. Cardinal Koenig said the affirmative support of the Pope would counter efforts by such a minority, and added:

"These trends cannot be reversed by mere administrative procedures. They will assert themselves more strongly once the measures the council has decided upon are applied and tested."

In Cardinal Koenig's opinion, the draft proposal on the Church is clearly the key document coming from the council. He commented:

"Its impact will be felt in a wide area of the life of the Church and its effects will be highly beneficial in bringing home to the faithful that they all are the people of God and that the Church sincerely desires to keep abreast of their spiritual needs in promoting what Pope Paul VI has aptly called the dialogue with the world."

Regarding draft proposal 13, on the position of the Church in the modern world, the cardinal was asked whether the fast pace the council has adopted might not jeopardize a careful enough examination of this vital schema.

"I don't think so," he said. "If we can now move ahead faster than before, this is due in large measure to the work done in previous sessions and especially in the council committees, which now bear fruit.

"At the same time perhaps, expectations in regard to schema 13 were too high all along. The schema cannot provide a cure-all for the world's ills. It can lay down certain principles, give some indications as to the direction one should pursue in dealing with contemporary problems, but it cannot possibly provide answers for all the questions raised.

"The problem of world poverty, for instance, certainly is one we should face realistically by expressing our concern for it and thereby inaugurate the sort of collective initiatives which eventually can lead to tangible results.

"All this requires time, and this also is the reason why, to my mind at least, a fourth council session will be necessary. We need more time to consider these matters and must not expect quick and easy solutions.

"However," Cardinal Koenig concluded, "there is every reason to be hopeful in regard to the council's further progress. I for one continue to be what you might call a moderate optimist when it comes to sizing up the accomplishments so far and the prospects of what remains to be done." FATHER PLACID JORDAN, O.S.B.

One of the most impressive ceremonies each day was the solemn enthronement of the Book of the Gospels. Here Bishop Paul Leonard Hagarty, O.S.B., of Nassau, Bahamas, carries the Gospels down the nave of St. Peter's basilica in the performance of that rite.

109th General Congregation

October 26, 1964

A Texas-born missionary bishop, telling the Second Vatican Council that he spoke in the name of millions who do not understand the Church's teaching on hell, deplored a "lack of proportion" between the sin of eating meat on Friday and the eternal hellfire which is its punishment.

By imposing such a heavy penalty for the breach of purely ecclesiastical laws, said Bishop Louis Morrow of Krishnagar, India, the Church puts a man who eats meat on Friday in the same category as an atheist or an adulterer.

The result is a dulling of the moral sense, Bishop Morrow asserted. Sanctions that are too heavy for the sin they punish actually defeat their own purpose, he said.

His appeal to the Church not to impose the pain of mortal sin too easily came during council debate on the introduction and chapters one, two and three of schema 13 on the Church in the modern world.

The same debate also heard a Yugoslav bishop, who had been imprisoned in the early years of communist rule, declare that the Church sometimes works better under an unfriendly government.

The Church should be wary of accepting too many privileges, warned Bishop Petar Cule of Mostar.

Like other speakers, he emphasized that the Church's activity in the world should be that of a leaven. Also like others, he warned that preaching has a hollow sound if Christians are no better than others.

Like other prelates from behind the Iron Curtain, he emphasized the Church's duty of proclaiming the primacy of spiritual values and the dignity of the person.

A Brazilian prelate, in a speech at once briskly humorous and passionately earnest, urged the council Fathers to throw off their gorgeous vestments and attend the council's next session dressed simply in black.

Archbishop Henrique Golland Trinidade of Botucatu noted that the council secretary general, Archbishop Pericle Felici, habitually addresses the council Fathers with the traditional Latin salute, "most adorned Fathers."

Yes, he said, we are indeed most adorned from top to toe as we walk to the council each morning, and we look like rich men instead of the Fathers we really are.

He emphasized, too, that good example must back up all preaching.

At the end of his speech, he suggested the Church set up a complaint bureau in the form of a "commission for dialogue." This commission would listen to anything anybody had to say to the Church.

In all, 18 speakers took part in the debate, nine on the introduction and chapter one, and nine on chapters two and three. Chapter one is on the vocation of the whole man; chapter two on the Church in the service of God and men; and chapter three on Christian conduct in today's world.

The 109th general council meeting began with Mass offered by Archbishop Custodio Alvim Pereira of Lourenco Marques, Mozambique. The Gospel was enthroned by Bishop Baltasar Alvarez Restrepo of Pereira, Colombia.

Leo Cardinal Suenens of Malines-Brussels was the moderator.

Archbishop Felici announced that 12 parish priests were to concelebrate Mass on the sixth anniversary of the election of Pope John XXIII (Oct. 28). His announcement was applauded warmly.

He asked the council Fathers to seek Pope John's intercession that the council's work might proceed tranquilly and with full harmony of minds.

He also announced that on Oct. 29, the 25th anniversary of the ordination of Julius Cardinal Doepfner of Munich, Germany, the cardinal would concelebrate Mass with the other council Fathers who would be celebrating the 25th anniversary of their consecration as bishops.

Paul Cardinal Leger of Montreal led off the debate on the schema's introduction and chapter one.

He said the root of every person's influence in the world is his vocation. Because the development of this vocation depends on both its natural and supernatural elements, man must achieve a proper balance between the two. It would be a grave mistake to give the impression that a Christian's first task is to despise the earth and desire only heavenly things, he said. He added that the text should say something on the problem of evil and the Christian concept of suffering.

Auxiliary Bishop Jan Pietraszko of Cracow, Poland, like others before him, urged the clarification of the term "the world." He also asked for a clearer explanation of man's vocation through a clearer explanation of the basis of that vocation. The document deals with the natural mystery of the world and the supernatural mystery of the Church, he said. While these are theological ideas, they should be expressed in a language that is not strictly theological, he stated. We must strive to fill the void of theological sense which is growing in the world, he said.

Abbot Jean Prou, O.P., president of the French Benedictine Congregation, urged that a sharper distinction be made by the schema between rational creatures who can be directed to Christ through grace, and irrational creatures which are incapable of grace. The council should carefully avoid prejudging any intricate theological problems, he said.

Auxiliary Bishop Jose Guerra Campos of Madrid said a large part of modern culture is pervaded by the Marxist notion that all religion is a denial of human nature. Without polemics or apologetics, he continued, the Church should make it very clear that religion is the dynamic expression of human perfection. The council should carefully avoid describing Christianity as an ideological system, he said.

Archbishop Josip Pogacnik of Ljubljana, Yugoslavia, suggested the schema could be improved by stating clearly just what the Church does for those living in misery. Referring to the schema's mention of the Biblical term "signs of the times," he said special emphasis should be put on atheism as a sign of the times. He said the Church has suffered from atheism both in the East and in the West. He asserted that God has permitted widespread apostasy because of the cosmic dimension of sin and in order to make everyone conscious of his own personal guilt. Resounding pastoral letters will be useless unless they are followed up by concrete action, he said. It is no secret that in some places government officials read Mater et Magistra before many bishops, he stated.

Auxiliary Bishop Heinrich Tenhumberg of Muenster, Germany, asserted that people often fail to recognize signs of the times because they lack spiritual intuition which, in turn, is due to a lack of practical devotion to the Holy Spirit. In explaining the Church's mission, the council must not fail to emphasize the task of bishops and of all who exercise authority in the Church, he declared.

Bishop Remi De Roo of Victoria, B.C., said he wanted the schema to instruct Christians to avoid any split between the natural and supernatural missions which are a part of their vocation. Christians should share in the world's struggles. Nobody can effectively collaborate in developing the Christian community unless he actively participates in building the human community, he stated.

Auxiliary Bishop Santo Quadri of Pinerolo, Italy, said the schema fails to give enough importance to work, whose place in man's complete vocation should be explained. Work is a biological need, since without it life cannot go on, he said. A Christian must recognize that in working he is collaborating with God. While work is neither the sole nor supreme value in life, we must have a clear notion of its spiritual value, he asserted.

Maronite-rite Archbishop Ignace Ziade of Beirut, Lebanon, urged that the document's arguments should appeal primarily to reason rather than to authority.

Auxiliary Bishop Alfred Ancel of Lyons, France, began debate on chapters two and three. The schema gives the impression that its sole aim is to build up the earthly city, he said. The schema should therefore take up the Church's essential mission of evangelization, he added.

Bishop Morrow said the mentality which expects God the Father to damn a man to hell for eating meat on Friday seems more legalistic than genuinely religious and makes the Church a laughing-stock for many.

Auxiliary Bishop Anthony Hacault of St. Boniface, Man., said that while the Church in this world cannot be expected to solve all the problems of all men, we must insist that constant efforts be made in this direction. The Church's closer contacts with men, a more vital dialogue and a more faithful awakening to the Holy Spirit will make it easier for the Church to complete its mission which is to lead all men to God through Christ, he stated.

Bishop Cule quoted the 19th century restorer of the Dominican Order in France, Father Lacordaire, to support his thesis that the Church runs a greater risk from a government which is too kindly disposed toward it than from a hostile government.

Archbishop Francois Marty of Rheims, France, deplored the schema's insufficient stress on the Church's vital presence in the world. He echoed Bishop Cule's point that the Church is a leaven in the world. In the Middle Ages the Church almost absorbed society, to the extent that the Church and society were then coterminous, he said.

Since the Church's presence in the world must be truly Catholic, all Western-mindedness should be eliminated from the schema, he went on. The Church's presence in the world is a duty not of the clergy and the hierarchy alone, nor of the laity alone, but of every member of the Church, he stated.

Bishop Otto Spuelbeck of Meissen, Germany, who holds a doctorate in science, declared that in speaking to scientists the Church often uses an archaic and moribund language. The council Fathers should examine their conscience to see if they are characterized by that ardent study which would enable them to understand today's problems and give adequate answers, he said.

How can we explain the influence of the late Father Pierre Teilhard de Chardin? he asked. We know he was a pious priest, and scientists tell us they felt close to him because he spoke their language. Some individuals today want him condemned, as though they were afraid of a concord between religion and science, he declared. This would be a repetition of the condemnation of Galileo and would not be without fault on our part, he said. Disagreement between science and faith has been caused not so much by ill will as by a lack of mutual understanding, he added.

Religious skepticism is growing among young students and could easily lead them into the ranks of unbelievers, he continued. It is our task to adopt an attitude that will enable us to maintain a spirit of comradeship in intellectual research without harm to the principles of faith, he said.

Bishop Michal Klepacz of Lodz, Poland, approached the achievements of science from a different tack. He said the glorification of scientific research and

discoveries has resulted in a genuine apotheosis of man and the construction of a new tower of Babel. Today's world is characterized by conflicting trends of exaggerated optimism and nihilistic pessimism, he said, and the Church must combat both of these destructive tendencies.

Bishop Rene Fourrey of Belley, France, criticized the schema's treatment of poverty. He said it is presented in a tone of spiritual exhortation and lacks a Scriptural base. Poverty afflicts not only individuals but countries and peoples, he noted. The Scriptural "Woe to the rich" is addressed not only to rich men but to rich nations, who have a duty to help the poor nations, he said. Yet the schema says nothing about collective poverty. Usury, which the speaker called the exploitation of want for purposes of gain, should be condemned in its many modern forms. Unless the council faces such concrete problems it will be straining out gnats and swallowing camels, he stated. The flower of real poverty is humble service of God and of man, he declared.

A total of 2,007 council Fathers attended the debate which ended at 12:15 because several speakers did not respond to the summons from Cardinal Suenens.

PATRICK RILEY

Bishop Wright Defends Schema 13

Bishop John J. Wright of Pittsburgh made a spirited defense of the council's schema 13 on the Church in the modern world and of the men who wrote it.

Without mentioning the name of Archbishop John C. Heenan of Westminster, England, the American prelate rebutted the archbishop's assault on the schema as a "set of platitudes" and his assault on the experts who helped prepare the schema as men who did not really know their subjects.

Bishop Wright spoke at a press conference (Oct. 24) two days after Archbishop Heenan's speech in the council hall. Bishop Wright pointed out that the schema has to lay down the general principles of the Church's engagement with the modern world. "General principles tend to be expressed in broad terms and therefore sometimes thought of as platitudes," he said.

He likened the principles laid down in the schema's introduction and the first two chapters to the principles set forth in the United Nations Charter, to the "revolutionary propositions" of the American Declaration of Independence, and to the Sermon on the Mount, "which I have heard described as platitudinous."

He protested that he could not fail to say "a word in tribute to the scholarly humility, the admirable patience, the loving faith and forebearance with which the overwhelming majority of periti (council experts) work."

Bishop Wright is a member of the mixed commission that drafted schema 13.

He maintained that the schema would not appeal to people who are preoccupied with the moral crisis of modern culture because it regards this moral crisis as merely symptomatic of a deeper crisis of ideas and therefore of dogma.

Noting that it is "always easier to call in the police" than to get at the root of a difficulty, Bishop Wright asserted that the men who must dig at the roots of our crisis are the thinkers and scholars—"and in terms of the council, the word for scholar is peritus."

When asked for his comment on Archbishop Heenan's speech, Bishop Wright said: "It is clear that he felt very deeply and personally about what he had to say, whatever it was he had to say."

Bishop Wright also noted that Archbishop Heenan was very anxious to have his speech known, for he provided "abundant translation" of it to newsmen.

A reporter asked Bishop Wright for comment on Archbishop Heenan's suggestion that the council create a new commission to rewrite the schema, and that the council meet in another three or four years to discuss it.

"I would be reluctant to believe that he wanted to bypass the schema entirely," Bishop Wright replied, "but that would be the effect."

Bishop Wright said three years and more had already gone into the preparation of the schema (including material prepared for the other schemata which have since been abandoned), and that Archbishop Heenan's suggestion would mean a total of seven or eight years in the preparation of the schema. PATRICK RILEY

Christian Responsibility and World Poverty

This is the text of an address, "Christian Responsibility and World Poverty," delivered by Father Arthur McCormack, M.H.M., to a meeting of the German bishops in Rome on Oct. 26.

I am an economist and a demographer. At the same time I am a priest. I would like to suggest, therefore, in considering the problems of world poverty, complicated by the population explosion, that to tackle these problems, we should "marry" the moral force, the moral indignation of the Christian conscience, in face of misery on a world-wide scale, with the exigencies of economics, to translate the Gospel "cup of cold water" into the realities of the economic situation in the 20th century.

We are the more able to do this now, because the world-renowned economists who treat of this subject no longer represent the old-fashioned school of laissez-faire economists, but are filled with the conviction that investment in human beings' social progress is not only in accord with the dignity of man and modern humanitarian ideals, but also with sound economic theory.

I feel abashed to speak before you, the bishops of Germany, who more than the others in the Church have not only realized the needs of the poorer countries, but have done something about them—something magnificent.

I have here the figures which tell the story of your Misereor, German Caritas, the Adveniat collections, 215 million marks ($54,000,000) was collected by Misereor, for example, between 1959 and the end of 1963. This amount of money represents astonishing generosity. It has been applied with thoroughness and care and, if I may say so, with a strategic sense which has assured that it really reaches the most need and does the most good.

I am not speaking as an armchair economist who looked up a few figures to prepare a talk. On a tour of South America in April I learned at first hand of the work of Misereor. The members of the DESAL organization (the movement for Socio-Economic Development in Latin America) helped me very much and allowed me to see the wonderful efforts stimulating self-help which DESAL is making, especially in Santiago, Chile. I spent several hours with the remarkable Father Vekkemans of the DESAL. It is no exaggeration to give to this team a great share of the credit for the election of

Eduardo Frei as president of Chile, with a program based on Catholic social principles which DESAL is constantly applying to the realities of the Chilean situation. DESAL is one of the several thousand projects financed by Misereor. Incidently, on the same tour I had the chance to go round the terrible slums of most of the big cities of South America, and see with my own eyes the statistics of world hunger and poverty in terms of human misery.

As an Englishman whose country has not done so much as yours, either with regard to private charity or governmental aid, I feel abashed. I have no right to speak to you; it is your kindness which has given me this opportunity. I welcome it very sincerely.

I feel that many in the Church have still not grasped the extent, the importance, and the urgency of these problems. By your example, and perhaps also by your words, you may be the means of making them aware. A revolution in this field is needed. Not indeed with regard to the teaching at the center. Mater et Magistra, Pacem in Terris, and the speeches of our present Holy Father are clear and detailed and splendid directives. But a revolution is needed in the appreciation of this teaching, so that it should reach all levels and all places and be a stimulus to action. "I was hungry and you formed a study group" could still be said of many in the Church.

The need for action is urgent. Perhaps you will bear with me while I sketch briefly that need.

The central problem of our age, one potentially as explosive as the bomb, is the division of the world into the "haves" and the "have nots." It is the existence of that "third world" where hunger and poverty are endemic and where, to use the words of the noted English economist Andrew Shonfield, "millions of people live lives well below what most of us would regard as the extreme limit of imaginable poverty."

Sober expert reports, such as those of P. V. Sukhatme of the F.A.O., estimate that half the world is suffering from lack of food sufficient in quantity and quality for a healthy existence, and that about one person in seven has literally not enough to eat. This would mean about 400 million people.

But hunger is, of course, only one of the evils summed up in the unemotional word "underdevelopment." The misery and degradation of acute poverty include many more human problems. Among the most pressing of these are lack of medical services, of basic education, and of adequate housing and clothing. People's inability to practice the simple rules of hygiene is another (though much progress has been made in this area in recent years, ironically bringing other problems by sparking off explosive population increase).

Again, there are industrial underdevelopment, lack of employment or concealed unemployment, and lack of the capital and savings to allow a breakthrough of the vicious circle of poverty breeding poverty. Finally, lack of opportunities for improvement and even absence of the desire to improve, caused by decades of malnutrition and disease, complete the picture.

It is estimated that 1¼ billion people in 100 countries have an annual income per head of only 400 marks [$100]. President Johnson said that anyone under 12,000 marks [$3,000] was in poverty in the United States.

Such poverty has always existed, indeed, in the past it has been worse than it is now. It has not been caused, as some imply, by this country's population explosion, nor will it be cured even by the most effective birth control campaigns. What is new, as Mr. Nehru has said, is not poverty and misery. The new thing is that people are now aware of their plight, and of the affluence of others, and are determined to correct the situation.

Since the end of World War II, there has been an awakening of the poorer half of the world of such magnitude as to justify Adlai Stevenson's phrase, "the revolution of rising expectations." Since then, one billion people have gained their independence. They have not done so in order to starve, but to win for themselves lives free from the degradation of poverty and worthy of their dignity as human beings.

The first action necessary is surely to make known these facts, as Pope John stressed in his speech to the FAO conference in April, 1960, when he said:

"Millions of human beings suffer hunger: others who do not strictly speaking go hungry, are underfed: these are the facts. They must be made known, they must be preached from the house-tops. Consciences must be awakened to a sense of responsibility that rests on the human community and on each individual, on the most privileged especially. We are all collectively responsible for the undernourished."

This Sunday, Oct. 25, the Italian television had a program on hunger and poverty throughout the world. Afterwards a reporter went out into the streets of Rome asking people did they know of these facts. Not one did. But when they were told, they all agreed it was their duty to help. There is, I believe, a vast potential of untapped generosity. In this sphere knowledge generates this generosity.

Of course, in face of the vastness of the problems, generosity alone is not enough. This vastness is, however, no reason for pessimism or despair. Leading economists and agriculturalists say that we have at last the means to wipe out poverty. Paul Hoffman, head of the U.N. Special Fund, has said:

"The most challenging, pervasive and explosive idea of this century is that poverty can be wiped out."

In parenthesis we may note that Lester Pearson of Canada has also said: "The grim fact is . . . that we prepare for war like precocious giants and for peace like retarded pigmies."

Barbara Ward, the world-famed economist (a very good Catholic and, I am proud to say, a good friend of mine), said at Oxford University last year:

"Even if the rate of population growth goes at its present dizzy speed, we can still feed the human race in the foreseeable future. Remember this is the first time in history that it has been possible to say this."

Dr. Lamartine Yates of FAO, after describing the advantages we now have in the war on want, said nearly 10 years ago—it is more true now:

"If this be a fair assessment, it is just about the most exciting prospect for a century-to-be, that mankind has ever faced. By comparison most of our other preoccupations appear puny indeed: cold war, class war, color prejudice and so on. What is almost within human grasp is nothing less than the abolition of poverty in the primary strongholds of poverty, the bringing of low income peoples, not to equality of income with the more prosperous countries, but to within hailing distance, so there is no longer a wide social and material gap between them."

There is no need to multiply expert testimony. The fact is that we have all the technical knowledge, all the material resources, all the financial potential to wipe poverty off the face of the earth in this century or at least in the next 50 years. What is lacking is a sense of urgency, a conviction that we can and must do it.

Can the Church do anything to hasten this? Should she do anything? Is it her role?

It may be well to recall that the First Vatican Council, though it was convened at the height of the industrial revolution, did not issue any guidance on social justice within the industrializing nations. There was no word of hope for the proletariat, for the victimized working class. They could hardly lift their eyes from their misery to rejoice in the definition of papal infallibility.

We may charitably suppose that, if the council

188

had continued, it would have issued a call for social justice. It would have been very remarkable if it had done so, however. Apart from that wonderful pioneer, Bishop von Ketteler of Mainz and some others, there had not up to then been very much interest among bishops in this subject. Indeed, even 20 years later, Pope Leo was ahead of his time when he issued Rerum Novarum, and yet he was too late to prevent the loss of the working class to the Church, in many countries, because it was thought that the Church was not concerned in its plight and was more interested in Church matters than in the world, with its harsh realities.

Today we face the same situation between nations as was faced 100 years ago within nations. Today there are proletariat nations. Vatican II has a magnificent chance, faces a stirring challenge to appeal for international social justice. The council could send forth a clarion call for an all-out war on want, a total war on the conditions that are the scandal of our age; the existence of grinding poverty in the midst of plenty, the fact that in this, the most properous century in world history, millions are living lives out of keeping with their human dignity.

Such an effort to mobilize the moral force of the Catholic Church behind a concerted drive to wipe out poverty would of its very nature find great support from other Christian bodies, indeed from all the major religions that believe in the brotherhood of man under the fatherhood of God. This would be ecumenical action about which there could be no controversy.

No one doubts the meaning of our Lord's injunction to feed the hungry and clothe the naked. In this way a "third world" of help would be mobilized to combat the poverty of the underprivileged "third world." All men of good will, even those who do not believe in God but are genuinely humane, could be invited to join this crusade. Of course, as I have already suggested, such an approach would have to be geared to the realities of economics and politics. The example of a newly awakened South America shows how this could be done.

I am not a peritus, so I can only wonder if Schema 13 gives the over-riding importance to this central problem of our age by a first high priority treatment of it, and whether concrete proposals, made with all due respect and deference, may be of interest:

1. To show the concern of the Church and the earnestness of her commitment, some ongoing structure, a sort of war cabinet, to direct this war on want for the Church could be set up. A cardinal of the stature of Cardinal Bea could head this structure. By his personality Cardinal Bea has come to symbolize the Church's ecumenical concern. In several years he has done much to revolutionize relations between the Churches. An outstanding cardinal as head of the organization I am suggesting could come to symbolize the Church's concern for world poverty. The functions of such a body would be manifold and vital. I would be willing to suggest some which have already been worked out.

2. The bishops in council could devote a solemn day to world poverty and pledge themselves to work to eliminate it, perhaps by some symbolic gesture.

3. The Church could give the moral force, the moral leadership which seems to be lacking, and ensure also that this war on want is not based on political expediency or economic self-interest, but on brotherly love and respect for the dignity of man.

4. The Church could see to it that a temporal messianism was not sought, that in finding bread for mankind, men would forget that man does not live by bread alone.

5. She could actively insist at every level that human dignity, the cultural and spiritual heritage of developing nations is not damaged in the urgent attempt to get rapid economic progress and development.

6. The Church could arrange for much greater use of her missionary personnel as stimulators of socioeconomic action. These missionaries form the biggest potential cadre of technical assistance in the world today by their knowledge of their people and their needs. This would need balance, of course; priests must do their spiritual duties. But one priest at least in each diocese could be an expert adviser to the bishop and fellow missionaries and indigenous clergy. Not only that: aid channeled through Church agencies and administered through missionaries is often the most effective, economical and secure way of giving help to those most in need.

7. The Church could preach in season and out of season the duty of the rich countries to share their prosperity, and the duty of the poorer countries to put themselves in a position to receive cooperative help by social reform, political stability, and real concern for the progress of all their people, and not the enrichment of a few.

Should the Church do this? Should priests be engaged in this work at all? This is not an idle question. Perhaps the best answer may be given by applying the parable of the Good Samaritan in modern language to the conditions of today. The priest and levite were hurrying to Jerusalem to take part in the liturgy of the People of God, the act of divine worship which is man's first and most important duty. They had not time—and it was not their job—to give emergency aid to the man lying injured by the roadside, still less to give him long-term socio-economic assistance by arranging for his lodging, etc. They might have missed the sacred ceremonies. They were apparently absolutely right—the only thing is: Our Lord did not think so!

110th General Congregation
October 27, 1964

Catholics are not contributing their share to the world's supply of scientists, a German bishop complained to the Second Vatican Council.

This reinforces a notion propagated through newspapers, television and other means of mass communications that religion is somehow hostile to science, Auxiliary Bishop Wilhelm Cleven of Cologne, Germany, noted.

He spoke during debate on chapters two and three of schema 13 on the Church in the modern world. The chapters deal with the Church in the service of God and men and on Christian conduct in today's world.

The day's debate heard renewed appeals for a fresh look at the heavy penalties attached to breaking some laws of the Church. Melkite-rite Patriarch Maximos IV Saigh of Antioch and Bishop Sergio Mendez Arceo of Cuernavaca, Mexico, in asking for a less rigidly legalistic attitude, echoed the speech made the previous day by American-born missionary Bishop Louis Morrow of Krishnagar, India.

Two cardinals also underlined the part poverty plays in the world, both as a plague afflicting mankind and, when voluntarily embraced, as a measure to help eradicate that plague.

Another group of council Fathers spoke of men's need to communicate with one another—or what has come to be called dialogue.

Bishop Cleven in his appeal to the council to reaffirm the Church's real teaching about science and its role in the life of man, asserted that the Church's list of forbidden books—the index—tends to deprive people of their confidence in Church authority. He said television shows and the like are making sure that men do not forget the Church's condemnation of the great scientist, Galileo.

Bishop Cleven began by referring to the passage in the chapter which treats of the attitude of Christians to the natural sciences. He said it is statistically certain that in most countries the proportion of Catholics among scientists is smaller than the proportion of Catholics among the total population.

This lack of full Catholic representation in the world of science should not be laid to any guile or ill will on the part of non-Catholics, he said.

He asserted that in an age when man's most basic needs, such as heat, water and bread, are brought to him through scientific discoveries, the relative scarcity of Catholic scientists is dangerous.

He appealed for a forthright declaration that the Church confidently expects that science will contribute to the spiritual mission of the Church itself. He said a clarifying note should be added that while Catholics should respect science and cooperate with it, they should not place their hope for salvation in science but in charity.

Raul Cardinal Silva Henriquez of Santiago, Chile, said the exercise of Christian poverty must be aimed at bringing about a more equitable distribution of the world's goods.

He said that while poverty can spring from grace, it can also be brought about by sin. This point was also made in a slightly different form by Antonio Cardinal Caggiano of Buenos Aires.

The Chilean cardinal noted that while God's perfection consists in what He is, man's perfection stems from what he has. He observed that this "having" can easily run riot.

He suggested that in order to make voluntary poverty socially effective, an organization should be set up to sponsor an annual worldwide collection for the poor. Such a collection—suggested by Protestant theologian Oscar Cullman, professor at the Universities of Paris and Basel, Switzerland, and a guest of the Secretariat for Promoting Christian Unity at the current council session—would be like "a sacramental of brotherhood."

Cardinal Caggiano asked that charity not be overemphasized in the schema at the expense of the virtue of justice. He said that if justice were respected, everyone would be given his due, and if everyone were given his due, there would be no vast armies of men without work.

We must follow Christ Crucified in a spirit of poverty, he said.

Bishop Charles-Marie Himmer of Tournai, Belgium, echoed this call for emphasis on the positive and constructive aspects of poverty. He said the schema must point out how this poverty is not sought for itself but as a means of building a better earthly city and eliminating poverty from the lives of those afflicted by it.

According to Bishop Himmer, all the problems of

this schema—from those of marriage to the eradication of hunger—demand the collaboration of men who are generous and really ready to help the poor. He asked for a clarification of the distinction between Christian poverty, which is essentially evangelical, and the detachment from earthly things sometimes practiced by non-Christians.

He also appealed for an investigation of modern society's economic and political structures to find means of a better sharing of wealth.

Bishop Mendez and Patriarch Maximos both laid the groundwork for their attacks on ecclesiastical legalism by emphasizing personal responsibility.

Bishop Mendez said efforts to nurture personal dignity and responsibility along with freedom are among the chief "signs of the times" of which the schema speaks. This insistence on liberty was anticipated by St. Paul who, the bishop said, was so fully convinced of his liberation from the Law of Moses.

While Church law should be so established as to promote a spirit of love, this is not always achieved by a multiplication of Church laws, he said. He added that the Church cannot afford to show a kindly face to those outside and a harsh face to its own children.

In a reference to the severe punishment attached to failure to observe certain Church laws, Bishop Mendez observed that if civil states imposed life imprisonment for small crimes, there would be no real understanding and cooperation between the authorities and citizens.

Patriarch Maximos also asserted that the Church's mind should be characterized by St. Paul's spirit of broad understanding. He said to state that missing Mass on a holy day or eating meat on Friday entails the guilt of mortal sin and can lead to eternal damnation is hardly reasonable.

The Church is a mother, he said, but he asked if even a stepmother would impose such punishments.

He suggested that a committee of moral theologians be set up to study the Church's commandments.

He also touched on the need for dialogue between the Church and its children, a dialogue that requires maturity on the part of Catholics.

Bishop Gerard Huyghe of Arras, France, also centered his speech on the need for a dialogue within the Church. Such internal dialogue is a necessary condition for a dialogue with those outside the Church, he said. The primary internal dialogue, he stated, is that of the individual with the Holy Spirit.

Bishop Huyghe returned to the question of Church law. He turned his fire on the petty laws and regulations which hobble the freedom of Catholics in their own fields of action. He said some theologians who were sincerely studying modern problems and trying to foster dialogue were condemned without a hearing. He declared this should not be.

Joseph Cardinal Frings of Cologne, Germany, began the day's debate with an address read by his secretary. His talk was basically a criticism of the schema for its emphasis on earthly goods at the expense of stress on the Cross and Redemption.

Cardinal Frings began with something of a concession to the schema's treatment, pointing out the dangers of the error of distinguishing too sharply between body and soul. Christ came to save not merely souls but the whole man, he said. Yet, he added, no matter how positive our approach to worldly progress, we must not forget that such progress does not of itself lead directly to the kingdom of God. While the Church and the world will be united when they achieve their final vocation at the end of time, on this earth they are irreducibly distinct, he stated.

Like Patriarch Maximos and Bishop Huyghe, Coadjutor Bishop Adrien Gand of Lille, France, spoke of the need for dialogue. Bishop Gand criticized the schema for not emphasizing this sufficiently.

Men tend to think of themselves as lost in an anonymous mass unless they are reminded that something is expected of each of them, he said.

Archbishop Elie Zoghbi, Melkite-rite patriarchal vicar for Egypt, said he wanted chapter two to take a new tack. It opens with a discussion of the Church's mission of service, he noted, and the Church is said to be in the world to bring the Gospel and salvation. Archbishop Zoghbi, however, suggested it would be more logical to start with the Church's mission of love. He pointed out that Christ started this way, healing the sick and feeding the hungry, thus preparing people to believe in His mission.

How many nursing Sisters have opened the way to God by ministering to sick bodies, he asked.

Saying that the council should state clearly that the Church is in the world for the sake of men, he said it would be good Church usage to avoid expressions smacking of temporal power or rule, such as "happily reigning" when referring to a pope.

Archbishop John Garner of Pretoria, South Africa, speaking in the name of 84 bishops of Europe and Latin America, said the Church should take advantage of the means for dialogue offered by modern tourism. He asked that it be mentioned in the text. Tourists, he said, make important contributions to world solidarity and peace.

Bishop Kazimierz Kowalski of Chelmo, Poland, asked for a fuller explanation of the text's reference to new modes of feeling, willing and acting. He said this new mode is a spirit of true penance or conversion of the heart.

The spirit of true penance consists less in deploring sins than in a continual and dynamic ascent to God, he added.

Auxiliary Bishop Franjo Kuheric of Zagreb, Yugoslavia, asked for a solemn council declaration on the relationship between science and revealed religion. He said that in countries under atheistic control, the Church is constantly being decried as an enemy of all progress and all science.

He also asked for a formal declaration on the inviolability of human life within the sanctuary of a mother's body to counter the plague of abortions which takes more lives than war.

Bishop Hermann Volk of Mainz, Germany, asked for a clearer outline of the role of the Lord's Day and of divine worship in showing Catholics how to play their role in the world.

Archbishop Enrico Nicodemo of Bari, Italy, suggested basing the schema's explanation of man's full vocation in the world on St. Paul's "recapitulation of all things in Christ." He said the text's treatment of atheism should affirm the transcendence of a personal God and the objective existence of moral evil. Individual responsibility should be emphasized, he stated.

Bishop Maurice Pourchet of Saint-Flour, France, suggested combining chapters two and three and giving them the same order of treatment followed in the schema on the nature of the Church: the mystery of the Church, of God, and the hierarchy. The Church's imminence in the world and the transcendence of its mission there should be made clear, he said.

Bishop Aurelio Sorrentino of Bova, Italy, asked that the schema be addressed not only to all men of good will but to all who do not refuse to listen. This is in the spirit of Christ and of St. Paul, he said.

The council's 110th general meeting began with a Maronite-rite Liturgy (Mass) concelebrated by Bishop Antoine Abed of Tripoli, Lebanon, and Fathers Michale Hokayem and Abdel Ahad Chanin. The Gospel was enthroned by Maronite-rite Archbishop Ignace Ziade of Beirut, Lebanon.

The day's moderator was Leo Cardinal Suenens of Malines-Brussels.

Chapter eight of the schema on the Church, which deals with Our Lady, was distributed. It was to take a single vote, which was expected on Oct. 29, on all the chapter's amendments.

PATRICK RILEY

Cardinal Suenens at Press Conference

The Church must walk with two legs—one ecumenism and the other evangelization—Leo Cardinal Suenens of Malines-Brussels told a press conference here.

Speaking on the coming council proposition on the missions, the cardinal pointed out that it must balance extensive talk thus far on ecumenism. Cardinal Suenens, one of the four council moderators, said:

"We discussed ecumenism at length. But the ecumenical approach is one-sided—an attempt to know each other better without the intention of conversion. We cannot, however, say conversion is no longer the duty of the Church. On the contrary, we must bring Christ to the whole world and this duty cannot be destroyed by ecumenical dialogues."

Ecumenism might give rise to the idea that now the Church should leave everyone to follow his own conscience, the cardinal said.

"Christ did not say this. He said to bring the Gospel to every creature—but with kindness. The priority of evangelization must be stressed, since this is what Christ wishes 'impatiently,' since love is impatient to communicate itself."

The cardinal said another coming council proposition, the one on seminaries and ecclesiastical formation, should be widened to include Religious scholasticates and even Sister formation centers. He said he would propose a new idea of seminaries based on the original idea of St. Charles Borromeo at the Council of Trent (1545-63), where seminary training was first formulated.

"Today the moment has arrived for a soulful examination," he said. "The Second Vatican Council must create a new kind of seminary in line with the needs of today. If there is one place where Pope John's updating is needed, it is here."

Using the new seminary in his own diocese as a pattern, he described his hopes. The new seminary should deal with the problems facing priests of today, who feel they are isolated from the current of the modern world as well as from the company of their fellow priests and even from God.

This last is true, he said, because seminary spirituality is not in line with the needs of the priest working in the world but is based more on monastic spirituality. He called for the formulation of a spirituality for an active life and said that unity between prayer and the apostolate is essential today.

"We must never stop stressing the need for prayer—but never in such a way that it is in opposition to the apostolate," he said. "The first 30 years of Christ's life were not contemplative. They were spent in normal labor. Contemplative preparation for the active ministry lasted 40 days, when Christ went into the desert."

Cardinal Suenens called for pastoral training throughout the seminary course, including active work among the laity. Since the priest today has a new dimension in serving the people of God, he said, "he has to learn how to pray, not instead of the people of God but at their head. The priest must learn to help the laity fulfil their apostolic mission."

Regarding the necessity of practical seminary training, the cardinal observed that "you need a swimming pool to learn how to swim." He suggested that seminarians spend two or three hours a week in active work under the guidance of pastoral experts and make reports on successes and failures. He added:

"An assignment of responsibility from the start is essential."

Speaking of a third document awaiting discussion by the council, the one on Religious, he said: "There is not much here on aggiornamento (updating)."

He called for putting Religious women on the same footing as Religious men and asked that "these million souls given to God must be used in a much more efficient way. Today women are ready to go to the moon. Why should they not be on the same footing of equality with men?"

FATHER JOHN P. DONNELLY

Bigger Church Role for Women Asked

"The Church must abandon the masculine superiority complex which ignores the spiritual power of women," said Leo Cardinal Suenens of Malines-Brussels in an interview here.

Asked to elaborate on his now famous council statement of last year that it sometimes seems as if the Church were paying no attention to "half of humanity," the cardinal, who is one of the four moderators of the ecumenical council, said:

"We must learn to respect woman in her true dignity and to appreciate her part in the plan of God.

"This is my firm conviction and is well founded on the Mariological teachings of the Church, which once again will be reflected in the council schema on the Church as theological principles of transcending importance.

"They also find a tangible expression in the presence of women auditors in council sessions, a presence of deeply symbolical significance inasmuch as it affirms an equality of all the people of God, be they women or men.

"The women auditors by their presence indicate clearly that we are slowly emerging from a state of affairs which was not doing justice to the feminine sex."

Would this, Cardinal Suenens was asked, also apply to the women Religious?

"Yes, indeed," replied the cardinal, "for by and large women Religious now have no opportunity to become articulate in the Church, to make their voices heard. This certainly is not in keeping with modern concepts of womanhood."

How could this situation be changed?

"By activating women Religious," said Cardinal Suenens. "By making them conscious of their place in the world, by letting them face the realities of life and become mature persons who can exercise a vital apostolate, especially among women, if they are properly equipped intellectually and so trained that they will gain in stature in their own consciousness and therefore be enabled to make contributions of their own toward the development of society."

The problems of marriage being of immediate concern of most women, what could the council contribute toward their solution, Cardinal Suenens was asked.

"We must be realists in this respect. Christian married couples do not always see things in the same light as theologians, who should be prepared to gain new perspectives in keeping abreast of specific situations.

"This does not mean that we should look for what might be called mechanical answers to so difficult a problem as birth control. We know it is being studied by theologians as well as by medical men. These studies must continue, and we should not be impatient, if tangible results are not immediately forthcoming. Once such results are obtained, it may well be possible to provide a guidance entirely acceptable by the standards of Church doctrine. In the meantime let us concentrate on what is most important, the kind of education and instruction of our own people which will make them realize more fully the preeminent factor of love, a love understood as Christian mutual charity."

Cardinal Suenens often has expressed the view that the life of the Church should be marked by greater simplicity. He was asked what his thoughts are now in this respect.

"Briefly," he replied, "I think we could easily do without all the things that smack of the style prevailing at former French imperial courts. Today we call it the curial style. This applies to titles, modes of dressing and other appurtenances not really in keeping with the spirit of the Gospel.

"Of course, I don't mean to refer to the liturgy of the Church. There solemnity must be preserved in a proper measure.

"In our day-to-day living, however, we should be as modest as possible and adapt our style of life to modern concepts."

In concluding the interview Cardinal Suenens spoke

of the council, its achievements so far and its prospects.

"Clearly," he said, "the first two sessions were in a sense preparatory. We now begin to garner the fruits of our labors.

"The schema on the Church, once adopted, will be a monumental acomplishment. Naturally, the principle of episcopal collegiality it proclaims will have to be applied in practice before we will experience its full import, and both theologians and pastors will find that for a long time to come it will offer food for thought. However, the groundwork is now done. The Holy Spirit has guided the council so that the high goal to complete what the First Vatican Council had begun could be achieved.

"Once this council is over, the post-conciliar commissions will go to work to implement our decisions, and then there is every reason to expect that the supreme council Pope Paul VI himself envisages as their crowning outcome will be set up to govern the universal Church in close union with the pontiff and under his direction. I personally hope it will not be too large a body, rather more of a working group representative of the whole Church.

"We must not expect spectacular developments. Progress will come about quietly, at times even unnoticed, and we should let things grow in the natural way, under the guidance of the Holy Spirit.

"Then, of course, there is that tremendously important development of ecumenism. Interfaith relations have gained an incentive through this council we never thought possible. This applies to our Protestant friends no less than to the Orthodox, although perhaps the prospects for reunion are more immediate in regard to the latter.

"We are now entering the phase of closer contacts with Orthodoxy when the separation that still stands between us will slowly be overcome, when we can talk to each other and understand one another better."

A last question was raised: how much longer might this council last?

"We will certainly be able to dispose of all that is on the agenda now by Nov. 20," replied Cardinal Suenens.

"Then the commissions will go to work again, and since they will have a great deal to do reworking such key schemata as the ones on the lay apostolate and the Church in the modern world, to mention just these two, I doubt that the fourth council session, which ought to be the last one, can be held before the fall of next year, probably in October, but it is likely to be short, lasting only four to six weeks.

"By that time I am convinced we will have accomplished what Pope John XXIII wanted us to do and what Pope Paul VI gave us the mandate to bring to a promising end."

(Giacomo Cardinal Lercaro of Bologna, Italy, another council moderator, said in his council address of Oct. 20 that in his opinion the fourth and closing session of the council should be held in 1966 in order to give ample time to the competent committees to rework the various draft proposals in the light of the recommendations made on the council floor.)

FATHER PLACID JORDAN, O.S.B.

*　*　*　*

Whether the Church will change its laws regarding abstinence from meat on Friday and church attendance on Sunday, it is already clear that some bishops want at least a change in attitude on these subjects.

This was the reaction of members of the U.S. bishops' press panel to references made in the council during discussion of the schema on the Church in the modern world.

Discussing the schema, several bishops used the examples of current Church laws of abstinence and Sunday Mass obligation under pain of mortal sin as indicating the need for reform in moral theology.

Father Charles Davis, British moral theologian, pointed out that the bishops' objection was not to the laws themselves but to the deeper question of the mentality of issuing such laws under pain of mortal sin.

"The simple statement of such binding force represents a primitive approach to morality," Father Davis said. "There is no recognition of the psychological working of consciences.

"Mortal sin comes about when an action performed embodies a fundamental rejection of God or a fundamental choice against Him. Development of conscience is demanded for an understanding of the positive precepts, which many do not have, and consequently they do not sin gravely in acting against such precepts."

Father Davis said statements saying that missing Mass on Sunday or eating meat on Friday damn one for eternity are "crude and confused," since they do not take into account the circumstances which can change the morality of an act and the degree of knowledge of an act's sinfulness required for sin.

"Hence authorities should not announce mortal sins —only God should do that. Church authorities should rather say they regard this or that matter as serious, something which cannot be ignored without turning away from God."

Father Francis J. Connell, C.SS.R., former dean of the School of Sacred Theology at the Catholic University of America, pointed out that the Church could change its abstinence and Sunday obligation laws, since they are "purely ecclesiastical, although connected with divine commands to fast and to worship God."

Regarding objections in the council that the Church

should not make such laws, he said he thought that another side to the argument might be the danger of the "wedge principle."

"If people are told that the obligation of Sunday Mass did not bind under pain of sin, how many would go to Mass?" he asked.

Another panel member, Msgr. George G. Higgins, director of the Social Action Department of the National Catholic Welfare Conference, said he did not think the specific examples used in the council chamber were anything more than examples. The main point, he said, was the theme which they represent—the mentality of binding under mortal sin in such cases. Any specific recommendations have been or will be referred to the commission on the revision of the Code of Canon Law, he stated.

"And I expect the whole system will be revised," Msgr. Higgins said.

Summary of Chapters 2 and 3
On the Church in the Modern World

These are the summaries of chapters two and three of the schema on the Church in the modern world that were released by the ecumenical council press office.

SUMMARY: CHAPTER 2

The Church in the Service of God and Men

Contacts between the Church and the world are necessary, inasmuch as the Church has been founded by Christ for the salvation of the world. Many of the difficulties issuing from her contacts with the world would be avoided or lessened if the value of the divine mission of the Church were understood.

Christ entrusted to His Church the task of evangelizing men. Religious liberty is indispensable, whether for the Church in order to be in a position to announce the Gospel, or for men for the acceptance of the message of salvation through a free act of Faith.

Since the Christian is at the same time a citizen of the world, he is bound to accept its laws, with the exception of those which may be in conflict with the law of God. The Church can only judge civil laws in the light of religious and moral principles, but she must not in any degree become involved in temporal things, and, much less, dominate them.

Without the presence of the Church there is realized no true progress in the world. Charity, as well as all the other virtues contained in it, will always be necessary for life. Thus the Church can always offer her own proper contribution to the unfolding of life in the world.

The concrete manifestation of charity will vary according to differences of time and circumstances, but the faithful must always act conformably to their own conscience, which in turn must be formed by the pastors of souls.

SUMMARY: CHAPTER 3

The Christians' Manner of Life in the World in Which They Live

It is God's will that men should not live the message of salvation only as individuals, but should also reflect it in their family and social background, in order to impregnate this background with the presence of Christ. The council sets itself to point out to the faithful how they are to be authentic Christians and at the same time citizens of the world.

Charity is the supreme law given by Christ, whether in relation to God or in relation to one's neighbor. It is charity which causes us to recognize as our neighbors those who suffer, putting ourselves under an obligation, through a pooling of forces, to assist in their needs both as individuals and peoples.

In the present-day circumstances, Christians are under obligation to accept offices in the temporal order, because otherwise they would fail to carry the influence of Christ into many sectors of life.

In order to achieve this mission it is necessary above all to follow Christ in a spirit of poverty, and then to know how to open dialogue with all men of good will, the kind of dialogue which aims at mutual understanding in view of brotherly cooperation. Solidity in Faith and the spirit of brotherhood make it possible for us to enter into dialogue in all fields, with all due regard for Christian prudence. This calls for a deep spirit of abnegation and humility.

As for the apostolate, in restricted fields, it is advisable not to multiply specifically Catholic organizations, except in case of absolute necessity. If contacts are established with organizations set up on a broader scale, in cooperation with believers of other religions or with Christians of other confessions, care must be taken in such associations to respect religious and moral freedom. With regard to associations on an international level, it is the duty of Catholics to collaborate with them both as individuals and as groups, with the intention of providing service and to make efforts to insure an ever greater expansion of the spirit of brotherhood and justice.

111th General Congregation

October 28, 1964

In the name of all the American Bishops in Rome for the ecumenical council, Archbishop Patrick A. O'Boyle of Washington urged the council to add a "forthright and unequivocal condemnation of racism in all its forms" to the schema on the Church in the modern world.

Racism is to be found throughout the world in some form and to some degree, the prelate told the 111th general council meeting.

He characterized racism as "first and foremost a moral and religious problem, and one of staggering proportions."

He said a clear-cut condemnation of all forms of racial injustice is the "very least" the council should undertake.

Archbishop O'Boyle proposed adding a "separate section in chapter four [of the schema] on the problem of racial discrimination and other forms of racial injustice."

The same debate on chapter four of the schema, which deals with the principal task of the Christian today, heard another powerful denunciation of racial discrimination from Bishop Andrew G. Grutka of Gary, Ind. He branded it a "challenge to Divine Providence."

Some form of hate or disrespect can be found in every act of racial segregation, Bishop Grutka said.

Every form of racial segregation and discrimination should be denounced with the strength of the trumpets of Jericho, he declared.

He singled out segregation in housing as a special evil. Decent housing is indispensable for good family life, he said, and the family is the foundation of society. "No one would look for beauty on a garbage dump, and no one can expect virtue in a slum," he declared, repeating this sentence in English for emphasis and clarity.

The work of priests is stymied when people flee a neighborhood at the first sign that families of another race are seeking homes there, he said.

Joseph Cardinal Ritter of St. Louis spoke on gaps in the text and ways of filling them. Bishop John J. Wright of Pittsburgh presented the commission's report on chapter four.

The council meeting opened with Mass concelebrated by Archbishop Pericle Felici, council secretary general, who was celebrating the anniversaries of his ordination and consecration, and 12 parish priests from 12 nations, including the U.S.

This concelebration was in honor of the sixth anniversary of the election of Pope John XXIII.

The Gospel was enthroned by Bishop Luigi Rosa of Bagnoregio, Italy.

The day's moderator, Gregorio Cardinal Agagianian, announced that "certain points" of the schema would not be discussed orally on the council floor. He said this measure was aimed at forestalling misinterpretation and misunderstanding on the part of outsiders ("inter profanos").

He did not specify what these "certain points" would be. However, it was generally understood he was referring to the schema's section dealing with birth control, and possibly the section on nuclear warfare.

(At the U.S. bishops' press panel, Msgr. George G. Higgins, director of the Social Action Department of the National Catholic Welfare Conference, noted that Cardinal Agagianian made no reference to any specific problem but seemed to be referring not so much to general problems as to particular points within these problems. "It is not a case of the moderators' imposing an unwelcome rule on bishops. Most national hierarchies I know of want to avoid descending into particulars," Msgr. Higgins said.

(Father Frederick R. McManus, canon law professor at the Catholic University of America, said he got the impression that Cardinal Agagianian was not imposing a rule, but making a strong exhortation.

(Father Arthur McCormack, a British Mill Hill missioner and an expert in social and demographic problems, said Cardinal Agagianian's intention was to exclude particulars, not subjects. "I do not think any subject will be excluded. In fact I know there will be interventions on all subjects contained in chapter four, and they will be forthright and open," he said.

(Father McCormack's idea of particulars was "this or that pill, for instance.")

Cardinal Agagianian emphasized that the council Fathers had full freedom to express themseves in writing on these unspecified points. He even urged the council Fathers to make their thoughts known to the commission in charge of amending schema 13. He assured the Fathers that their written observations would be given full consideration in the final revision of the text.

Bishop Wright, in presenting the commission's report on chapter four, noted that it takes up some key themes in the life of the world today. He called these ideas "the master-knots of human fate."

Among them he listed the nature and dignity of the human person, the nature of holiness and difficulties of family life, economic and social problems, cultural values closely connected with human life, peace and world security.

It is not our task to find clever answers to all these problems, Bishop Wright said. This would take years. But we must exert every effort to apply the Church's ancient wisdom to the new and previously unheard of conditions harassing the human conscience today, he said.

The Church does not pronounce the last word on these problems, he said, only the first word of a dialogue. It would be a mistake to ask too much of a schema which has no precedent in conciliar history, he declared.

He replied directly to a head-on attack made on the schema the previous week by Archbishop John C. Heenan of Westminster, England.

We cannot search all the signs of the times, Bishop Wright said. This would take many years. To do as Archbishop Heenan admonished us to do would require a team of sociologists. It could not be done by the council, he stated.

Bishop Wright assured the Fathers that a special commission had already been set up to receive observations from every source, particularly from the less fully developed countries of the world not in the mainstream of the Christian tradition.

Bishop Wright concluded with a declaration that any attack on the social order is ultimately an attack on man and his dignity. Taking a line from the poet, Oliver Goldsmith, he said the council must concentrate on keeping the earth from becoming a place "where wealth accumulates and men decay."

The Fathers received copies of the changes made by the Theological Commission in chapter one of the schema on the nature of the Church. A vote on the amended chapter as a whole, which deals with the mystery of the Church, was to be taken Oct. 29. It was announced it would be only a yes or no vote, since the purpose was to determine whether the council agreed with the way the commission handled the suggested corrections.

Only two Fathers, Bishop Marcello Gonzales Martin of Astorga, Spain, and Coptic-rite Bishop Isaac Ghattas of Thebes, Egypt, spoke on the fourth chapter of schema 13 in general.

Bishop Gonzales complained that the text fails to tell Catholics how they are to be prepared for the grave tasks awaiting them. In past centuries, the Church universities were training grounds and in more modern times papal encyclicals have served this purpose, he said. He also noted that before the Church can hope to be heard by those outside it, it must renew itself within.

Bishop Ghattas said the chapter lacks a clear idea of the political value of the nation or fatherland. Catholics, he stated, are looking for concrete directives regarding their nations. While nationalism is an evil, the love of a country is a virtue, he said. The Christian who criticizes his country when it needs criticism is a dutiful son of his country, he declared.

Cardinal Ritter's criticism centered on the way the dignity of the human person is approached in the schema. He suggested that the section should first say something on how human dignity is to be understood and fostered; that it should be reorganized to state the problem at the outset, then enunciate pertinent principles and finally draw conclusions; and that it should aim at a recognition of the dignity of the human person.

He said each individual must recognize his own dignity before he can recognize the dignity of others.

The cardinal said man must overcome his natural passivity to exercise his responsibilities in private and public life.

Canadian and African bishops pleaded for full recognition of the dignity of women.

Bishop Gerard Coderre of Saint-Jean de Quebec urged that the schema throw a brighter light on the personality and role of women in the world, which have been obscured by the prevailing mistaken idea of the basic inferiority of women. Today's growing recognition of the dignity of women is among the signs of the times to be scrutinized by the schema, he said.

He proposed that the schema state that women are necessary for the completion of the divine plan for man's perfection, for the perfection of the family and for that of society. It should also ask men to strive to give women their proper place in the world.

Archbishop Joseph Malula of Leopoldville, the Congo, said that in Africa the work of freeing slaves must be completed now by freeing women. Women must be brought to a full acknowledgment of their own responsibility, he said. Woman is not just a servant, a handmaid, a mother or an instrument of pleasure, but man's helpmate and companion, he stated.

Archbishop Malula also touched on discrimination, but in a different context from Archbishop O'Boyle and Bishop Grutka. He said that in Africa tribalism is racism on a minor scale. It affects Christians, causing hatred and fear, and should be declared a serious sin against charity, he said.

Archbishop Dominic Athaide of Agra, India, also spoke of slavery, asserting that it exists even today. Men are being bought and sold and deprived of rights, he said. Often, through a policy of apartheid, they are victimized by discrimination on the basis of color. The council must take a strong stand on this because all men are awaiting liberation from this new slavery, he declared.

He praised the late Mahatma Ghandi's lifetime of work for 60 million outcasts in his own country. He also praised the late President John F. Kennedy. He recalled that Pope Paul VI, in a recent private audience with the American Negro leader, Dr. Martin Luther King, encouraged him in his peaceful crusade for racial equality, explicitly praising his policy of peaceful resistance.

Another Indian, Auxiliary Bishop Duraisamy Lourduswamy of Bangalore, spoke in the name of all 60 Indian bishops at the council. He urged that in giving help to individuals or nations, the person or nation giving aid avoid having or showing feelings of superiority. The distribution of aid should not be over-organized, since that prevents heart-to-heart contact, he said.

Auxiliary Bishop Georges Bejot of Rheims, France, urged the council to make three statements in order to emphasize the dignity of the human person:

The first would explain in the light of the faith just what human dignity consists of.

The second would point out how Christ promoted human dignity.

The third would indicate how the Church sees the signs of the time in men's aspirations.

Bishop Stjepan Bauerlein of Djakovo i Srijem, Yugoslavia, asked the text to specify the errors it alludes to. He said the text fails to give a complete view of Christian marriage and the dangers it is exposed to. The text gives insufficient emphasis to the role of civil and religious liberty for the education and development of the family, he said.

Bishop Pablo Barrachina Estevan of Orihuela-Alicante, Spain, said human dignity cannot be recognized without a correct evaluation of the human person. Despite the importance of psychological data in evaluating a personality, care must be taken not to think of man simply as a heap of psychological data, he said.

Auxiliary Bishop Eduard Schick of Fulda, Germany, praised the schema for hurling no accusations and passing no judgments, but examining the world situation to see what help the Church can offer. Men listen to the Church more readily today than in past decades, especially when the Church echoes Christ's charity, he said. He urged that the schema be given a deeper theological basis through more liberal use of Holy Scripture. He also urged that the schema be altered lest it give the impression of presenting Christianity as simply one ideology among many.

Bishop Pierre de la Chanonie of Clermont, France, urged the council to take up the special problem of bringing the Gospel to children who are handicapped physically or psychologically, morally or socially. He said that in France such handicapped youths make up almost one-fourth of the nation's adolescents and that in other countries their proportion is still greater.

Noting that the Church declares itself the mother of the poor, he asserted these children are the poorest of all. Despite their afflictions, they too have a right to fulfil their own human vocation in both the natural and supernatural order, he said.

Bishop Stefan Lazlo of Eisenstadt, Austria, urged the text provide a more detailed treatment of the notion of real liberty. Only thus can it forestall a false use of liberty, he said. Many things done in the name of liberty really conflict with genuine liberty. Such deeds diminish the dignity of the human person, he stated.

PATRICK RILEY

* * * *

In the light of what has been said in the ecumenical council, is the Congregation of the Holy Office obsolete in the modern Church?

This question, raised by a reporter at the U.S. bishops' press panel, drew a unanimous "no" from panel members, though several said the congregation needs considerable updating.

"As long as the Church continues to be a teacher, the need for such an office will exist," said Father John J. King, O.M.I., of Lowell, Mass., superior of the General House of Studies in Rome for Oblate priests.

How the Holy Office should operate is another question, Father King added. He stated: "Men should always be free to investigate and learn to apply the Faith. It is in keeping with the nature of such a body that this freedom be recognized as a positive necessity in order to promote understanding, but there is no contradiction between this office and the need for freedom."

Father Charles Davis, English moral theologian and temporary panel member, agreed that the Holy Office is not on its way out. "Nothing that has been said in the council removes the place of the pope as supreme authority in the Church, and in this capacity he will need such an office," he said.

Father Davis foresaw, however, that relations between this congregation and any future senate of bishops which may result from the council's teaching on collegiality would have to be investigated. He said:

"Bishops should exercise collegiality at the local level in doctrine before a matter reaches the central and more authoritative decision-making body. Collegiality supposes this doctrinal activity on local levels, making more mature the decisions later at the central level."

Msgr. George W. Shea, rector of Immaculate Conception Seminary, Darlington, N.J., pointed out that bishops sometimes fail to make such decisions. He referred to a recent communication from the Holy Office to bishops which expressed concern that bishops had not been more active at the local level. For instance, they were said to be giving approval for publication of books which contained doctrinal errors.

"The Holy Office is not unaware of the principle of subsidiarity," he said. Often less severe warnings are issued through local or national channels before outright condemnations are publicized, he said.

"You do not hear about many cases where the Holy Office was right in its condemnation and the Faith was safeguarded as a result. If such a body did not exist, we would have to invent one," he stated.

Father Roberto Tucci, S.J., editor of the Rome Jesuit review, Civilta Cattolica, and temporary panel member, agreed with Father Davis on the need for the local exercise of collegiality "provided the local bishop or national conference are not more severe than the Holy Office."

Father Francis J. Connell, C.SS.R., former dean of the School of Sacred Theology at the Catholic University of America, said: "There is as much need for the Holy Office as there is for the Supreme Court in the United States."

"There will always be a necessity for a doctrinal authority," said Father Francis J. McCool, S.J., of the faculty of the Pontifical Biblical Institute in Rome, "but it must be in tune with the ideas of the world it is trying to reach, such as what the world thinks of liberty, and so forth. The Holy Office was founded in the Middle Ages when these ideas were not so clear."

The Holy Office is not only concerned with doctrine, noted Msgr. Mark J. Hurley, chancellor of the Stockton, Calif., diocese. It also handles matters concerning marriage, the index of forbidden books, Eucharistic worship and fasting, some of which might possibly be given to other congregations, he said.

Reviewing the history of the congregation from its beginnings during the Renaissance, Msgr. Shea noted that the invention of moveable type and the consequent beginnings of literacy among peoples brought the need for the Holy Office. He said the congregation is not so much concerned with scholars as with popularizers of new theories in theology and Scripture, who present theories as fact.

Responding to this, Father Davis said: "The whole set-up of guarding the Faith by protecting people from ideas belongs to an earlier age. Whether we like it or not, modern society is such that people will be exposed to ideas. To guard against this will not work. There were advantages to a paternalistic state at one time — but there are also advantages to democracy. The Holy Office is obsolete regarding methods, which in this age must be designed to strengthen the Faith of those exposed to the new ideas." FATHER JOHN P. DONNELLY

Archbishop O'Boyle

This is the text of the remarks of Archbishop Patrick A. O'Boyle of Washington, D.C., at the ecumenical council's discussion (Oct. 28) of the schema on the Church in the modern world.

I speak in the name of all the bishops of the United States gathered in Rome for the present session of the council.

Schema 13 in general I accept. Indeed the general spirit or tone of the schema pleases me very much. Its spirit or tone is very positive and constructive. It reflects the same sympathetic interest in and concern for true human values which characterized the two great social encyclicals of Pope John XXIII, of happy memory —Mater et Magistra and Pacem in Terris. Like the more recent encyclical of Pope Paul VI, Ecclesiam Suam, it also emphasizes the need for a continuing dialogue between the Church and the world and indicates a number of ways in which this dialogue, so rich with promise for the future, can be carried on more effectively not only by the hierarchy but, even more importantly, by the faithful ad quos uti Caput "De Laicis" in Schemate "De Ecclesia" bene notat, "peculiari modo spectat res temporales omnes, quibus arcte conjunguntur, ita illuminare et ordinare, ut secundum Christum jugiter fiant et crescant et sint in laudem Creatoris et Redemptoris" [. . . even more importantly, by the faithful, referred to especially by the chapter on the laity in the schema on the nature of the Church when it says that the layman, looking in a special way at all temporal things with which he is involved, should so clarify and order them that all things may have their beginning, their growth and existence according to Christ in the praise of the Creator and the Redeemer.]

In a word, Schema 13, if adopted with whatever changes the Fathers may desire to make in the present text, will do much to advance the aggiornamento which good Pope John so auspiciously and so providentially inaugurated in convening this historic council.

In this intervention I do not intend to suggest any specific changes in the text of the schema or any deletions. Rather, I wish to propose the addition of a separate section in Chapter IV on the problem of racial discrimination and other forms of racial injustice. Racism, which, in various forms and in varying degrees, is to be found in almost every region of the world, is not merely a social or cultural or political problem. It is, first and foremost, a moral and religious problem and one of staggering proportions.

The present text of Schema 13 refers to the problem two or three times, but only incidentally and in passing. What I am proposing is that it be treated formally and explicitly as a separate problem, not merely from the sociological point of view, but from the point of view of morality and religion. Our treatment of this problem in Schema 13 need not be very long, nor should it attempt to offer detailed solutions to specific social problems in particular countries or regions of the world. At the very least, however, it should include a forthright and unequivocal condemnation of racism in all its forms and should outline, if only in general terms, the theological basis for this condemnation. It should also emphasize the obligation which rests upon all the members of the Church to do everything within their power to eliminate the cancerous evil of racial injustice and to advance, through all available means, the cause of interracial brotherhood under the fatherhood of God. I might add, in this connection, that our own experience in the United States suggests that this is one area of social action which calls for the closest possible cooperation between Catholics, Protestants, and Jews and all other men of good will.

In our judgment, racism is one of the most serious moral and religious problems of our times. If we fail to give it separate and adequate treatment, I fear that the world will conclude that we are very poorly informed about the signs of the time, or, worse than that, that we are insensitive to the tragic plight of the millions of innocent men and women all over the world who are the victims of racial pride and racial injustice.

In closing, permit me to quote, in my own native language, a brief excerpt from an address delivered in that language by Pope Pius XII, of happy memory, to a group of Negro publishers from the United States: All men are brothered in Jesus Christ; for He, though God, became also man, became a member of the human family, a brother of all. This fact, the expression of infinite universal love, is the true bond of fraternal charity which unites men and nations. May it be welded even more firmly through the efforts of all men of good will.

Unless I am mistaken, the whole world is looking to us to reaffirm this simple, but very profound truth in a solemn conciliar statement and to do so unequivocally and with all the clarity, precision, and forcefulness at our command.

Facilities for press coverage of the third session were under the general supervision of Archbishop Martin J. O'Connor, center, president of the Council's Press Commission and former rector of the North American College in Rome. Msgr. Fausto Vallainc, left, is director of the Council Press Office and Father Edward Heston, C.S.C., right, is head of the English-language section of the press office. Archbishop O'Connor is also head of the Pontifical Commission for the Communications Media.

112th General Congregation

October 29, 1964

The ecumenical council has begun discussion of the long-awaited subject of marriage and birth control, but has sidestepped the particular question of birth-control pills.

Pope Paul VI has reserved this question to himself, said Archbishop John F. Dearden of Detroit in presenting the report on the treatment of family life in schema 13 on the Church in the modern world.

This document, as drafted by the commission, lays down the principle that fecundity in marriage should be both generous and conscious, Archbishop Dearden said.

Judgment about how many children a couple should have belongs to the partners in the marriage, he said. Their decision on whether to restrict the number of children should be made with a correctly formed conscience.

Judgment about the means of limiting offspring, he said, must be made according to the mind of the Church. He said this leaves no room for subjectivism.

Archbishop Dearden explained that the question of the pills had been avoided not only because the Pope had reserved it to himself, but because it is such an intricate problem that discussion on the council floor would be unable to settle it.

He pointed out that in the brief treatment of marriage presented in the schema's article 21, a full treatment of the nature, holiness and properties of marriage could not be expected. The text provides only a synthesis of doctrine to enable Christians today to achieve a better understanding of the dignity and holiness of their state, he continued.

He said a true understanding of conjugal love is to be understood in the context of the dignity given it by the collaboration of parents with God in rearing a family.

Ernesto Cardinal Ruffini of Palermo, Italy, led off debate on the section on family life at the council's 112th general meeting. He lamented the text's omission of any mention of the nobility of Christian marriage. The unity and indissolubility of marriage must be safeguarded at all costs, he said.

He took up the passage where the text states that married couples with sufficiently serious reasons to limit the number of their children must still manifest tender love to each other. He commented that the text fails to explain how such love can be expressed, and that Catholic teaching has always maintained that in such circumstances the use of marriage is unlawful.

Cardinal Ruffini also asserted the text leaves the door open to all sorts of abuses by leaving the final judgment on this important problem to the interested individuals.

St. Augustine wrote some very harsh passages on certain aspects of married life in his day, and this shows that our own age is not so different, he said.

Cardinal Ruffini concluded by expressing the hope that the commission, in revising the text, will follow the authentic teaching of Pope Pius XI's encyclical on marriage and Pope Pius XII's 1951 speech to midwives. These two documents, he said, provide us with all the principles needed for the solution of this problem.

Leo Cardinal Suenens of Malines-Brussels appeared to reply to Cardinal Ruffini directly when he said we have learned much since the time of Aristotle—here the Belgian Cardinal paused—and even since the time of St. Augustine.

Urging the council to be courageous in facing pastoral demands for an objective study of the theology of marriage, Cardinal Suenens asserted there are grounds for thinking that the traditional outlook has been too one-sided.

The council press office paraphrased him as saying:

"Our insistence on the command 'to increase and multiply' may have caused us to forget that this is not the only text in Sacred Scripture and that another passage, stating that a husband and wife 'become two in one flesh,' is also contained in Revelation and thus is equally divine in origin.

"We still have much to learn. No one can ever presume to exhaust the inexhaustible riches of Christ.

"We may well wonder if our theology texts have gone into every last detail and exhausted every possibility."

It was here that he mentioned Aristotle and St. Augustine.

"It is true that the Church cannot abandon a doctrine which has been accepted and which clearly comes from Revelation. But there is nothing to prevent the

Church from making a thorough inquiry to see if all facets of a problem have been sufficiently explored.

"Modern science may well have much to tell us in this connection and we should keep a ready ear. The council should take care to avoid a new 'Galileo' case. One such case in the history of the Church is quite enough!

"There are no grounds for being afraid. The Holy Father has set up his commission to study this all important problem, and the competent commission of the council should work in close collaboration with it. The council commission should be made up of men of all ranks and walks of life in such a way as to represent the entire people of God. It would be well for the names of the members of this commission to be made available to the public."

Council Fathers applauded Cardinal Suenens' speech.

Paul Cardinal Leger of Montreal, who followed Cardinal Ruffini, noted that the text takes up serious problems which as yet have had no satisfactory answer.

He noted that some people seem to fear any revision of the theology of marriage. They fear the Church will be accused of opportunism in undertaking such a study. But, he said, we cannot forget that this review has been provoked by the worries of some of the faithful and that its only purpose is to protect the holiness of marriage.

He said difficulties in this field could have arisen from inadequate explanations in theological manuals concerning the purposes of marriage, explanations not based on Holy Scripture but dictated by an unduly pessimistic mentality.

In this connection, Cardinal Leger praised the schema for avoiding the old terminology of the primary and secondary purposes of marriage. He also praised the schema for stating that marital fecundity must be governed by prudence and generosity.

He asserted that it is not sufficient merely to establish the specific purposes of marriage, but more attention must be paid to the purpose of individual acts. This would only elevate into the order of principles what has long been a part of the Church's teaching, especially concerning the lawfulness of conjugal love despite sterility. With such principles, moralists, physicians and psychologists will be in a position to deal with further details.

Cardinal Leger's address was also applauded.

Melkite-rite Patriarch Maximos IV Saigh of Antioch, like Cardinal Suenens who directly preceded him, called on the council to have the courage to take up the problems of the hour.

The council press office paraphrased his speech, also applauded, as follows:

"There is a question of a break between the official doctrine of the Church and the contrary practice of the immense majority of Christian couples. The authority of the Church is called into question on a vast scale. We must have the courage to approach a solution to this problem without prejudice.

"Frankly, the official position of the Church on this matter should be revised on the basis of modern theological, medical, psychological and sociological science.

"In marriage, the development of personality and its integration into the creative plan of God are all one. Thus, the ends of marriage should not be divided into 'primary' and 'secondary' ends."

The 85-year-old patriarch said he wondered whether official positions might not derive from what he called a "bachelor psychosis" on the part of persons "unfamiliar with marriage."

He suggested, as the council press office paraphrased his speech, that "perhaps unwillingly, we are setting up a Manichean conception of man and the world, in which the work of the flesh, vitiated in itself, is tolerated only in view of children." (Manicheans held that all matter, and therefore all flesh, is intrinsically evil.)

Patriarch Saigh called for study by theologians, physicians, psychologists and sociologists to find proper moral solutions.

The Church's duty, he said, is to educate the moral sense of its children, not to bind them in a net of prescriptions which they must blindly obey. He said the Church's mission in the world is at stake.

Bishop Eugenio Beitia Aldazabal of Santander, Spain, asked for more clarity in the schema's teaching on fecundity in marriage. He also asked that the term "contract" and its implications be used in the schema regarding marriage. This, he said, is called for by the Church's traditional teaching on marriage.

Archbishop Tulio Botero Salazar of Medellin, Colombia, asked for a clear stand on the Church's position on birth control and the means used for it. He said it is a mistake to think that poverty is the only reason for the practice of birth control. God foresaw the difficulties connected with procreation, and he has certainly provided the necessary spiritual help. The schema must fearlessly reject any means of birth limitation which gives priority to instinct and diverts married couples from the obligation flowing from their true and noble love, he said.

Bishop Paulus Rusch of Innsbruck-Feldkirch, Austria, urged that the schema insist on the deep significance of those laws of the Church which seem to cause difficulty. He said the defense of these laws is a great contribution to the welfare of all mankind, as millions of "orphans of divorce" can bear witness. If God's laws had been followed in the homes where they were born, their lives would not be so blighted, he stated.

He also appealed for a statement on the condition of youth, especially in industrialized countries where young people spend most of their time away from home.

Bishop Rudolf Staverman for Sukarnapura, Indonesia, urged that the schema avoid a false dualism in describing marriage. He said this would be detrimental to the full integrity of the physical and the spiritual in Christian marriage.

Before the debate began on marriage and its problems, the council concluded discussion of articles 19 and 20 of the schema on the Church in the modern world. These articles deal with the dignity of the human person.

Bishop Josef Stimpfle of Augsburg, Germany, said he saw difficulties arising from the exhortation to the faithful to change social conditions which are not in keeping with Christian principles. He pointed out that while slavery existed in the time of Christ, neither Christ nor the apostles openly opposed it. St. Peter urged the slaves to be obedient to their masters, he said, and St. Paul sent a newly baptized slave, Onesimus, back to his master, Philemon. Bishop Stimpfle asserted that the attitude of the early Christians gradually spread, thus bringing about the gradual elimination of slavery.

He also urged that the schema give importance to the role of liberty in education and scientific research. Top administrators should also have their subordinates free to act, he said.

Auxiliary Bishop Santo Quadri of Pinerolo, Italy, asked that the schema outline the Church's social doctrine concisely. He also urged prudence and care in the schema's defense of the rights of women, lest the council be accused of either feminism or anti-feminism.

Auxiliary Bishop Augustin Frotz of Cologne, Germany, said that just as the Church once failed to perceive the deep problems of labor in modern life, the Church has not yet become aware of the worldwide implications of the changed position of women in modern society. Women should be accepted as the Church's grown-up daughters, not just children. In the liturgy they should be addressed directly as "sisters" and not just submerged in the salute "brother."

Bishop Gilles Barthe of Frejus-Toulon, France, asked for the insertion of a paragraph describing the standards of man's dignity according to Catholic teaching. Freedom, he said, has become an absolute today. Man ascribes his entire dignity to his autonomy.

Increasing liberty is a good thing, but it often means an increasing spirit of domination and of egoism. Man's fullest freedom consists in his subjection to God and God's laws, and this fullest freedom will circumscribe the domination and egoism which stem from a narrower idea of freedom. In subjection to God men find their true dignity, he said.

Maurice Cardinal Feltin of Paris was allowed to anticipate debate on article 25 (world peace) because of his imminent departure from Rome.

Cardinal Feltin said world opinion expects the council to be as forthright on the question of peace and war as Pope John XXIII was in Pacem in Terris. Public opinion expects in particular a definite condemnation of modern war and all its terror, he said.

He asserted that the text is sufficient already to outlaw atomic, bacteriological and chemical warfare, but said there must be a concerted effort to outlaw all armaments.

Cardinal Feltin said work for peace must become part of the Church's ordinary pastoral work.

The changes proposed by the Theological Commission for chapter two of the schema on the nature of the Church were distributed in the council. Archbishop Pericle Felici, council secretary general, announced that a vote on the procedure and decisions of the commission would be taken Oct. 30.

Gregorio Cardinal Agagianian was the day's moderator.

The meeting opened with Mass concelebrated by Julius Cardinal Doepfner of Munich, Germany, who was marking the silver jubilee of his ordination, and 12 other council Fathers. All were celebrating some anniversary. Among them were Bishop Cuthbert O'Gara of Yuanling, China, now living in Union City, N.J., a Canadian missioner who was imprisoned by the Chinese Reds and then expelled, and U.S.-born Bishop Louis Morrow of Krishnagar, India.

The Gospel was enthroned by the apostolic administrator of the Montevideo, Uruguay, archdiocese, Bishop Antonio Corso.

The ecumenical council, avoiding any appearance of settling disputed questions about the Blessed Virgin's role as "Mother of the Church," is steering clear of that title.

The chapter of the schema on the nature of the Church dealing with the Blessed Virgin, as rewritten by the Theological Commission according to the virtually unanimous agreement of the council Fathers, simply affirms the Church's devotion to Mary "as a most-loved Mother."

This formula, said Archbishop Maurice Roy of Quebec in explaining the commission's revisions to the council Fathers, is an equivalent expression of Mary's motherly role in the Church.

He asserted that the amended text provides a better explanation of Mary's motherhood in the order of grace.

Regarding the title "mediatrix," which was questioned in the council debate as tending, unless very carefully explained or properly understood, to detract from Christ as the sole mediator, the amended text contents itself with stating that Mary has been invoked under this title.

Archbishop Roy said the commission was in almost unanimous agreement that this and other titles such as "advocate" and "helper" are perfectly faithful to Holy Scripture.

Such an enumeration of various titles, he said, deliberately avoids theological controversy and simply affirms the fact of this widespread invocation and devotion.

The council Fathers passed the amended chapter by an ample majority. A total of 1,559 council Fathers voted their unqualified approval. With 2,091 votes cast, the required majority was 1,394.

There were only 10 "no" votes.

However, 521 Fathers voted qualified approval, that is, approval with changes to be made. One vote was null.

The chapter was enlarged in the commission to explain how all apostolic activity in the Church regards the Mother of God and the Mother of men as a perfect model.   PATRICK RILEY

*   *   *   *

Coffee bars were virtually deserted and council Fathers listened in silence as debate began on marriage and the family.

The applause greeting some of the speeches was the most enthusiastic heard so far in the council. Thus the members of the U.S. bishops' press panel described the electrifying effects of the explosive issue in the schema on the Church in the modern world as debate on it began, with its attendant discussion on the population expansion and birth control.

"Today represents a turning point whose impact can hardly be overestimated," Father Charles Davis, editor of the Westminster Clergy Review and dogmatic theologian at St. Edmund's Seminary, Ware, England, said.

"Although there has been a feeling that the Church needs a change of thinking on these matters, there has until now been uncertainty whether such a change was allowable. Now the suggestion has been made in the council of a re-thinking—not on the (progesterone) pill only—but on the whole general doctrine on marriage. The authority of the speakers today shows it can be said those who think a change is needed have support."

An English Mill Hill priest, Father Arthur McCormack, an expert on population problems and editor of World Justice magazine, agreed. But he cautioned that a broader view of today's talks is necessary. He said:

"The old view that married couples were to have as many children as possible already had been changing before this morning. But the applause given the talk of Cardinal Suenens indicated authoritative backing for the need for this change in thinking. All should rejoice that it has been said in the council that the personal relationship in marriage is equal to the procreative function.

"Cardinal Suenens by the exalted nature of his talk brought out strongly that the Church is not talking to prostitutes in this, but to respectable families who are kept from the sacraments because of this problem."

Father John J. King, O.M.I., of Lowell, Mass., superior of the General House of Studies in Rome for Oblate priests, also said he felt that the day's speeches "marked the beginning of a new era and attitude." But he added that such a change was inevitable and predictable because of changed circumstances today and the change in general thought on family life.

"Objections that have been raised against the Church's position demanded such a response, and Cardinal Suenens has presented a balanced and Catholic attitude toward such objections. He called for an investigation in the light of Faith necessitated by changing circumstances, and he asked that this be done through scientific examination of the circumstances.

"But do not anticipate, because of any prejudice, the ultimate outcome of this investigation. Possibly the Church will find there is no answer available today," he warned.

Others on the panel did not agree that the day's speeches represented any great change or turning point.

Archbishop Joseph T. McGucken of San Francisco said he did not feel we were in any new position. "These subjects have been discussed for a long time.

"We hope the current study will be broad and deep. Marriage is plagued with many problems, even problems deeper than contraception. Broken homes, abandoned children are all part of the problems of marriage. The true nature of love as discussed today has broader and wider application than merely the problem of birth control," the archbishop said.

"I do not think the discussion today has changed things in the slightest," Auxiliary Bishop Philip M. Hannan of Washington said. He referred to the study begun several years ago at Georgetown University on the same point and indicated that Archbishop Patrick A. O'Boyle of Washington and himself had helped to set it up.

Referring to the recent statement by the European Economic Community, that European industry needs a greater population, he said that this side of the population problem must be considered.

Msgr. George W. Shea, rector of Immaculate Conception Seminary, Darlington, N.J., said he felt the newness of the ideas expressed in the day's council meeting were "perhaps exaggerated."

"The personal relationship between spouses has been discussed by many authors, by the catechism of the Council of Trent and by the papal encyclical on marriage, Casti Conubii," he said. "This aspect of matrimony has never quite been lost sight of."

The practical conclusion of this doctrine, he said, "is that parenthood must be responsible, and there is a place for planning. But we must not be too hasty in drawing conclusions regarding the means to be used in this planning. Chemical and mechanical means still have not been given the green light. Casti Conubii bases arguments against these means on the foundation of the Church's tradition, and it is doubtful whether we are free to debate these means outside the council—especially in light of Pope Paul's mandate not to debate them publicly, at least until the special commission he has set up finishes its work."

Msgr. George G. Higgins, director of the Social Action Department of the National Catholic Welfare Conference, said the morning's speeches had an importance "far beyond family regulation. They include the whole question on whether there has been sufficient freedom in the Church to debate debatable issues. Cardinal Suenens asked the members of the Pope's commission and any others that may be organized on this topic be made a matter of public record. This may also be a minor turning point."

Father Francis J. Connell, C.SS.R., former dean of the School of Theology at Catholic University of America, reminded that the "development of doctrine does not mean the denial of doctrine."

He added: "If contraception were the only answer to family problems, then its increased use today should mean there would be a decline in divorce and broken homes. But this just isn't so."

FATHER JOHN P. DONNELLY

Interview With Father Kueng

The accelerated progress of Vatican Council II gives real cause to expect that four schemas will be adopted before the end of this current session, according to Father Hans Kueng.

The Swiss-born theologian, a council expert, asserted in an interview with the N.C.W.C. News Service that the council drafting committees were making major strides forward in the last days of October, partly as a result of their "burning the midnight oil."

"We can be fairly certain," Father Kueng said, "that the council will approve the final texts of the schemas on Divine Revelation, the nature of the Church, on ecumenism, and on the pastoral duties of bishops. The Jewish statement is now likely to be incorporated in the schema on the Church without detracting from its original intent. And the religious liberty statement—after final consultation about it between Augustin Cardinal Bea's Secretariat (for Promoting Christian Unity) and the Theological Commission—is now about ready to go to press. Thus all these documents may soon be approved on the council floor."

Father Kueng said that this would be a notable achievement for the third session in itself. But he added: "There is more than that, as I see it. Great progress already has been secured by this council in these specific respects:

"1. The council has clearly upheld the goals set by Pope John by refraining from doctrinal definitions which might have closed doors to further dialogue.

"2. Numerous doors have been opened through the unfettered council debates with the whole world listening in, which was certainly not possible before the council opened.

"3. A broad spiritual opening has occurred within the Church, especially in regard to other Christians, to Jews and non-Christians generally.

"4. The liturgical reform inaugurated in the first session is now sealed by decrees which will go far toward providing new incentives for the meaningful participation by the faithful in worship everywhere. The schemas to be adopted in this session will further accentuate these gratifying trends which are bound to promote ecumenism in all fields through Scriptural grounds.

"5. There can no longer be any standstill, because the movement toward renewal, now initiated with such vigor and determination, will be carried on toward even greater progress by its own power.

"6. The supreme world council of bishops under and with the Pope is certain to come into being, and will bring about the much-desired internationalization and decentralization of the Roman curia. The whole Church as represented in the council—and a large sector of the other Christian Churches as well as public opinion the world over—is backing the initiatives of this council. This will help promote the effectiveness and ultimate success of such a bishops' council."

Father Kueng concluded: "We can be confident that the council's decisions will not remain just dead letters. We now stand at the beginning of a hopeful new epoch of the Church." FATHER PLACID JORDAN, O.S.B.

Cardinal Suenens

This is a translation of the Latin-language address made by Leo Cardinal Suenens of Malines Brussels (Oct. 29) at the ecumenical council on the problems of marriage and the family.

I should like to make a few observations on . . . the dignity of marriage and the family.

We all know how crucial the question of marriage, and particularly that of birth control, is for the world and for the Church. Consequently,

1) It seems to me necessary to add to the text certain elements of doctrine found in the appendices. This implies recasting the text so as to present a doctrinal synthesis at the same time more profound, more consistent and Biblical. I am presenting a sample of such a synthesis to the commission in writing.

2) It seems to me equally necessary for the council commission to work in close harmony with the commission which His Holiness the Pope has happily set up for a broad and detailed examination of these problems.

3) May I be allowed to voice the hope that this commission will make a very broad enquiry among renowned moralists from every corner of the world, intellectuals and university faculties of various disciplines, among the laity both men and women, and among Christian married couples.

One would wish that the names of the members of this commission were well known so that they could receive the most ample information and truly be representatives of the People of God.

4) In order that this commission know the spirit with which the council views these problems, it seems essential to me to formulate some basic orientation for the success of its work.

a) In the realm of Faith:

The primary task of this commission is to be found in the realm of Faith and must consist in this: to find out whether we have to date thrown sufficient light on all aspects of the Church's teaching on marriage.

There is certainly no question of modifying or of doubting the truly traditional teachings of the Church. That would be folly! It is a question of knowing if we are going to open our hearts entirely to the Holy Spirit so as to understand divine Truth.

The Gospel remains the same always. But no age can boast of having fully perceived the unfathomable riches of Christ. The Holy Spirit was promised us to introduce us gradually into the fulness of Truth.

In fact, the Church never has to repudiate a truth once it is taught, but, as she progresses in the more profound examination of the Gospel, she can and must integrate this Truth into a richer synthesis and reveal the fuller wealth of these same principles. In this way the Church draws from its treasury some things new and some old.

Granting this, it is necessary to examine whether we have kept all the dimensions of the teaching of the Church on marriage in perfect balance. It may be we have stressed the words of Scripture: "Increase and multiply" to the point of leaving in the shadow the other divine statement: "And they will be two in one flesh." These two truths are central and both are Scriptural. They must clarify each other in the light of the fulness of truth revealed to us by Our Lord Jesus Christ. St. Paul has, in fact, spoken of the very love of Christ for His Church as the archetype for Christian marriage. This "two in one" is a mystery of inter-personal communion ratified and sanctified by the sacrament of marriage. And this union is so strong that divorce can never sever the two whom God has joined together.

Therefore it will be the task of the commission to tell us whether we have not laid too much stress on the primary purpose, which is procreation, to the detriment of an equally imperative purpose, which is growth in conjugal unity.

Likewise, it will be the task of the commission to respond to the immense problem posed by the present demographic explosion and over-population in many regions of the earth. This is the first time we have had to undertake such an examination in the light of the Faith. The matter is difficult, but in this field the world, more or less consciously, expects the Church to express its thought and be the "light of nations."

Let it not be said that we are thus opening the way to moral laxity. The problem is incumbent upon us, not because the faithful try to satisfy their passions and their selfishness, but because the best among them are trying with anguish to observe a twofold fidelity—to the doctrine of the Church and to the demands of conjugal and parental love.

b) In the realm of natural ethics and of science:

The second task of the commission lies in the field of scientific progress and of a deeper knowledge of natural ethics. The commission will have to examine whether classical doctrine, and particularly that contained in manuals, takes sufficiently into account the new data of modern science.

We have come a long way since Aristotle. We have discovered the complexity of reality whereby the biological touches upon the psychological, the conscious, the unconscious. New possibilities are constantly discovered in man regarding his power to direct the course of nature. Hence comes a deeper knowledge of man's unity of being as a spirit incarnate, as well as of the dynamism of his whole life, a unity which is at the heart of Thomist anthropology. From this comes a more exact assessment of the rational power over the world which is entrusted to him. How could anyone help seeing that we might thus be led to further research on the question of what is "according to or against nature"? We shall follow the progress of science.

I implore you, brothers, let us avoid another Galileo trial. One is enough for the Church.

It will be the task of the commission to include new elements in the overall view and to submit conclusions to the Supreme Teaching Authority. Let it not be said that by this new synthesis we make concessions to so-called situation morality. It is proper for the exposition of doctrine, immutable in its principles, to take into account factors that are contingent or evolving in the course of history. This is what the popes did who wrote successively Rerum Novarum, Quadragesimo Anno and Mater et Magistra in order to express with greater precision the same principles in relation to new times.

Venerable brothers, we do not have the right to remain silent. Let us not be afraid to approach the study of these problems. The salvation of souls, of our families, as well as of the world, is at stake. Let us heed the Holy Spirit and accept fully every particle of truth suggested to us, remembering the words of the Lord: the truth—natural as well as supernatural—the truth—total and vital—will set you free.

Patriarch Maximos IV Saigh

This is a translation of the, ecumenical council speech (Oct. 29) on schema 13, article 21, "Dignity of Marriage and the Family," by Melkite-rite Patriarch Maximos IV Saigh of Antioch.

Today I would like to draw the attention of your venerable assembly to a special aspect of morals: the regulation of birth.

The fundamental virtue which imposes itself on us, we shepherds gathered in a council that wishes to be pastoral, is the courage to approach squarely present day problems in the love of God and of souls. Now, among the anguishing and sorrowful problems which agitate the human masses today, there emerges the problem of birth regulation, a problem most urgent since it is at the bottom of a grave crisis of the Catholic conscience. There is here a conflict between the official doctrine of the Church and the contrary practice of the vast majority of Christian families. The authority of the Church is once more questioned on a large scale. The faithful are reduced to living outside the law of the Church, far from the sacraments, in constant anguish, unable to find a working solution between two contradictory imperatives, conscience and the normal conjugal life.

On the other hand, on the social plane, the demographic growth in certain countries, and particularly in the great agglomerations, prevents under present circumstances any improvement in the standard of living and condemns hundreds of millions of human beings to a shameless and hopeless misery. The council must give it a valid solution. It is its pastoral duty. It must say whether God really wants this depressing and antinatural blind alley.

Venerable fathers, you who in the Lord, Who died and resurrected for the salvation of men, are conscious of the sorrowful conscience crisis of our faithful, let us have the courage to approach it without bias. Frankly, should not the official positions of the Church regarding this matter be revised in the light of modern science, theological as well as medical, psychological and sociological? In marriage, the development of the person and his integration in the creating plan of God forms a whole. The purpose of marriage therefore must not be dissected into primary and secondary purposes. This consideration opens up a horizon on new perspectives regarding the morality of conjugal behavior as a whole. And then, do we not have the right to ask ourselves whether certain official positions are not subordinated to obsolete conceptions and possibly even to the psychosis of bachelors who are strangers to this sector of life? Are we not, unwittingly, weighed down by this Manichean conception of man and of the world whereby the carnal act vitiated in itself, is tolerated only for the sake of the child? Is the external biological rectitude of the acts the only criteria of morality, independent of the life of the home and of its conjugal and familial moral climate, and of the grave imperatives of prudence, the basic rule of all our human activity?

On the other hand, does not present day exegesis commit us to more prudence in the inter-reorientation of two passages of Genesis: "Grow and multiply" and that of Onan, which have been used for so long as a classical Scriptural testimony of radical rebuking of anti-conception acts?

How relieved did the Christian conscience feel when Paul VI announced to the world that the problem of the regulation of births and of family morals "is being studied, a study as wide and profound as possible, that is to say, as grave and honest as is demanded by the great importance of this matter. The Church will have to proclaim this law of God in the light of scientific, social and psychological truths which, lately, have been the object of study and of documentation."

Because of this, in view of the extent and gravity of this problem, which concerns the whole world, we ask that the study should be conducted by theologians, doctors, psychologists and sociologists, in order to find the normal solution which imposes itself. The collaboration of exemplary Christian married people also seems necessary. In addition, is it not in line with the ecumenism of this council to start a dialogue on this matter with the other Christian churches and even with thinkers of other religions?

Why remain closed within ourselves? Do we not have before us a problem common to all mankind? Must not the Church open herself to the Christian as well as to the non-Christian world? Is it not the leaven which is to raise the dough? Also, it is necessary that it should achieve in this, as well as in all other sectors which concern mankind, positive results which will give peace of conscience.

Far be it from me to minimize the delicacy and gravity of the matter and of the possible abuses. But here as elsewhere is it not the duty of the Church to educate the moral sense of its children, to train them in personal and community moral responsibility, profoundly mature in Christ, rather than enveloping them in a network of prescriptions and commandments, and purely and simply asking them to conform to them blindfold? And we ourselves, let us open our eyes and be practical. Let us see things as they are and not as we would wish them to be. Otherwise, we risk talking in a desert. The future of the mission of the Church in the world is at stake.

Let us therefore put into practice, loyally and effectively, the declaration of His Holiness Paul VI at the opening of the second session of the Council:

"May the world know that the Church looks at it with profound understanding, with a sincere admiration, sincerely disposed, not to subjugate it but to serve it, not to deprecate it but to appreciate it, not to condemn it but to sustain and save it."

Summary of Chapter 4
On the Church in the Modern World

Following is the summary of Chapter 4 of the schema on the Church in the modern world released by the ecumenical council press office.

SUMMARY: CHAPTER 4

The Principal Tasks of Christians Today

This chapter is a practical application of the principles enunciated in the three previous chapters.

a) *The dignity of the human person*:

All men must be treated alike, without regard for race, sex or social condition. It is not enough for this equality to be recognized only theoretically, but it must be translated into action. Much has been done for the advancement of man but even today there are some concrete realities which offend against his dignity.

b) *Marriage and the family*:

In what regards the family, the following truths must be kept in mind:

1. The supernatural, and not only the natural, ends of marriage;

2. Marriage is based on genuine love, constituted by fidelity and indissolubility;

3. Marriage is not only a means of procreation, but it is the way which normally leads to procreation, which is not dictated by blind instinct, but by a sense of responsibility enlightened by Christian principles;

4. The Church is aware of the difficulties of those Christian couples who want to respect the law of God in regard to birth control but—while still hoping for better solutions founded on scientific and theological studies—has no other course but to recommend the spirit of sacrifice in continence.

c) *Culture*:

1. As we dedicate ourselves to human activities, we are following the commandment of God whereby man was given all power over the earth, and at the same time we are contributing to the enhancement of the dignity of the human person.

2. It must be borne in mind that all must observe the hierarchy of values and it is evident that spiritual values must occupy first place. Nevertheless there are concrete situations in which the first duty is to satisfy material needs.

3. Wherever cultures meet, this means the beginning of a dialogue in which the first requirement is mutual respect.

4. In the accomplishment of her mission the Church also exercises a cultural function and this is demonstrated by the great number of artistic works which have sprung from Christian civilization.

d) *Economic life*:

1. Economic progress tends toward an equitable distribution of wealth, in such a way as to make man's daily life more human.

2. The Church shows no preference for one or other of the different economic systems.

3. We must ultimately achieve the elimination of all social differences, without prejudice to the respect due to the characteristic gifts and rights of individuals.

4. There must be recognition of the rights of workingmen in so far as they are sharers and collaborators in one common undertaking.

5. Catholics must enter into economic and social life, occupying the places belonging to them in view of the common welfare.

e) *The solidarity of the human race*:

1. Economic development must keep pace with the cultural development of a nation.

2. Underdeveloped nations have the obligation to do everything in their power to make progress.

3. Especially today the more developed countries have an obligation to assist poorer nations.

4. Assistance to emerging countries is a very serious duty of justice and charity.

5. There must be generous international collaboration for the solution of the demographic problem. Immoral solutions of the problem, that is to say, solutions which run counter to the divine law, may not be propagated.

6. Peace is in strict relationship with the independence of people.

7. In our times international organizations are really necessary, especially those whose aim is to establish harmony among peoples.

8. Participation by Catholics in this field is indispensable and urgently necessary. It must be a concrete manifestation of each one's own Christian Faith.

f) *Peace*:

1. True peace consists in friendship among peoples and in a balance of power.

2. International controversies must be solved peacefully. Especially, in no case should there be recourse to nuclear arms, since there is no proportion between the good which might be obtained and a war carried on by these means and the evil effects which would be caused for the entire human race.

3. Those international organizations are deserving of support which aim at eliminating the cause of war and the armaments race.

4. No effort and no sacrifice should be omitted for the attainment of genuine peace.

CONCLUSIONS:

Catholics must collaborate with all men for the attainment of the common welfare:

—with Christian non-Catholics;

—with the adorers of one God;

—with whoever, even though not a believer, is working for the welfare of humanity;

—also with those who oppose the Church, by means of prayer and the spirit of pardon.

Auditors at the Vatican Council — lay men and women — received Holy Communion during the Liturgy celebrated in the Ethiopian Rite in St. Peter's basilica. James J. Norris of the United States is first among the men approaching the altar. Pope Paul VI kneels in prayer at the left. Council Fathers are in the background.

113th General Congregation

October 30, 1964

The ecumenical council heard the Church's Dutch cardinal declare that "an honest doubt" is arising among married people and theologians on whether the rhythm method of birth control is the only moral way to reconcile the demands of married love with the other needs of married life.

The "precise question," said Bernard Cardinal Alfrink of Utrecht, "is this: in performing this one and the same act a moral conflict has arisen. For if in this act a couple wants to preserve its biological purpose, their human duty of the human and Christian education of future and present offspring is compromised.

"If, on the other hand, they wish to preserve the good of fidelity and the good of education, then (outside of periodic continence, which is exercised by many spouses with great Christian virtue, but more often is tried with great inconveniences, or outside of complete continence, which . . . demands greater moral strength than a couple normally is supposed to have) only one solution is open to them: namely, performing the marriage act while excluding offspring, at least in this concrete act."

Cardinal Alfrink said it is evident that if this exclusion were accomplished "by the use of means which without any doubt are intrinsically evil, the Church can never admit the sacrifices of a particular value in order to save the value of the whole marriage."

Here he added a crucial sentence:

"But with our new understanding of the science of man, and especially with our growing understanding of the essential distinction between merely biological sexuality and human sexuality, an honest doubt is arising among many couples and among scientists and some theologians about the arguments produced to demonstrate that in such conflicts in the married life of the faithful of good will, complete or periodic continence is the sole solution which is entirely efficacious, moral and Christian."

The Cardinal said the Church should be solicitous for the purity of the observance of divine law, but it must also be solicitous for human problems. He added:

"The Church must in a holy and diligent way so search that all Christians may know that the Church, whatever the answer may be, has studied the problem with great charity with all the means which the various sciences can bring."

He suggested creating a permanent commission to follow the growth of problems treated by the council's schema on the Church in the modern world.

Cardinal Alfrink's carefully prepared speech was followed by a virtually extemporaneous plea from Alfredo Cardinal Ottaviani, secretary of the Congregation of the Holy Office, that the council not leave the role of Divine Providence out of the schema's treatment of marriage problems.

He said he had no text, since he had expected to speak later. (It is believed that the moderators warned him they planned to ask for a cloture vote, which, in fact, was passed by a great majority.)

Then the cardinal, who has risen to one of the highest offices in the Church, recalled his childhood in Rome's tough Trastevere district.

"I come from a family of 12 children," the cardinal began.

"My father was a workingman, not an owner or manager. I was the 10th child.

"Never did my parents have any doubts about Divine Providence."

He quoted Christ's words: "Look at the birds of the air: they do not sow, or reap, or gather into barns; yet your heavenly Father feeds them. Are you not of much more value than they?"

"We are forgetting Divine Providence," he declared.

He asserted that the text insinuates that the Church has erred in the past on a grave moral problem. He said that if such is the case, the commission now drafting the text on the Church's indefectibility in doctrine should revise its text.

Cardinal Ottaviani said the council cannot possibly approve the freedom granted by the schema to married couples to judge for themselves the number of children they should have.

The Scriptural command to increase and multiply, he said, is not in opposition to the other text which speaks of married couples as two in one flesh.

Cardinal Ottaviani said that Michael Cardinal Browne, O.P., of the Roman curia, would emphasize the doctrinal points which he too felt should be emphasized.

Cardinal Browne first noted that he was a member of the mixed commission which had drafted the schema. He said that he therefore had at one time decided not to speak. But he added that he felt that certain things should be said which until then had not been said.

"My purpose in asking to speak was to offer witness on things that cannot usefully be argued about," Cardinal Browne said.

Some things are certain, he said, from both the Church's teaching authority and the classical schools of theologians. The primary end of marriage is the procreation and education of children. Other considerations of mutual help and the satisfaction of desires must not be lost sight of, but they are secondary ends.

He made the classical distinction between the love of desire, in which the lover desires his own good, and the love of friendship, in which the lover desires the good of the beloved.

"The love needed in marriage to keep it firm, stable and deep is the love of friendship," he said.

"In married life there is indeed sense pleasure. Yet it is natural that the more one party is moved by desire, the more the other party loses the love of friendship. Therefore, care should be taken in demanding marriage rights."

He said the teaching that the conjugal act must conform to nature and remains lawful in sterile periods can be found in the works of Popes Leo XIII, Pius XI and Pius XII. There are and always will be difficulties which must be solved by scientific discoveries rather than by theological discussion, he said, and added that the Church can only await the outcome of present research.

If, with the Pope's consent, the council also occupies itself with problems about the infertile period, this should be done through a commission, he said.

Auxiliary Bishop Joseph Reuss of Mainz, Germany, speaking in the name of 145 bishops of many countries, echoed Cardinal Alfrink's emphasis on the distinction between merely biological sex and human sex. He asked that the text be amended to include this emphasis.

Bishop Reuss said the schema should say that human sexuality involves the whole person. He asked for a forthright statement that married people must realize that they are called to procreation and not just to the selfish use of marriage.

Archbishop Joseph Urtasun of Avignon, France, deplored the text's silence on divorce, which he called a plague of modern life. He pointed to the dangers to children involved in divorce. He said the schema should include a passage on the social implications of chastity and its importance in helping to choose a marriage partner.

He said he entirely agreed with Cardinal Alfrink.

Bishop Abilio del Campo y de la Barcena of Cala-

horra, Spain, said some parts of the text conflict with the traditional doctrine on conjugal love and imply approval of errors which have been condemned by the Church. This means a danger of scandal both inside and outside the Church, he said.

Like Cardinal Ottaviani, he criticized the schema's failure to mention spiritual supports in the difficulties of married life. He said the text implies that it is almost impossible to keep God's laws.

Bishop Joseph Nkongolo of Luebo, the Congo, said the big problems affecting marriage in Africa are the lack of free consent on the girls' part and polygamy. He said the schema should state the most basic requirements for a valid marriage and should insist on its unity and indissolubility.

Bishop Francisco Rendeiro of Faro, Portugal, asserted that it is the state's duty to safeguard the sanctity of family life, especially through movies, radio and TV. He said it is an inescapable fact that the theme of most shows in these media is human love, and that these do not always treat love with proper reverence. Youths must be protected, he said.

Bishop Pietro Fiordelli of Prato, Italy, urged that the text deal with the problem of abortion and asked that something be said about how to help young people of courting age. Special attention should be devoted to illegitimate children, who are deprived both of their name and a home, he stated.

Bishop Fiordelli said the council should not concern itself in detail with methods of birth control but should follow the Pope's example and put the question into the hands of a commission of experts.

Bishop Juan Hervas y Benet for Ciudad Real, Spain, complained that the schema, though basically good, reflects one viewpoint among many.

He said that there was no mention of the influence of the supernatural life, of trust in Providence, of the love and acceptance of the Cross. He urged that the schema provide a more positive outlook on marriage, praising its virtues and encouraging married people to accept children with faith and joy. He said that psychologists and sociologists are generous in praising large families for their mutual help. Large families are also a source of priests and Religious, he said.

Archbishop Bernard Yago of Abidjan, Ivory Coast, urged the council to say something clear on the problems of tribalism. He criticized the schema's silence on the modern cult of sensuality and on polygamy.

Like Bishop Nkongolo, he asked for a statement on the need for free consent in marriage. He also asked for a statement on the abuses of the dowry system and on divorce.

Gregorio Cardinal Agagianian, moderator of the day, announced that the moderators considered debate had been sufficient on the subject of family life (Article 21).

He put it to a vote. An overwhelming majority approved.

Then Giacomo Cardinal Lercaro of Bologna, Italy, took over as the moderator for debate on article 22 dealing with the promotion of culture.

Father Joao Ferreira, prefect apostolic of Portuguese Guinea, complained that the schema used the word "culture" dozens of times but in different ways. He urged greater precision.

Bishop Roger Johan of Agen, France, said all the faithful are witnesses of the truth and have a real vocation in the promotion of culture.

Auxiliary Bishop Bohdan Bejze of Lodz, Poland, complained that the text is silent on the role of philosopy and the promotion of culture. He pointed to the influence of such philosophies as Hegelianism, Marxism and existentialism, and urged the text to emphasize Christian philosophy and the importance of Christian philosophers in culture.

Underlining the role of the saints in shaping culture, he suggested that Pope John XXIII be enrolled on the Church's list of saints.

Bishop Stanislaus Lokuang of Tainan, Formosa, said that in mission countries the Church cannot make its presence felt by preaching its social doctrine. The small number of Catholics make their influence too weak, he said. However, institutions such as universities, the Catholic press and organized works of charity bring the Church's influence to bear in a country, he noted.

Father Aniceto Fernandez, O.P., master general of the Dominican Order, criticized the text for its failure to emphasize the role of theology in promoting the progress of human culture. Theology can forestall the danger of mistaken orientation, especially in society, he said. The Church's contribution to culture will be in the foundation of universities to promote understanding of integral truth, he stated.

Coadjutor Bishop Pablo Munoz Vega of Quito, Ecuador, said the Church's mission demands that it have professors as well as pastors. Before the Reformation, Church universities kept the Church in touch with culture, he said. Today, we must show our trust in genuine science by directing serious universities worthy of the name, he noted.

He pointed out that in Latin America one of the greatest sources of Marxist infection is in academic life, especially the universities. Catholic universities must be the means of combating this evil, he said.

The council was adjourned until Nov. 4 at the close of the day's meeting. During the debate the Fathers voted on the way the Theology Commission had handled changes in chapters one and two of the schema on the Church.

The vote on changes in chapter one was 1,903 "yes" to 17 "no," with 17 votes of qualified approval and four null votes.

The vote on changes in chapter two was 1,893 "yes" to 19 "no" with three null votes.

The day's opening Mass was offered by Bishop Jean Gay of Basse-Terre and Pointe-a-Pitre, Guadaloupe. The Gospel was enthroned by the abbot general of the Premonstratensian Fathers, Abbot Norbert Calmels.

PATRICK RILEY

Cardinal Alfrink

This is a translation of the ecumenical council speech (Oct. 30) on schema 13, article 21, "Dignity of Marriage and the Family," by Bernard Cardinal Alfrink of Utrecht, the Netherlands.

All priests having the care of souls are beset with the anxieties and tremendous difficulties involved in the matrimonial life of so many of the faithful of good will who desire generously to follow the moral obligations of their state. Not rarely these difficulties give occasion for some alienation from the Church. The spiritual struggle can furthermore become so debilitating that it can no longer be tolerated without detriment to human values, and most of all, that highest value of matrimony (bonum fidei) fidelity which is placed in danger.

It is clearly evident that the Church, guardian of divine law, can never change that law because of human difficulties, no matter how great, adapting it to human incapacity. It is further evident that sociological analyses of these difficulties cannot lessen anything which pertains to the moral character of human acts. The Church cannot indulge in situation ethics, by which the absolute norm of morality is considered to lose its force in certain determined circumstances. Further, the Church always professes that sacrifice and self-denial pertain to the essence of the Christian life. However, not only the Cross but also the Resurrection pertains to the essence of Christian life and God is not pleased with the straits of men.

This being so, the difficulties of married life are often of such a nature that in fact a difficult conflict of conscience arises between two matrimonial values, that is, between the value of procreation and that of the human and Christian education of offspring, which is possible only when conjugal love is present between the parents, a love which is normally supported and increased by carnal relations. This conflict is not one between two separate values. For without conjugal love and fidelity renewed through the "cult of love" (as the schema rightly says) the very motive of procreation is virtually endangered.

The precise question then is this: a moral conflict arises in performing one and the same act. If in this act the spouses wish to preserve biological finality, then the human duty of providing for the human and Christian education of present and future offspring is harmed. If on the other hand they wish to preserve fidelity and assure their children's education, then aside from periodic continence, which is practiced by many spouses with great Christian virtue but often not without grave inconvenience, or aside from complete continence which indeed, not to mention other things, demands of the spouses greater moral strength than normally is presumed to be present, only one solution can remain and that is performing the act of the marriage contract while excluding (the possibility of) children at least in this concrete case.

It is evident that if the act is performed while excluding the possibility of children by the use of means which are certainly *intrinsically* evil, the Church can never allow the sacrifice of a particular value at the expense, so to speak, of the whole of matrimony.

However, with renewed anthropological knowledge, especially arising from knowledge of the essential distinction between merely biological sexuality and human sexuality, an *honest doubt* in fact arises among many married couples, among men dedicated to science and among theologians, relative at least to the argument put forth to demonstrate that in such conflicts arising among married faithful of good will complete or periodic abstinence is the only solution altogether efficacious, moral and Christian.

The situation or condition of the problem is of too much importance for the Church to solve this real conflict by decree precipitously and perhaps prematurely. The Church must be solicitous also concerning human problems and must sensibly and diligently investigate so that all the Christian faithful can know that, whatever response must be forthcoming, she has investigated the matter with great charity and with all the means the various fields of science can offer. For this reason, we must rejoice over the establishment of the commission of chosen experts which is examining this matter.

Only if real certitude eventually arises concerning knowledge of the authentic content of divine law, however, can and must the Church bind or loose the consciences of her faithful.

Finally, because of the very swift progress of science—especially medicine and the other sciences concerned with human life—which scientific progress daily creates new ethical and moral problems, the question can be asked whether the Church of today does not indeed need some permanent commission of experts in the fields of philosophy and theology as well as in the sciences, which would accompany the evolution of these sciences immediately and in an up-to-date manner with the insight of pastoral concern, lest the Church ever be too late in investigation and in effort to solve new problems.

114th General Congregation

November 4, 1964

The council's 114th meeting approved proposals to establish a central commission of bishops to assist the pope in Church government and to reorganize the Roman curia in the light of present-day needs.

The council Fathers, back from a four-day break in daily meetings, were asked by Pope Paul VI to pray for the success of the Pan-Orthodox Conference in Rhodes. They also heard strong pleas for a clear declaration on the necessity of liberty for scientific research.

Approval of the so-called senate of bishops and reorganization of the curia were voted by overwhelming majorities during a series of votes on amendments to the schema on the pastoral duties of bishops.

The Fathers, however, showed disfavor with one change that had been made in the text dealing with the collegiality of the bishops.

As expressed in chapter three of the schema on the nature of the Church, the text reads that the college of bishops together with the pope exercises "supreme and full power over the universal Church."

However, as several members of the U.S. bishops' press panel pointed out, this was not the text quoted in the present schema on the duties of bishops. Rather, another text from the schema on the Church was used which omits the word "full." The council secretary general, Archbishop Pericle Felici, said the omission was made so that the text used in this schema would correspond to the phrasing found in the schema on the Church.

What was not explained immediately is why the verbatim quotation from chapter three of the schema on the Church was not used instead of the other quotation from another section of the same document, which some Fathers regard as ambiguous.

As a result, many Fathers chose to vote with reservations on the schema on bishops when the entire introduction and first chapter came up for a vote. The vote was 1,030 in favor, 77 against, and 852 in favor with reservations.

This was the largest number of favorable-with-reservations votes in the history of the council. One council spokesman said the great majority of the reservations centered on the omission of the word "full." As a result of the vote, Archbishop Felici announced,

the chapter must be sent back to commission and the Fathers' reservations studied. The chapter will again have to come before a general council meeting after it has been processed by the commission.

The meeting began with Mass in the Ambrosian rite celebrated by Milan-born Efrem Cardinal Forni of the Roman curia in honor of St. Charles Borromeo's feast. The Ambrosian rite is a Latin rite used only in the Milan, Italy, archdiocese. It is named for St. Ambrose, fourth century bishop of the See, which was also headed centuries later by St. Charles. The Gospel was enthroned by Bishop Charles-Marie Himmer of Tournai, Belgium. Giacomo Cardinal Lercaro of Bologna, Italy, was moderator.

Coadjutor Archbishop Pierre Veuillot of Paris reported on the amendments to the schema on bishops before the voting took place. He noted that 102 bishops had made more than 400 suggested changes. He said that the policy guiding the commission in revising the schema was to set down principles rather than provide for specific details. The aim was to supply principles for pastoral activity and the role of the bishop in the world today.

The theological basis of the schema is to be found in the schema on the nature of the Church, he said. Such problems as suggestions to abolish titular Sees were not dealt with, he said, as they are not concerned with pastoral activities of bishops.

Bishop Joseph Gargitter of Bolzano-Bressanone, Italy, delivered the report on the first chapter of the schema dealing with relations between bishops and the Roman curia and with the principles relating to the role of bishops in the universal Church. In referring to collegiality, Bishop Gargitter said that the present text has omitted repeated references to the authority of the pope because this has been clearly stated from the outset.

The concept of a central commission of bishops, he said, has been included in the amended text. It should not be regarded as a representative body of bishops, he noted, but rather as a symbolic sign of the council Fathers' desire to cooperate with the pope.

The text, he said, now urges reorganization of the Roman curia in view of modern needs, but it does not make explicit recommendations for such offices as the Congregation of the Holy Office or apostolic nuncio and delegates because it was the mind of the drafting commission that all these matters would be within the competence of the reorganizing committee.

After these two reports, five series of votes were taken on the revised schema on bishops. The Fathers also continued debating the schema on the Church in the modern world. Voting results were:

Vote one — on the introduction and articles one to three regarding the general contents of the schema: "yes" 1,908; "no" 101.

Vote two — on article four regarding the application and exercise of collegiality: "yes" 1,782; "no" 225.

(It was in this article that the word "full" was omitted, but the Fathers decided to register their disfavor with the omission not in the vote on the article itself, which would have meant an outright negative vote, but to wait until the overall vote was taken which permits favorable-with-reservations votes.)

Vote three — on articles five to seven regarding the establishment of a central commission of bishops to assist the pope and its role in the Church; "yes" 1,912; "no" 81.

(Bishop Gargitter in his report said that in article six a phrase which described the college of bishops as "successors of the apostles" had been omitted. This omission, he said, was not deliberate and was due to a typographical error.)

Vote four — on article eight regarding the authority of a bishop in his diocese: "yes" 1,880; "no" 81.

Vote five was the vote on the chapter as a whole: "yes" 1,030; "no" 77; "yes with reservations" 852.

Strong pleas for declarations on the freedom of scientific investigation and study were voiced during the debate on the schema on the Church in the modern world by Auxiliary Bishop Leon Elchinger of Strasbourg, France, and by Mexican Bishop Manuel Talamas Camandari of Ciudad Juarez.

Bishop Elchinger said the schema's section dealing with the Church's relation to culture will appear to learned men as mere pious exhortations, since many leaders of cultural movements of the present time have for the most part abandoned Christian beliefs or are actively opposed to them.

To overcome much of public opinion's distrust of the Church's attitude toward culture, he said, it is necessary to overcome "dogmatic imperialism," a tendency to judge all things as if theology gives a universal competence over all other fields of human learning. The Church is too bound up in classical and Western culture and shows too little openness of mind, he said.

As an example, he cited the case of Galileo. He noted that this year is the celebration of the fourth centenary of the birth of Galileo, but pointed out that there has been no retraction on the part of the Church of his "miserable and unjust condemnation." To offset this, he said, the Church must take a positive approach to the problem of culture and view it with an open and benevolent mind, recognizing freedom of investigation and study even in the religious sciences.

Bishop Talamas called for a declaration of the freedom of study and research as means of refuting the charge that the Church favors obscurantism. Even when it appears that a scholar is at variance or in conflict with Revelation, the Church should not condemn him or force him to make a retraction, but should rather encourage investigation until all facets of the matter are completed. This, he said, would work toward a synthesis of science and philosophy and closer collaboration between Church and scientists.

The day's first speaker was Giacomo Cardinal Lercaro of Bologna, Italy, who spoke on article 22 of the schema on the Church in the modern world. Article 22 treats of the Church's relation to culture. It was Cardinal Lercaro's contention that the Church should place greater stress on evangelical poverty.

He stated the Church has many riches and treasures from other ages that do not fit in the modern world, such as the medieval philosophy and terminology coming from the culture of the past. While they have value and significance, the Church should not boast of these as if they are all it has to offer to the world today.

He called for greater magnimininity toward the culture of today and urged the Church to go back to the treasures of the Bible and the early Fathers, who were bishops and teachers in the true sense. Man today does not want a philosophical system but a supernatural and spiritual dynamism from the Church, he said.

Italian Bishop Luigi Carli of Segni said the schema was incomplete in describing culture and put too much stress on material things, without warning of the dangers that can arise from modern culture. Among these dangers he listed "technicism," in which man is often considered only a tool within the larger social unity and also the danger of the suffocation of true culture by technicism, which leaves man passive.

Archbishop Charles De Provencheres of Aix, France, also warned of the dangers and weaknesses of modern culture which are brought about when the more backward cultures of newly emerging countries clash with richer cultures which are strongly influenced by technical advance and progress.

Archbishop Jean Zoa of Yaounde, Cameroun, criticized the schema for having no sense of the objectivity of the world. Therefore, he said, it would have a significance for modern Africa. What Africa needs, he declared, is for the institutions of the Church to free the

African people from superstition by legitimate science. Moreover, the need for a deeper sense of God should be an element of culture, he declared.

Ecuadorian Bishop Leonidas Proano Villalba of Riobamba, speaking in the name of 70 bishops, said he wanted great stress on the need for basic education. He said that in Latin America 80 million people out of a total population of 200 million are illiterate and that 600,000 teachers are needed today to combat this situation. He appealed to the council to work "to remove this crying shame."

After Bishop Proano finished, discussion was shifted to the schema's article 23 which deals with socio-economic matters.

Stefan Cardinal Wyszynski of Warsaw, speaking for the Polish bishops, said they had sent detailed suggestions on this portion of the schema to the drafting commission earlier, but that he wanted to repeat that the Church must protect Catholics against civic and economic systems which are wrong or oppressive. He said the methods and modes of some economic systems cannot be accepted since they are harmful to the individual and nation. They are systems that spread atheism, and the Church must show more concern for the poor and the working classes.

Paul Cardinal Richaud of Bordeaux, France, said he wanted more attention paid to the problems of workers' security and unemployment. He called for a condemnation of exaggerated profits from speculation and blamed many social problems on the inequality of the distribution of riches. The Church should face these problems with justice and without fear, he said.

Bishop Angel Herrera y Oria of Malaga, Spain, also expressed concern about the workers' plight. The social question cannot be passed over in silence, he said, and the council must take its stand by issuing concrete directives and norms. He called for collaboration of workers, management, the state and the Church in social activity to be carried out in the charity of Christ.

Colombian Bishop Raul Zambrano Camader of Facatativa stressed the Church is not bound to one economic system and that economic systems are not fixed and unchanging but are constantly undergoing alterations. He also asked that the document repeat the basic concept of property which has been taught by the Church in the past.   James C. O'Neill

Interview With Miss Pilar Bellosillo

"Catholic women the world over will be delighted to hear of the pronouncements on their behalf by four council Fathers," said Miss Pilar Bellosillo, president of the World Union of Catholic Women's Organizations, whose home is in Madrid and who is here as a woman council auditor.

The union is made up of 115 Catholic women's organizations in 82 countries and counts a total membership of 36 million.

Miss Bellosillo said in an interview:

"To hear one bishop after another address the council in the course of debate on schema 13, which deals with the position of the Church in the modern world, and take a stand in full recognition of the personal dignity of woman and of her role in the Church, as well as in human society at large, was indeed a joyful experience."

Which statements specifically did she have in mind, Miss Bellosillo was asked.

"The ones by Bishop Gerard Coderre of Saint-Jean de Quebec, on behalf of 40 Canadian bishops, and by Archbishop Joseph Malula of Leopoldville, the Congo — both of whom spoke on Oct. 28 — and of Auxiliary Bishop Augustin Frotz of Cologne, Germany, and Aux-iliary Bishop Santo Quadri of Pinerolo, Italy — both of whom spoke on Oct. 29.

"Just take these key sentences of Bishop Coderre: 'Man and woman while different in their specific make-ups, own human nature in its fulness and integrity. Woman has her own and necessary task to perform in the realization of God's plans on both the natural and the supernatural level. Without a real contribution of woman, human society, and even the kingdom of God, would not achieve their perfection and their fulness. The Church is duty bound to promote woman's calling in every possible way.'

"Or hear what Bishop Frotz has to say: 'Modern women expect to be accepted as equal partners of men in intellectual and cultural life, and the Church should set herself to promote the spiritual interests of woman, in order that she may gain the opportunity to apply her unique gifts to the Church's apostolate, for the benefit of all society.'

"Archbishop Malula, of course, spoke mainly of African women and condemned in no uncertain terms the slavery of women. Other bishops expressed themselves in similar terms.

"We women auditors, both Religious and lay, were

particularly impressed and pleased by these utterances because to our mind schema 13 as now presented does not give sufficient consideration to the equal rights of the sexes which are so firmly stated in Pacem in Terris and other papal documents."

Miss Bellosillo then spoke of the function of women auditors in the council and said:

"We are not limited to a mere presence in silence. We make our own contribution in various committees where it can truly be effective."

Will this participation of women in the council have direct practical consequences?

"I certainly hope so," Miss Bellosillo replied, "for a great deal remains to be done, especially in legislation in various countries, to give proper recognition to woman in society. The Church, too, has so far not always promoted women's interests sufficiently. We of the World Union of Catholic Women's Organizations are trying to exercise our influence in order that these situations may be corrected. It is gratifying that our efforts are now gaining such influential support on the part of council Fathers whose competence ought to impress public opinion.

"These bishops and other council Fathers who have given recognition to women help us greatly in creating a climate which will encourage women to assume greater responsibilities than up to now they were able to assume.

"To my mind, this will at the same time contribute toward a more active participation of women in Catholic activities because they will no longer feel restricted to a merely passive role in the Church.

"As Bishop Frotz aptly expressed it: 'Times change and women change, too!' Modern women, he said, especially those who have no families of their own, should be given their proper share in the life of the Church. Then they would see in the Church the true guardian of their personal dignity."

FATHER PLACID JORDAN, O.S.B.

115th General Congregation

November 5, 1964

For its debate on what the Church can and should do about world poverty, the Second Vatican Council brought before it an American layman who has immersed himself in the problem for decades.

James J. Norris, in the flawless Latin of a former classics professor, pictured the specter of hunger-ridden poverty that breeds disease and despair and finds relief only in death.

The white-haired, youthful-appearing president of the International Catholic Migration Commission urged the council to "secure full Catholic participation in the worldwide attack on poverty."

He described today's community of nations as "lopsided," with nations representing 16% of the world's population holding 70% of the world's wealth, and three-quarters of the human race existing "in a state of poverty bordering on or below subsistence level."

Worse yet, the rich are growing richer and the poor are growing poorer in this single world community, said Norris, who is also assistant to the executive director of Catholic Relief Services—National Catholic Welfare Conference.

"This is a wholly unprecedented historical fact, and it presents the Christian conscience of the Western nations with a challenge," Norris declared.

He pinpointed this new challenge: "For the first time in history it is accepted as a fact that, given time, they have the means to wipe out poverty in the rest of the world."

It is meaningless to profess Christianity without remembering that wealth is a trust "and that riches on the scale of the West's modern riches must be redeemed by generosity," he asserted.

While a number of agencies—private, governmental, ecclesiastical and international—have been attempting to alleviate poverty in the world, Norris said, the constantly widening gap between the rich and the poor demands now a sustained, realistic, dedicated campaign to bring full Christian activity to bear upon these problems.

"All Christian communions are involved and therefore the opportunity is offered to all to unite in these efforts and bring joint influence to bear to encourage governments to continue and expand their policies for providing capital and technical assistance.

"No other group is likely to have the staying power needed for this long, arduous and often disappointing work," he continued.

He warned that world poverty will not be eradicated quickly.

"But the goal will be reached if in each wealthy country there is brought into being a strong, committed, well-informed and courageous group of men of good will who are prepared to see world poverty as one of the great central concerns of our time and press steadily and vocally for the policies in aid, in trade and in the transfer of skills that will lessen the widening gap between the rich and the poor."

Although Norris spoke at an hour when many council Fathers usually step out of the council hall for a cup of coffee and a brief chat, the benches of the vast basilica were full.

The council Fathers listened intently to Norris as he listed some of the human sufferings that are inevitably brought in the wake of dire poverty:

— "A constant gnawing hunger that is never satisfied day or night."

— "Disease that cannot be cured because there are no medical services."

— "Illiteracy in lands where the great majority of people cannot read or write."

— "Slums that breed crime and sin."

He then spoke of one of the most poignant of tragedies: "Poverty means that a mother looks at her newborn infant knowing that it will probably die before the year is out."

Norris concluded: "From this ecumenical council could come a clarion call for action which would involve the creation of a structure that would devise the kind of institutions, contacts, forms of cooperation and policy, which the Church can adopt to secure full Catholic participation in the worldwide attack on poverty."

The Fathers applauded loud and long when Norris quoted Pope Paul VI's Christmas message of last year in Italian: "We make our own the sufferings of the poor. And we hope that this sympathy of ours may itself become capable of enkindling that new love which, through a specially planned economy, will multiply the bread needed to feed the world."

222

Norris was the second lay auditor to address a working session of the council. Patrick Keegan of Britain, head of the International Federation of Christian Workers Movements, spoke in English on Oct. 13.

Technically, the address Norris gave was a report on article 24 of the schema on the Church in the modern world. While such reports are officially presented on behalf of the commission which drafted the schema, the mixed commission which drafted this schema passed the Norris report virtually without alteration.

(Expanding later on his suggestion for "a structure that would devise the kind of institutions, contacts, forms of cooperation and policy which the Church can adopt," Norris said he envisages a central coordinating group for the Church's national social programs already in existence. These, he said, would enmesh their work with the predominantly Protestant and Orthodox World Council of Churches and similar organizations.)

Almost as if to take up Norris' suggestion and make it concrete, Joseph Cardinal Frings of Cologne, Germany, suggested creation of a general secretariat to coordinate Catholic efforts and maintain contact with international agencies such as the United Nations Food and Agricultural Organization, the United Nations Children Fund and the World Health Organization.

Bishops, he said, should engage in such activities "with modesty," divesting themselves of what he called "triumphal clothing."

(Norris later said that Cardinal Frings told him he had in mind a secretariat in Geneva, Switzerland, which would not only coordinate activity but exchange information and stimulate research in the war on want.)

Bishop Jean Rupp of Monaco, emphasizing that in his diocese there are lots "of good, honest people nobody has ever heard about," proceeded to give the council some of the suggestions his people had given him.

Some of them had declared their conviction that there can be no Christian order where hunger reigns. More energy, they had said, should be devoted to uprooting this evil than to denouncing it.

In conjunction with this, Bishop Rupp suggested that the schema emphasize the solidarity of Christians in eradicating evils such as hunger. It should be borne in mind, however, that the word Christian has been so watered down that it tends to lose its meaning, he said.

Bishop Rupp criticized the style of the article as wordy and swollen, too prudent, too diplomatic, too political. He said his criticism could be summed up in a phrase: "too feminine."

He ended his address: "My children have spoken, I have spoken."

Bishop Antonio Pildain y Zapiain of the Canary Islands framed the problem in simple terms. Some "apparently Christian" nations are wealthy, he said, while others are deprived of basic necessities. He said the remedy is not communism but a "Christian communitarianism" founded on the rule that in dire necessity all things are in common — the principle of moral theology that a man in dire need may take from the abundance of another. Liberal capitalism detests this principle, he said.

Nobody has the right to luxury while others are in need, he declared. This applies to nations as well as individuals.

Auxiliary Bishop Edward E. Swanstrom of New York, executive director of Catholic Relief Services-National Catholic Welfare Conference, said that as director of the American Bishops' foreign relief program he has the "privilege of cooperating with many of you in your efforts to assist the poor and afflicted in your areas."

He said that in his travels through the "misery-scourged corners" of the world he has seen the Biblical story of the rich man Dives and the poor man Lazarus enacted over and over again.

"I saw Lazarus most obviously in a leprous beggar dragged in a cart on a begging journey around the streets of Calcutta," he said.

"I saw him too in the refugee who had escaped from mainland China in 1961 and who had been caught up and deposited in the Fan Ling transit camp. I went up to this camp and saw thousands of unfortunates who had risked their lives to escape, but were allowed to sit at the gates of the free world for a few days, and then herded into trucks to be returned to China. There was no inn for them in the towns and cities of our Western civilization."

(Here he seemed to echo a cry of Bishop Rupp against "the scandal of Christian nations which close their doors to immigrants from the poor countries.")

Bishop Swanstrom declared with Pope Paul VI that the first of the world's needs is hunger. He said that a great gulf exists between the hungry nations and the well fed nations which is "clearly in the eternal order," like the gulf that the Bible speaks of between the souls of Lazarus and Dives.

Bishop Swanstrom asked how, for example, the Church can meet the critical shortage of native priests where decent standards of life and education have not been achieved.

"Poverty, hunger and disease are afflictions as old as man himself. But in our time and in this age there has been a change. Change is not so much in the realities of life, but in the hopes and expectations of the future. If mens' hopes are not obtainable by a peaceful revolution, a violent revolution is inevitable," he warned.

Bishop Swanstrom said chapter 24 speaks in broad terms of what governments and laymen should do. He urged that it be rewritten "to emphasize also the tremendous responsibility placed upon bishops and priests in our day and age to participate most actively in programs to assist the people of God to raise themselves out of the abyss of poverty and degradation."

Syro-Malankar Archbishop Gregorios Thangalathil of Trivandrum, India, said that without the basic needs of life, man is forever exposed to the dangers of sin. The problem of hunger has its repercussions in the moral order, he noted.

He pointed to economists who say that every nation that hopes to progress economically must reinvest 12% of its national income. But how, he asked, can this be done by nations which have barely enough to live on?

Archbishop Pericle Felici, council secretary general, opened the council business by announcing the death of Bishop Giuseppe Gagnor of Alessandria, Italy.

He said Pope Paul would personally attend the following day's meeting, which was to take up the schema on the missions before returning to schema 13.

The Pope would sit among the council presidents, he said, not on his special throne.

This would be the first time the Pope had been present at a debate of the Second Vatican Council.

Archbishop Felici also announced the Pope desired to meet all the council Fathers before the end of the session. The bishops would be received in national or linguistic groups, and appointments would be announced regularly in the council hall.

The day's moderator, Giacomo Cardinal Lercaro of Bologna, Italy, then asked for a standing vote to close debate on schema 13's article 23. The cloture vote was passed.

Auxiliary Bishop Benitez Avalos of Asuncion, Paraguay, in the name of 105 Latin American bishops, complained that the schema had taken too theoretical an approach to the concrete problems it hopes to help solve. Latin America has one-third of the world's Catholic population. Its population was 200 million in 1960 and this is expected to triple by the end of the century, he noted. Economically, the annual per capita income in Latin America does not exceed $200, which is about 10% of that of more productive countries. The economy suffers from a lack of capital and bad distribution of the means of production, he pointed out. These countries are too dependent upon the richer nations. For years Latin America has had no middle class, and this has meant a certain torpor among the lower classes, who need to be roused to a desire for self-betterment, he said.

On the political plane, most nations are ruled by oligarchies, he stated. Even when a government wants to make needed changes, it may lack the authority to achieve them. The Church's grave responsibility is to form competent laymen who will be able to train others, he declared.

Mexican Bishop Jose Alba Palacios of Tehuantepec said the Pope must be heeded regarding the problems of marriage and family life even when he does not use his full teaching authority. The bishop urged full freedom for scientific research which will prepare the way for the Church's mature judgments.

Archbishop Paul Zoungrana of Ouagadougou, Upper Volta, in the name of 70 bishops of Africa and Brazil, spoke of the so-called third world. The council cannot afford to ignore this underdeveloped third group of nations, he said. Their population will double before the end of the century in all the poorer areas of the world. These countries lack land, investment and education. Competent experts should revise article 23 to make it pertinent to the underdeveloped nations, he said.

Through a mixup, Bernard Cardinal Alfrink of Utrecht, the Netherlands, was called upon to speak on Article 25. He urged the council to show great concern for all who are persecuted for religion, especially under communism. But he did not think that the council should formally condemn Marxism, since this would be a simple repetition of what the pope and bishops have already done. A condemnation, he said, would touch atheistic materialism of the theoretical variety only, and this is not any more dangerous than atheistic materialism of the practical variety.

Instead, Cardinal Alfrink suggested, the council should encourage a dialogue between well prepared Christians and individual Marxists. Such contacts, he said, would be like Christ's night-time conversation with Nicodemus.

Bishop Luigi Carli of Segni, Italy, presented the first report on the second chapter of the schema on the pastoral duties of bishops, confining his report to articles one and two.

He said that the commission had attempted to give a definition of a disease based on its intrinsic elements, rather than on its territorial limits. This allowed formulation of a theology of the individual church and put the bishop's pastoral activity in a brighter light. It also allows room for the so-called personal diocese, he said.

The report affirms the absolute independence of bishops from civil power and the Church's full freedom to appoint bishops. However, the Holy See's freedom to appoint bishops, as explained in the schema, does not exclude the possibility of concessions to various authorities.

Bishop Carli said that while the resignation of a bishop may be strongly recommended, it is not absolutely imposed. The schema allows room for competent authority's suggestion that a bishop resign if he is unable to fulfill his duties.

Bishop Narciso Jubany Arnau of Gerona, Spain, read the substance of the report on the schema's article three (chapter two). He said that the commission agreed that coadjutor and auxiliary bishops should be preserved and that their authority should be consistent with their dignity as members of the episcopal college. They could be appointed either as vicars general, he said, or a new canonical position could be introduced, that of episcopal vicar.

Voting on the schema on bishops continued:

Articles 11 to 18 on the duties of bishops: 2,040 "yes," 22 "no."

Articles 19 and 20 on freedom of bishops and their appointment: 2,055 "yes," 8 "no."

Article 21 on retirement of bishops: 1,986 "yes," 57 "no."

Articles 22 to 24 on diocesan boundaries: 1,979 "yes," 12 "no."

Articles 25 and 26 on coadjutor and auxiliary bishops: 1,982 "yes," 22 "no."

Articles 27 to 29 on organization of chanceries: 1,956 "yes," 25 "no."

Articles 30 to 32 on pastors, their duties and appointment and retirement: 1,950 "yes," 14 "no."

Articles 33 to 35 on religious: 1,801 "yes," 172 "no."

The council meeting opened with Mass celebrated by Auxiliary Bishop Clemens Chabukasansha of Fort Rosebery, Zambia. Archbishop Mariano Rossel y Arellana of Guatemala City enthroned the Gospel.

PATRICK RILEY

* * * *

It was stated at the U.S. bishops' press panel following the council debate:

"For two and one-half years the Second Vatican Council has been considering the Church's internal structure. Now in two and a half hours it has considered the central problem of our age—world poverty. Only the level of talks today saved this contrast from being too painful."

This was the assessment of an English Mill Hill priest, Father Arthur McCormack, editor of World Justice magazine and population expert.

He called for the Church to set up a "war cabinet" in the form of a new secretariat to wage "total war on poverty." He suggested that a cardinal head the new office to give the program identity, just as Augustin Cardinal Bea, S.J., embodies the entire work of the Secretariat for Promoting Christian Unity.

Bishop Swanstrom, a panel guest following his council talk the same morning on poverty, urged going slow on forming such an organization as Father McCormack suggested.

Msgr. George G. Higgins, director of the Social Action Department of the National Catholic Welfare Conference, pointed out that schema 13 sets a new pattern for forming Catholic organizations.

"It goes further than any other Catholic document I know of in promoting cooperation with the best equipped existing organizations. It also sets down the principle that the Church should not start Catholic organizations unless they are absolutely necessary, and then by way of exception. Such a principle would put a damper on a situation which has befuddled the Church's work for the past 100 years," he said.

Referring to the relationship between birth control and world poverty, Father McCormack said: "If you invented a [contraceptive] pill which would serve the millions who need or want it, you still would not solve the problem of world hunger or abolish its root causes."

James Norris, after his council speech the same morning, told the panel audience that the American people need much education regarding social welfare programs. He said they must be convinced that not everything in foreign aid programs is bad or "money down a rathole. No developing country ever developed in less than 50 years. We need to be patient," he said.

James J. Norris

This is a translation of the Latin-language speech delivered at the Nov. 5 ecumenical council meeting by James J. Norris, president of the International Catholic Migration Commission and assistant to the executive director of Catholic Relief Services—National Catholic Welfare Conference.

In the last decade the problem of poverty—one of the oldest and deepest that confronts the Christian conscience—has taken on a new shape, new dimensions and new urgency. "The poor you have always with you" —yes, but today the poor are with us in a new and revolutionary context, because modern science, medicine and technology have helped to bring about a single economy, a neighborhood that is interdependent, but largely lacking the institutions and the policies that express solidarity, compassion and human obligation.

In this lopsided community, one small group of nations have become immensely wealthy. These nations represent 16% of the world's peoples, and they own 70% of its wealth. They are the nations grouped around the North Atlantic, which are Christian by tradition, if not always in practice. For the first time in history they foresee rising prosperity—rich today, they will be richer tomorrow.

Meanwhile, three-quarters of the human race live in a state of poverty bordering on or below the subsistence level.

The gap between the rich and the poor is rapidly widening—side by side the rich grow richer and the poor grow poorer, in a single world community. This is a wholly unprecedented historical fact, and it presents the Christian conscience of the western nations with a challenge, because for the first time in history it is accepted as a fact that, given time, they have the means to wipe out poverty in the rest of the world.

There will be no meaning to their Christian profession or humane traditions if they forget that wealth is a trust and that property carries social obligations and that riches on the scale of the West's modern riches must be redeemed by generosity.

A number of Church, private, governmental and international agencies have been attempting to alleviate the problems of poverty and hunger in the world; nevertheless, the constantly widening gap between the rich and the poor demands now a sustained, realistic, dedicated campaign to bring full Christian activity to bear upon these problems.

All Christian communions are involved and therefore the opportunity is offered to all to unite in these efforts and bring joint influence to bear to encourage governments to continue and expand their policies for providing capital and technical assistance. No other group is likely to have the staying power needed for this long, arduous and often disappointing work.

World poverty will not be wiped out speedily, nor will the problem of development be solved in anything short of several generations. Our Christian peoples must not become weary of well doing.

But the goal will be reached if in each wealthy country there is brought into being a strong, committed, well-informed and courageous group of men of good will who are prepared to see world poverty as one of the great central concerns of our time and press steadily and vocally for the policies in aid, in trade and in the transfer of skills, that will lessen the widening gap between the rich and the poor.

This problem is not only the concern of the wealthy nations. In our complex 20th-century world, the developing nations, to progress effectively, need the capital, the knowledge, and the technical assistance of the more economically developed countries, but as wise leaders in those countries insist, the development must come from the local resources, both material and human, which God has given these lands.

Recently, a bishop from one of these lands said to me, "My people live not only in poverty but in permanent misery." This type of utter poverty brings with it other human sufferings. The first is hunger—a constant, gnawing hunger that is never satisfied day or night. Poverty brings diseases that cannot be cured because there are no medical services. Poverty brings illiteracy in lands where the great majority of people cannot read or write. Poverty brings bad housing "slums" that breed crime and sin. Poverty means that a mother looks at her new-born infant knowing that it will probably die before the year is out. For millions of people, poverty means that life expectancy is 35 years. For millions of people, living in this kind of poverty, death is a sweet release.

A loving human family does not permit its members to suffer in this way. When all the members of our Christian family become aware of the extent of suffering and privation among the poor of the world surely they will make certain that their wealthy lands will not fail to respond to their Christian obligation.

From this ecumenical council could come a clarion call for action which would involve the creation of a structure that would devise the kind of institutions, contacts, forms of cooperation and policy, which the Church can adopt, to secure full Catholic participation in the world-wide attack on poverty.

This great gathering of bishops represents every continent and every country on earth. Since world poverty affects all humanity, the great contribution of our universal Church can be a world-encircling manifestation of brotherly love, bringing effectively to bear the social teaching of the Church on the problem which our beloved Holy Father discussed in his Christmas message last year when he said that hunger is the principal problem in the world today and concluded with these words: "Unless this heart-rending situation is relieved, we must foresee that it will grow worse, not better . . . . Even though we are not given Christ's miraculous power of materially multiplying bread for the world's hunger, still we can take to heart the plea that rises from the masses, still oppressed and languishing with misery, and to feel it vibrate in us with the very pity which was felt by the heart of Christ which is both divine and completely human: Misereor super turbam . . . 'I have compassion on the multitude . . . . They have nothing to eat.'

"We make our own the sufferings of the poor. And we hope that this our sympathy may itself become capable of enkindling that new love which, by means of a specially planned economy, will multiply the bread needed to feed the world."

Bishop Swanstrom

This is a translation of the Latin-language speech delivered at the Nov. 5 ecumenical council meeting by Auxiliary Bishop Edward E. Swanstrom of New York, executive director of Catholic Relief Services—National Catholic Welfare Conference.

As the director of the American bishops' foreign relief program which now encompasses 73 countries of the world, I have the privilege of cooperating with many of you in your efforts to assist the poor and afflicted in your areas. In carrying out that responsibility I have naturally had occasion to visit most of the countries of Europe, the Middle East, Africa, Asia and the Far East, and Latin America.

For those of us who live in America, the world still presents a face of some calm and orderliness. Our lives have not been caught up in the incessant upheavals that have afflicted so many human beings whose fate it was to be thrust over frontiers as refugees or to be part of the post-colonial areas battling their way into freedom and struggling for some semblance of stability.

Even though there are some very threatening clouds on our own horizon, life in America is in sharp contrast to all the unrest, the homelessness, the hunger and anguish that I have witnessed all over the world in the past several years.

We all remember with poignant clarity the Gospel stories of need and suffering that were taught to us even in the years of our childhood. The story of Lazarus and the rich man has always retained a special poignancy for me. As I have traveled about the world—to its misery-scourged corners—I have seen Lazarus in my mind's eye over and over again.

I saw him most obviously in a leprous beggar dragged in a cart on a begging journey around the streets of Calcutta, a city whose streets teem with millions of people, many of them refugees. I saw him, too, in the refugee who had escaped from the mainland of China in 1961 and who had been caught up and deposited in the Fan Ling transit camp.

I went up to this camp and saw thousands of unfortunates who had risked their lives to escape, but were allowed to sit at the gates of the free world for a few days, then were herded into trucks to be returned to China. There was no inn for them in the towns and cities of our western civilization.

In the giant slums which have mushroomed around Latin America's proudest cities—Rio de Janeiro, Santiago, Lima, Bogota—I have seen countless men waiting at the gate of the world for the opportunity to take part in productive life and waiting in vain.

The Lazarus of the Gospel sat at the gate longing for "the crumbs that fell from the rich man's table." But the rich man "who used to clothe himself in purple and fine linen, and who feasted every day in fine fashion," turned away from Lazarus and gave him no aid. Poor Lazarus died, and went from the gate where "the dogs licked his sores" to the peace of Abraham's bosom in heaven. When the rich man died, he went to—well, somewhere else—and he cried for Lazarus to come down and put a drop of water on his tongue in his place of torment.

But as the Gospel tells us, "a great gulf" had been placed between them. The gulf that the rich man had chosen to maintain between him and the poor while on earth was continued for all eternity. It gives us pause to realize that no other sin is imputed to the rich man, merely that he did not perform the works of mercy in his power. He did not feed the hungry.

It is in such Gospel stories as this that we see the real meaning of Pope Paul's message of last Christmas when he told us that world hunger was the most urgent of the world's problems. In talking about the needs of the world, "a question that makes one dizzy," said our Holy Father, "because the needs are so vast, so manifold, so immeasurable," he states very definitely, "the first is hunger."

We know that it existed, he went on to say, "but today it has been recognized. It has now been scientifically proven to us that more than half the human race has not enough food. Entire generations of children, even today, are dying or suffering because of indescribable poverty." How true are his words!

The great gulf that exists between the hungry and the well-fed, between the rich and poor nations, is one that is dangerous, not only in the temporal order, but quite clearly in the eternal order.

If we are our brother's keeper, we must bear witness to this fact. It is not as simple any more as leaving our home and finding a Lazarus at our gate. Since Vatican Council II is concerned with updating every aspect of the Church's mission to make the Gospel of Christ relevant to 20th century life, we must update our expression of concern for our brother in the world in which we find ourselves. In our day and age, the social mission of the Church must be our great concern, perhaps for some of us a primary concern.

How for example are we to meet the critical problem of a shortage of native priests in many areas until we help lift the social and economic status of our people to a point where there is adequate provision for a decent standard of living and for the primary and secondary education of their children, so essential for candidates for the priesthood?

It is not that there is anything new about the situation we find in the world today. Poverty, hunger and disease are afflictions as old as man himself. But in our time and in this age there has been a change. The change is not so much in the realities of life, but in the hopes and expectations of the future. If men's hopes are not obtainable by a peaceful revolution, a violent revolution is inevitable.

The present world situation has created a worldwide boom of vast portent which has come to be known as the "revolution of rising expectations." The meaning of this revolution is very simple. It means that people all over the world want for themselves the same things that they know others have and which all of us want for our loved ones, for our friends and for our children and that many of us have already.

They intend that their families shall live a decent life and that they have a job that gives them survival and dignity. They intend that their children shall be taught to read and write, they intend that the hungry shall be fed and the sick shall be treated. They intend to take their place in the great movement of modern society, to take their share in the benefits of that society.

These just desires, once unleashed, can never again be stifled. The people in the developing world are on the march and certainly we, as the leaders of the Catholic Church throughout the world, must be beside them on that march.

In his great encyclical "Mater et Magistra," which Pope John of blessed memory issued shortly before this ecumenical council convened, he states, "we are all equally responsible for the undernourished peoples," and again, "now justice and humanity require that these richer countries come to the aid of those in need."

I am sure we all realize that in the encyclical Ma-

ter et Magistra our Holy Father is just making an effort to apply the teaching of our Lord and Saviour, Jesus Christ, to our own times. Christ says He is the light of the world. He makes plain His concern also for the earthly needs of men, not only by His words, but also in the deeds of His life, as when to alleviate the hunger of a crowd, He more than once miraculously multiplies bread.

Every man created by God has a right to the indispensable means of human subsistence, to sufficient food and clothing for his body, to housing, to employment, to suitable leisure and even to decent recreation. What our Holy Father tries to make clear to us is that if our brothers in any land are lacking any such necessities they are our responsibility as much as anyone else's.

In our modern civilization, it is worthy of note that many governments have now turned their full attention to the tragic problems of poverty and destitution in the world. Even though their motivation may be largely political and their chief desire is to prevent revolution and war, it is the charity in the hearts of most of their people that is behind this endeavor to spread the world's wealth and goods among all nations. Surely it is our function as the bishops of the Church established by Christ Himself to exhort, stimulate and encourage our governments in this endeavor to assist them in shaping policies and join with them in distributing food and clothing and the means of earning a livelihood among those less fortunate than ourselves, and most particularly among the destitute and the starving.

Paragraph 24 talks largely about what governments and laity should do. It should be rewritten to emphasize also the tremendous responsibility placed upon bishops and priests in our day and age to participate most actively in programs to assist the people of God to raise themselves out of the abyss of poverty and degradation. Since we are other Christs, like Christ Himself, we must carry out our social as well as our spiritual mission.

We, too, must stand before the judgment seat of God and we will want Him to say to us, "Amen I say to you when you did this to one of the least of my brethren, you did it unto Me."

116th General Congregation
November 6, 1964

Pope Paul VI, breaking age-old tradition by presiding over a working session of an ecumenical council, threw his own influence behind the council's draft document on mission work.

It had been expected that the drastically abbreviated series of propositions on the missions would encounter heavy weather in the council hall. Many missionary bishops and missionary superiors were known to be dissatisfied with it. At least two substitute documents on the missions were on the sidelines ready to be offered to the council in place of the official document.

The Pope, however, said that in examining the document which actually had been put before the council: "We have found many things worthy of our praise, both for its content and its order of exposition."

In his brief address while appearing on the council floor, he stated: "We therefore believe that the text will be approved by you easily, although after undergoing some final necessary adjustments."

What pleased him the most about the schema, the Pope said, was its constant emphasis that the entire Church should be missionary, and that, so far as possible, individual members of the Church should be missionary in mind and deed.

He called the missionary apostolate "the most excellent of all in importance and efficacy."

The Pope told the Fathers that he had decided to preside over at least one of the council's general congregations. What prompted him to choose the congregation dealing with the missions was "the grave and singular importance of the topic."

In fact, the council interrupted its debate on its schema on the Church in the modern world to introduce the schema on the missions on the day of the Pope's visit.

Pope Paul did not remain at the session for the debate itself—which developed some strong criticism of details of the schema. However, none of the day's five speakers attacked the substance of the schema.

Augustin Cardinal Bea, S.J., who was the last of the four cardinals to speak, defended the Church's missionary activity against those who think the Church should concentrate its energies and expend its resources on other things.

Cardinal Bea, who as president of the Secretariat for Promoting Christian Unity practically personifies Catholic ecumenism, urged a rebirth of missionary zeal.

Missionary activity, he said, is part of the Church's very nature. Thus the council must instill new missionary drive throughout the Church.

He said the schema tries to answer those who doubt whether missionary activity, strictly so called, is timely today.

Cardinal Bea took up the objection that since hierarchies have been erected in almost every country, and since so-called Christian countries have in many instances fallen into neo-paganism, it hardly seems worthwhile to send missioners to new countries. He replied that while work in Christian countries can never be underestimated, the proclamation of the Gospel to those who have never heard the name of Christ has always been dear to the Church.

The German-born cardinal moved for inclusion in the schema of a brief statement affirming that missionary activity is necessary. He asked that it be so phrased that it can easily be understood by modern man.

Bishop Stanislaus Lokuang of Tainan, Formosa, presented the report on the schema on behalf of the council's Commission on the Missions, which drafted it. Speaking immediately after the Pope's departure from the hall, he said that the schema had been reduced considerably by the time it was distributed to the council Fathers last January. But before the observations and recommendations sent in by the bishops could be taken into consideration, he said, the council Coordinating Commission issued orders to reduce the material concerning the missions to a simple series of propositions.

The Commission on the Missions had no choice but to obey, Bishop Lokuang continued. But he said that in view of the importance of the matter, it would gladly have worked out a more detailed text. Because of the importance of the subject, he said, the draft can hardly be viewed as satisfactory in its present reduced state.

Noting that the revised text now comprises 13 propositions, he proceded to explain how various parts of the original schema had been synthesized into the new document.

Bishop Lokuang said that the missions commission

refrained from any attempt to define missionary activity. He said the reason for this is that missiologists have not reached agreement on the subject.

Paul-Emile Cardinal Leger of Montreal led off the debate on the missions schema. He first took up the question of a "central mission board" as proposed by the text.

Bishop Lokuang had reported that the men who drew up the text had deliberately refrained from pinpointing relationship of such a board with the Holy See's Congregation for the Propagation of the Faith. The reason behind this deliberate vagueness was the desire to leave this decision up to the Pope, he said.

Cardinal Leger, however, asked that the text clearly specify that this board be integrated into the Congregation for the Propagation of the Faith as that mission body's supreme council.

(According to the draft document, this central mission board or central council of evangelization would be comprised of representatives of those actually working in the missions. Its task would be to work out common plans through which the Church's missionary activity would be directed. These plans, after being approved by the Pope, would be put into execution by the Congregation for Propagation of the Faith.)

Cardinal Leger asserted that the new liberty accorded to bishops as a result of this council is nowhere more necessary than in the missions. Bishops must be free to adapt the Gospel message to individual peoples, Cardinal Leger said, and the schema should be strengthened on this point.

He also urged that the schema speak out on the importance of the confronting not only of cultures (on which it already has something to say) but also on the importance of the encounter with various religions.

In a like vein, Peter Cardinal Doi of Tokyo complained that the schema treats of the missions only as they exist among non-Christian peoples of primitive (or evolving) cultures. He suggested that the schema turn its attention also to other non-Christian peoples of ancient culture and high educational level.

Laurian Cardinal Rugambwa of Bukoba, Tanganyika, pleaded for a more flexible spirit of adaptability in the mission field. He said St. Paul wrote the Magna Carta for all apostles when he declared that he had become all things to all men in order to save all. Only when the Church achieves an understanding of and a reverence for individual nations will what Cardinal Rugambwa called the "splendor of diversity" shine forth from the Church.

Cardinal Rugambwa urged that missionaries have a real respect for local laws. He said missionaries should adopt God's command to Abraham—to "go out of thy land and away from thy relatives"—making of his apostolic field a new home and a new fatherland.

Cardinal Bea then spoke.

The final speaker was Father Martino Legarra, O.R.S.A., prelate nullius of Bocas del Toro, Panama, who said he was voicing the ideas of "several" bishops. His point was that those special, and usually small, ecclesiastical territories known as prelatures nullius should receive the same treatment as all other mission fields. He feared that the terminology of the schema is open to misunderstanding on the point. He said such prelatures do not receive the same regular financial support as other mission territories, simply because they are not called missions. This, he said, makes it very difficult to plan ahead.

Cardinal Agagianian, in introducing the schema, gave a brief outline of the changes in the Church's missionary activities in the past century. He pointed out that in 1870 there was not a single native bishop in the Church's mission territories, while today there are 167, including four cardinals.

Even within the past 15 years, he said, the number of Catholics in territories subject to Propaganda Fide has almost doubled, jumping from 28 million to 50 million.

Cardinal Agagianian paid tribute to the valuable work of lay missionaries.

Voting on the schema on the pastoral duties of bishops continued throughout the debate on the missions schema.

The first vote was on the whole of Chapter II. Although only 19 council Fathers voted against the chapter, 889 expressed a desire to see changes (placet juxta modum). A total of 1,219 Fathers expressed their unqualified approval.

The chapter therefore was approved, but must still be amended.

(Archbishop Joseph T. McGucken of San Francisco later expressed the opinion that most of those who want the chapter changed object to the passage making all Religious—members of religious communities—subject to local bishops in public worship, in education and in other fields. He said most Religious working in the missions might want autonomy for certain charitable and cultural works.)

Seven other votes were taken on articles or groups of articles of the schema on the pastoral duties of bishops. The results of only three of them were available by the time the council Fathers arose to leave:

—Articles 36 and 37 (on synods and particular councils, and the concept of national episcopal conferences), "yes" 2,000, "no" 11.

—Article 38 (the structure, competence and collaboration of episcopal conferences), "yes" 1,948, "no" 71.

—Articles 39 to 41 (the division of ecclesiastical provinces and erection of ecclesiastical territories), "yes" 1,998, "no" 27.

—Articles 42 and 43 (bishops with interdiocesan

functions [such as military ordinaries and directors of national societies]), "yes" 2,053, "no" 11.

—Article 44 (exhortation to bishops on pastoral duties), "yes" 2,049, "no" 15.

—On the whole of chapter III (on the cooperation of bishops for the common good of their churches), "yes" 1,582, "no" 15, "yes with reservations" 496.

The votes of unqualified approval carried this chapter by more than the required two-thirds majority (with four null votes there was a total of 2,070 votes). But council officers have repeatedly stated that the commission will take suggestions of the council Fathers into account in the final draft of the schema, even when a two-thirds majority has been reached.

Archbishop Herman Schaeufele of Freiburg, Germany, gave the report on Chapter III, on whose articles the votes were taken. He said the commission agreed not to state that national episcopal conferences are an expression of the power of the college of bishops. The schema bases them not on the principle of collegiality but on the need for collaboration and the need to share inspirations of prudence.

He said differences between the Oriental and Latin Rite Churches prevented a formulation of norms common to all. This is why the schema recommends that various rites within the same territory assemble to promote the best interests of all.

Although several council Fathers had asked for the total elimination of the term "nation," he said this had proved impossible since most episcopal conferences represent the hierarchy of an entire nation.

The commission tackled three main problems concerning the organization of national episcopal conferences: what bishops have a right to belong to a conference, the kind of vote enjoyed by the members, and just how extensive is the juridical authority of such conferences.

It was decided:

— that all local Ordinaries of whatever rite would be members of the conferences.

— that all local Ordinaries and coadjutors would have a deliberative vote, while the conference might grant a deliberative vote to other bishops such as auxiliaries.

— that the judicial authority of episcopal conferences would extend to matters committed to them by common law, to those left in their hands by the Apostolic See or expressly given to them by the Apostolic See.

The day's meeting opened with Mass in the Ethiopian Rite celebrated by Bishop Haile Cahsay of Adigrat, Ethiopia. The music and singing were provided by students from the Pontifical Ethiopian College here. The Gospel book was enthroned by Bishop Ghebre Jacob, Ordaining Bishop in Rome for the Ethiopian Rite, accompanied by a solemn hymn sung by Ethiopian students to the accompaniment of their bells and drums.

The moderator of the day was Julius Cardinal Doepfner of Munich, Germany.   PATRICK RILEY

*   *   *   *

It was a red letter day at the ecumenical council. For the first time since the Council of Trent, a pope personally presided over an assembly of the world's hierarchy, implicity confirming by his presence the principle of the collegiality of bishops.

When the Pope entered St. Peter's at 9:10 a.m. the council Fathers had taken their seats. On ordinary days they usually swarmed over the aisles engaged in animated conversation. The Pope was greeted with enthusiastic applause.

Accompanied by Eugene Cardinal Tisserant, dean of the college of cardinals; Paolo Cardinal Marella, archpriest of St. Peter's; Archbishop Pericle Felici, the council's secretary general; and Archbishop Enrico Dante, secretary of the Congregation of Rites, the Pope went directly to a seat in front of the altar where an Ethiopian-rite prelate started Mass.

The Ethiopian-rite Liturgy lasted a whole hour. Then the Pope was led by Archbishop Felici to the presidents' rostrum where the center seat had been reserved for him amidst the 12 cardinals—a bishop among bishops.

The council moderators remained in their seats in the cardinals' stalls except for Julius Cardinal Doepfner of Munich, Germany, who took over after the Gospel had been enthroned.

"The moderators have been moderated," quipped one of the bishops. It was understood that when the Pontiff was present he would act as moderator himself.

After Archbishop Felici had read the names of five cardinals and 14 bishops listed as speakers on the schema dealing with missions, the Pope delivered a brief address. It was noted that he spoke of himself as St. Peter's successor and of "you bishops, successors of the apostles," thus confirming the principle of episcopal collegiality adopted earlier by the council.

Pope Paul listened to the report on the mission schema given by Gregorio Cardinal Agagianian, prefect of the Congregation for the Propagation of the Faith. Then he rose, gave his apostolic blessing to all council Fathers present and their faithful, and left the hall on foot.

While going out he greeted the cardinals, patriarchs, and especially Ukrainian-rite Major Archbishop Josyf Slipyi of Lvov, released in 1963 from a Soviet prison. The applause of the bishops echoed through the hall. When he reached the lower end of the hall, the Pope turned around once more, lifting both hands in a gesture as though he meant to embrace the whole assembly.

FATHER PLACID JORDAN, O.S.B.

Pope Paul

This is a translation of the speech in Latin delivered on Nov. 6 in the ecumenical council hall by Pope Paul VI.

You may be sure, beloved brothers, that it would be our most ardent desire to be present at the assembly of the ecumenical council gathered together in this sacred hall of the Vatican basilica.

Having determined to preside at at least some of your general congregations we have desired to be present today when your attention is turned on the schema of the missions. The grave and singular importance of the matter which at the moment occupies your souls and minds has led us to this decision. In us, the successor of the blessed Peter, and in you, the successors of the apostles, the words of the divine mandate re-echo: "Go forth into the whole world and preach the Gospel to every creature." The salvation of the world depends on the fulfillment of this mandate.

Among other things, the illustrious task of preparing new roads, of devising new means, of stimulating new energies for a more efficacious and wider diffusion of the Gospel is entrusted to this sacred synod.

Examining the schema which you have in your hands, in which this subject is treated, we have found many things worthy of our praise, both as to the contents as well as to the order of their presentation. We believe, therefore, that the text will be easily approved by you even after having noted the necessity of final improvement.

The pondered suggestions contained in the schema, the initiatives displayed, the attitudes and indications illustrated for such a high end can arouse a fervor of action for a more intense spreading of the kingdom of God on earth. They can offer the evangelical seed the possibility of a more abundant harvest.

Above all we like what is constantly anticipated in the text—that all the Church be missionary, that even the individual faithful, as far as possible, become missionaries in the spirit and in deeds. Those who are enriched with the ineffable gift of the Faith, those who are enlightened by the splendor of the Gospel, those who are part of the royal priesthood of the holy people of God, give thanks continually to the Most High for such a gift and offer prayers, exercises of piety and material aid in generous help for the assistance of the heralds of the Gospel.

Because there is nothing so healthy for men nor more suitable to the glory of God than the courageous effort for the spreading of the Faith, may those who dedicate themselves to the missionary apostolate—the most excellent of all for its importance and efficaciousness—commit themselves to spread the true spirit of piety with every most noble effort, surrendering to Providence and trusting in the mercy of God who is "your benefactor who wants you to be munificent and He who lavishes gifts on you, wants you to possess them and distribute them, saying 'give and it will be given to you.'" (St. Leo the Great).

The evangelical field, however, even if diligently cultivated produces fruit in happy quantity only if watered by the grace of God. Therefore, prayers for the missionaries rise to God more fervently, reinforced by alms and by good works. "O God, You desire that all men should be saved and come to the knowledge of Your truth. Send, we pray You, laborers into Your harvest and grant them grace to speak Your word with all confidence, that Your word may issue forth and be glorified and that all nations may know You, the one true God, and Him, whom You sent, Jesus Christ, Your Son Our Lord who, being God, lives and reigns."

Before ending our brief talk, with a paternal soul we desire to acknowledge in a special way the Fathers of the ecumenical council who work for the kingdom of Christ in the lands of the missions. Besides them, our thought, with all good wishes, go out to the priests, the auxiliary missioners of both sexes, to the catechists, to all those who assist the missionaries and to those who offer concrete help to the missions and who aid the missionary enterprises.

Our apostolic blessing which we impart to all of you with paternal affection confirms these wishes.

Summary of Council Propositions on the Missions

This is the summary of the ecumenical council propositions on the missions released by the council press office.

SUMMARY 14

Series of Propositions on the Missionary Activity of the Church

INTRODUCTION:

This schema is composed of an Introduction and of 13 Propositions. The Introduction recalls the evangelical message which must reach all men, even to the utmost ends of the earth. Present-day circumstances—the spread of the Gospel in recently emerged nations, the de-Christianization of so-called Christian nations, scientific progress, the evolution of social conditions, the ever-increasing ecumenical awareness of the Church—demand reorganization of the work of evangelization and of the missionary apostolate.

The following propositions are applicable only to those countries where the ecclesiastical hierarchy has not yet been organized and for those areas where the Christian community is not yet self-sufficient.

PROPOSITIONS:

1. The Church is the universal means of salvation willed by Christ Himself. Hence the explicit duty to announce the Gospel to all men.

2. a) The bishops, in union with the pope and under his authority, have the task of sending messengers of the Gospel everywhere.

b) It is necessary that, in addition to episcopal conferences, there should be established conferences composed of religious men and women belonging to a particular area. All the conferences should propose to the Holy See new rules to determine the relationships between Religious and their own bishop, who is the head and the leader of all apostolates.

c) Always under the direction of the bishop, close collaboration should be established between missionary institutes.

d) Before preaching the Gospel by word of mouth, missionaries should first undertake to preach it through example, through a life of humility, simplicity and poverty.

3. In the task of establishing the Church in a given country, attention should be paid to the various stages of evangelization:

a) Finding in the cultural patrimony of each country, elements which are in harmony with the Gospel message. Then, through works, making known the charity of Christ, His meekness and profound humanness.

b) Preaching the message of a living God, and of Christ who is "the Way, the Truth, and the Life."

c) Inducing converts to lead an authentic life of Faith and charity, through Baptism, Confirmation, and the Eucharist.

d) Continuing the instruction of new Christians through appropriate instructions, enabling them to participate actively in the life of the Christian community, through the liturgy, Catholic Action, etc. In this way the new community will become missionary-minded itself and will be a sign of the presence of God in the world.

e) In countries where complete evangelization is not possible, teaching at least those religious and moral truths which derive from the natural law.

4. There should be organized at the Congregation for the Propagation of the Faith a "Central Evangelization Board" to unite all (bishops of all rites, religious and pontifical organizations) engaged in missionary activity.

a) The task of this board will be to draw up a body of directive principles governing all the missionary activity of the Church.

b) It will be assisted by a secretariat composed of experts, with the task of keeping it informed on the religious situation in the world, and on methods of evangelization in view of promoting better missionary cooperation, e.g., assistance to poor churches.

5. Bishops should remember that, by virtue of their episcopal consecration, they are at the service of the Universal Church. Hence they must be interested in:

a) sending some priests from their diocese into mission territories;

b) promoting the recruitment of vocations for missionary institutes;

c) providing financial assistance for the missions;

d) supporting and developing pontifical missionary organizations in their own dioceses.

Missionary bishops should remember they are not to devote all their time and strength only to those who have been converted.

6. Priests, both diocesan and Religious, who are the ministers of the sacraments, especially the Eucharist, must feel inspired to participate in the work of evangelization. They must take measures to stir up missionary vocations among the faithful, especially in youth organizations and Catholic schools.

7. Contemplative Religious must always bear in mind that the salvation of a multitude of men depends on their prayers and sacrifices. The Church expects from contemplatives more far-reaching collaboration in the task of evangelizing the world. The superiors of active congregations should see to the adaptation of their form of the religious life to local culture and conditions.

8. The laity must provide for the missions their own contribution of prayer, sacrifice and material assistance. All those who have been moved by the desire to collaborate in various social activities in emerging countries are strongly urged to collaborate with Christians of other confessions, with non-Christians and with international organizations, acting always in such a way that social progress will contribute to regenerating the human race in Christ.

9. Catholics must collaborate not only with Christians of other churches, conformably to the directives laid down in the Constitution on Ecumenism, but also with non-Christians.

10. Precisely because she is catholic, the Church is never a stranger anywhere. Consequently, she must diffuse a Christian culture adapted to every country and every locality. Scientific institutes have the task of adapting catechetics, the ascetical life and the liturgy, as well as studies and culture. Theological students shall be provided with thorough training in the culture of their country, especially its philosophical and theological thought, in order to make useful comparisons with the Christian religion.

11. Missionaries must have a solid technical and scientific formation in order the better to know the people among whom they carry on their apostolate and in order to make better use of the means of the apostolate at their disposal.

12. This proposition takes up the work of catechists in the mission field.

13. The last proposition deals with the erection of institutes of higher study with the special task of studying the sociology of countries to be evangelized.

117th General Congregation
November 7, 1964

Despite Pope Paul VI's personal intervention in behalf of the council's drastically reduced document on the missions, council Fathers handled it roughly.

Eight Fathers, including two cardinals, declared that the propositions on the missions are unsatisfactory. Several others, while not assaulting the propositions head on, called for extensive revision and enlargement.

Pope Paul, the day before (Nov. 6), had told council Fathers that in his opinion they could "easily approve" the propositions before them with some final and necessary touching up.

Joseph Cardinal Frings of Cologne, Germany, led off the debate (Nov. 7) by asserting that important subjects such as the Church's missionary life cannot be compressed into just a few propositions.

Bernard Cardinal Alfrink of Utrecht, the Netherlands, said practically the same thing, asserting that the missionary vocation cannot be treated in a few propositions. He called for extensive treatment.

Bishop Paternus Geise of Bogor, Indonesia, speaking for all the bishops of Indonesia, said the product of the Mission Commission's long labors reminded him of the Latin poet Horace's line about mountains being in labor and producing a mouse.

In the name of the bishops of Thailand, Bishop Peter Carretto for Rajaburi said they were as disappointed with the new text as they had been delighted with the earlier one (now drastically cut down).

Bishop John Velasco of Amoy, China, expelled from his See and now episcopal vicar for Chinese in the Philippines, said it would be better to say nothing at all than to say so little about such an important subject.

Father Giocondo Grotti, head of the independent prelature of Acre and Purus, Brazil, speaking for Brazil's 38 independent prelates, said that while the commission's work was praiseworthy, what it produced was not.

Bishop Guy-Marie Riobe of Orleans, France, asked for a new text based on observations which the council Fathers, during the interim period between sessions, had sent to Rome about the former text.

Bishop James Moynagh of Calabar, Nigeria, branded the propositions as inadequate and declared they must be redone entirely.

The most rousing speech of the day — to judge by the reaction of the council Fathers — was perhaps the most diplomatic, since it criticized the document powerfully without actually rejecting it.

The speech came from Bishop Donal Lamont, O. Carm., of Umtali, Rhodesia. It was punctuated throughout by burst after burst of applause from council Fathers.

Bishop Lamont said he spoke in the name of "many" of the bishops of Africa. He said missionary bishops had expected "not bare, simple propositions, but a schema of fully sound doctrine and practical proposals."

He emphasized the present document's good points. "It is positive in its approach. The propositions are useful. They are necessary. But they are not enough," he said.

The Irish-born missioner said the Pope's visit to the council the previous day "is a consolation far beyond anything we had hoped for."

He said all missionary bishops were thrilled to see "the first missionary sitting among us, and for this we offer him from our hearts our most profound thanks."

Bishop Lamont said it would be "a dreadful disappointment" to missionaries and their people "if the glorious missionary work of the Church is to be compressed into a few naked propositions."

He likened the propositions to "dry bones" and said they recall Ezechiel's vision of a valley of dry bones. The Lord asked Ezechiel whether these bones would live, and Ezechiel answered that only God knew, he noted.

Bishop Lamont said only God knows whether the propositions on the missions will ever live or not.

He asked the bishops whether the propositions before them had inspired any of them to sacrifice or to a new effort for missions.

"If the schema has not moved the bishops, much less can we expect it to move generals of orders and congregations. I am certain this cold list of propositions will never inspire superior generals of religious orders of men or (which is perhaps something more) superior generals of nuns, to send their subjects on missions, filling their places in schools and hospitals at home with suitable lay people."

He said missionaries had expected a "Pentecostal light" from the council and had been offered "this little candle."

Missionaries had asked for modern weapons and had been offered a document of "bows and arrows."

"We asked for bread and they gave us, I do not say a stone, but a few cold propositions from a tract on missiology," he continued.

He returned to Ezechiel's vision of the bones. "I am convinced that we can and we will put flesh and nerves on the bones contained in this schema. Do not leave them here as they are. Breathe into them the breath of life," he urged.

Then the eloquent Irishman drew on the eloquence of the Bible.

"Ezechiel saw and 'beheld the sinews and the flesh came upon them and the skin was stretched over them, and the Lord said: Come Spirit, from the four winds and blow upon these slain and let them live again . . . And the Spirit came into them, and they lived; and they stood upon their feet, an exceeding great army.'"

While council Fathers clapped and shouted their appreciation, the day's moderator, Joseph Cardinal Doepfner of Munich, Germany, interrupted to remark dryly that the speaker should deal with specific points and council Fathers should refrain from applause.

(Several German bishops later protested to Cardinal Doepfner about his remarks. It was pointed out that debate was on the mission document in general.)

The day's meeting opened with a Mass of the Blessed Virgin celebrated by Archbishop Carlos Jurgens Byrne of Cuzco, Peru. Music was provided by students of the Latin American College. The Gospel was enthroned by Archbishop John McCarthy of Kaduna, Nigeria.

The council secretary general, Archbishop Pericle Felici, told the assembly he had received a letter from a council Father asking why no public recognition had been made of the dedicated and tireless ushers of the council. Archbishop Felici replied that since these ushers are members of his secretariat, it seemed poor taste for him to praise his own staff publicly. Nonetheless, he said, he wished to give homage to their work. Council Fathers applauded.

At the end of the day's debate Archbishop Felici announced that discussion on the Church's missionary activity would wind up on Nov. 9 and that the council would resume its interrupted debate on schema 13 on the Church in the modern world.

(It was stated at the U.S. bishops' press panel that a vote would be taken Nov. 9 on whether the text should be sent back to commission. If council Fathers vote not to send it back to commission for revision, a vote would then be taken on the schema itself.)

Cardinal Frings, after asserting that the Church's missionary life cannot be compressed into a few propositions, suggested that the subject be given "vaster" treatment and held for discussion until the council's fourth session.

He urged that the term "mission" be used in one sense only, not analogically. He would reserve its use for areas where Christ is being preached for the first time and not apply it to de-Christianized areas of the Church.

He backed the idea of a central mission board (or mission senate) advanced in the document, and urged annual worldwide collections for the missions.

Cardinal Alfrink complained that the schema treats the missionary vocation briefly and in passing. He said that the matter is treated more adequately in the schema on the nature of the Church. The work of evangelization has hardly begun, he said, pointing to two billion human beings who have not learned of Christ. The cardinal also pointed out that missionary vocations have decreased in recent years.

Leo Cardinal Suenens of Malines-Brussels requested the revision and strengthening of several points of the document. He lamented the dearth of mention of the laity in the text, and its silence on the need for forming a self-sufficient local laity, with missionaries progressively loosening their grip on local responsibility.

Bishop Dieudonne Yougbare of Koupela, Upper Volta, asked for a real dialogue between those who provide for the missions and those who receive. He said such a dialogue should take place in an atmosphere of real equality, not smacking of a rich man speaking to a beggar.

He called for the creation of a pontifical institute for the formation of catechists, to be named after St. Paul (just as the pontifical institute for the formation of native priests is named after St. Peter).

Archbishop Bernardin Gantin of Cotonou, Dahomey, returned to the often discussed problem of the relation of missionary effort to local cultures. The African prelate said that while the Church cannot be bound by any one culture, it must make a contribution to the culture of the country in which it is working, and in turn receive benefits from that same culture.

Bishop Geise asked the council Fathers to charge the Commission on Missions with preparing a completely new schema, taking into account the observations offered by the Fathers between the second and third sessions.

He said this desire is shared by 75 superior generals of missionary congregations and 25 episcopal conferences.

Auxiliary Bishop Cipriano Kihangire of Gulu, Uganda, echoed Bishop Yougbare's plea for fuller training of catechists, whom he described as the ears, eyes and hands of the priests. Catechists are a question of life or death in many places, he said. He asked for a pontifical association for catechists.

Bishop Pietro Massa, exiled from the Nanyang diocese in China, also said catechists deserve more than just two lines in the text. The Italian missionary prelate described the text as "good but only juxta modum" (with reservations). Like several others in this debate, he touched on the need for allowing converts to preserve whatever is good in their culture.

Bishop Carretto lamented the disappearance from the text of the proposal that dioceses in Christian countries adopt "twin" dioceses in mission countries.

Bishop Peter Moors of Roermond, the Netherlands, speaking for the Dutch hierarchy, asked for a theological treatment of missionary activity which, he said, is lacking in the text.

Bishop Velasco suggested that if the document must remain in its abbreviated form, it should be incorporated into the schema on the pastoral duties of bishops. He also urged great tact in all expressions referring to the people with whom missioners come in contact.

Father Grotti criticized the mission document for a tendency to shy away from a direct solution to a problem. He recalled that the commission's reporter had explained the previous day that the document avoided the definition of a mission because the experts could not agree. He suggested that the experts be sent to the missions for a while and then they will know what a mission is.

He also suggested a rearrangement of the Church's central administration of the missions, with the Consistorial Congregation working in closer collaboration with the Congregation for the Propagation of the Faith. He also suggested that the latter be renamed the Congregation for New Churches.

Bishop Jean Gahamanyi of Butare, Rwanda, emphasized that a bishop must be the center of unity in his diocese. While he must recognize the spirit of each religious institute in his diocese, Religious in turn must train their people to recognize the bishop as the head and center of all apostolic activity.

Bishop Riobe replied to a remark of Father Grotti that some diocesan priests and laymen in the missions have proved to be tourists rather than real missioners. He said several bishops who are Religious and several who are not wished to express their regret at that remark.

He called the mission text acceptable provided it could be explained by a supplementary decree drawn up from the observations which bishops had sent in on the earlier schema.

Bishop Moynagh, after saying that the document is not adequate and should be redone, also appeared to reply to Father Grotti, saying his diocese was staffed by 150 Irish diocesan priests. He said public thanks should be given to the Congregation for the Propagation of the Faith, to hierarchies at home, for the hidden sacrifices of the faithful, to families who have given sons and daughters to the missions.

Bishop Stanislaus Lokuang of Tainan, Formosa, who had given the commission's report on the document to the council, said that while it was not usual for the reporter to speak on his own document, he thought some observations on conversions and faith might be useful.

He said the problem of conversion is fundamental because it touches the very nature of the apostolate and explains many of the difficulties arising in some new Christian communities. Although conversion by nature involves some break with the past, this need not entail a break with the national culture as such, but only with elements that are out of harmony with the Christian religion. Faith, he said, progresses through instruction and grace grows through the sacraments.

PATRICK RILEY

* * * *

A cardinal interrupted ecumenical council discussion in an effort to clarify a speech he had made on marriage problems and to deny that he had questioned authentic Church teaching in this field.

Leo Cardinal Suenens of Malines-Brussels said that a "misunderstanding in public opinion" had led many to interpret his council talk of Oct. 29 as an affirmation that Church teaching on birth control would be changed.

A report on that talk by the council press office described the Belgian cardinal as asserting that there is reason to believe that the Church's traditional outlook on marriage problems has been too one-sided.

The council press bulletin paraphrased him as saying:

"Our insistence on the command 'to increase and multiply' may have caused us to forget that this is not the only text in Sacred Scripture and that another passage, stating that a husband and wife 'become two in one flesh,' is also contained in Revelation and thus is equally divine in origin.

"We still have much to learn. No one can ever presume to exhaust the inexhaustible riches of Christ. We may well wonder if our theology texts have gone into every last detail and exhausted every possibility."

Cardinal Suenens returned to this subject in an aside to a talk on mission problems. He declared:

"May I be permitted on this occasion to reply briefly to certain reactions of public opinion which interpreted my speech on the ethics of marriage as if I affirmed that the Church's doctrine and discipline had been changed.

"As regards doctrine, as was clearly stated, there was question only of a study to be made in this connection, not to re-elaborate what has already been authentically and definitively proclaimed by the Church's teaching authority, but rather in view of formulating a synthesis of all principles governing this subject.

"On the question of discipline, the conclusions of the commission will have to be submitted to the Holy Father and judged by his supreme authority, as was expressly stated.

"Hence it is obvious that the methods to be followed in these studies and research depend solely on this same authority. All this is said to dissipate any misunderstanding in public opinion."

Bishop Lamont

This is a translation of the address by Bishop Donal Lamont, O.Carm., of Umtali, Rhodesia, delivered (Nov. 7) during the Second Vatican Council discussion of the document on the missions.

I speak in the name of many of the bishops of Africa. The schema as it stands immediately reveals the grave difficulties involved in its preparation. It had a difficult birth, the details of which the relator has been kind enough to explain to us. To him and to all the members of the commission we offer our thanks. As is well known, those children who are born in difficulty and in great pain are more than normally loved, and are even regarded as more beautiful than others born with less hazard. However, the missionary bishops, although they are sensitive of the sufferings of others, expected something else, not bare, simple propositions, but a schema full of sound doctrine and practical proposals, capable of producing in missionaries new energies worthy of their apostolate.

I don't say there is nothing good in the schema. On the contrary, it has much to recommend it. It is positive in its approach; the propositions are useful; they are necessary; but they are not enough. They could be compared to the substructure of an electricity system comprising pylons, and yet still not connected with the central dynamo, or as if the dynamo itself had not yet been switched on.

The discussion which has here taken place will certainly bring some consolation to us missionary bishops. Yes, the very presence of the Supreme Pontiff yesterday in the aula is a consolation far beyond anything we had hoped for. We missionaries were all thrilled to see His Holiness, the first missionary, sitting amongst us, and for this we offer him from our hearts our most profound thanks. But it will be a dreadful disappointment to us, to our people, and to our missionaries if the glorious missionary work of the Church is to be compressed into a few, naked propositions.

As it stands, the schema will not do. Instead of a strong and virile support, we have nothing in it but dry bones. It brings to mind the vision which the Lord showed to Ezechiel: "The valley was full of bones — and there were very many upon the valley; and lo, they were very dry" (Ez. 37, 1-3). May I ask of you what the Lord asked of Ezechiel: "Son of man, can these bones live? And I answered, Oh Lord God thou knowest." Dry bones without flesh, without nerves — only God knows whether they will ever live or not.

With all possible reverence may I say that this schema should be completely overhauled. Something better is wanted. We need something alive; something worthy of the Second Pentecost. Without it the whole missionary activity of the Church will lack the dynamism which we expect from the council. It helps us little to tell us that many aspects of missionary activity have been treated elsewhere by the council. What a pity it is that this schema on the missions was prepared before the fundamental schema on the Church, a schema that illuminates all the others. Therefore I say, let it be done over again.

The whole Church now examining itself is waiting for a renewal of the first impulse of the divine command given to the apostles to conquer the world for Christ. We, whose honor and privilege it is to work in the mission countries, we expect from the council a new pledge of serious purpose from all the bishops; a new infusion of zeal; new ardor; new hope of universal cooperation. Forgive me, you theologians, if I still use the term "mission territory." How can we not speak of the missionary world when four-fifths of the world's populations have not yet heard of Christ?

Let me ask you, Venerable Fathers, if this document has already inspired anyone of you to any sacrifice or to any new effort on behalf of the missions? If the schema has not moved the bishops, much less can we expect it to move the generals of orders and congregations. I am certain that this cold list of propositions will never inspire the superior generals of religious orders of men or (which is perhaps something more) the superior generals of nuns, to send their subjects on the missions, filling their places in schools and hospitals at home with suitable layfolk.

Of what use are vague, juridical propositions? Will they fill the hearts of the young with zeal or generosity or a spirit of sacrifice? Did not Our Lord say: "I have come to cast fire upon the earth, and what will I but that it be kindled"? (Luke 12, 49). This document will set nothing on fire.

Frankly, we are quite disappointed. We hoped to hear the united voice of the council Fathers ringing out to the uttermost ends of the earth in this document; but for that purpose the schema, as it exists now, is as useless as would be a single human voice trying to reach the remote corners of this vast basilica without the aid of a microphone.

We looked to the council for a Pentecostal light which would illumine the minds of men throughout the world—they have lighted this little candle for us!

We asked for modern weapons against the fiery darts of paganism—they offered us in this schema bows and arrows.

We asked for bread and they gave us, I do not say a stone, but a few cold propositions from a tract on missiology.

Venerable Fathers, we want from this Second Vatican Council the inspiration of the Gospel, new apostolic vision, new drive, new united effort. We want to be so filled with zeal that we shall be able to set others on fire. We, the true successors of the apostles, are gathered together here in the Holy Spirit to carry on the very same work which the Lord committed to them. How can we possibly leave this council satisfied with coexistence with a pagan world daily increasing in numbers?

Forgive me, Venerable Fathers, if finally I turn once more to the simile of the bones. I am convinced that we can and will put flesh and nerves on the bones contained in this schema. Do not leave them here as they are. Breathe into them the breath of life. Give us something worthy of this Second Pentecost so that, filled with the Holy Spirit in this Council, we may go out from it as did the apostles in the First Pentecost, renewed in strength and faith, to proclaim the wonderful works of God to the farthest corners of the earth.

Ezechiel saw and: "Behold, the sinews and the flesh came up upon them, and the skin was stretched out over them—and the Lord said: Come, Spirit, from the four winds and blow upon these slain and let them live again . . . and the Spirit came into them, and they lived; and they stood up upon their feet, an exceeding great army" (Ez. 37, 8-10).

This is my hope. This is the work that lies before us.

Dixi.

The first working session attended by Pope Paul VI was the general congregation on Nov. 6, 1964. The Holy Father is seen here, standing among the members of the Council of the Presidency, leading the Council Fathers in prayer. The Holy Father's presence, he told the council, indicated his great interest in the missions.

118th General Congregation

November 9, 1964

Pleas to ban all use of nuclear weapons, and a vote which sent the propositions on the missions back to commission for complete revision, highlighted the ecumenical council's 118th meeting as it began its second to last week of discussions of the third session.

Bernard Cardinal Alfrink of Utrecht, the Netherlands, called on the council to adopt a statement on nuclear weapons and the end of the arms race as strong as that contained in Pope John XXIII's encyclical, Pacem in Terris.

Auxiliary Bishop Alfred Ancel of Lyons, France, went even further and asked the council to propose that all nations renounce the right to make war and entrust weapons of war to an international authority which would have the task of defending individual countries from attackers.

With less than two full weeks to go before the third session is adjourned, the council heard further criticism of the missions document and then closed debate on it. Bishop Stanislaus Lokuang of Tainan, Formosa, presented a wrapup report of the debate and asked the bishops to vote to send the whole document back to the Commission on the Missions for revision.

The request came in the wake of three days of criticism of the propositions, which were contained in only five and a half pages of text, a drastic reduction from the former text. There was also the element of Pope Paul VI's speech on Nov. 6 in which he expressed the belief that the council Fathers might be able to approve the text easily, although only with revisions.

When the bishops were asked to send it back for revision, they approved this action by 1,601 votes to only 311 votes to accept the document as it stood.

Auxiliary Bishop Fulton J. Sheen of New York said that Pope Paul had recognized the need for revision in his speech and the bishop asked that the word "mission" be given a broader concept. He asked it not be limited to the Church's endeavors in non-Christian countries, but be extended to all areas wherever true missionary activity is necessary.

During the same meeting, Bishop Floyd L. Begin of Oakland, Calif., rose to urge favorable support of tithing. Speaking on article 24 of schema 13 on the Church in the modern world, which deals with human solidarity, Bishop Begin said the council should not lose sight of the economic system referred to in the Bible as tithing. He said if it were adopted, it would solve the world's poverty problem.

The meeting opened with Mass celebrated by Benedetto Cardinal Aloisi Masella, Archpriest of St. John Lateran's basilica, on the Roman feast day of its dedication. The Bible was enthroned by Bishop Thomas Parker of Northampton, England.

The main interest of the day centered on four Fathers who spoke on schema 13's article 25 dealing with peace and war. Three of these speeches pinpointed the problems raised by nuclear warfare.

Cardinal Alfrink was the first to speak. Citing the example of Pacem in Terris, he called for a council denunciation of the arms race. He also objected to the part of the text which could be interpreted as denouncing the "dirty bomb," whose effects are not controllable by science, and yet permitting the newly developed "clean nuclear bombs," whose effects can be controlled.

The Dutch cardinal urged that no room for misunderstanding be left in the final document and that use of all nuclear arms be denounced. He quoted the late President John F. Kennedy that "unless we destroy our arms they will destroy us."

He also objected to the portion of the text which acknowledged the right of a just war and said it could be implied that the use of nuclear weapons in a just defensive war would be justified.

Bishop Ancel also objected to this "internal contradiction" which seems to affirm the lawfulness of the use of nuclear weapons defensively while condemning the use of nuclear weapons in general.

To remedy the obvious difficulty of how a country attacked by nuclear weapons could defend itself, he offered two propositions. First, for the good of the human family, all nations definitely and absolutely renounce the right to make war, including all weapons, keeping only those necessary for maintaining civil order. Secondly, an international authority should have whatever weapons are necessary to prevent wars and protect the individual nations from aggression. He said these proposals are not in conflict with the schema but only carry it a step further.

Bishop Michel Ntuyahaga of Usumbura, Burundi, said the problems of peace and war can only be resolved in terms of brotherly love. The African prelate said the document should reflect this and asked the council to call for special prayers to be offered throughout the world for peace.

Bishop Jacques Guilhem of Laval, France, said the disproportion of the consequences of nuclear weapons is the greatest injury against God and humanity and urged the council to raise its voice "against this form of genocide." To achieve success in banning nuclear weapons, it is necessary to have discussion and dialogue, and public opinion must be formed among Catholics to support civil leaders in disarmament.

Before discussion on the missions project came to an end, six speakers took the floor. The first was Bishop Lawrence Picachy of Jamshedpur, India, speaking for all the bishops of India and for others from Pakistan, Burma and Malaysia.

He said the bishops he was speaking for did not approve of the reduction of the mission schema to a series of propositions. He said he wanted stress placed on how much the missions contribute to the whole life of the Church, fostering as they do vitality, fervor and increased awareness of Catholicism.

A Belgian missionary, Bishop Xavier Geeraerts, former apostolic vicar of Bukavu, the Congo, spoke in the name of 75 missionary bishops. He said he wanted more stress on the theology of the missionary apostolate and not just a juridical view of the situation. Moreover, he said, he wanted it made clear that missions are not distinct from the life of the Church in Christian countries but proceed from the living Church.

This unity of the Church and missions was also stressed by Spain's Archbishop Segundo Garcia de Sierra y Mendez of Burgos who said all bishops have a missionary role even if missionary work is not carried on within the diocese. Such bishops can set up mission seminaries or promote those already in existence. National episcopal conferences are to coordinate these efforts.

Archbishop Elie Zoghbi, Melkite-rite patriarchal vicar for Egypt, recommended that the council take into account the mystique of the Eastern Church which in its past had a missionary apostolate. The East, he said, considered the missions as an outpouring of faith in Christ, a planting of the seed of the word of God. It is not good to impose a prefabricated Christ on other cultures, but the Church should make it possible through the missions for people to reincarnate Christ in the light of their own cultures, he said.

Ghana's Archbishop John Kodwo Amissah of Cape Coast called for a complete revision of the document which, he said, pays no attention to the new phenomenon of the rise of new churches headed by native bishops. He urged religious institutes in mission territories and bishops to work in harmony. Lastly, he said, the mission document should be accorded as much attention as was given the one on the lay apostolate.

Bishop Sheen was the last speaker on the document of missions.

With the close of debate and vote to return the document to committee, the council turned its attention again to discussion of schema 13, resuming debates on article 24 on human solidarity.

The lead-off speaker, Laurean Cardinal Rugambwa of Bukoba, Tanzania, insisted that the principles contained in this section should be more concrete and practical. Real love will always be reflected in concrete action, he stated.

Father Gerald Mahon, superior general of the Mill Hill Fathers, asked for more extended treatment of the problems of hunger, world poverty and the population explosion. He asked for a "clarion call for an all-out war on want" and urged that abolition of world hunger and world poverty be given prominence as one of the main themes.

Father Mahon declared that "today inequalities between nations in the world community are as glaring as they formerly were between classes within nations. Today it is not the proletarian classes but proletarian nations that await the outcome of this council."

The importance of the statement on emigration was stressed by Archbishop Franjo Seper of Zagreb, Yugoslavia. Many social problems today cannot be solved within the boundaries of a single country, he said. He added that the council should publicly proclaim the right to emigrate, to return later and to be protected against discrimination for having chosen to emigrate for a while.

Bishop Begin stated that tithing was established by God Himself in the Old Testament and no one was excepted. Even the poor had to tithe. Tithing, he said, would help alleviate the world's misery since much of it is due to the inequitable distribution of goods and wealth.

Moreover, he said, the practice of tithing increases the spirit of penance and abnegation and will develop a host of Christian virtues.

Paul Cardinal Richaud of Bordeaux, France, was the last speaker on article 24. He called attention to the existence of Caritas Internationalis, established by Pius XII in 1950, in which 73 national relief organizations cooperate. He singled out generous examples of the National Catholic Welfare Conference and its Canadian and German counterparts. He urged the council work for the education of Catholics in a spirit of charity and to produce leaders in this field.

Before the discussion began, Archbishop Pericle Felici, council secretary general, informed the council that the agenda for projects not yet introduced to the council floor will come up in the following order—on Religious, on priestly formation, on Catholic education and on matrimony.

Archbishop Felici announced the death of Archbishop Joseph F. Rummel of New Orleans. The council Fathers recited the De Profundis and prayers for the dead.

* * * *

At the U.S. bishops' press panel, Msgr. George G. Higgins, director of the Social Action Department of the National Catholic Welfare Conference, defended the schema's treatment of war—especially atomic war—from the accusation hurled in the council that it is weaker than Pacem in Terris and should ban nuclear war.

His own impression, Msgr. Higgins said, is that the schema is merely shorter than Pacem in Terris, not weaker.

Msgr. Mark J. Hurley, chancellor of the diocese of Stockton, Calif., said in comparing the pertinent passages of both the documents, that the only perceptible difference between the two is that the encyclical specifically asks for a reciprocal and effective control in disarmament.

As for the request that the council document brand all nuclear weapons immoral, Msgr. Higgins said the schema aims at achieving a situation where even defensive warfare would be unnecessary.

"Beyond that, it is hard to see what the council could say without being demagogic. It would be nothing short of demagogic for the council to attempt to solve this exceedingly difficult question in a simple conciliar statement of a few words."

Msgr. Higgins said he knows that a group of laymen who have devoted years to studying this question has sent a letter to the competent council commission, saying it would be naive for the council to speak of nuclear weapons without the necessary refinements. This letter claims the schema does not take into sufficient account the actual state of nuclear weaponry.

Msgr. George W. Shea, rector of Immaculate Conception Seminary in Darlington, N.J., and Father Roberto Tucci, S.J., editor of the Rome Jesuit review, La Civilta Cattolica, pointed to what Msgr. Higgins described as the "crucial passage" of the schema's section on warfare:

"Although after all helps to peaceful discussion have been exhausted, it may not be illicit, when one's rights have been unjustly trammeled, to defend those rights against such unjust aggression by violence and force, nevertheless, the use of arms, especially nuclear weapons whose effects are greater than can be imagined and therefore cannot be reasonably regulated by men, exceeds all just proportion and therefore must be judged most wicked before God and man."

Msgr. Shea and Father Tucci asserted that the schema does not say all nuclear weapons are wrong.

JAMES C. O'NEILL

* * * *

You could have heard a pin drop in St. Peter's when Bishop Fulton Sheen rose to address the ecumenical council on the subject of the missions.

For days, the bishops of the world had been awaiting the views of the American whose work for the missions has made his name almost universally known.

So when the Auxiliary Bishop of New York who heads the Society for the Propagation of the Faith in the U.S. arose to speak the other Fathers gave rapt attention. The man who has been a popular radio-TV speaker in his own country made an impassioned plea that the concept of missionary activity be enlarged to embrace not only territories under the Congregation for the Propagation of the Faith, but also the poor throughout the world, especially in Latin America.

Bishop Sheen used the microphone in the council section where he had his seat. His voice was perfectly modulated, rising and falling in accordance with the exigencies of his text. He followed his custom of accompanying his statements with dramatic gestures. He spoke slowly, using elegant Latin which was perfectly understandable even to those who sometimes experience difficulty following American speakers when they use the council's official language.

The council Fathers had delayed their usual coffee breaks so as not to miss this famous speaker. When he concluded, the members of his audience—one of a kind he had never before faced—expressed their appreciation by spontaneous applause.

It was the first time Bishop Sheen had spoken during the three council sessions. Although he spoke overtime, the moderator did not cut him off.

Bishop Sheen was the last speaker scheduled to talk about the missions. Immediately after his address, it was decided by an overwhelming vote to send the curtailed missions schema back to committee for a complete rewriting in the light of the critical observations that had been made on the council floor.

The keynote of Bishop Sheen's talk was when he expressed full approval of Pope Paul's plea the previous week that the mission schema be polished and developed.

"In place of the theological question, 'What are the missions?', I would suggest that we turn to the practical question 'Where are the missions?'," he said. He went on:

"Are missions exclusively in those territories where there are non-Christians? Or are they also in those regions where there are few priests, few churches, great poverty? The simple answer is the missions are both."

Bishop Sheen then explained that it is souls, not territories, that make missions. Then he gave his full sup-

244

port to the proposal that a central council be formed for dealing with all missionary problems. Such a council, he said, should be one "transcending all juridical distinctions about congregations, and giving flexibility to missionary effort according to diverse circumstances."

With a voice almost trembling with emotion, Bishop Sheen then concluded by appealing to the council that "the notion of poverty be strongly affirmed—the spirit of poverty should be the fruit of this council. If we have an ecumenical spirit to the brothers outside the Church, then let us be charitable about the missions."

As the bishops filed out of the meeting at noon, Bishop Sheen's talk was the main topic of their conversation. Said one prominent mission bishop: "This was one of the council's greatest days, thanks to Fulton Sheen."

FATHER PLACID JORDAN, O.S.B.

Bishop Begin

This is the summary of the ecumenical council speech (Nov. 9) of Bishop Floyd L. Begin of Oakland, Calif., as released by the council press office bulletin.

For the solution of the problem of poverty in the world we have within our reach an economic system which is really of divine institution. Tithing was established by God Himself in the Old Testament and from this obligation none was excepted. Even the poor were under obligation to provide the first fruits of their fields and of their flocks. We have the poor with us always, not because means of livelihood are wanting, but because they are not properly distributed.

Tithing was approved by Our Lord although He condemned the injustice of the system as practiced by the Pharisees. The practice was very much in vogue in the Church for centuries. Even now the ritual for the consecration of a church contains an eloquent exhortation addressed by the consecrating pontiff to the surrounding faithful urging them to give tithes and other offerings.

The practice of tithing will increase the spirit of penance and the abnegation of the material, develop a host of Christian virtues and teach a right appreciation of material things. It also leads to a new insight into spiritual values.

Bishop Sheen

This is a translation of the speech which Auxiliary Bishop Fulton J. Sheen of New York, national director in the U.S. of the Society for the Propagation of the Faith, delivered in the Second Vatican Council on Nov. 9, 1964. The council was debating the schema on the Missions.

Paul the Sixth, reigning as a missionary pontiff, has suggested to the council that our schema be polished and developed. Let us do this, at the same time granting to every member of the commission the right to choose his own "expert."

In place of the theological question *"What* are missions?" I would suggest that we turn to the practical question: *"Where* are the missions?"

Are the missions exclusively in those territories where there are non-Christians?

or

Are the missions also in those regions, where there are few priests, few churches and great poverty?

The simple answer to this question is: The missions are both.

I am a servant of the missions under the Propaganda. But during three sessions of this council, many bishops who are living in great poverty, come to my seat in the council hall. They come from territories, which are not under the Propaganda, but from areas where there are only seven to ten priests to care for 50,000 square miles.

I ask, Is it Christian? Is it Catholic? Is it worthy of the charity of Christ to say to them: "You do not belong to mission territory?"

Is it not true that the doctrine of the collegiality of bishops imposes on us a missionary responsibility, not only for territories which were defined as missionary 300 years ago, but also "for the salvation of the whole world"? (Number 4 of the Schema).

Why does Paul the Sixth, reigning as a pastor, in his encyclical letter Ecclesiam Suam so rarely use the word "mission"?

What other word does he use in its place?

Dialogue.

And he uses that word 77 times. To him dialogue is the showing of the love and charity of Christ to all men.

We bishops in this council must not enter into a dispute about what is a missionary territory and what is not, or who belongs to this congregation or to that congregation, saying: "I am one of Paul's men," "I am one of Apollo's," or "I am one of Cephas'"; while some one else says "I owe my faith to Christ alone." What are you saying? Is there more than one Christ? (1 Cor. 1:12).

Let us not be like the priest and the levite in the parable of the Good Samaritan, who passed by the wounded man saying: "He does not belong to our congregation."

In the Body of Christ there are no "new churches," there are no "old churches," for we are all living cells in that Body dependent on one another.

It is souls, not territories, which make the missions. The missions must not be the one aspect of the life of the Church which admits of no "aggiornamento."

What God has joined together — the Church and the missions — let no schema separate.

The true Catholic solution to this problem of the diversity of missions is to be found in Number Four of the schema, where there is proposed a "Central Council for Spreading the Gospel." This council transcends all juridical distinctions about congregations and gives flexibility to missionary effort, according to diverse circumstances.

Let no one fear that he will receive less aid if some help is given to a needy brother. In the early Church, just as soon as there was "one heart and one soul," then they began to "consider all property in common" (Acts 3:32). Furthermore, if we share, then as we read in the Epistle to the Corinthians:

"He that gathered much had nothing over
He that gathered little had no lack" (2 Cor. 8:15).

Second Observation

One of the conciliar Fathers has asked that all reference to poverty be taken out of this schema.

I beg you most earnestly, Venerable Fathers, that the notion of poverty be strongly affirmed in this council.

Put your finger on the 30th Parallel; run it around a globe of the earth, lifting it slightly above China. What do you find?

Practically all of the prosperity is above the 30th Parallel, and the greater part of the poverty of the world is beneath the 30th Parallel, that is in Africa, Asia and Latin America.

As chastity was the fruit of the Council of Trent, and obedience the fruit of the First Vatican Council, so may the spirit of poverty be the fruit of this Second Vatican Council.

We live in a world, in which 200 million people would willingly take the vow of poverty tomorrow, if they could live as well, eat as well, be clothed as well, and be housed as well as I am — or even some who take the vow of poverty.

The greater number of bishops in this council are living in want or in persecution, and they come from all peoples and all nations.

As only a wounded Christ could convert a doubting Thomas, so only a Church wounded by poverty can convert a doubting world.

Conclusion

If we have an ecumenical spirit to brothers that are outside the Church, then let us have an ecumenical spirit to brothers who are inside the Church. Let us be charitable about the missions, remembering that the Lord who said: "Go teach all nations" (Cong. of the Propaganda) is the same Lord who bewailed: "I have mercy on the multitudes" (Latin America).

Mass in the Armenian rite was offered in the presence of Pope Paul VI, right foreground, in St. Peter's basilica on Nov. 18, 1964. Armenian Patriarch Ignace Pierre XVI Batanian was the celebrant. Non-Catholic observers can be seen in the tribune in the upper lefthand corner. Patriarchs at the council are seen upper center.

119th General Congregation
November 10, 1964

A defense of the possible just use of limited nuclear weapons in self-defense and renewed appeals to ban all use of such weapons were voiced during the second and last day of the ecumenical council debate on war and peace.

Auxiliary Bishop Philip M. Hannan of Washington, at the 119th council meeting, took issue with the statement in schema 13 on the Church in the modern world that any use of nuclear weapons is unjust because of their incalculable disastrous effects. Instead he called for a clear statement on a nation's right to defend itself from aggression and a thorough knowledge of the various types of nuclear weapons, including those with a known limited potential.

"Certainly we hold war in horror, but we must state with precision what is prohibited in waging war to those who justly and laudably defend liberty," Bishop Hannan stated.

Pointing out that there are some nuclear weapons "which have a very precise limit of destruction," Bishop Hannan declared: "Although even a low yield nuclear weapon inflicts great damage, still it cannot be said that its 'effects are greater than what can be imagined (or estimated).'

"Its effects are very well calculated and can be foreseen. Furthermore, it may be permitted to use these arms with their limited effect against military objectives in a just war according to theological principles."

Bishop Hannan complained that schema 13's section on war and peace "seems to ignore the common teaching of the Church and the norms to be applied to the conduct of a just war."

On the other hand, Melkite-rite Patriarch Maximos IV Saigh of Antioch urged the council to raise its voice "and change the course of history" by going on record against any form of nuclear warfare. Declaring that national sovereignties must restrict their power because of the dire consequence of nuclear warfare to humanity, he asked for a solemn and clear denunciation of the ABC weapons—atomic, bacteriological and chemical.

After 11 Fathers spoke, debate on schema 13 ended and the council turned to the propositions on Religious. This document was introduced by Bishop Joseph McShea of Allentown, Pa. The only Father to speak on

it during the Nov. 10 meeting was Francis Cardinal Spellman of New York, who warned against putting too great a load on the Religious who are already engaged in various apostolates and against underestimating the contribution which contemplative Religious make to the Church.

The meeting opened with Mass celebrated by Archbishop Louis Mathias of Madras, India, on the 30th anniversary of his consecration. The Bible was enthroned by Bishop Thomas Fernando of Tuticorin, India.

Before the debate began, the council secretary general, Archbishop Pericle Felici, announced that there would be another Saturday session on Nov. 14. This was done because on Friday, Nov. 13, there was to be no regular meeting. Instead there was to be an Eastern-rite Liturgy (Mass) concelebrated by Patriarch Maximos and other Eastern prelates in the presence of Pope Paul VI.

In commenting on the schema 13 section dealing with peace, Bishop Hannan first pointed out the need to distinguish clearly "between the aspirations of the Church for the establishment of peace and the requirements of the moral theology of the Church on conducting a just war."

After suggesting various changes in the text, Bishop Hannan pointed out the existence of limited nuclear weapons and defended their use in just self-defense. Criticizing the document for ignoring the Church's teachings on just war, he added that it "would seem to imply that all nations have been equally negligent in securing international peace. This is a cruel injustice to many nations and to heads of governments who have expanded great efforts toward securing peace; it is especially cruel to nations which are now suffering invasion and unjust aggression from that force which has so far prevented peace. The whole world knows the source of aggression."

In conclusion, Bishop Hannan said "since this schema deals with practical matters, we should at least say a word about the defense of liberty and a word of praise in favor of those who defend liberty as well as those who freely offered their lives so that we may enjoy freedom as the sons of God. Therefore, in my humble judgment, the whole paragraph should be completely revised."

Speaking in the name of a number of bishops of England and Wales, Archbishop George Beck of Liverpool noted that Popes Pius XII and John XXIII condemned the use of any weapon whose effect cannot be estimated or controlled. He added:

"I would suggest, however, that it is important to make clear that this is not a universal condemnation of the use of nuclear weapons . . . If legitimate targets for nuclear weapons may in fact exist, the council should not condemn the possession and the use of these weapons as essentially and necessarily evil."

Archbishop Beck gave an example of what might be a legitimate target of nuclear weapons. He said: "To attack a ballistic missile or a satellite missile in the outer atmosphere would be, for example, a legitimate act of defense and, with just proportion duly preserved, it might require the use of a weapon of vast power."

Archbishop Beck said the council "has the duty to express sympathy and consideration to those who carry the heavy burden" of exercising supreme authority of the state and with whom responsibility for the use of nuclear weapons rests.

"Let us not too readily condemn those governments which succeed and which have succeeded in keeping peace, however tentative, in the world by the use of such means" as the threat to use nuclear weapons as a deterrent against unjust aggression, he said.

During the meeting the Fathers voted approval of the commission's handling of the suggested changes made in the introduction and chapter one of the ecumenism schema. The vote was 2,068 to 47.

Patriarch Maximos, the day's first speaker, declared the threat of destruction hovers over the human race more heavily than ever because of nuclear weapons. He said the voices of 2,000 bishops could change the course of history and would be listened to by the world's leaders. Therefore, he declared, the council should declare nuclear warfare absolutely unlawful. The billions now spent on armaments could be better devoted to solving poverty and other world problems, he said.

German Bishop Franz Hengsbach of Essen urged the fostering and encouragement of national and international organizations to work for peace. He noted that many people are discussing peace but do not always share the same principles. If politicians and military men are not guided by moral principles, then in coming years it will be more than difficult to avoid nuclear warfare. Therefore, organizations are needed to promote a dialogue and Catholics should work with those of other faiths to achieve peace.

After Bishop Hannan's talk, eight other Fathers took the floor to speak in the name of 70 or more bishops. The first of these was Costa Rican Bishop Romano Arrieta Villalobos of Tilaran, who asked the council to approve and bless solemnly any effort to promote culture, especially by drastic reduction of military expenses. He pointed to the example of his own country, whose constitution forbids the formation or maintenance of an army.

After Archbishop Beck's speech, Bishop Candido Rada Senosiain of Guaranda, Ecuador, reminded the Fathers that in its dialogue with the modern world, the Church is often talking with atheists and therefore it is necessary for the Church to insist with them on the affirmation of the human values of freedom.

Bishop Rada said that all Christian dialogue must show how Christianity helps to liberate man, not always in the terms of earthly values but at least in the light of a supernatural ideal. This entails a spirit of poverty in the Church to maintain the primacy of the supernatural, he added.

Melkite-rite Bishop Georges Hakim of Acre, Israel, called for a condemnation of practical as well as theoretical materialism and atheism. This condemnation should not include all socialistic governments, he said. He also called for a council condemnation of ABC weapons.

French Bishop Maurice Rigaud of Pamiers also insisted on the importance of international organizations, but called for an overhauling of the structures of many of them to increase their effectiveness. International Catholic organizations should be encouraged to a greater spirit of mutual cooperation and priests should be trained in these movements and to form public opinion within the Church, he said.

It is not enough to preach charity when people have an urgent need for the basic necessities of life, said Bishop Luis Yanez Ruiz Tagle of Los Angeles, Chile. Fundamental justice is needed, he said, and it should be admitted that many have forgotten the social teaching of Pope Pius XI's encyclical, Quadragesimo Anno.

Bishop Marco McGrath of Santiago de Veraguas, Panama, told the council Fathers that while they were discussing in the council hall, the world was letting them know what it thinks. Noting that in the past, the world has been deaf or indifferent to the Church's actions, he said that this has changed because from Pope Leo XIII on, the popes have continually spoken out on human values. The council should continue this and avoid preaching and moralizing, he said. The Church cannot be passive in the presence of the day's problems. Marxists know history and they also know how to act here and now, he stated.

The last speaker on schema 13 was Vietnamese Bishop Michel Nguyen Khac Ngu of Long-Xuyen, who complained that many students who go abroad for higher studies lose their faith and become indifferent to their national tradition and heritage.

Prof. Juan Vazquez of Argentina, president of the International Federation of Catholic Youth Organizations, addressed the council in Spanish. He expressed the lay auditor's satisfaction that the debate on schema 13 showed the Fathers affirming the positive natural and supernatural values of man's vocations.

Vazquez said laymen had been used in the preparation of the schema and that they would cooperate in its revision and in implementing its final results in the Church throughout the world.

Following Vazquez, Bishop Emilio Guano of Leghorn, Italy, read a report concluding discussion of the schema. He said that at some later date a series of declarations will be submitted to the Fathers to be voted on so that the commission on revising schema 13 will have some guidelines for future work.

Bishop McShea then introduced the propositions on Religious. He noted the text had been boiled down to four pages from an earlier draft of 30 pages, which in turn had been drawn from the original text of 100 pages.

Cardinal Spellman was the only speaker on the propositions because of the press of time. He expressed satisfaction with the text.

The following is the full text of the council press bulletin report on the Cardinal's talk:

"However caution must be observed in any discussion of this 'renovation' of religious life and activity because renovation is not infrequently used as a pretext for the introduction of elements which could eventually lead to a weakening of the religious life.

"There are some people today who want all Religious without exception to be engaged in the external apostolate.

"They forget that the whole life of a Religious is an apostolate. We cannot ask our teaching Sisters and our nursing Sisters after their difficult days in their respective apostolates to go out and engage in other works. If we want Religious to take over direction of Catholic Action, to visit the sick, take the parish census, visit families and the like, then special institutes must be founded or individual Religious must be provided with special formation.

"These are worries which are of concern to many Mother Superiors today. Nothing which would ultimately tend to the weakening of religious discipline and spirit would produce any lasting good for the Church. In the United States, traditionally known for its activism, contemplative Religious are making tremendous contributions to the effectiveness of the apostolate of the Church. Without unduly lengthening the text, a passage could be inserted at the beginning of proposition 5 to make it very clear how much the council counts on

the contribution of contemplative Religious."

JAMES C. O'NEILL

✤ ✤ ✤ ✤

Bishop Joseph McShea of Allentown, Pa., introduced the commission report on the document on Religious to council Fathers with an apology for its brevity.

This brevity was the result of strict order from the council's directive organisms, he said.

Religious are discussed in several council documents because they belong so intimately to the life of the Church, he said. Nevertheless, he declared, a separate schema was thought necessary to consider religious life, in and by itself, in a more practical and up-to-date way.

He remarked that many bishops had been astonished by the schema's brevity. But in view of the directives from above, he stated, the commission had set forth brief propositions of the religious life as essential points.

The original text had covered 100 pages. This in turn was cut to 30 pages, while the present text covers five pages, he noted.

Much of what was omitted will be of use to the commission revising canon law, he told the Fathers.

The actual implementation of the schema's recommendations is up to Religious superiors and to Religious themselves, he pointed out.

Bishop McShea said the title had been changed to "On Religious" from "On the States of Perfection to be Acquired" because this was considered in fuller keeping both with tradition and with the other council documents.

Under the headings of religious life and of Religious, he said, the schema includes all those pursuing perfection through the profession of an evangelical counsel.

To forestall confusion among societies of common life and secular institutes, the schema specifies that every institute is to carry out the schema's provisions "without prejudice to its own character," the bishop said.

The schema, as summarized by the council press office, consists of an introduction and 19 propositions.

The introductory paragraph states that in keeping with the teaching of the schema on the nature of the Church, the pursuit of perfection through the profession of the evangelical counsels derives from Christ's teaching and example.

The first proposition—on the basic principle of renovation—asserts that the spiritual and religious renovation of every religious institute and their adaption to modern requirements are to be pursued under the Church's guidance, with the Gospel and the imitation of Christ as the supreme rule, and with due consideration for the aims of their founders.

The second proposition says that renovation must be reconciled with loyalty to the institute.

The third is on the competent authority for this renovation and states that no effective adaption can be achieved without the cooperation of all the Religious of an institute under the guidance of legitimate authority.

The fourth says that perfect love of God and neighbor is the chief goal.

The fifth is on contemplative institutes and says they retain their role in the Mystical Body of Christ and produce rich fruits of holiness for the Church and that they too are to see to their own renovation.

The sixth is on the coordination of the active institutes.

The seventh is on renewal in the spirit of the evangelical counsels.

The topic of the eighth is renewal in individual poverty, meaning poverty in spirit as well as dependence upon superiors for the use of temporal goods.

The ninth deals with renewal in collective poverty, saying that property of religious institutes is a sacred patrimony to be used for the benefit of the Church and the needy, avoiding every suspicion of luxury, excessive profit or accumulation of wealth.

The 10th is on common life. It says that those known as "lay Religious" should be given a close share in the life and activities of the institute while the institutes of women should work toward the elimination of class distinctions.

The 11th deals with the cloister. It declares that aside from strictly contemplative nuns, other nuns engaged in outside activities should be exempted from enclosure and should be governed by special constitutions.

The 12th says the religious habit should be simple, modest, poor, yet becoming, hygienic, up-to-date and practical. Habits which, in the Holy See's judgment, do not conform to these standards will be changed.

The 13th treats of the training of candidates. It states that Religious not destined for the priesthood should not be assigned to the apostolate immediately after the novitiate, but should be assured of special training in special houses.

The 14th is on new institutes and notes that the future usefulness and prospects of growth should be considered.

The 15th topic is the preservation, adaptation and abandonment of works. It says institutes should preserve works proper to the institute, adapt them to needs, use whatever new methods are called for, and drop whatever activities are not in keeping with the spirit and authentic character of institutes.

The 16th deals with decadent monasteries and institutes. It says that when the Holy See sees no hope for growth, no further novices shall be admitted and the monastery or institute shall be united with a more flourishing establishment of similar character.

The 17th is on furthering union among institutes. It encourages federations or outright union.

The 18th treats of conferences of major superiors. These are encouraged by the council for their potentialities of help to individual institutes and more effective cooperation for the Church's interests.

The 19th—on recruitment of vocations—says priests, teachers and preachers should foster religious vocations and that parents, by providing the proper kind of education, shall nurture and safeguard vocations among their children. It says institutes have the right to publish information on themselves and their activities and to recruit vocations, provided this is done with due prudence and in obedience to the Holy See's directives.

PATRICK RILEY

Archbishop Beck

This is a translation of the speech by Archbishop George Andrew Beck of Liverpool, England, delivered Nov. 10 during the Second Vatican Council discussion of Paragraph 25 of Schema 13 on the Church in the Modern World.

I speak in the name of a number of bishops from England and Wales. About Paragraph 25 of the schema entitled "De Pace Firmanda," I wish to make three short points.

1. In the first place, we agree that the text of the schema is generally satisfactory, being both balanced and objective. We agree, however, as has been said for other points, that the presentation of the council statement is set out better in the appendix than in the text which we are discussing.

Great clarity and exactness are needed in Paragraph 2, p. 31, especially 11, 4-10, in connection with the use of nuclear weapons from which the present problem of peace and war derives its gravity and urgency: since, in the words of Pope John XXIII, "people live in constant fear lest the storm that every moment threatens should break upon them with dreadful violence." The council must, of course, maintain the traditional doctrine that indiscriminate destruction in which the direct killing of the innocent is sought and achieved must be condemned as murder and as something intrinsically evil. There is place in the schema for some reference to the teaching of Pope Pius XII with regard to biological and chemical warfare which do not receive mention in the text.

The draft statement does in fact repeat the condemnation of Pope Pius XII and of Pope John XXIII (Pacem in Terris, A.A.S. 1963, pp. 286-7), of any weapon whose effect cannot be estimated and controlled. I would suggest, however, that it is important to make clear that this is not a universal condemnation of the use of nuclear weapons. There may well exist objects which in a just war of defense are legitimate targets of nuclear weapons even of vast force. To attack a ballistic missile or a satellite missile in the outer atmosphere would, for example, be a legitimate act of defense and with just proportion duly preserved, it might require the use of a weapon of vast power. If, as I think is correct, legitimate targets for nuclear weapons may in fact exist, the council should not condemn the possession and use of these weapons as essentially and necessarily evil.

2. In the second place, we must remember that responsibility for the use of nuclear weapons and for all decisions concerning peace and war rests with those who exercise supreme authority in the state. The council has a duty to express sympathy and consideration for those who carry the heavy burden of this responsibility. The government of a country has the duty to protect not only the lives and the property of its citizens but even more the spiritual and cultural values, which are the inheritance of a people or a nation. The government of a country has a grave duty to do everything in its power to promote justice and prevent war. It must do this by peaceful means to the limit of its

power but it may be true that in certain circumstances peace can be assured only by what has been called "the balance of terror" by the threat of the use of nuclear weapons as a deterrent against unjust aggression. Let us not too readily condemn these governments which succeed and which have succeeded in keeping peace however tentative in the world by the use of such means. Millions of people owe them gratitude. Let the council make clear, therefore, that it does not demand of governments that they decide on a unilateral abandonment of nuclear weapons merely because of the very real and possibly proximate danger that these weapons may be used in an unjust and immoral way. To turn the other cheek is a counsel of perfection addressed to individuals, not to governments who have a grave duty to defend the citizens entrusted to their authority.

3. In the third place, I hope that the text of the schema, in 11, 25-35, will be strengthened. The first duty and one of the utmost gravity for all governments is to work in an active and practical way for the establishment of an international order in which war is outlawed as an instrument of policy.

The council must repeat the teaching of Pope Pius XII and Pope John XXIII about the duty of all governments to work toward organic, progressive and mutually agreed disarmament, so that in Pope John XXIII's words weapons may be reduced on both sides, simultaneously.

The council must emphasize that equal security must be given to all peoples (Pope Pius XII, Christmas message, 1955). Above all, it must emphasize the duty which all men must accept of striving to establish the order of justice among nations, and of setting up juridical and administrative machinery for the peaceful solution of international differences.

Bishop Hannan

This is a translation of an intervention by Auxiliary Bishop Philip M. Hannan of Washington, D.C., delivered Nov. 10 as the Second Vatican Council debated Schema 13 on the Church in the Modern World.

Paragraph 25 should be corrected and rewritten so that it clearly distinguishes between the aspirations of the Church for the establishment of peace and the requirements of moral theology of the Church on conducting a just war. If there is a treatment of the moral theology of conducting warfare, it should be written by very competent moral theologians; these theologians must be acquainted with the facts about modern weapons, including nuclear weapons, or they must be willing to secure the facts. With all our heart we desire peace—

peace with justice and complete liberty. Certainly we hold war in horror, but we must state with precision what is prohibited in waging war to those who justly and laudably defend liberty.

The following are defects in the Paragraph:

1. In Section 1, the first sentence fails to mention the most important foundation of peace, namely, justice — "peace, the work of justice" (the motto of Pius XII). Thus, the first sentence ignores the definition of peace in Paragraph 2 where it rightly defines peace.

2. In Section 1, the following erroneous sentence occurs, "Therefore, everything that unfortunately divides rather than unites must be adjudged as opposed to peace. . . ." The sentence should read, "Therefore those things that are unjust or evil must be adjudged as opposed to peace. . . ." Injustice is the cause of divisions.

3. In Section 2, there is a grave mistake of fact in regard to nuclear weapons, and therefore a false conclusion is reached. In the second sentence of this section it is stated, ". . . the use of arms, especially nuclear weapons, whose effects are greater than can be imagined and therefore cannot be reasonably regulated by men, exceeds all just proportion and therefore must be judged before God and man as most wicked." Contrary to this statement, there now exists nuclear weapons which have a very precise limit of destruction. Some of these weapons are mobile; obviously, if they did not have a limited field of destruction they would kill the soldiers who fired them. There is a weapon now in use which has a range of 1.3 to 2.5 miles whose missile has a force of 40 tons of TNT. These weapons were developed to avoid the huge destruction of larger nuclear explosions and to destroy individual military targets.

Although even a low-yield nuclear weapon inflicts great damage, still it cannot be said that its "effects are greater than what can be imagined (or estimated)." Its effects are very well calculated and can be foreseen. Furthermore, it may be permitted to use these arms, with their limited effect, against military objectives in a just war according to theological principles.

The whole paragraph therefore seems to ignore the common teaching of the Church and the norms to be applied to the conduct of a just war.

4. The whole paragraph would seem to imply that all nations have been equally negligent in securing international peace. This is a cruel injustice to many nations and heads of governments who have expended great efforts toward securing peace; it is especially cruel to the nations which are now suffering invasion and unjust aggression from that force which has so far prevented peace. The whole world knows the source of aggression.

The question of the greatest importance, now and for the future, is to avoid war and to defend liberty, both national and personal. We must have complete and actual liberty to carry on a dialogue with militant atheists. No dialogue is possible if we fall into slavery. Because liberty is the foundation of human life, those who defend liberty should be praised.

Therefore, since this schema deals with practical matters, we should at least say a word about the defense of liberty and a word of praise in favor of those who defend liberty as well as those who freely offered their lives so that we may enjoy the freedom of the sons of God.

Therefore, in my humble judgment, the whole paragraph should be completely revised.

Cardinal Spellman

This is a translation of the speech of Francis Cardinal Spellman of New York delivered Nov. 10 at the opening of debate in the Second Vatican Council on the schema dealing with religious life in the Church.

In general the schema meets with my approval. With certain modifications and definite clarification on some fundamental points, it can be accepted by the council and used as a basis of sincere renewal of religious life in the Church.

This schema is important, Venerable Fathers, since, in the words of Pope Paul VI, "the Church receives a great part of her power in the world from the flourishing condition of the religious life. . . . The work of religious institutes is wholly necessary for the Church in these days" (L'Osservatore Romano, 24 May 1964). Therefore this schema deals with matters of no less vital interest for the welfare of the Mystical Body of Christ than those we have been discussing in the council up to the present.

A renewal of the religious life both as regards its internal constitution and its external apostolate as well as an adaptation to modern condition is necessary in many instances. This work of "aggiornamento" has been going on for many years and will gather momentum from the encouragement which we give it in this council. But this "aggiornamento" presupposes that the true nature of the religious life and its essential function in the Church is both appreciated and safeguarded. There is question of adaptation only of external forms and accidentals. There is no question of changing the nature of the religious life. We must beware "lest our youth, becoming confused while thinking of their choice of a state of life, should be hindered in any way from having a clear and distinct vision of the special function and immutable importance of the religious state within the Church" (Paul VI).

The religious life is a life of entire dedication to God and the things of God; it is a life of prayer and union with God; it is a life of sacrifice and self-abnegation; it is a public testimony that the Kingdom of God is not of this world (John 18:36), a testimony of which the Church has special need today. It is a serious error then to think of the religious life as though it were nothing more than a kind of lay apostolate, differing from the ordinary lay apostolate only by the fact that Religious take vows. This would be to confuse two testimonies — the testimony of the baptized Christian who lives and acts in the world and the deeper testimony of the Religious, who even when acting in the world, must be seen to transcend it. "The profession of the evangelical vows is a super-addition to that consecration which is proper to Baptism. It is indeed a special consecration which perfects the former one, inasmuch as by it the follower of Christ totally commits and dedicates himself to God, thereby making his entire life a service to God alone" (Pope Paul VI).

Now, certain things have been said and written regarding the religious life and its adaptation to modern conditions which seem to involve this confusion; they seem to overlook and almost deny the special witness which is given to Christ by the religious life. Suggestions have been made for modernizing religious life which tend to deprive it of its specific nature, which tend, in fact, to destroy it. Religious life must be modernized — though the need for this can be exaggerated — and Religious orders must adapt their special apostolate to cope with modern needs, but nothing must be suggested and nothing must be done in the name of modernization or of apostolic efficiency, which would prevent Religious from bearing their essential witness to Christ by their vows, by their life of union with God, by their life of detachment from the world and the things of the world, by their wholehearted spirit of abnegation and self-renunciation which unites them to Christ in His Redemption.

Certain things which have been said and written, Venerable Fathers, have not been merely inadequate in theory, but, I say it with all possible conviction, they have been seriously harmful in practice. In not a few cases they have disturbed the mind and spirit of Religious men and women, indeed of whole Religious communities, causing them to doubt whether their life of dedication, of poverty, of chastity and obedience, of prayer and penance in its present form, is of value for the Church. Not a few have been so disturbed that they have desired to leave Religious life.

In my diocese there are over 5,000 Religious women alone. These excellent Religious have borne and bear their own special testimony to Christ and that testimony has been fruitful among the Catholics of my diocese and has excited the admiration and reverence of non-Catholics as well. Without the testimony of these Religious men and women, my diocese would be much poorer spiritually; no amount of lay Catholic activity, however excellent in itself, could compensate this loss. Yet even in my diocese not a few Religious have been disturbed by confused writings and speeches on the modernization of religious life in the Church.

I must therefore ask that the council in its statement on religious life emphasize its special nature and insist on the special testimony that it gives to Christ in the Church. This council should hold up before the world the essential values of genuine religious obedience, religious poverty, and consecration to God by chastity; it should make clear the necessity of the lives of sacrifice, of prayer, of self-abnegation and penance which genuine Religious lead. The work of modernization and adaptation should proceed under proper guidance but nothing must be done under the plea of aggiornamento which empties the religious life of its purpose and significance. We must hold up the religious life for what it is and not condone, or seem to condone, any ideas which confuse it or would reduce it to the level of other forms of Christian life in the Church, however excellent.

This plea I make in the deepest sincerity since I owe it as a public tribute to the Religious men and women of my diocese and as an acknowledgment of their profound religious spirit.

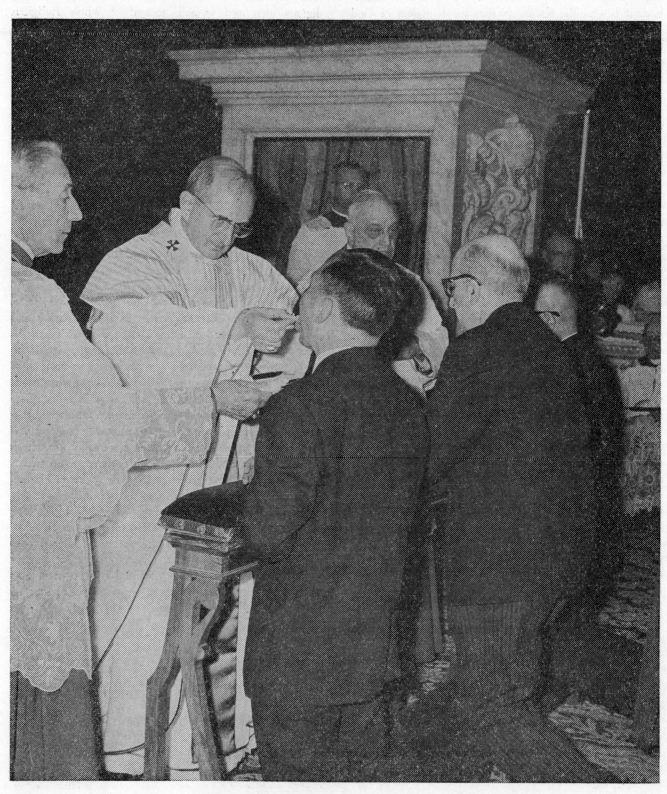

On the closing day of the third session Pope Paul VI personally gave Holy Commun-
ion to auditors and auditresses invited to the session. Archbishop Enrico Dante, left,
assists the Holy Father.

120th General Congregation
November 11, 1964

Archaic religious habits, the excessive cost of the clothing ceremonies of some religious orders, and the requirement that nuns be accompanied by a companion Sister when outside a convent were criticized as the ecumenical council discussed how to adapt religious orders and congregations to the needs of the modern world.

Seven cardinals and three superior generals of religious communities were among the 17 Fathers who spoke on the council propositions on Religious at the 120th general council meeting. In general, most of them agreed that the propositions could be acceptable but needed lots of revision. But one—Leo Cardinal Suenens of Malines-Brussels—declared that he did not like the schema at all and called for a new document.

It was Cardinal Suenens who raised objections to various religious habits. "These are a cause for ridicule for nuns in the street," he said. Objecting particularly to various forms of garments devised in the last century, the cardinal asked that they be suppressed. He also suggested doing away with the Sister-companion requirement which, he said, is no longer needed.

Cardinal Suenens' speech, however, was not restricted to specific points. He said that what he wants most of all is a schema that will foster training and community life in which Sisters and nuns will act as adult women capable of responding to the needs of today's world. He stated that he wants a theology of the vows of poverty, chastity and obedience to be explicitly spelled out in positive terms.

The cardinal further warned against two dangers in some convents. One is a paternalism on the part of major superiors which permits little community participation or representation in the life of a convent. The other is a result of this first problem, namely, that subjects in a convent resign themselves to obedience in a completely passive way almost bordering on infantilism.

To counteract these tendencies, he urged that canon law experts be put to the task of restructuring constitutions and forms of government so that all members of a community can take part in community life in an adult and responsible way.

The clothing ceremonies of some congregations came under fire from Indian Archbishop Dominic Athaide of Agra, who said that they are often marred by undue pomp and expense. As a result, he said, some postulants remain in the convent even though they do not have a vocation because they feel so much has been expended on them.

In place of this, he proposed that such ceremonies be carried out with a solemn simplicity and with stress on the fact that the ceremony marks only a beginning, not a definitive accomplishment. The same, he said, applies to the ceremony at the making of a temporary profession.

Only when it is a case of making perpetual vows, he declared, should a ceremony take on splendor, and then it should be joyous rather than funereal, as it often is among various orders and congregations.

The day's meeting began with Mass celebrated by Archbishop Louis Ferrand of Tours, France, on the feast of St. Martin of Tours. The Gospel was enthroned by Bishop Sandor Kovacs of Szombatheley, Hungary, the birthplace of St. Martin.

Archbishop Pericle Felici, council secretary general, asked for a vote on the commission's handling of amendments on chapter two of the ecumenism schema. This was approved by a vote of 2,021 to 85.

Among the changes in the second chapter was a sentence which had previously placed responsibility for the implementation of ecumenical practices, such as reciting common prayers with non-Catholics, on local bishops. As approved on Nov. 11, the sentence says that this responsibility rests with local episcopal authority unless it is decided otherwise by a national episcopal conference or the Holy See.

During the debate, Father Joseph Buckley, S.M., Minnesota-born prepositor general of the Marist Fathers, objected that the mission proposition contained "no gesture of friendship toward the diocesan clergy." He declared that it is time "we recognized that diocesan priests have their own sound spirituality. There is much in common between them and Religious."

Among the common bonds, Father Buckley listed the facts that diocesan priests often live in common, have a duty of obedience to their bishop and pastor, share a poverty similar to that of Religious and engage in the same kind of apostolic ministry. "It is safe to say," he stated, "that Religious priests in active life are closer to diocesan priests than they are to contemplative Religious."

Father Buckley suggested removing the distinction between orders and congregations and said that the section dealing with religious obedience seems "to apply to everyone the religious concept of obedience, which may be all right for monks but is not what the apostolic Religious need today."

He said that the crisis in obedience today seems to him to concern superiors rather than subjects, since "today's young people do not swallow archaic formulas like 'the will of the superior is exactly the same as the will of God.'"

Like Cardinal Suenens, Father Buckley held that many superiors "do not even understand proper and efficient procedure for running a . . . meeting" of a religious council and that superiors often do not consult their councils.

The day's first speaker was Jaime Cardinal de Barros Camara of Rio de Janeiro, who spoke in the name of 103 Brazilian bishops. He said that the document can only treat of the general principles governing Religious and that details should be worked out by a post-council commission. There is need in the text for a statement of the importance of religious life in the structure of the Church, he said. He added that the text should show a great knowledge of the history of Religious and that an effort should be made to safeguard the variety of religious institutes.

He said he was also interested in some treatment of non-clerical Religious, such as Brothers and Sisters, and asked for encouragement for major superiors' conferences and cooperation between them and national bishops' conferences. In regard to the renovation of religious organizations, he asked that the text state clearly what authority is to be given competence in this matter so that anarchy may not reign in religious communities.

The same view was taken by Ernesto Cardinal Ruffini of Palermo, Italy, who specifically urged that this authority be lodged with the Holy See. He warned against unrestricted renovation which could give rise to a wild desire for excessive change and called for fidelity to the spirit of the founders of the various religious institutes.

Another Father who called for caution in the authorization of renovation was Father Anastasio Ballestrero, O.C.D., prepositor general of the Discalced Carmelite Fathers. He urged that renovation be based on a return to the first fervor of the community and to the intentions of its founder, thus avoiding "an itch for novelty." He warned against the mentality that considers that everything old is bad and everything new is good. Speaking in the name of 185 Fathers, he asked for the addition of a doctrinal introduction.

Paul Cardinal Richaud of Bordeaux, France, suggested that the title of the schema be changed since it covers many dedicated people who are not Religious in the canonical sense. He said he would like to have it called "Christians Especially Dedicated to God and Souls."

The French cardinal asked for a better treatment of the differences between contemplative and active Religious, noting that all contemplatives are active in some respects and that no amount of activity is effective without contemplative foundations. He said he found the text too juridical in spirit and said the cloister should not be regarded as a separation from the world but as a protection from it. He also suggested that permission to leave the cloister should be left up to the superior of the house rather than to the bishop.

Juan Cardinal Landazuri Ricketts, O.F.M., of Lima, Peru, called for a more ample treatment of the topic and said he wanted a clear statement on the role of contemplatives in the Church as well as consideration given to the question of perseverence in the religious life.

Too many Religious are leaving the religious life, many becoming diocesan priests unsuccessfully, the Franciscan cardinal said. This is due, he continued, to a superficial knowledge of what religious life is. Many in religion fail to understand that religious life is not only an organization but is a form of exercising the apostolate, he stated. He called for a statement of praise for the contribution Religious have made to the Church, noting that there are 1.2 million women and 800,000 priests and Brothers in religion. He was given warm applause at the conclusion of his speech.

Following Cardinal Suenens, Augustin Cardinal Bea, S.J., rose to urge that inspiration for the religious life be drawn from the liturgy and Bible and also from a missionary and ecumenical spirit.

The Jesuit president of the Secretariat for Promoting Christian Unity stressed that Religious should realize that they are not only members of an institute but members of the Church, and that while it is necessary for a community to preserve the gifts of its founder, it must also cooperate with other religious institutes to live and feel with the Church.

Bishop Andre Charue of Namur, Belgium, said the document's treatment of the renovation of religious life was too generic and not sufficiently specific. It lacks stress on the need for cooperation between Religious and bishops, he said.

Then speaking in the name of Belgium's bishops, he said that the right of Religious to recruit vocations should be recognized, but that emphasis on priestly vocations as such should be insisted on. He said some exaggerations on religious vocations have been made in the past and that bishops' rights in the field of vocations should be protected.

Father Aniceto Fernandez, O.P., master general of

the Dominican Order, said he wanted more attention paid to the training of novice masters and mistresses and suggested an international school be established to train them. He called for more and better training of Religious women for the apostolate, saying that what the Council of Trent did for the clergy by establishing seminaries, the Second Vatican Council should do for Sisters.

Agreeing with Francis Cardinal Spellman of New York, who had spoken the previous day on the generosity of Religious, Father Fernandez asked that a suggestion contained in the earlier draft of the document on Religious—that national conferences of religious superiors meet and work with national conferences of bishops—be returned to the text under discussion.

Dutch Bishop Petrus Moors of Roermond said he wanted stress on the fact that the adaptation of religious life should not be presented only in the light of modern needs but more in terms of the demands of the Gospel, and that adaptation should be a return to the Gospel counsels of poverty, chastity and obedience.

A complaint that poverty and its spirit is almost negligible today in many orders was voiced by Coadjutor Bishop Andrea Sol of Amboina, Indonesia. Speaking in the name of Indonesia's bishops, he expressed regret at the condensation of the document but said he accepted it because it was the Pope's wish. He called, however, for a better theological foundation and for a section to point out that fidelity to one's institute can mean not standing still but evolving. He also called for greater stress on the missionary spirit within religious institutes.

Archbishop Pacifico Perantoni, O.F.M., of Lanciano, Italy, former Franciscan minister general, speaking in the name of 370 Fathers, said the text was acceptable but that revision is needed to clarify the actuality and necessity of the religious life today in terms of its special contribution to the Church. The multiplicity of religious institutes should be regarded as a sign of special gifts of the Holy Spirit in the Church, he said. He also said he wanted specific praise of the role of Brothers and emphasis on vocation needs.

A French prelate, retired Archbishop Victor Sartre, S.J., of Tananarive, Malagasy Republic, speaking in the name of 265 Fathers and more than 200 mother generals, complained that too often diocesan priests harm vocations to the religious life by emphasizing to inquiring youngsters the values of the lay apostolate, of living in the world and of Catholic Action. He called this a downgrading of the religious life and harmful to the Church. He also said he wanted the document to reaffirm the primacy of the element of consecration in religious life.

Bishop Richard Guilly, S.J., of Georgetown, British Guiana, said he wanted to know why so little had been said about the contemplative life and its value. Contemplatives are eminently apostolic and they should avoid those forms of the apostolate that harm their essential structure, he said. He called for a declaration on contemplative life.   JAMES C. O'NEILL

*   *   *   *

America's nun auditor at the ecumenical council, Sister Mary Luke, has stated that women Religious would like to have "some representation in the bodies which govern their lives."

The Sister of Loreto, who is president of the Conference of Major Superiors of Women Religious in the U.S., spoke as a guest panelist of the U.S. bishops' press panel here.

Such representation, she said on the day the council was debating the schema on Religious, is an example of what nuns hope for from "aggiornamento"—the updating of the Church launched by Pope John XXIII and being pursued by the council he convoked. She did not elaborate, but it seemed that she was referring to the Church's central administration in Rome—the Roman curia—and the Congregation of Religious in particular.

Another hope of nuns, she said, is that the "theology of the council might in some way be integrated into their lives."

Sister Mary Luke said that there is "more room than people think" within the present framework of canon law for updating religious communities of women.

"Most of the outmoded customs are not demanded by canon law," she said.

"All of us in active communities have been alerted . . . to the possibility that we could enter more fully into the apostolate," she continued. She cited the possibility that teaching nuns could also work with adult study groups or visit the families of their pupils, "especially in deprived areas."

She also called for "some means of communication between women Religious and bishops on a national or regional level." For this purpose she suggested the creation of liaison committees.   PATRICK RILEY

Father Buckley

This is a translation of the ecumenical council speech made Nov. 11 on the schema on Religious by Father Joseph Buckley, S.M., superior general of the Marist Fathers.

I would like to begin by thanking the 130 council Fathers who signed my request to speak.

There are some good aspects of this latest schema on Religious. It insists on the renewal which is the chief aim of this Second Vatican Council. It expressly pursues the adaptation which the Sacred Congregation of Religious began as far back as 1950 and has continued to push ever since.

But there are many defects in the schema:

1. For instance there is no gesture of friendship toward the diocesan clergy. It can be objected that this kind of gesture does not belong to a schema on the renewal of Religious life. But the disagreements between Religious, and bishops and diocesan priests, are a serious difficulty in the Church.

Bishops want to exercise a greater authority over the Religious in their diocese. Religious are worried about this. But we Religious might as well face up to the fact that some of our habits irritate the diocesan clergy; for example, our inclination to talk as if we were the only ones in the state of perfection.

It is time we recognized that diocesan priests have their own sound spirituality. There is much in common between them and Religious. In many places they live in community. They observe the same chastity as we do. They all have to obey their bishop and assistants have to obey their pastor. Their poverty is often not much different from ours. They carry out the same kinds of apostolic ministry in the same way. It is safe to say that Religious priests of active life are closer to diocesan priests than they are to contemplative Religious.

Even though we have to make a canonical distinction we don't have to insist on it in practice. "What unites us is more important than what separates us" is good philosophy.

I put these ideas to Pope John in an audience. With that spontaneity of his he replied immediately, "Adesso c'intendiamo"—"That's what I think too."

2. The same principle of removing unnecessary differences suggests another step in renewing religious life: remove the distinctions between orders and congregations.

Congregations have already proved their worth in the Church. It is time to stop thinking of their members as second class Religious, poor relations—"dei parenti poveri." We are very grateful to the Holy Fathers John XXIII and Paul VI that the superior generals of congregations are members of the council, provided they have a thousand priests in their congregation. On the other hand, superior generals of orders that do not even have 100 priests are members of the council, not to mention bishops with less than 10 diocesan priests in their diocese.

It seems to me that a step in the renovation of the congregations, at least the congregations of men, is to grant them power of jurisdiction and faculties for the exercise of the sacred ministry in their own houses for their own subjects, without the obligation of continually asking for indults.

3. Number eight of the new schema is on religious obedience. This seems to apply to all religious a concept of obedience which might be all right for monks but it is not what the active-apostolic Religious need today.

Some superiors are always talking about the crisis in obedience. My opinion is that the crisis is with the superiors, not with the subjects. The truth is that today's young people don't swallow archaic formulas like "the will of the superior is exactly the same as the will of God."

Nothing is said in the schema about the obligation of superiors to consult their council—local or provincial or general. There are many superiors, particularly among the nuns, among the men, too, who do not even understand the proper and efficient procedure for running a council meeting. I suggest that renovation of religious life is more a matter of the formation and efficiency of superiors than of greater obedience in the subject.

For these reasons, and others there is no time for now, it appears to me that the present schema does not give us a full response to the modern problems of Religious life.

Another revision, still more favorable to aggiornamento, is called for. I doubt if it can come from the commission unless new periti are added to it.

121st General Congregation

November 12, 1964

Council Fathers decided by a narrow majority to vote on the propositions on Religious after eight speakers, speaking in the name of hundreds of others, pronounced it inadequate. They then moved on to the discussion of the propositions on seminary training, which fared better at the hands of the day's speakers.

Three of the speakers on the propositions on Religious were superiors of religious communities and five were bishops. In general they said the text is out of date and avoids the important issues of the exemption of religious orders from episcopal regulation and the modernization of the Religious apostolate.

But in spite of this, the Fathers approved by a vote of 1,155 to 882 a motion to take a vote on the propositions rather than return them to commission for revision. The second vote was to be taken Nov. 14.

Albert Cardinal Meyer of Chicago said much in the seminary propositions is good, but added that he wanted a clearer statement of what is common to all seminary training and what is adaptable to local circumstances and needs. The cardinal, a former seminary professor, said he was pleased that the text makes national episcopal conferences competent to make adaptations for their areas subject to the approval of the Holy See.

To provide for a clear vision of unity for the priestly apostolate, he suggested that the propositions on seminary training be combined with those on the priesthood to form one expanded schema.

The good priest must first of all be a good man, Cardinal Meyer said, strong in the virtues of veracity, sincerity, courage and justice. Therefore it is necessary that norms for all Christian education be applied likewise to seminary training.

He said the grace of the priesthood is grace for others, not medicinal grace for the priest's own defects, and that the text must clearly reflect this.

Another former seminary professor also expressed pleasure with the propositions. Archbishop Giovanni Colombo of Milan, a seminary rector for 20 years, said the text assures the formation of priests who are mature men and not narrowminded.

Though the reduction of the text from a schema to propositions has narrowed argument, he said, we still

have an effective weapon against two major defects of present seminaries. Against the defect of a lack of organic unity of spiritual, intellectual and cultural formation, the text centers all these disciplines in the "mystery of Christ," he said. Without the love of Christ there is no genuine progress in training, he added. Against the defect of a lack of "human formation," he said, the text stresses norms of psychology in formation and provides for the interruption of the curriculum to expand the spiritual and pastoral training of students during their seminary life.

He cautioned against "prophylactic training" in which emphasis on preserving seminaries from the "contagion of the world" leads to passivity toward the world and its problems.

Stressing freedom of choice as an absolute necessity for a priestly candidate, he urged that the Church assure that students will be free to leave the seminary at any time, if they feel they lack a vocation, without the fear of being accused of being unfaithful to the grace of God, disloyalty to the family, ingratitude and the like. To make the transfer easier in such cases, he said, the curriculum, particularly of minor seminaries, should be carefully coordinated with that of other schools.

Another prelate with 20 years of seminary experience called for a clarification of the word "vocation." Jose Cardinal Bueno y Monreal of Seville, Spain, said the text is acceptable but that the Fathers must add a clearer notion of "vocation" as applied to the priesthood, which is distinct from the other vocations. He said the role of the minor seminary is to help youngsters discover whether they have this vocation. He suggested that formation here might be broader so that it would be a preparation for life in the world if the youngster decides he has no vocation.

The 121st general council meeting opened with Mass offered by exiled Auxiliary Bishop Jazeps Rancans of Riga, Latvia. The Gospel was enthroned by Bishop Antonio Bagnoli of Fiesole, Italy. Leo Cardinal Suenens of Malines-Brussels was the moderator.

During the meeting a brochure was distributed containing the qualifications of those who had voted qualified approval on chapter three of the ecumenism schema. It was announced a vote would be taken on

Nov. 14 on how the Secretariat for Promoting Christian Unity had handled these qualifications.

Leading off the discussion on the propositions on Religious, Bishop Gerard Huyghe of Arras, France, set the keynote for the other speakers by branding the text as insufficient.

"It is without a soul, too juridical, too occidental," he said. "Its doctrine on the Church is precouncil. A new text must be prepared to put religious life in proper perspective in the life of the whole Church."

This must be done, he said, by showing the relation of religious life both to other states inside the Church and in the outside world. It should not regard the religious life as almost another Church, but should stress its "ecumenical role" within the Church as a witness to the Church's inner unity in perfection and as an example to all.

Toward the outside world, he said, the text must stress the role of Religious as "soldiers of Christ" in the missionary apostolate, whether their life is active or contemplative. To carry out this missionary task, new forms of religious life are needed, forms which will be simpler, give more stress to poverty and be more flexible regarding residences, clothing and the cloister. Special care must be taken to avoid thrusting Western forms on Eastern communities, he stated.

Calling the present schema "incurable," he asked that a new one be formulated with the help of the Sisters who are council auditors.

In the name of more than 140 council Fathers, including 43 superior generals of religious congregations, Father Germain-Marie Lalande, C.S.C., also called the text "insufficient." The superior general of the Congregation of Holy Cross said that if the traditions of the Church must be imbued with a dynamic and progressive spirit, this is all the more true of the traditions of individual institutes.

The text appears too juridical, he said, and lacks a pastoral spirit and concreteness. Its effect can be no more than an external accommodation on the part of Religious, he stated.

Vocations to the religious life are perhaps in crisis today because these institutions seem too traditionalistic and not in accord with modern times, he said. He added that the text must show how the authentic practice of the vows of poverty, chastity and obedience can combat the modern evils of materialism, sensualism, lust for power and riches, and the deification of liberty, or reckless individualism, which is so common.

He called for the appointment of new council experts to the Commission on Religious who are more modern in their outlook and who have greater experience, particularly with youth.

Speaking in the name of all the bishops of Poland, Archbishop Antoni Baraniak of Poznan said that if the present text is passed, "it will slight a large number of men who have undertaken an extensive effort on behalf of the Church. It is thin and faulty and an amputation which leaves only the remains of the former schema."

He pointed out that atheistic regimes try above all to destroy religious orders in their war on the Church, preventing them from working among the faithful, depriving them of property, schools and even homes. Such hostile aggression shows that Religious are the Church's "front line" and that this should be recognized in the schema, he declared.

By its "solemn silence" on the Religious who works in the half of the world under atheistic regimes, the council could be interpreted as pronouncing a "death sentence and preparing for burial," he stated.

He called for a reexamination of the whole concept of the exemption of Religious, observing that it is not right for Religious to disclaim dependence on the local bishop in some things and then come to him for favors in others. He asked particularly that Ordinaries have control over studies of Religious students.

Regarding the text's statement on poverty, he asked that it be made clear that this does not exclude the right of Religious to own property and institutions. He observed that confiscations behind the Iron Curtain are often based on this excuse.

Father Joseph Van Kerckhoven, M.S.C., superior general of the Sacred Heart Missioners, said the active apostolate is part of the essence of religious congregations (presumably in contrast to the largely contemplative religious order) and that the apostolate should not be regarded as a danger to the spiritual life but rather as a positive means for personal holiness. There is a great danger in separating the spiritual life from the apostolate, he said. Modifications of the religious life should be made according to circumstances, he stated, such as modification of the community life of Religious when they are working in the mission field.

Bishop Pietro Fiordelli of Prato, Italy, urged that more be said on secular institutes than the passing phrase with which the present schema dismisses them. The title of the schema can remain the same despite the fuller treatment of secular institutes which is demanded by their important role in the modern Church, he said.

Bishop Smiljan Cekada of Skoplje, Yugoslavia, after protesting his warm friendship for Religious, launched into an attack on the exemptions given to certain communities (especially the older orders) of Religious. He pointed out that exemptions do not exist in the Eastern Church. He asserted that they occasion many clashes between bishops and Religious because they involve an overlapping of jurisdictions. He said the schema on the pastoral duties of bishops has made a good start in providing remedies and that they should be vigorously pursued.

Auxiliary Bishop James Carroll of Sydney, Australia, requested special treatment in the schema for Brothers and Sisters.

Bishop Carroll said the entirely lay structure of institutes of Brothers need not be altered to provide for the promotion of some members to the priesthood or diaconate. Their flourishing history justifies their lay structure, he said.

He asked that members of such congregations be brought to the council and their opinions be sought in matters in which they are competent by virtue of their work.

Father Paul Hoffer, S.M., superior general of the Marianist Society, who rules a congregation which promotes some Brothers to the priesthood, complained that the schema considers the religious life exclusively under its internal aspect. But many Religious, including teaching Brothers, live the religious life under the aspect of a dialogue with the world, he said.

Teaching Brothers have made the sacrifices of the religious life without the consolations of the priesthood, he said. Their ultimate goal is the conversion to God of their charges and themselves. They aim at giving even the poorest of their pupils the opportunity to achieve perfection, he said. Thus the goal of their lives is not in themselves but in God. Notwithstanding failures, they will always be ready to work for the Church's interests, he said.

When Cardinal Suenens, the moderator, put the debate on Religious up for cloture, an overwhelming majority agreed to cut off debate. All of the speakers listed to express the mind of several Fathers or more had been heard, and those remaining on the list were scheduled to speak in their own name only.

Before voting on whether to send the schema back to the commission for radical revision or vote on it as it stood, the council Fathers heard a report on the commission's stand by the schema's relator, Bishop Joseph McShea of Allentown, Pa.

The bishop stated that many of the reasons put forward in the council for a complete revision of the text had been weighed and rejected by the commission itself. He said its theological aspects had been treated elsewhere, leaving the schema free to restrict itself to more juridical considerations. This, he said, explains the schema's strong juridical character which was criticized in the council.

As for the schema's brevity, that can be rectified by restoring many of the things omitted in the process of abbreviating it, Bishop McShea said. He added that there is still no possibility of discussing everything in detail, such as the color and shape of nuns' habits.

Before beginning the debate on the propositions on priestly formation, which is a highly compressed and reworked version of an earlier schema on seminaries,

the council Fathers heard the commission's report on it.

The reporter, Bishop Giuseppe Carraro of Verona, Italy, called attention to the close connection between these propositions and the teaching of the schema on the nature of the Church. He said the mystery of Christ cannot be understood without the priesthood of Christ, not only in the constitutive order but even in the practical order. The titles sometimes applied to a priest—man of God, good shepherd, wise master and so forth—all demand a solid formation for the priest if he is to live up to them. Everything in the formation of a priest depends on the spirit in which it is imparted, he said.

He added that elements of the schema include accommodation to modern times, accommodation to persons and places, and a balanced synthesis and timely renovation.

He concluded by stating that while the commission is fully aware that its work must be perfected through the observations of the council Fathers, the Fathers are requested not to load the commission down unduly with suggestions.

Besides Cardinals Meyer and Bueno and Archbishop Colombo, only one other speaker was heard on priestly training before the meeting closed. Auxiliary Bishop Jozef Drzazga of Gniezno, Poland, complained that the principles laid down in the text were too abstract and therefore insufficient for today's needs. Local authorities, he said, are not in a sufficiently good position to establish norms for seminary training. These norms should come from the Holy See, he stated. Subsequent discussion, he said, would throw light on the text's basic defects.

FATHER JOHN P. DONNELLY

* * * *

Obstacles mounting in the path of the Vatican Council's ecumenism schema and its related declarations on the Jews and religious liberty made the promulgation of these documents less and less likely as the third session of the council neared its final week of work.

One problem with the religious liberty schema itself was that a key passage is based on the concept of collegiality, and collegiality itself still had not been brought before the council Fathers in its final form. The crucial third chapter of the schema on the Church, the chapter outlining the doctrine on collegiality, had been bottled up in committee for weeks. There was still doubt it would emerge in time for the final two votes—private and public—by the council Fathers.

The text on religious liberty had been printed as the next to the last week ended, and there seemed to be time for voting on it in the final week. However, the possibility loomed that some bishops would demand a fresh debate since the new text has a strikingly different structure. However, this new look had been given the text as a result of the demands of the council Fathers themselves.

Of the three, the text on Christian-Jewish relations seemed farthest behind on the road to promulgation. It was behind the religious liberty declaration in the printing schedule, but of course could catch up on voting. One advantage it held over the religious liberty document was that it had been assigned a place in a broader document on non-Christians, while the religious liberty schema still had not found a home. It seemed quite possible the religious liberty document would not be attached to any other bigger document, but would be proclaimed separately. However, to make this decision could consume enough time to require postponing promulgation until the next session.

Father Thomas F. Stransky, C.S.P., a member of the unity secretariat, suggested that the Theological Commission might want to include the text on religious liberty within the schema on the nature of the Church. If this schema were promulgated this session, the religious liberty text—the dark horse—might cross the finish line on the coat tails of "De Ecclesia" before the texts on the Jews and ecumenism itself.

Father Stransky told the U.S. bishops' press panel that the new text on the Jews is "stronger" even than the original. This presumably meant that the passage acquitting the Jews of the charge of deicide, which had been omitted from the schema that was put before the third session, had at last been restored. PATRICK RILEY

* * * *

Interfaith relations have gained considerable incentive during the third session of the ecumenical council, but it remains to be determined how the various Christian denominations will be able to cooperate in the future.

This was stated by Dr. Lukas Vischer of Geneva, the official observer-delegate of the World Council of Churches at the council, in a talk at the German press center here.

"Clearly a new situation in interchurch relations has arisen," he said, "inasmuch as changes of far-reaching import have taken place in the Catholic Church and as its desires to meet with other Christian churches become constantly more articulate."

Vischer stressed that the Catholic Church now recognizes the necessity of its inner renewal and that it has something to learn from other churches. Although dividing issues remain, especially regarding papal primacy, Vischer said all churches are now convinced they no longer dare to remain in isolation, and non-Catholic churches realize they need to examine their own consciences to bring about renewal.

"The ecumenism schema," said Vischer, "is really only a beginning. We must undertake a dialogue about the dialogue, as it were. Now that we are closer to one another, the vista through the doors that are half opened must lead to our opening them altogether in a joint effort."

At a press conference, Prior Roger Schutz of the Protestant monastery in Taize, France, suggested the publication of an "ecumenical edition" of the New Testament of which a million copies could be distributed in Latin America.

Prior Schutz described the ecumenism schema as "a new spring," but he stressed it should be implemented by Christian solidarity in the relief of world poverty, such as proposed by the American layman James J. Norris on the council floor the previous week. Norris is assistant to the executive director of the Catholic Relief Services—National Catholic Welfare Conference.

122nd General Congregation

November 14, 1964

Vatican council Fathers moved into the final week of their current session by clearing the way for the promulgation of the schema on ecumenism.

This action was taken with an affirmative vote of 1,870 to 82 on the third chapter of the ecumenism schema. All other chapters had been previously approved.

In other events at the council's 122nd general congregation the council Fathers greeted with groans an announcement that they would probably be asked to attend double sessions on some of the days of the final week, in order to complete work on some of the most important schemata.

Council officials explained informally that there would probably be afternoon sessions, from 5 to 7 p.m., on one or two days, scheduled mainly for voting rather than debate.

After the last working days, Monday through Friday, the third session concludes with a public plenary session scheduled on Saturday, Nov. 21, in the presence of Pope Paul VI for the formal promulgation of new decrees and constitutions. Since not one document had reached its final form at the end of the ninth week, a crowded and demanding schedule awaited the final tenth week's developments.

Although the double daily sessions were greeted with groans, the Fathers applauded loudly when informed that the amended chapters three to eight of the schema on the nature of the Church — including the all-important chapter on collegiality — were to be distributed in the council hall and that voting on them would be held Tuesday and Wednesday. This announcement meant that the long-awaited chapters which are the keystone of the work of the Second Vatican Council will reach the floor for the crucial vote needed to ready them for promulgation Saturday.

When the third chapter of the ecumenism schema was approved it meant that the complete document on ecumenism had cleared all major hurdles and can be readied for promulgation Nov. 21.

Also brought to the floor were six votes on various propositions in the document on the Religious. Although the document had been accepted in general by an earlier vote rather than being thrown out completely, Saturday's six votes on individual sections of the proposi-

tions showed great dissatisfaction with the present form and meant that the propositions in general will have to be revised entirely according to the suggestions submitted with the votes.

Once the voting was out of the way, discussion reopened on the propositions dealing with seminaries. Two major currents of debate were easily observed. One centered on whether or not the philosophy and theology of St. Thomas Aquinas should be given special reverence in the curriculum of seminaries. The second revolved around the provision in the document permitting seminary training to be interrupted to give seminarians time out of the seminary to live in the world in order to gain better experience for the exercise of their future ministry as priests.

The session began with Mass celebrated by Archbishop Gabriel Bukatko of Belgrade, Yugoslavia. The previous day he had been one of the celebrants in a Byzantine Liturgy, but Saturday he offered Mass in the Latin rite since, because of pastoral considerations in Yugoslavia, he can offer Mass in both liturgies. Archbishop Franjo Seper of Zagreb, Yugoslavia, enthroned the Bible and Gregory Cardinal Agagianian of the Roman curia was the session's moderator.

The votes on the propositions on the Religious showed great dissatisfaction with individual propositions, as five out of six votes were cast with heavy "yes, but" reservations. This means the commission has to revise the document extensively before it can be brought back at a future session.

The balloting was as follows:

Vote one — Introduction and Articles 1 to 3 concerning the principles governing renovation of the Religious, criteria to be used and what authority is to have competence — affirmative, 871, negative, 77, yes with reservations, 1,005.

Vote two — Article 4 stating the perfection of the religious life is to be found in the love of God and neighbor — affirmative, 1,049, negative, 64, yes with reservations, 845.

Vote three — Articles 5 and 6 on encouragement of contemplatives and of right organization of the active life institutes — affirmative, 883, negative, 77, yes with reservations, 987.

Vote four — Articles 7 to 10 on the observance of the Evangelical Counsels, especially poverty, chastity and obedience — affirmative, 907, negative, 66, yes with reservations, 975.

Vote five — Articles 11 to 13 on the common life, enclosure of nuns and Religious habits or garments — affirmative, 940, negative, 56, yes with reservations, 947.

Vote six — Article 14 on training of candidates for the religious life — affirmative, 1,076, negative, 65, yes with reservations, 103.

Three additional votes were to be taken Monday to complete voting on these propositions.

The day's debate on the propositions on seminary training was opened by Jaime Cardinal de Barros Camara of Rio de Janeiro. He said that the propositions were good and that it was more a question of how to go about the renovation of seminaries rather than of dealing with specifics. He urged that general principles be dealt with and that a careful study based on sound psychological principles be devoted to the problem.

The debate over St. Thomas' role in the theological and philosophical curriculum of the seminary was begun by Ernesto Cardinal Ruffini of Palermo.

Noting that he had been 30 years in the seminary as a student and as a professor and was secretary of the congregation of seminaries for 18 years, he deplored the slighting mention given to St. Thomas. He pointed to the example of 80 Popes since the 13th century and particularly to Leo XIII and Paul VI who have held St. Thomas' teaching in great regard.

A greater mention of St. Thomas does not neglect other Fathers, he said, but gives him his rightful place. Cardinal Ruffini also supported the existence of minor seminaries as being as valid today as in the time of the Council of Trent, and added, "I am an old man and you can't put old wine into new bottles but don't forget the ancient truth."

Canada's Paul Emile Cardinal Leger of Montreal took an opposite stand. He began by taking issue with a phrase in the text which recommends teaching the "perennial philosophy" of the Church in seminaries.

Cardinal Leger said if this refers to scholastic philosophy then it is ambiguous, since historians of philosophy have shown that there is not one scholastic system but many. Moreover, to teach one philosophy, he said, conflicts with the nature of philosophy itself which does not proceed from authority but from investigation into reality.

The end of philosophy is not to say what authors have written or thought, he commented, but to say what things are. He also warned of the danger of imposing a system of Western philosophy on non-Western seminarians.

It is not the council's role, he said, to impose one philosophical system or another on the students but to assure them of a philosophical formation that is sound, correct and useful.

As for theological formation, Cardinal Leger objected specifically to teaching only Thomistic theology. "Woe to the Church of one teacher," he declared, and urged that a phrase in the text which placed theological formation "under the guidance of St. Thomas" be removed.

Instead he proposed that St. Thomas be offered as a teacher and model for all — not his system but himself — in light of his ability to put the science of his time at the service of the Gospel.

Cardinal Leger further warned against building up an artificial world and living inside as in a cloister, saying that dialogue with the Middle Ages is not dialogue with today. He called for revision of moral theology texts because they are too juridical, legalistic and casuistic, whereas they should be more closely related with dogma and Scripture.

Disagreeing with Cardinal Leger and agreeing with Cardinal Ruffini was Archbishop Dino Staffa, secretary of the Congregation on Seminaries. Speaking in the name of several Latin and Eastern-rite Fathers, he called for closer reliance on St. Thomas in the schema, saying that it would not do to separate what is new from what is true. Hailing St. Thomas "as a man of all hours," and one who "transcends space and time," Archbishop Staffa said St. Thomas is as valid for men of today as for those of his own time. Moreover, Eastern tradition can accept St. Thomas, even though he is Western, because he teaches truth, and truth is everywhere the same, never changing. Thomism, he said, is not an element of division.

The second major current of the day's debate centered on the proposal to permit some period of time during the seminary training for students to be outside the seminary to get better orientation and appreciation of the world's problems before completing studies.

Cardinal Ruffini was the first to speak out against this idea. He said too much worldly contact would weaken discipline and harm the unity of seminary life. Instead he suggested that necessary contacts with the world could be provided in a period of pastoral apprenticeship after ordination, suggesting as much as two years of apprenticeship.

Julius Cardinal Doepfner of Munich, Germany, in passing, supported the idea of a period of pastoral apprenticeship. He said such a period would make young priests more humanly, spiritually and pedagogically equal to their task.

Bishop Paul Sani of Den Pasar, Indonesia, and Archbishop Joseph Mark Gopu of Hyderabad, India, speaking in the name of all India's bishops, opposed breaking up the seminary cycle but urged vacation periods to be used to provide practical experience.

Cardinal Doepfner said the text had been improved by being reduced to propositions and steered a middle course by retaining long-standing principles while also taking decisive steps toward bringing seminary formation up to date. He called for coordination of the norms of national bishops' conferences with competent offices of the Holy See, and said all efforts should be directed to developing a sense of personal responsibility.

Regarding minor seminaries, while commending them, he cautioned that they are not the only source of vocations, since many vocations come from colleges and go directly into higher studies. Thus the Christian families in which these vocations grow should be made aware of their responsibility, he said, and more stress should be put on contacts with the laity to offset exaggeration of the isolation of clerical life.

Leo Cardinal Suenens of Malines-Brussels, Belgium, asked for a special commission to study overall reorganization of seminaries on the grounds that promulgation of texts is not enough to ensure pastoral renewal. The Council of Trent, 400 years ago, established seminaries to meet the difficulties of its time, and now seminaries must be integrated in the movement of renovation that is going on within the Church, he declared.

Cardinal Suenens said we must hold fast to traditions which call for union with God through prayer, self-denial and zeal, but he said most seminaries are based in some degree on the general structure of religious houses, which does not provide diocesan priests with the spirituality fitted to their needs. He further called for reorganization of theological studies, better instruction in preaching, better leadership instruction and the pastoralization of the whole seminary cycle.

Bishop Manuel Fernandez Conde of Cordoba, Spain, called for special attention to be paid to training seminarians in the natural virtues, such as gravity, responsibility, and approachability. He said the whole edifice of evangelical formation must be built on the foundation of the natural virtues.

Bishop Sani objected to the practice of educating seminarians abroad, since today many mission countries have adequate seminaries. Being educated abroad, he said, leaves many seminarians dissatisfied and they are no longer native priests. Also, by taking the best students for education in Europe, the standards of the local seminaries are lowered.

European influence was also decried by Archbishop Gopu, who said it was a mistake to turn mission seminaries into slavish imitations of European seminaries. He also asked that the propositions apply to religious seminaries as well as diocesan, and that there should be special emphasis on the interior life as the soul of the apostolate.

Archbishop Lorenz Jaeger of Paderborn, Germany, said he felt the text as it stands avoids the possibility of exaggeration of uniformity of training because it recognizes national and regional differences. But he wanted emphasis placed on the interior and personal development of priest-candidates and not merely passive formation. He asked that material contained in the earlier text be added to the present text to round it out.

A genuine family spirit within seminary walls was called for by Archbishop Tulio Botero Salazar of Medellin, Colombia. He asked that the rector be a real father, particularly to avoid a too abrupt transition from family life to that of the seminary and especially for the very young.

Christ must be the center of the seminary and the seminary must recognize that the first apostolate is that to their own souls. Priests, he said, must remember their grave responsibility to be kindly and fatherly with the faithful.

Spain's Bishop Jaime Florez Martin of Barbastro wanted attention paid to the exercise of authority and obedience within the seminary. It is necessary to reaffirm the principles of authority and the need of obedience, he said, particularly in the light of some things said in the council. Authority should show itself kind, approachable and interested in the unfolding personality and the development of initiative and personal responsibility, he declared.

The last speaker of the day, Bishop Jean Sauvage of Annecy, France, said philosophy in the seminary should not be regarded as a necessary evil but as a means of dialogue between priests and the world. Seminaries should be regarded as the heart of priestly training, and it is important for seminary authorities to encourage a spirit of mutual trust and confidence between superiors and subjects, he said. It will be impossible to promote any dialogue with those outside unless priests have first learned to carry on fruitful dialogue among themselves, he asserted.

Summary of the Schema on Seminaries

The schema on the formation of priests, as it reached the floor of the Second Vatican Council, was reduced from a lengthy treatise entitled "On Seminaries" to 22 propositions with a brief introduction.

This, however, represented an expansion upon an earlier set of 19 propositions to which the original version had been reduced by order of the council's coordinating commission.

The introduction to the revised schema insists that the renewal of the entire Church depends in large part on the clergy. Therefore the training of priests is of first importance.

The first proposition, in view of local diversity of peoples and conditions, merely sets forth general laws. Individual conferences of bishops are charged with drawing up programs for priestly formation — to be periodically revised and submitted to the Holy See for approval. In this way, the universal laws will be adapted to the needs and characteristics of individual peoples and countries.

The second proposition: The entire Christian community, especially parents and priests, should foster vocations to the priesthood by prayer, penance, good example and other means. Vocations should be fostered to meet not only local needs but also those of the Church everywhere.

Third: Minor seminaries should respect the norms of sound psychology. Students should not be too isolated from the world and their families. The curriculum should be planned to allow those who leave the seminary to continue their studies elsewhere without difficulty. Seminaries for late vocations are to be promoted.

Fourth: Training for the priesthood must be markedly pastoral, especially in major seminaries.

Fifth: Superiors and professors of major and minor seminaries should be chosen from among the most capable priests and should be especially prepared for their jobs.

Sixth: Ever greater care must be exercised in screening vocations.

Seventh: Interregional seminaries should be organized where a satisfactory diocesan seminary cannot be organized. Large seminaries should group their students to allow more attention to the personal formation of each individual student.

Eighth: Spiritual formation in seminaries must be solid and Christ-centered. It must be aimed at acquiring priestly virtues.

Ninth: A deep sense of the Church must create in priests a spirit of unity, service, obedience and abnegation.

Tenth: Priestly chastity should be inculcated, and students should be warned and equipped against modern dangers to chastity.

Eleventh: Priestly formation must apply all norms of Christian education, taking advantage of progress in psychology and pedagogy — the art of teaching.

Twelfth: Bishops must allow vocations to mature in young men, using all the means and time necessary or opportune.

Thirteenth: A solid scientific and humanistic preparation shall precede ecclesiastical studies.

Fourteenth: Ecclesiastical studies will begin with an introduction to the mystery of Christ, which will recapitulate the history of humankind and will serve as a center of all priestly formation.

Fifteenth: Seminarians should be given a clear and coherent grasp of the principles of traditional philosophy. They should also learn about other philosophical systems, especially modern ones, and about scientific advances, so as to understand and answer the questions of modern man.

Sixteenth: Theological education should enable the student, under the guidance of the Church's teaching authority, to grasp Revelation. Holy Writ must be the soul of all theological studies in such a way as to become also the soul of all priestly life. Seminarians should also learn of the Christian communities separated from the Holy See and of non-Christian religions, too.

Seventeenth: Teaching methods should be revised and modernized, subjects and class hours should be kept at a minimum, and obsolete questions should be eliminated.

Eighteenth: Bishops are to send their more talented candidates for special training not only in sacred studies but also in other fields to meet the needs of the apostolate.

Nineteenth: Special attention should be paid to pastoral formation.

Twentieth: Such broad and modern pastoral formation must have a universal spirit.

Twenty-first: This pastoral formation is to be practical as well as theoretical and is to be accompanied by apostolic training.

Twenty-second: Episcopal conferences will study the most effective means of enabling priests to pursue their formation after the seminary.

123rd General Congregation

November 16, 1964

The importance of choosing the right people to staff seminaries and of training them adequately was insisted on at the council's 123rd session before debate on the document on the renovation of seminaries was closed.

Twelve speakers took the council floor during the session to air their thoughts on how seminaries and priestly training can be modernized to meet the needs of the day. Two of them made it a point to answer Paul-Emile Cardinal Leger of Montreal, who two days earlier had recommended a deemphasis on Thomistic philosophy and theology.

Enthusiastic applause filled the council chamber when the secretary general, Archbishop Pericle Felici, announced that the moderators after long deliberation had decided that no afternoon sessions would be held during this last week of this session. However, he informed them regular morning sessions might be prolonged from noon until 1 p.m. to deal with the press of work.

During the day's session three votes on the propositions on Religious life were taken. This concluded for this session the council's handling on the draft document. The results are as follows:

Vote seven—Articles 15 through 17, on the foundation of new institutes, adaptation or suppression of the undertakings proper to existing religious institutes and abandonment of decadent institutes—"yes" 1,833, "no" 63, "yes" with reservations, 226.

Vote eight—Articles 18 and 19, on the promotion of cooperation and unity among institutes and on national conferences of major superiors—"yes" 1,936, "no" 50, "yes" with reservations, 131.

Vote nine—Article 20, on the promotion of Religious vocations—"yes" 1,639, "no" 50, "yes" with reservations, 419.

Before the day's debate opened, Archbishop Felici told the Fathers that there was a typographical error in the booklet containing the changes in the third chapter on the nature of the Church which gave the impression the Fathers would have to vote on each and every change. Instead, he said, they would be asked to vote only to accept or reject the theological commission's method of handling the changes suggested earlier on the floor.

He took time out to pay tribute to the Vatican Press printers who had been working round-the-clock to ready documents for distribution on the council floor during the final week of meetings.

He also assured the Fathers that all procedural rules for handling documents had been observed and there were no grounds for the complaints that some had voiced. Furthermore, he answered the question raised by many who wanted to know what precise value would be attributed to the declaration on the Church if it were passed by the council and promulgated by Pope Paul.

He said there is no question of an infallible definition unless that is specifically stated, which the document does not do.

The question of value centered essentially on the doctrine of episcopal collegiality, and Archbishop Felici took the opportunity to read an explanatory note accompanying the text. This note, which had been contested by some, was an attempt to describe relations of the college of bishops to the Pope and served as a defense of the primacy and independent authority of the Pope.

Archbishop Felici also warned the Fathers to expect many series of votes, and said that although they might be confusing, he hoped that the Fathers would be patient.

He said many bishops had asked what they could do to emulate the example of the Pope's donation of his triple crown for the poor on Nov. 13. Archbishop Felici said that if they wished, they could help by sending aid to the Pope so he could make further contributions to the poor.

Debate opened with Antonio Cardinal Caggiano of Buenos Aires declaring that one of the main points of the schema on seminaries was on how to reorganize ecclesiastical studies to permit the integral formation of seminarians as men and priests. He said it was a problem of choosing to keep the good qualities of the older concepts and yet to add what is useful and valuable from new techniques so that seminaries could meet the demands of the times.

Cardinal Caggiano was the first speaker to stress the need for teaching of Thomistic methods and principles. While asserting that the outer covering of the body of teaching of St. Thomas is clothed in scholastic terms, he said that the inner marrow is what is important, and that it is this that should be preserved.

An even stronger defense of St. Thomas came from Antonio Cardinal Bacci of the Roman curia, who said he was dismayed by comments on St. Thomas which almost belittled the great doctor of the Church. Citing the writings of 80 popes, including Paul VI, Cardinal Bacci said that if the council were to deemphasize St. Thomas' place in the curriculum of seminaries, it would appear that the council would be placing itself above or against the Pope.

Persons present in the council hall said that when Cardinal Bacci made this statement, a rumble of noise was heard from the bishops' benches.

Cardinal Bacci proposed that a new paragraph be inserted in the text insisting on the rightful place of Thomism as the perennial philosophy of the Church, as is evident from the mind of the popes. This, he said, would not mean neglect of the other Church Fathers and doctors.

Three council Fathers rose to speak on the need of selecting the faculty of seminaries carefully and for special training of this personnel.

The first to broach the subject was Bishop Antonio Anoveros of Cadiz, Spain, who said the success of a seminary's training depends on the men in charge. Train superiors well and be careful not to choose men too young, he advised. He said that otherwise there is a risk that they will mistake what he called the crisis of adolescence to be a lack of vocation. Many vocations are lost because of this mistake, he said. He also recommended that seminaries be regional rather than diocesan, since it is easier to find competent personnel from a greater area, and money can be saved by cooperative effort.

Poland's Bishop Antoni Pawlowski of Wloclawek cautioned that a seminary should not be run by the rector alone, but needs the cooperation of the members of the faculty. Thus it is important to pick the right type of men for seminary assignments to get the best results, he said. He also cautioned against introducing changes too frequently or too suddenly. This could lead to a mentality of relativism on the part of students and faculty, he said.

Bishop Jean Weber, S.S., for Strasbourg, France, also stressed the need for the proper type of men on seminary faculties. He asked the council to avoid two extremes in proposing changes—iconoclasm, the destruction of everything done by the Council of Trent, and immobilism, which, he said, would be turning a deaf ear to the crying needs of our times.

Auxiliary Bishop Jacobus Komba for Peramiho, Tanzania, speaking for 40 missionary bishops, wanted the title changed to "The training of future priests," because, he said, the present title would include the training of priests even after their ordination.

He also wanted it urged that there should be perfect coordination between the curriculum of the seminaries and with the educational requirements of the countries in which they are located, so that priest-graduates would be entitled to the diplomas and academic ratings demanded by the state.

Archbishop Denis E. Hurley, O.M.I., of Durban, South Africa, praised the text, stating it tries to correct two defects found in many seminaries: a lack of organic unity, and a lack of truly human formation. The first aim of a seminary, he said, is to provide for the pastoral training of future priests and therefore the Bible should be at the heart of the seminary training. From this there should be developed a dynamic and organic knowledge of the Church Fathers, scholastic philosophers and theologians, he said.

Pastoral training should complement ecclesiastical studies and there should be a relationship between doctrinal and pastoral studies within the framework of spiritual formation, which essentially should be based on the word of God. Seminarians should prepare for their life of preaching of the word of God and thus must learn self-control, how to use liberty well, how to use initiative and develop themselves to working for the poor, Archbishop Hurley said.

Speaking for 102 Brazilian and other bishops, Bishop Benedito Zorzi of Caxias asked for inclusion of statements on the need for studying Latin and also on the need for devotion to Mary. He warned against spiritual avarice on the part of dioceses rich in vocations. He pointed to his diocese as one of the less poor dioceses among very poor ones. His diocese is open to all religious houses which want to come, he said, and also sends priests to help the poorer dioceses. Yet his diocese has not suffered from a lack of vocations. Twisting the Gospel a bit, he said: Give unto them and it will be given unto us.

France's Bishop Paul Schmitt of Metz said the main problem is how to adapt seminaries to the conditions of modern times, as the cultural world of many of the older seminaries is that of the Middle Ages. The question is furthermore one of whether diocesan seminaries are to be like religious houses or more like parish houses in which seminarians are to live in the future.

Bishop Schmitt said positive formation should be stressed. He urged that religious superiors take seriously the doubts and problems of their seminarians and that they concentrate on the good qualities of their students instead of concentrating only on the defects. To modernize seminaries, he said, lay experts in the educational field should be consulted.

Auxiliary Bishop Arturo Rivera of San Salvador, El Salvador, declared that the council should not be afraid to say unpleasant things about the need for discipline in the seminary. Too often discipline is rejected by the young as hampering the development of the personality. This cannot be left uncorrected, he said.

Bishop Andre Charue of Namur, Belgium, wanted concentration on the need for a deep spiritual formation. While there is a spirituality of activity, he said, it must be based on a spirituality coming from intimate unity with Christ. The spirituality of the clergy should not be just a happy transition of monastic spirituality to a worldly situation but rather it should be spirituality proper to its situation.

The day's last speaker was Coadjutor Bishop Emilio Benavent of Malaga, Spain. He supported the suggestion that seminarians have a period of pastoral experience before being ordained.

He urged that after completing theological studies, seminarians be sent out to parishes for two years for practical and personal experience in pastoral and social activities under the direction of the pastors. He also suggested that it would be good if seminarians spent their summers working with the poor.

Gregorio Cardinal Agagianian, one of the four council moderators, asked the Fathers to approve closing debate on the propositions. Cloture was approved by a standing vote. A vote was to be taken the next day as to whether the council should immediately proceed to vote on individual propositions of the schema on seminaries. If approved, the proposition would be submitted to the Fathers in a series of seven votes.

The day began with Mass celebrated by Bishop Sebastian Valloppilly of Tellicherry, India, in the Malabar Rite. The book of the Gospels was enthroned by Bishop Matthew Potanamuzhi of Kothamangalam, India.

The explanation of episcopal collegiality which the council's doctrinal commission sent along with the revised text of the document on collegiality rules out the idea that collegiality is a vague charitable affinity among bishops.

Instead, according to the commission's explanatory note, the college of the Church's bishops is a stable body whose structure is explained through Revelation, which is the Church's heritage.

This college is a dynamic reality demanding juridical form, the note said. But the note insisted that it is not to be understood in the strictly juridical sense of a group of equals who delegate power to a president.

Membership in the college is achieved through episcopal consecration plus hierarchical communion with the head and other members of the college. (Deliberately left to one side is the question of the powers of the bishops of the separated Churches of the East.)

In explaining the schema's teaching that the college, with its head and never separated from it, is the subject of full and supreme authority over the Universal Church, the commission made the operative distinction not between the Roman pontiff on the one hand and the other bishops on the other, but between the Roman pontiff on the one hand and the Roman pontiff with the bishops on the other.

Father Charles Davis, English theologian who summarized the commission's note at a meeting of the American bishops' press panel, commented that this seems at first glance to favor the theory that supreme authority in the Church resides in a "double subject": the Pope on one hand and the college on the other. But Father Davis pointed out that the commission states expressly that it is not entering into the question of whether there is a single subject of supreme power or two subjects incompletely distinct. He said the commission's handling of the "modi"—changes suggested by the council Fathers—bears this out.

The commission also explained that the Pope is able to exercise his power at will. However, the college of bishops, while it always exists, is not always "in full act." It acts only with the consent of its head.

This part of the commission's note dealt with a change which the commission had made in the text as a result of the debate on the document on the council floor. This removed the statement that collegial power cannot be exercised "independently," leaving out the question of the dependence of the college on its head and making the relation between pope and college one of communion.   JAMES C. O'NEILL

Fourteen Eastern rite prelates took part in the concelebration of Divine Liturgy in the Byzantine Rite on Nov. 13, 1964, in St. Peter's basilica. Pope Paul VI, at the far right, and the Council Fathers attended. Ukrainian Rite Archbishop Maxim Hermaniuk, C.SS.R., of Winnipeg, Man., and Bishop Nicholas T. Elko of the Byzantine Rite Diocese of Pittsburgh were among the concelebrants.

124th General Congregation

November 17, 1964

Francis Cardinal Spellman of New York has called on the ecumenical council to declare that since it is the function of the state to facilitate civil freedoms, "justice and equity demand that a due measure of public aid be available to parents in support of the schools they select for their children."

The cardinal was the first of five Fathers to take the floor when the council's 124th meeting turned its attention to a declaration on Christian education.

He was joined by Joseph Cardinal Ritter of St. Louis, Archbishop John P. Cody of New Orleans and by two French bishops.

Cardinal Ritter rejoiced that the declaration was not limited only to Catholic schools, since "most of the Catholic children and students in the world are in state schools and must be, in fact, the object of the solicitude of the Church, the family and especially the teachers in these schools for their religious education."

During the day's session, chapter three of the schema on the nature of the Church, which is the chapter containing the key concept of the collegiality of the bishops, was passed in its final form by a large majority. When passage was announced, the news was greeted with warm applause. Two other chapters of the schema on the Church were also approved with great majorities. This left only three remaining chapters of the document to be voted on Nov. 18 before it was ready for promulgation at a plenary public meeting on Nov. 21.

At the Nov. 17 meeting the new text of the declaration on religious liberty was distributed. It was announced that voting was to begin on it on Nov. 19. The Fathers, moreover, voted to accept the propositions on seminaries and gave overwhelming approval to the first three propositions in separate votes.

Although discussion on the seminary propositions had been closed at the end of the previous day's meeting, three Fathers took the floor in the first part of the Nov. 17 meeting to speak in the name of 70 or more Fathers. Two of them said they wanted positive consideration of the celibacy of the clergy and that it must not be looked on as a "sort of admission ticket" to Holy Orders.

The opening Mass, celebrated by Latin-rite Patriarch Alberto Gori, O.F.M., of Jerusalem, was offered for all the sick and particularly for sick bishops. The Gospel

was enthroned by Abbot Anselmo Tranfaglia, O.S.B., head of the independent abbey of Monte Vergine, Italy.

Cardinal Spellman told the assembly that the "direct intention of the schema is to affirm the rights of children and their parents, not necessarily to seek money from the public treasury for religious schools." Noting that in many nations the school support question is difficult for historical, sociological and political reasons, he proposed the following change in the text:

"Parents should be free to choose the schools they wish for their children. They should not in consequence of this choice be subject to unjust economic burdens which would infringe upon this freedom of choice. Since it is the function of the state to facilitate civil freedoms, justice and equity demand that a due measure of public aid be available to parents in support of the schools they select for their children.

"Moreover, if these schools serve the public purpose of popular education, the fact that they may be religious in their orientation should not exclude them from a rightful measure of public support."

Cardinal Spellman said he proposed this amendment to make the council's intention "clearly apparent, and accordingly I hope that useless quarrels over the words of the schema may be avoided in the future."

He also warmly favored the text's proposal to establish a postconciliar commission to study further the intricate problems of Christian education because, "in my opinion, considering the variety of schools from place to place, with the consequent diversity of problems, no commission can decide all particular norms for the whole world or give definitive answers to the schools of all nations and their problems."

The cardinal urged that the postconciliar commission be composed of representatives from major areas of the world and also "truly expert members from all phases of education, including laymen along with priests and Religious men and women." He said he also liked the fact that practical application of general principles is to be left in the hands of the national episcopal conferences.

Cardinal Ritter expressed satisfaction that the text provides for a postconciliar commission "to make necessary surveys and research in a professional manner to pro-

272

duce a document on education not only worthy of the council but of real and genuine value to men of good will everywhere."

Commenting on the fact that the title of the declaration had been changed from one on Catholic schools to a larger concept of Christian education, Cardinal Ritter praised this decision to give it "a much wider term." He also asked the council to give a "ringing endorsement" to the work of the laity in such organizations as the Confraternity of Christian Doctrine, schools of religion, and Newman clubs.

Cardinal Ritter said that in addition to affirming the freedom of parents to select schools of their choice, the Church must also insist on freedom within its schools. "Within their own walls Catholic schools must be models of Christian freedom in their administration, their teaching and particularly in the interpersonal relationships among teachers, pupils and parents," he said.

The cardinal said that since truth is one, "our schools and their professors and students must pursue the truth boldly and freely without fear, confident that the truth they seek is none other than Christ, who described Himself as the way, the truth and the light, that the truth they seek is the truth which the Sacred Scriptures declare will make us free."

Lastly, the cardinal asked that the document emphasize the fact that Catholic schools by their nature "must be of substantial benefit to the entire community where they serve and to society itself."

Catholic schools do not exist to serve "narrow sectarian purposes nor to protect the selfish interests of the Church . . . Rather they stand as an expression of the free choice and liberal sacrifice not only of parents but of priests, Religious and devoted laymen and lay women for God and country as well as for families and the Church itself."

Archbishop Cody of New Orleans, who spoke in the name of several American and other bishops, is a member of the commission which drafted the document and president of the National Catholic Educational Association.

Archbishop Cody noted that today the greatest national expenditures are for defense and education, which shows the importance of this document to the world. The Church carries on its teaching mission and the schema reflects this mission, he said. It would be offensive to priests, Religious and laymen and all those in the Catholic educational field if the council did not speak out on the subject, he stated. The declaration will come as a joy to U.S. Catholics, he declared, including the 161,000 priests, Brothers and teachers engaged in the field.

Archbishop Cody reported that the text originally had been 16 pages long and then had been reduced to the propositions which had been sent to the bishops. The bishops reacted unfavorably to these, and so the com-

mission redrafted the document, making it a declaration three pages long. Because of the many difficulties in the educational field, such as evergrowing teaching methods, the commission decided to leave the more profound work to the post-conciliar commission and the specifics to national bishops' conferences.

Two French bishops were not quite as warm in praise of the document as their American confreres.

Coadjutor Bishop Leon Elchinger of Strasbourg said he felt the text had been drafted too early and therefore did not reflect the council's spirit to be found in the perfected texts of the schemas on the nature of the Church, on the lay apostolate and on the Church in the modern world. Saying it was the goal of the document to transmit the council's spirit to the youth of today, he called for considerable revision.

Christian education, he said, should inculcate the missionary spirit, personal faith and a faith that communicates itself to others, opening the way for dialogue and conversation with those seeking the truth. The document further should speak of the rights and duties of the state in education and make it clear that no state or family owns the child and that no single ideology or totalitarianism can be taught in the schools at the state's dictation.

Lastly, he said he wanted emphasis on the family's role in education which, in the Christian sense, goes deeper than the school. To reorganize Christian education properly, he declared there is a need for "wise audacity."

Archbishop Paul Gouyon of Rennes also wanted emphasis placed on the first of educators—parents—and also on the duty of Christian education to transmit the Faith and encourage personal faith and prayer, which is not the same as the mere multiplication of the exercise of pious practices. Education should encourage personal attention and initiation in the apostolate and membership in Catholic Action, he said.

In a report on the schema before the education discussion began, Bishop Jules Daem of Antwerp, Belgium, explained the change of title from "On Catholic Schools" to "On Christian Education." The change had been made, he said, because Catholic schools embrace too vast a field of problems and because the Church's teaching mission goes beyond Catholic schools.

In the day's votings, the first on the list were votes on chapters three, four and five of the schema on the Church. Chapter three, dealing with collegiality, was approved 2,099 to 46. Chapter four was approved 2,135 to 8, and chapter five was approved 2,142 to 4.

Asked if they were willing to vote on the propositions on seminaries, the Fathers approved the motion by a vote of 2,076 to 41. They then voted on groups of articles of the propositions.

Vote one was on the introduction and article one

dealing with seminary training, the importance and powers of national conferences—affirmative 1,707, negative 3, affirmative with reservations 120.

Vote two was on articles two and three dealing with vocation recruitment and the role of minor seminaries—affirmative 1,721, negative 10, affirmative with reservations 149.

Vote three was on articles four through seven dealing with the organization of minor seminaries—affirmative 1,808, negative 4, affirmative with reservations 154.

Three council Fathers, speaking in the name of 70 or more bishops, spoke on the seminaries schema. Archbishop Gabriel Garrone of Toulouse, France, led off by stating that it was good that authority for seminary training was left with national bishops' conferences, but said that this will require closer cooperation between conferences and Rome to facilitate coordination of the various regions.

He called for renovation of the Congregation of Seminaries to make it capable of meeting the needs of the hour and to keep up with modern developments. Up to now, it has been too negative and detached from the times, he said. He also said the congregation should be in contact with the congregation dealing with priests so that it knows what problems priests have and thus can prepare students for the future. He suggested it might be profitable to merge these two congregations.

Bishop Sergio Mendez Arceo of Cuernavaca, Mexico, asked for an organic and vital treatment of clerical celibacy. He urged that celibacy be treated in the terms of St. Paul in which it is seen as apostolic celibacy. He warned

against the dangers of loneliness and urged not only that common life be recommended but also that fraternal contacts among fellow priests be encouraged to offset this danger. He also asked that bishops be given the faculty to dispense unfaithful priests from celibacy and to reduce them to the lay state under certain circumstances. However, he asked that discussion on this point be held off until the fourth session.

Auxiliary Bishop Joseph Reuss of Mainz, Germany, also wanted celibacy considered in its positive aspects. He said it is a mistake to look on celibacy as nothing more than a renunciation or as a necessary admission ticket to Holy Orders. It must be regarded in the positive light of the imitation of Christ.

A summation was delivered by Bishop Giuseppe Carraro of Verona, Italy, in the name of the commission which drafted the propositions. He promised that all suggestions made would be reviewed and the best ideas incorporated into the revised text.

Before debate opened on education, a Spanish priest, Father Luis Marcos of Madrid, addressed the council in the name of the pastors who had been invited to attend the council by the Pope. He thanked the Fathers for rejecting the schema on the priesthood and sending it back so that a genuine and complete statement could be produced. Among other things pastors would welcome, Father Marcos said, was the right to administer Confirmation where it is necessary for the good of souls and to hear confessions everywhere, or at least everywhere within national boundaries.

JAMES C. O'NEILL

Council Document On Education

The spectacle of nations throughout the world which are spending every effort to bring education to their people has spurred the Second Vatican Council to speak on the Church's own responsibilities in the field of education.

This is the explanation given in the council hall by the representative of the council's Commission on Education in presenting the draft document on Christian education to the council Fathers.

Bishop Jules Daem of Antwerp, Belgium, pointed out that education is part of the Church's general mission, which is the sanctification of the world and of life. He said this sanctification presupposes a synthesis between human things and divine things, and that modern science and techniques have made this synthesis available to all, especially youth.

Bishop Daem, touching on the history of the schema, said its previous title "On Catholic Schools" was dropped in favor of the present title "On Christian Education" because the Church's educational mission could not be circumscribed by academic education alone. Much of Christian education is given outside of the school, for example in the family, he noted.

The immensity of the field of education also prompted the commission to avoid details, leaving them to a postconciliar commission which would undertake a thorough study and reach reliable conclusions, he said.

(At the U.S. bishops' press panel, Msgr. Mark J. Hurley, chancellor of the diocese of Stockton, Calif., pointed out that when the commission's members arrived at the third session they were presented with a schema in the form of a set of propositions, which they found inadequate. The result is an expanded schema. It is no longer a set of mere propositions, but a draft declaration, he said.)

As for the human and social dimensions of education, Bishop Daem said, the task of the Church is to work for the formation of a society where all men live together peacefully. The Church's means are the message of Christ's salvation and the witness of His life. The Church must also emphasize every human and divine value. The Church must give its approval to every valid effort in education from whatever source it comes, he stated.

In the apostolic dimension of education, the Church aims at forming perfect Christians and making them conscious of the apostolate to be carried on in the world.

This requires close cooperation between families and educational institutions, he went on.

Still within this same apostolic dimension, the Church must follow Christ's example in its special love for children, delinquent youth, the poor and the sick, he said.

The relator (as the commission's representative is called) said that regarding the juridical dimension of education, the commission wanted to draw attention to rights and duties. History teaches how much humankind has suffered, and suffers even now, from a lack of tolerance or from outright contempt of rights, he stated.

The text, therefore, speaks of the inalienable rights of parents and of the Church to educate their children and to start schools, with due regard for the requirements of civil society and of the common good.

The schema, said Bishop Daem, speaks of the rights of parents to entrust their children to the schools selected by their own free choice. Mention is also made of the duty of civil society, without prejudice to its own rights, to help parents discharge their duty in this regard.

Other points made by the schema, aside from those indicated by the relator, can be summed up as follows:

It suggests that an ad hoc committee be created to draw up principles concerning Catholic education. This committee is to draw on the help of experts, including laymen.

Application of these principles is to be left to the bishops' conference of each country.

The Church, realizing the importance of education, wants to be at the service of society. Catholics must therefore cooperate and see that good schools and teachers are provided.

The Church will use all means of social communications in the apostolate of education.

Because of the primary right of parents to educate their children and therefore to choose their own schools, they should be treated equally by the law of the land. There should be no monopoly of education.

The schema speaks of the serious obligation of parents to see to the religious education of all their children who are not getting a formal religious education at school.

The states which help in this matter are to be praised. Wherever possible, children should be sent to Catholic schools.

Schools are a real apostolate worthy of priests, men and women Religious, and lay people.

The Church favors so-called special schools such as those for the handicapped, for adult education, and for remedial training.

Universities and colleges should enjoy freedom of scientific enquiry.

One of the tasks of higher institutes is to show the concord between religion and science.

In education, quantity must not be achieved at the expense of quality.

There should be cooperation at the national and international level among institutions of higher learning.

At the end, the schema reiterated that Christian education, especially schools, is a great apostolate to be recommended highly for priests, Religious and lay people.

Msgr. Hurley, a member of the press panel, said three cardinal points of the schema were:

—Emphasis on the rights of parents in education, including the right to select the school for their children.

"The schema does not ask the state to give money for the Church school," Msgr. Hurley said. "It asks for recognition of the right of parents to equal treatment under the law."

—Emphasis on concern for the religious education of children studying in non-religious schools. This is the duty of the parents primarily, although the Church stands ready to cooperate in this.

—Emphasis on the genuine worth of schools as an apostolic activity. The schema states that this apostolate is worthy of all: priests, Religious and lay people.

A vital part of the schema, according to Msgr. Hurley, is its recommendation that an ad hoc committee be set up to establish further principles and particulars.   PATRICK RILEY

Cardinal Spellman

This is a translation of the speech made in the ecumenical council Nov. 17 by Francis Cardinal Spellman of New York on the education schema.

In accord with the purpose of this schema as is noted in the proemium itself, namely, to set forth "certain fundamental principles" on Christian education, we wish to say how excellently the commission has attained this purpose.

I propose one verbal emendation so that the intention of the council may be more clearly apparent from the text.

The direct intention of the schema is to affirm the rights of children and their parents, not necessarily to seek money from the public treasury for religious schools. In many nations, for historic, sociological and political reasons, the question of the support of schools is a difficult and complicated one. Therefore, I propose the following emendation to be added to paragraph four on page 12 of the declaratio:

"Parents should be free to choose the schools they wish for their children. They should not in consequence of their choice be subject to unjust economic burdens which would infringe upon this freedom of choice. Since it is the function of the state to facilitate civil freedoms, justice and equity demand that a due measure of public aid be available to parents in support of the schools they select for their children.

"Moreover, if these schools serve the public purpose of popular education, the fact that they may be religious in their orientation should not exclude them from a rightful measure of public support."

I propose this emendation so that the intention of the council may be more clearly apparent, and accordingly I hope that useless quarrels over the words of the schema may be avoided in the future.

There remains, however, a more fundamental question. Is it possible really that this council or some post-conciliar commission or a Commission for the Revision of the Code of Canon Law could recommend norms which will apply the fundamental principles to all the actual problems of Catholic schools and Christian education?

In my opinion, considering the variety of schools from place to place with a consequent diversity of problems, no commission can decide all the particular norms for the whole world or give definitive answers to the schools of all nations and their problems.

Therefore, I commend the commission warmly for proposing a practical solution in the proemium, namely, the establishing of a special post-conciliar commission to study further the intricate problems of Christian education. This commission must not only have representation from the major areas of the world, but as well have truly expert members from all phases of education and include laymen along with priests and Religious men and women. I commend the suggestion, also, that the practical application of these general principles be placed in the hands of the conferences of bishops around the world in accord with the instructions of the Holy See.

Therefore, this declaration, with some changes in expression, merits in my opinion a vote of placet [approval].

Cardinal Ritter

This is an English text of the intervention of Joseph Cardinal Ritter of St. Louis Nov. 17 on the "Declaration on Christian Education" proposed to the Second Vatican Council.

The "Declaration on Christian Education" is very pleasing to me. The importance of the subject, Christian Education, can scarcely be exaggerated since it involves the command of Christ to go forth and teach all nations. The subject itself, as is quite evident, deserves a much fuller treatment than was possible in the "Declaration."

Not only is the subject itself a very complex one involving a theology of education, a philosophy of education, and indeed special professional competence in the field of schools and universities, but it is made more complex by reason of its universal world-wide importance and interest. No statement in detail could possibly be applicable to all countries or even almost all countries with their diverse cultures, standards of living, and legal status for schools and the Church itself.

Of particular moment in complicating the problems of such a document is the relationship of Church and State in each country, a delicate matter better solved country-by-country. Indeed, the school question with its diverse ramifications has become in many states the special practical test, the cause celebre, in the matter of the relationship between the Church and the State, between citizens and their government, between families and the society in which they live.

Rightly then does the Declaration call for a post-conciliar "ad hoc" committee to make the necessary surveys and research in a professional manner to produce a document on education not only worthy of the Council but of real and genuine value to men of good will everywhere. The commission rightly and laudably has eschewed a facile solution by compromise which would fit no country, help no nation, nor be of real value to any people, and indeed might even compromise the very freedom of education which all men of good will desire.

This post-conciliar "ad hoc" committee, if approved, deserves not only the support of the bishops but their cooperation in the research that they will make as a basis for a document suitable to our Vatican council. I wish to affirm my wholehearted support for this solution proposed by the Commission on Schools and Universities. Also, the commission proposes to leave to episcopal conferences themselves the specific application of the questions of Christian education in their own countries. This is certainly worthy of praise for the reasons I have already mentioned above.

I. It is noteworthy that the title of this Declaration has been changed from "De scholis catholicis" to "De educatione christiana," a much wider term. The Catholic school is not and must not be the only concern of the Church. Most of the Catholic children and students in the world are in state schools and must be in fact the object of the solicitude of the Church, the family, and especially the teachers in these schools for their religious education.

This Synod should give a ringing endorsement to the work, particularly of the devoted laity of Christian education as effected by the Confraternity of Christian Doctrine, the Schools of Religion, the Newman Foundations, the Young Christian Students, and similar organizations around the world devoted to the religious education of students not receiving formal religious education in state or secular or neutrally religious schools.

II. Rightly does the "Declaratio" affirm the freedom of parents to choose the schools they wish for their children. However, freedom must extend not only to the choice of schools but to the schools themselves. Within their own walls the Catholic schools must be models of Christian freedom in their administration, their teaching, and particularly in the interpersonal relationships among teachers, pupils, and parents.

The matter extends, too, to the pursuit of learning. Often have we heard in the aula of the unity of the Church, of the unity of the people and family of God; there is also a unity of truth. Truth is one, integral, and whole because ultimately with its source in the One God, truth cannot and does not in fact contradict itself. Consequently our schools and their professors and students must pursue the truth boldly and freely without fear, confident that the truth they seek is none other than Christ Who described Himself as the way, the truth and the life, that the truth they seek is the truth which the Sacred Scriptures declare will make us free.

Therefore Catholic schools and colleges and universities must not only be free from unjust external coaction and coercion but must be models of Christian freedom within their own walls.

III. Our document on Christian education must emphasize that the Catholic schools do not exist to serve narrow sectarian purposes, nor to protect selfish interests of the Church as if they were weapons of defense, nor to shield boys and girls from the marketplace (forum) and public life. Rather they stand as an expression of the free choice and liberal sacrifice not only of parents but of priests, Religious, and devoted laymen and laywomen, for God and for country as well as for the families and the Church itself. Catholic schools indeed are and of their very nature must be of substantial benefit to the entire community where they serve and to society itself. Otherwise they would stand self-condemned and be unworthy of the title "Catholic."

CONCLUSION:

I warmly approve the solutions proposed in the "Declaratio" for a fuller schema and urge you, Venerable Brothers, to accord it a "placet" vote. Dixi.

Interview With Bishop Sheen

"Pope John did what the Risen Lord did. The Church has been behind closed doors for centuries. He said: 'Open the doors! There is a world waiting for salvation. Go into it!' The Lord is again appearing behind the closed doors of the council as we debate and discuss, and there is no stepping back as we hear Him say, in the words of the Apocalypse: 'I have set before you an open door, and let no man close it'."

In these words Auxiliary Bishop Fulton J. Sheen of New York, who is director in the United States of the Society for the Propagation of the Faith, summed up his impressions at the end of the third council session.

Bishop Sheen's recent speech in the council debate on the missions met with a wide echo. He expanded on his ideas in an interview given to this correspondent.

What will come of the council, he was asked.

"This council," he replied, "is the battleground of what might be called a communion-istic revolution. There is a war not against truth, which is revealed and held in common, but against entrenched modes of thinking, patterns of administration, nationalistic hoardings and antiquated mental heirlooms. Those who are fashioned in these molds often are no more willing to give them up than the rich landowners of Latin America.

"But from all over the world came the communionists with a new revolution, asking that the Church adapt itself to the world, enlarge its offices to embrace all nations and acknowledge that there are other civilizations besides the Western.

"This revolution took place in the council between a minority group with entrenched ideological capital and a new majority group made up of many nationalistics.

"We must understand that there can be not only a capitalism of money, but also of ideas. The communion-istic revolution now is dividing the intellectual wealth and distributing it to the Church all over the world."

He was asked: Will not such an ideological division cause unrest in the Church?

"I don't think so," said Bishop Sheen. "The council needs both tendencies, and so does the Church. The minority group softened the ideas of the majority group in the council, and this will give the latter balance, make their definitions more precise, prevent them from throwing out the baby with the bath.

"On the other hand, the majority group gave a breath of fresh air to the stuffy air of the past cen-

turies, enlarged the horizons of those who lived close to the Mediterranean and made them conscious that the men and women outside the Church are not enemies but friends.

"The two groups—the minority and the majority—are like a weight on a fly-wheel. Without the weight the fly-wheel would fly off the axle; with the weight the fly-wheel goes faster. The two mentalities are necessary like the subject and predicate of a sentence."

"But," this correspondent said, "the result might be a mere compromise."

"On the surface," replied Bishop Sheen, "it may seem as if there is compromise between the two, but there is not. There actually is a synthesis. Take infallibility as defined by the First Vatican Council. That was only one side of the Church and the Scriptures. It needed to be combined with the doctrine of the collegiality of bishops, for Peter, the supreme pontiff, was chosen from among the twelve.

"As I see it, the equilibrium which is coming out of this council, as it builds up its doctrine and practice, is something wonderful to behold."

Which issue stands out among those that came up during the third council session, Bishop Sheen was asked.

"I think," he said, "the one note that rang out in the council was that the Church is to be the Church of the poor. The magnificent gesture of the Holy Father in surrendering his triple tiara symbolized it. The council actually has discovered another presence of Christ. Besides the Eucharistic presence in the tabernacle there is also the presence of Christ in the poor.

"This affects also the priesthood. Priests will no longer be like gasoline station attendants caring only for the regular clients who come in weekly for refueling.

"They will also be explorers digging for the Holy Spirit in the souls of their fellowmen. It likewise affects religious congregations inasmuch as it will cure them from organizational sclerosis, as they begin to have dialogue with one another and serve with bishops for the glory of the entire Church.

"In this light one of the principal fruits of the council is the practical realization that we are all living cells in the Mystical Body of Christ.

"The bishops from comfortable dioceses have become uncomfortable at the sight of their impoverished brethren from Latin America, Africa and Asia. The unstudious bishops have become conscious that they have missed much of their episcopal vocation in counting and administration. On the other hand, the experts in the council have realized how far removed they sometimes were from the dust of human lives.

"It really is like a new Pentecost. Each was going his own way. Now they have, as the Acts of the Apostles state, 'one mind and one heart'."

A last question came from this correspondent as to whether this impact of the new Pentecost will last beyond the council, once it has adjourned?

"Of this," Bishop Sheen replied, "I have no doubt whatsoever. The impulse is so strong it is bound to remain effective. The various local conferences of bishops will grow in stature. There will be independent initiatives which all will fit into the general pattern of that inner renewal of the Church Pope John has initiated, and Pope Paul now is promoting with the best of intentions.

"The doors have been opened wide, much too wide to be closed again." FATHER PLACID JORDAN, O.S.B.

125th General Congregation

November 18, 1964

The ecumenical council should support full freedom in scientific investigation, including research and study on Church sciences, within Catholic universities, Paul Cardinal Leger of Montreal told the Fathers during the second day of debate on the document on Christian education.

The Canadian cardinal's speech echoed the sentiments voiced by Joseph Cardinal Ritter of St. Louis on the previous day. But unlike Cardinal Ritter, who accepted the document in principle, Cardinal Leger called for its outright rejection. He urged that it be sent back for complete redrafting so that the council could present to the world at the next session a significant "modern charter of Christian education."

During the 125th meeting of the council, the Fathers voted overwhelmingly to approve the changes made in the three final chapters of the schema on the nature of the Church, thus assuring its promulgation on Nov. 21, although they were to vote once more on the schema as a whole at the Nov. 19 session. The announcement by Archbishop Pericle Felici, council secretary general, that all the chapters had been approved was greeted with loud applause.

Chapter six was approved by a vote of 2,114 to 12. Chapter seven was approved by 2,127 to 4, and chapter eight was approved 2,096 to 23.

While the schema on the Church sailed through with ease, the declaration on religious liberty ran into a last minute complication. Archbishop Felici announced that several Fathers had asked for more time to study the document, which had been distributed on Nov. 17 and which was scheduled to be voted on at the Nov. 19 meeting. The delay was asked on the grounds that the document as it now stands is a new document and considerably different from the previous one, and that its theological implications and importance require further examination.

As a result, the council presidency and moderators decided to put this point to a vote on Nov. 19, leaving it up to the Fathers themselves to determine if they wanted to go ahead with voting or to delay a decision until future sessions.

The council declaration on non-Christians, including the Jews, was distributed during the meeting and was to be voted on Nov. 20. It laments past and present persecutions and warns against Catholics' presenting the Jews as rejected by God or as cursed or guilty of deicide (God-killing).

Among the speakers of the day was Auxiliary Bishop James William Malone of Youngstown, Ohio, who was especially interested in emphasizing the distinction between society and the state. He defined society as a social concept, as the people. The state is a narrower political concept, he said. Society determines the power of the state, but the state does not determine the power of the people, he said. The terms society and state are not the same, he added.

If this distinction is insisted on, he said, much of the confusion on the matters of the rights of people, parents, the Church, teachers, government and students themselves can be cleared up.

Support of the previous day's statement by Francis Cardinal Spellman of New York was voiced in the session when English Archbishop George Beck of Liverpool declared that Catholic parents as citizens and taxpayers have rights that should be recognized by the public authorities. "In fact, in many parts of the world they are recognized, at least to some extent, so that Catholic parents are able with a quiet conscience to send their children to Catholic schools without an unfair or too heavy financial burden being imposed on them."

Moreover, said Archbishop Beck, governments should recognize the contribution which Catholic schools make to the good of society. This argument, he said, is a "further argument for assistance, at least in part, from public funds. It is not indeed an argument based on justice but on the recognition of the service which such schools give to the state."

Pope Paul VI surprised the council Fathers by attending the morning Mass, which was offered at the beginning of the 50th anniversary year of the slaughter of the Armenians in 1915 during World War I. The Pope entered the basilica with a small group of his household and left immediately after Mass without making any statements or greeting anyone.

Mass was offered by Armenian-rite Patriarch Ignace Pierre XVI Batanian of Cilicia. The Gospel was en-

280

throned by Armenian-rite Archbishop Nerses Tayroyan of Baghdad, Iraq.

Cardinal Leger opened the day's discussions by calling for the return of the schema on Christian education to commission for complete revision. He said the Fathers had not had the time or strength to work out a suitable document that could be a veritable charter for Christian education and higher studies in the years to come.

He chose to concentrate on two problems involved with higher education. First, he called for better co-operation and coordination between various Catholic universities and said this should be the main concern of the congregation of the Holy See in charge of the supervision of studies.

Secondly, he said he wanted a clear statement on the freedom of scientific investigation and particularly that the schema should emphasize liberty of research in the sacred sciences. Noting that the Church's teaching power, or magisterium, is a necessary and useful element, he said that the Church should not be over-anxious to take positions or issue decisions until there has been full freedom of investigation of a given topic.

Bishop Malone asked for a "clear and explicit distinction" between "society itself and the state or government, which is society's political arm or instrument." He said it is not enough to stress the rights of the Church in education but "it is equally necessary to give the reasons why" these are rights.

Beyond asserting the right of parents to choose schools and their right to equal treatment under the law, and rejecting all monopoly of education, he said it is also necessary to "put in prospective the delicate and complex relationships among all those agents with rights in education: the Church, state, family, private associations, schools, teachers, administrators and students themselves."

Bishop Malone said each "agent in education has a proper and legitimate interest in the education of its children" and therefore it is important to distinguish between society itself and the state. He said that society "is a social concept which describes the community itself; society means 'the people,' as we say in English, 'we the people.'"

On the other hand, the state or government "is an instrument of society, the political arm of society and its functions and specific duties must be determined by the consent of the people."

Bishop Malone insisted on this distinction because "confusion in education in most countries of the world, whether of the Occident or Orient, stems largely from confusion of the bases upon which each agent in education vindicates its rights and duties. The theory of state monopoly in education is based upon total identification of society and the state. We cannot answer that mo-

nopoly with a theory of family monopoly or Church monopoly in the 20th century."

Auxiliary Bishop Arturo Rivera Damas of San Salvador, speaking for 40 bishops, expressed disappointment with the schema's soft-pedaling of the importance of Catholic schools. Calling the text weak and sickly, he urged that a new text be drawn up to state firmly and clearly the Church's rights in this field. The present schema's timidity can do the Church much harm, he said, since it is an open provocation to abuse and makes us ridiculous in the eyes of our enemies.

Nigerian Bishop Luke Olu Nwaezeapu of Warri said he also felt the text was not strong enough on the role of Catholic schools, especially in missionary areas. Such schools often form the nucleus of the Catholic community and are not just another form of proselytizing, since non-Catholics are not required to study religion, he said.

Auxiliary Bishop Luis Henriquez Jimenez of Caracas, Venezuela, also rejected the text because, he said, it sidetracks important questions and practically canonizes whatever has been done up to now without contributing anything new. He called for a serious study of the entire question of Catholic schools which, he said, have the goal of spreading the Gospel. Given the fact that the majority of Catholic children are not in Catholic schools and that the children of the poor find it increasingly difficult to enter Catholic schools, he asked if it is not possible that some other method of evangelization might be more effective. Schools are a means, not an end in themselves, and if they are not doing the job, he said, then there should be a major restudy of the role of Catholic schools in the Church's program of evangelization.

Archbishop Beck said he found the schema "short and uneven" and added he wanted to give a more prominent place to the right of parents to educate their children according to their conscience. He said this is necessary for two practical reasons.

First, he said, it is necessary in the present age for the Church to show itself as the defender of the rights of all parents, not just Catholics. Secondly, he said, the rights of Catholic parents as citizens and taxpayers should be recognized by the public authorities.

Pointing out that many countries today do recognize the contribution which Catholic and other denominational schools make to the nation, Archbishop Beck said "we should therefore express our gratitude to those governments which recognize the value of Christian education today and offer financial assistance to Catholic schools," including England, Scotland, Ireland and the Netherlands.

Speaking in the name of the bishops of Indonesia, Archbishop Nicolas Schneiders of Makassar asked that a post-conciliar commission study in depth the serious problem of the loss of faith and indifferentism to be found among so many graduates of Catholic schools in order to discover the root of this weakness in Catholic education. He also called for a clarification of the aims of Christian education, especially regarding training in the use of liberty.

Bishop Simon Hoa Nguyen-van Hien of Dalat, Vietnam, said he wanted stress placed on the fact that Catholic schools are effective means of the apostolate in missionary countries and that they attract non-Catholics, who admire Christian morality and ideals and who become defenders of Catholics against detractors. But he warned that standards must be kept high.

The day's last speaker was Coadjutor Bishop Pablo Munoz Vega of Quito, Ecuador, who said three major problems need to be treated. The first, he said, is the importance and decisive influence attached to education today.

The second is a tendency of modern governments to establish educational monopolies. The last is the divorce of science and religion. Unfortunately, the drastic reduction and simplification of the scehma has made the correct treatment difficult, he stated.

Votes were taken on four groups of articles in the proposition on seminaries:

Articles 8 through 12, dealing with the insistence on the spiritual life in seminaries: 1,773 "yes," 10 "no," 213 "yes with reservations."

Articles 13 through 15, dealing with classical and scientific studies, coordination of ecclesiastical studies and the importance of philosophy: 1,618 "yes," 5 "no," 319 "yes with reservations."

Articles 16 through 18, dealing with the integration of theological formation and bishops' responsibilities to provide the opportunity for higher studies: 1,740 "yes," 8 "no," 307 "yes with reservations."

Articles 19 through 22, dealing with the need of pastoral training in seminaries and steps to encourage priests who are ordained to perfect their seminary learning: 1,845 "yes," 6 "no," 93 "yes with reservations."

Articles 1 through 7 were voted on the previous day.

JAMES C. O'NEILL

Bishop Malone

This is a translation of the ecumenical council speech made Nov. 18 on the schema on Christian education by Auxiliary Bishop James William Malone of Youngstown, Ohio.

Within the limits of its reduced form, this declaration on Christian education "placet." All will concede that the declaration must be amplified, enlarged upon, and expanded into a full document, as the commission which drew up the schema suggests. Thus we suggest a fundamental proposition to undergird and to support our treatment of education, namely that a clear and explicit distinction be elucidated between society itself and the state or government which is society's political arm or instrument.

It is not sufficient simply to affirm the rights of the Church in education, to proclaim the rights of the family, to delineate the rights of the state and its correlative duties. It is equally necessary to give the reasons why these rights and corresponding duties are what they are; to present both a theological and philosophical basis for the claims we make; to fashion a coherent synthesis that makes sense not only to our own people but to all men of good will.

Our document justly affirms the rights of parents to choose the schools they wish for their children; their right to equal treatment under the laws of a nation in the matter of education; and equally rejects all monopoly of education as contrary to these parental rights.

But the schema must go deeper and put into perspective the delicate and complex relationships among all those agents with rights in education: Church, state, family, private associations, schools, teachers and administrators and the students themselves. The respective relationships put into focus in modern times by Pope Pius XI in his great encyclical on education, Divini Illius Magistri, must be developed further. We cannot rest our case simply on the affirmation of rights.

The school is not "simpliciter" the extension of the home or family; the teachers are not "simpliciter" delegates of the parents or even of the Church. Neither is the school "simpliciter" the agent, much less the servant of the state. Each agent in education has a proper and legitimate interest in the education of its children, but each from its own point of view and within the limits of its own competence.

Consequently, the full schema must include the fundamental distinction between society itself and the state. Society is a social concept which describes the community itself; society means "the people," as we say in English, "we the people," whereas in contrast the state is a political concept, much narrower in meaning. The state or the government is an instrument of society, the political arm of society, and its functions and specific duties must be determined by the consent of the people, i.e., by society itself. Society then must be distinguished from the state or government precisely because it is not coterminous with it either in extension or in fundamental rights.

Contrary to some prevalent theories of the state, the government is not and must not become the master of the people but rather its servant. In the field of education, the government must not be the official teacher and arbiter of religion, science, art, literature, music or culture. Rather the state must be the servant of the expressed will and consent of the people with its unquestioned right to see to it that its citizens are fully equipped to fulfil their obligations as citizens and members of the body politic within the field of its proper competence.

Having made this fundamental point, the schema may then proceed to the general principles in education which concern man in the exercise of his highest faculties and in his dignity as a free person. The right of a family to equal treatment under the laws of a state or nation; the repudiation of all monopoly in education as an offense against the dignity of a parent to choose the school he wishes for his children; the right of equal justice in relationship to government subsidies in pluralistic societies; the duties of the Church and the state alike to foster and assist parents in their task and duty; will be brought into clearer focus.

The confusion in education today in most countries of the world, whether of the Occident or Orient, stems largely from a confusion of the bases upon which each agent in education vindicates its rights and duties.

The theory of state monopoly in education is based upon the total identification of society and the state. We cannot answer that monopoly with a theory of family monopoly, or Church monopoly, in the 20th century.

This basic distinction between the people and its political arm, the state, will go a long way toward clearing up this confusion in the field of education.

We plead therefore for the freedom of man in the field of education and indeed as a prime test of the freedom of religion.

Declaration on the Church's Relations With Non-Christians

This is a summary of the ecumenical council's declaration on the Church's relations with non-Christians.

Preliminary note: The new text has about 1,200 words, with the structure: 1) Introduction; 2) The Diverse Non-Christian Religions; 3) The Moslems; 4) The Jews; 5) Universal Brotherhood, Without Discrimination.

I. Introduction.

The community of all peoples is one. One is their origin, for God made the entire human race live on all the face of the earth. One, too, is their ultimate end, God. Men expect from the various religions answers to the riddles of the human condition: What is man? What is the meaning and purpose of our lives? What is the moral good and what is sin? What are death, judgment, and retribution after death?

II. The Diverse Non-Christian Religions.

Ever since primordial days, numerous peoples have had a certain perception of that hidden power which hovers over the course of things and over the events that make up the lives of men; some have even come to know of a Supreme Being and Father. Religions in an advanced culture have been able to use more refined concepts and a more developed language in their struggle for an answer to man's religious questions.

In Hinduism, men use myths and philosophical ways in the effort to fathom the divine mystery; they seek freedom from the anguish of our human condition through ascetical methods, meditation, and a flight to God.

Buddhism realizes the radical inadequacy of this changeable world. It teaches the way of liberation, through self-denial and inner purification, in order to attain a state of lasting rest.

Other religions counter the restlessness of the human heart by proposing ways, that is to say, doctrines, rules of life and sacred rites.

Nothing that is true and holy in these religions is scorned by the Catholic Church. Ceaselessly the Church proclaims Christ, "the Way, the Truth, and the Life," in whom God reconciled all things to Himself. The Church regards with sincere reverence those ways of action and of life, precepts and teachings which, although they differ from the ones she sets forth, reflect nonetheless a ray of that Truth which enlightens all men.

The Church, therefore, admonishes Catholics that they converse and collaborate with the followers of other religions in order to serve, indeed, advance those spiritual and moral goods as well as those socio-cultural values that have a home among men of other religious traditions.

III. The Moslems.

The Church esteems the Moslems: they adore the one God who is a living and all-powerful God, the Creator of heaven and earth who has spoken to men. They strive to obey even His incomprehensible decrees, just as Abraham did, to whose faith they like to link their own. Though Moslems do not acknowledge Jesus as God, they revere Him as a Prophet. They also honor Mary, His Virgin-Mother; at times they even call on her with devotion. They await the day of judgment when God will reward all those who have risen. They worship God through prayer, almsgiving, and fasting. They seek to make the moral life — be it that of the individual or that of the family and society — conform to His will.

In the past many quarrels and hostilities have arisen between Christians and Moslems. The council urges all not only to forget the past but also to work honestly for mutual understanding and to further as well as guard together social justice, all moral goods, especially peace and freedom, so that mankind may benefit.

IV. The Jews.

The council searches into the mystery of the Church. The Church of Christ gratefully acknowledges that, according to God's saving design, the beginnings of her faith and her election were already among the patriarchs, Moses and the prophets. All Christians — Abraham's sons according to faith — were included in the same patriarch's call. The Church cannot forget that she received the revelation of the Old Testament from the people with whom God in His mercy concluded the former Covenant. The Church believes that by His Cross Christ reconciled Jews and Gentiles, making both one.

The Church keeps in mind what St. Paul says about his kinsmen: "Theirs is the sonship, the glory, the covenants, the giving of the law, the worship, and the promises. Theirs are the patriarchs, and of them is the Christ according to the flesh" (Rom. 9, 4-5), the Son of Mary the Virgin. The apostles, as well as most of the early disciples, sprang from the Jewish people.

Even though a large part of the Jews did not accept the Gospel, they remain dear to God for the sake of the patriarchs. God's gifts and call are irrevocable (cf. Rom. 11, 28f). The Church awaits that day, known to God alone, on which all peoples will address the Lord in a single voice and "serve Him shoulder to shoulder" (Soph. 3, 9).

The spiritual patrimony common to Christians and Jews is very rich. Thus, the council supports and recommends their mutual knowledge and respect — the fruit, above all, of biblical and theological studies, as well as of fraternal dialogue. The council, in her rejection of any injustice, is mindful of this common patrimony between Christians and Jews. Thus, the council deplores and condemns hatred and persecution of Jews, whether they arose in former or in our own days.

Nothing in catechetical work or preaching should teach anything that could give rise to hatred or contempt of Jews in the hearts of Christians. The Jewish people should never be presented as one rejected, cursed or guilty of deicide. What happened to Christ in His Passion cannot be attributed to the whole people then alive, much less to that of today. Besides, the Church held and holds that Christ underwent His Passion and death freely, because of the sins of all men and out of infinite love. Christian preaching proclaims the Cross of Christ as the sign of God's all-embracing love and as the fountain from which every grace flows.

V. Universal Brotherhood, Without Discrimination.

We cannot address God, the Father of us all, if we refuse to treat some men or other in a brotherly way. "He who does not love does not know God" (I John 4, 8). Any theory or practice that, so far as their human dignity is concerned, discriminates between man and man or people and people, creating a different set of rights for each of them, has no foundation. All men, especially Christians, must refrain from discrimination against, or harassment of, others because of their race, color, creed, or walk of life. Catholics should "maintain good conduct among the Gentiles" (I Pet. 2, 12) and live, so far as it depends on them, in peace with all men, so that they may really be sons of the Father who is in heaven.

To show his concern for the poor Pope Paul VI gave his coronation tiara to charity. In a symbolic gesture on Nov. 13, 1964, the Holy Father carried the triple crown to an altar in the council hall. Shown with him on this occasion are Archbishop Enrico Dante (right) and Alberto Cardinal Di Jorio, left.

126th General Congregation
November 19, 1964

The next to last working meeting of the ecumenical council's third session exploded in controversy and confusion as Eugene Cardinal Tisserant, dean of the council presidency, announced that no vote would be taken on the document on religious liberty at this session.

This followed the previous day's contradictory statement by the council secretary general, Archbishop Pericle Felici.

Immediate reaction registered all over the council hall. Albert Cardinal Meyer of Chicago, one of the council presidents, was taken completely by surprise. He left his seat and gathered groups of bishops around him. Joseph Cardinal Ritter of St. Louis, Paul Cardinal Leger of Montreal and Bernard Cardinal Alfrink of Utrecht, the Netherlands, joined him and a protest movement began.

"Almost from nowhere petitions sprouted like mushrooms around the council hall," an American bishop said afterward. "Before the morning was over, perhaps 1,000 signatures from bishops all over the world had been collected."

The petition was reliably reported to have asked Pope Paul VI "urgently, more urgently, most urgently" to intervene in the council and assure a vote on religious liberty the following day in spite of the announcement by Cardinal Tisserant.

That such was the will of the majority became clear later at the meeting when Bishop Emile De Smedt of Bruges, Belgium, read according to schedule the report on the controversial document. He was applauded wildly five times during his speech and for several minutes afterwards. The day's moderator, Julius Cardinal Doepfner of Munich and Freising, Germany, tried to silence the forbidden applause, but soon gave up.

Almost overlooked in the confusion was another milestone of the Second Vatican Council as the Fathers accepted in its entirety one of the council's most important documents, the constitution on the nature of the Church, by an overwhelming vote of 2,134 to 10. One vote was null. The only step left was a formal vote and its promulgation by Pope Paul at the Nov. 21 closing meeting.

During the meeting, the Fathers also accepted the declaration on Catholic schools for voting and began to vote on its various sections after eight Fathers spoke.

Then the report was given on the last document of the council to reach the floor for discussion, that on the sacrament of Matrimony. One speaker, Norman Cardinal Gilroy of Sydney, Australia, praised the document in general outlines before the stormy meeting came to its close.

Cardinal Tisserant's announcement came after a hurried consultation with other presidents and Archbishop Felici. Then Cardinal Doepfner introduced him.

"Many Fathers have objected that there is not sufficient time to consider the new text on religious liberty before voting," Cardinal Tisserant said, "especially since the text presents a new structure, which the Secretariat for Promoting Christian Unity admits.

"It seems proper to the presidency that this cannot be decided by a vote of a general congregation [meeting]. There will not, therefore, be a vote. The Fathers are invited to submit their observations on the text to the unity secretariat before Jan. 31, 1965."

A council official pointed out that "vigorous applause from a very few bishops" followed the announcement.

That there had been changes in the document since it left the council floor several weeks ago was admitted by Bishop De Smedt in his report. He said the unity secretariat had "amplified the treatment, presenting the practical consequences of religious liberty in a broader setting." It was presumed that Cardinal Tisserant referred to these.

However, Bishop De Smedt also said "none of the changes affect the substance. It is the same doctrine as before." On the basis of this, he said, the Fathers can vote wisely, informatively and prudently.

Regarding the declaration itself, Bishop De Smedt said "it cannot but happen that the Church will win over its adversaries among men of good will, not by force or political means, but with the arms of justice and the power of God."

During the morning the amended text and observations of the council Fathers on the propositions on the Eastern Churches were distributed and it was announced that a vote on these would be taken on Nov. 20.

The Fathers also decided by a vote of 1,457 to 419 to begin voting on various sections of the declaration on Catholic education, following the speeches on it by seven speakers and a summary of the discussion given by Bishop Jules Daem of Antwerp, Belgium. The first balloting covered the introduction and first three chapters, which received 1,592 affirmative votes, 157 negative votes and 140 votes of qualified approval.

Although balloting took place on three other sections of this document, the results were not announced.

The document on the sacrament of Matrimony has the unique title of a "votum" (that is, an expression of the will of the council) and is described as containing suggestions for future canonical legislation on matrimony, to be taken up by the commission for Revision of Canon Law. It was introduced by Benedetto Cardinal Aloisi Masella, president of the council's commission on the Discipline of the Sacraments.

After pointing out that the text deals only with matrimony in its disciplinary aspects, he listed the subjects on which the preparatory commission had presented its findings. These were matrimonial impediments, mixed marriages, matrimonial consent, the form of celebration of marriage, and the basic principles which should govern a reorganization of the handling of marriage cases. Since the time of the preparatory commission's work, he said, a chapter has been added on preparation of couples for marriage and on pastoral concern for their conjugal happiness.

Then Archbishop Joseph Schneider of Bamberg, Germany, gave the official report, explaining that the present form of the document was a "result of directives received from higher authority."

He said the text was intended to list various points on which it is necessary or advisable to adapt matrimonial legislation to the needs of the times. Several Fathers, he said, had found the original text too brief and not sufficiently concrete, and for this reason the commission had recast the text at a meeting held on Oct. 14. The result of this revision was the text presented for consideration, he said.

Noting that several Fathers had asked for treatment on birth control in this document, he said the commission had decided that subject was beyond its competence, since the subject pertains to faith and morals and not to the discipline of the sacraments.

Birth control had already been debated on the council floor during the discussion of the schema on the Church in the modern world, and was sent back to commission for revision and further discussion.

Praising the document's practical suggestions aimed at avoiding frequent invalid marriages, Cardinal Gilroy added several suggestions of his own. He said the impediment of disparity of cult, forbidding marriages between a Catholic and non-baptized person unless a dispensation has been granted, should no longer invalidate a marriage.

He asked for a stronger statement urging Catholics not to contract mixed marriages but suggested there be no absolute prohibition unless there is danger to the faith of the Catholic party. Regarding the promises required in a mixed marriage, he suggested they be made before the local pastor to insure moral certainty that they are sincere.

Civil marriages, even of Catholics, should be recognized as valid, although unlawful, he said, provided the civil ceremony can be proven with documents. But even so, a couple should be denied the sacraments until they have taken steps to rectify their situation.

For mixed marriages, he suggested a nuptial Mass be allowed, but not prescribed.

The 126th general meeting of the council opened with Mass celebrated by Bishop Joseph Ijjas, apostolic administrator of Csanad, Hungary, one of the five Hungarian bishops recently appointed and consecrated in Budapest. It was the feast of St. Elizabeth of Hungary. The Gospel was enthroned by Bishop Charles Lemaire, P.I.M.E., superior general of the Paris Foreign Mission Society.

Archbishop Felici announced the death of Bishop Augustin Olbert, S.V.D., former Bishop of Tsingtao, China.

A mimeographed sheet was distributed in the council hall indicating certain modifications introduced by the unity secretariat over and above the formal reservations on the ecumenism schema which would be given a final vote the following day. A council press office bulletin said these modifications had been made "conformable to authoritative suggestions made by competent persons."

(At a meeting of the U.S. bishops' press panel the same day, Father Thomas F. Stransky, C.S.P., a member of the unity secretariat, said these changes were actually made by the Pope "acting as the head of the council."

(The unity secretariat cannot have approved them, he said, because it has not held a plenary meeting since the suggestions were made. In all, 19 changes have been submitted. They will be incorporated into a printed text to be passed out to the council Fathers on Nov. 20. They will not be voted on as such, but simply included in the entire text to be voted on, Father Stransky said. If the Fathers disapprove of them, they will have to vote against the entire schema.

(He added that most of the changes are "definitely clarifications" and a few of them on "very subtle points." Some deal with points which the council has already altered through qualified votes. One has to do with the way non-Catholic Christians find—or seek to find—God speaking to them in Holy Scripture, he said, and another with the Eucharist and non-Catholic Christians.)

The first speaker on Christian education was Bishop Johannes Pohlschneider of Aachen, Germany. The document should have been the kind that makes history, he said. He added that he wondered why it had been reduced to a few propositions. He urged that it be prefaced by a theological and Biblical introduction and that it stress man's twofold task of subjecting the earth to himself and of reaching his eternal goal through a Christian life.

The state should follow the principle of subsidiarity in the field of education, he said, and the text must clearly affirm that distributive justice obliges the state to support all private schools provided they attain the same standards as public schools. Secularism in state schools must be avoided at all costs, he said. It is the "great heresy of our times."

Though the state is entitled to control the external aspects of education, such as housing, public health and the like, he said, it must leave internal principles and religious foundations to the consciences of parents.

Bishop Godfrey Okoye of Port Harcourt, Nigeria, observed that the aim of marriage is the procreation and education of children. Since parents cannot provide alone for proper education, schools become necessary, he said, and the quality of education is of supreme importance.

The school must include some spiritual and religious training in order to serve as a continuation of the home, he said, and the state has no right to impose on parents schools which they may regard as harmful for their children. The state must provide assistance for the schools chosen by parents because they pay taxes; therefore the text should strongly affirm the right of the Church to found and direct schools and the right of parents to financial assistance, he concluded.

Maronite-rite Archbishop Antoine Abed of Tripoli, Lebanon, said the need for schools flows from the very nature of the Church's educational mission. He said he wanted included in the schema a declaration of criteria whereby a truly Catholic education can be recognized. It cannot be a purely commercial institution, he said, but must have moral aims as well and meet the needs of the whole person and community. The text should demand for private schools the same type of assistance provided for government schools.

He called for an international commission to study educational problems and draw conclusions which will "prescind from any one state or form of government."

Bishop Anthony Nwedo of Umahia, Nigeria, asked that lay instructors replace priests as far as possible in Catholic schools, so that priests can give more time to the "ministry, strictly so-called."

There should be no blanket prohibition against Catholic students attending non-Catholic schools, he urged, since this is often the only place they can get the particular education they want.

"In a pluralistic society, our students must learn to live with everyone and thus there will be less danger of perversion in faith when they reach the university level."

By a standing vote the council then decided to cut off debate on education, but three more speakers were allowed to address the council Fathers since they were speaking in the name of more than 70 others.

The first of these was Father Aniceto Fernandez, O.P., master general of the Dominican Fathers, who spoke for 120. He objected to the use of the phrase "Catholic university," since it puts all other universities under the purely negative heading of "non-Catholic universities."

He said that it was helpful to study natural and sacred sciences in one and the same university center, and asked that in every Catholic university philosophy and theology be taught according to the principles of St. Thomas Aquinas. He observed, however, that devotion to his fellow Dominican "is not devotion to a person but to things; it is not a question of who but of what." This, he said, saves the Church from the danger of being a "one doctor church." St. Thomas (a doctor of the Church) did not preach himself, Father Fernandez said, but ideas.

In the name of the bishops of Poland, Auxiliary Bishop Bohdan Bejze of Lodz said that the fate of the world depends on youth, and the fate of youth is closely bound up with its education. The schema needs to be reworked by qualified experts, he said, in order to face serious challenges of the world today. Included in this, he said, should be an attempt to frame a curriculum characterized by a certain progress in the sciences and by emphasizing the harmony between faith and reason.

The aim of all study should be to arouse in students the desire for what is divine, he concluded.

The former rector of Belgium's Louvain University, Auxiliary Bishop Honore Van Waeyenbergh of Malines-Brussels, said that the mission of the Catholic university demands progressive coordination in the light of the unity of truth. The Church must always make it its duty to serve the cause of human knowledge, he said, and he called for a briefer, clearer and more concrete text.

In his summary of the debate, Bishop Daem recalled that the first title of the schema had been "On Catholic Schools," and that it had been changed only when the new form of the schema had been "imposed on the commission." He said that the observations of the speakers clearly showed how varied conditions are in different countries, and that this fact emphasized the wisdom of the commission's decision not to attempt a definitive statement in the council, but to leave more detailed declarations to the postconciliar commission.

In the name of the commission, he proposed that the council Fathers call for a more complete document from the postconciliar commission, accept the present schema as the basis for further and more complete work by the commission, with a view to restoring the text to the original form, and make concrete suggestions by attaching them to the vote in different propositions.

FATHER JOHN P. DONNELLY

*   *   *   *

With wave after wave of irresistible applause, the Fathers of the Second Vatican Council thundered their support for the redrafted declaration on religious liberty despite an earlier anouncement that because of doubts it would not be voted on at this session.

The applause punctuated a report on the new draft delivered by the representative of the commission which drew it up, the Secretariat for Promoting Christian Unity, headed by Augustin Cardinal Bea, S.J. When Bishop Emile De Smedt of Bruges, Belgium, finished delivering his report—which amounted to an impassioned plea for the right of men to worship God according to their best lights—council Fathers broke into the loudest and longest clapping heard during the council's three sessions.

The day's moderator, Julius Cardinal Doepfner of Munich and Freising, Germany, holding up his hand for order, seemed like a new King Canute trying to hold back the waves of the sea. With the storm of applause bursting over his head, even the iron-willed German cardinal admitted defeat. He watched passively while the applause at length spent itself.

Bishop De Smedt's report—although prepared long before the announcement by Eugene Cardinal Tisserant, dean of the council presidency, that it had decided to delay the vote on the text—anticipated the very argument given to justify this delay.

Cardinal Tisserant—like Archbishop Pericle Felici, council secretary general, the day before—said several council Fathers had complained that the text was entirely new and therefore more time was needed to study it.

Bishop De Smedt's reply was that although the text had been rearranged and reconstructed, it incorporated the same substantial teaching. He pointed out further that it had been redrawn along lines suggested by the council Fathers themselves in their written "modi" or proposed amendments.

Even while Bishop De Smedt spoke, council Fathers were feverishly collecting signatures for a petition to be taken to Pope Paul VI himself. This asked the Pope to countermand the council presidency's decision to put off the vote on the religious liberty document until next session. Ironically, the leader among those collecting signatures was Albert Cardinal Meyer of Chicago, a member of the presidency in whose name Cardinal Tisserant had spoken.

As if to stress the urgency of the document, Bishop De Smedt said the world is watching and waiting for the Church's reply to the great question of religious liberty.

Religious liberty, he said, is necessary in modern society if the Faith is to make progress.

The effective test of the truth of the Gospel, he said, will be if the Church puts its faith in its truth by espousing religious freedom.

The Church will win its adversaries over to its side, he said, not by force, not by political means, but by the arms of the justice and the power of God.

Bishop De Smedt, widely considered to be among the council's handful of genuine orators, summoned all his rhetorical powers in defending man's right to freedom from coercion in matters religious. Several times his voice, surcharged with emotion, seemed about to break.

But at the end his voice dropped to a virtual whisper when, as if replying to the argument that the document had been presented too late, he ticked off a list of dates.

On Oct. 16, he said, the president of the Coordinating Commission, Amleto Cardinal Cicognani, gave the order that the teachings of the already-prepared document be examined by five members of the Doctrinal Commission. (Four of the five approved the document, while one withheld his approval.)

On Oct. 24, the unity secretariat gave its final and unanimous approval to the declaration on religious liberty.

On Nov. 9, at the order of Cardinal Cicognani, still acting in his capacity as president of the Coordinating Commission, the document was examined by the entire Theological Commission.

(According to American Father John Courtney Murray, S.J., the vote was 12 for approval, 9 for qualified approval, and 8 for disapproval. This meant approval by well over the required two-thirds majority.)

Bishop De Smedt's meaning was clear: the document had been ready in plenty of time, but had been subject to administrative delay. The unity secretariat, said Bishop De Smedt, had complied with changes suggested by the Theological Commission where these changes did not run counter to the expressed will of the council Fathers as conveyed in qualifications of votes. The schema, thus amended, had been ready but was not brought before the council when ready.

In the body of his report, Bishop De Smedt said that objections to the previous text fell into two categories—objections against the presentation or against the arguments sustaining the doctrine, and objections against the doctrine itself. He said these objections were answered in another part of his report, which he did not read but which was contained in the printed text circulated to the council Fathers.

The declaration avoids the question of Church-State

relations. It avoids inquiry into the theological problem of the Church's right and duty of preaching the Gospel.

It also avoids moral teaching on the standards guiding the Christian in his contacts with non-Christians. On all these points, said Bishop De Smedt, the Church's teaching must be faithfully carried out.

To modern man's question about the Church's attitude toward modern systems of religious pluralism, the schema answers that no man can be coerced by others in religious matters. Religion is above the competence of the state, it declares. The state must recognize and defend the free exercise of religion by all its citizens.

On the difficult question of the limits to the right of external manifestations of religion, the reporter said that it is difficult to find formulas which cannot be abused by public authority. The schema states two principles, one moral and one juridical.

The moral principle asserts that in the external exercise of religious liberty no one may violate the rights of others. The juridical principle is that no one may exercise his religion in such a way as to cause a great disturbance of public order.

Bishop De Smedt defended the Church against the charge of opportunism—that it is proclaiming religious liberty simply because such a declaration happens to be advantageous to the Church now. Civil authorities, he said, have shifted their ground on this matter.

The sum of the bishop's reply to such an accusation was that the Church recognizes the maturing of the human conscience and approves the religious liberty claimed by society.

The affirmation of religious liberty does not prejudice the Church's rights, Bishop De Smedt asserted, for what is more dignified than that the Church should carry out its divine mission freely and independently.

Nor does it prevent the Catholic Church from having a privileged status where Catholics are in the majority, he said, since such privileged status is not opposed to religious liberty provided that non-Catholics are not coerced.

Bishop De Smedt's peroration brought rousing applause. He said the Church does not put its trust in the power of the civil authorities. In its difficulties it must not run to them for help. The Church's most effective witness to the truth of the Gospel will be in putting its confidence in the power of truth itself.

However, in his spoken address Bishop De Smedt omitted one significant line from his printed report. This line said that despite the delays to which the schema had been subjected, "not all hope has vanished" for a vote on religious liberty in this session. PATRICK RILEY

Council Votum
On Matrimony

This is the text of the summary issued by the council press office of the council votum (suggestions for canonical legislation) on matrimony.

The Commission for the Discipline of the Sacraments had prepared a schema on marriage in 1963, in the period between the first and second session of the council, summarizing and synthesizing the studies on this point carried out by the Preparatory commission. In January, 1964, the Coordinating Commission decided to reduce and transform the schema into a simple presentation of suggestions, containing clear directives for a reform of canon law on marriage along the lines of pastoral exigencies. It must be borne in mind that, although this does not take up the question of marriage as a sacrament in explicit terms, the topic is discussed in the schema on the Church, in the one on the apostolate of the laity and also in the schema on the Church in the modern world.

The text now presented to the Fathers, compressed into a little more than two pages, is subdivided into five paragraphs, which are in turn divided into three parts.

Part I recalls a certain number of fundamental principles, such as the sacred character of marriage considered in its entirety, the holiness of marriage contracted between two baptized persons as members of Christ whose union is in close relationship with that of Christ and His Church, the competence of the Church for the safeguarding of the integrity of the sacrament of Matrimony and, consequently, her right to legislate in this connection.

The second part contains directives for the revision of canon law in view of the special needs of our times. The proposition underlines the new conditions which have been created, e.g., by the phenomenon of emigration and the creation of new states. Legislation concerning impediments is to be simplified, e.g., the suppression of all impediments known as "minor." Among these are consanguinity in the third degree of the collateral line, affinity in the second degree of the collateral line, spiritual relationship arising from being sponsor for Baptism or Confirmation.

As regards the impediments of mixed religion (between a Catholic and a baptized non-Catholic) and disparity of worship (between a Catholic and an unbaptized person) the future legislation shall be guided by the provisions of the council concerning ecumenism.

Steps shall likewise be taken to simplify the formalities hitherto required for the celebration of marriage in the presence of a priest duly authorized to bless the marriage. There shall also be a closer control in the part of the bishop over the cases involving marriage contracted with what is known as the "extraordinary form," that is to say, in cases when the presence of a priest is impossible.

Lastly, steps shall be taken to simplify the procedure in marriage cases and provisions must be made to assure the selection of competent judges as well as the gratuitous services of a lawyer.

In the last part, the proposition mentions prepara-tion for marriage as a serious duty for pastors of souls. Whenever necessary, pastors shall seek out the collaboration of other priests or competent lay people—men and women—for instruction and preparation in view of marriage. They shall endeavor to come to know the fiances through personal contacts in order to strengthen them in Christian faith and life.

Pastors shall likewise observe scrupulously the rules governing the prenuptial investigation and shall never permit the celebration of the sacrament of Matrimony if they are not fully convinced of the free consent of the parties. Finally, they shall see to it that the marriage ceremony reflects the profound significance of the sacrament and that those assisting at the ceremony have the opportunity to participate actively in the liturgy.

Pastors of souls must continue their attentive interest even after marriage, assisting the newlyweds to live in the fulness of the grace of the sacrament their life as two in one, and counseling them on the new problems which will arise in the education of their children.

Schema 13 Will Be Drastically Revised

The schema on the Church in the Modern World, which underwent almost three weeks of sharp debate, inevitably will receive drastic revision between now and the fourth session of the Second Vatican Council.

The lively discussion on the schema in the council hall made it very clear that, in the opinion of the council Fathers, the present draft does not present a completely adequate theology of the Church and the world. However, this is not surprising in view of the fact that no previous council of the Church ever addressed itself to this subject and in view of the further fact that contemporary theology has yet to arrive at a consensus on the subject.

On the other hand, there can be little doubt that the present schema marks a historic step in the right direction. It can and will be improved substantially in the light of the oral and written interventions of the Fathers and, while no one expects the final draft to say the last word on the subject of the Church and the world, we can be certain that it will be a document worthy of a council which was called not to settle disputed questions in speculative theology, but rather to bring about an "aggiornamento" (updating) in the pastoral life of the Church.

Refinements in the speculative theology of the Church and the world will come in due time from scholars in the field of the sacred sciences who can now be expected, under the stimulus of schema 13, to give greater attention than ever before to this all-important subject. It goes without saying that they will need to cooperate as closely as possible with competent scholars in every pertinent branch of secular learning.

The document has a fourfold purpose:

1. To instruct all men how they should view and perform even their temporal duties in the light of their one true vocation (Chapter 1).

2. To have the Church order its relations with the world so as not only to manifest the spiritual nature of its mission, but also its contribution to the common good of all humanity (Chapter 2).

3. To persuade every Christian and all Christian communities that they should make known Christ living in the midst of His brethren by their honest and generous cooperation with all men in a spirit of brotherhood, poverty and service (Chapter 3).

4. To urge all Christians without exception to apply themselves energetically to the solution of the most urgent problems of the day and at the same time to lay down certain basic moral principles pointing toward a sound solution of these problems (Chapter 4).

The outside world has tended to concentrate almost exclusively on the last of these four purposes of the schema and has given only passing attention to the first three. This is understandable, but in many ways also regrettable. The basic problem confronting the Church in its relations with the world is not to solve specific problems in the temporal order—important as these problems are—but rather to develop what might be called a theology of temporal or terrestrial values and to motivate the faithful to fulfill their own obligatory role in the temporal order in the light of this theology.

This means, for example, that the Church must, in the first instance, formulate as clearly as possible its own theology of the world, the nature and the limitations of its own role as an institution in the temporal order, and finally the duties of the faithful in the world. It is only after it has completed this preliminary spade work that the Church can address itself meaningfully to specific problems in the temporal order.

With regard to the fourth section of the schema, which received the major part of public attention given the schema, it is well to emphasize that it was never the intention of the council to settle any or all of the specific problems confronting the world at the present time. Bishop John J. Wright of Pittsburgh made this point emphatically in his official introduction of the schema to the council Fathers.

"It is not therefore our intention," he told the Fathers, "to bring up and settle individual points in detail, or to attempt easy and over-simplified answers which could be only glib and, in the long run, deceptive." He added that the "signs of the times" are offered as points of reflection for the Fathers, both in the council and afterwards, working with sociologists and other experts in a common search for adequate answers.

"In no way does our chapter pretend to be either exhaustive or definitive," Bishop Wright said. "It ought not to be the last word in our dialogues with the modern world, but rather the first word, or the beginning, from our side, of an entirely new dialogue."

The importance of Bishop Wright's cautionary explanation of the precise purpose of chapter 4 of schema 13 can hardly be exaggerated. There are those who will disagree with the bishop and will argue that the council should at least attempt to say the last word on the morality of nuclear warfare, for example, or on the morality of the pill. But this does not appear to be the opinion of the majority of the council Fathers as expressed in the council debate.

What the Church can be expected to do is to begin to clarify the theology of its own role—and the role of its individual members—in the modern world. It can also be expected to state as clearly as possible its own understanding of the moral law as it applies to some of the major problems of the day. But the world is doomed to be disillusioned if it expects the Church to do much more than that at the present time.

MSGR. GEORGE G. HIGGINS

Msgr. Higgins is director of the Social Action Department of the National Catholic Welfare Conference and a council expert who assisted in the preparation of a substantial amount of the material covered by the schema.

127th General Congregation
November 20, 1964

The final working day of the third session of the ecumenical council ended as a large majority approved the declaration on the Church's relations with non-Christians, which includes a strong and clear statement on the Jews.

But the Fathers did not have enough time to cast the declaration in its final form for promulgation at this session.

At the same time, it was announced in the name of Pope Paul VI that the decision not to vote on the religious liberty declaration was upheld in order to give the Fathers sufficient time to study it. It was stated that if at all possible it will be the first order of business at the fourth session, which probably will be called for the fall of 1965.

The final working meeting, which was the 127th to be held since the council opened in October, 1962, also saw final voting on the schemas on the Eastern churches and ecumenism, thus clearing the way for their promulgation at the plenary council session in the Pope's presence on Nov. 21. One other schema became an official act of the council as a result of this third session, the one on the nature of the Church.

At the end of the debate on the document on matrimony, the Fathers voted to send it to the Pope for his action because they felt the problems are so in need of immediate action that it would be wrong to have to wait on the long and complex process of the council and a new codification of canon law.

Three votes were taken on the declaration on the Church's relations with non-Christians. The entire text was approved 1,651 to 99, with 242 other Fathers voting in favor of the declaration but with reservations. It was the favorable-with-reservations votes that made it impossible to promulgate the declaration at this session, since each of the reservations must be studied by the commission to see if they can significantly add to the final document.

In addition to the overall vote on the declaration, two other votes on its various sections were cast. The first vote was on the introduction and first three articles, dealing with non-Christians in general and particularly with Moslems. These were approved 1,838 to 136. The second vote covered articles four and five dealing with the Jews

and the affirmation of universal brotherhood. These were approved 1,770 to 185.

Among the speakers on the document on matrimony were Joseph Cardinal Ritter of St. Louis and Auxiliary Bishop John M. Fearns of New York, who delivered the text prepared for Francis Cardinal Spellman of New York, who had left Rome the previous day. Archbishop John J. Krol of Philadelphia also was among the 13 speakers of the day.

Cardinal Ritter said he was "highly pleased" with the matrimony document, particularly with the provision dealing with mixed marriages. He singled out the document's proposed change of Church law, which at present requires both parties in a mixed marriage to give promises to baptize their children as Catholics and rear and educate them as Catholics. The document proposed that only the Catholic party be required to make these promises.

"Adaptation of the suggested proposal would strengthen respect for divine law by stressing more emphatically the role of personal responsibility. Responsibility for the security of his own faith as well as for the Catholic education of their children is rightly placed on the Catholic party. In this way, we can lessen the possibility of offense to the consciences of our separated brethren."

Cardinal Ritter also favored the proposal to authorize certain changes in the form of mixed marriages, which now must be contracted before a Catholic priest only and in the presence of witnesses.

He said the schema "supports the general retention of the canonical form of marriage for validity in such cases" and that, in light of the "high incident of early and hasty marriages with a probability of subsequent divorce," this retention is justified.

However, he said, "to demonstrate our respect for human dignity and to reduce the principles of ecumenism to practice, it is apparent that in some cases the Ordinary must be empowered to grant a dispensation from the form." Lastly, he said, "for the sake of honesty and justice those baptized in the Catholic Church who have been reared without a Catholic education must not be bound by the canonical form of marriage nor restricted by any impediments of merely ecclesiastical law."

Bishop Fearns took the floor immediately after Cardinal Ritter to deliver Cardinal Spellman's statement in the name of more than 100 American bishops. The speech commended the text when it sought to protect the dignity and sanctity of matrimony, but declared some of the proposals will serve as a vast mandate for sanctioning dangerous changes. Even if the changes might be beneficial in some countries, there is no reason to impose them on other nations, it said.

The council Fathers should have had time to consult their pastors on such important matters, and the commission which drew up this document should have consulted pastors who know the problems. In short, it was declared, the text has so many and such important defects that it should be revised completely.

If dispensation from the marriage form is allowed in mixed marriages, it was stated, a decrease in the peoples' respect for marriage will result. It will also deprive couples of the counsel and guidance of pastors.

Catholic people demand the presence of the priest at a marriage and do not approve of mixed marriages in non-Catholic churches or civil registry offices, it said. Even state authorities recognize this in the U.S. and couples married in a Catholic church are not required to go through another ceremony elsewhere, it was declared.

The speech also said the text was vague regarding the reasons that could be advanced for asking for a dispensation from the marriage form. It would be enough for one party to object to a marriage before a priest, it said. This deprives couples of pastoral guidance and gives no assurance of the baptism and education of the children, the speech continued. The text does not take into account the good accomplished by the present regulations, and it is necessary for a mixed-marriage couple to appreciate the problems before, not after, marriage.

Archbishop Krol was the third American to speak at the session. He warned of the dangers of indifference and secularism in the U.S. where 60 million people profess no religion or only the vaguest concept of religion.

Archbishop Krol declared the Church cannot confirm anyone in indifferentism and that it is necessary to go carefully in the matter of mixed marriages. Regarding the form of a mixed marriage, Archbishop Krol said that in general a priest should be present, but that the Ordinary could have the power to dispense from this for ecumenical reasons.

As for the priest who is to be present, he said he wanted a clearer qualification of the type of priest who would be a witness at a mixed marriage. As the text stands, he said, any priest, even an excommunicated one, could officiate. Archbishop Krol asked that the text specify that the priest involved should be at least known to ecclesiastical authorities.

The final session opened with a Mass celebrated by Archbishop John Heenan of Westminster, England, who was also one of the day's speakers. The Gospel was en-

throned by Bolivian Bishop Luis Rodriguez Pardo of Santa Cruz de la Sierra. Julius Cardinal Doepfner of Munich and Freising, Germany, moderated.

Archbishop Pericle Felici, council secretary general, announced that the Fathers were to be given gold medals honoring Our Lady presented by anonymous donors. It was also announced that the Pope had granted faculties to superior generals of congregations and orders similar to those granted to bishops at the end of the last session, giving them increased authority without having recourse to Ordinaries or Rome in various matters.

Copies of the new texts on divine Revelation and on the priestly life were distributed. The Fathers can make observations on them up to Jan. 31, 1965. The Fathers were also informed that one chapter of the schema on the pastoral duties of bishops had been finished by the commission, but had not been printed as yet and therefore the schema could not be promulgated at this session.

Eugene Cardinal Tisserant, dean of the council presidency, rose to state that since a number of Fathers were greatly disappointed by the failure to vote on the religious liberty schema, they had petitioned the Pope to bring the declaration to the floor for a vote. Cardinal Tisserant said, speaking in the name of the Pope, that the council presidency in agreeing to delay a vote to permit greater study of the declaration had acted in accordance with the procedural rules.

The delay, Cardinal Tisserant said, also was a sign of respect for the individual Fathers' wishes. However, the declaration will come up for discussion and a vote at the next session of the council and, if possible, will have priority on the agenda.

This wrote the end to an attempt by hundreds of Fathers, including many Americans, to bring the declaration to the floor before the end of the third session.

Debate on the matrimony schema was begun by Ernesto Cardinal Ruffini of Palermo, Italy, who called for a clear delineation of the respective roles of Church and state in marriage. The state is competent only in what concerns the purely civil effects of marriage, he said.

He added that it may be advisable to abrogate the excommunication—now contained in canon law—of Catholics who go through the marriage ceremony before non-Catholic ministers. But, he said, if excommunication is removed, the text should contain a stringent prohibition against such an act. He further expressed surprise that anyone would propose as valid for Catholics a marriage contracted contrary to the laws of the Church before a civil magistrate or a non-Catholic minister. Such a proposal is at first sight well nigh unthinkable, he stated.

Jose Cardinal Bueno y Monreal of Seville, Spain, took an opposite view. He said that a mixed marriage contracted before a civil magistrate or a minister should be regarded as valid, but that the parties involved should remain outside of ecclesiastical communion until they repent and make peace with the Church.

He also said he wanted it left to national bishops' conferences to determine such questions as impediments of consanguinity. Furthermore, he said, the impediment of Holy Orders should derive only from priestly ordination and not be applied to subdeacons and deacons or to those with solemn vows.

Cardinal Doepfner proposed sending the whole matter to the Pope. He said that since the question of mixed marriages is extremely urgent and the code of canon law cannot be revised for at least some years, the council should ask the Pope to take steps immediately to implement the legislation proposed in this schema. This was his sole oral suggestion. He submitted his other remarks in writing to save the council's time.

After all the speeches had been given for the day, the moderators put Cardinal Doepfner's suggestion to a vote and it was approved by 1,092 to 427.

Following Cardinal Doepfner, Cardinal Ritter, Bishop Fearns and Archbishop Krol took the floor. They were followed by French Bishop Alexandre Renard of Versailles, who spoke of the problems posed by baptized Catholics who have little or no knowledge of their faith or the sacramental character of marriage. Some priests refuse outright to admit such couples to a marriage before the Church, while others sanction these marriages for fear of further alienating the couples, he said. To remedy this, the council should give pastoral directives on the practical preparation of couples for marriage, he urged. Ordinaries should also have the faculty, he concluded, to permit a marriage to be contracted without any religious rite but only in the presence of a priest and witnesses in cases in which the rite would be offensive.

Switzerland's Bishop Francois Charriere of Lausanne, Geneva and Fribourg declared that mixed marriages are among the greatest pastoral problems of the day and since the times have changed, the Church's legislation should also change. He stated that the promises required by the Church should be abolished because they alienate people. Baptism of the children is a divine duty for the Catholic party, he stated.

He said there should be no prohibition against the parties of a mixed marriage after a Catholic ceremony going to the church or the minister of the non-Catholic party, not to enter into a new contract, but to pray for God's blessing. We must use every means to safeguard family peace in a mixed marriage, he said.

Bishop Paul Yoshigoro Taguchi of Osaka, Japan, agreed that promises should not be demanded of the non-Catholic party and, like the previous speaker, Bishop Charriere, he said mixed marriages should be allowed to take place with Mass. He also said the canonical form should not be essential for the validity of the marriage.

Archbishop Heenan welcomed the proposals for future celebration of mixed marriages. "Until now in many places the ceremonies of a mixed marriage were so stripped of solemnity and joy they were more suitable for a funeral than a wedding. There was no ring, no candles or flowers and—what used to make the bride burst into tears—there was no organ."

By sanctioning more ceremonies, the Church will show it is concerned not only for the Catholic but also for the non-Catholic party. Regarding the usual promises, he said that in general he favored retaining them since the non-Catholic partner is rarely an active member of any religious community and therefore the promise to bring the children up as Catholics rarely causes difficulties.

However, in cases involving non-Catholic partners who cannot in good conscience bring up their children as Catholics, there should be no coercion.

He said it is enough for the non-Catholic party simply not to object to that promise being made by the Catholic party.

He also agreed with the idea that there should be no objection in mixed marriages if the couple, after marriage in a Catholic church, go to the church of the non-Catholic partner to pray and receive a blessing.

Speaking in the name of the Dutch hierarchy, Bishop Petrus Moors of Roermond, the Netherlands, said the Church should try to harmonize its marriage laws with the civil law of the country when possible. He cited the minimum age as an example and asked that no worldwide age be set down because of different conditions throughout the world.

Archbishop William Conway of Armagh, Northern Ireland, declared that the Church's tendency should be to prohibit mixed marriages rather than favoring them in any way. Saying that he was born and raised among the Protestants of North Ireland, he added that non-Catholic Christians share this viewpoint on the inadvisability of mixed marriages for the same reasons as do Catholics. He said it was not a matter of kindliness or diplomacy but of the essential welfare of the Church.

He cautioned against being too hasty in introducing changes in canonical form and promises. He objected that the Fathers had hardly more than a few hours to discuss such a grave problem and said no parliament in the world would act so hastily to change serious and traditional law. Applause greeted this last declaration.

The last speaker of the session was Archbishop Adrianus Djajasepoetra of Jakarta, Indonesia, who said the main element to be stressed about marriage is not the contractual element but rather the element of permanent association for life. Many do not marry for love, but are in love because they are married. Love cannot be regarded as the main element because very often the chief reason for marriage is the aim to have a family.

Midway through the list of speakers, Augustin Cardinal Bea, S.J., president of the Secretariat for Promoting Christian Unity, was called to the rostrum to deliver a report on the declaration on non-Christians. One of his main points was that the declaration is to be attached to the schema on the nature of the Church as an appendix. He said this decision stresses the declaration's religious character and frees it of political aspects and also stresses the importance which the Church accords to other religions.

During the final session, several series of votes were taken. Also announced on Nov. 20 were the results of three votes taken on the Christian education schema on Nov. 19, when the results of only one out of four votes were announced. The remaining three were announced Nov. 20 and all registered great majorities.

The vote on the complete text on ecumenism was 2,054 "yes", 64 "no", and 6 "favorable with reservations."

There were also three votes on the document on the Eastern churches. The first vote—on the introduction and articles two, three and four—was "yes" 1,841, "no" 283. The second vote—on the approval of the general amendments—"yes" 1,923, "no" 188. The third vote was the overall vote on the document. It passed 1,964 "yes" to 135 "no" and one "favorable with reservations."

The declaration on non-Christians which the council approved at its final meeting of the third session is like the mustard seed in that it has grown from a brief statement on the Jews into a treelike document in which all non-Christian religions are finding their place.

That is the way Cardinal Bea described the evolution of the declaration that is to be promulgated at the next session in 1965.

Promulgation was held up because approval came only on the last day of the third session and there are still some 200 written commentaries that have to be studied before the final form is given to it.

Cardinal Bea reported that the council presidency, the Coordinating Commission and the council moderators wanted the declaration to be closely coordinated with the schema on the nature of the Church. But since that schema was to be promulgated at the plenary meeting closing the third council session on Nov. 21, it was decided to add the declaration later as an appendix to the dogmatic constitution on the nature of the Church.

Cardinal Bea said the declaration now has a broader scope than it had in its early forms, since it aims to take in the whole field of relationships of the Church with non-Christian religions. Cardinal Bea acknowledged it was not possible to please everyone, but said that in the declaration the Fathers are dealing with God's plan of salvation, recognizing His benefits, condemning past hatred and injuries and avoiding the same in the future. Thus the Church too, and not just the council, must carry out its mission and may not remain silent.

Cardinal Bea said it is of the greatest importance that the Church, the Christian world and public opinion should have their attention called to the problems set forth in this declaration. The importance and extreme value of the declaration are found in the fruits that are to be hoped will come out of it in the future, he said.

For the first time in the history of ecumenical councils, the principles dealing with non-Christians are set forth in solemn form. The Church has a serious obligation to initiate a dialogue with the one billion men who do not know Christ or His work of redemption, he said. It is the task of the Church to assist them in reaching a full share in the riches of Christ, he concluded.

JAMES C. O'NEILL

Outlines Document On Marriage

The suggestions for canonical legislation on marriage which the council has sent to Pope Paul VI for his own consideration take up little more than two pages of printed text.

But if accepted and enacted, they could give the Church's matrimonial laws a much milder countenance.

All so-called "minor" impediments to marriage would be suppressed.

Future legislation on marriage between Catholics and baptized non-Catholics, or between Catholics and unbaptized persons, would be oriented along the council's guidelines on ecumenism.

The legal procedure in marriage cases would be streamlined. All persons would be assured the help of a qualified lawyer without cost.

The original schema on marriage was drawn up in 1963 during the interim between the council's first and second sessions. The Commission on Discipline of the Sacraments prepared this document by synthesizing the extensive studies on marriage carried out by its predecessor, the preparatory commission.

However, in January of 1964, the Coordinating Commission decided to reduce the schema to a simple series of suggestions for reform of the Church's law on marriage. Such reform would be determined by the demands of the care of souls, or what is called the pastoral ministry.

Marriage as a sacrament is not treated in detail by this set of suggestions. However, the sacrament of Matrimony is touched upon by the council's documents on the nature of the Church, on the apostolate of the laity, and on the Church in the modern world.

The present text is divided into three parts:

The first part recalls a number of basic principles, such as Matrimony's sacred character and holiness of marriage contracted between two baptized persons as members of Christ. Their union can be closely related to Christ's union with His Church, it says.

It touches on the Church's competence in safeguarding the integrity of the sacrament of Matrimony and its consequent right to make laws on marriage.

The second part offers guidelines for a revision of Church law in view of the needs of our times, especially those created by more fluid emigration and the emergence of new states.

It suggests suppression of minor impediments, among which are consanguinity in the third degree of the collateral line, affinity in the second degree of the collateral line, and spiritual relationships arising from sponsorship in Baptism or Confirmation.

It recommends simplification of the formalities required for marriage in the presence of a priest authorized to bless the marriage. The local bishop will have closer control over the so-called extraordinary form of marriage, that is, when the presence of a priest is impossible.

The third and last part urges pastors of souls to regard preparation for marriage as a serious duty of their ministry. Pastors should seek the collaboration of other priests or competent lay persons, both men and women, in this instruction and preparation for marriage. They should try to know the engaged couple personally in order to strengthen them in Christian faith and Christian living. Pastors should carefully carry out the required premarriage investigation and never permit a marriage unless they are fully convinced that both parties have given full consent. They should make sure the marriage ceremony reflects the deep meaning of the sacrament, allowing those at the ceremony to participate actively in the liturgy.

Pastors should continue their interest in the couple even after their marriage, counseling them on new problems that will arise in the education of their children.

Cardinal Ritter

This is the text of the address delivered by Joseph Cardinal Ritter of St. Louis in the ecumenical council Nov. 20 on the document on matrimony.

I am highly pleased by the votum "On the Sacrament of Matrimony" and more particularly on the suggested dispositions affecting inter-confessional marriages.

In its fifth paragraph the proposed votum would introduce two very important departures from the present legislation: the one concerns the premarital guarantees, the other the canonical form.

The new approach to the guarantees, it seems to me, is particularly praiseworthy in that it serves both truth and charity. Herein the Church is concerned with the observance of divine law and the safeguarding of personal right. It is evident that the new disposition would safeguard the right to marry more realistically than the present law. Moreover, the new approach would more effectively secure respect for the divine law. The norms of the Code of Canon Law often enough obscure the existence of a divine law, and by insisting over much on juridical procedure, emphasize ecclesiastical law beyond measure. Adoption of the suggested proposal would strengthen respect for divine law, by stressing more emphatically the role of personal responsibility. Responsibility for the security of his own faith as well as for the Catholic education of children is rightly placed on the Catholic party. In this way we can lessen the possibility of offense to the consciences of our separated brethren.

The schema proceeds wisely and prudently in its approach to the canonical form. It offers a middle course between the extremes of inflexible retention and complete relaxation of the form. Although each extreme has its adherents, I believe that this compromise affords the best response to the needs of our time. On the side the schema supports the general retention of the canonical form of marriage for validity in such cases. Not a few Fathers will find this displeasing and they can point out that the clandestinity of marriage, which the Tridentine legislation was intended to counteract, is no longer a problem. However, a new pastoral problem has presented itself in some countries—the high incidence of early and hasty marriage with a probability of subsequent divorce—which recommends the retention of the form for validity.

Nonetheless, to demonstrate our respect for human dignity and to reduce the principles of ecumenism to practice, it is apparent that in some cases, the Ordinary must be empowered to grant dispensation from the form. This disposition is closer to the spirit of Trent than the existing norms. It would be well to remember that in the decree "Tametsi," the Council of Trent, treating of clandestine marriages already contracted, stated:

"Inasmuch as we must not doubt that clandestine marriages contracted by the consent of the parties are true marriages as long as the Church did not make them invalid; they are rightly condemned who deny that these are true and valid marriages, and this Sacred Synod so condemns them. . . . (Denz 990)."

Finally for the sake of honesty and justice, those baptized in the Catholic Church who have been reared without Catholic education must not be bound by the canonical form of marriage, nor restricted by any impediments of merely ecclesiastical law.

I conclude by asking that these norms which answer so well the pressing needs of many persons be enacted and promulgated without delay. In serving the cause of truth and charity we must transcend considerations of our own convenience and procedural efficiency.

Closing of Council's Third Session

November 21, 1964

With the proclamation of the constitution on the nature of the Church and the decrees on ecumenism and the Eastern Churches, Pope Paul VI solemnly brought the third session of the ecumenical council to a close in the presence of the entire body of the Church's bishops.

During the course of the ceremony he proclaimed Mary "Mother of the Church" and announced that the council will have its "definitive conclusion in the fourth session." The date for this session was not announced, and speculation in council circles has ranged all the way from March of next year to a date sometime during 1966.

In a surprise move, Pope Paul VI changed the Eucharistic fast regulations, reducing the time of fasting from solid foods before Communion from three hours to one hour.

Archbishop Pericle Felici, secretary general of the council, made the announcement during the council's closing session. He said the new relaxation applies to priests as well as to the faithful, and was made "at the request of bishops of many countries."

The proclamation of the council's most important document on the Church came immediately after a Mass concelebrated by Pope Paul and 24 council Fathers. Each of them has within his diocese a major Marian shrine and was chosen to concelebrate for this reason. The Mass was that of the day's feast — the Presentation of Mary in the Temple. Among the celebrants was Archbishop Patrick A. O'Boyle of Washington, in whose diocese the National Shrine of the Immaculate Conception is located.

After Archbishop Felici briefly read from the beginning and end of each chapter, a formal vote on the constitution was taken. The results were tabulated almost immediately: 2,151 affirmative to five negative.

The bishops were directed to stand and remove their mitres, and Pope Paul began:

"In the name of the Holy and Undivided Trinity, the Father, Son and Holy Spirit. The dogmatic Constitution on the Church, which has now been read in brief in this sacred and universal Second Vatican Synod,

lawfully assembled, has pleased the Fathers. And we, by the apostolic authority given to us by Christ, together with the venerable Fathers, in the Holy Spirit approve, decree and enact this constitution and command that what has been thus enacted in the synod be promulgated for the glory of God."

Thunderous applause broke out in the basilica.

The same formula was carried through for the two decrees, first that on the Eastern Churches, then on ecumenism. The first was affirmed by a vote of 2,110 to 39, and the second by 2,137 to 11.

In obvious deference to the patriarchs of the Eastern Churches who are mentioned prominently in the decree, Pope Paul then announced through Archbishop Felici that its implementation was to take place in two months, but he granted to the patriarchs "the faculty of reducing or prolonging this time for just cause."

Each proclamation was followed by prolonged applause.

Concluding the ceremony, the Pope spoke for a half hour, praising the assembly for having "studied and described the doctrine on the Church, thus completing the doctrinal task of this Second Vatican Council . . . .

"Henceforth it will be possible to have a fuller understanding of the thought of God in relation to the Mystical Body of Christ, and we shall be able to draw therefrom clearer and surer norms for the life of the Church, greater strength in order to lead men to salvation, better hopes for the progress of the Kingdom of Christ in the world . . . .

"We are very pleased that this doctrine has been studied with an abundance of documentation and careful study and has been brought to clear conclusions. It is a duty to do this, to complete the teaching of the First Vatican Council. It was the time to do it, because of advances of theological studies in modern times, because of the spread of the Church throughout the world, and the problems encountered by ecclesiastical government in the daily life of the Church, and because of the expectations of many bishops who are anxiously awaiting a clarification of the Church's doctrine pertaining to them."

This was a reference to the most hotly debated issue contained in the document, the third chapter's doctrine of "collegiality" of bishops, which states that they are successors of the apostles as the Pope is the successor of St. Peter, and that together with the Pope as their head they exercise "full and supreme authority over the Church."

It was not the Pope's intention, nor that of the council, to proclaim a solemn infallible doctrine by this constitution. This was made clear throughout the last days of council voting, and was reiterated by the Pope in his talk.

This constitution "was the way to handle this question," he said. "And thus we do not hesitate, bearing in mind the explanation furnished on the doctrine and the terminology to be used, as also the theological qualification which the council intends to give to its teachings, to promulgate this present constitution on the Church."

The "theological qualification" was clearly stated a few days before in the council session: "supreme teaching authority but not infallible."

"The best commentary on this doctrine is that through it nothing is really changed in the doctrine of the Church. What Christ wanted, we want also. What was present remains. What the Church taught for centuries we teach also. The only difference is that what was simply lived previously is now expressed; what was uncertain and not clear, what was meditated on and discussed and in some part a point of controversy has now reached a calm formulation."

The last chapter of the document contains a glowing tribute to Mary and clarifies her role in the Church's makeup and life. Referring to this chapter, the Pope pointed out that it is "the first time an ecumenical council presents such a vast synthesis of the place of Mary in the mystery of Christ and the Church , . . ."

"In fact, the reality of the Church is not exhausted through her hierarchical structure, her sacraments, her juridical ordinances. Her intimate essence and the explanation of her fecundity are to be searched for in her close union with Christ, a union which cannot be separated from her who is the mother of the Word Incarnate and whom Jesus Christ Himself wanted so near to Himself in the mystery of our salvation . . . knowledge of the exact doctrine of the Church on Mary will always be the key to a precise understanding of the mystery of Christ and His Church."

These things make us feel, the Pope said, "that this is the most solemn and appropriate moment to accede to a desire which has called for an explicit declaration during this council of the maternal role of the Virgin over the Christian people. To achieve this end we have felt it opportune to consecrate in this public session a title suggested from various parts of the Christian world and which is particularly dear to us, because in a marvelous synthesis it sums up the privileged position recognized by the council for the Virgin Mary in the Holy Church.

"For the glory of the Virgin Mary and for our own consolation, we proclaim Mary the Mother of the Church, that is of the whole People of God, of the faithful as well as of the pastors, and we wish that through this title the Mother of God should be still more honored and invoked by the entire Christian people."

Twice during this announcement the Pope was interrupted by applause. When he finished, a standing ovation signified warm assent by the council Fathers.

It was not the only applause during his talk, however. Clapping also followed the Pope's clear indication that he would make use of the long-discussed "senate" or permanent council of bishops in conjunction with a newly reformed Roman Curia.

"The constant recurrence of new problems in the modern world will make us even more disposed than we are now to convoke and to consult at determined times some of your number, venerable brothers (of the council), designated in ways to be determined, in order to have around us the comfort of your presence, the help of your experience, the support of your counsel and the assistance of your authority. This will be useful also because the reorganization of the Roman Curia, which is now undergoing careful study, will be able to profit from the experience and help of diocesan bishops, thus integrating its organization and drawing help from their wisdom and their charity.

"This plurality of studies and discussions will undoubtedly entail practical difficulties. Collective action is always more difficult than individual action. But we shall endeavor in a spirit of charity and mutual collaboration to overcome all the obstacles."

He spoke of the work still remaining on the council's agenda, particularly the schema under revision on the Church in the modern world and the declaration on religious liberty. The latter was blocked from its first vote at the eleventh hour of this session, just two days before, by a vastly unpopular decision of the council's presidency.

Of the former he said: "The Church is for the world. The Church seeks no other earthly power for herself than that which will make it possible for her to serve and to love. As she perfects her thought and her structure, the Church does not aim to separate herself from the experience of individual men but rather endeavors to understand them better while sharing their sufferings and their aspirations. This place of the Church in the world, studied and discussed already in this session, will find its complete development in the next and last session."

The religious liberty text, he said, "only because

of lack of time at the end of this session could not be brought to a conclusion." It was on this basis, and because of the claim by a reported 100 council Fathers that the redrafted text was too drastically revised to vote intelligently in such a short time, that Eugene Cardinal Tisserant the previous Thursday had announced that the vote would be held over until the fourth session.

Almost 1,000 Fathers appealed to the Pope for a reversal of this decision, but according to reliable sources he refused to interfere with the council presidents, who have the authority to make such agenda changes by council rules.

Turning to another aspect of religious liberty, Pope Paul paid tribute to those suffering persecution for their Faith, a recurring theme during the third session's deliberations.

"We are consoled by the thought of those of our brothers and sons who live in areas where they are denied sufficient and dignified liberty of religion, to the point that they must be numbered in the ranks of the Church of Silence and Tears. Their sufferings and their fidelity offer a stupendous witness to the Church as they imitate Christ, the Victim for the salvation of the world."

He linked the decree on ecumenism, opening vast new possibilities for Catholics to work together with non-Catholics in areas which do not compromise belief, with the Constitution on the Church.

"We trust this doctrine (on the Church) will be kindly and favorably received by Christians as yet separated from us. May it have for them the role of a stimulus to that revision of ideas and attitudes which may bring them closer to our communion and finally, God willing, make them one with us. In this doctrine they can know that the Church, as she traces the outlines of her own image, does not restrict but rather widens the confines of her charity and does not slow down the march of her progressive, multiform and inviting catholicity.

"At this point we wish to express our reverent greeting to the observers representing Christian churches or confessions separated from us. We thank them for assisting at the council sessions, and extend our warmest greetings for their Christian prosperity."

In conclusion the Pope announced his intention to send a special mission in the near future to Fatima, Portugal, "to carry a golden rose to the sanctuary of Fatima, dear not only to the noble Portuguese people—always, but particularly today, dearest to us — but also known and venerated by the faithful throughout the entire Catholic world."

"In this manner," he said, "we intend to entrust to the care of this heavenly mother the entire human family with its problems and worries, with its lawful aspirations and ardent hopes."

The golden rose is a traditional sign of personal tribute by a pope to a nation, organization, or members of a particular Church. The gesture of sending it to the Portuguese shrine at this particular time struck many Vatican observers as a gentle answer by Pope Paul to severe criticism from Portuguese sources of his coming trip to India in early December to attend the International Eucharistic Congress in Bombay.

Relations between India and Portugal have been severed since the Indians forcibly took over Portugal's longtime Indian colony of Goa more than three years ago. Portuguese authorities have suppressed all public comment on the Eucharistic Congress and the Pope's trip. In one recent incident the government seized copies of a Catholic magazine that carried an article on the congress, indefinitely suspended its license to publish, and withdrew its recognition of its publisher, a missionary community, as a missionary congregation.

In all the Pope was interrupted seven times by warm and prolonged applause, increasing in intensity as the speech progressed.

The beginning of the morning's ceremonies was silent, however. Contrary to his usual custom in Rome, the Pope entered the basilica on his gestatorial chair without any greeting or applause from the congregation. The recessional at the end was quite different, in fact, tumultuous, with cheers and shouts, sustained clapping and cries of "Viva il Papa."

When he entered, the bishops were already in their usual places in the temporary stands erected for the council down the center portion of the basilica. They were dressed in cope and mitre. The cardinals and patriarchs entered in the papal procession and took their places at the front of the hall.

The Mass began immediately. It was a high Mass, sung in familiar chants by the council Fathers and virtually the entire congregation. The Epistle and the Gospel were recited from the high altar facing the congregation, while the Pope sat on his portable throne below and in back. After the Creed was sung the Pope recited the newly introduced "Prayer of the People," which according to the new Liturgy introduced at the council's last session, varies with the occasion.

He prayed: "Let us, beloved brothers, ask God the Father Almighty suppliantly that He who has gathered the pastors of the Church in the Holy Spirit may abundantly pour out on them all the gifts of His love, through His only begotten Son."

The Julian Choir took up the prayer and intoned verses from the Litany of the Saints.

Then the concelebrants, who had been ranged around the foot of the altar in a semicircle up to this point, mounted the altar steps and continued the mutual offering of the Mass with the Pope.

Their voices could be heard one after another

as the mircrophone was moved around the altar — except during the Consecration when the basilica's organ burst forth, accompanied by golden trumpets.

Concelebrants of the day were:

Latin-rite Patriarch Alberto Gori of Jerusalem, whose jurisdiction includes the basilica of the Annunciation at Nazareth; Archbishop Primo Principi, Pontifical administrator of Loreto sanctuary in Italy; Bishop Pierre Theas of Tarbes and Lourdes, France; Bishop Joao Pereira Venancio of Leiria, Portugal, whose jurisdiction includes the shrine of Fatima; Archbishop Pedro Cantero Cuadrado of Zaragoza, Spain, with its shrine of Our Lady of the Pilar.

Abbot Raymond Tschudy, O.S.B., of the independent abbey of the Most Holy Virgin Mary of Einsiedeln, Switzerland; Bishop Thomas Leo Parker of Northhampton, England, with the shrine of Our Lady of Walsingham; Bishop Stefan Barela of Czestochowa, Poland; Bishop Joseph Schoiswohl of Graz-Seckau, Austria, representing the shrine of Our Lady of Mariazell; Bishop Matthias Wehr of Trier, Germany, representing the shrine of Maria Laach; Archbishop Joseph Walsh of Tuam, Ireland, representing the sanctuary of Our Lady of Knock; Archbishop Michael Gonzi of Malta, representing the shrine of Melheha; Bishop Andre Marie Charue of Namur, representing all the Marian shrines of Belgium;

Jose Cardinal Garibi y Rivera of Guadalajara, Mexico, representing the shrine of Our Lady of Guadalupe; Coadjutor Archbishop Pablo Munoz Vega of Quito, Ecuador, representing the shrine of Our Lady of El Quinche; Archbishop Abel Antezana y Rojas of La Paz, Bolivia, representing the shrine of Our Lady of Copacabana; Bishop Luis Tome of Mercedes, Argentina, representing the Shrine of Our Lady of Lujan; Auxiliary Bishop Antonio Ferreira de Macedo of Sao Paulo, Brazil, representing the shrine of the Aparecida; Archbishop Patrick A. O'Boyle of Washington, representing the National Shrine of the Immaculate Conception; Archbishop Leon Duval of Algiers, representing the shrine of Our Lady of Africa; Bishop Michel Ntuyahaga of Usumbura, Burundi, representing the shrine of Mugera; Bishop Rajarethinam Sundaram of Tanjore, India, representing the Shrine of Velangani; and Archbishop Thomas Cooray of Colombo, Ceylon, representing the shrine of Tewatta.

The rest of the ceremony followed the pattern of the third session's opening concelebrated Mass according to the newly devised rite of concelebrations.

After the Mass the papal throne was set up in front of the high altar and the choir sang the hymn "Christus Vincit" (Christ Conquers).

The patriarchs and two representatives of the cardinals paid tribute to the Pope, kneeling before him and kissing his ring, after which he led the assembly in the prayer regularly recited at the beginning of each council session.

Then followed the singing of "Come Holy Spirit," alternating between the choir and the congregation.

Taking his usual position at the rostrum in the body of the basilica, Archbishop Felici began to read the documents, pausing before each to refer to the Pope as "Paul, bishop, one of the council Fathers."

This was another outright expression of the collegiality proclaimed in the constitution on the Church and referred to over and over again in the Pope's speech.

"We cannot thank God enough," the Pope said, "for having granted to us the happy lot of honoring the sacred character of your ministry, O Venerated Brothers, the fulness of your priesthood, and recognizing the solidarity that exists between you and us.

"We have been edified to read how the primary, singular and worldwide mission entrusted by Christ to Peter and to his successors, the Roman pontiffs, has been amply and repeatedly recognized in this solemn document on the Church.

"This is not because of the prestige thereby deriving to our poor person, but because of the honor rendered to the word of Christ from the coherence manifested with the teaching and tradition of the Church, and from the effective harmony and government of the Church.

"It was important that this recognition of the prerogatives of the Sovereign Pontiff should come at a time when the question of episcopal authority was being discussed in the Church, in order that this authority would not be in contrast with the power of the Pope but should stand out in full harmony with the Vicar of Christ as head of the Apostolic College.

"Thus the power of the episcopate finds in the successor of St. Peter, not power diverse and extrinsic to its own, but rather its center and head. This in turn makes us anxious to laud your own prerogatives and to set them off in their proper light, so as to integrate them with our own. In this we fear no diminishing of our authority. Rather are we strengthened in the task of governing the Church by knowing that you are closely united with us and that all of us are closely united in the name of Christ."   FATHER JOHN P. DONNELLY

Council Box Score

Here is a box score on Second Vatican Council accomplishments through the first three sessions.

Council acts debated, amended and promulgated:

The Constitution on the Liturgy and the Decree on Communications Media, in the second session (1963).

The Constitution on the Nature of the Church and Decrees on Ecumenism and the Eastern Churches, in the third session (1964).

Schemata debated, amended, but not voted upon in final form:

The Pastoral Duties of Bishops, and the statement on non-Christians, including Jews. This statement is to be an appendix to the Constitution on the Nature of the Church.

Schemata debated and sent back for amendment, but still completely in commission hands:

Divine Revelation, Religious, Seminaries, the Church in the Modern World, Christian Education, Lay Apostolate.

Schemata debated and sent back for complete revision:

Missions, Priestly Life and Ministry.

Schemata not brought to the floor after being debated and sent back for amending:

Religious Liberty.

Schemata transferred from conciliar authority and placed in the hands of the Pope:

Matrimony.

Pope Paul's Speech At Closing Session

This is a translation of the speech delivered Nov. 21 by Pope Paul VI at the closing session of the ecumenical council's third session.

After two months of intense brotherly effort, we render thanks to God for the happy celebration of this Second Vatican Ecumenical Council, of which we conclude today the third session with this solemn and sacred assembly. Truly indeed, we must offer God the expression of our grateful and rejoicing souls for having granted us the great fortune of being present and, what is more, the fortune of ourselves giving consistency, meaning and fulness to this historic and providential event as humble and happy protagonists. Truly we may regard as spoken for us today the words of the Gospel: "Blessed are the eyes that see what you see and the ears that hear what you hear" [Matt. 13, 16].

Here is present before us, in the persons of its shepherds followed by their respective flocks, the Holy Church of God, called together by Him through our voice. Here is the Catholic hierarchy on whom it is incumbent to form and guide the holy People of God, gathered together in one place, in one sentiment, with one prayer, one faith, one charity on their lips and in their hearts.

We shall never tire of admiring, nor shall we ever forget this incomparable assembly entirely intent on proclaiming the glory of the Father, the Son and the Holy Spirit, concerned only with re-evoking the blessed words of revelation and penetrating into their true and deep sense.

This is an assembly of men free like none other from self-interest and engaged in giving witness to divine truths; men as we are, weak and fallible, but convinced of being able to pronounce truths that admit neither contradiction nor termination; men who are sons of our own times and our own earth, yet above time and above earth in order to take upon our shoulders the burdens of our brothers and to lead them to spiritual salvation. This we do with a love greater than these same hearts that house it, with a strained effort that might seem foolhardy, but is full of serene trust in its search for the meaning of human life and history to give it value, greatness, beauty, union in Christ, only in Christ Our Lord!

Brethren, the fact that you are here is stupendous. It is stupendous for those who behold us from the outside. Never shall we behold a scene more impressive, more pious, more dramatic or more solemn.

Our happiness increases as, in this final moment of the council session we are about to close, we recall the things that have been discussed, the things finally approved. The doctrine on the Church has been described and studied, and thus the doctrinal task of the First Vatican Ecumenical Council has been completed. The mystery of the Church was explored, and the divine plan of its fundamental constitution was outlined.

Once again we thank God for this happy result and we allow our souls to be filled with legitimate bliss. From now on we can enjoy greater understanding of divine thought relative to the Mystical Body of Christ, and from this we can draw clearer and safer rules for the life of the Church, greater energy for her incessant effort to lead men to salvation, further hope for the progress of the reign of Christ in the world. Let us bless the Lord.

Too much would need to be said on the work accomplished. Deserving of special mention are the reverent and exacting studies to make this doctrine conform perfectly with Biblical truth and the genuine tradition of the Church; the efforts made to discover the innermost significance and substantial truth of the constitutional law of the Church herself, to determine what is immobile and certain therein and what is a derivation by a process of natural and authoritative evolution from basic principles. The purpose of this has been to provide a fair treatment of every part, every function and every aim of the Mystical Body. It remains true that the most difficult and most memorable part of these spiritual efforts revolved around the doctrine on the episcopate. And on this point alone we should like to dwell briefly.

We shall say only that we are satisfied that this doctrine has been enacted with sufficient breadth of study and discussion and with similar clarity of conclusion. It was a duty to do this, being a completion of the First Vatican Ecumenical Council. It was the time to do it because of the advance of theological studies in modern times; because of the spread of the Church throughout the world; because of the problems encountered by ecclesiastical government in the daily life of the Church, and because of the expectations of many bishops who were anxiously awaiting a clarification of the Church's doctrine pertaining to them. That was also the way to handle the question. Thus we do not hesitate—bearing in mind the explanations furnished both on the interpretation to be given the terms used, as well as the theological qualification which this council intends to give to the doctrine discussed—we do not hesitate, with the help of God, to promulgate the present constitution On the Nature of the Church.

It would seem to us that the best commentary is that through this promulgation nothing in traditional doctrine is really changed. What Christ wants, we also want. That which was remains. What the Church has taught for centuries, we likewise teach. The only difference is that what was simply lived previously is now declared expressly; what was uncertain has been clarified; what was meditated on, discussed and in part disagreed with now reaches a serene formulation.

Truly we can say that Divine Providence has prepared a shining hour for us; yesterday slowly maturing, today resplendent, tomorrow surely rich in teachings, to stimulate and improve the life of the Church.

We also say we are happy this constitution renders honor also to the People of God. Nothing can give us greater pleasure than to see proclaimed the dignity of all our brothers and sons who make up the Holy People of God, to whose vocation, to whose sanctification, to whose salvation and guidance the hierarchical ministry is oriented.

How happy we are also to see the constitution proclaim the dignity of our brothers in the episcopate, honor their role in the Church and recognize their powers. We cannot thank God sufficiently for having granted us the privilege of honoring the sacred character of your ministry and the fulness of your priesthood, beloved and venerated brothers, to acknowledge the loyalty that binds you to each other and to us.

We have observed with edification how the principal, unique and universal mission entrusted to Peter by Christ and transmitted to his successors, the Roman Pontiffs, whose authority we today hold, unworthy as we are, is fully and repeatedly recognized and venerated in this solemn document which we have just promulgated.

We cannot fail to be pleased by this, not for the prestige deriving from it to our person, since we are fearful rather than eager for such a mission, but for the honor rendered to the word of Christ, for the consistency manifested with the teaching and the tradition of the Church, for the guarantee assured for the unity of the Church itself and the harmonious and secure effectiveness assured to her government. It was of highest importance that this recognition of the prerogatives of the office of the sovereign pontiff should be stated explicitly at this time when the question of episcopal authority in the Church was to be dealt with in order that this authority would not be in contrast with the power of the pope but should stand out in full harmony with the vicar of Christ as head of the apostolic college.

And it is this intimate and essential relation that makes a unified assembly of the episcopate, that finds in the successor of Peter, not different and extraneous, but rather its center and head. This in turn makes us anxious to laud your prerogatives with ours, to rejoice in their exaltation, to vindicate their excellence, so as to integrate them with our own. Thus acknowledging the episcopal mission in its fulness, we feel the communion of faith, of charity, of co-responsibility, of collaboration increasing around us.

We do not fear that our authority will be lessened nor hampered while we acknowledge and extol yours; but rather we feel stronger because of the tie that draws us together; we feel more able to guide the universal Church with the knowledge that each of you is working toward the same end; we feel more trustful in the help of Christ because we are and want to be all gathered together more closely in His name.

It is not easy to say what practical consequences these doctrinal clarifications may have, but it is not difficult to foresee that they will be fruitful in spiritual insights and canonical ordinances.

The ecumenical council will have its definite conclusion with the fourth session. But the application of its decrees will involve a network of post-conciliar commissions in which the collaboration of the bishops will be indispensable; as likewise the occurrence of questions of general interest to the modern world will make us even more disposed than we now are, venerable brothers, to call some of you, designated, at the proper time, together and consult you at determined times, in order to have around us the comfort of your presence, the help of your experience, the support of your counsel, the assistance of your authority. This will be useful also because the reorganization of the Roman Curia, which is now undergoing careful study, will be able to profit from the experienced help of diocesan bishops, thus integrating its organization, already so efficient in faithful service, with bishops from various countries bringing the help of their wisdom and charity. This plurality of studies and discussions may entail some practical difficulties. Collective action is more complicated than individual action, but if it better serves the monarchical and hierarchical character of the Church, and comforts our labor with your cooperation, we shall be able to overcome with prudence and charity the obstacles inherent in a more complex organization of ecclesiastical government.

We like to think that the doctrine of the mystery of the Church, illustrated and proclaimed by this council will, from this moment, find a positive echo in the minds of Catholics. Especially it will let the faithful see the real face of the bride of Christ more fully delineated and revealed; it will let them see the beauty of their mother and teacher; the simplicity and the majesty of the lines of such a venerable institution; it will let them admire a prodigy of historical fidelity, of stupendous sociology, of outstanding legislation, a forward-moving realm in which divine and human elements blend in order to reflect on believing humanity the outlines of the Incarnation and the Redemption—the whole Christ Our Saviour, to use the expression of St. Augustine.

May this spectacle bring intoxicating joy especially to those whose only and constant profession is the search of Christian perfection. We mean the Religious, who are the exemplary members of the Church, its generous supporters, its dearest sons.

And may joy and consolation come also to those our brothers and sons who live in places where sufficient and dignified religious liberty is still denied to them or is so restricted that we have to number them in ranks of the Church of silence and tears. Let them rejoice in the doctrinal splendor that illuminates Holy Church, to which their suffering and fidelity offers stupendous witness, thereby deserving for themselves the greater glory—that of Christ, victim for the salvation of the world.

We also hope that the same doctrine of the Church will be benevolently and favorably considered by the Christian brothers who are still separate from us. We wish that this doctrine, completed by the declarations contained in the schema On Ecumenism, likewise approved by this council, might have in their souls the power of a loving leaven for the revision of thoughts and attitudes which may draw them closer to our communion, and finally, God willing, may merge them in it. To us this same doctrine gives the surprising joy of observing how the Church, by precisely tracing its own outlines, does not restrict, but widens the boundaries of its charity and does not check the movement of its multiform progress, inviting catholicity.

May we be allowed at this point to express, on this occasion also, our reverent greeting to the observers who are here representing Christian Churches or confessions separate from us, our thanks for their welcome assistance at the conciliar meetings, and our warmest wishes for their Christian prosperity.

And finally we should like the doctrine of the Church to radiate some attractive light on the profane world in which it lives and by which it is surrounded. It must appear like a sign raised among the peoples [Is. 5,26] to offer orientation to all on their way toward truth and life. In fact as anyone can see, while the elaboration of this doctrine observes the theological rigor that justifies and magnifies it, it never forgets mankind which assembles in the Church and which constitutes the historical and social environment in which its mission is exercised. The Church is for the world. The Church does not desire any other earthly power for itself than that which enables it to serve and to love. By perfecting its thought and its structure, the Church does not aim at estranging itself from the experience which is proper to the men of its time, but it aims rather at understanding them better, at sharing better in their sufferings and their good aspirations, at better sustaining the effort of modern man toward his prosperity, his liberty, his peace. But this recurrent theme will have its development at the end of the council when the schema on religious liberty, which will crown the work of the council, and which, only because of lack of time at the end of this session, could not be ended, and the one on relations between the Church and the world, which has already been deliberated on at the present session, will be finally and completely treated at the next session.

And now, in conclusion, another thought strikes us. Our thought, venerable brothers, cannot but rise with sentiments of sincere and filial gratitude to the Holy Virgin. Also, to her whom we like to regard as the protectress of the present council, the witness of our toil, our most kindly adviser, because it is to her, as a heavenly patron, together with St. Joseph, that the work of our ecumenical assembly was entrusted by Pope John XXIII right from the start.

Moved by these same sentiments, last year we offered to the Most Blessed Mary a solemn act of common homage, by gathering in the Liberian basilica, round the image venerated with the glorious title of "Salus Populi Romani" (Salvation of the Roman people).

This year, the homage of our council appears much more precious and significant. By the promulgation of today's constitution, which has as its crown and summit a whole chapter dedicated to Our Lady, we can rightly affirm that the present session ends as an incomparable hymn of praise in honor of Mary.

It is the first time, in fact—and saying it fills our souls with profound emotion—that an ecumenical council presents such a vast synthesis of the Catholic doctrine regarding the place which the Blessed Mary occupies in the mystery of Christ and of the Church.

This corresponds to the aim which this council set itself of manifesting the countenance of the Holy Church, to which Mary is closely linked, and of which, as it has been authoritatively affirmed, she is "portio maxima, portio optima, portio praecipua, portio electissima" [greatest, finest, principal, most elect part] (Rupert, in Apc. I,VII, c 12, P.L. 169,10434).

Truly, the reality of the Church is not exhausted in its hierarchial structure, in its liturgy, in its sacraments, in its juridical ordinances. The intimate, the primary source of its sanctifying effectiveness are to be sought in its mystic union with Christ; a union which we cannot conceive as separate from her who is the Mother of the Word Incarnate and whom Jesus Christ Himself wanted closely united to Himself for our salvation. Thus the loving contemplation of the marvels worked by God in His Holy Mother must find its proper perspective in the vision of the Church. And knowledge of the true Catholic doctrine on Mary will always be a key to the exact understanding of the mystery of Christ and of the Church.

Meditation on these close relationships between Mary and the Church, so clearly established in today's conciliar Constitution, makes us feel that this is the most solemn and appropriate moment to fulfill a wish which, after we mentioned it at the end of the preceding session, very many council Fathers made their own, pressing for an explicit declaration at this council of the Motherly role of the Virgin among the Christian people.

To achieve this aim, we have felt it opportune to consecrate in this very public session, a title which was suggested in honor of the Virgin from various parts of the Catholic world and which is particularly dear to us because it sums up in an admirable synthesis the privileged position recognized by the council for the Virgin in the Holy Church.

Therefore, for the glory of the Virgin Mary and for our own consolation, we proclaim the Most Blessed Mary Mother of the Church, that is to say of all the people of God, of the faithful as well as of the pastors, who call her the most loving Mother. And we wish that the Mother of God should be still more honored and invoked by the entire Christian people by this most sweet title.

This is a title, venerable brothers, not new to Christian piety; it is precisely by this title, in preference to all others, that the faithful and the Church address Mary. It truly is part of the genuine substance of devotion to Mary, finding its justification in the very dignity of the Mother of the word Incarnate.

Just as, in fact, the divine maternity is the basis for her special relationship with Christ, and for her presence in the economy of salvation brought about by Jesus Christ, thus it also constitutes the principal basis for the relations between Mary and the Church, since she is the mother of Him who, right from the time of His Incarnation in her virginal bosom, joined to Himself as head His Mystical Body which is the Church. Mary, then as mother of Christ, is mother also of all the faithful and of all the pastors.

It is therefore with a soul full of trust and filial love that we raise our glance to her, despite our unworthiness and weakness. She, who has given us in Jesus the fountainhead of grace, will not fail to succor the Church, now flourishing through the abundance of the gifts of the Holy Ghost and setting herself with new zeal to the fulfilment of its mission of salvation.

And our trust is even more lively and fully corroborated if we consider the very close links between this heavenly Mother of ours and mankind. Although adorned by God with the riches of admirable prerogatives, to make her a worthy Mother of the Word Incarnate, she is nevertheless very close to us. Daughter of Adam, like ourselves, and therefore our sister through ties of nature, she is, however, the creature who was preserved from original sin in view of the merits of the Saviour, and who possesses besides the privileges obtained the personal virtue of a total and exemplary faith, thus deserving the evangelical praise "beata quae credidisti (blessed art thou who believed). In her earthly life, she realized the perfect image of the disciple of Christ, reflected every virtue, and incarnated the evangelical beatitudes proclaimed by Christ. Therefore in her, the entire Church, in its incomparable variety of life and of work, attains the most authentic form of the perfect imitation of Christ.

We trust then, that with the promulgation of the Constitution On the Church, sealed by the proclamation of Mary as Mother of the Church, that is to say of all the faithful and all the pastors, the Christian people may, with greater ardor, turn to the Holy Virgin and render to her the honor and devotion due to her.

As for ourselves, just as at the invitation of Pope John XXIII we entered the council hall, along with "Mary, the Mother of Jesus," so at the close of the third session we leave this temple with the most holy and sweet name of Mary, Mother of the Church.

As a sign of gratitude for her loving assistance, lavished on us during this last conciliar period, let each of you, venerable brothers, pledge himself to hold high among the Christian people the name and the honor of Mary, indicating in her the model of faith and of the full response to any call from God, the model of the full assimilation of the teaching of Christ and of His charity, so that all the faithful, united in the name of the common Mother, may feel themselves ever more firmly rooted in the faith and in union with Jesus Christ, and at the same time fervent in charity toward the brothers, promoting love for the poor, dedication to justice and defense of peace. As the great St. Ambrose exhorted: "sit in singulis Mariae anima ut magnificet Dominum; sit in singulis spiritus Mariae et exultet in Deo" [Let the soul of Mary be in individuals, that it may magnify the Lord; let the spirit of Mary be in individuals, that it may rejoice in the Lord] (St. Ambrose, Exp. in Luc. II, 26, 15, 1642).

Above all, we desire that it should be made clear that Mary, the humble handmaid of the Lord, exists only in relation to God and to Christ, our sole Mediator and Redeemer. And likewise, may the true nature and the aims of the Marian veneration in the Church be illustrated, particularly where there are many separated brothers, so that those who are not part of the Catholic community may understand that devotion to Mary, far from being an end in itself, is instead a means essentially ordained to orient souls to Christ and thus unite them with the Father in the love of the Holy Ghost.

While we turn in ardent prayer to the Virgin, that she may bless the ecumenical council and the entire Church, hastening the hour of the union of all Christians, our glance opens on the endless horizons of the whole world, the object of the most lively care of the ecumenical council, and which our venerated predecessor, Pius XII of venerated memory, not without inspiration from on high, solemnly consecrated to the Immaculate Heart of Mary. Today, we consider it particularly opportune to recall this act of consecration. Bearing this

in mind, we have decided to send a special mission to Fatima in the near future in order to carry the Golden Rose to the sanctuary of Fatima, more dear than ever not only to the people of the noble Portuguese nation—always, but particularly today, dear to us—but also known and venerated by the faithful throughout the entire Catholic world. In this manner we intend to entrust to the care of this heavenly Mother the entire human family, with its problems and anxieties, with its legitimate aspirations and ardent hopes.

O, Virgin Mary, Mother of the Church, to you we recommend the entire Church and our ecumenical council!

You, "auxilium Episcoporum," aid of bishops, protect and assist the bishops in their apostolic mission, and all those priests, Religious and laymen, who help them in their arduous work.

You who were presented by your Son Himself, at the moment of His redeeming death, as Mother to His best-loved disciple, remember the Christian people who entrust themselves to you.

Remember all your sons; support their prayers to God, preserve their faith, strengthen their hope, increase their charity.

Remember those who are in tribulation, in need, in danger and particularly those who suffer persecution and who are in prison because of their faith. For these, O Virgin, obtain fortitude and hasten the desired day of just freedom.

Look with benign eyes on our separate brothers and condescend to unite us, you who brought forth Christ as a bridge of unity between God and men.

O, temple of light without shadow and without blemish, intercede with your only Son, mediator of our reconciliation with the Father (cf. Rom. 5, 11) that He may have mercy on our shortcomings and may dispel any difference between us, giving us the joy of loving.

To your Immaculate Heart, O Mary, we finally recommend the entire human race. Lead it to the knowledge of the sole and true Saviour, Jesus Christ; protect it from the scourges provoked by sin, give to the entire world peace in truth, in justice, in liberty and in love.

And let the entire Church, by celebrating this great ecumenical assembly, raise to the God of mercy the majestic hymn of praise and thanksgiving, the hymn of joy and of exultation, because the Lord has worked great things through you, O clement, O pious, O sweet Virgin Mary.

Closing the third session as he had opened it, Pope Paul VI concelebrated Mass with a score of Council Fathers. This time, the Holy Father invited prelates to join him who have major Marian shrines within their ecclesiastical jurisdictions. Archbishop Patrick A. O'Boyle of Washington, D.C., was one of these. The National Shrine of the Immaculate Conception is in his see. The Pope also proclaimed Mary "Mother of the Church."

Constitution on the Church

This is an unofficial English translation of the text of the Second Vatican Council's Constitution on the Church, proclaimed by Pope Paul VI on Nov. 21, 1964.

1. Christ is the Light of nations. Because this is so, this Sacred Synod gathered together in the Holy Spirit eagerly desires, by proclaiming the Gospel to every creature (cf. Mark 16, 15), to bring the light of Christ to all men, a light brightly visible on the countenance of the Church. Since the Church is in Christ like a sacrament or as a sign and instrument both of a very closely knit union with God and of the unity of the whole human race, it desires now to unfold more fully to the faithful of the Church and to the whole world its own inner nature and universal mission. This it intends to do following faithfully the teaching of previous councils. The present-day conditions of the world add greater urgency to this work of the Church so that all men, joined more closely today by various social, technical and cultural ties, might also attain fuller unity in Christ.

Chapter I: The Mystery of the Church

2. The eternal Father, by a free and hidden plan of His own wisdom and goodness, created the whole world. His plan was to raise men to a participation of the divine life. God the Father did not leave men, fallen in Adam, to themselves, but ceaselessly offered helps to salvation, in view of Christ, the Redeemer "who is the image of the invisible God, the firstborn of every creature" (Col. 1,15). All the elect, before time began, the Father "foreknew and predestined to become conformed to the image of His Son, that he should be the firstborn among many brethren" (Rom. 8,29). He planned to assemble in the holy Church all those who would believe in Christ. Already from the beginning of the world the foreshadowing of the Church took place. It was prepared in a remarkable way throughout the history of the people of Israel and by means of the Old Covenant[1]. In the present era of time the Church was constituted and, by the outpouring of the Spirit, was made manifest. At the end of time it will gloriously achieve completion, when, as is read in the Fathers, all the just, from Adam and "from Abel, the just one, to the last of the elect"[2], will be gathered together with the Father in the universal Church.

3. The Son, therefore, came, sent by the Father. It was in Him, before the foundation of the world, that the Father chose us and predestined us to become adopted sons, for in Him it pleased the Father to re-establish all things (cf. Eph. 1. 4-5 and 10). To carry out the will of the Father Christ inaugurated the Kingdom of heaven on earth and revealed to us the mystery of that kingdom. By His obedience He brought about redemption. The Church, or, in other words, the kingdom of Christ now present in mystery, grows visibly through the power of God in the world. This inauguration and this growth are both symbolized by the Blood and Water which flowed from the open side of the crucified Jesus (cf. John 19, 34), and are foretold in the words of the Lord referring to His death on the Cross: "And I, if I be lifted up from the earth will draw all things to myself" (John 12, 32). As often as the sacrifice of the cross in which Christ our Passover was sacrificed (I Cor. 5, 7) is celebrated on the altar, the work of our redemption is carried on, and, in the sacrament of the eucharistic bread, the unity of all believers who form one body in Christ (cf. I Cor. 10, 17) is both expressed and brought about. All men are called to this union with Christ, who is the light of the world, from whom we go forth, through whom we live, and toward whom our whole life strains.

4. When the work which the Father gave the Son to do on earth (cf. John 17, 4) was accomplished, the Holy Spirit was sent on the day of Pentecost in order that He might continually sanctify the Church, and thus, all those who believe would have access through Christ in one Spirit to the Father (cf. Eph. 2, 18). He is the Spirit of Life, a fountain of water springing up to life eternal (cf. John 4, 14; 7, 38-39). To men, dead in sin, the Father gives life through Him, until, in Christ, He brings to life their mortal bodies (cf. Rom. 8, 10-11). The Spirit dwells in the Church and in the hearts of the faithful, as in a temple (cf. Cor. 3, 16; 6, 19). In them He prays on their behalf and bears witness to the fact

that they are adopted sons (cf. Gal. 4, 6; Rom. 8, 15-16 and 26). The Church, which the Spirit guides in the way of all truth (cf. John 16, 13) and which He unified in communion and in works of ministry, He both equips and directs with hierarchical and charismatic gifts and adorns with His fruits (cf. Eph. 4, 11-12; I Cor. 12, 4; Gal. 5, 22). By the power of the Gospel He makes the Church keep the freshness of youth. Uninterruptedly He renews it and leads it to perfect union with its Spouse (3). The Spirit and the Bride both say to Jesus, the Lord, "Come!" (cf. Apoc. 22, 17).

Thus, the Church has been seen as "a people made one with the unity of the Father, the Son and the Holy Spirit" (4).

5. The mystery of the holy Church is manifest in its very foundation. The Lord Jesus set it on its course by preaching the Good News, that is, the coming of the Kingdom of God, which, for centuries, had been promised in the Scriptures: "The time is fulfilled, and the kingdom of God is at hand" (Mark 1, 15; cf. Matt. 4, 17). In the word, in the works, and in the presence of Christ, this kingdom was clearly open to the view of men. The Word of the Lord is compared to a seed which is sown in a field (Mark 4, 14); those who hear the Word with faith and become part of the little flock of Christ (Luke 12, 32), have received the Kingdom itself. Then, by its own power the seed sprouts and grows until harvest time (cf. Mark 4, 26-29). The Miracles of Jesus also confirm that the Kingdom has already arrived on earth: "If I cast out devils by the finger of God, then the kingdom of God has come upon you" (Luke 11, 20; cf. Matt. 12, 28). Before all things, however, the Kingdom is clearly visible in the very Person of Christ, the Son of God and the Son of Man, who came "to serve and to give His life as a ransom for many" (Mark 10, 45).

When Jesus, who had suffered the death of the cross for mankind had risen, He appeared as the one constituted as Lord, Christ and eternal Priest (cf. Acts 2,36; Hebr. 5,6; 7,17-21), and He poured out on His disciples the Spirit promised by the Father (cf. Acts 2,33). From this source the Church, equipped with the gifts of its Founder and faithfully guarding His precepts of charity, humility and self-sacrifice, receives the mission to proclaim and to spread among all peoples the Kingdom of Christ and of God and to be, on earth, the initial budding forth of that kingdom. While it slowly grows, the Church strains toward the completed Kingdom and, with all its strength, hopes and desires to be united in glory with its King.

6. In the Old Testament the revelation of the Kingdom is often conveyed by means of metaphors. In the same way the inner nature of the Church is now made known to us in different images. Taken either from tending sheep or cultivating the land, from building or even from family life and from betrothals, the images receive preparatory shaping in the books of the Prophets.

The Church is a Sheepfold whose one and indispensable door is Christ (John 10, 1-10). It is a flock of which God Himself foretold He would be the shepherd (cf. Is. 40, 11; Ex. 34, 11f), and whose sheep, although ruled by human shepherds, are nevertheless continuously led and nourished by Christ Himself, the Good Shepherd and the Prince of the shepherds, (cf. John 10, 11; I Peter 5, 4), who gave His life for the sheep (cf. John 10, 11-15).

The Church is a piece of land to be cultivated, the Tillage of God (I Cor. 3, 9). On that land the ancient olive tree grows whose holy roots were the Prophets and in which the reconciliation of Jews and Gentiles has been brought about and will be brought about (Rom. 11, 13-26). That land, like a choice vineyard, has been planted by the heavenly Husbandman (Matt. 21, 33-43; cf. Is. 5, 1f.) The true vine is Christ who gives life and the power to bear abundant fruit to the branches, that is, to us, who through the Christ remain in Christ without whom we can do nothing (John 15, 1-5).

Often the Church has also been called the Building of God (I Cor. 3, 9). The Lord Himself compared Himself to the stone which the builders rejected, but which was made into the cornerstone (Mt. 21, 42; cf. Acts 4, 11; I Peter 2,7; Ps. 117, 22). On this foundation the Church is built by the apostles (cf. I Cor. 3, 11), and from it the Church receives durability and consolidation. This edifice has many names to describe it: the house of God (I Tim. 3,15) in which dwells His Family; the household of God in the Spirit (Eph. 2, 19-22); the dwelling place of God among men (Apoc. 21, 3); and, especially, the holy Temple. This Temple, symbolized in places of worship built out of stone, is praised by the Holy Fathers and, not without reason, is compared in the liturgy to the Holy City, the New Jerusalem (5). As living stones we here on earth are built into it (I Peter 2, 5). John contemplates this holy city coming down from heaven at the renewal of the world as a bride made ready and adorned for her husband (Apoc. 21 1 f).

The Church, further, "that Jerusalem which is above" is also called "our mother" (Gal. 4, 26; cf. Apoc. 12, 17). It is described as the spotless Spouse of the spotless Lamb (Apoc. 19, 7; 21, 2 and 9; 22, 17), whom Christ "loved and for whom He delivered Himself up that He might sanctify her" (Eph. 5, 26), whom He unites to Himself by an unbreakable covenant, and whom He unceasingly "nourishes and cherishes" (Eph. 5, 29) and whom, once purified, He willed to be cleansed and joined to Himself, subject to Him in love and fidelity (cf. Eph. 5, 24), and whom, finally, He filled with heavenly gifts for all eternity, in order that we may know the love of God and of Christ for us, a love which surpasses all knowledge (cf. Eph. 3, 19). The

Church, while on earth it journeys in a foreign land away from the Lord (cf. II Cor. 5, 6), is like an exile. It seeks and experiences those things which are above, where Christ is seated at the right-hand of God, where the life of the Church is hidden with Christ in God until it appears in glory with its Spouse (cf. Col. 3, 1-4).

7. In the human nature united to Himself the Son of God, by overcoming death through His own death and resurrection, redeemed man and re-molded him into a new creation (cf. Gal. 6, 15; II Cor. 5, 17). By communicating His Spirit, Christ made His brothers, called together from all nations, mystically the components of His own Body.

In that Body the life of Christ is poured into the believers who, through the sacraments, are united in a hidden and real way to Christ who suffered and was glorified [6]. Through Baptism we are formed in the likeness of Christ: "For in one Spirit we were all baptized into one body" (I Cor. 12, 13). In this sacred rite a oneness with Christ's death and resurrection is both symbolized and brought about: "For we were buried with Him by means of Baptism into death"; and if "we have been united with Him in the likeness of His death, we shall be so in the likeness of His resurrection also" (Rom. 6, 4-5). Really partaking of the body of the Lord in the breaking of the eucharistic bread, we are taken up into communion with Him and with one another. "Because the bread is one, we though many, are one body, all of us who partake of the one bread" (I Cor. 10, 17). In this way all of us are made members of His Body (cf. I Cor. 12, 27), "but severally members one of another" (Rom. 12, 5).

As all the members of the human body, though they are many, form one body, so also are the faithful in Christ (cf. I Cor. 12, 12). Also, in the building up of Christ's Body various members and functions have their part to play. There is only one Spirit who, according to His own richness and the needs of the ministries, gives His different gifts for the welfare of the Church (cf. I Cor. 12, 1-11). What has a special place among these gifts is the grace of the apostles to whose authority the Spirit Himself subjected even those who were endowed with charisms (cf. I Cor. 14). Giving the body unity through Himself and through His power and inner joining of the members, this same Spirit produces and urges love among the believers. From all this it follows that if one member endures anything, all the members co-endure it, and if one member is honored, all the members together rejoice (cf. I Cor. 12, 26).

The Head of this Body is Christ. He is the image of the invisible God and in Him all things came into being. He is before all creatures and in Him all things hold together. He is the head of the Body which is the Church. He is the beginning, the first born from the dead, that in all things He might have the first place

(cf. Col. 1, 15-18). By the greatness of His power He rules the things in heaven and the things on earth, and with His all-surpassing perfection and way of acting He fills the whole body with the riches of His glory [7] (cf. Eph. 1, 18-23).

All the members ought to be molded in the likeness of Him, until Christ be formed in them (cf. Gal. 4, 19). For this reason we, who have been made to conform with Him, who have died with Him and risen with Him, are taken up into the mysteries of His life, until we will reign together with Him (cf. Phil. 3, 21; II Tim. 2, 11; Eph. 2, 6; Col. 2, 12 etc.). On earth, still as pilgrims in a strange land, tracing in trial and in oppression the paths He trod, we are made one with His sufferings like the body is one with the Head, suffering with Him, that with Him we may be glorified (cf. Rom. 8, 17).

From Him "the whole body, supplied and built up by joints and ligaments, attains a growth that is of God" (Col. 2, 19). He continually distributes in His body, that is, in the Church, gifts of ministries in which, by His own power, we serve each other unto salvation so that, carrying out the truth in love, we might through all things grow unto Him who is our Head (cf. Eph. 4, 11-16.).

In order that we might be unceasingly renewed in Him (cf. Eph. 4, 23), He has shared with us His Spirit who, existing as one and the same being in the Head and in the members, gives life to, unifies and moves through the whole body. This He does in such a way that His work could be compared by the holy Fathers with the function which the principle of life, that is, the soul, fulfills in the human body [8].

Christ loves the Church as His bride, having become the model of a man loving his wife as his body (cf. Eph. 5, 25-28); the Church, indeed, is subject to its Head (Eph. 23-24). "Because in Him dwells all the fulness of the Godhead bodily" (Col. 2, 9), He fills the Church, which is His body and His fulness, with His divine gifts (cf. Eph. 1, 22-23) so that it may expand and reach all the fulness of God (cf. Eph. 3, 19).

8. Christ, the one Mediator, established and continually sustains here on earth His holy Church, the community of faith, hope and charity, as an entity with visible delineation [9] through which He communicated truth and grace to all. But, the society structured with hierarchical organs and the Mystical Body of Christ are not to be considered as two realities, nor are the visible assembly and the spiritual community, nor the earthly Church and the Church enriched with heavenly things; rather they form one complex reality which coalesces from a divine and a human element. [10] For this reason, by no weak analogy, it is compared to the mystery of the incarnate Word. As the assumed nature inseparably united to Him, serves the divine Word as a living

organ of salvation, so, in a similar way, does the visible social structure of the Church serve the Spirit of Christ, who vivifies it, in the building up of the body (cf. Eph. 4, 16) [11].

This is the one Church of Christ which in the Creed is professed as one, holy, catholic and apostolic, [12] which our Saviour, after His Resurrection, commissioned Peter to shepherd (John 21, 17), and him and the other apostles to extend and direct with authority (cf. Matt. 28, 18, etc.), which He erected for all ages as "the pillar and mainstay of the truth" (1 Tim. 3, 15). This Church constituted and organized in the world as a society, subsists in the Catholic Church, which is governed by the successor of Peter and by the Bishops in communion with him, [13] although many elements of sanctification and of truth are found outside of its visible structure. These elements, as gifts belonging to the Church of Christ, are forces impelling toward catholic unity.

Just as Christ carried out the work of redemption in poverty and persecution, so the Church is called to follow the same route that it might communicate the fruits of salvation to men. Christ Jesus, "though He was by nature God . . . emptied Himself, taking the nature of a slave" (Phil. 2, 6), and "being rich, became poor" (II Cor. 8, 9) for our sakes. Thus, the Church, although it needs human resources to carry out its mission, is not set up to seek earthly glory, but to proclaim, even by its own example, humility and self-sacrifice. Christ was sent by the Father "to bring good news to the poor, to heal the contrite of heart" (Luke, 4, 18), "to seek and to save what was lost" (Luke, 19, 10). Similarly, the Church encompasses with love all who are afflicted with human suffering and in the poor and afflicted sees the image of its poor and suffering Founder. It does all it can to relieve their need and in them it strives to serve Christ. While Christ, holy, innocent and undefiled (Hebr. 7, 26) knew nothing of sin (II Cor. 5, 21), but came to expiate only the sins of the people (cf. Hebr. 2, 17), the Church, embracing in its bosom sinners, at the same time holy and always in need of being purified, always follows the way of penance and renewal. The Church, "like a stranger in a foreign land, presses forward amid the persecutions of the world and the consolations of God" [14], announcing the cross and death of the Lord until He comes (cf. I Cor. 11, 26). By the power of the risen Lord it is given strength that it might, in patience and in love, overcome its sorrows and its challenges, both within itself and from without, and that it might reveal to the world, faithfully though darkly, the mystery of its Lord until, in the end, it will be manifested in full light.

Chapter II: On the People of God

9. At all times and in every race God has given welcome to whosoever fears Him and does what is right cf. Acts 10, 35). God, however, does not make men holy and save them merely as individuals, without bond or link between one another. Rather has it pleased Him to bring men together as one people, a people which acknowledges Him in truth and serves Him in holiness. He therefore chose the race of Israel as a people unto Himself. With it He set up a covenant. Step by step He taught and prepared this people, making known in its history both Himself and the decree of His will and making it holy unto Himself. All these things, however, were done by way of preparation and as a figure of that new and perfect covenant, which was to be ratified in Christ, and of that fuller revelation which was to be given through the Word of God Himself made flesh. "Behold the days shall come, saith the Lord, and I will make a new covenant with the House of Israel, and with the house of Judah . . . I will give my law in their bowels, and I will write it in their heart, and I will be their God, and they shall be my people . . . For all of them shall know Me, from the least of them even to the greatest, saith the Lord" (Jer. 31-34). Christ instituted this new covenant, the new testament, that is to say, in His Blood (cf. I Cor. XI, 25), calling together a people made up of Jew and gentile, making them one, not according to the flesh but in the spirit. This was to be the new People of God. For those who believe in Christ, who are reborn not from a perishable but from an imperishable seed through the word of the living God (cf. I Peter 1, 23), not from the flesh but from water and the Holy Spirit (cf. John III, 5-6), are finally established as "a chosen race, a royal priesthood, a holy nation, a purchased people . . . who in times past were not a people, but are now the people of God" (I Peter II, 9-10).

That messianic people has Christ for its head, "Who was delivered up for our sins, and rose again for our justification" (Rom. IV, 25), and now, having won a name which is above all names, reigns in glory in heaven. The state of this people is that of the dignity and freedom of the sons of God, in whose hearts the Holy Spirit dwells as in His temple. Its law is the new commandment to love as Christ loved us (cf. John 13,34). Its end is the kingdom of God, which has been begun by God Himself on earth, and which is to be further extended until it is brought to perfection by Him at the end of time, when Christ, our life (cf. Col. III, 4), shall appear, and "creation itself will be delivered from its slavery to corruption into the freedom of the glory of the sons of God" (Rom. VIII, 21). So it is that that messianic people, although it does not actually include all men, and at times may look like a small flock, is nonetheless a lasting and sure seed of unity, hope and salvation for the whole human race. Established by Christ as a communion of life, charity and truth, it is also used by Him as an instrument for the redemption of all, and is sent forth into the whole world as the light of the world and the salt of the earth (cf. Matt. V, 13-16).

Israel according to the flesh, which wandered as an exile in the desert, was already called the Church of God (cf. 2 Esdr. 13, 1; Num. XX, 4; Deut. XXIII 1 sq). So likewise the new Israel which while living in this present age goes in search of a future and abiding city (cf. Heb. XIII, 14) is called the Church of Christ (cf. Matt. 16, 18). For He has bought it for Himself with His blood (cf. Acts XX, 28), has filled it with His Spirit and provided it with those means which befit it as a visible and social union. God gathered together as on all those who in faith look upon Jesus as the author of salvation and the source of unity and peace, and established them as the Church, that for each and all it may be the visible sacrament of this saving unity [1]. While it transcends all limits of time and confines of race, the Church is destined to extend to all regions of the earth and so enters into the history of mankind. Moving forward through trial and tribulation, the Church is strengthened by the power of God's grace, which was promised to her by the Lord, so that in the weakness of the flesh she may not waver from perfect fidelity, but remain a bride worthy of her Lord, and moved by the Holy Spirit may never cease to renew herself, until through the Cross she arrives at the light which knows no setting.

10. Christ the Lord, High Priest taken from among men (Heb. V, 1-5), made the new people "a kingdom and priests to God the Father" (Apoc. 1, 6; V, 9-10). The baptized, by regeneration and the anointing of the Holy Spirit, are consecrated as a spiritual house and a holy priesthood, in order that through all those works which are those of the Christian man they may offer spiritual sacrifices and proclaim the power of Him who has called them out of darkness into His marvelous light (cf. I Peter II, 4-10). Therefore all the disciples of Christ, persevering in prayer and praising God (cf. Acts II, 42, 47), should present themselves as a living sacrifice holy and pleasing to God (cf. Rom. XII, 1). Everywhere on earth they must bear witness to Christ and give an answer to those who seek an account of that hope of eternal life which is in them (cf. 1 Peter III, 15).

Though they differ from one another in essence and not only in degree, the common priesthood of the faithful and the ministerial or hierarchical priesthood are nonetheless interrelated: each of them in its own special way is a participation in the one priesthood of Christ. [2] The ministerial priest, by the sacred power he enjoys, teaches and rules the priestly people; acting in the person of Christ, he makes present the eucharistic sacrifice, and offers it to God in the name of all the people. But the faithful, in virtue of their royal priesthood, join in the offering of the Eucharist [3]. They likewise exercise that priesthood in receiving the sacraments, in prayer and thanksgiving, in the witness of a holy life, and by self-denial and active charity.

11. It is through the sacraments and the exercise of the virtues that the sacred nature and organic structure of the priestly community is brought into operation. Incorporated in the Church through baptism, the faithful are destined by the baptismal character for the worship of the Christian religion; reborn as sons of God they must confess before men the faith which they have received from God through the Church [4]. They are more perfectly bound to the Church by the sacrament of Confirmation, and the Holy Spirit endows them with special strength so that they are more strictly obliged to spread and defend the faith, both by word and by deed, as true witnesses of Christ [5]. Taking part in the eucharistic sacrifice, which is the fount and apex of the whole Christian life, they offer the Divine Victim to God, and offer themselves along with It [6]. Thus both by reason of the offering and through Holy Communion all take their dual part in this liturgical service, not indeed, all in the same way but each in that way which is proper to himself. Strengthened in Holy Communion by the Body of Christ, they then manifest in a concrete way that unity of the people of God which is suitably signified and wondrously brought about by this most august sacrament.

Those who approach the sacrament of Penance obtain pardon from the mercy of God for the offense committed against Him and are at the same time reconciled with the Church, which they have wounded by their sins, and which by charity, example, and prayer seeks their conversion. By the sacred anointing of the sick and the prayer of her priests the whole Church commends the sick to the suffering and glorified Lord, asking that He may lighten their suffering and save them (cf. Jas. 5, 14-16); she exhorts them, moreover, to contribute to the welfare of the whole people of God by associating themselves freely with the passion and death of Christ (cf. Rom. 8, 17; Col. I, 24; II Tim. 2, 11-12; I Peter 4, 13). Those of the faithful who are consecrated by Holy orders are appointed to feed the Church in Christ's name with the word and the grace of God. Finally, Christian spouses, in virtue of the sacrament of matrimony, whereby they signify and partake of the mystery of that unity and fruitful love which exists between Christ and His Church (cf. Eph. 5, 32), help each other to attain to holiness in their married life and in the rearing and education of their children. By reason of their state and rank in life they have their own special gift among the people of God (cf. I Cor. 7, 7) [7]. From the wedlock of Christians there comes the family, in which new citizens of human society are born, who by the grace of the Holy Spirit received in baptism are made children of God, thus perpetuating the people of God through the centuries. The family is, so to speak, the domestic Church. In it parents should, by their word and example, be the first preachers of the faith to their children; they should encourage them in the vocation which is proper to each of them, fostering with special care vocation to a sacred state.

Fortified by so many and such powerful means of salvation, all the faithful, whatever their condition or state, are called by the Lord, each in his own way, to that perfect holiness whereby the Father Himself is perfect.

12. The holy people of God shares also in Christ's prophetic office; it spreads abroad a living witness to Him, especially by means of a life of faith and charity and by offering to God a sacrifice of praise, the tribute of lips which give praise to His name (cf. Heb. 13, 15). The entire body of the faithful, anointed as they are by the Holy One (cf. John 2, 20, 27), cannot err in matters of belief. They manifest this special property by means of the whole peoples' supernatural discernment in matters of faith when "from the Bishops down to the last of the lay faithful" [8] they show universal agreement in matters of faith and morals. That discernment in matters of faith is aroused and sustained by the Spirit of truth.

It is exercised under the guidance of the sacred teaching authority, in faithful and respectful obedience to which the people of God accepts that which is not just the word of men but truly the word of God (cf. I Thess. 2, 13). Through it, the people of God adheres unwaveringly to the faith given once and for all to the saints (cf. Jud. 3), penetrates it more deeply with right thinking, and applies it more fully in its life.

It is not only through the sacraments and the ministries of the Church that the Holy Spirit sanctifies and leads the people of God and enriches it with virtues, but "alloting his gifts to everyone according as He wills" (1 Cor. 12, 11), He distributes special graces among the faithful of every rank. By these gifts He makes them fit and ready to undertake the various tasks and offices which contribute toward the renewal and building up of the Church, according to the words of the Apostle: "The manifestation of the Spirit is given to everyone for profit" (I Cor. 12, 7). These charisims, whether they be the more outstanding or the more simple and widely diffused, are to be received with thanksgiving and consolation for they are perfectly suited to and useful for the needs of the Church. Extraordinary gifts are not to be sought after, nor are the fruits of apostolic labor to be presumptuously expected from their use; but judgment as to their genuinity and proper use belongs to those who are appointed leaders in the Church, to whose special competence it belongs, not indeed to extinguish the Spirit, but to test all things and hold fast to that which is good (cf. I Thess. 5, 12, 19-21).

13. All men are called to belong to the new people of God. Wherefore this people, while remaining one and only one, is to be spread throughout the whole world and must exist in all ages, so that the decree of God's will may be fulfilled. In the beginning God made human nature one and decreed that all His children, scattered as they were, would finally be gathered together as one (cf. John 11, 52). It was for this purpose that God sent His Son, whom He appointed heir of all things (cf. Heb. 1, 2), that He might be teacher, king and priest of all, the head of the new and universal people of the sons of God. For this too God sent the Spirit of His Son as Lord and Life-giver. He it is who brings together the whole Church and each and every one of those who believe, and who is the well-spring of their unity in the teaching of the apostles and in fellowship, in the breaking of bread and in prayers (cf. Acts 2, 42).

It follows that though there are many nations there is but one people of God, which takes its citizens from every race, making them citizens of a kingdom which is of a heavenly rather than of an earthly nature. All the faithful, scattered though they be throughout the world, are in communion with each other in the Holy Spirit, and so "he who dwells in Rome knows that the people of India are his members" [9]. Since the kingdom of Christ is not of this world (cf. John 18, 36) the Church or people of God in establishing that kingdom takes nothing away from the temporal welfare of any people. On the contrary it fosters and takes to itself, insofar as they are good, the ability, riches and customs in which the genius of each people expresses itself. Taking them to itself it purifies, strengthens, elevates and ennobles them. The Church in this is mindful that she must bring together the nations for that King to whom they were given as an inheritance (cf. Ps. 2, 8) and to whose city they bring gifts and offerings (cf. Ps. 71, (72) 10; Is. 60, 4-7; Apoc. 21, 24). This characteristic of universality which adorns the people of God is a gift from the Lord Himself. By reason of it, the Catholic Church strives constantly and with due effect to bring all humanity and all its possessions back to its source in Christ, with Him as its head and united in His Spirit [10].

In virtue of this catholicity each individual part contributes through its special gifts to the good of the other parts and of the whole Church. Through the common sharing of gifts and through the common effort to attain fulness in unity, the whole and each of the parts receive increase. Not only, then, is the people of God made up of different peoples but in its inner structure also it is composed of various ranks. This diversity among its members arises either by reason of their duties, as is the case with those who exercise the sacred ministry for the good of their brethren, or by reason of their condition and state of life, as is the case with those many who enter the religious state and, tending toward holiness by a narrower path, stimulate their brethren by their example. Moreover, within the Church particular Churches hold a rightful place; these Churches retain their own traditions, without in any way opposing the primacy of the Chair of Peter, which presides over the whole assembly of charity [11] and protects legitimate differences, while at the same time assuring that such differences do not hinder unity but rather contribute toward it. Between all the parts of the Church there remains a bond of close communion whereby they share spiritual riches, apostolic workers and temporal resources. For the members of the people of God are called to share these goods in common, and of each of the Churches the words of the Apostle hold good: "According to the gift that each has received, administer it to one another as good stewards of the manifold grace of God" (I Peter 4, 10).

All men are called to be part of this catholic unity of the people of God which in promoting universal peace presages it. And there belong to or are related to it in various ways, the catholic faithful, all who believe in Christ, and indeed the whole of mankind, for all men are called by the grace of God to salvation.

14. This sacred council wishes to turn its attention firstly to the Catholic faithful. Basing itself upon Sacred Scripture and Tradition, it teaches that the Church, now sojourning on earth as an exile, is necessary for salvation. Christ, present to us in His Body, which is the Church, is the one Mediator and the unique way of salvation. In explicit terms He Himself affirmed the necessity of faith and baptism (cf. Mark 16, 16; John 3, 5) and thereby affirmed also the necessity of the Church, for through baptism as through a door men enter the Church. Whosoever, therefore, knowing that the Catholic Church was made necessary by Christ, would refuse to enter it or to remain in it, could not be saved.

They are fully incorporated in the society of the Church who, possessing the Spirit of Christ, accept her entire system and all the means of salvation given to her, and are united with her as part of her visible bodily structure and through her with Christ, who rules her through the Supreme Pontiff and the bishops. The bonds which bind men to the Church in a visible way are profession of faith, the sacraments, and ecclesiastical government and Communion. He is not saved, however, who, though part of the body of the Church, does not persevere in charity. He remains indeed in the bosom of the Church, but, as it were, only in a "bodily" manner and not "in his heart" [12]. All the Church's children should remember that their exalted status is to be attributed not to their own merits but to the special grace of Christ. If they fail moreover to respond to that grace in thought, word and deed, not only shall they not be saved but they will be the more severely judged [13].

Catechumens who, moved by the Holy Spirit, seek with explicit intention to be incorporated into the Church are by that very intention joined with her. With love and solicitude Mother Church already embraces them as her own.

15. The Church recognizes that in many ways she is linked with those who, being baptized, are honored with the name of Christian, though they do not profess the faith in its entirety or do not preserve unity of communion with the successor of Peter [14]. For there are many who honor Sacred Scripture, taking it as a norm of belief and a pattern of life, and who show a sincere zeal. They lovingly believe in God the Father Almighty and in Christ, the Son of God and Saviour [15]. They are consecrated by baptism, in which they are united with Christ. They also recognize and accept other sacraments within their own Churches or ecclesiastical communities. Many of them rejoice in the episcopate, celebrate the Holy Eucharist and cultivate devotion toward the Virgin Mother of God [16]. They also share with us in prayer and other spiritual benefits. Likewise we can say that in some real way they are joined with us in the Holy Spirit, for to them too He gives His gifts and graces whereby He is operative among them with His sanctifying power. Some indeed He has strengthened to the extent of the shedding of their blood. In all of Christ's disciples the Spirit arouses the desire to be peacefully united, in the manner determined by Christ, as one flock under one shepherd, and He prompts them to pursue this end [17]. Mother Church never ceases to pray, hope and work that this may come about. She exhorts her children to purification and renewal so that the sign of Christ may shine more brightly over the face of the earth.

16. Finally, those who have not yet received the Gospel are related in various ways to the people of God [18]. In the first place we must recall the people to whom the testament and the promises were given and from whom Christ was born according to the flesh (cf. Rom. 9, 4-5). On account of their fathers this people remains most dear to God, for God does not repent of the gifts He makes nor of the calls He issues (cf. Rom. 11, 28-29). But the plan of salvation also includes those who acknowledge the Creator. In the first place amongst these there are the Mohammedans, who, professing to hold the

faith of Abraham, along with us adore the one and merciful God, who on the last day will judge mankind. Nor is God far distant from those who in shadows and images seek the unknown God, for it is He who gives to all men life and breath and all things (cf. Acts 17, 25-28), and as Saviour wills that all men be saved (cf. I Tim. 2, 4). Those also can attain to salvation who through no fault of their own do not know the Gospel of Christ or His Church, yet sincerely seek God and moved by grace strive by their deeds to do His will as it is known to them through the dictates of conscience[19]. Nor does Divine Providence deny the helps necessary for salvation to those who, without blame on their part, have not yet arrived at an explicit knowledge of God and with His grace strive to live a good life. Whatever good or truth is found amongst them is looked upon by the Church as a preparation for the Gospel[20]. She knows that it is given by Him who enlightens all men so that they may finally have life. But often men, deceived by the Evil One, have become vain in their reasonings and have exchanged the truth of God for a lie, serving the creature rather than the Creator. Or some there are who, living and dying in this world without God, are exposed to final despair. Wherefore to promote the glory of God and procure the salvation of all of these, and mindful of the command of the Lord, "Preach the Gospel to every creature" (Mark 16, 16), the Church fosters the missions with care and attention.

17. As the Son was sent by the Father (cf. John 20, 21), so He too sent the apostles, saying: "Go, therefore, make disciples of all nations, baptizing them in the name of the Father and of the Son and of the Holy Spirit, teaching them to observe all things whatsoever I have commanded you. And behold I am with you all days even to the consummation of the world" (Matt. 21, 18-20). The Church has received this solemn mandate of Christ to proclaim the saving truth from the apostles and must carry it out to the very ends of the earth (cf. Acts 1, 8). Wherefore she makes the words of the Apostle her own: "Woe to me, if I do not preach the Gospel" (I Cor. 9, 16), and continues unceasingly to send heralds of the Gospel until such time as the infant churches are fully established and can themselves continue the work of evangelizing. For the Church is compelled by the Holy Spirit to do her part that God's plan may be fully realized, whereby He has constituted Christ as the source of salvation for the whole world. By the proclamation of the Gospel she prepares her hearers to receive and profess the faith. She gives them the dispositions necessary for baptism, snatches them from the slavery of error and of idols and incorporates them in Christ so that through charity they may grow up into full maturity in Christ. Through her work, whatever good is in the minds and hearts of men, whatever good lies latent in the religious practices and cultures of diverse peoples, is not only saved from destruction but is also cleansed, raised up and perfected unto the glory of God, the confusion of the devil and the happiness of man. The obligation of spreading the faith is imposed on every disciple of Christ, according to his state[21]. Although, however, all the faithful can baptize, the priest alone can complete the building up of the Body in the eucharistic sacrifice. Thus are fulfilled the words of God, spoken through His prophet: "From the rising of the sun until the going down thereof my name is great among the gentiles, and in every place a clean oblation is sacrificed and offered up in my name" (Mal. 1, 11)[22]. In this way the Church both prays and labors in order that the entire world may become the People of God, the Body of the Lord and the Temple of the Holy Spirit, and that in Christ, the Head of all, all honor and glory may be rendered to the Creator and Father of the Universe.

Chapter III: On the Hierarchical Structure Of the Church and in Particular on the Episcopate

18. For the nurturing and constant growth of the People of God, Christ the Lord instituted in His Church a variety of ministries, which work for the good of the whole body. For those ministers, who are endowed with sacred power, serve their brethren, so that all who are of the People of God, and therefore enjoy a true Christian dignity, working toward a common goal freely and in an orderly way, may arrive at salvation.

This sacred council, following closely in the footsteps of the First Vatican Council, with that council teaches and declares that Jesus Christ, the eternal Shepherd, established His holy Church, having sent forth the apostles as He himself had been sent by the Father (John 20, 21); and He willed that their successors, namely the bishops, should be shepherds in His Church even to the consummation of the world. And in order that the episcopate itself might be one and undivided, He placed Blessed Peter over the other apostles, and instituted in him a permanent and visible source and foundation of unity of faith and communion[1]. And all this teaching about the institution, the perpetuity, the meaning and reason for the sacred primacy of the Roman Pontiff and of his infallible magisterium, this sacred council again proposes to be firmly believed by all the faithful. Continuing in that same undertaking, this council is resolved to declare and proclaim before all men the doctrine concerning bishops, the successors of the apostles, who together with the successor of Peter, the Vicar of Christ [2], the visible Head of the whole Church, govern the house of the living God.

19. The Lord Jesus, after praying to the Father, calling to Himself those whom He desired, appointed 12 to be with Him, and whom He would send to preach the Kingdom of God (Mark 3, 13-19; Matt. 10, 1-42); and these apostles (Luke 6, 13) He formed after the manner of a college or a stable group, over which He placed Peter chosen from among them (John 21, 15-17). He sent them first to the children of Israel and then to all nations (Rom. 1, 16), so that as sharers in His power they might make all peoples His disciples, and sanctify and govern them (Matt. 28, 16-20; Mark 16, 15; Luke 24, 45-48; John 20, 21-23), and thus spread His Church, and by ministering to it under the guidance of the Lord, direct it all days even to the consummation of the world (Matt. 28, 20).

And in this mission they were fully confirmed on the day of Pentecost (Acts 2, 1-26) in accordance with the Lord's promise: "You shall receive power when the Holy Spirit comes upon you, and you shall be witnesses for me in Jerusalem, and in all Judea and in Samaria, and even to the very ends of the earth" (Acts 1,8). And the apostles, by preaching the Gospel everywhere (Mark 16, 20), and it being accepted by their hearers under the influence of the Holy Spirit, gather together the universal Church, which the Lord established on the Apostles and built upon blessed Peter, their chief, Christ Jesus Himself being the supreme cornerstone (Apoc. 21, 14; Matt. 16, 18; Eph. 2, 20) [3].

20. That divine mission, entrusted by Christ to the apostles, will last until the end of the world (Matt. 28, 20), since the Gospel they are to teach is for all time the source of all life for the Church. And for this reason the apostles, appointed as rulers in this society, took care to appoint successors.

For they not only had helpers in their ministry [4], but also, in order that the mission assigned to them might continue after their death, they passed on to their immediate cooperators, as it were, in the form of a testament, the duty of confirming and finishing the work begun by themselves [5], recommending to them that they attend to the whole flock in which the Holy Spirit placed them to shepherd the Church of God (Acts 20, 28). They therefore appointed such men, and gave them the order that, when they should have died, other approved men would take up their ministry [6]. Among those vari-

ous ministries which, according to tradition, were exercised in the Church from the earliest times, the chief place belongs to the office of those who, appointed to the episcopate, by a succession running from the beginning [7], are passers-on of the apostolic seed [8]. Thus, as St. Irenaeus testifies, through those who were appointed bishops by the apostles, and through their successors down to our own time, the apostolic tradition is manifested [9] and preserved [10].

Bishops, therefore, with their helpers, the priests and deacons, have taken up the service of the community [11], presiding in place of God over the flock [12], whose shepherds they are, as teachers for doctrine, priests for sacred worship, and ministers for governing [13]. And just as the office granted individually to Peter, the first among the apostles, is permanent and is to be transmitted to his successors, so also the apostles' office of nurturing the Church is permanent, and is to be exercised without interruption by the sacred order of bishops [14]. Therefore, the sacred council teaches that bishops by divine institution have succeeded to the place of the apostles [15], as shepherds of the Church, and he who hears them, hears Christ, and he who rejects them, rejects Christ and Him who sent Christ (cf. Luke 10,16) [16].

21. In the bishops, therefore, for whom priests are assistants, Our Lord Jesus Christ, the Supreme High Priest, is present in the midst of those who believe. For sitting at the right hand of God the Father, He is not absent from the gathering of His high priests [17] but above all through their excellent service He is preaching the word of God to all nations, and constantly administering the sacraments of faith to those who believe; by their paternal functioning (cf. 1 Cor. 4, 15). He incorporates new members in His body by a heavenly regeneration, and finally by their wisdom and prudence He directs and guides the People of the New Testament in their pilgrimage toward eternal happiness. These pastors, chosen to shepherd the Lord's flock of the elect, are servants of Christ and stewards of the mysteries of God (cf. 1 Cor. 4,1), to whom has been assigned the bearing of witness to the Gospel of the grace of God (cf. Rom. 15,16; Acts 20,24), and the ministration of the Spirit and of justice in glory (cf. 2 Cor. 3, 8-9).

For the discharging of such great duties, the apostles were enriched by Christ with a special outpouring of the Holy Spirit coming upon them (cf. Acts 1,8; 2,4; John 22,23), and they passed on this spiritual gift to their helpers by the imposition of hands (cf. 1 Tim. 4,14; 2 Tim. 1, 6-7), and it has been transmitted down to us in episcopal consecration [18]. And the sacred council teaches that by episcopal consecration the fulness of the sacrament of Orders is conferred, that fulness of power, namely, which both in the Church's liturgical practice and in the language of the Fathers of the Church is called the high priesthood, the supreme

power of the sacred ministry [19]. But episcopal consecration, together with the office of sanctifying, also confers the office of teaching and of governing, which,
however, of its very nature, can be exercised only in
hierarchial communion with the head and the members
of the college. For from the tradition, which is expressed
especially in liturgical rites and in the practice of both
the Church of the East and of the West, it is clear
that, by means of the imposition of hands and the
words of consecration, the grace of the Holy Spirit is
so conferred [20], and the sacred character so impressed
[21], that bishops in an eminent and visible way sustained the roles of Christ Himself as Teacher, Shepherd
and High Priest, and that they act in His person [22].
Therefore it pertains to the bishops to admit newly
elected members into the episcopal body by means of
the sacrament of Orders.

22. Just as in the Gospel, the Lord so disposing, St.
Peter and the other apostles constitute one apostolic
college, so in a similar way the Roman Pontiff, the successor of Peter, and the bishops, the successors of the
apostles, are joined together. Indeed, the very ancient
practice whereby bishops duly established in all parts
of the world were in communion with one another and
with the Bishop of Rome in a bond of unity, charity
and peace [23] and also the councils assembled together
[24] in which more profound issues were settled in common [25], the opinion of the many having been prudently considered, [26] both of these factors are already an
indication of the collegiate character and aspect of the
episcopal order; and the ecumenical councils held in the
course of centuries are also manifest proof of that same
character. And it is intimated also in the practice, introduced in ancient times, of summoning several bishops
to take part in the elevation of the newly elected to the
ministry of the high priesthood. Hence, one is constituted
a member of the episcopal body in virtue of sacramental
consecration and hiearchical communion with the head
and members of the body.

But the college or body of bishops has no authority
unless it is understood together with the Roman pontiff,
the successor of Peter as its head. The pope's power of
primacy over all, both pastors and faithful, remains whole
and intact. In virtue of his office, that is as Vicar of
Christ and pastor of the whole Church, the Roman
pontiff has full, supreme and universal power over the
Church. And he is always free to exercise this power.
The order of bishops, which succeeds to the college of
apostles and gives this apostolic body continued existence,
is also the subject of supreme and full power over the
universal Church, provided we understand this body
together with its head the Roman pontiff and never
without this head [27]. This power can be exercised only
with the consent of the Roman pontiff. For Our Lord
placed Simon alone as the rock and the bearer of the

keys of the Church (Matt. 16, 18-19), and made him
shepherd of the whole flock (John 21, 15); it is evident,
however, that the power of binding and loosing, which
was given to Peter (Matt. 16, 19), was granted also to
the college of apostles, joined with their head (Matt.
18, 18; 28, 16-20) [28]. This college, insofar as it is composed of many, expresses the variety and universality of
the people of God, but insofar as it is assembeld under
one head, it expresses the unity of the flock of Christ. In
it, the bishops, faithfully recognizing the primacy and pre-
eminence of their head, exercise their own authority for
the good of their own faithful, and indeed of the whole
Church, the Holy Spirit supporting its organic structure
and harmony with moderation. The supreme power in
the universal Church, which this college enjoys, is exercised in a solemn way in an ecumenical council. A council is never ecumenical unless it is confirmed or at least
accepted as such by the successor of Peter; and it is prerogative of the Roman pontiff to convoke these councils,
to preside over them and to confirm them [29]. This
same collegiate power can be exercised together with the
pope by the bishops living in all parts of the world, provided that the head of the college calls them to collegiate
action, or at least approves of or freely accepts the united
action of the scattered bishops, so that it is thereby made
a collegiate act.

23. This collegial union is apparent also in the
mutual relations of the individual bishops with particular churches and with the universal Church. The Roman
pontiff, as the successor of Peter, is the perpetual and
visible principle and foundation of unity of both the
bishops and of the faithful [30]. The individual bishops,
however, are the visible principle and foundation of
unity in their particular churches, [31] fashioned after
the model of the universal Church, in and from which
churches comes into being the one and only Catholic
Church [32]. For this reason the individual bishops represent each his own church, but all of them together
and with the Pope represent the entire Church in the
bond of peace, love and unity.

The individual bishops, who are placed in charge
of particular churches, exercise their pastoral government over the portion of the People of God committed
to their care, and not over other churches nor over the
universal Church. But each of them, as a member of the
episcopal college and legitimate successor of the apostles,
is obliged by Christ's institution and command to be
solicitous for the whole Church [33] and this solicitude,
though it is not exercised by an act of jurisdiction, contributes greatly to the advantage of the universal Church.
For it is the duty of all bishops to promote and to safeguard the unity of faith and the discipline common to
the whole Church, to instruct the faithful to love for the
whole Mystical Body of Christ, especially for its poor
and sorrowing members and for those who are suffering

persecution for justice's sake (Matt. 5, 10), and finally to promote every activity that is of interest to the whole Church, especially that the faith may take increase and the light of full truth appear to all men. And this also is important, that by governing well their own church as a portion of the universal Church, they themselves are effectively contributing to the welfare of the whole Mystical Body, which is also the body of the churches [34].

The task of proclaiming the Gospel everywhere on earth pertains to the body of pastors, to all of whom in common Christ gave His command, thereby imposing upon them a common duty, as Pope Celestine in his time recommended to the Fathers of the Council of Ephesus [35]. From this it follows that the individual bishops, insofar as their own discharge of their duty permits, are obliged to enter into a community of work among themselves and with the successor of Peter, upon whom was imposed in a special way, the great duty of spreading the Christian name [36]. With all their energy, therefore, they must supply to the missions both workers for the harvest and also spiritual and material aid, both directly and on their own account, as well as by arousing the ardent cooperation of the faithful. And finally, the bishops, in a universal fellowship of charity, should gladly extend their fraternal aid to other churches, especially to neighboring and more needy dioceses in accordance with the venerable example of antiquity.

By divine Providence it has come about that various churches, established in various places by the apostles and their successors, have in the course of time coalesced into several groups, organically united, which, preserving the unity of faith and the unique divine constitution of the universal Church, enjoy their own discipline, their own liturgical usage, and their own theological and spiritual heritage. Some of these churches, notably the ancient patriarchal churches, as parent-stocks of the Faith, so to speak, have begotten others as daughter churches, with which they are connected down to our own time by a close bond of charity in their sacramental life and in their mutual respect for their rights and duties [37]. This variety of local churches with one common aspiration is splendid evidence of the catholicity of the undivided Church. In like manner the episcopal bodies of today are in a position to render a manifold and fruitful assistance, so that this collegiate feeling may be put into practical application.

24. Bishops, as successors of the apostles, receive from the Lord, to whom was given all power in heaven and on earth, the mission to teach all nations and to preach the Gospel to every creature, so that all men may attain to salvation by faith, baptism and the fulfillment of the commandments (cf. Matt. 28, 18; Mark 16, 15-16; Acts 26, 17 sq.). To fulfill this mission, Christ the Lord promised the Holy Spirit to the Apostles, and on Pentecost day sent the Spirit from heaven, by whose power they would be witnesses to Him before the nations and peoples and kings even to the ends of the earth (Acts 1, 8; 2, 1 ff; 9, 15). And that duty, which the Lord committed to the shepherds of His people, is a true service, which in sacred literature is significantly called "diakonia" or ministry (Acts 1, 17, 25; 21, 19; Rom. 11, 13; 1 Tim. 1, 12).

The canonical mission of bishops can come about by legitimate customs that have not been revoked by the supreme and universal authority of the Church, or by laws made or recognized by that same authority, or directly through the successor of Peter himself; and if the latter refuses or denies apostolic communion, such bishops cannot assume any office [38].

25. Among the principal duties of bishops the preaching of the Gospel occupies an eminent place [39]. For bishops are preachers of the faith, who lead new disciples to Christ, and they are authentic teachers, that is, teachers endowed with the authority of Christ, who preach to the people committed to them the faith they must believe and put into practice, and by the light of the Holy Spirit illustrate that faith. They bring forth from the treasury of Revelation new things and old (Matt. 13, 52), making it bear fruit and vigilantly warding off any errors that threaten their flock (2 Tim. 4, 1-4). Bishops, teaching in communion with the Roman pontiff, are to be respected by all as witnesses to divine and Catholic truth. In matters of faith and morals, the bishops speak in the name of Christ and the faithful are to accept their teaching and adhere to it with a religious assent. This religious submission of mind and will must be shown in a special way to the authentic magisterium of the Roman pontiff, even when he is not speaking ex cathedra; that is, it must be shown in such a way that his supreme magisterium is acknowledged with reverence, the judgments made by him are sincerely adhered to, according to his manifest mind and will. His mind and will in the matter may be known either from the character of the documents, from his frequent repetition of the same doctrine, or from his manner of speaking.

Although the individual bishops do not enjoy the prerogative of infallibility, they nevertheless proclaim Christ's doctrine infallibly whenever, even though dispersed through the world, but still maintaining the bond of communion among themselves and with the successor of Peter, and authentically teaching matters of faith and morals, they are in agreement on one position as definitely to be held [40]. This is even more clearly verified when, gathered together in an ecumenical council, they are teachers and judges of faith and morals for the universal Church, whose definitions must be adhered to with the submission of faith [41].

And this infallibility with which the Divine Redeemer willed His Church to be endowed in defining doctrine of faith and morals, extends as far as the deposit of Revelation extends, which must be religiously guarded and faithfully expounded. And this is the infallibility which the Roman pontiff, the head of the college of bishops, enjoys in virtue of his office, when, as the supreme shepherd and teacher of all the faithful, who confirms his brethren in their faith (cf. Luke 22, 32), by a definitive act he proclaims a doctrine of faith or morals [42]. And therefore his definitions, of themselves, and not from the consent of the Church, are justly styled irreformable, since they are pronounced with the assistance of the Holy Spirit, promised to him in blessed Peter, and therefore they need no approval of others, nor do they allow an appeal to any other judgment. For then the Roman pontiff is not pronouncing judgment as a private person, but as the supreme teacher of the universal Church, in whom the charism of infallibility of the Church itself is individually present, he is expounding or defending a doctrine of Catholic faith [43]. The infallibility promised to the Church resides also in the body of Bishops, when that body exercises the supreme magisterium with the successor of Peter. To these definitions the assent of the Church can never be wanting, on account of the activity of that same Holy Spirit, by which the whole flock of Christ is preserved and progresses in unity of faith [44].

But when either the Roman pontiff or the Body of Bishops together with him defines a judgment, they pronounce it in accordance with Revelation itself, which all are obliged to abide by and be in conformity with, that is, the Revelation which as written or orally handed down is transmitted in its entirety through the legitimate succession of bishops and especially in care of the Roman pontiff himself, and which under the guiding light of the Spirit of truth is religiously preserved and faithfully expounded in the Church [45]. The Roman pontiff and the bishops, in view of their office and the importance of the matter, by fitting means diligently strive to inquire properly into that revelation and to give apt expression to its contents [46]; but a new public revelation they do not accept as pertaining to the divine deposit of faith [47].

26. A bishop marked with the fulness of the sacrament of Orders, is "the steward of the grace of the supreme priesthood"[48], especially in the Eucharist, which he offers or causes to be offered[49], and by which the Church continually lives and grows. This Church of Christ is truly present in all legitimate local congregations of the faithful which, united with their pastors, are themselves called churches in the New Testament[50]. For in their locality these are the new People called by God, in the Holy Spirit and in much fulness (cf. 1 Thes. 1,5). In them the faithful are gathered together by the preaching of the Gospel of Christ, and the mystery of the Lord's Supper is celebrated, that by the food and blood of the Lord's body the whole brotherhood may be joined together [51]. In any community of the altar, under the sacred ministry of the bishop[52], there is exhibited a symbol of that charity and "unity of the Mystical Body, without which there can be no salvation"[53]. In these communities, though frequently small and poor, or living in the Diaspora, Christ is present, and in virtue of His presence there is brought together one, holy, catholic and apostolic Church[54]. For "the partaking of the body and blood of Christ does nothing other than make us be transformed into that which we consume" [55].

Every legitimate celebration of the Eucharist is regulated by the bishop, to whom is committed the office of offering the worship of Christian religion to the Divine Majesty and of administering it in accordance with the Lord's commandments and the Church's laws, as further defined by his particular judgment for his diocese.

Bishops thus, by praying and laboring for the people, make outpourings in many ways and in great abundance from the fulness of Christ's holiness. By the ministry of the word they communicate God's power to those who believe unto salvation (cf. Rom. 1,16), and through the sacraments, the regular and fruitful distribution of which they regulate by their authority[56], they sanctify the faithful. They direct the conferring of baptism, by which a sharing in the kingly priesthood of Christ is granted. They are the original ministers of confirmation, dispensers of Sacred Orders and the moderators of penitential discipline, and they earnestly exhort and instruct their people to carry out with faith and reverence their part in the liturgy and especially in the holy sacrifice of the Mass. And lastly, by the example of their way of life they must be an influence for good to those over whom they preside, refraining from all evil and, as far as they are able with God's help, exchanging evil for good, so that together with the flock committed to their care they may arrive at eternal life[57].

27. Bishops, as vicars and ambassadors of Christ, govern the particular churches entrusted to them[58] by their counsel, exhortations, example, and even by their authority and sacred power, which indeed they use only for the edification of their flock in truth and holiness, remembering that he who is greater should become as the lesser and he who is the chief become as the servant (cf. Luke 22, 26-27). This power, which they personally exercise in Christ's name, is proper, ordinary and immediate, although its exercise is ultimately regulated by the supreme authority of the Church, and can be circumscribed by certain limits, for the advantage of the Church or of the faithful. In virtue of this power, bishops have the sacred right and the duty before the Lord to make laws for their subjects, to pass judgment on them and to moderate everything pertaining to the ordering of worship and the apostolate.

The pastoral office or the habitual and daily care of

their sheep is entrusted to them completely; nor are they to be regarded as vicars of the Roman pontiffs, for they exercise an authority that is proper to them, and are quite correctly called "prelates," heads of the people whom they govern[59]. Their power, therefore, is not destroyed by the supreme and universal power, but on the contrary it is affirmed, strengthened and vindicated by it[60], since the Holy Spirit unfailingly preserves the form of government established by Christ the Lord in His Church.

A bishop, since he is sent by the Father to govern his family, must keep before his eyes the example of the Good Shepherd, who came not to be ministered unto but to minister (Matt. 20,28; Mark 10,45), and to lay down his life for his sheep (John 10,11). Being taken from among men, and himself beset with weakness, he is able to have compassion on the ignorant and erring (Heb. 5, 1-2). Let him not refuse to listen to his subjects, whom he cherishes as his true sons and exhorts to cooperate readily with him. As having one day to render an account for their souls (Heb. 13, 17), he takes care of them by his prayer, preaching, and all the works of charity, and not only of them but also of those who are not yet of the one flock, who also are commended to him in the Lord. Since, like Paul the Apostle, he is debtor to all men, let him be ready to preach the Gospel to all (Rom. 1, 14-15), and to urge his faithful to apostolic and missionary activity. But the faithful must cling to their bishop, as the Church does to Christ, and Jesus Christ to the Father, so that all may be of one mind through unity[61], and abound to the glory of God (2 Cor. 4,15).

28. Christ, whom the Father has sanctified and sent into the world (John 10,36), has through His apostles, made their successors the Bishops partakers of His consecration and His mission [62]. They have legitimately handed on to different individuals in the Church various degrees of participation in this ministry. Thus the divinely established ecclesiastical ministry is exercised on different levels by those who from antiquity have been called bishops, priests and deacons[63]. Priests, although they do not possess the highest degree of the priesthood, and although they are dependent on the bishops in the exercise of their power, nevertheless they are united with the bishops in sacerdotal dignity[64]. By the power of the sacrament of Orders[65], in the image of Christ the eternal high Priest (Heb. 5,1-10; 7,24; 9, 11-28), they are consecrated to preach the Gospel and shepherd the faithful and to celebrate divine worship, so that they are true priests of the New Testament[66]. Partakers of the function of Christ the sole Mediator (1 Tim. 2,5) on their level of ministry, they announce the divine word to all. They exercise their sacred function especially in the Eucharistic worship or the celebration of the Mass by which acting in the person of Christ[67] and proclaiming His Mystery, they unite the prayers of the faithful with the sacrifice of their Head and renew and apply[68] in the sacrifice of the Mass until the coming of the Lord (1 Cor. 11, 26) the only sacrifice of the New Testament, namely that of Christ offering Himself once for all a spotless Victim to the Father (cf. Heb. 9, 11-28). For the sick and the sinners among the faithful, they exercise the ministry of alleviation and reconciliation and they present the needs and the prayers of the faithful to God the Father (Heb. 5, 1-4). Exercising within the limits of their authority the function of Christ as Shepherd and Head[69], they gather together God's family as a brotherhood all of one mind[70], and lead them in the Spirit, through Christ, to God the Father. In the midst of the flock they adore Him in spirit and in truth (John 4, 24). Finally, they labor in word and doctrine (1 Tim. 5,17), believing what they have read and meditated upon in the law of God, teaching what they have believed, and putting in practice in their own lives what they have taught[71].

Priests, prudent cooperators with the episcopal order[72], its aid and instrument, called to serve the people of God, constitute one priesthood[73] with their bishop although bound by a diversity of duties. Associated with their bishop in a spirit of trust and generosity, they make him present in a certain sense in the individual local congregations, and take upon themselves, as far as they are able, his duties and the burden of his care, and discharge them with a daily interest. And as they sanctify and govern under the bishop's authority, that part of the Lord's flock entrusted to them, they make the universal Church visible in their own locality and bring an efficacious assistance to the building up of the whole body of Christ (Eph. 4, 12). Intent always upon the welfare of God's children, they must strive to lend their effort to the pastoral work of the whole diocese, and even of the entire Church. On account of this sharing in their priesthood and mission, let priests sincerely look upon the bishop as their father and reverently obey him. And let the bishop regard his priests as his co-workers and as sons and friends, just as Christ called His disciples now not servants but friends (John 15, 15). All priests, both diocesan and religious, by reason of Orders and ministry, fit into this body of bishops and priests, and serve the good of the whole Church according to their vocation and the grace given to them.

In virtue of their common sacred ordination and mission, all priests are bound together in intimate brotherhood, which naturally and freely manifests itself in mutual aid, spiritual as well as material, pastoral as well as personal, in their meetings and in communion of life, of labor and charity.

Let them, as fathers in Christ, take care of the faithful whom they have begotten by baptism and their teaching (1 Cor. 4, 15; 1 Peter 1, 23). Becoming from the heart a pattern to the flock (1 Peter 5, 3), let them so lead and serve their local community that it may worthily be called by that name, by which the one and entire people of God is signed, namely, the Church of God (1 Cor. 1, 2; 2 Cor. 1, 1). Let them remember that by their daily life and interests they are showing the face of a truly sacerdotal and pastoral ministry to the faithful and the infidel, to Catholics and non-Catholics, and that to all they bear witness to the truth and life, and as good shepherds go after those also (Luke 15, 4-7), who though baptized in the Catholic Church have fallen away from the use of the sacraments, or even from the faith.

Because the human race today is joining more and more into a civic, economic and social unity, it is that much the more necessary that priests, by combined effort and aid, under the leadership of the bishops and the Supreme Pontiff, wipe out every kind of separateness, so that the whole human race may be brought into the unity of the family of God.

29. At a lower level of the hierarchy are deacons, upon whom hands are imposed "not unto the priesthood, but unto a ministry of service"[74]. For strengthened by sacramental grace, in communion with the bishop and his group of priests they serve in the diaconate of the liturgy, of the word, and of charity to the people of God. It is the duty of the deacon, according as it shall have been assigned to him by competent authority, to administer baptism solemnly, to be custodian and dispensor of the Eucharist, to assist at and bless marriages in the name of the Church, to bring Viaticum to the dying, to read the Sacred Scripture to the faithful, to instruct and exhort the people to preside over the worship and prayer of the faithful, to administer sacramentals, to officiate at funeral and burial services. Dedicated to duties of charity and of administration, let deacons be mindful of the admonition of Blessed Polycarp: "Be merciful, diligent, walking according to the truth of the Lord, who became the servant of all"[75].

Since these duties, so very necessary to the life of the Church, can be fulfilled only with difficulty in many regions in accordance with the discipline of the Latin Church as it exists today, the diaconate can in the future be restored as a proper and permanent rank of the hierarchy. It pertains to the competent territorial bodies of bishops, of one kind or another, with the approval of the Supreme Pontiff, to decide whether and where it is opportune for such deacons to be established for the care of souls. With the consent of the Roman Pontiff, this diaconate can, in the future, be conferred upon men of more mature age, even upon those living in the married state. It may also be conferred upon suitable young men, for whom the law of celibacy must remain intact.

Chapter IV: The Laity

30. Having set forth the functions of the hierarchy, the Sacred Council gladly turns its attention to the state of those faithful called the laity. Everything that has been said above concerning the People of God is intended for the laity, religious and clergy alike. But there are certain things which pertain in a special way to the laity, both men and women, by reason of their condition and mission. Due to the special circumstances of our time the foundations of this doctrine must be more thoroughly examined. For their pastors know how much the laity contribute to the welfare of the entire Church. They also know that they were not ordained by Christ to take upon themselves alone the entire salvific mission of the Church toward the world. On the contrary they understand that it is their noble duty to shepherd the faithful and to recognize their ministries and charisms, so that all according to their proper roles may cooperate in this common undertaking with one mind. For we must all "practice the truth in love, and so grow up in all things in Him who is head, Christ. For from Him the whole body, being closely joined and knit together through every joint of the system, according to the functioning in due measure of each single part, derives its increase to the building up of itself in love" (Eph. 4, 15-16).

31. The term laity is here understood to mean all the faithful except those in holy orders and those in the state of religious life specially approved by the Church. These faithful are by baptism made one body with Christ and are constituted among the People of God; they are in their own way made sharers in the priestly, prophetical, and kingly functions of Christ; and they carry out for their own part the mission of the whole Christian people in the Church and in the world.

What specifically characterizes the laity is their secular nature. It is true that those in holy orders can at times be engaged in secular activities, and even have a secular profession. But they are by reason of their particular vocation especially and professedly ordained to the sacred ministry. Similarly, by their state in life, religious give splendid and striking testimony that the world cannot be transformed and offered to God without the spirit of the beatitudes. But the laity, by their very vocation, seek the kingdom of God by engaging in temporal affairs and by ordering them according to the plan of God. They live in the world, that is, in each and in all of the secular professions and occupations. They live in the ordinary circumstances of family and social life, from which the very web of their existence is woven. They are called there by God that by exercising their proper function and led by the spirit of the Gospel they may work for the sanctification of the world from within as a leaven. In this way they may make Christ known to others, especially by the testimony of a life resplendent in faith, hope and charity. Therefore, since they are tightly bound up in all types of temporal affairs it is their special task to order and to throw light upon these affairs in such a way that they may come into being and then continually increase according to Christ to the praise of the Creator and the Redeemer.

32. By divine institution Holy Church is ordered and governed with a wonderful diversity. "For just as in one body we have many members, yet all the members have not the same function, so we, the many, are one body in Christ, but severally members one of another" (Rom. 12:4-5). Therefore, the chosen People of God is one: "one Lord, one faith, one baptism" (Eph. 4:5); sharing a common dignity as members from their regeneration in Christ; having the same filial grace and the same vocation to perfection; possessing in common one salvation, one hope and one undivided charity. There is, therefore, in Christ and in the Church no inequality on the basis of race or nationality, social condition or sex, because "there is neither Jew nor Greek: there is neither bond nor free: there is neither male nor female. For you are all 'one' in Christ Jesus" (Gal. 3:28; cf. Col. 3:11).

If therefore in the Church everyone does not proceed by the same path, nevertheless all are called to sanctity and have received an equal privilege of faith through the justice of God (cf. 2 Peter 1:1). And if by the will of Christ some are made teachers, pastors and dispensers of mysteries on behalf of others, yet all share a true equality with regard to the dignity and to the activity common to all the faithful for the building up of the Body of Christ. For the distinction which the Lord made between sacred ministers and the rest of the People of God bears within it a certain union, since pastors and the other faithful are bound to each other by a mutual need. Pastors of the Church, following the example of the Lord, should minister to one another and to the other faithful. These in their turn should enthusiastically lend their joint assistance to their pastors and teachers. Thus in their diversity all bear witness to the wonderful unity in the Body of Christ. This very diversity of graces, ministries and works gathers the children of God into one, because "all these things are the work of one and the same Spirit" (1 Cor. 12:11).

Therefore, from divine choice the laity have Christ for their brother, who though He is the Lord of all, came

not to be served but to serve (cf. Matt. 20:28). They also have for their brothers those in the sacred ministry who by teaching, by sanctifying and by ruling with the authority of Christ feed the family of God so that the new commandment of charity may be fulfilled by all. St. Augustine puts this very beautifully when he says: "What I am for you terrifies me; what I am with you consoles me. For you I am a bishop; but with you I am a Christian. The former is a duty; the latter a grace. The former is a danger; the latter, salvation"[1].

33. The laity are gathered together in the People of God and make up the Body of Christ under one head. Whoever they are they are called upon, as living members, to expend all their energy for the growth of the Church and its continuous sanctification, since this very energy is a gift of the Creator and a blessing of the Redeemer.

The lay apostolate, however, is a participation in the salvific mission of the Church itself. Through their baptism and confirmation all are commissioned to that apostolate by the Lord Himself. Moreover, by the sacraments, especially holy Eucharist, that charity toward God and man which is the soul of the apostolate is communicated and nourished. Now the laity are called in a special way to make the Church present and operative in those places and circumstances where only through them can it become the salt of the earth[2]. Thus every layman, in virtue of the very gifts bestowed upon him, is at the same time a witness and a living instrument of the mission of the Church itself "according to the measure of Christ's bestowal" (Eph. 4:7).

Besides this apostolate which certainly pertains to all Christians, the laity can also be called in various ways to a more direct form of cooperation in the apostolate of the hierarchy[3]. This was the way certain men and women assisted Paul the Apostle in the Gospel, laboring much in the Lord (cf. Phil. 4:3; Rom. 16:3 ff). Further, they have the capacity to assume from the hierarchy certain ecclesiastical functions, which are to be performed for a spiritual purpose.

Upon all the laity, therefore, rests the noble duty of working to extend the divine plan of salvation to all men of each epoch and in every land. Consequently, may every opportunity be given them so that, according to their abilities and the needs of the times, they may zealously participate in the saving work of the Church.

34. The supreme and eternal Priest, Christ Jesus, since He wills to continue His witness and service also through the laity, vivifies them in this Spirit and increasingly urges them on to every good and perfect work.

For besides intimately linking them to His life and His mission, He also gives them a sharing in His priestly function of offering spiritual worship for the glory of God and the salvation of men. For this reason the laity, dedicated to Christ and anointed by the Holy Spirit, are marvelously called and wonderfully prepared so that ever more abundant fruits of the Spirit may be produced in them. For all their works, prayers and apostolic endeavors, their ordinary married and family life, their daily occupations, their physical and mental relaxation, if carried out in the Spirit, and even the hardships of life, if patiently borne—all these become "spiritual sacrifices acceptable to God through Jesus Christ" (1 Peter 2:5). Together with the offering of the Lord's body, they are most fittingly offered in the celebration of the Eucharist. Thus, as those everywhere who adore in holy activity, the laity consecrate the world itself to God.

35. Christ, the great Prophet, who proclaimed the Kingdom of His Father both by the testimony of His life and the power of His words, continually fulfills His prophetic office until the complete manifestation of glory. He does this not only through the hierarchy who teach in His name and with His authority, but also through the laity whom He made His witnesses and to whom He gave understanding of the faith (sensu fidei) and an attractiveness in speech (cf. Acts 2: 17-18; Apoc. 19:10) so that the power of the Gospel might shine forth in their daily social and family life. They conduct themselves as children of the promise, and thus strong in faith and in hope they make the most of the present (cf. Eph. 5:16; Col. 4:5), and with patience await the glory that is to come (cf. Rom. 8:25). Let them not, then, hide this hope in the depths of their hearts, but even in the program of their secular life let them express it by a continual conversion and by wrestling "against the world-rulers of this darkness, against the spiritual forces of wickedness" (Eph. 6:12).

Just as the sacraments of the New Law, by which the life and the apostolate of the faithful are nourished, prefigure a new heaven and a new earth (cf. Apoc. 21: 1), so too the laity go forth as powerful proclaimers of a faith in things to be hoped for (cf. Heb. 11:1), when they courageously join to their profession of faith a life springing from faith. This evangelization, that is, this announcing of Christ by a living testimony as well as by the spoken word, takes on a specific quality and a special force in that it is carried out in the ordinary surroundings of the world.

In connection with the prophetic function, that state of life which is sanctified by a special sacrament is obviously of great importance, namely, married and family life. For where Christianity pervades the entire mode of family life, and gradually transforms it, one will find there both the practice and an excellent school of the lay apostolate. In such a home husbands and wives find their proper vocation in being witnesses of the faith and love of Christ to one another and to their children. The Christian family loudly proclaims both the present virtues of the Kingdom of God and the hope of a blessed life to come. Thus by its example and its witness it ac-

cuses the world of sin and enlightens those who seek the truth.

Consequently, even when preoccupied with temporal cares, the laity can and must perform a work of great value for the evangelization of the world. For even if some of them have to fulfill their religious duties on their own, when there are no sacred ministers or in times of persecution; and even if many of them devote all their energies to apostolic work; still it remains for each one of them to cooperate in the external spread and the dynamic growth of the Kingdom of Christ in the world. Therefore, let the laity devoutedly strive to acquire a more profound grasp of revealed truth, and let them insistently beg of God the gift of wisdom.

36. Christ, becoming obedient even unto death and because of this exalted by the Father (cf. Phil. 2:8-9), entered into the glory of His kingdom. To Him all things are made subject until He subjects Himself and all created things to the Father that God may be all in all (cf. 1 Cor. 15:27-28). Now Christ has communicated this royal power to His disciples that they might be constituted in royal freedom and that by true penance and a holy life they might conquer the reign of sin in themselves (cf. Rom. 6:12). Further, He has shared this power so that serving Christ in their fellow men they might by humility and patience lead their brethren to that King for whom to serve is to reign. But the Lord wishes to spread His kingdom also by means of the laity, namely, a kingdom of truth and life, a kingdom of holiness and grace, a kingdom of justice, love and peace[4]. In this kingdom creation itself will be delivered from its slavery to corruption into the freedom of the glory of the sons of God (cf. Rom. 8:21). Clearly then a great promise and a great trust is committed to the disciples: "All things are yours, and you are Christ's, and Christ is God's" (1 Cor. 3:23).

The faithful, therefore, must learn the deepest meaning and the value of all creation, as well as its role in the harmonious praise of God. They must assist each other to live holier lives even in their daily occupations. In this way the world may be permeated by the spirit of Christ and it may more effectively fulfill its purpose in justice, charity and peace. The laity have the principal role in the overall fulfillment of this duty. Therefore, by their competence in secular training and by their activity, elevated from within by the grace of Christ, let them vigorously contribute their effort, so that created goods may be perfected by human labor, technical skill and civic culture for the benefit of all men according to the design of the Creator and the light of His Word. May the goods of this world be more equitably distributed among all men, and may they in their own way be conducive to universal progress in human and Christian freedom. In this manner, through the members of the Church, will

Christ progressively illumine the whole of human society with His saving light.

Moreover, let the laity also by their combined efforts remedy the customs and conditions of the world, if they are an inducement to sin, so that they all may be conformed to the norms of justice and may favor the practice of virtue rather than hinder it. By so doing they will imbue culture and human activity with genuine moral values; they will better prepare the field of the world for the seed of the Word of God; and at the same time they will open wider the doors of the Church by which the message of peace may enter the world.

Because of the very economy of salvation the faithful should learn how to distinguish carefully between those rights and duties which are theirs as members of the Church, and those which they have as members of human society. Let them strive to reconcile the two, remembering that in every temporal affair they must be guided by a Christian conscience, since even in secular business there is no human activity which can be withdrawn from God's dominion. In our own time, however, it is most urgent that this distinction and also this harmony should shine forth more clearly than ever in the lives of the faithful, so that the mission of the Church may correspond more fully to the special conditions of the world today. For it must be admitted that the temporal sphere is governed by its own principles, since it is rightly concerned with the interests of this world. But that ominous doctrine which attempts to build a society with no regard whatever for religion, and which attacks and destroys the religious liberty of its citizens, is rightly to be rejected [5].

37. The laity have the right, as do all Christians, to receive in abundance from their spiritual shepherds the spiritual goods of the Church, especially the assistance of the word of God and of the sacraments [6]. They should openly reveal to them their needs and desires with that freedom and confidence which is fitting for children of God and brothers in Christ. They are, by reason of the knowledge, competence or outstanding ability which they may enjoy, permitted and sometimes even obliged to express their opinion on those things which concern the good of the Church [7]. When occasions arise, let this be done through the organs erected by the Church for this purpose. Let it always be done in truth, in courage and in prudence, with reverence and charity toward those who by reason of their sacred office represent the person of Christ.

The laity should, as all Christians, promptly accept in Christian obedience the decisions of their spiritual shepherds, since they are representatives of Christ as well as teachers and rulers in the Church. Let them follow the example of Christ, who by His obedience even unto death, opened to all men the blessed way of the liberty of the children of God. Nor should they omit to pray for those placed over them, for they keep watch as having to render an account of their souls, so that they may do this with joy and not with grief (cf. Heb. 13,17).

Let the spiritual shepherds recognize and promote the dignity as well as the responsibility of the laity in the Church. Let them willingly employ their prudent advice. Let them confidently assign duties to them in the service of the Church, allowing them freedom and room for action.

Further, let them encourage lay people so that they may undertake tasks on their own initiative. Attentively in Christ, let them consider with fatherly love the projects, suggestions and desires proposed by the laity [8]. However, let the shepherds respectfully acknowledge that just freedom which belongs to everyone in this earthly city.

A great many wonderful things are to be hoped for from this familiar dialogue between the laity and their spiritual leaders: in the laity a strengthened sense of personal responsibility; a renewed enthusiasm; a more ready application of their talents to the projects of their spiritual leaders. The latter, on the other hand, aided by the experience of the laity, can more clearly and more incisively come to decisions regarding both spiritual and temporal matters. In this way, the whole Church, strengthened by each one of its members, may more effectively fulfill its mission for the life of the world.

38. Each individual layman must stand before the world as a witness to the resurrection and life of the Lord Jesus and a symbol of the living God. All the laity as a community and each one according to his ability must nourish the world with spiritual fruits (cf. Gal. 5:22). They must diffuse in the world that spirit which animates the poor, the meek, the peace makers—whom the Lord in the Gospel proclaimed as blessed (cf. Matt. 5:3-9). In a word, "Christians must be to the world what the soul is to the body." [9]

Chapter V

The Universal Call to Holiness in the Church

39. The Church, whose mystery is being set forth by this sacred synod, is believed to be indefectibly holy. Indeed Christ, the Son of God, who with the Father and the Spirit is praised as "uniquely holy" [1] loved the Church as His bride, delivering Himself up for her. He did this that He might sanctify her (cf. Eph. 5, 25-26). He united her to Himself as His own body and brought it to perfection by the gift of the Holy Spirit for God's glory. Therefore in the Church, everyone whether belonging to the hierarchy or being cared for by it, is called to holiness, according to the saying of the Apostle: "For this is the will of God, your sanctification" (1 Thess. 4,3; Eph. 1,4). However, this holiness of the Church is unceasingly manifested, and must be manifested, in the fruits of grace which the Spirit produces in the faithful; it is expressed in many ways in individuals, who in their walk of life, tend toward the perfection of charity, thus causing the edification of others; in a very special way this (holiness) appears in the practice of the counsels, customarily called "evangelical." This practice of the counsels, under the impulsion of the Holy Spirit, undertaken by many Christians, either privately or in a Church-approved condition or state of life, gives and must give in the world an outstanding witness and example of this same holiness.

40. The Lord Jesus, the divine Teacher and Model of all perfection, preached holiness of life to each and everyone of His disciples of every condition. He Himself stands as the author and consumator of this holiness of life: "Be you therefore perfect, even as your heavenly Father is perfect" (Matt. 5, 48) [2]. Indeed He sent the Holy Spirit upon all men that He might move them inwardly to love God with their whole heart and their whole soul, with all their mind and all their strength (cf. Mark 12, 30) and that they might love each other as Christ loves them (cf. John 13, 34; 15, 12). The followers of Christ are called by God, not because of their works, but according to His own purpose and grace. They are justified in the Lord Jesus, because in the baptism of faith they truly become sons of God and sharers in the divine nature. In this way they are really made holy. Then too, by God's gift, they must hold on to and complete in their lives this holiness they have received. They are warned by the Apostle to live "as becomes saints" (Eph. 5, 3), and to put on "as God's chosen ones, holy and beloved, a heart of mercy, kindness, humility, meekness, patience" (Col. 3, 12), and to possess the fruit of the Spirit in

holiness (cf. Gal. 5, 22; Rom. 6, 22). Since truly we all offend in many things (cf. James 3, 2) we all need God's mercies continually and we all must daily pray: "Forgive us our debts" (Matt. 6, 12) [3].

Thus it is evident to everyone, that all the faithful of Christ of whatever rank or status, are called to the fulness of the Christian life and to the perfection of charity; [4] by this holiness as such a more human manner of living is promoted in this earthly society. In order that the faithful may reach this perfection, they must use their strength accordingly as they have received it, as a gift from Christ. They must follow in His footsteps and conform themselves to His image, seeking the will of the Father in all things. They must devote themselves with all their being to the glory of God and the service of their neighbor. In this way, the holiness of the People of God will grow into an abundant harvest of good, as is admirably shown by the life of so many saints in Church history.

41. In the various classes and differing duties of life, one and the same holiness is cultivated by all, who are moved by the Spirit of God, and who obey the voice of the Father and worship God the Father in spirit and in truth. These people follow the poor Christ, the humble and cross-bearing Christ in order to be worthy of being sharers in His glory. Every person must walk unhesitatingly according to his own personal gifts and duties in the path of living faith, which arouses hope and works through charity.

In the first place, the shepherds of Christ's flock must holily and eagerly, humbly and courageously carry out their ministry, in imitation of the eternal high Priest, the Shepherd and Guardian of our souls. They ought to fulfill this duty in such a way that it will be the principal means also of their own sanctification. Those chosen for the fulness of the priesthood are granted the ability of exercising the perfect duty of pastoral charity by the grace of the sacrament of Orders. This perfect duty of pastoral charity [5] is exercised in every form of episcopal care and service, prayer, sacrifice and preaching. By this same sacramental grace, they are given the courage necessary to lay down their lives for their sheep, and the ability by their daily example, having become a pattern for their flock (1 Peter 5,3).

Priests, who resemble bishops to a certain degree in their participation of the sacrament of Orders, form the spiritual crown of the bishops. [6] They participate in the grace of their office and they should grow daily in their love of God and their neighbor by the exercise of their office through Christ, the eternal and unique Mediator. They should preserve the bond of priestly communion, and they should abound in every spiritual good and thus present to all men a living witness to God.[7] All this they should do in emulation of those priests who often, down through the course of the centuries, left an outstanding example of the holiness of humble and hidden service. Their praise lives on in the Church of God. By their very office of praying and offering sacrifice for their own people and the entire people of God, they should rise to greater holiness. Keeping in mind what they are doing and imitating what they are handling,[8] these priests, in their apostolic labors, rather than being ensnared by perils and hardships, should rather rise to greater holiness through these perils and hardships. They should ever nourish and strengthen their action from an abundance of contemplation, doing all this for the comfort of the entire Church of God. All priests, and especially those who are called "diocesan priests," due to the special title of their ordination, should keep continually before their minds the fact that their faithful loyalty toward and their generous cooperation with their bishop is of the greatest value in their growth in holiness.

Ministers of lesser rank are also sharers in the mission and grace of the Supreme Priest. In the first place among these ministers are deacons, who, in as much as they are dispensers of Christ's mysteries and servants of the Church[9] should keep themselves free from every vice and stand before men as personifications of goodness and friends of God (cf. 1 Tim. 3, 8-10 and 12-13). Clerics, who are called by the Lord and are set aside as His portion in order to prepare themselves for the various ministerial offices under the watchful eye of spiritual shepherds, are bound to bring their hearts and minds into accord with this special election (which is theirs). They will accomplish this by their constancy in prayer, by their burning love, and by their unremitting recollection of whatever is true, just and of good repute. They will accomplish all this for the glory and honor of God. Besides these already named, there are also laymen, chosen of God and called by the bishop. These laymen spend themselves completely in apostolic labor, working the Lord's field with much success[10].

Furthermore, married couples and Christian parents should follow their own proper path (to holiness) by faithful love. They should sustain one another in grace throughout the entire length of their lives. They should embue their offspring, lovingly welcomed as God's gift, with Christian doctrine and the evangelical virtues. In this manner, they offer all men the example of unwearying and generous love; in this way they build up the brotherhood of charity; in so doing, they stand as the witnesses and cooperators in the fruitfulness of Holy Mother Church; by such lives, they are a sign and a participation in that very love, with which Christ loved His Bride and for which He delivered Himself up for her[11]. A like example, but one given in a different way, is that offered by widows and single people, who are able to make great contributions toward holiness and apostolic endeavor in the Church. Finally, those who engage in labor — and frequently it is of a heavy nature — should better themselves by their human labors. They should be of aid to their fellow citizens. They should raise all of society, and even creation itself, to a better mode of existence. Indeed, they should imitate by their lively charity, in their joyous hope and by their voluntary sharing of each others' burdens, the very Christ who plied His hands with carpenter's tools and Who in union with His Father, is continually working for the salvation of all men. In this, then, their daily work, they should climb to the heights of holiness and apostolic activity.

May all those who are weighed down with poverty, infirmity and sickness, as well as those who must bear various hardships or who suffer persecution for justice sake — may they all know they are united with the suffering Christ in a special way for the salvation of the world. The Lord called them blessed in His Gospel and they are those whom "the God of all graces, who has called us unto His eternal glory in Christ Jesus, will Himself, after we have suffered a little while, perfect, strengthen and establish" (1 Peter 5, 10).

Finally all Christ's faithful, whatever be the conditions, duties and circumstances of their lives — and indeed through all these, will daily increase in holiness, if they receive all things with faith from the hand of their heavenly Father and if they cooperate with the divine will. In this temporal service, they will manifest to all men the love with which God loved the world.

42. "God is love, and he who abides in love, abides in God, and God in Him" (1 John 4, 16). But, God pours out his love into our hearts through the Holy Spirit, Who has been given to us (cf. Rom. 5, 5); thus the first and most necessary gift is love, by which we love God above all things and our neighbor because of God. Indeed, in order that love, as good seed may grow and bring forth fruit in the soul, each one of the faithful must willingly hear the Word of God and accept His Will, and must complete what God has begun by their own actions with the help of God's grace. These actions consist in the use of the sacraments and in a special way the Eucharist, frequent participation in the sacred action of the Liturgy, application of oneself to prayer, self-abnegation, lively fraternal service and the constant exercise of all the virtues. For charity, as the bond of perfection and the fulness of the law (cf. Col. 3,14; Rom. 13,10) rules over all the means of attaining holiness and gives life to these same means [12]. It is charity which

guides us to our final end. It is the love of God and the love of one's neighbor which points out the true disciple of Christ.

Since Jesus, the Son of God, manifested His charity by laying down His life for us, so too no one has greater love than he who lays down his life for Christ and His brother (cf. 1 John 3, 16; John 15, 13). From the earliest times, then, some Christians have been called upon — and some will always be called upon — to give the supreme testimony of this love to all men, but especially to persecutors. The Church, then, considers martyrdom as an exceptional gift and as the fullest proof of love. By martyrdom a disciple is transformed into an image of his Master by freely accepting death for the salvation of the world — as well as his conformity to Christ in the shedding of his blood. Though few are presented such an opportunity, nevertheless all must be prepared to confess Christ before men. They must be prepared to make this profession of faith even in the midst of persecutions, which will never be lacking to the Church, in following the way of the cross.

Likewise, the holiness of the Church is fostered in a special way by the observance of the counsels proposed in the Gospel by Our Lord to His disciples[13]. An eminent position among these is held by virginity or the celibate state (cf. 1 Cor. 7, 32-34). This is a precious gift of divine grace given by the Father to certain souls (cf. Matt 19, 11; 1 Cor. 7, 7), whereby they may devote themselves to God alone the more easily, due to an undivided heart[14]. This perfect continency, out of desire for the kingdom of heaven, has always been held in particular honor in the Church. The reason for this was and is that perfect continency for the love of God is an incentive to charity, and is certainly a particular source of spiritual fecundity in the world.

The Church continually keeps before it the warning of the Apostle which moved the faithful to charity, exhorting them to experience personally what Christ Jesus had known within Himself. This was the same Christ Jesus, who "emptied Himself, taking the nature of a slave . . . becoming obedient to death" (Phil. 2, 7-8), and because of us "being rich, he became poor" (2 Cor. 8, 9). Because the disciples must always offer an imitation of and a testimony to the charity and humility of Christ, Mother Church rejoices at finding within her bosom men and women who very closely follow their Saviour who debased Himself to our comprehension. There are some who, in their freedom as sons of God, renounce their own wills and take upon themselves the state of poverty. Still further, some become subject of their own accord to another man, in the matter of perfection for love of God. This is beyond the measure of the commandments, but is done in order to become more fully like the obedient Christ[15].

Therefore, all the faithful of Christ are invited to strive for the holiness and perfection of their own proper state. Indeed they have an obligation to strive. Let all then have care that they guide aright their own deepest sentiments of soul. Let neither the use of the things of this world nor attachment to riches, which is against the spirit of evangelical poverty, hinder them in their quest for perfect love. Let them heed the admonition of the Apostle to those who use this world; let them not come to terms with this world; for this world, as we see it, is passing away (cf. 1 Cor. 7, 31 ff)[16].

Chapter VI: Religious

43. The evangelical counsels of chastity dedicated to God, poverty and obedience are based upon the words and examples of the Lord. They were further commended by the apostles and Fathers of the Church, as well as by the doctors and pastors of souls. The counsels are a divine gife, which the Church receives from its Lord and which it always safeguards with the help of His grace. Church authority has the duty, under the inspiration of the Holy Spirit, of interpreting these evangelical counsels, of regulating their practice and finally to build on them stable forms of living. Thus it has come about that, as if on a tree which has grown in the field of the Lord, various forms of solitary and community life, as well as various religious families have branched out in a marvelous and multiple way from this divinely given seed. Such a multiple and miraculous growth augments both the progress of the members of these various religious families themselves and the welfare of the entire Body of Christ[1]. These religious families give their members the support of a more firm stability in their way of life and a proven doctrine of acquiring perfection. They further offer their members the support of fraternal association in the militia of Christ and of liberty strengthened by obedience. Thus these religious are able to tranquilly fulfill and faithfully observe their religious profession and so spiritually rejoicing make progress on the road of charity[2].

From the point of view of the divine and hierarchical structure of the Church, the religious state of life is not an intermediate state between the clerical and lay states. But, rather, the faithful of Christ are called by God from both these states of life so that they might enjoy this particular gift in the life of the Church and thus each in one's own way, may be of some advantage to the salvific mission of the Church[3].

44. The faithful of Christ bind themselves to the three aforesaid counsels either by vows, or by other sacred bonds, which are like vows in their purpose. By such a bond, a person is totally dedicated to God, loved beyond all things. In this way, that person is ordained to the honor and service of God under a new and special title. Indeed through Baptism a person dies to sin and is consecrated to God. However, in order that he may be capable of deriving more abundant fruit from this baptismal grace, he intends, by the profession of the evangelical counsels in the Church, to free himself from those obstacles, which might draw him away from the fervor of charity and the perfection of divine worship. By his profession of the evangelical counsels, then, he is more intimately consecrated to divine service[4]. This consecration will be the more perfect, in as much as the indissoluble bond of the union of Christ and His bride, the Church, is represented by firm and more stable bonds.

The evangelical counsels which lead to charity[5] join their followers to the Church and its mystery in a special way. Since this is so, the spiritual life of these people should then be devoted to the welfare of the whole Church. From this arises their duty of working to implant and strengthen the Kingdom of Christ in souls and to extend that Kingdom to every clime. This duty is to be undertaken to the extent of their capacities and in keeping with the proper type of their own vocation. This can be realized through prayer or active works of the apostolate. It is for this reason that the Church preserves and fosters the special character of her various religious institutes.

The profession of the evangelical counsels, then, appears as a sign which can and ought to attract all the members of the Church to an effective and prompt fulfillment of the duties of their Christian vocation. The people of God have no lasting city here below, but look forward to one that is to come. Since this is so, the religious state, whose purpose is to free its members from earthly cares, more fully manifests to all believers the presence of heavenly goods already possessed here below. Furthermore, it not only witnesses to the fact of a new and eternal life acquired by the redemption of Christ, but it foretells the future resurrection and the glory of the heavenly kingdom. Christ proposed to His disciples this form of life, which He, as the Son of God, accepted in entering this world to do the will of the Father. This same state of life is accurately exemplified and perpetually made present in the Church. The religious state clearly manifests that the Kingdom of God and its needs, in a very special way, are

raised above all earthly considerations. Finally it clearly shows all men both the unsurpassed breadth of the strength of Christ the King and the infinite power of the Holy Spirit marvelously working in the Church.

Thus, the state which is constituted by the profession of the evangelical counsels, though it is not the hierarchial structure of the Church, nevertheless undeniably belongs to its life and holiness.

45. It is the duty of the ecclesiastical hierarchy to regulate the practice of the evangelical counsels by law, since it is the duty of the same hierarchy to care for the People of God and to lead them to most fruitful pastures (Ezech. 34, 14). The importance of the profession of the evangelical counsels is seen in the fact that it fosters the perfection of love of God and love of neighbor in an outstanding manner and that this profession is strengthened by vows[6]. Furthermore, the hierarchy, following with docility the prompting of the Holy Spirit, accepts the rules presented by outstanding men and women and authentically approves these rules after further adjustments. It also aids by its vigilant and safeguarding authority those institutes variously established for the building up of Christ's Body in order that these same institutes may grow and flourish according to the spirit of the founders. Any institute of perfection and its individual members may be removed from the jurisdiction of the local Ordinaries by the Supreme Pontiff and subjected to himself alone. This is done in virtue of his primacy over the entire Church in order to more fully provide for the necessities of the entire flock of the Lord and in consideration of the common good[7]. In like manner, these institutes may be left or committed to the charge of the proper patriarchial authority. The members of these institutes, in fulfilling their obligation to the Church due to their particular form of life, ought to show reverence and obedience to bishops according to the sacred canons. The bishops are owed this respect because of their pastoral authority in their own churches and because of the need of unity and harmony in the apostolate[8].

The Church not only raises the religious profession to the dignity of a canonical state by her approval, but even manifests that this profession is a state consecrated to God by the liturgical setting of that profession. The Church itself, by the authority given to it by God, accepts the vows of the newly professed. It begs aid and grace from God for them by its public prayer. It commends them to God, imparts a spiritual blessing on them and accompanies their self-offering by the Eucharistic sacrifice.

46. Religious should carefully keep before their minds the fact that the Church presents Christ to believers and non-believers alike in a striking manner daily through them. The Church thus portrays Christ in con-

templation on the mountain, in His proclamation of the kingdom of God to the multitudes, in His healing of the sick and maimed, in His work of converting sinners to a better life, in His solicitude for youth and His goodness to all men, always obedient to the will of the Father who sent Him [9].

All men should take note that the profession of the evangelical counsels, though entailing the renunciation of certain values which are to be undoubtedly esteemed, does not detract from a genuine development of the human persons, but rather by its very nature is most beneficial to that development. Indeed the counsels, voluntarily undertaken according to each one's personal vocation, contribute a great deal to the purification of heart and spiritual liberty. They continually stir up the fervor of charity. But especially they are able to more fully mold the Christian man to that type of chaste and detached life, which Christ the Lord chose for Himself and which His Mother also embraced. This is clearly proved by the example of so many holy founders. Let no one think that Religious have become strangers to their fellowmen or useless citizens of this earthly city by their consecration. For even though it sometimes happens that religious do not directly mingle with their contemporaries, yet in a more profound sense these same Religious are united with them in the heart of Christ and spiritually cooperate with them. In this way the building up of the earthly city may have its foundation in the Lord and may tend toward Him, lest perhaps those who build this city shall have labored in vain [10].

Finally, this sacred synod encourages and praises the men and women, Brothers and Sisters, who in monasteries, or in schools and hospitals, or in the missions, adorn the Bride of Christ by their unswerving and humble faithfulness in their chosen consecration and render generous services of all kinds to mankind.

47. Let each of the faithful, called to the profession of the evangelical counsels, therefore, carefully see to it that he persevere and ever grow in that vocation God has given him. Let him do this for the increased holiness of the Church, for the greater glory of the one and undivided Trinity, which in and through Christ is the fount and the source of all holiness.

Chapter VII

The Eschatological Nature of the Pilgrim Church And Its Union With the Church in Heaven

48. The Church, to which we are all called in Christ Jesus, and in which we acquire sanctity through the grace of God, will attain its full perfection only in the glory of heaven, when there will come the time of the restoration of all things (Acts 3, 21). At that time the human race as well as the entire world, which is intimately related to man and attains to its end through him, will be perfectly re-established in Christ (Eph. 1, 10; Col. 1, 20; II Peter 3, 10-13).

Christ, having been lifted up from the earth has drawn all to Himself (John 12, 32). Rising from the dead (Rom. 6, 9) He sent His life-giving Spirit upon His disciples and through Him has established His Body which is the Church as the universal sacrament of salvation. Sitting at the right hand of the Father He is continually active in the world that He might lead men to the Church and through it join them to Himself and that He might make them partakers of His glorious life by nourishing them with His own Body and Blood. Therefore the promised restoration which we are awaiting has already begun in Christ, is carried forward in the mission of the Holy Spirit and through Him continues in the Church in which we learn the meaning of our terrestrial life through our faith, while we perform with hope in the future the work committed to us in this world by the Father, and thus work out our salvation (Phil. 2, 12).

Already the final age of the world has come upon us (1 Cor. 10, 11) and the renovation of the world is irrevocably decreed and is already anticipated in some kind of a real way; for the Church already on this earth is signed with a sanctity which is real although imperfect. However, until there shall be new heavens and a new earth in which justice dwells (2 Peter 3, 13) the pilgrim Church in her sacraments and institutions which pertain to this present time, has the appearance of this world which is passing and she herself dwells among creatures who groan and travail in pain until now and await the revelation of the sons of God (Rom. 8, 19-22.

Joined with Christ in the Church and signed with the Holy Spirit "who is the pledge of our inheritance"

(Eph. 1, 14), truly we are called and we are sons of God (I John 3, 1) but we have not yet appeared with Christ in glory (Col. 3, 4), in which we shall be like to God, since we shall see Him as He is (I John 3, 2). And therefore "while we are in the body, we are exiled from the Lord (II Cor. 5, 6) and having the first-fruits of the Spirit we groan within ourselves (Rom. 8, 23) and we desire to be with Christ" (Phil. 1, 23). By that same charity however, we are urged to live more for Him, who died for us and rose again (2 Cor. 5, 15). We strive therefore to please God in all things (2 Cor. 5, 9) and we put on the armor of God, that we may be able to stand against the wiles of the devil and resist in the evil day (Eph. 6, 11-13). Since however we know not the day nor the hour, on Our Lord's advice we must be constantly vigilant so that, having finished the course of our earthly life (Heb. 9, 27) we may merit to enter into the marriage feast with Him and to be numbered among the blessed (Matt. 25, 31-46) and that we may not be ordered to go into eternal fire (Matt. 25, 41) like the wicked and slothful servant (Matt. 25, 26), into the exterior darkness where "there will be the weeping and the gnashing of teeth" (Matt. 22, 13 and 25, 30). For before we reign with Christ in glory, all of us will be made manifest "before the tribunal of Christ, so that each one may receive what he has won through the body, according to his works, whether good or evil" (2 Cor. 5, 10) and at the end of the world "they who have done good shall come forth unto resurrection of life; but those who have done evil unto resurrection of judgment" (John 5, 29; Matt. 25, 46). Reckoning therefore that "the sufferings of the present time are not worthy to be compared with the glory to come that will be revealed in us" (Rom. 8, 18; 2 Tim. 2, 11-12) strong in faith we look for the "blessed hope and the glorious coming of our great God and Saviour, Jesus Christ" (Tit. 2, 13) "who will refashion the body of our lowliness, conforming it to the body of His glory" (Phil. 3, 21) and who will come "to be glorified in His saints and to be marveled at in all those who have believed" (2 Thess. 1, 10).

49. Until the Lord shall come in His majesty, and all the angels with Him (Matt. 25, 31) and death being destroyed, all things are subject to Him (I Cor. 15, 26-27), some of His disciples are exiles on earth, some having died are purified, and others are in glory beholding "clearly God Himself triune and one, as He is";[1] but all in various ways and degrees are in communion in the same charity of God and neighbor and all sing the same hymn of glory to our God. For all who are in Christ, having His Spirit, form one Church and cleave together in Him (Eph. 4, 16). Therefore the union of the wayfarers with the brethren who have gone to sleep in the peace of Christ is not in the least weakened or interrupted, but on the contrary, according to

the perpetual faith of the Church, is strengthened by a communication of spiritual goods[2]. For by reason of the fact that those in heaven are more closely united with Christ, they establish the whole Church more firmly in holiness, lend nobility to the worship which the Church offers to God here on earth and in many ways contribute to its greater edification (I Cor. 12, 12-27)[3]. For after they have been received into their heavenly home and are present to the Lord (II Cor. 5, 8), through Him and with Him and in Him they do not cease to intercede with the Father for us[4], showing forth the merits which they won on earth through the one Mediator between God and man (1 Tim. 2, 5), serving God in all things and filling up in their flesh those things which are lacking of the sufferings of Christ for His Body which is the Church (Col. 1, 24)[5]. Thus by their brotherly interest our weakness is greatly strengthened.

50. Fully conscious of this communion of the whole Mystical Body of Jesus Christ, the pilgrim Church from the very first ages of the Christian religion has cultivated with great piety the memory of the dead[6], and "because it is a holy and wholesome thought to pray for the dead that they may be loosed from their sins" (2 Mach. 12, 46), also offers suffrages for them. The Church has always believed that the apostles and Christ's martyrs who had given the supreme witness of faith and charity by the shedding of their blood, are closely joined with us in Christ, and she has always venerated them with special devotion, together with the Blessed Virgin Mary and the holy angels[7]. The Church has piously implored the aid of their intercession. To these were soon added also those who had more closely imitated Christ's virginity and poverty[8], and finally others whom the outstanding practice of the Christian virtues[9] and the divine charisms recommended to the pious devotion and imitation of the faithful[10].

When we look at the lives of those who have faithfully followed Christ, we are inspired with a new reason for seeking the City that is to come (Heb. 13, 14; 11, 10) and at the same time we are shown a most safe path by which among the vicissitudes of this world, in keeping with the state in life and condition proper to each of us, we will be able to arrive at perfect union with Christ, that is, perfect holiness[11]. In the lives of those who, sharing in our humanity, are however more perfectly transformed into the image of Christ (II Cor. 3, 18), God vividly manifests His presence and His face to men. He speaks to us in them, and gives us a sign of His Kingdom[12], to which we are strongly drawn, having so great a cloud of witnesses over us (Heb. 12, 1) and such a witness to the truth of the Gospel.

Nor is it by the title of example only that we cherish the memory of those in heaven, but still more in order that the union of the whole Church may be strengthened in the Spirit by the practice of fraternal charity (Eph. 4, 1-6). For just as Christian communion among wayfarers brings us closer to Christ, so our companionship with the saints joins us to Christ, from whom as from its Fountain and Head issues every grace and the very life of the people of God[13]. It is supremely fitting, therefore, that we love those friends and co-heirs of Jesus Christ, who are also our brothers and extraordinary benefactors, that we render due thanks to God for them[14] and "suppliantly invoke them and have recourse to their prayers, their power and help in obtaining benefits from God through His Son, Jesus Christ, who is our Redeemer and Saviour.[15]" For every genuine testimony of love shown by us to those in heaven, by its very nature tends toward and terminates in Christ who is the "crown of all saints,"[16] and through Him, in God Who is wonderful in His Saints and is magnified in them[17].

Our union with the Church in heaven is put into effect in its noblest manner especially in the sacred Liturgy, wherein the power of the Holy Spirit acts upon us through sacramental signs. Then, with combined rejoicing we celebrate together the praise of the divine majesty;[18] then all those from every tribe and tongue and people and nation (Apoc. 5, 9) who have been redeemed by the blood of Christ and gathered together into one Church, with one song of praise magnify the one and triune God. Celebrating the Eucharistic sacrifice therefore, we are most closely united to the Church in heaven in communion with and venerating the memory first of all of the glorious ever-Virgin Mary, of Blessed Joseph and the blessed apostles and martyrs and of all the saints[19].

51. This sacred council accepts with great devotion this venerable faith of our ancestors regarding this vital fellowship with our brethren who are in heavenly glory or who having died are still being purified; and it proposes again the decrees of the Second Council of Nicea[20], the Council of Florence[21] and the Council of Trent[22]. And at the same time, in conformity with our own pastoral interests, we urge all concerned, if any abuses, excesses or defects have crept in here or there, to do what is in their power to remove or correct them, and to restore all things to a fuller praise of Christ and of God. Let them therefore teach the faithful that the authentic cult of the saints consists not so much in the multiplying of external acts, but rather in the greater intensity of our love, whereby, for our own greater good and that of the whole Church, we seek from the saints "example in their way of life, fellowship in their communion, and aid by their intercession."[23] On the other hand, let them teach the faithful that our communion with those in heaven, provided that it is understood in the fuller light of faith according to its genuine nature, in no way weakens, but conversely, more thoroughly enriches the latreutic worship we give to God the Father, through Christ, in the Spirit[24].

For all of us, who are sons of God and constitute one family in Christ (Heb. 3, 6), as long as we remain in communion with one another in mutual charity and in one praise of the most holy Trinity, are corresponding with the intimate vocation of the Church and partaking in foretaste the liturgy of consummate glory[25]. For when Christ shall appear and the glorious resurrection of the dead will take place, the glory of God will light up the heavenly City and the Lamb will be the lamp thereof (Apoc. 21, 24). Then the whole Church of the saints in the supreme happiness of charity will adore God and "the Lamb who was slain" (Apoc. 5, 12), proclaiming with one voice: "To Him who sits upon the throne, and to the Lamb blessing, and honor, and glory, and dominion forever and ever" (Apoc. 5, 13-14).

Chapter VIII

The Blessed Virgin Mary, Mother of God, In the Mystery of Christ and the Church

I. Introduction

52. Wishing in His supreme goodness and wisdom to effect the redemption of the world, "when the fulness of time came, God sent His Son, born of a woman, . . . that we might receive the adoption of sons" (Gal. 4, 4-5). "He for us men, and for our salvation, came down from heaven, and was incarnate by the Holy Spirit from the Virgin Mary."[1] This divine mystery of salvation is revealed to us and continued in the Church, which the Lord established as His body. Joined to Christ the Head and in the unity of fellowship with all His saints, the faithful must in the first place reverence the memory "of the glorious ever Virgin Mary,

Mother of our God and Lord Jesus Christ" (Gal. 4, 4-5)[2].

53. The Virgin Mary, who at the message of the angel received the Word of God in her heart and in her body and gave Life to the world, is acknowledged and honored as being truly the Mother of God and Mother of the Redeemer. Redeemer by reason of the merits of her Son and united to Him by a close and indissoluble tie, she is endowed with the high office and dignity of being the Mother of the Son of God, by which account she is also the beloved daughter of the Father and the temple of the Holy Spirit. Because of this gift of sublime grace she far surpasses all creatures, both in heaven and on earth. At the same time, however, because she belongs to the offspring of Adam she is one with all those who are to be saved. She is "the mother of the members of Christ . . . having cooperated by charity that faithful might be born in the Church, who are members of that Head."[3] Wherefore she is hailed as a preeminent and singular member of the Church, and as its type and excellent examplar in faith and charity. The Catholic Church, taught by the Holy Spirit, honors her with filial affection and piety as a most beloved mother.

54. Wherefore this holy synod, in expounding the doctrine on the Church, in which the divine Redeemer works salvation, intends to describe with diligence both the role of the Blessed Virgin in the mystery of the Incarnate Word and the Mystical Body, and the duties of redeemed mankind toward the Mother of God, who is mother of Christ and mother of men, particularly of the faithful. It does not, however, have it in mind to give a complete doctrine on Mary, nor does it wish to decide those questions which the work of theologians has not yet fully clarified. Those opinions therefore may be lawfully retained which are propounded in Catholic schools concerning her, who occupies a place in the Church which is the highest after Christ and yet very close to us.[4]

II. The Role of the Blessed Mother in the Economy of Salvation

55. The Sacred Scriptures of both the Old and the New Testament, as well as ancient Tradition show the role of the Mother of the Saviour in the economy of salvation in an ever clearer light and draw attention to it. The books of the Old Testament describe the history of salvation, by which the coming of Christ into the world was slowly prepared. These earliest documents, as they are read in the Church and are understood in the light of a further and full revelation, bring the figure of the woman, Mother of the Redeemer, into a gradually clearer light. When it is looked at in this way, she is already prophetically foreshadowed in the promise of victory over the serpent which was given to our first parents after their fall into sin (cf. Gen. 3, 15).

Likewise she is the Virgin who shall conceive and bear a son, whose name will be called Emmanuel (cf. Is. 7, 14; Mich. 5, 2-3; Matt. 1, 22-23). She stands out among the poor and humble of the Lord, who confidently hope for and receive salvation from Him. With her the exalted Daughter of Sion, and after a long expectation of the promise, the times are fulfilled and the new Economy established, when the Son of God took a human nature from her, that He might in the mysteries of His flesh free man from sin.

56. The Father of mercies willed that the incarnation should be preceded by the acceptance of her who was predestined to be the mother of His Son, so that just as a woman contributed to death, so also a woman should contribute to life. That is true in outstanding fashion of the mother of Jesus, who gave to the world Him who is Life itself and who renews all things, and who was enriched by God with the gifts which befit such a role. It is no wonder therefore that the usage prevailed among the Fathers whereby they called the mother of God entirely holy and free from all stain of sin, as though fashioned by the Holy Spirit and formed as a new creature.[5] Adorned from the first instant of her conception with the radiance of an entirely unique holiness, the Virgin of Nazareth is greeted, on God's command, by an angel messenger as "full of grace" (Luke 1, 28), and to the heavenly messenger she replies: "Behold the handmaid of the Lord, be it done unto me according to thy word" (Luke 1, 38). Thus Mary, a daughter of Adam, consenting to the divine Word, became the mother of Jesus, the one and only Mediator. Embracing God's salvific will with a full heart and impeded by no sin, she devoted herself totally as a handmaid of the Lord to the person and work of her Son, under Him and with Him, by the grace of almighty God, serving the mystery of redemption. Rightly therefore the holy Fathers see her as used by God not merely in a passive way, but as freely cooperating in the work of human salvation through faith and obedience. For, as St. Irenaeus says, she "being obedient, became the cause of salvation for herself and for the whole human race."[6] Hence not a few of the early Fathers gladly assert in their preaching: "The knot of Eve's disobedience was untied by Mary's obedience; what the virgin Eve bound through her unbelief, the Virgin Mary loosened by her faith."[7] Comparing Mary with Eve, they call her "the Mother of the living,"[8] and still more often they say: "death through Eve, life through Mary."[9]

57. This union of the Mother with the Son in the work of salvation is made manifest from the time of Christ's virginal conception up to His death. It is shown first of all when Mary, arising in haste to go to visit Elizabeth, is greeted by her as blessed because of her belief in the promise of salvation and the precursor leaped with joy in the womb of his mother (cf. Luke 1,

41-45). This union is manifest also at the birth of Our Lord, who did not diminish His mother's virginal integrity but sanctified it,[10] when the Mother of God joyfully showed her firstborn Son to the shepherds and Magi. When she presented Him to the Lord in the temple, making the offering of the poor, she heard Simeon foretelling at the same time that her Son would be a sign of contradiction and that a sword would pierce the mother's soul, that out of many hearts thoughts might be revealed (cf. Luke 2, 34-35). When the Child Jesus was lost and they had sought Him sorrowing, His parents found Him in the temple, taken up with the things that were His Father's business; and they did not understand the word of their Son. His mother indeed kept these things to be pondered over in her heart (cf. Luke 2, 41-51).

58. In the public life of Jesus, Mary makes significant appearances. This is so even at the very beginning, when at the marriage feast of Cana, moved with pity, she brought about by her intercession the beginning of miracles of Jesus the Messiah (cf. John 2, 1-11). In the course of her Son's preaching she received the words whereby, in extolling a kingdom beyond the calculations and bonds of flesh and blood, He declared blessed (cf. Mark 3, 35; Luke 11, 27-28) those who heard and kept the word of God, as she was faithfully doing (cf. Luke 2, 19, 51). After this manner, the Blessed Virgin advanced in her pilgrimage of faith, and faithfully persevered in her union with her Son unto the cross, where she stood, in keeping with the divine plan (cf. John 19, 25), grieving exceedingly with her only begotten Son, uniting herself with a maternal heart with His sacrifice, and lovingly consenting to the immolation of this Victim which she herself had brought forth. Finally, she was given by the same Christ Jesus dying on the cross as a mother to His disciple, with these words: "Woman, behold thy son" (John 19, 26-27).[11]

59. But since it has pleased God not to manifest solemnly the mystery of the salvation of the human race before He would pour forth the Spirit promised by Christ, we see the apostles before the day of Pentecost "persevering with one mind in prayer with the women and Mary the Mother of Jesus, and with His brethren" (Acts 1, 14), and Mary by her prayers imploring the gift of the Spirit, who had already overshadowed her in the Annunciation. Finally, the Immaculate Virgin, preserved free from all guilt of original sin,[12] on the completion of her earthly sojourn, was taken up body and soul into heavenly glory,[13] and exalted by the Lord as Queen of the universe, that she might be the more fully conformed to her Son, the Lord of lords (cf. Apoc. 19, 16) and the conqueror of sin and death.[14]

III. On the Blessed Virgin and the Church

60. There is but one Mediator as we know from the words of the apostle, "for there is one God and one mediator of God and men, the man Christ Jesus, who gave himself a redemption for all" (1 Tim. 2, 5-6). The maternal duty of Mary toward men in no wise obscures or diminishes this unique mediation of Christ, but rather shows His power. For all the salvific influence of the Blessed Virgin on men originates, not from some inner necessity, but from the divine pleasure. It flows forth from the superabundance of the merits of Christ, rests on His mediation, depends entirely on it and draws all its power from it. In no way does it impede, but rather does it foster the immediate union of the faithful with Christ.

61. Predestined from eternity to be the Mother of God by that decree of divine providence which determined the incarnation of the Word, the Blessed Virgin was on this earth the virgin Mother of the Redeemer, and above all others and in a singular way the generous associate and humble handmaid of the Lord. She conceived, brought forth, and nourished Christ, she presented Him to the Father in the temple, and was united with Him by compassion as He died on the Cross. In this singular way she cooperated by her obedience, faith, hope and burning charity in the work of the Saviour in giving back supernatural life to souls. Wherefore she is our mother in the order of grace.

62. This maternity of Mary in the order of grace began with the consent which she gave in faith at the Annunciation and which she sustained without wavering beneath the cross, and lasts until the eternal fulfilment of all the elect. Taken up to heaven she did not lay aside this salvific duty, but by her constant intercession continued to bring us the gifts of eternal salvation.[15] By her maternal charity, she cares for the brethren of her Son, who still journey on earth surrounded by dangers and difficulties, until they are led into the happiness of their true home. Therefore the Blessed Virgin is invoked by the Church under the titles of Advocate, Auxiliatrix, Adjutrix, and Mediatrix.[16] This, however, is to be so understood that it neither takes away from nor adds anything to the dignity and efficaciousness of Christ the one Mediator.[17]

For no creature could ever be counted as equal with the Incarnate Word and Redeemer. Just as the priesthood of Christ is shared in various ways both by the ministers and by the faithful, and as the one goodness of God is really communicated in different ways to His creatures, so also the unique mediation of the Redeemer does not exclude but rather gives rise to a manifold cooperation which is but a sharing in this one source.

The Church does not hesitate to profess this subordinate role of Mary. It knows it through unfailing experience of it and commends it to the hearts of the faithful, so that encouraged by this maternal help they may the more intimately adhere to the mediator and Redeemer.

63. By reason of the gift and role of divine maternity, by which she is united with her Son, the Redeemer, and with His singular graces and functions, the Blessed Virgin is also intimately united with the Church. As St. Ambrose taught, the Mother of God is a type of the Church in the order of faith, charity and perfect union with Christ.[18] For in the mystery of the Church, which is itself rightly called mother and virgin, the Blessed Virgin stands out in eminent and singular fashion as exemplar both of virgin and mother.[19] By her belief and obedience, not knowing man but overshadowed by the Holy Spirit, as the new Eve she brought forth on earth the very Son of the Father, showing an undefiled faith, not in the word of the ancient serpent, but in that of God's messenger. The Son whom she brought forth is He whom God placed as the first-born among many brethren (cf. Rom. 8, 29), namely the faithful, in whose birth and education she cooperates with a maternal love.

64. The Church indeed, contemplating her hidden sanctity, imitating her charity and faithfully fulfilling the Father's will, by receiving the word of God in faith becomes herself a mother. By her preaching she brings forth to a new and immortal life the sons who are born to her in baptism, conceived of the Holy Spirit and born of God. She herself is a virgin, who keeps the faith given to her by her Spouse whole and entire. Imitating the mother of her Lord, and by the power of the Holy Spirit, she keeps with virginal purity an entire faith, a firm hope and a sincere charity. [20]

65. But while in the most holy Virgin the Church has already reached that perfection whereby she is without spot or wrinkle, the followers of Christ still strive to increase in holiness by conquering sin (cf. Eph. 5, 27). And so they turn their eyes to Mary who shines forth to the whole community of the elect as the model of virtues. Piously meditating on her and contemplating her in the light of the Word made man, the Church with reverence enters more intimately into the great mystery of the Incarnation and becomes more and more like her Spouse. For Mary, who since her entry into salvation history unites in herself the greatest teachings of the Faith she is being proclaimed and venerated, calls the faithful to her Son and His sacrifice and to the love of the Father. Seeking after the glory of Christ, the Church becomes more like her exalted Type, and continually progresses in faith, hope and charity, seeking and doing the will of God in all things. Hence the Church, in her apostolic work also, justly looks to her, who brought forth Christ, who was conceived of the Holy Spirit and who was born of the Virgin that through the Church He may be born and may increase in the hearts of the faithful also. The Virgin in her own life lived an example of that maternal love, by which it behooves that all should be animated who cooperate in the apostolic mission of the Church for the regeneration of men.

IV. *The Cult of the Blessed Virgin in the Church.*

66. Placed by the grace of God, as God's Mother, next to her Son, and exalted above all angels and men, Mary intervened in the mysteries of Christ and is justly honored by a special cult in the Church. Clearly from earliest times the Blessed Virgin is honored under the title of Mother of God, under whose protection the faithful took refuge in all their dangers and necessities.[21] Hence after the Synod of Ephesus the cult of the people of God toward Mary wonderfully increased in veneration and love, in invocation and imitation, according to her own prophetic words: "All generations shall call me blessed, because He that is mighty hath done great things to me" (Luke 1, 48). This cult, as it always existed, although it is altogether singular, differs essentially from the cult of adoration which is offered to the Incarnate Word, as well to the Father and the Holy Spirit, and it is most favorable to it. The various forms of piety toward the Mother of God, which the Church within the limits of sound and orthodox doctrine, according to the conditions of time and place, and the nature and ingenuity of the faithful has approved, bring it about that while the Mother is honored, the Son, through whom all things have their being (cf. Col. 1, 15-16) and in whom it has pleased the Father that all fulness should dwell (cf. Col. 1, 19), is rightly known, loved and glorified and that all His commands are observed.

67. This most holy synod deliberately teaches this Catholic doctrine and at the same time admonishes all the sons of the Church that the cult, especially the liturgical cult, of the Blessed Virgin, be generously fostered, and the practices and exercises of piety, recommended by the magisterium of the Church toward her in the course of centuries be made of great moment, and those decrees, which have been given in the early days regarding the cult of images of Christ, the Blessed Virgin and the saints, be religiously observed.[22] But it exhorts theologians and preachers of the divine word to abstain zealously both from all gross exaggerations as well as from petty narrowmindedness in considering the singular dignity of the Mother of God.[23] Following the study of Sacred Scripture, the Holy Fathers, the doctors and liturgy of the Church, and under the guidance of the Church's magisterium, let them rightly illustrate the duties and privileges of the Blessed Virgin which always look to Christ, the source of all truth, sanctity and piety. Let them assiduously keep away from whatever, either by word or deed, could lead separated brethren or any other into error regarding the true

doctrine of the Church. Let the faithful remember moreover that true devotion consists neither in sterile or transitory affection, nor in a certain vain credulity, but proceeds from true faith by which we are led to know the excellence of the Mother of God, and we are moved to a filial love toward our mother and to the imitation of her virtues.

V. *Mary the sign of created hope and solace to the wandering people of God.*

68. In the interim just as the Mother of Jesus, glorified in body and soul in heaven, is the image and beginning of the Church as it is to be perfected in the world to come, so too does she shine forth on earth, until the day of the Lord shall come (cf. II Peter 3, 10), as a sign of sure hope and solace to the people of God during its sojourn on earth.

69. It gives great joy and comfort to this holy and general synod that even among the separated brethren there are some who give due honor to the Mother of Our Lord and Saviour, especially among the Orientals, who with devout mind and fervent impulse give honor to the Mother of God, ever virgin. [24] The entire body of the faithful pours forth instant supplications to the Mother of God and Mother of men that she, who aided the beginnings of the Church by her prayers, may now, exalted as she is above all the angels and saints, intercede before her Son in the fellowship of all the saints, until all families of people, whether they are honored with the title of Christian or whether they still do not know the Saviour, may be happily gathered together in peace and harmony into one people of God, for the glory of the Most Holy and Undivided Trinity.

Footnotes on the Constitution on the Church

Chapter I

The Mystery of the Church

[1] Cfr. S. Cyprianus, *Epist.* 64, 4: PL 3, 1017. CSEL (Hartel) III B, p. 720. S. Hilarius Pict., *In Mt.* 23, 6: PL 9, 1047. S. Augustinus, *passim.* S. Cyrillus Alex., *Glaph. in Gen.* 2, 10: PG 69, 110 A.

[2] Cfr. S. Gregorius M., *Hom. in Evang.* 19, 1: PL 76, 1154 B. S. Augustinus, *Serm.* 341, 9, 11: PL 39, 1499 s. S. Io. Damascenus, *Adv. Iconocl.* 11: PG 96, 1357.

[3] Cfr. S. Irenaeus, *Adv. Haer.* III, 24, 1: PG 7, 966 B; Harvey 2, 131; ed. Sagnard, *Sources Chr.*, p. 398.

[4] S. Cyprianus, *De Orat. Dom.* 23: PL 4, 553; Hartel, III A, p. 285, S. Augustinus, *Serm.* 71, 20, 33: PL 38, 463 s. S. Io. Damascenus, *Adv. Iconocl.* 12: PG 96, 1358 D.

[5] Cfr. Origenes, *In Matth.* 16, 21: PG 13, 1443 C; Tertullianus, *Adv. Marc.* 3, 7: PL 2, 357 C; CSEL 47, 3 p. 386. Pro documentis liturgicis, cfr. *Sacramentarium Gregorianum*: PL 78, 160 B. Vel C. Mohlberg, *Liber Sacramentorum romanae ecclesiae*, Romae 1960, p. 111, XC: "Deus, qui ex omni coaptacione sanctorum aeternum tibi condis habitaculum . . ." Hymnus *Urbs Ierusalem beata* in Breviario monastico, et *Coelestis urbs Ierusalem* in Breviario Romano.

[6] Cfr. S. Thomas, *Summa Theol.* III, q. 62, a. 5, ad 1.

[7] Cfr. Pius XII, Litt. Encycl. *Mystici Corporis*, 29 iun. 1943: *AAS* 35 (1943), p. 208

[8] Cfr. Leo XIII, Epist. Encycl. *Divinum illud*, 9 maii 1897: *AAS* 29 (1896-97) p. 650. Pius XII, Litt. Encycl. *Mystici Corporis*, l. c., pp. 219-220; Denz. 2288 (3808). S. Augustinus, *Serm.* 268, 2: PL 38, 1232, et alibi. S. Io. Chrysostomus, *In Eph.* Hom. 9, 3: PG 62, 72. Didymus Alex., *Trin.* 2, 1: PG 39, 449 s. S. Thomas, *In Col.* 1, 18, lect. 5; ed. Marietti, II, n. 46: "Sicut constituitur unum corpus ex unitate animae, ita Ecclesia ex unitate Spiritus . . ."

[9] Leo XIII, Litt. Encycl. *Sapientiae christianae*, 10 ian. 1890: *AAS* 22 (1889-90) p. 392. Id., Epist. Encycl. *Satis cognitum*, 29 iun. 1896: *AAS* 28 (1895-96) pp. 710 et 724 ss. Pius XII, Litt. Encycl. *Mystici Corporis*, l. c., pp. 199-200.

[10] Cfr. Pius XII, Litt. Encycl. *Mystici Corporis*, l. c., p. 221 ss. Id., Litt. Encycl. *Humani generis*, 12 aug. 1950: *AAS* 42 (1950) p. 571.

[11] Leo XIII, Epist. Encycl. *Satis cognitum*, l. c., p. 713.

[12] Cfr. *Symbolum Apostolicum*: Denz. 6-9 (10-13); *Symb. Nic.-Const.*: Denz. 86 (150); coll. *Prof. fidei Trid.*: Denz. 994 et 999 (1862 et 1868).

[13] Dicitur "Sancta (catholica apostolica) Romana Ecclesia": in *Prof. fidei Trid.*, l. c. et Conc. Vat. I, Sess. III, Const. dogm. *de fide cath.*: Denz. 1782 (3001).

[14] S. Augustinus, *Civ. Dei*, XVIII, 51, 2: PL 41, 614.

Chapter II

On the People of God

[1] Cfr. S. Cyprianus, *Epist.* 69, 6: PL 3, 1142 B; Hartel 3 B, p. 754: "inseparabile unitatis sacramentum."

[2] Cfr. Pius XII, Alloc. *Magnificate Dominum*, 2 nov. 1954: AAS 46 (1954) p. 669. Litt Encycl. *Mediator Dei*, 20 nov. 1947: *AAS* 39 (1947) p. 555.

[3] Cfr. Pius XI, Litt. Encycl. *Miserentissimus Re-*

demptor, 8 maii 1928: *AAS* 20 (1928) p. 171 s. Pius XII, Alloc. *Vous nous avez*, 22 sept. 1956: *AAS* 48 (1956) p. 714.

(4) Cfr. S. Thomas, *Summa Theol.* III, q. 63, a. 2.

(5) Cfr. S. Cyrillus Hieros., *Catech.*, 17, de Spiritu Sancto, II, 35-37: PG 33, 1009-1012. Nic. Cabasilas, *De vita in Christo*, lib. III, de utilitate chrismatis: PG 150, 569-580. S. Thomas, *Summa Theol.* III, q. 65, a. 3 et q. 72, a. 1 et 5.

(6) Cfr. Pius XII, Litt. Encycl. *Mediator Dei*, 20 nov. 1947: *AAS* 39 (1947), praesertim p. 552 s.

(7) *1 Cor.* 7, 7: "Unusquisque proprium donum (idion charisma) habet ex Deo: alius quidem sic, alius vero sic". Cfr. S. Augustinus, *De Dono Persev.* 14, 37: PL 45, 1015 s.: "Non tantum continentia Dei donum est, sed coniugatorum etiam castitas".

(8) Cfr. S. Augustinus, *De Praed. Sanct.* 14, 27: PL 44, 980.

(9) Cfr. S. Io. Chrysostomus, *In Io.* Hom. 65, 1: PG 59, 361.

(10) Cfr. S. Irenaeus, *Adv. Haer*, III, 16, 6; III, 22, 1-3: PG 7, 925 C-926 A et 955 C-958 A; Harvey 2, 87 s. et 120-123; Sagnard, Ed. *Sources Chrét.*, pp. 290-292 et 372 ss.

(11) Cfr. S. Ignatius M., *Ad Rom., Praef.*: Ed. Funk, I. p. 252.

(12) Cfr. S. Augustinus, *Bapt. c. Donat.* V. 28, 39: PL 43, 197: "Certe manifestum est, id quod dicitur, in Ecclesia intus et foris, in corde, non in corpore cogitandum". Cfr. *ib.*, III, 19, 26: col. 152; V, 18, 24: col. 189; *In Io.* Tr. 61, 2: PL 35, 1800, et alibi saepe.

(13) Cfr. *Lc.* 12, 48: "Omni autem, cui multum datum est, multum quaeretur ab eo." Cfr. etiam *Mt.* 5, 19-20; 7, 21-22; 25, 41-46; *Iac.* 2, 14.

(14) Cfr. Leo XIII, Epist. Apost. *Praeclara gratulatinis*, 20 iun. 1894; *ASS* 26 (1893-94) p. 707.

(15) Cfr. Leo XIII, Epist. Encycl. *Satis cognitum*, 29 iun. 1896: *ASS* 28 (1895-96) p. 738. Epist. Encycl. *Caritatis stadium*, 25 iul. 1898: *ASS* 31 (1898-99) p. 11. Pius XII, Nuntius radioph. *Nell'alba*, 24 dec. 1941: *ASS* 34 (1942) p. 21.

(16) Cfr. Pius XI, Litt. Encycl. *Rerum Orientalium*, 8 sept. 1928: *AAS* 20 (1928) p. 287. Pius XII, Litt. Encycl. *Orientalis Ecclesiae*, 9 apr. 1944: *AAS* 36 (1944) p. 137.

(17) Cfr. Inst. S.S.C.S. Officii, 20 dec. 1949: *AAS* 42 (1950) p. 142.

(18) Cfr. S. Thomas, *Summa Theol.* III, q. 8, a. 3, ad 1.

(19) Cfr. *Epist.* S.S.C.S. Officii ad Archiep. Boston.: Denz. 3869-72.

(20) Cfr. Eusebius Caes., *Praeparatio Evangelica*, 1, 1: PG 21, 28 AB.

(21) Cfr. Benedictus XV, Epist. Apost. *Maximum illud*: *AAS* 11 (1919) p. 440, praesertim p. 451 ss. Pius

XI, Litt. Encycl. *Rerum Ecclesiae*: *AAS* 18 (1926) p. 68-69. Pius XII, Litt. Encycl. *Fidei Donum*, 21 apr. 1957: *AAS* 49 (1957) pp. 236-237.

(22) Cfr. *Didachè*, 14: ed. Funk, I, p. 32. S. Iustinus, *Dial.* 41: PG. 6, 564. S. Irenaeus, *Adv. Haer.* IV, 17, 5; PG 7, 1023; Harvey, 2, p. 199 s. Conc. Trid., Sess. 22, cap. 1; Denz. 939 (1742).

Chapter III
On the Hierarchical Structure of the Church
And in Particular on the Episcopate

(1) Cfr. Conc. Vat. I, Sess. IV, Const. Dogm. *Pastor aeternus*: Denz. 1821 (3050 s.).

(2) Cfr. Conc. Flor., Decretum pro Graecis: Denz. 694 (1307) et Conc. Vat. I, ib.: Denz. 1826 (3059).

(3) Cfr. *Liber sacramentorum* S. Gregorii, Praefatio in Cathedra S. Petri, in natali S. Mathiae et S. Thomas: PL 78, 50, 51 et 152. S. Hilarius, *In Ps.* 67, 10: PL 9, 450; CSEL 22, p. 286. S. Hieronymus, *Adv. Iovin.* 1, 26: PL 23, 247 A. S. Augustinus, *In Ps.* 86, 4: PL 37, 1103. S. Gregorius M., *Mor. in Iob*, XXVIII, V: PL 76, 455-456. Primasius, *Comm. in Apoc.* V: PL 68, 924 BC. Paschasius Radb., *In Matth.* L. VIII, cap. 16: PL 120, 561 C. Cfr. Leo XIII, Epist. *Et sane*, 17 dec. 1888: *ASS* 21 (1888) p. 321.

(4) Cfr. *Act.* 6, 2-6; 11, 30; 13, 1; 14, 23; 20, 17; *1 Thess.* 5, 12-13; *Phil.* 1, 1; *Col.* 4, 11, et passim.

(5) Cfr. *Act.* 20, 25-27; *2 Tim.* 4, 6 s. coll. c. *1 Tim.* 5, 22; *2 Tim.* 2, 2; *Tit.* 1, 5; S. Clem. Rom., *Ad Cor.* 44, 3; ed. Funk, I, p. 156.

(6) S. Clem. Rom., *Ad Cor.* 44, 2; ed. Funk, I, p. 154 s.

(7) Cfr. Tertull., *Praescr. Haer*, 32; PL 2, 52 s.; S. Ignatius M., passim.

(8) Cfr. Tertull., *Praescr. Haer.* 32; PL 2, 53.

(9) Cfr. S. Irenaeus, *Adv. Haer.* III, 3, 1; PG 7, 848 A; Harvey 2, 8; Sagnard, p. 100 s.: "manifestatam."

(10) Cfr. S. Irenaeus, *Adv. Haer.* III, 2, 2; PG 7, 847; Harvey 2, 7; Sagnard, p. 100: "custoditur", cfr. ib. IV, 26, 2; col. 1053; Harvey 2, 236, necnon IV, 33, 8; col. 1077; Harvey 2, 262.

(11) S. Ign. M., *Philad.* Praef.; ed. Funk, I, p. 264.

(12) S. Ign. M., *Philad.*, 1, 1; *Magn.* 6, 1; Ed. Funk, I, pp. 264 et 234.

(13) S. Clem. Rom., l. c., 42, 3-4; 44, 3-4; 57, 1-2; Ed. Funk, I, 152, 156, 171 s. S. Ign. M., *Philad.* 2; *Smyrn.* 8; *Magn.* 3; *Trall.* 7; Ed. Funk, I, p. 265 s.; 282; 232; 246 s. etc.; S. Iustinus, *Apol.*, *1*, 65; PG 6, 428; S. Cyprianus, *Epist.* passim.

(14) Cfr. Leo XIII, Epist. Encycl. *Satis cognitum*, 29 iun. 1896: *ASS* 28 (1895-96) p. 732.

(15) Cfr. Conc. Trid., Sess. 23, Decr. *de sacr. Ordinis*, cap. 4: Denz. 960 (1768); Conc. Vat. I, Sess. 4, Const. Dogm. *1 De Ecclesia Christi*, cap. 3: Denz. 1828 (3061). Pius XII, Litt. Encycl. *Mystici Corporis*, 29 iun.

1943: *ASS* 35 (1943) pp. 209 et 212. *Cod. Iur. Can.*, c. 329 § 1.

(16) Cfr. Leo XIII, Epist. *Et sane,* 17 dec. 1888: *ASS* 21 (1888) p. 321 s.

(17) S. Leo M., *Serm.* 5, 3: PL 54, 154.

(18) Conc. Trid., Sess. 23, cap. 3, citat verba 2 *Tim.* 1, 6-7, ut demonstret Ordinem esse verum sacramentum: Denz. 959 (1766).

(19) In *Trad. Apost.* 3, ed. Botte, *Sources Chr.,* pp. 27-30, Episcopo tribuitur "primatus sacerdotii". Cfr. *Sacramentarium Leonianum,* ed. C. Mohlberg, *Sacramentarium Veronense,* Romae, 1955, p. 119: "ad summi sacerdotii ministerium . . . Comple in sacerdotibus tuis mysterii tui summam" . . . Idem, *Liber Sacramentorum Romanae Ecclesiae,* Romae, 1960, pp. 121-122: "Tribuas eis, Domine, cathedram episcopalem ad regendam Ecclesiam tuam et plebem universam." Cfr. PL 78, 224.

(20) *Trad. Apost.* 2, ed. Botte, p. 27.

(21) Conc. Trid., Sess. 23, cap. 4, docet Ordinis sacramentum imprimere characterem indelebilem: Denz. 960 (1767). Cfr. Ioannes XXIII, Alloc. *Iubilate Deo,* 8 maii 1960: *AAS* 52 (1960) p. 466. Paulus VI, Homelia in Bas. Vaticana, 20 oct. 1963: *AAS* 55 (1963) p. 1014.

(22) S. Cyprianus, *Epist.* 63, 14: PL 4, 386; Hartel, III B, p. 713: "Sacerdos vice Christi vere fungitur." S. Io. Chrysostomus, *In 2 Tim.* Hom. 2, 4: PG 62, 612: Sacerdos est "symbolon" Christi. S. Ambrosius, *In Ps.* 38, 25-26: PL 14, 1051-52: CSEL 64, 203-204. Ambrosiaster, *In 1 Tim.* 5, 19: PL 17, 479 C et *In Eph.* 4, 11-12: col. 387. C. Theodorus Mops., *Hom. Catech.* XV, 21 et 24: cd. Tonneau, pp. 497 et 503. Hesychius Hieros., *In Lev.* L. 2, 9, 23: PG 93, 894 B.

(23) Cfr. Eusebius, *Hist. Eccl.,* V, 24, 10: GCS II, 1, p. 495; ed. Bardy, *Sources Chr.* II, p. 69. Dionysius, apud Eusebium, *ib.* VII, 5, 2: GCS II, 2, p. 638 s.; Bardy, II, p. 168 s.

(24) Cfr. de antiquis Conciliis, Eusebius, *Hist. Eccl.* V, 23-24: GCS II, 1, p. 488 ss.; Bardy, II, p. 66 ss. et passim. Conc. Nicaenum. Can. 5: *Conc. Oec. Decr.* p. 7.

(25) Tertullianus, *De Ieiunio,* 13: PL 2, 972 B; CSEL 20, p. 292, lin. 13-16.

(26) S. Cyprianus, *Epist.* 56, 3: Hartel, III, B, p. 650; Bayard, p. 154.

(27) Cfr. Relatio officialis Zinelli, in Conc. Vat. I: Mansi 52, 1109 C.

(28) Cfr. Conc. Vat. I, Schema Const. dogm. II, *de Ecclesia Christi,* c. 4: Mansi 53, 310. Cfr. Relatio Kleutgen de Schemate reformato: Mansi 53, 321 B-322 B et declaratio Zinelli: Mansi 52, 1110 A. Vide etiam S. Leonem M., *Serm.* 4, 3: PL 54, 151 A.

(29) Cfr. *Cod. Iur. Can.,* c. 227.

(30) Cfr. Conc. Vat. I, Const. Dogm. *Pastor aeternus*: Denz. 1821 (3050 s.).

(31) Cfr. S. Cyprianus, *Epist.* 66, 8: Hartel III, 2, p. 733: "Episcopus in Ecclesia et Ecclesia in Episcopo."

(32) Cfr. S. Cyprianus, *Epist.* 55, 24: Hartel, p. 642, lin. 13: "Una Ecclesia per totum mundum in multa membra divisa." *Epist.* 36, 4: Hartel, p. 575, lin. 20-21.

(33) Cfr. Pius XII, Litt. Encycl. *Fidei Donum,* 21 apr. 1957: *AAS* 49 (1957) p. 237.

(34) Cfr. S. Hilarius Pict., *In Ps.* 14, 3: PL 9, 206; CSEL 22, p. 86.—S. Gregorius M., *Moral.* IV, 7, 12: PL 75, 643 C. Ps.—Basilius, *In Is.* 15, 296: PG 30, 637 C.

(35) S. Coelestinus, *Epist.* 18, 1-2, ad Conc. Eph.: PL 50, 505 AB; Schwartz, *Acta Conc. Oec.* I, 1, 1, p. 22. Cfr. Benedictus XV, Epist. Apost. *Maximum illud*: *AAS* 11 (1919) p. 440, Pius XI. Litt. Encycl. *Rerum Ecclesiae,* 28 febr. 1926: *AAS* 18 (1926) p. 69. Pius XII, Litt. Encycl. *Fidei Donum,* 1. c.

(36) Leo XIII, Litt. Encycl. *Grande munus,* 30 sept. 1880: *ASS* 13 (1880) p. 145. Cfr. *Cod. Iur. Can.,* c. 1327; c. 1350 § 2.

(37) De iuribus Sedium patriarchalium, Cfr. Conc. Nicaenum, can. 6 de Alexandria et Antiochia, et can. 7 de Hierosolymis: *Conc. Oec. Decr.,* p. 8.—Conc. Later. IV, anno 1215, Constit. V: *De dignitate Patriarcharum*: ibid. p. 212.—Conc. Ferr.-Flor.: ibid. p. 504.

(38) Cfr. *Cod Iuris pro Eccl. Orient.,* c. 216-314: de Patriarchis; c. 324-399: de Archiepiscopis maioribus; c. 362-391: de aliis dignitariis; in specie, c. 238 § 3; 216; 240; 251; 255: de Episcopis a Patriarcha nominandis.

(39) Cfr. Conc. Trid., Decr. de reform., Sess. V, c. 2, n. 9; et Sess. XXIV, can. 4; *Conc. Oec. Decr.* pp. 645 et 739.

(40) Cfr. Conc. Vat. I, Const. dogm. *Dei Filius,* 3: Denz. 1712 (3011). Cfr. nota adiecta ad Schema I de Eccl. (desumpta ex. S. Rob. Bellarmino): Mansi 51, 579 C; necnon Schema reformatum Const. II de Ecclesia Christi, cum commentario Kleutgen: Mansi 53, 313 AB. Pius IX, Epist. *Tuas libenter*: Denz. 1683 (2879).

(41) Cfr. *Cod. Iur. Can.,* c. 1322-1323.

(42) Cfr. Conc. Vat. I, Const. dogm. *Pastor Aeternus*: Denz. 1839 (3074).

(43) Cfr. explicatio Gasser in Conc. Vat. I: Mansi 52, 1213 AC.

(44) Gasser, ib.: Mansi 1214 A.

(45) Gasser, ib.: Mansi 1215 CD, 1216-1217 A.

(46) Gasser, ib.: Mansi 1213.

(47) Conc. Vat. I, Const. dogm. *Pastor Aeternus,* 4: Denz. 1836 (3070).

(48) Oratio consecrationis episcopalis in ritu byzantino: *Euchologion to mega,* Romae, 1873, p. 139.

(49) Cfr. S. Ignatius M., *Smyrn* 8, 1: ed. Funk, I, p. 282.

(50) Cfr. *Act.* 8, 1; 14, 22-23; 20, 17, et passim.

(51) Oratio mozarabica: PL 96, 759 B.

(52) Cfr. S. Ignatius M., *Smyrn.* 8, 1: ed. Funk, I, p. 282.

(53) Cfr. S. Thomas, *Summa Theol.* III, q. 73, a. 3.

(54) Cfr. S. Augustinus, *C. Faustum*, 12, 20: PL 42, 265; *Serm.* 57, 7: PL 38, 389, etc.

(55) S. Leo M., *Serm.* 63, 7: PL 54, 357 C.

(56) *Traditio Apostolica Hippolyti*, 2-3: ed Botte, pp. 26-30.

(57) Cfr. textus *examinis* in initio consecrationis episcopalis, et *Oratio* in fine Missae eiusdem consecrationis, post *Te Deum.*

(58) Benedictus XIV, Br. *Romana Ecclesia*, 5 oct. 1752, § 1: *Bullarium Benedicti XIV*, t. IV, Romae, 1758, 21: "Episcopus Christi typum gerit, Eiusque munere fungitur." Pius XII, Litt. Encycl. *Mystici Corporis*, l. c., p. 211: "Assignatos sibi greges singuli singulos Christi nomine pascunt et regunt."

(59) Leo XIII, Epist. Encycl. *Satis cognitum*, 29 iun. 1896: *ASS* 28 (1895-96) p. 732. Idem, Epist. *Officio sanctissimo*, 22 dec. 1887: *ASS* 20 (1887) p. 264. Pius IX, Litt. Apost. ad Episcopos Germaniae, 12 mart. 1875, et Alloc. Consist., 15 mart. 1875: Denz. 3112-3117, in nova ed. tantum.

(60) Conc. Vat. I, Const. dogm. *Pastor aeternus,* 3: Denz. 1828 (3061). Cfr. Relatio Zinelli: Mansi 52, 1114 D.

(61) Cfr. S. Ignatius M., *Ad Ephes.* 5, 1: ed. Funk, I, p. 216.

(62) Cfr. S. Ignatius M., *Ad Ephes*, 6, 1: ed. Funk, I, p. 218.

(63) Cfr. Conc. Trid., Sess. 23, *De sacr. Ordinis,* cap. 2: Denz. 958 (1765), et can. 6: Denz. 966 (1776).

(64) Cfr. Innocentius I, *Epist. ad Decentium*: PL 20, 554 A; Mansi 3, 1029; Denz. 98 (215): "Presbyteri, licet secundi sint *sacerdotes*, pontificatus tamen *apicem* non habent." S. Cyprianus, *Epist.* 61, 3: ed. Hartel, p. 696.

(65) Cfr. Conc. Trid., l. c., Denz 956a-968 (1763-1778), et in specie can. 7: Denz. 967 (1777). Pius XII, Const. Apost. *Sacramentum Ordinis*: Denz. 2301 (3857-61).

(66) Cfr. Innocentius I, l. c.—S. Gregorius Naz., *Apol.* II, 22: PG 35, 432 B. Ps.-Dionysius, *Eccl. Hier.*, 1, 2: PG 3, 372 D.

(67) Cfr. Conc. Trid., Sess. 22: Denz. 940 (1743). Pius XII, Litt. Encycl. *Mediator Dei*, 20 nov. 1947: *AAS* 39 (1947) p. 553; Denz. 2300 (3850).

(68) Cfr. Conc. Trid. Sess. 22: Denz. 938 (1739-40). Conc. Vat. II, Const. *De Sacra Liturgia*, n. 7 et n. 47.

(69) Cfr. Pius XII, Litt. Encycl. *Mediator Dei*, l. c., sub. n. 67.

(70) Cfr. S. Cyprianus, *Epist.* 11, 3: PL 4, 242 B; Hartel, II, 2, p. 497.

(71) *Ordo consecrationis sacerdotalis*, in impositione vestimentorum.

(72) *Ordo consecrationis sacerdotalis*, in praefatione.

(73) Cfr. S. Ignatius M., *Philad.* 4: ed. Funk, I, p. 266. S. Cornelius I, apud S. Cyprianum, *Epist.* 48, 2: Hartel, III, 2, p. 610.

(74) *Constitutiones Ecclesiae aegyptiacae*, III, 2: ed. Funk, *Didascalia*, II, p. 103. *Statuta Eccl. Ant.* 37-41: Mansi 3, 954.

(75) S. Polycarpus, *Ad Phil.* 5, 2: ed. Funk, I, p. 300: Christus dicitur "omnium diaconus factus." Cfr. Didachè, 15, 1: ib., p. 32. S. Ignatius M., *Trall.* 2, 3: ib., p. 242. *Constitutiones Apostolorum*, 8, 28, 4: ed. Funk, *Didascalia*, I, p. 530.

Chapter IV

The Laity

(1) S. Augustinus, *Serm.* 340, 1: PL 38, 1483.

(2) Cfr. Pius XI, Litt. Encycl. *Quadragesimo anno*, 15 maii 1931: *ASS* 23 (1931) p. 221 s. Pius XII, Alloc. *De quelle consolation*, 14 oct. 1951: *ASS* 43 (1951) p. 790 s.

(3) Cfr. Pius XII, Alloc. *Six ans se sont écoulés*, 5 oct. 1957: *AAS* 49 (1957) p. 927. De "mandato" et missione canonica, Cfr. Decretum *De Apostolatu laicorum*, cap. IV, n. 16, cum notis 12 et 15.

(4) Ex *Praefatione* festi Christi Regis.

(5) Cfr. Leo XIII, Epist. Encycl. *Immortale Dei*, 1 nov. 1885: *AAS* 18 (1885) p. 166 ss. Idem, Litt. Encycl. *Sapientiae christianae*, 10 ian. 1890: *AAS* 22 (1889-90) p. 397 ss. Pius XII, Alloc. *Alla vostra filiale*, 23 mart. 1958: *AAS* 50 (1958) p. 220: "la legittima sana laicita dello Stato."

(6) *Cod. Iur. Can.*, can. 682.

(7) Cfr. Pius XII, Alloc. *De quelle consolation*, l. c., p. 789: "Dans les batailles décisives, c'est parfois du front que partent les plus heureuses initiatives . . ." Idem, Alloc. *L'importance de la presse catholique*, 17 febr. 1950: *AAS* 42 (1950) p. 256.

(8) Cfr. *1 Thess.* 5, 19 et *1 Io.* 4, 1.

(9) *Epist. ad Diognetum*, 6: ed. Funk, I, p. 400, Cfr. S. Io. Chrysostomus, *In Matth.* Hom. 46 (47), 2: PG 58, 478, de fermento in massa.

Chapter V

The Universal Call to Holiness in the Church

(1) *Missale Romanum*, *Gloria in excelsis.* Cfr. *Lc.* 1, 35; *Mc.* 1, 24; *Lc.* 4, 34; *Io.* 6, 69 (ho hagios tou Theou); *Act.* 3, 14; 4, 27 et 30; *Hebr.* 7, 26; *1 Io.* 2, 20; *Apoc.* 3, 7.

(2) Cfr. Origenes, *Comm. Rom.* 7, 7: PG 14, 1122 B. Ps.-Macarius, *De Oratione*, 11: PG 34, 861 AB. S. Thomas, *Summa Theol.* II-II, q. 184, a. 3.

(3) Cfr. S. Augustinus, *Retract.* II, 18: PL 32, 637 s.—Pius XII, Litt. Encycl. *Mystici Corporis,* 29 iun. 1943: *AAS* 35 (1943) p. 225.

(4) Cfr. Pius XI, Litt. Encycl. *Rerum omnium,* 26 ian. 1923: *AAS* 15 (1923) p. 50 et pp. 59-60. Litt. Encycl. *Casti Connubii,* 31 dec. 1930: *AAS* 22 (1930) p. 548. Pius XII, Const. Apost. *Provida Mater,* 2 febr. 1947: *AAS* 39 (1947) p. 117. Alloc. *Annus sacer,* 8 dec. 1950: *AAS* 43 (1951) pp. 27-28. Alloc. *Nel darvi,* 1 iul. 1956: *AAS* 48 (1956) p. 574 s.

(5) Cfr. S. Thomas, *Summa Theol.* II-II, q. 184, a. 5 et 6. *De perf. vitae spir.,* c. 18. Origenes, *In Is.* Hom. 6, 1: PG 13, 239.

(6) Cfr. S. Ignatius M., *Magn.* 13, 1: ed. Funk, I, p. 241.

(7) Cfr. S. Pius X, Exhort. *Haerent animo,* 4 aug. 1908: *ASS* 41 (1908) p. 560 s. *Cod Iur. Can.,* can. 124. Pius XI, Litt. Encycl. *Ad catholici sacerdotii,* 20 dec. 1935: *AAS* 28 (1936) p. 22 s.

(8) *Ordo consecrationis sacerdotalis,* in Exhortatione initiali.

(9) Cfr. S. Ignatius M., *Trall.* 2, 3: ed. Funk, I, p. 244.

(10) Cfr. Pius XII, Alloc. *Sous la maternelle protection,* 9 dec. 1957: *AAS* 50 (1958) p. 36.

(11) Pius XI, Litt. Encycl. *Casti Connubii,* 31 dec. 1930: *AAS* 22 (1930) p. 548 s. Cfr. S. Io Chrysostomus, *In Ephes.* Hom. 20, 2: PG 62, 136 ss.

(12) Cfr. S. Augustinus, *Enchir.* 121, 32: PL 40, 288. S. Thomas, *Summa Theol.* II-II, q. 184, a. 1. Pius XII, Adhort. Apost. *Menti nostrae,* 23 sept. 1950: *AAS* 42 (1950) p. 660.

(13) De consiliis in genere, Cfr. Origenes, *Comm. Rom.* X, 14: PG 14, 1275 B. S. Augustinus, *De S. Virginitate,* 15, 15: PL 40, 403. S. Thomas, *Summa Theol.* I-II, q. 100, a. 2 C (in fine); II-II q. 44, a. 4, ad 3.

(14) De praestantia sacrae virginitatis, Cfr. Tertullianus, *Exhort. Cast.* 10: PL 2, 925 C. S. Cyprianus, *Hab. Virg.* 3 et 22: PL 4, 443 B et 461 A s. S. Athanasius (?), *De Virg.*: PG 28, 252 ss. S. Io. Chrysostomus, *De Virg.*: PG 48, 533 ss.

(15) De spirituali *paupertate et oboedientia* testimonia praecipua S. Scripturae et Patrum afferuntur in Relatione pp. 152-153.

(16) De praxi effectiva consiliorum quae non omnibus imponitur, Cfr. S. Io. Chrysostomus, *In Matth.* Hom. 7, 7: PG 57, 81 s. S. Ambrosius, *De Viduis,* 4, 23: PL 16, 241 s.

Chapter VI

Religious

(1) Cfr. Rosweydus, *Vitae Patrum,* Antwerpiae, 1628. *Apophtegmata Patrum*: PG 65. Palladius, *Historia Lausiaca*: PG 34, 995 ss.; ed. C. Butler, Cambridge 1898

(1904). Pius XI, Const. Apost. *Umbratilem,* 8 iul. 1924: *AAS* 16 (1924) pp. 386-387. Pius XII, Alloc. *Nous sommes heureux,* 11 apr. 1958: *AAS* 50 (1958) p. 283.

(2) Paulus VI, Alloc. *Magno gaudio,* 23 maii 1964: *AAS* 56 (1964) p. 566.

(3) Cfr. *Cod Iur. Can.,* c. 487 et 488, 4⁰. Pius XII, Alloc. *Annus sacer,* 8 dec. 1950: *AAS* 43 (1951) p. 27 s. Pius XII, Cons. Apost. *Provida Mater,* 2 febr. 1947: *AAS* 39 (1947) p. 120 ss.

(4) Paulus VI, 1. c., p. 567.

(5) Cfr. S. Thomas, *Summa Theol.* II-II, p. 184, a. 3 et q. 188, a. 2. S. Bonaventura, Opusc. XI, *Apologia Pauperum,* c. 3, 3: ed. Opera, Quaracchi, t. 8, 1898, p. 245 a.

(6) Cfr. Conc. Vat. I, Schema *De Ecclesia Christi,* cap. XV, et Adnot. 48: Mansi 51, 549 s. et 619 s. - Leo XIII, Epist. *Au milieu des consolations,* 23 dec. 1900: *ASS* 33 (1900-01) p. 361. Pius XII, Const. Apost. *Provida Mater,* 1. c., p. 114 s.

(7) Cfr. Leo XIII, Const. *Romanos Pontifices,* 8 maii 1881: *ASS* 13 (1880-81) p. 483. Pius XII, Alloc. *Annus sacer,* 8 dec. 1950: *AAS* 43 (1951) p. 28 s.

(8) Cfr. Pius XII, Alloc. *Annus sacer,* 1. c., p. 28. Pius XII, Const. Apost. *Sedes Sapientiae,* 31 maii 1956: *AAS* 48 (1956) p. 355. Paulus VI, 1. c., pp. 570-571.

(9) Cfr. Pius XII, Litt. Encycl. *Mystici Corporis,* 29 iun. 1943: *AAS* 35 (1943) p. 214 s.

(10) Cfr. Pius XII, Alloc. *Annus sacer,* 1. c., p. 30. Alloc. *Sous la maternelle protection,* 9 dec. 1957: *AAS* 50 (1958) p. 39 s.

Chapter VII

The Eschatological Nature of the Pilgrim Church and Its Union With the Church in Heaven

(1) Conc. Florentinum, *Decretum pro Graecis*: Denz. 693 (1305).

(2) Praeter documenta antiquiora contra quamlibet formam evocationis spirituum inde ab Alexandro IV (27 sept. 1258), Cfr. Encycl. S.S.C.S. Officii, *De magnetismi abusu,* 4 aug. 1856: *ASS* (1865) pp. 177-178, Denz. 1653-1654 (2823-2825); responsionem S.S.C.S. Officii, 24 apr. 1917: *AAS* 9 (1917) p. 268, Denz. 2182 (3642).

(3) Videatur synthetica expositio huius doctrinae paulinae in: Pius XII, Litt. Encycl. *Mystici Corporis*; *AAS* 35 (1943) p. 200 et passim.

(4) Cfr., i. a., S. Augustinus, *Enarr. in Ps.* 85, 24: PL 37, 1099. S. Hieronymus, *Liber contra Vigilantium,* 6: PL 23, 344. S. Thomas, *In 4m Sent.,* d. 45, q. 3, a. 2. S. Bonaventura, *In 4m Sent.,* d. 45, a. 3, q. 2; etc.

(5) Cfr. Pius XII, Litt. Encycl. *Mystici Corporis*: *AAS* 35 (1943) p. 245.

(6) Cfr. Plurimae inscriptiones in Catacumbis romanis.

(7) Cfr. Gelasius I, Decretalis *De libris recipiendis,* 3: PL 59, 160, Denz. 165 (353).

(8) Cfr. S. Methodius, *Symposion*, VII, 3: GCS (Bonwetsch), p. 74.

(9) Cfr. Benedictus XV, *Decretum approbationis virtutum in Causa beatificationis et canonizationis Servi Dei Ioannis Nepomuceni Neumann*: AAS 14 (1922) p. 23; plures Allocutiones Pii XI de Sanctis: *Inviti all'eroismo*. Discorsi . . . t. I-III, Romae 1941-1942, passim; Pius XII, *Discorsi e Radiomessaggi*, t. 10, 1949, pp. 37-43.

(10) Cfr. Pius XII, Litt. Encycl. *Mediator Dei*: AAS 39 (1947) p. 581.

(11) Cfr. *Hebr*. 13, 7: *Eccli*. 44-50; *Hebr*. 11, 3-40. Cfr. etiam Pius XII, Litt. Encycl. *Mediator Dei*: AAS 39 (1947) pp. 582-583.

(12) Cfr. Conc. Vaticanum I, Const. *De fide catholica*, cap. 3: Denz. 1794 (3013).

(13) Cfr. Pius XII, Litt. Encycl. *Mystici Corporis*: AAS 35 (1943) p. 216.

(14) Quaod gratitudinem erga ipsos Sanctos, Cfr. E. Dichl, *Inscriptiones latinae christianae veteres*, I, Berolini, 1925, nn. 2008, 2382 et passim.

(15) Conc. Tridentinum, Sess. 25, *De invocatione... Sanctorum*: Denz. 984 (1821).

(16) Breviarium Romanum, *Invitatorium in festo Sanctorum Omnium*.

(17) Cfr. v. g., 2 *Thess*. 1, 10.

(18) Conc. Vaticanum II, Const. *De Sacra Liturgia*, cap. 5, n. 104.

(19) *Canon* Missae Romanae.

(20) Conc. Nicaenum II, Act. VII: Denz. 302 (600).

(21) Conc. Florentinum, *Decretum pro Graecis*: Denz. 693 (1304).

(22) Conc. Tridentinum, Sess. 35, *De invocatione, veneratione et reliquiis Sanctorum et sacris imaginibus*: Denz. 984-988 (1821-1824); Sess. 25, *Decretum de Purgatorio*: Denz. 983 (1820); Sess. 6, *Decretum de iustificatione*, can. 30: Denz. 840 (1580).

(23) Ex *Praefatione*, alliquibus dioecesibus concessa.

(24) Cfr. S. Petrus Canisius, *Catechismus Maior seu Summa Doctrinae christianae*, cap. III (ed. crit. F. Streicher), pas I, pp. 15-16, n. 44 et pp. 100-101, n. 49.

(25) Cfr. Conc. Vaticanum II, Const. *De Sacra Liturgia*, cap. 1, n. 8.

Chapter VIII

The Blessed Virgin Mary, Mother of God, in the Mystery of Christ and the Church

(1) *Credo* in Missa Romana: Symbolum Constantinopolitanum: Mansi 3, 566. Cfr. Conc. Ephesinum, ib. 4, 1130 (necnon ib. 2, 665 et 4, 1071); Conc. Chalcedonense, ib. 7, 111-116; Conc. Constantinopolitanum II, ib. 9, 375-396.

(2) *Canon* Missae Romanae.

(3) S. Augustinus, *De S. Virginitate*, 6: PL 40, 399.

(4) Cfr. Paulus Pp. VI, *Allocutio in Concilio*, die 4 dec. 1963: AAS 56 (1964) p. 37.

(5) Cfr. S. Germanus Const., *Hom. in Annunt. Deiparae* PG 98, 328 A; In Dorm. 2: col. 357.—Anastasius Antioch., *Serm. 2 de Annunt.*, 2: PG 89, 1377 AB; *Serm*. 3, 2: col. 1388 C. — S. Andreas Cret., *Can. in B. V. Nat.* 4: PG 97, 1321 B. *In B. V. Nat.*, 1: col. 812 A. *Hom. in dorm.* 1: col. 1068 C. — S. Sophronius, *Or. 2 in Annunt.*, 18: PG 87 (3), 3237 BD.

(6) S. Irenaeus, *Adv. Haer*. III, 22, 4: PG 7, 959 A; Harvey, 2, 123.

(7) S. Irenaeus, *ib.*; Harvey, 2, 124.

(8) S. Epiphanius, *Haer*. 78, 18: PG 42, 728 CD—729 AB.

(9) S. Hieronymus, *Epist*. 22, 21: PL 22, 408. Cfr. S. Augustinus, *Serm*. 51, 2, 3: PL 38, 335; *Serm*. 232, 2: col. 1108.—S. Cyrillus Hieros., *Catech*. 12, 15: PG 33, 741 AB.—S. Io. Chrysostomus, *In Ps.* 44, 7: PG 55, 193. —S. Io. Damascenus, *Hom. 2 in dorm. B.M.V.*, 3: PG 96, 728.

(10) Cfr. Conc. Lateranense anni 649, Can. 3: Mansi 10, 1151. — S. Leo M., *Epist. ad Flav.*: PL 54, 759.—Conc. Chalcedonese: Mansi 7, 462.—S.Ambrosius, *De inst. virg.*: PL 16, 320.

(11) Cfr. Pius XII, Litt. Encycl. *Mystici Corporis*, 29 iun. 1943: AAS 35 (1943) pp. 247-248.

(12) Cfr. Pius IX, *Bulla Ineffabilis*, 8 dec. 1854: *Acta Pii IX*, 1, I, p. 616; Denz. 1641 (2803).

(13) Cfr. Pius XII, Const. Apost. *Munificentissimus*, I nov. 1950: AAS 42 (1950); Denz. 2333 (3903). Cfr. S. Io. Damascenus, *Enc. in dorm. Dei genitricis*, Hom. 2 et 3: PG 96, 721-761, speciatim col. 728 B. — S. Germanus Constantinop., *In S. Dei. gen. dorm.* Serm. 1: PG 98 (6), 340-348; Serm. 3: col. 361. — S. Modestus Hier., *In dorm. SS. Deiparae*: PG 86 (2), 3277-3312.

(14) Cfr. Pius XII, Litt. Encycl. *Ad coeli Reginam*, 11 oct. 1954: AAS 46 (1954), pp. 633-636; Denz. 3913 ss. Cfr. S. Andreas Cret., *Hom. 3 in dorm. SS. Deiparae*: PG 97, 1089-1109.—S. Io. Damascenus, *De fide orth.*, IV, 14: PG 94, 1153-1161.

(15) Cfr. Kleutgen, textus reformatus *De mysterio Verbi incarnati*, cap. IV: Mansi 53, 290. Cfr. S. Andreas Cret., *In nat. Mariae*, sermo 4: PG 97, 865 A.—S. Germanus Constantinop., *In annunt. Deiparae*: PG 98, 321 BC. *In dorm. Deiparae*, III: col. 361 D.—S. Io. Damascenus, *In dorm. B.V. Mariae*, Hom. 1, 8: PG 96, 712 BC —713 A.

(16) Cfr. Leo XIII, Litt. Encycl. *Adiutricem populi*, 5 sept. 1895: ASS 15 (1895-96), p. 303.—S. Pius X, Litt. Encycl. *Ad diem illum*, 2 febr. 1904: *Acta*, I p. 154; Denz. 1978 a (3370).—Pius XI, Litt. Encycl. *Miserentissimus*, 8 maii 1928: AAS 20 (1928) p. 178.— Pius XII, *Nuntius Radioph.*, 13 maii 1946: AAS 38 (1946) p. 266.

(17) S. Ambrosius, *Epist*. 63: PL 16, 1218.

(18) S. Ambrosius. *Expos. Lc.* II, 7: PL 15, 1555.

(19) Cfr. Ps.-Petrus Dam., *Serm.* 63: PL 144, 861 AB.—Godefridus a S. Victore, *In nat. B. M.*, Ms. Paris, Mazarine, 1002, fol. 109 r.—Gerhohus Reich., *De gloria et honore Filii hominus,* 10: PL 194, 1105 AB.

(20) S. Ambrosius, *l. c. et Expos. Lc.* X, 24-25: PL 15, 1810.—S. Augustinus, *In Io.* Tr. 13, 12: PL 35, 1499. Cfr. *Serm.* 191, 2, 3: PL 38, 1010; etc. Cfr. etiam Ven. Beda, *In Lc. Expos.* I, cap. 2: PL 92, 330.—Isaac de Stella, *Serm.* 51: PL 194, 1863 A.

(21) "Sub tuum praesidium."

(22) Conc. Nicaenum II, anno 787: Mansi 13, 378-379; Denz. 302 (600-601).—Conc. Trident., sess. 25: Mansi 33, 171-172.

(23) Cfr. Pius XII, *Nuntius radioph.*, 24 oct. 1954: *AAS* 46 (1954) p. 679. Litt. Encycl. *Ad coeli Reginam,* 11 oct. 1954: *AAS* 46 (1954) p. 637.

(24) Cfr. Pius XI, Litt. Encycl. *Ecclesiam Dei,* 12 nov. 1923: *AAS* 15 (1923) p. 581.—Pius XII, Litt. Encycl. *Fulgens corona,* 8 sept. 1953: *AAS* 45 (1953) pp. 590-591.

Decree on Ecumenism

This is an unofficial English translation of the text of the Second Vatican Council's decree on Ecumenism which was proclaimed by Pope Paul VI on Nov. 21, 1964.

Introduction

1. The RESTORATION OF UNITY among all Christians is one of the principal concerns of the Second Vatican Council. Christ the Lord founded one Church and one Church only. However, many Christian communions present themselves to men as the true inheritors of Jesus Christ; all indeed profess to be followers of the Lord but differ in mind and go their different ways, as if Christ Himself were divided (cf. 1 Cor. 1,13). Such division openly contradicts the will of Christ, scandalizes the world, and damages the holy cause of preaching the Gospel to every creature.

But the Lord of Ages wisely and patiently follows out the plan of His grace on our behalf, sinners that we are. In recent times He has begun to bestow more generously upon divided Christians remorse over their divisions and a longing for unity. Everywhere large numbers have felt the impulse of this grace, and among our separated brethren also there increases from day to day the movement, fostered by the grace of the Holy Spirit, for the restoration of unity among all Christians. This movement toward unity is called "ecumenical." Those belong to it who invoke the Triune God and confess Jesus as Lord and Saviour, doing this not merely as individuals but also as corporate bodies. For almost everyone regards the body in which he has heard the Gospel as his Church and indeed, God's Church. All however, though in different ways, long for the one visible Church of God, a Church truly universal and set forth into the world that the world may be converted to the Gospel and so be saved, to the glory of God.

The sacred council gladly notes all this. It has already declared its teaching on the Church, and now, moved by a desire for the restoration of unity among all the followers of Christ, it wishes to set before all Catholics guidelines, helps and methods by which they too can respond to this grace and to this divine call.

Chapter I

Catholic Principles on Ecumenism

2. What has revealed the love of God among us is that the Father has sent into the world His only-begotten Son, so that, being made man, He might by His redemption give new life to the entire human race and unify it (cf. 1 John 4, 9; Col. 1, 18-20; John 11, 52). Before offering Himself up as a spotless victim upon the altar, Christ prayed to His Father for all who believe in Him: "that they all may be one; even as thou, Father, art in me, and I in thee, that they also may be one in us, so that the world may believe that thou has sent me" (John 17, 21). In His Church He instituted the wonderful sacrament of the Eucharist by which the unity of His Church is both signified and made a reality. He gave His followers a new commandment to love one another (cf. John 13, 34), and promised the Spirit, their Advocate (cf. John 16,7), who, as Lord and life-giver, should remain with them forever.

After being lifted up on the cross and glorified, the Lord Jesus poured forth His Spirit as He had promised, and through the Spirit He has called and gathered together the people of the New Covenant, which is the Church, into a unity of faith, hope and charity, as the Apostle teaches us: "There is one body and one Spirit, just as you were called to the one hope of your calling; one Lord, one faith, one Baptism" (Eph. 4, 4-5). For "all you who have been baptized into Christ have put on Christ . . . for you are all one in Christ Jesus" (Gal. 3, 27-28). It is the Holy Spirit, dwelling in those who believe and pervading and ruling over the Church as a whole, who brings about that wonderful communion of the faithful and joins them together so intimately in Christ that He is the principle of the Church's unity. By distributing various kinds of spiritual gifts and ministries (cf. 1 Cor. 12, 4-11), He enriches the Church of Jesus Christ with different functions "in order to equip the saints for the work of service, so as to build up the body of Christ" (Eph. 4, 12).

In order to establish this His holy Church everywhere in the world till the end of time, Christ entrusted to the College of the Twelve the task of teaching, ruling and sanctifying (cf. Matt. 28, 18-20, collato John 20, 21-23). Among their number He selected Peter, and after his confession of faith determined that on him He would build His Church. Also to Peter He promised the keys of the kingdom of heaven (cf. Matt. 16, 18, collato Matt. 18, 18), and after His profession of love, entrusted all His sheep to him to be confirmed in faith (cf. Luke 22, 32) and shepherded in perfect unity (cf. John 21, 15-18). Christ Jesus Himself was forever to remain the chief cornerstone (cf. Eph. 2, 20) and shepherd of our souls (cf. 1 Peter 2, 25; conc. Vaticanum I, Sess. IV (1870), Constitutio Pastor Acternus: Collac 7, 482 a).

Jesus Christ, then, willed that the apostles and their successors—the bishops with Peter's successor at their head—should preach the Gospel faithfully, administer the sacraments, and rule the Church in love. It is thus, under the action of the Holy Spirit, that Christ wills His people to increase, and He perfects His people's fellowship in unity: in their confessing the one faith, celebrating divine worship in common, and keeping the fraternal harmony of the family of God.

The Church, then, is God's only flock; it is like a standard lifted high for the nations to see it (cf. Is. 11, 10-12): for it serves all mankind through the Gospel of peace (cf. Eph. 2,17-18, collato Mark 16, 15) as it makes its pilgrim way in hope toward its goal, the fatherland above (cf. 1 Peter 1, 3-9).

This is the sacred mystery of the unity of the Church, in Christ and through Christ, the Holy Spirit energizing its various functions. It is a mystery that finds its highest exemplar and source in the unity of the Persons of the Trinity: the Father and the Son in the Holy Spirit, one God.

3. Even in the beginnings of this one and only Church of God there arose certain rifts (cf. 1 Cor. 11, 18-19; Gal. 1, 6-9; 1 John 2, 18-19), which the Apostle strongly condemned (cf. 1 Cor. 1, 11 sqq; 11, 22). But in subsequent centuries much more serious dissensions appeared and quite large communities separated from full communion with the Catholic Church—for which, often enough, men of both sides were to blame. However, one cannot charge with the sin of the separation those who at present are born into these communities and in them are brought up in the faith of Christ, and the Catholic Church accepts them with respect and affection as brothers. For men who believe in Christ and have been properly baptized are brought into a certain, though imperfect, communion with the Catholic Church. Without doubt the differences that exist in varying degrees between them and the Catholic Church—whether in doctrine and sometimes in discipline, or concerning the structure of the Church—do indeed create many obstacles, sometimes serious ones, to full ecclesiastical communion. The ecumenical movement is striving to overcome these obstacles. But even in spite of them it remains true that all who have been justified by faith in baptism are members of Christ's body (cf. Conc. Florentinum, Sess. VIII (1439), Decretum Exultate Deo: Mansi 31, 1055 A), and have a right to be called Christain, and so are with good reason accepted as brothers by the children of the Catholic Church (cf. S. Agustinus, In Ps. 32, Enarr. II, 29: PL 36, 299).

Moreover, some, even very many of the significant elements and endowments which together go to build up and give life to the Church itself, can exist outside the visible boundaries of the Catholic Church: the written word of God; the life of grace; faith, hope and charity, with the other interior gifts of the Holy Spirit, and visible elements too. All of these, which come from Christ and lead back to Christ, belong by right to the one Church of Christ.

The brethren divided from us also use many liturgical actions of the Christian religion. These most certainly can truly engender a life of grace in ways that vary according to the condition of each Church or community. These liturgical actions must be regarded as capable of giving access to the community of salvation.

It follows that the separated Churches (cf. Conc. Lateranense IV (1215) Constitutio IV: Mansi 22, 990; Conc. Lugdunense II (1274), Professio fidei Michaelis Palaeologi: Mansi 24, 71 E; Conc. Florentinum, Sess. VI (1439), Definitio Laetentur caeli: Mansi 31, 1026 E.) and communities as such, though we believe them to be deficient in some respects, have been by no means deprived of significance and importance in the mystery of salvation. For the Spirit of Christ has not refrained from using them as means of salvation which derive their efficacy from the very fulness of grace and truth entrusted to the Catholic Church.

Nevertheless, our separated brethren, whether considered as individuals or as communities and Churches, are not blessed with that unity which Jesus Christ wished to bestow on all those who through Him were born again into one body, and with Him quickened to newness of life—that unity which the Holy Scriptures and the ancient Tradition of the Church proclaim. For it is only through Christ's Catholic Church, which is "the all-embracing means of salvation," that they can benefit fully from the means of salvation. We believe that Our Lord entrusted all the blessings of the New Covenent to the apostolic college alone, of which Peter is the head, in order to establish the one Body of Christ on earth to which all should be fully incorporated who belong in any way to the people of God. This people of God, though still in its members liable to sin, is ever growing in Christ during its pilgrimage on earth, and is guided by God's gentle wisdom, according to His hidden designs, until it shall happily arrive at the fulness of eternal glory in the heavenly Jerusalem.

4. Today, in many parts of the world, under the inspiring grace of the Holy Spirit, many efforts are being made in prayer, word and action to attain that fulness of unity which Jesus Christ desires. The sacred council exhorts all the Catholic faithful to recognize the signs of the times and to take an active and intelligent part in the work of ecumenism.

The term "ecumenical movement" indicates the initiatives and activities planned and undertaken, according to the various needs of the Church and as opportunities offer, to promote Christian unity. These are: first, every effort to avoid expressions, judgments and actions which do not represent the condition of our separated brethren with truth and fairness and so make mutual relations with them more difficult. Then, "dialogue" between competent experts from different Churches and communities; in their meetings, which are organized in a religious spirit, each explains the teaching of His communion in greater depth and brings out clearly its distinctive features. In such dialogue, everyone gains a truer knowledge and more just appreciation of the teaching and religious life of both communions. In addition, the way is prepared for cooperation between them in the duties for the common good of humanity which are demanded by every Christian conscience; and, wherever this is allowed, there is prayer in common. Finally, all are led to examine their own faithfulness to Christ's will for the Church and, wherever necessary, undertake with vigor the task of renewal and reform.

When such actions are carried out prudently and patiently by the Catholic faithful, with the attentive guidance of their bishops, they promote justice and truth, concord and collaboration, as well as the spirit of brotherly love and unity. This is the way that, when the obstacles to perfect ecclesiastical communion have been gradually overcome, all Christians will at last, in a common celebration of the Eucharist, be gathered into the unity of the one and only Church, which Christ bestowed on His Church from the beginning. We believe that this unity subsists in the Catholic Church as something she can never lose, and we hope that it will continue to increase until the end of time.

However, it is evident that, when individuals wish for full Catholic communion, their preparation and reconciliation is an undertaking which of its nature is distinct from ecumenical action. But there is no opposition between the two, since both proceed from the marvelous ways of God.

Catholics, in their ecumenical work, must assuredly be concerned for their separated brethren, praying for them, keeping them informed about the Church, making the first approaches toward them. But their primary duty is to make a careful and honest appraisal of whatever needs to be done or renewed in the Catholic household itself, in order that its life may bear witness more clearly and faithfully to the teachings and institutions which have come to it from Christ through the hands of the apostles.

For although the Catholic Church has been endowed with all divinely revealed truth and with all means of grace, yet its members fail to live by them with all the fervor that they should. As a result the radiance of the Church's face shines less brightly in the eyes of our separated brethren and of the world at large, and the growth of God's kingdom is delayed. All Catholics must therefore aim at Christian perfection (cf. James 1,4; Rom. 12, 1-2) and, each according to his station, play his part that the Church may daily be more purified and renewed. For the Church must bear in her own body the humility and dying of Jesus (cf. 2 Cor. 4, 10; Phil. 2, 5-8), against the day when Christ will present her to Himself in all her glory without spot or wrinkle (cf. Eph. 5,27).

All in the Church must preserve unity in essentials. But let all, according to the gifts they have received enjoy a proper freedom, in their various forms of spiritual life and discipline, in their different liturgical rites, and even in their theological elaborations of revealed truth. In all things let charity prevail. If they are true to this course of action, they will be giving ever better expression to the authentic catholicity and apostolicity of the Church.

On the other hand, Catholics must gladly acknowledge and esteem the truly Christian endowments from our common heritage which are to be found among our separated brethren. It is right and salutary to recognize the riches of Christ and virtuous works in the lives of others who are bearing witness to Christ, sometimes even to the shedding of their blood. For God is always wonderful in His works and worthy of all praise.

Nor should we forget that anything wrought by the grace of the Holy Spirit in the hearts of our separated brethren can contribute to our own edification. Whatever is truly Christian is never contrary to what genuinely belongs to the faith; indeed, it can always bring a deeper realization of the mystery of Christ and the Church.

Nevertheless, the divisions among Christians prevent the Church from attaining the fulness of catholicity proper to her, in those of her sons who, though attached to her by baptism, are yet separated from full communion with her. Furthermore, the Church herself finds it more difficult to express in actual life her full catholicity in all its aspects.

This sacred council is gratified to note that the participation by the Catholic faithful in ecumenical work is growing daily. It commends this work to the bishops everywhere in the world to be vigorously stimulated by them and guided with prudence.

Chapter II

The Practice of Ecumenism

5. The attainment of union is the concern of the whole Church, faithful and shepherds alike. This concern extends to everyone, according to his talent, whether it be exercised in his daily Christian life or in his theological and historical research. This concern itself reveals already to some extent the bond of brotherhood between all Christians and it helps toward that full and perfect unity which God in His kindness wills.

6. Every renewal of the Church (cfr. Conc. Lateranse V, Sess, XII (1517), Constitutio Constituti: Mansi 32, 988 B-C) is essentially grounded in an increase of fidelity to her own calling. Undoubtedly this is the basis of the movement toward unity.

Christ summons the Church to continual reformation as she goes her pilgrim way. The Church is always in need of this, in so far as she is an institution of men here on earth. Thus if, in various times and circumstances, there have been deficiencies in moral conduct or in church discipline, or even in the way that church teaching has been formulated—to be carefully distinguished from the deposit of faith itself—these can and should be set right at the opportune moment and in the proper way.

Church renewal has therefore notable ecumenical importance. Already in various spheres of the Church's life, this renewal is taking place. The Biblical and liturgical movements, the preaching of the word of God and catechetics, the apostolate of the laity, new forms of religious life and the spirituality of married life, and the Church's social teaching and activity—all these should be considered as promises and guarantees for the future progress of ecumenism.

7. There can be no ecumenism worthy of the name without a change of heart. For it is from renewal of the inner life of our minds (cf. Eph. 4, 24), from self-denial and an unstinted love that desires of unity take their rise and develop in a mature way. We should therefore pray to the Holy Spirit for the grace to be genuinely self-denying, humble, gentle in the service of others, and to have an attitude of brotherly generosity towards them. St. Paul says: "I, therefore, a prisoner for the Lord, beg you to lead a life worthy of the calling to which you have been called, with all humility and meekness, with patience, forbearing one another in love, eager to maintain the unity of the spirit in the bond of peace" (Eph. 4, 1-3). This exhortation is directed especially to those raised to sacred orders precisely that the work of Christ may be continued. He came among

us "not to be served but to serve" (Matt. 20, 28).

The words of St. John hold good about sins against unity: "If we say we have not sinned, we make him a liar, and his word is not in us" (1 John 1, 10). So we humbly beg pardon of God and of our separated brethren, just as we forgive them that trespass against us.

The faithful should remember that the more effort they make to live holier lives according to the Gospel, the better will they further Christian unity and put it into practice. For the closer their union with the Father, the Word, and the Spirit, the more deeply and easily will they be able to grow in mutual brotherly love.

8. This change of heart and holiness of life, along with public and private prayer for the unity of Christians, should be regarded as the soul of the whole ecumenical movement, and merits the name, "spiritual ecumenism."

It is a recognized custom for Catholics to have frequent recourse to that prayer for the unity of the Church which the Saviour Himself on the eve of His death so fervently appealed to His Father: "That they may all be one" (John 17, 20).

In certain special circumstances, such as in prayer services "for unity," and during ecumenical gatherings, it is allowable, indeed desirable that Catholics should join in prayer with their separated brethren. Such prayers in common are certainly an effective means of obtaining the grace of unity, and they are a true expression of the ties which still bind Catholics to their separated brethren. "For where two or three are gathered together in my name, there am I in the midst of them" (Matt. 18, 20).

Yet worship in common (communicatio in sacris) is not to be considered as a means to be used indiscriminately for the restoration of Christian unity. There are two main principles governing the practice of such common worship: first, the bearing witness to the unity of the Church, and second, the sharing in the means of grace.

Witness to the unity of the Church very generally forbids common worship to Christians, but the grace to be had from it sometimes commends this practice. The course to be adopted, with due regard to all the circumstances of time, place, and persons, is left to the prudent decision of the local episcopal authority, unless otherwise provided for by the Bishops Conference according to its statutes, or by the Holy See.

9. We must get to know the outlook of our sep-

arated brethren. To achieve this purpose, study is of necessity required, and this must be pursued with a sense of realism and good will. Catholics, who already have a proper grounding, need to acquire a more adequate understanding of the respective doctrines of our separated brethren, their history, their spiritual and liturgical life, their religious psychology and cultured background. Most valuable for this purpose are meetings of the two sides—especially for discussion of theological problems—where each can treat with the other on an equal footing—provided that those who take part in them are truly competent and have the approval of the bishops.

From such dialogue will emerge still more clearly what the situation of the Catholic Church really is. In this way too the outlook of our separated brethren will be better understood, and our own belief more aptly explained.

10. Sacred theology and other branches of knowledge, especially of an historical nature, must be taught with due regard for the ecumenical point of view, so that they may correspond as exactly as possible with the facts.

It is most important that future shepherds and priests should have mastered a theology that has been carefully worked out in this way and not polemically, especially with regard to those aspects which concern the relations of separated brethren with the Catholic Church.

This importance is the greater because the instruction and spiritual formation of the faithful and of religious depends so largely on the formation which their priests have received.

Moreover, Catholics engaged in missionary work in the same territories as other Christians ought to know, particularly in these times, the problems and the benefits in their apostolate which derive from the ecumenical movement.

II. The way and method in which the Catholic faith is expressed should never become an obstacle to dialogue with our brethren. It is, of course, essential that the doctrine be clearly presented in its entirety. Nothing is so foreign to the spirit of ecumenism as a false irenicism, in which the purity of Catholic doctrine suffers loss and its genuine and certain meaning is clouded.

At the same time, the Catholic faith must be explained more profoundly and precisely, in such a way and in such terms as our separated brethren can also really understand.

Furthermore, in ecumenical dialogue, Catholic theologians, standing fast by the teaching of the Church, yet searching together with separated brethren into the divine mysteries, should do so with love for the truth, with charity, and with humility. When comparing doctrines with one another, they should remember that in Catholic doctrine there exists a "hierarchy" of truths, since they vary in their relation to the fundamental Christian faith. Thus the way will be opened by which through "fraternal rivalry" all will be stirred to a deeper understanding and a clearer presentation of the unfathomable riches of Christ (cf. Eph. 3,8).

12. Before the whole world let all Christians confess their faith in God, one and three, in the incarnate Son of God, our Redeemer and Lord. United in their efforts, and with mutual respect, let them bear witness to our common hope which does not play us false. In these days when cooperation in social matters is so widespread, all men without exception are called to work together, with much greater reason all those who believe in God, but most of all, all Christians in that they bear the name of Christ. Cooperation among Christians vividly expresses that bond which already unites them, and it sets in clearer relief the features of Christ the Servant. Such cooperation which has already begun in many countries, should be developed more and more, particularly in regions where a social and technical evolution is taking place. It should contribute to a just evaluation of the dignity of the human person, to the establishment of the blessings of peace, the application of Gospel principles to social life, and the advancement of the arts and sciences in a truly Christian spirit. It should also be intensified in the use of every possible means to relieve the afflictions of our times, such as famine and natural disasters, illiteracy and poverty, lack of housing, and the unequal distribution of wealth. All believers in Christ can, through this cooperation, be led to acquire a better knowledge and appreciation of one another, and pave the way to Christian unity.

Chapter III

Churches and Ecclesial Communities Separated From the Roman Apostolic See

13. We now turn our attention to the two chief types of division as they affect the seamless robe of Christ.

The first divisions occurred in the East, when the dogmatic formulae of the Councils of Ephesus and Chalcedon were challenged, and later when ecclesiastical communion between the Eastern Patriarchates and the Roman See was dissolved.

Other divisions arose more than four centuries later in the West, stemming from the events which are usually referred to as "The Reformation." As a result, many communions, national or confessional, were separated from the Roman See. Among those in which Catholic traditions and institutions in part continue to exist, the Anglican communion occupies a special place.

These various divisions differ greatly from one another not only by reason of their origin, place and time, but especially in the nature and seriousness of questions bearing on the faith and the structure of the Church. Therefore, without minimizing the differences between the various Christian bodies, and without overlooking the bonds between them which exist in spite of divisions, this holy council decides to propose the following considerations for prudent ecumenical action.

I. The Special Position of the Eastern Churches

14. For many centuries the Church of the East and that of the West each followed their separate ways though linked in a brotherly union of faith and sacramental life; the Roman See by common consent acted as moderator when disagreements arose between them over matters of faith or discipline. Among other matters of great importance, it is a pleasure for this council to remind everyone that there flourish in the East many particular or local Churches, among which the Patriarchial Churches hold first place, and of these not a few pride themselves in tracing their origins back to the apostles themselves. Hence a matter of primary concern and care among the Easterns in their local churches, has been, and still is, to preserve the family ties of common faith and charity which ought to exist between sister Churches.

Similarly it must not be forgotten that from the beginning the Churches of the East have had a treasury from which the Western Church has drawn extensively —in liturgical practice, spiritual tradition, and law. Nor must we undervalue the fact that it was the ecumenical councils held in the East that defined the basic dogmas of the Christian faith, on the Trinity, on the Word of God, who took flesh of the Virgin Mary. To preserve this faith these Churches have suffered and still suffer much.

However, the inheritance handed down by the apostles was received with differences of form and manner, so that from the earliest times of the Church it was explained variously in different places, owing to diversities of genius and conditions of life. All this, quite apart from external causes, prepared the way for divisions arising also from a lack of charity and mutual understanding.

For this reason the council urges all, but especially those who intend to devote themselves to the restoration of the full communion that is desired between the Churches of the East and the Catholic Church, to give due consideration to this special feature of the origin and growth of the Eastern Churches, and to the character of the relations which obtained between them and the Roman See before separation. They must take full account of all these factors and, where this is done, it will greatly contribute to the dialogue that is looked for.

15. Everyone knows with what great love the Christians of the East celebrate the sacred liturgy, especially the eucharistic mystery, source of the Church's life and pledge of future glory, in which the faithful, united with their bishop, have access to God the Father through the Son, the Word made flesh, Who suffered, and has been glorified, and so, in the outpouring of the Holy Spirit, they enter into communion with the most holy Trinity, being made "shares of the divine nature" (2 Peter 1, 4). Hence, through the celebration of the Holy Eucharist in each of these churches, the Church of God is built up and grows in stature (cf. S. Ioannes Chrysostomos, In Ioannem Homelia XLVI PG 59,260-262) and through concelebration, their communion with one another is made manifest.

In this liturgical worship, the Christians of the East pay high tribute, in beautiful hymns of praise, to Mary ever Virgin, whom the ecumenical Council of Ephesus solemnly proclaimed to be the holy Mother of God, so that Christ might be acknowledged as being truly Son of God and Son of Man, according to the Scriptures. Many also are the saints whose praise they sing, among them the Fathers of the universal Church.

These Churches, although separated from us, yet possess true sacraments and above all, by apostolic succession, the priesthood and the Eucharist, whereby they are linked with us in closest intimacy. Therefore some worship in common (communicatio in sacris), given suitable circumstances and the approval of Church authority, is not merely possible but to be encouraged.

Moreover, in the East are to be found the riches of those spiritual traditions which are given expression especially in monastic life. From the glorious times of the holy Fathers, monastic spirituality flourished in the East, which later flowed over into the Western world, and there provided a source from which Latin monastic life took its rise and has drawn fresh vigor ever since. Catholics therefore are earnestly recommended to avail themselves of the spiritual riches of the Eastern Fathers which lift up the whole man to the contemplation of the divine.

The rich liturgical and spiritual heritage of the Eastern Churches should be known, venerated, preserved and cherished by all. They must recognize that this is of supreme importance for the faithful preservation of the fulness of Christian tradition, and for bringing about reconciliation between the Eastern and Western Christians.

16. From the earliest times the Eastern Churches followed their own forms of ecclesiastical law and custom, which were sanctioned by the approval of the Fathers of the Church, of synods, and even of ecumenical councils. Far from being an obstacle to the Church's unity, such diversity of customs and observances only adds to her comeliness, and is of great help in carrying out her mission, as has already been stated. To remove, then, all shadow of doubt, this holy council solemnly declares that the Churches of the East, while remembering the necessary unity of the whole Church, have the power to govern themselves according to the disciplines proper to them, since these are better suited to the character of their faithful, and more for the good of their souls. The perfect observance of this traditional principle, not always indeed carried out in practice, is one of the essential prerequisites for any restoration of unity.

17. What has just been said about the lawful variety that can exist in the Church must also be taken to apply to the differences in theological expression of doctrine. In the study of revelation East and West have followed different methods, and have developed differently their understanding and confession of God's truth. It is hardly surprising, then, if from time to time one tradition has come nearer to a full appreciation of some aspects of a mystery of revelation than the other, or has expressed them in a better manner. In such cases, these various theological expressions are to be considered often as mutually complementary rather than conflicting. Where the authentic theological traditions of the Eastern Church

are concerned, we must recognize the admirable way in which they have their roots in Holy Scripture, and how they are nurtured and given expression in the life of the liturgy. They derive their strength too from the living tradition of the apostles and from the works of the Fathers and spiritual writers of the Eastern Churches. Thus they promote the right ordering of Christian life and, indeed, pave the way to a full vision of Christian truth.

All this heritage of spirituality and liturgy, of discipline and theology, in its various traditions, this holy synod declares to belong to the full Catholic and apostolic character of the Church. We thank God that many Eastern children of the Catholic Church, who preserve this heritage, and wish to express it more faithfully and completely in their lives, are already living in full communion with their brethren who follow the tradition of the West.

18. After taking all these factors into consideration, this sacred council solemnly repeats the declaration of previous councils and Roman pontiffs, that for the restoration or the maintenance of unity and communion one must "impose no burden beyond what is essential" (Acts 15, 28). It is the council's urgent desire that, in the various organizations and living activities of the Church, every effort should be made toward the gradual realization of this unity, especially by prayer, and by fraternal dialogue on points of doctrine and the more pressing pastoral problems of our time. Similarly, the council commends to the shepherds and faithful of the Catholic Church to develop closer relations with those who are no longer living in the East but are far from home, so that friendly collaboration with them may increase, in the spirit of love, to the exclusion of all feeling of rivalry or strife. If this cause is wholeheartedly promoted, the council hopes that the barrier dividing the Eastern and Western Church will be removed, and that at last there may be but the one dwelling, firmly established on Christ Jesus, the cornerstone, who will make both one (cf. Conc. Florentinum, Sess. VI (1439), Definitio Laetentur caeli: Mansi 31 1026 E).

II. Separated Churches and Ecclesial Communities in the West

19. In the great upheaval which began in the West toward the end of the Middle Ages, and in later times too, Churches and ecclesial communities came to be separated from the Apostolic See of Rome. Yet they have retained a particularly close affinity with the Catholic Church as a result of the long centuries in which all Christendom lived together in ecclesiastical communion.

But since these Churches and ecclesial communities on account of their different origins, and different teachings in matters of doctrine on the spiritual life, vary considerably not only with us, but also among themselves, the task of describing them at all adequately is extremely difficult; and we have no intention of making such an attempt here.

Although the ecumenical movement and the desire for peace with the Catholic Church have not yet taken hold everywhere, it is our hope that ecumenical feeling and mutual esteem may gradually increase among all men.

It must however be admitted that in these Churches and ecclesial communities there exist important differences from the Catholic Church, not only of a historical, sociological, psychological and cultural character, but especially in the interpretation of revealed truth. To make easier the ecumenical dialogue in spite of these differences, we wish to set down some considerations which can, and indeed should, serve as a basis and encouragement for such dialogue.

20. Our thoughts turn first to those Christians who make open confession of Jesus Christ as God and Lord and as the sole mediator between God and men, to the glory of the one God, Father, Son and Holy Spirit. We are aware indeed that there exist considerable divergences from the doctrine of the Catholic Church concerning Christ Himself, the Word of God made flesh, the work of redemption, and consequently, concerning the mystery and ministry of the Church, and the role of Mary in the plan of salvation. But we rejoice to see that our separated brethren look to Christ as the source and center of Church unity. Their longing for union with Christ inspires them to seek an ever closer unity, and also to bear witness to their faith among the peoples of the earth.

21. A love and reverence of Sacred Scripture which might be described as devotion leads our brethren to a constant meditative study of the sacred text. For the Gospel "is the power of God for salvation to every one who has faith, to the Jew first and then to the Greek" (Rom. 1, 16).

While invoking the Holy Spirit, they seek in these very Scriptures God as it were speaking to them in Christ, Whom the prophets foretold, Who is the Word of God made flesh for us. They contemplate in the Scriptures the life of Christ and what the Divine Master taught and did for our salvation, especially the mysteries of His death and resurrection.

But while the Christians who are separated from us hold the divine authority of the Sacred Books, they differ from ours—some in one way, some in another—regarding the relationship between Scripture and the Church.

For, according to Catholic belief, the authentic teaching authority of the Church has a special place in the interpretation and preaching of the written word of God.

But Sacred Scriptures provide for the work of dialogue an instrument of the highest value in the mighty hand of God for the attainment of that unity which the Saviour holds out to all.

22. Whenever the Sacrament of Baptism is duly administered as Our Lord instituted it, and is received with the right dispositions, a person is truly incorporated into the crucified and glorified Christ, and reborn to a sharing of the divine life, as the Apostle says: "You were buried together with Him in baptism, and in Him also rose again—through faith in the working of God, who raised Him from the dead" (Col. 2, 12; cf. Rom. 6, 4).

Baptism therefore establishes a sacramental bond of unity which links all who have been reborn by it. But of itself baptism is only a beginning, an inauguration wholly directed toward the fulness of life in Christ. Baptism, therefore, envisages a complete profession of faith, complete incorporation in the system of salvation such as Christ willed it to be, and finally toward a complete integration into eucharistic communion.

Though the ecclesial communities which are separated from us lack the fulness of unity with us flowing from Baptism, and though we believe they have not retained the proper reality of the eucharistic mystery in its fulness, especially because of the absence of the sacrament of Orders, nevertheless when they commemorate His death and resurrection in the Lord's Supper, they profess that it signifies life in communion with Christ and look forward to His coming in glory. Therefore the teaching concerning the other sacraments, worship, and the ministry of the Church, must be the subject of the dialogue.

23. The daily Christian life of these brethren is nourished by their faith in Christ and strengthened by the grace of baptism and by hearing the word of God. This shows itself in their private prayer, their meditation on the Bible, in their Christian family life, and in the worship of a community gathered together to praise God. Moreover, their form of worship sometimes displays notable features of the liturgy which they shared with us of old.

Their faith in Christ bears fruit in praise and thanksgiving for the benefits received from the hands of God. Among them, too, is a strong sense of justice and a true charity toward others. This active faith has been responsible for many organizations for the relief of spiritual and material distress, the furtherance of the education of youth, the improvement of the social conditions of life, and the promotion of peace throughout the world.

While it is true that many Christians understand the moral teaching of the Gospel differently from Catholics, and do not accept the same solutions to the more difficult problems of modern society, nevertheless they share our desire to stand by the words of Christ as the source of Christian virtue, and to obey the command of the Apostle: "And whatever you do, in word or in work, do all in the name of the Lord Jesus Christ, giving thanks to God the Father through Him" (Col. 3, 17). For that reason an ecumenical dialogue might start with discussion of the application of the Gospel to moral conduct.

24. Now that we have briefly set out the conditions for ecumenical action and the principles by which it is to be directed, we look with confidence to the future. This sacred council exhorts the faithful to refrain from superficiality or imprudent zeal, for these can hinder real progress toward unity. Their ecumenical action must be fully and sincerely Catholic, that is to say, faithful to the truth which we have received from the apostles and Fathers of the Church, in harmony with the faith which the Catholic Church has always professed, and at

the same time directed toward that fulness to which Our Lord wills His Body to grow in the course of time.

This sacred council firmly hopes that the initiatives of the sons of the Catholic Church joined with those of the separated brethren will go forward, without obstructing the ways of divine Providence, and without prejudging the future inspirations of the Holy Spirit. Further, this council declares that it realizes that this holy objective—the reconciliation of all Christians in the unity of the one and only Church of Christ—transcends human powers and gifts. It therefore places its hope on the prayer of Christ for the Church, on our Father's love for us, and on the power of the Holy Spirit. "And hope does not disappoint, because God's love has been poured into our hearts through the Holy Spirit, who has been given to us" (Rom. 5,5).

Decree on the Eastern Churches

This is an unofficial English translation of the text of the decree on the Catholic Eastern Churches, passed by a vote of 2,110 to 39 by Vatican Council II on Nov. 21 and promulgated by Pope Paul VI the same day.

Preamble

1. The Catholic Church holds in high esteem the institutions, liturgical rites, ecclesiastical traditions and the established standards of the Christian life of the Eastern Churches, for in them, distinguished as they are for their venerable antiquity, there remains conspicuous the tradition that has been handed down from the Apostles through the Fathers, [1] and that forms part of the divinely revealed and undivided heritage of the

universal Church. This Sacred Ecumenical Council, therefore, in its care for the Eastern Churches which bear living witness to this tradition, in order that they may flourish and with new apostolic vigor execute the task entrusted to them, has determined to lay down a number of principles, in addition to those which refer to the universal Church; all else is remitted to the care of the Eastern synods and of the Holy See.

The Individual Churches or Rites

2. The Holy Catholic Church, which is the Mystical Body of Christ, is made up of the faithful who are organically united in the Holy Spirit by the same faith, the same sacraments and the same government and who, combining together into various groups which are held together by a hierarchy, form separate Churches or Rites. Between these there exists an admirable bond of union, such that the variety within the Church in no way harms its unity; rather it manifests it, for it is the mind of the Catholic Church that each individual Church or Rite should retain its traditions whole and entire and likewise that it should adapt its way of life to the different needs of time and place. [2]

3. These individual Churches, whether of the East or the West, although they differ somewhat among themselves in rite (to use the current phrase), that is, in liturgy, ecclesiastical discipline, and spiritual heritage, are, nevertheless, each as much as the others, entrusted to the pastoral government of the Roman Pontiff, the divinely appointed successor of St. Peter in primacy over the universal Church. They are consequently of equal dignity, so that none of them is superior to the others as regards rite and they enjoy the same rights and are under the same obligations, also in respect of preaching the Gospel to the whole world (cf. Mark 16, 15) under the guidance of the Roman Pontiff.

4. Means should be taken therefore in every part of the world for the protection and advancement of all the individual Churches and, to this end, there should be established parishes and a special hierarchy where the spiritual good of the faithful demands it. The hierarchs of the different individual Churches with jurisdiction in one and the same territory should, by taking common counsel in regular meetings, strive to promote unity of action and with common endeavor to sustain common tasks, so as better to further the good of religion and to safeguard more effectively the ordered way of life of the clergy.[3]

All clerics and those aspiring to sacred orders should be instructed in the rites and especially in the practical norms that must be applied in interritual questions. The laity, too, should be taught as part of its catechetical education about rites and their rules.

Finally, each and every Catholic, as also the baptized of every non-Catholic church or denomination who enters into the fulness of the Catholic communion, must retain his own rite wherever he is, must cherish it and observe it to the best of his ability,[4] without prejudice to the right in special cases of persons, communities or areas, of recourse to the Apostolic See, which, as the supreme judge of interchurch relations, will, acting itself or through other authorities, meet the needs of the occasion in an ecumenical spirit, by the issuance of opportune directives, decrees or rescripts.

Preservation of the Spiritual Heritage Of the Eastern Churches

5. History, tradition and abundant ecclesiastical institutions bear outstanding witness to the great merit owing to the Eastern Churches by the universal Church.[5]

The Sacred Council, therefore, not only accords to this ecclesiastical and spiritual heritage the high regard which is its due and rightful praise, but also unhesitatingly looks on it as the heritage of the universal Church. For this reason it solemnly declares that the Churches of the East, as much as those of the West, have a full right and are in duty bound to rule themselves, each in accordance with its own established disciplines, since all these are praiseworthy by reason of their venerable antiquity, more harmonious with the character of their faithful and more suited to the promotion of the good of souls.

6. All members of the Eastern Rite should know and be convinced that they can and should always preserve their legitimate liturgical rite and their established way of life, and that these may not be altered except to obtain for themselves an organic improvement. All these, then, must be observed by the members of the Eastern rites themselves. Besides, they should attain to an ever greater knowledge and a more exact use of them, and, if in their regard they have fallen short owing to contingencies of times and persons, they should take steps to return to their ancestral traditions.

Those who, by reason of their office or apostolic ministries, are in frequent communication with the Eastern Churches or their faithful should be instructed according as their office demands in the knowledge and veneration of the rites, discipline, doctrine, history and character of the members of the Eastern Rites.[6] To enhance the efficacy of their apostolate, Religious and associations of the Latin Rite working in Eastern countries or among Eastern faithful are earnestly counseled to found houses or even provinces of the Eastern rite, as far as this can be done.[7]

Eastern Rite Patriarchs

7. The patriarchate, as an institution, has existed in the Church from the earliest times and was recognized by the first ecumenical councils.[8]

By the name Eastern patriarch, is meant the bishop to whom belongs jurisdiction over all bishops, not excepting metropolitans, clergy and people of his own territory or rite, in accordance with canon law and without prejudice to the primacy of the Roman Pontiff.[9]

Wherever a hierarch of any rite is appointed outside the territorial bounds of the patriarchate, he remains attached to the hierarchy of the patriarchate of that rite, in accordance with canon law.

8. Though some of the patriarchates of the Eastern Churches are of earlier and some of later date, nonetheless all are equal in respect of patriarchal dignity, without however prejudice to the legitimately established precedence of honor.[10]

9. By the most ancient tradition of the Church

the patriarchs of the Eastern Churches are to be accorded special honor, seeing that each is set over his patriarchate as father and head.

This sacred council, therefore, determines that their rights and privileges should be re-established in accordance with the ancient tradition of each of the Churches and the decrees of the ecumenical councils. [11]

The rights and privileges in question are those that obtained in the time of union between East and West, though they should, however, be adapted somewhat to modern conditions.

The patriarchs with their synods are the highest authority for all business of the patriarchate, including the right of establishing new eparchies and of nominating bishops of their rite within the territorial bounds of the patriarchate, without prejudice to the inalienable right of the Roman Pontiff to intervene in individual cases.

10. What has been said of patriarchs is valid also, in harmony with the canon law, in respect to major archbishops, who rule the whole of some individual church or rite. [12]

11. Seeing that the patriarchal office in the Eastern Church is a traditional form of government, the Sacred Ecumenical Council ardently desires that new patriarchates should be erected where there is need, to be established either by an ecumenical council or by the Roman Pontiff. [13]

The Discipline of the Sacraments

12. The Sacred Ecumenical Council confirms and approves the ancient discipline of the sacraments existing in the Oriental Churches, as also the ritual practices connected with their celebration and administration and ardently desires that this should be re-established if circumstances warrant it.

13. The established practice in respect of the minister of Confirmation that has obtained from most early times in the Eastern Church should be fully restored. Therefore, priests validly confer this sacrament, using chrism blessed by a patriarch or a bishop. [14]

14. All Eastern Rite priests, either in conjunction with Baptism or separately from it, can confer this sacrament validly on all the faithful of any rite including the Latin; licitly, however, only if the regulations both of the common and the particular law are observed. [15] Priests, also, of Latin Rite, in accordance with the faculties they enjoy in respect of the administration of this sacrament, validly administer it also to the faithful of Eastern Churches; without prejudice to the rite, observing in regard to licitness the regulations both of the common and of the particular law. [16]

15. The faithful are bound to take part on Sundays and feast days in the Divine Liturgy or, according to the regulations or custom of their own rite, in the celebration of the Divine Office. [17] That the faithful may be able more easily to fulfil their obligation, it is laid down that the period of time within which the precept should be observed extends from the Vespers of the vigil to the end of the Sunday or the feast day. [18] The faithful are earnestly exhorted to receive Holy Communion on these days, and indeed more frequently — yes, even daily. [19]

16. Owing to the fact that the faithful of the different individual churches dwell intermingled with each other in the same area or Eastern territory, the faculties for hearing confessions duly and without restriction given to priests of any rite by their own hierarchs extend to the whole territory of him who grants them and also to the places and faithful of any other rite in the same territory, unless the hierarch of the place has expressly excluded this for places of his rite. [20]

17. In order that the ancient established practice of the Sacrament of Orders in the Eastern Churches may flourish again, this sacred council ardently desires that the office of the permanent diaconate should, where it has fallen into disuse, be restored. [21] The legislative authorities of each individual church should decide about the subdiaconate and the minor orders and the rights and obligations that attach to them. [22]

18. To obviate invalid marriages when Eastern Catholics marry baptized Eastern non-Catholics and in order to promote fidelity in and the sanctity of marriage, as well as peace within the family, the sacred council determines that the canonical "form" for the celebration of these marriages is of obligation only for liceity; for their validity the presence of a sacred minister is sufficient, provided that other prescriptions of laws are observed. [23]

Divine Worship

19. It belongs only to an ecumenical council or to the Apostolic See to determine, transfer or suppress feast days common to all the Eastern Churches. On the other hand, to determine, transfer or suppress the feast days of any of the individual churches is within the competence not only of the Apostolic See but also of the patriarchal or archiepiscopal synod, due regard being had to the whole area and the other individual churches. [24]

20. Until such time as all Christians are agreed on a fixed day for the celebration of Easter, with a view meantime to promoting unity among the Christians of the same area or nation, it is left to the patriarchs or supreme authorities of a place to come to an agreement by the unanimous consent and combined counsel of those affected to celebrate the feast of Easter on the same Sunday. [25]

21. Individual faithful dwelling outside the area or territory of their own rite may follow completely the established custom of the place where they live as regards the law of the sacred seasons. In families of mixed rite it is permissible to observe this law according to one and the same rite. [26]

22. Eastern clerics and Religious should celebrate in accordance with the prescriptions and traditions of their own established custom the Divine Office, which from ancient times has been held in high honor in all Eastern Churches. [27] The faithful too should follow the example of their forbears and assist devoutly as occasion allows at the Divine Office.

23. It belongs to the patriarch with his synod, or to the supreme authority of each church with the council of the hierarchs to regulate the use of languages in the sacred liturgical functions and, after reference to the Apostolic See, of approving translations of texts into the vernacular. [28]

Relations With the Brethren Of Separated Churches

24. The Eastern Churches in communion with the Apostolic See of Rome have a special duty of promoting the unity of all Christians, especially Eastern Christians, in accordance with the principles of the decree, "About Ecumenism," of this sacred council, by prayer in the first place, and by the example of their lives, by religious fidelity to the ancient Eastern traditions, by a greater knowledge of each other, by collaboration and a brotherly regard for objects and feelings. [29]

25. If any separated Eastern Christian should, under the guidance of the grace of the Holy Spirit, join himself to the unity of Catholics, no more should be required of him than what a bare profession of the Catholic faith demands. Eastern clerics, seeing that a valid priesthood is preserved among them, are permitted to exercise the Orders they possess on joining the unity of the Catholic Church, in accordance with the regulations established by the competent authority. [30]

26. Common participation in worship (communicatio in sacris) which harms the unity of the Church or involves formal acceptance of error or the danger of aberration in the faith, of scandal and indifferentism, is forbidden by divine law. [31]

On the other hand, pastoral experience shows clearly that, as regards our Eastern brethren, there should be taken into consideration the different cases of individuals, where neither the unity of the Church is hurt nor are verified the dangers that must be avoided, but where the needs of the salvation of souls and their spiritual good are impelling motives. For that reason the Catholic Church has always adopted and now adopts rather a mild policy, offering to all the means of salvation and an example of charity among Christians, through participation in the sacraments and in other sacred functions and things. With this in mind, "lest because of the harshness of our judgment we be an obstacle to those seeking salvation" [32] and in order more and more to promote union with the Eastern Churches separated from us, the sacred council lays down the following policy.

27. Without prejudice to the principles noted earlier, Eastern Christians who are in fact separated in good faith from the Catholic Church, if they ask of their own accord and have the right dispositions, may be admitted to the sacraments of Penance, the Eucharist and the Anointing of the Sick. Further, Catholics may ask for these same sacraments from those non-Catholic ministers whose churches possess valid sacraments, as often as necessity or a genuine spiritual benefit recommends such a course and access to a Catholic priest is physically or morally impossible. [33]

28. Further, given the same principles, common par-

ticipation by Catholics with their Eastern separated brethren in sacred functions, things and places is allowed for a just cause.[34]

29. This conciliatory policy with regard to "communicatio in sacris" (participation in things sacred) with the brethren of the separated Eastern Churches is put into the care and control of the local hierarchs, in order that, by combined counsel among themselves and, if need be, after consultation also with the hierarchs of the separated churches, they may by timely and effective regulations and norms direct the relations among Christians.

Conclusion

30. The sacred council feels great joy in the fruitful zealous collaboration of the Eastern and the Western Catholic Churches and at the same time declares: All these directives of law are laid down in view of the present situation till such time as the Catholic Church and the separated Eastern Churches come together into complete unity.

Meanwhile, however, all Christians, Eastern as well as Western, are earnestly asked to pray to God fervently and assiduously, nay, indeed daily, that, with the aid of the most holy Mother of God, all may become one. Let them pray also that the strength and the consolation of the Holy Spirit may descend copiously upon all those many Christians of whatsoever church they be who endure suffering and deprivations for their unwavering avowal of the name of Christ.

"Love one another with fraternal charity, anticipating one another with honor" (Rom. 12, 10).

Footnotes on Decree on the Eastern Churches

[1] Leo XIII, Litt. Ap. *Orientalium dignitas*, 30 nov. 1894, in Leonis XIII Acta, vol. XIV, pp. 201-202.

[2] S. Leo IX, Litt. *In terra pax*, an. 1053: "Ut enim"; Innocentius III, Synodus Lateranensis IV, an. 1215, cap. IV: "Licet Gracos"; Litt. *Inter quatuor*, 2 aug. 1206: "Postulasti postmodum"; Innocentius IV, Ep. *Cum de cetero*, 27 aug. 1247; Ep. *Sub catholicae*, 6 mart. 1254, proem.; Nicolaus III, Instructio *Istud est memoriale*, 9 oct. 1278; Leo X, Litt. Ap. *Accepimus nuper*, 18 maii 1521; Paulus III, Litt. Ap. *Dudum*, 23 dec. 1534; Pius IV, Const. *Romanus Pontifex*, 16 febr. 1564, § 5; Clemens VIII, Const. *Magnus Dominus*, 23 dec. 1595, § 10; Paulus V, Const. *Solet circumspecta*, 10 dec. 1615, § 3; Benedictus XIV, Ep. Enc. *Demandatam*, 24 dec. 1743, § 3; Ep. Enc. *Allatae sunt*, 26 iun. 1755, §§ 3, 6-19, 32; Pius VI, Litt. Enc. *Catholicae communionis*, 24 maii 1787; Pius IX, Litt. *In suprema*, 6 ian. 1848, § 3; Litt. Ap. *Ecclesiam Christi*, 26 nov. 1853; Const. *Romani Pontificis*, 6 ian. 1862; Leo XIII, Litt. Ap. *Praeclara*, 20 iun. 1894, n. 7; Litt. Ap. *Orientalium dignitas*, 30 nov. 1894, proem.; etc.

[3] Pius XII, Motu proprio *Cleri sanctitati*, 2 iun. 1957, can. 4.

[4] Pius XII, Motu proprio *Cleri sanctitati*, 2 iun. 1957, can. 8: "sine licentia Sedis Apostolicae", sequendo praxim saeculorum praecedentium; item quoad baptizatos acatholicos in can. 11 habetur: "ritum quem maluerint am plecti possunt"; in textu proposito disponitur modo positivo observantia ritus pro omnibus et ubique terrarum.

[5] Cfr. Leo XIII, Litt. Ap. *Orientalium dignitas*, 30 nov. 1894; Ep. Ap. *Praeclara gratulationis*, 20 iun. 1894, et documenta in nota 2 allata.

[6] Cfr. Benedictus XV, Motu proprio *Orientis catholici*, 15 oct. 1917; Pius XI, Litt. Enc. *Rerum orientalium*, 8 sept. 1928, etc.

[7] Praxis Ecclesiae catholicae temporibus Pii XI, Pii XII, Ioannis XXIII motum hunc abunde demonstrat.

[8] Cfr. Synodum Nicaenam I, can. 6; Constantinopolitanam I, can. 2 et 3; Chalcedonensem, can. 28; can. 9; Constantinopolitanam IV, can. 17; can. 21; Lateranensem IV, can. 5; can. 30; Florentinam, Decr. pro. Graecis; etc.

[9] Cfr. Synodum Nicaenam I, can. 6; Constantinopolitanam I, can. 3; Constantinopolitanam IV, can. 17; Pius XII, Motu proprio *Cleri sanctitati*, can. 216, § 2, 1°.

[10] In Synodis Oecumenicis: Nicaena I, can. 6; Constantinopolitana I, can. 3; Constantinopolitana IV, can. 21; Lateranensi IV, can. 5; Florentina, decr. pro Graecis, 6 iul. 1439, § 9. Cfr. Pius XII, Motu proprio *Cleri sanctitati*, 2 iun. 1957, can. 219, etc.

[11] Cfr. supra, nota 8.

[12] Cfr. Synodum Ephesinam, can. 8; Clemens VII, *Decet Romanum Pontificem*, 23 febr. 1596; Pius VII, Litt. Ap. *In universalis Ecclesiae*, 22 febr. 1807; Pius XII, Motu proprio *Cleri sanctitati*, 2 iun. 1957, can. 324-327; Syn. Carthaginen., an. 419, can. 17.

[13] Syn. Carthaginen., an. 419, can. 17 et 57; Chalcedonensis, an. 451, can. 12; S. Innocentius I, Litt. *Et onus et honor*, a. c. 415: "Nam quid sciscitaris"; S. Ni-

colaus I, Litt. *Ad consulta vestra,* 13 nov. 866: "A quo autem"; Innocentius III, Litt. *Rex regum,* 25 febr. 1204; Leo XII, Const. Ap. *Petrus Apostolorum Princeps,* 15 aug. 1824; Leo XIII, Litt. Ap. *Christi Domini,* an. 1895; Pius XII, Motu proprio *Cleri sanctita,* 2 iun. 1957, can. 159.

(14) Cfr. Innocentius IV, Ep. *Sub catholicae,* 6 mart. 1264, § 3, n. 4; Syn. Lugdunensis II, an. 1274 (professio fidei Michaelis Palaeologi Gregorio X oblata); Eugenius IV, in Syn. Florentina, Const. *Exsultate Deo,* 22 nov. 1439, § 11; Clemens VIII, Instr. *Sanctissimus,* 31 aug. 1595; Benedictus XIV, Const. *Etsi pastoralis,* 26 maii 1742, § II, n. 1, § III, n. 1, etc.; Synodus Laodicena, an. 347/381, can. 48; Syn. Sisen. Armenorum, an. 1342; Synodus Libanen. Maronitarum, an. 1736, P. II, Cap. III, n. 2, et aliae Synodi particulares.

(15) Cfr. S.C.S. officii, Instr. (ad Ep. Scepusien.), an. 1783; S.C. de Prop. Fide (pro Coptis), 15 mart. 1790, n. XIII; Decr. 6 oct. 1863, C. a; S.C. pro Eccl. Orient., 1 maii 1948; S.C.S. Officii, resp. 22 apr. 1896 cum litt. 19 maii 1896.

(16) CIC, can. 782, § 4; S.C. pro Eccl. Orient., Decretum *"de Sacramento Confirmationis administrando etiam fidelibus orientalibus a presbyteris latini ritus, qui hoc indulto gaudeant pro fidelibus sui ritus",* 1 maii 1948.

(17) Cfr. Syn. Laodicen., an. 347/381, can. 29; S. Nicephorus CP., cap. 14; Syn. Duinen. Armenorum, an. 719, can. 31; S. Theodorus Studita, sermo 21; S. Nicolaus I, Litt. *Ad consulta vestra,* 13 nov. 866: "In quorum Apostolorum"; "Nos cupitis"; "Quod interrogatis"; "Praeterea consulitis"; "Si die Dominico"; et Synodi particulares.

(18) Novum quid, saltem ubi viget obligatio audiendi S. Liturgiam; ceterum cohaeret diei liturgicae apud Orientales.

(19) Cfr. Canones Apostolorum, 8 et 9; Syn. Antiochena, an. 341, can. 2; Timotheus Alexandrinus, interrogat, 3; Innocentius III, Const. *Quia divinae,* 4 ian. 1215; et plurimae Synodi particulares Ecclesiarum Orientalium recentiores.

(20) Salva territorialitate iurisdictionis, canon providere intendit, in bonum animarum pluralitati iurisdictionis in eodem territorio.

(21) Cfr. Syn. Nicaena I, can. 18; Syn. Neocaesarien., an. 314/325, can. 12; Syn. Sardicen., an. 343, can. 8; S. Leo M., Litt. *Omnium quidem,* 13 ian. 444; Syn. Chalcedonen., can. 6; Syn. Constantinopolitana IV, can. 23, 26; etc.

(22) Subdiaconatus consideratur apud Ecclesias Orientales plures Ordo minor, sed Motu proprio Pii XII, *Cleri sanctitati,* ei praescribuntur obligationes Ordinum maiorum. Canon proponit ut redeatur ad disciplinam antiquam singularum Ecclesiarum quoad obligationes subdiaconorum, in derogationem iuris communis *"Cleri sanctitati".*

(23) Cfr. Pius XII, Motu proprio *Crebrae allatae,* 22 febr. 1949, can. 32, § 2, n. 5° (facultas patriarcharum dispensandi a forma); Pius XII, Motu proprio *Cleri sanctitati,* 2 iun. 1957, can. 267 (facultas patriarcharum sanandi in radice); S.C. S. Offici et S.C. pro Eccl. Orient., an. 1957 concedunt facultatem dispensandi a forma et sanandi ob defectum formae (ad quinquennium): "extra patriarchatus, Metropolitis, ceterisque Ordinariis locorum. . . qui nullum habent Superiorem infra Sanctam Sedem".

(24) Cfr. S. Leo M., Litt. *Quod saepissime,* 15 apr. 454; "Petitionem autem"; S. Nicephorus CP., cap. 13; Syn. Sergii Patriarchae, 18 sept. 1596, can. 17; Pius VI, Litt. Ap. *Assueto paterne,* 8 apr. 1775; etc.

(25) Cfr. Syn. Vaticana II, Const. *De Sacra Liturgia,* 4 dec. 1963.

(26) Cfr. Clemens VIII, Instr. *Sanctissimus,* 31 aug. 1595, § 6: "Si ipsi graeci"; S.C.S. Officii, 7 jun. 1673, ad 1 et 3; 13 mart. 1727, ad 1; S.C. de Prop. Fide, Decret. 18 aug. 1913, art. 33; Decret. 14 aug. 1914, art. 27; Decret. 27 mart. 1916, art. 14; S.C. pro Eccl. Orient., Decret. 1 mart. 1929, art. 36; Decret. 4 maii 1930, art. 41.

(27) Cfr. Syn. Laodicen., 347/381, can. 18; Syn. Mar Issaci Chaldaeorum, an. 410, can. 15; S. Nerses Glaien. Armenorum, an. 1166; Innocentius IV, Ep. *Sub catholicae,* 6 mart. 1254, § 8; Benedictus XIV, Const. *Etsi pastoralis,* 26 maii 1742, § 7, n. 5; Inst. *Eo quamvis tempore,* 4 maii 1745, § § 42 ss.; et Synodi particulares recentiores: Armenorum (1911), Coptorum (1898), Maronitarum (1736), Rumenorum (1872), Ruthenorum (1891), Synorum (1888).

(28) Ex traditione orientali.

(29) Ex tenore Bullarum unionis singularum Ecclesiarum orientalium catholicarum.

(30) Obligatio synodalis quoad fratres seiunctos Orientales et quoad omnes Ordines cuiuscumque gradus tum iuris divini tum ecclesiastici.

(31) Haec doctrina valet etiam in Ecclesiis seiunctis.

(32) S. Basilius M., *Epistula canonica ad Amphilochium,* PG. 32, 669 B.

(33) Fundamentum mitigationis consideratur: 1) validitas sacramentorum; 2) bona fides et dispositio; 3) necessitas salutis aeternae; 4) absentia sacerdotis proprii; 5) exclusio periculorum vitandorum et formalis adhaesionis errori.

(34) Agitur de s. d. "communicatione in sacris extrasacramentali". Concilium est quod mitigationem concedit, servatis servandis.

Cardinal Bea on Statement on the Jews

This is a translation of a statement by Augustin Cardinal Bea, president of the Secretariat for Promoting Christian Unity, which appeared in L'Osservatore Romano Dec. 1 and in which he asserted the council's declaration on non-Christian religions should not be given a political interpretation.

In the [ecumenical council's] 127th general congregation on Nov. 20 the declaration on the Church's relations to non-Christian religions was approved by a large majority. (Out of the 1,906 Fathers present, 1,651 voted "yes," 242 "yes with reservations" and 99 "no.")

The official reporter explicitly emphasized this year, as he did last year also, that the declaration does not admit of any political interpretation, but is of a purely religious character. This exclusively religious character of the declaration is even more accentuated, in the text submitted for the vote, by the fact that, meanwhile, it had been decided that it should form an appendix to the Constitution on the Church, and that it concerns not only the Jews but all non-Christians.

Just as the passages on the Hindus, Buddhists and Moslems have nothing to do with politics, which is evident, so also the passage on the Jews is extraneous from any political interpretation. In fact, it deals only with the relation existing between the religion of the Old Testament and the Christian, and, in addition, with the doctrine of St. Paul regarding the future religious fate of the people of Israel. It does not even mention explicitly the question of the guilt of those who played an active part in the condemnation of Jesus. It only affirms that this condemnation cannot be attributed to the four million and more Jews who in those days lived outside Palestine — in the diaspora — and even less to the Jews of our time. The pastoral outcome of these facts also concerns the religious field alone.

After all these measures and declarations, cautious and objective, it may be justifiably hoped that the declaration may be rightly interpreted and serenely assessed; and that therefore inferences may be disregarded which have been echoed in the press these past few days regarding political intentions and designs. Otherwise the affirmations made in the declaration would be interpreted in an arbitrary and distorted manner, misrepresenting the intentions of the council and of a conciliar document inspired by motives of truth, justice and Christian charity, evidently in full accordance with the Gospel. It is a religious matter in which the council has no other intention than to foster peace everywhere, hoping that religion may not be exploited to justify discrimination and political prejudice.

Index

E

East, development of theology in, 111
Eastern Churches, 12, 111; amended text distributed, 285; and Roman Churches, similarities, 111; debate on, 133, 136, 137, 138, 141, 142, 143, 159, 160, 163, 165; decree proclaimed, 299; decree on, 303; decree on (text), 353; discipline, 111, 137; document approved, 296; final summary on, 165; married deacons, 76; most crucial problem—more than one jurisdiction within territory of the same diocese, 141; patriarchs of, 299; preservation of spiritual patrimony, 168; proposition on, 126, described, 136; sacraments and worship in, 118; schema approved, 293; traditional practice of, 122; unity, 137; value and importance of rights and traditions, 168; vote on sections of proposition on, 167, 168; voting completed on proposition, 171
Eastern hierarchy, establishment of, 161
Eastern rites, and Orthodox, exchange of sacraments, 142; and "over-zealous Latinizers," 142; areas, revision asked on schema, 33; bishops, 68; Catholic and Orthodox Christians, contact between, 171; Catholics, esteem and love for, 143; Catholics persecuted, 141, danger of "proselytizing" members of, 141; discipline of the sacraments, 168; laity and clergy in, 120; liturgy, 171; sacraments from Orthodox priests, 137; special vocation for, 142; patriarchs, 137, 138, 165, 168, 354; persecution of, 142; sacramental discipline, reform in, 160; suffer from "Latinizers," 141
Eastern studies, progress by modern scholars, 97
Ecclesiam Suam, 62, 132, 171, 177, 200, 244
Ecclesiastical, benefices, asks revision of, 131; formation, council proposition on, 192; functionaries, priests as, 131; legalism, 190; "prisons," 129; provinces, division of, vote on, 230; studies, associations which encourage, 134, studies, reorganization of, 267; territories, vote on erection of, 230
"Ecclesio-typical" Mariologists, 50, 51, 52
Ecclesiology, 121
Economic, and biological idolatry, 169; and social life, 164; and social problems, 198; life, 211; systems, no preference for one or other, 211
Economical order and social justice, 179
Ecuador, 47
Ecumenical, action, 188; activity and apostolate of conversion, no opposition between, 99; council, an exceptional moment in Church's life, 1, principal task, 3, regular meetings urged, 24, supreme power exercised in, 38, third session opens, 3, true representation of universal Church, 1, universal prayers for successful outcome, 2
Ecumenical movement, Catholics to engage actively in, 99, 100; object of, 82
Ecumenical Patriarchate of Constantinople, 49
Ecumenical, practices, responsibility for implementation of, 255; training, especially in seminary, 103
Ecumenism, 60, 192; Church's stand on, 143, 144; constitution on, 234; decree on, 301, 303, 343; decree, changes approved, 99; decree, proclaimed, 299; Holy Spirit's role in, 100; how Catholics can participate in, 103; nature of, 64; proposed directory, 103, 106; schema, 89, 91, 138, 207, 261, approved handling of suggested changes, 248, 293, booklet on chapter 3, 259, changes approved, 103, changes, vote on, 99, discussion on, 59, 62, 64, 78, 143, modifications introduced by the Unity Secretariat, 286, religious liberty declaration taken from, 40, report on chapter 1, 99, text approved, 296, third chapter approved, 263, vote on, 78, 111, 115, voting method, 95, voting on chapter 2, 255, votes on chapters, 103; spirit, some seems infantilism and romanticism, 105
Edelby, Archbishop Neophytos, 101, 161
Educated laity, 118
Education, and youth, 287; apostolic dimension of, 274; juridical dimension of, 274; importance and decisive influence attached to, 281; parents inalienable rights, 274; part of Church's general mission, 273; family's role in, 272; freedom of, 45, 205; need for basic, 219; no monopoly of, 274; public aid to parents, 271; quality of supreme importance, 287; quality not quantity, 274; rejects monopoly of, 280; religious, of children, 274; rights of parents in, 276; specialists, greater use of contemplated, 173; suggests committee be appointed to draw up principles, 274; schema, report on, 272; summary of council document on, 273, 274
Educational, field, difficulties in, 272; mission, nature of, 287; monopolies, tendency of modern governments to establish, 281
80th general congregation, 11; 81st, 15; 82nd, 19; 83rd, 23; 84th, 27; 85th, 31; 86th, 35; 87th, 43; 88th, 55; 89th, 67
Einsiedeln, Switzerland, 302
Elchinger, Bishop Leon, 12, 75, 167, 169, 218, 272
Elko, Bishop Nicholas T., 178
El Quinche, Our Lady of, 302
Ember days, sanctification of, 2
Emigration, importance of statement on, 242
Emmenegger, Msgr. Joseph E., 127, 129
Encyclical, papal, 175
Encyclicals of modern popes, 164
England, 64, 177, 280; and Wales, bishops of, 67, 81; Bishop John, 117
Enormous intensification of life of Church, possibility opens, 30
Enrique y Terancon, Archbishop Vicente, 117
Episcopacy, a sacrament, 31; prerogatives, 5; voting on chapter on, 122
Episcopal, appointments, 38; authority, 3; college, 224, voting on chapter on, 122; collegiality, 267, and episcopate, objection to concepts of sacramentality of, 27, defense sent to council Fathers, 269, expressed in 3rd chapter, 25, statement distributed on Biblical basis for, 21; vicar, 224
Episcopal conferences, 133, 233; competence of, 24; formation of, 44; national, Religious on, 32; structure, competence and collaboration of, vote on, 230
Episcopal consecration, confers powers of teaching and ruling, 31; imposition of hands in, 152
Episcopate, apostles as founders of, 96; and Holy see, relations between, 8; constitutional prerogatives, 5, 8; divine origin of, 31; nature and function, 5, 8; pope's duty of heading, 5; pope's tribute to, 9; role and mandate, 9; vote on articles on nature of, 84
Epistle to the Romans, 61
Equal treatment in education, parents right to, 280
Erroneous conscience, 45, 66; as a divine vocation, 48
Error, objective rights of, 43; no right to persuade men to, 45
Eschatological, demands of Christian life, 121; nature of our calling, 11; nature of the pilgrim Church and its union with the Church in heaven, 330
Eschatology, chapter on, 11; last things, 15
Establishment of religion, 47
Estrada, Mother, 41
Etchmiadzin Catholicate, 49
Eucharist, fast reduced, 299; most holy mystery of, 150; reservation of, 155
Eucharistic worship, 200
Eulogius, Bishop of Alexandria, 8
Europe, 226
European, bishops, 190; nations, three, have had 90% of canonizations, 16
Evangelical, formation, 265; Church (Lutheran) of Germany, 49
Evangelisti, Archbishop Joseph, 130
Evangelization, 192; church's mission of, 168, 184; stages of, 233; work of, 37
Evolution, treatment of, 168
Exaggerated freedom given to Biblical scholars, 97
Exaltation of the Holy Cross, feast of, 4
Exegesis, problems of modern, 97
Exempt religious orders, schema's treatment of, 24
Exemption from local bishops authority of religious communities, 23
Exemption of Religious, asks re-examination of, 260
Existence and eternity of hell, 12
Existentialism, 215
Expenditures, greatest national, for defense and education, 271
Experts, council, 171, 172, 175, 185; consulted on schema 13, 178; norms for, 13; restrictions on, 13; of council violating restrictions, 27

F

Fairweather, Rev. Eugene, 49
Faith, and science, disagreement between, 185; freedom of, 57; historical foundation for, 104; loss of, study in depth of, 281; no one can be forced to embrace, 92
Faithful, joining spiritually in council, 1; places of, 155; prayer of, 151
Fallen priests, need for merciful attention to, 29
Falls, Father Thomas B., 127, 129
False irenicism, 103, 104
Families, large 214
Family, chief function procreation and education of children, 127; morals, study of, 210; regulation, 207; role in education, 272
Family life, 168, 171, 175, 178, 198; and movies, 214; and radio, 214; and television, 214; apostolic significance of, 84; in Schema 13, 203; sanctity of, 214
F.A.O., 186, 187
Far East, 226
Fares, Archbishop Armando, 25, 91, 104, 131
Farren, Bishop Niel, 95
Fast before Communion reduced, 299
Fasting, 200
Fatima, Pope sends golden rose to, 301; shrine of, 302
Fearns, Bishop John M., 293, 295
Fecundity in marriage, 204
Felici, Archbishop Pericle, 4, 6, 11, 13, 15, 19, 21, 24, 27, 28, 44, 56, 68, 70, 74, 84, 89, 95, 115, 125, 126, 129, 133, 134, 135, 143, 159, 164, 177, 183, 197, 205, 217, 223, 231, 236, 242, 243, 247, 255, 267, 279, 285, 286, 288, 294, 299, 302
Feltin, Maurice Cardinal, 205
Feminism, 205
Fernandes, Archbishop Angelo, 113
Fernandez, O.P., Father Aniceto, 20, 55, 56, 57, 111, 173, 215, 256, 287
Fernandez Conde, Bishop Manuel, 265
Fernando, Bishop Thomas, 247
Forni, Efrem Cardinal, 217
Ferraira, O.F.M., Father Joao, 105, 215
Ferrand, Archbishop Louis, 255
Ferreira de Macedo, Archbishop Antonio, 126, 134, 302
Financial aid, distribution of, 134
Financial assistance for missions, 233
Fiordello, Bishop Pietro, 260
First Vatican Council, 1, 3, 4, 7, 8, 28, 31, 33, 85, 86, 89, 90, 96, 142, 187, 193, 299; completes work of, 29
Flahiff, Archbishop George B., 96
Flores Martin, Bishop Jaime, 100, 138, 265
Florit, Archbishop Ermenegildo, 83, 85
Foeley, Bishop Brian, 25
Forbidden books, Church's list of, 189
Foreign aid programs, 224
Formation for and with Church, 125
"Forthbringer of God," 51
Fougerat, Bishop Andre, 125
Fourth session of council, 160, 163, 171, 172, 177, 181, 194, 236, 273, 293, 299
France, bishops of, 32, 67
Franic, Bishop Frane, 24, 27, 28, 83, 85, 173
Free choice of schools, 45
Free consent in marriage, 214
Free exercise of religion, 37
Freedom, affirmation of human values of, 248; Church insists on her own, 39; denied because of religion, 167; Church champions for others, 39; from religion, 44; from social coercion, 55; is highest political end, 39; of bishops and their appointment, vote on, 224; of choice necessity for priestly candidate, 259; of civil liberty, 36; of conscience and consciences, distinction needed, 56; of education, 45; of faith, 57; of individual conscience, 174; of non-belief, 35; of non-believers, 36; of scientific inquiry, 274; of scientific investigation and study, 218; offends totalitarianism, 44; to profess religion, 37; within schools, 271
Freemasonry, 69
Frei, Eduardo, 186
Frey, Msgr. Gerard L., 127, 129
Friends World Committee, 50
Frings, Joseph Cardinal, 23, 69, 190, 222, 235, 236
Frotz, Bishop Augustin, 205, 219, 220
Function and nature of episcopate, 8
Future priests, training of, 268

G

Gagnor, Bishop Giuseppe, 223
Gahamanyi, Bishop Jean, 85, 237
Galileo, 185, 189, 204, 209, 218
Gand, Bishop Adrien, 190
Gantin, Archbishop Bernardin, 236
Gaona Sosa, S.D.B., Bishop Emilio, 68
Garaygordobil Berrizbeitia, Bishop Victor, 135
Garcia de Sierra y Mendez, Archbishop Segundo, 12, 179, 242
Garcia y Garcia de Castro, Archbishop Rafael, 19, 21, 101
Gargitter, Bishop Joseph, 217, 218
Garibi y Rivera, Jose Cardinal, 302
Garner, Archbishop John, 190
Garrone, Archbishop Gabriel, 20, 56, 138, 273
Gasbarri, Bishop Primo, 19, 21, 100
Gawlina, Archbishop Jozef, 19, 27, 33
Gay, Bishop Jean, 215
Geeraerts, Bishop Xavier, 242
Geise, Bishop Paternus, 235, 236
Georgetown University, 206
German bishops, 16, 85, 101, 186, 236; Caritas, 186; conferences, 242; council press center, 22, 174, 262
German-language bishops, 115
Germany, 82
Ghandi, Mahatma, 199
Ghanem, Mother Marie Henriette, 41
Ghattas, Bishop Isaac, 142, 198
Gilroy, Norman Cardinal, 285
Gold medals honoring Our Lady given council Fathers, 294
Golden rose to Fatima, Pope sends, 301
"Golden rule" of religion and catechetical instruction, 125
Goldie, Rosemary, 41
Goldsmith, Oliver, 198
Gomes dos Santos, Archbishop Fernando, 133
Good priest, the, 259
Gonzales Martin, Bishop Marcello, 133, 198
Gonzalez Arbelaez, Archbishop Juan, 105
Gonzalez Moralejo, Bishop Rafael, 38, 178
Gonzi, Archbishop Michele, 134, 302
Good Samaritan, parable of, 188
Gopu, Archbishop Joseph Mark, 264, 265
Gori, O.F.M., Patriarch Alberto, 12, 142, 271, 302
Gospels, development of, 97; historical character of, 87, 100, 101, 105; historicity of, 91, 99; modern scientific research in interpreting, 99
Gouyon, Archbishop Paul, 178, 272

101, 106, 113, 120, 166, 219, 243, 249, 257, 269, 273, 281, 296
Only truth has rights, 37
Optimism, exaggerated, 185
Orbegozo y Giocoes, Bishop Ignacio, 120
Orders and congregations, asks removing distinctions from, 256, 258
Organ, place of, 155
Organic unity, lack of, 268
Organizations, new pattern in forming, 224; of chanceries, vote on, 224; to coordinate providing priests for needy dioceses, 130; too much emphasis on, 120
Organized apostolate, importance of, 108
Oriental Churches, see Eastern Churches
Oriental Studies, Dominican Institute for, 62; White Fathers of the Pontifical Institute of, 62
Origin of episcopate, 8
Original sin, 126, 168
Orthodox, 193; and Roman Catholics, cooperation between, 111; Christians, gesture of brotherhood, 35; Church of Georgia, 49; churches, 85; churches, position in Catholic Church, 160; Mary as bridge to, 20; Patriarchate of Constantinople, 77; priests validly ordained, 137; theological institute, 50
Ottaviani, Alfredo Cardinal, 35, 37, 173, 213, 214
Our Lady (see Virgin Mary, Mary), 15; chapter on, 83; schema dealing with, distributed, 181
Outler, Rev. Albert C., 49
Overpopulation, 208

P

Pacem in Terris, 36, 39, 44, 48, 65, 186, 200, 205, 241, 243, 251
Padin, Bishop Candido, 126
Paganism, attitude toward, 75
Pagans, 67
Pan-Orthodox conference, 217
Papal encyclical on marriage, 206
Papal encyclicals, 198
Papal infallibility, 142
Papal primacy, teaching of First Vatican Council, 28
Pardons those who have offended Catholic Church, 103
Parecattil, Archbishop Joseph, 75
Parental love, 208
Parente, Archbishop Pietro, 23, 27, 28, 29, 43, 44
Parents, first of educators, 272; inalienable rights in education, 274; public aid to, for education, 271; right to educate children according to their conscience, 280
Parish census and religious, 249
Parish parliaments, 117
Parker, Bishop Thomas, 241, 302
Parliament of laity, 118
Parochial ministry, preeminence of, 134
Pastor, must serve everyone, 32; petitions that one be invited to address council, 134
Pastoral, apprenticeship, 264; care of souls, 25; duties of bishops, 181, debate on, 29, report on chapter dealing with, 223, schemata on, 15, 23, 303, voting on, 217, 218; experience for seminarians, 269; needs of Church today, 130; problems, conference on, 129; sociology chapter on, asked, 25, diocesan commissions on, 25; theology, asks declaration on, 33, study of, 131; training, 268, throughout seminary course, 192
Pastoralization of whole seminary cycle, 265
Pastors, and apostolate of laity, 108; and laity belong to People of God, 20; country, 130; their duties, appointment and retirement, vote on, 224; laity's cooperation and loyalty to, 84; nature and mission of, 5, 8; respect due, 113; rural, 130
Paternalism, in hierarchy outmoded, 27; of hierarchy or clergy rejected, 29; on part of major superiors, 255
Patras, Greece, 35
Patriarchal Conference of the Chaldean Rite, 159
Patriarchal dignity, restoration of, 138
Patriarchal system, 142, 160, 165
Patriarchate of Moscow, 49
Patriarchates called anachronism, 159
Patriarchs, schema's treatment of, 159
Paul VI, Pope, 3, 4, 6, 19, 30, 35, 51, 53, 59, 66, 76, 77, 90, 99, 103, 121, 127, 132, 134, 144, 145, 156, 160, 171, 181, 186, 193, 194, 199, 203, 204, 207, 210, 217, 221, 222, 223, 226, 229, 232, 235, 241, 244, 245, 247, 252, 253, 263, 264, 276, 285, 294, 299, 300, 301, 302, 303
Pawley, Rev. Bernard C., 49
Pawlowski, Bishop Antoni, 268
Peace, 164, 179, 198, 211; and war, 241, question of, 205; asks special prayers for, 242; encouragement of national and international organizations to work for, 248; work of justice, 251
Peaceful crusade for racial equality, 199
Pearson, Lester, 187
Pedicini, Bishop Gioacchino, 115
Pellanda, Bishop Geraldo, 32
Penalties for breach of purely ecclesiastical laws, 183
Penance and prayer contributing to council, 1

Pensions for disabled priests, 130
People of God, pastors and laity belong to, 20
People without fixed residence, special attention for, 29
Peoples, community of, 179
Perantoni, O.F.M., Archbishop Pacifico, 257
Pereira, Bishop Joao, 302
Pereira, Bishop Manuel, 135
Periodic continence, 216
Periti, 171, 185
Permanent Committee for International Congresses of the Lay Apostolate, 41
Perris, Archbishop Giovanni, 130, 131
Persecuted Eastern rite Catholics, plea for, 141
Persecution, and hatred should be rejected, 69; of nationality or race condemned, 62; those suffering for the Faith, 301
Perseverance in the religious life, consideration of question of, 256
Person, dignity of, 183
Personal, diocese, 223; liberty in religion, 48; religious liberty, foundation of, 45; responsibility, 190, development of, 265
Peruvian bishops, 89
Pessimism, nihilistic, 185
Philbin, Bishop William, 101
Philippine bishops, 179
Philosophy and theology, taught in every Catholic university according to principles of St. Thomas Aquinas, 287
Philosophy, end of, 264; role of, 215
Picachy, Bishop Lawrence, 242
Pietraszko, Bishop Jan, 184
Piety, personal exercises of, 130
Pilar, Our Lady of the, 302
Pildain Zapain, Bishop Antonio, 24, 222
Pill, progesterone, 206
Pious practices, 83
Pironio, Bishop Eduardo, 120
Pius X, Pope, 19, 25, 52
Pius XI, Pope, 52, 82, 119, 168, 203, 214, 248, 281
Pius XII, Pope, 9, 19, 28, 43, 44, 46, 65, 76, 81, 115, 119, 140, 201, 203, 214, 248, 251
"Placet juxta modum," 70; avoidance of voting, asked, 15
Platitudes, set of, 175
Plumey, Bishop Yves, 74
Pluta, Bishop Wilhelm, 32, 125
Pocock, Archbishop Philip F., 69
Podesta, Bishop Jeronimo, 76
Pogacnik, Archbishop Josip, 184
Pogodin, Archimandrite Ambrose, 49
Pohlschneider, Bishop Johannes, 44, 45, 287
Poland, 82
Polish bishops, 89, 219, 260, 287; ask title of Mother of the Church for Mary, 16
Political, stability, 188; value of the nation or fatherland, 198
Politics, laity active part in, 172
Polygamy, 214
Pont y Gol, Bishop Jose, 12
Pontifical Biblical Commission, 28, 100, 101, 140; instruction, 87
Pontifical Biblical Institute, 21
Pontifical Commission for Biblical Studies instruction, 97
Pontifical Ethiopian college, 231
Pontifical institute for formation of catechists asked, 236
Pontifical missionary organizations, 233
Poor, and rich, gap widening, 221, 225; church, 172; parishes, international organizations to relieve, 1; world-wide collection for, 189
Pope, and title of Mary as Mother of the Church, 19; authority of, 3, 217; donation of tiara to the poor, 267; duty of heading episcopate, 5; full, supreme and universal power emphasized, 28; infallibility of teaching, 4, 8; primacy, 31, 33; primacy and infallibility of, 3; primacy, collegiality of bishops would diminish, 28; primacy of jurisdiction, 4, 8; primacy, whether collegiality endangers, 27; successor of St. Peter, vote on, 27; supremacy, 122; supreme power remains intact, 28; teaching authority, 171, 175; to meet all council Fathers, 223
Population, expansion, 206; explosion, 186, 242, increase explosive, 187
Post-apostolic tradition, 89
Potanamuzhi, Bishop Matthew, 269
Potter, Rev. Philip, 49
Pourchet, Bishop Maurice, 191
Poverty, 178, 181, 186, 187, 188, 222; abolition of, 187; and birth control, 204; and its spirit, 257; and the priest, 129, 135; asks "war cabinet" to wage total war on, 224; Christian, 189, 190; collective, 185; concerted drive to wipe out, 188; in the mission schema, 245; in the world, 189; means to wipe out, 221; more stress on, 260; of diocesan priests, 258; problem of, 224; schema 13's spirit of, 185; spirit of, 245, 248; three-fourths of human race live in, 225; voluntary, 189; vows of, 260; Western nations have means to wipe out, 225; world, and birth control, 224; world, and Christian responsibility, 186; world's concern for, 188; world, debate on, 221

Power, Bishop William, 125

Power, of binding and loosing, 28; of the episcopate, 8, 24
Practice of ecumenism, 346
Prayer, and penance contributing to council, 1; of the faithful, 151
Prayers, and services in common, 112; of expiation and supplication for council, 2
Preaching, and moralizing, council should avoid, 248; better instruction in, 265; mission comes from episcopal consecration, schema's presupposition that, 24
Prelatures nullius, 230
Prerogatives, of the episcopate, 5, 8; of pope, 8
Presbyterian Church of Scotland, 49
Preservation of spiritual heritage of Eastern Churches, 354
Press panel, U.S. bishops, see U.S. bishops' press panel
Priests, advisory council of, 133; adequate compensation of, 131; and bishops, relations between, 32, 133; and evangelical counsels of poverty, chastity and obedience, 135; and faithful, relationship between, 129; and the missions, 234; as ecclesiastical functionaries, 131; asked to have greater confidence in their people, 116; associations which pool funds for social security for, 134; better distribution of, 134, 135; charity in life of, 129; common life for, 130; consultative board of, 135; country, 129; draft on called inadequate, 129; discussion of proposition on, 137, 138, 139; excommunicated, could witness mixed marriage, 294; further training of, 134; health insurance, 135; international training center for, 119; intimate union with Christ, 130; invited to attend council, 127; last wills, 131; lay garb, 133; medical care, 129, 130; mission, 138; missionary spirit, 130; monthly days of recollection, 134; natural virtues emphasized, 129; need for holiness, 135; need for spiritual exercises, 134; normal compensation for work, 136; obedience in life of, 129; pensions for disabled, 130; political questions, 134; poverty in life of, 129; psychologically disturbed, 129; psychotic, 129; reduction of inequalities between, 32; relations with laity, 135; reorganization of texts on, 32; retirement pensions, 129, 130; salaries, 129, 130; sick, 130; social security, 135; spiritual and economic rights, recognition of, 134; spirituality, 129; supernatural virtues required of, 129; to be admitted to discussion of priesthood proposition, 103; to leave their property to good works in diocese, 131; training, 130; unfaithful, 273; with mental illness, 130
Priesthood, asks more emphasis on dignity and sublimity of, 134; asks revision of schema on, 133; called divine vocation, 48; holiness of, 134; proposition sent back for revision, 159; rejecting candidates for, 133; report on proposition on, 129; schema on, 126; spirituality of diocesan, 134; value of suffering in, 131
Priestly formation, agenda for, 243; proposition reported and discussed, 261
Priestly life and ministry, 126, 127, 129, 130, 131, 133, 134, 135, 136; schemata on, 303; twelve council propositions on, 135; new text distributed, 294
Priestly studies, 135; training, proposition called too abstract, 261; virtues, 134; vocations, emphasis on, 256
Primacy, and infallibility of pope, 3; of consecration in religious life, 257; of jurisdiction of pope, 4, 8; of love in schema 13, 174; of pope, 31, 33
Primeau, Bishop Ernest J., 43, 44, 46
Principal task of council, 3
Principal tasks of Christians today, 180, 210
Principi, Archbishop Primo, 302
Printesis, Archbishop Benedictos, 172
Privileges, Church should be wary of accepting, 183
Proano Villalba, Bishop Leonidas, 33, 135, 219
Problem of our age, central, 186
Problems that concern men, transition of council to treatment of, 163
Procreation, value of, 215
Profession of faith, 9
Programs to assist people of God to raise themselves out of abyss of poverty and degradation, 227
Proletariat nations, 188
Propaganda Fide, 230
Propagation of error, 81
Property, basic concept of, 219; carries social obligations, 225
"Prophylactic training" in seminaries, 259
Proposition, definition of council, 21
Proselytism, 73, 93; and religious liberty, 37; condemned, 40; defined, 40
Protection of marriage, 37
Protestant, churches, 85; Federation of France, 50
Prou, O.P., Abbot Jean, 184
Providence, and marriage proposition, 213; divine, 213; role of, 168
Pseudo-mysticism, 48
Psychological data, importance of, 199

T

U